7th Edition

GOVERNING
An Introduction to Political Science

Austin Ranney
University of California, Berkeley

PRENTICE-HALL, Upper Saddle River, New Jersey 07458

Library of Congress Cataloging–in–Publication Data

Ranney, Austin.
   Governing: an introduction to political science / Austin Ranny.
   —7th ed.
      p.   cm.
   Includes bibliographical references and index.
   ISBN 0–13–326216–2
   1. Political science.   I. Title.
JA66.R298   1996
320—dc20   95–22602
                                            CIP

Acquisitions editor: Jennie Katsaros
Editorial/production supervision and interior design: Serena Hoffman
Buyer: Bob Anderson
Copy editor: Nancy Marcello
Photo researcher: Dallas Chang
Cover design: Bruce Kenselaar
Cover art: Peter Gridley, FPG International

 © **1996, 1993, 1990 by Prentice-Hall, Inc.**
Simon & Schuster/A Viacom Company
Upper Saddle River, New Jersey 07458

Printed in the United States of America
10 9 8 7 6 5 4 3 2 1

ISBN: 0-13-326216-2

Prentice-Hall International (UK) Limited, *London*
Prentice-Hall of Australia Pty. Limited, *Sydney*
Prentice-Hall Canada Inc., *Toronto*
Prentice-Hall Hispanoamericana, S.A., *Mexico*
Prentice-Hall of India Private Limited, *New Delhi*
Prentice-Hall of Japan, Inc., *Tokyo*
Simon & Schuster Asia Pte. Ltd., *Singapore*
Editora Prentice-Hall do Brasil, Ltda., *Rio de Janeiro*

Contents

PREFACE   xiii

Part One: Politics, Governments, and People ———————————————

1 **POLITICS IN HUMAN LIFE**   1
What Is Politics?   1
    "Politics" in Everyday Conversation   1
    Politics as Policy Making   2
Some Universal Characteristics of Politics   4
    Politics Is Conflict   4
    Group Conflict in Politics   5
    Tactics of Political Action   8
    Who Uses Which Tactics?   17
Some Characteristics of Political Conflict   18
    Multiplicity   18
    Opposition   19
    Overlapping Memberships   20
    Imperfect Mobilization   20
Politics and Government   21
For Further Reading   23 / *Notes*   24

2 **GOVERNMENTS AND GOVERNING**   25
What Governments Do   25
    In Primitive Societies   25
    In "Advanced/Industrialized" Societies   26
What Is Government?   27
    Government and Other Organizations   27
    Government Defined   27

How Government Differs from Other Social Organizations   28
    Comprehensive Authority   28
    Involuntary Membership   29
    Authoritative Rules   29
    Legitimate Monopoly of Overwhelming Force   30
    Highest Stakes   30
Basic Tasks and Tools of Government   31
    Interest Articulation   31
    Interest Aggregation   32
    Coercion and Compromise   32
An Illustration: The American Conflict over Abortion   34
    The "Pro-life" Side   35
    The "Pro-choice" Side   35
    Where Things Stand   37
    Some Lessons for the Study of Governing   38
Nationalism and the Birth and Death of Nations   39
    Nature of Nations   39
    The Birth of Nations   41
    The Death of Nations   41
For Further Reading   43 / Notes   44

3

POLITICAL PSYCHOLOGY, SOCIALIZATION, AND CULTURE   **45**
Political Psychology: What Forms People's Political Beliefs and
    Behavior?   45
    Biological Nature and Needs   45
    Psychological Processes and Cognitive Maps   46
    Group Memberships and Pressures to Conform   48
Political Socialization   55
    Concept   55
    Profile of the Developing Political Self   55
    Agents of Socialization   58
Political Culture   62
    Components   62
    Some Differences Among Political Cultures   64
For Further Reading   67 / Notes   69

4

MODERN POLITICAL IDEOLOGIES   **70**
Nature of Ideologies   70
    What Is an Ideology?   70
    Intellectual Components of an Ideology   71
    Types of Ideologies   73
Ideologies of Limits on Government   74

Constitutionalism and Classical Liberalism   74
Totalitarianism   77
Ideologies of Economic Control   79
Capitalism and Laissez Faire   79
Socialism   81
Political Ideologies, American Style   87
Modern American Liberalism   88
Modern American Conservatism   89
For Further Reading   91 / Notes   92

5   DEMOCRACY AND AUTHORITARIANISM: PRINCIPLES AND MODELS   93

Principles for a Working Definition of Democracy   94
Popular Sovereignty   94
Political Equality   95
Popular Consultation   96
Majority Rule   96
Models of Democracy   99
The Nature and Uses of Models in Social Science   99
Participatory and Accountable-Elites Models   102
Presidential and Parliamentary Models   104
Majoritarian and Consensual Models   104
Authoritarianism and Dictatorship   105
Classifying Actual Governments   109
Surge of Democracy   110
For Further Reading   111 / Notes   112

Part Two: Politics Outside Formal Governments

6   PUBLIC OPINION IN DEMOCRATIC SYSTEMS   113

Nature of Public Opinion   114
Definition   114
Dimensions of Public Opinion: Preference and Intensity   115
Measurement by Public Opinion Polls   116
Opinion Distributions in Western Democracies   123
What Concerns People?   123
Ideology   125
Domestic Policy: Economic and Social Responsibilities of Government   127
Foreign Policy   130
Conclusion   130
For Further Reading   131 / Notes   131

7

POLITICAL COMMUNICATION   **132**

Nature of Political Communication   133
    What Is Communication?   133
    Elements of Political Communication   134
Mass Communications Media   136
    Television   136
    Newspapers   144
    Radio   146
Political Impact of Mass Communications   146
    On Mass Publics   146
    On Political and Governmental Leaders   151
Communications Revolutions, Past and Future   155
For Further Reading   156 / Notes   157

8

THE ELECTORAL PROCESS   **158**

Elections in Democratic Systems   158
    Essential Characteristics of Free Elections   159
    Qualifications for Voting   160
    Nonvoting and Compulsory Voting   162
    Nominations and Candidate Selection   165
Principal Democratic Electoral Systems   168
    Single-Member-District Systems   168
    Multi-Member-Proportional Systems   170
    Political Effects of Electoral Systems   173
    The German Hybrid   175
Apportionment of Electoral Districts   177
    Problems   177
    Procedures   178
Referendum Elections   179
    Rationale   179
    Organization   180
    Results and Evaluation   181
For Further Reading   186 / Notes   187

9

VOTING BEHAVIOR   **188**

Intervening Variables in Voting Behavior   189
    Party Identification   191
    Issue Orientation   195
    Candidate Orientation   197
For Further Reading   200 / Notes   201

10 **POLITICAL PARTIES AND PARTY SYSTEMS** **202**
Political Parties in Democratic Systems   202
  What Is a Political Party?   202
  Party Identification and Membership   203
  Principal Activities of Parties   206
Differences Among Parties in Democratic Systems   208
  In the Nature and Role of Ideology   208
  In Centralization   212
  In Discipline   213
  In Cohesion   214
Fractionalization of Democratic Party Systems   215
  Measurement: Rae's Index of Fractionalization   215
  Characteristics of the More Fractionalized Systems   216
  Characteristics of the Less Fractionalized Systems   219
Authoritarian One-Party Systems   220
  Monoparty Systems   220
  Dominant Party Systems   224
For Further Reading   226 / *Notes*   227

Part Three: Governmental Structures, Authorities, and Processes

11 **THE LEGISLATIVE PROCESS** **228**
Presidential And Parliamentary Democracies   228
  Doctrine of Separation of Powers   229
  Separation of Powers in Presidential Democracies   229
  Fusion of Powers in Parliamentary Democracies   230
  Crossing Boundaries   231
Functions of Legislatures   232
  Statute Making   232
  Constitution Making and Amending   232
  Electoral Functions   233
  Financial Functions   233
  Quasi-Executive Functions   233
  Quasi-Judicial Functions   234
  Investigative Functions   235
  Informational Functions   235
Structure and Procedures of Legislatures   236
  Number of Houses   236
  Main Steps in Handling Bills   237
  Legislative Committees   240
  Party Organization   242

Legislative Ways of Life   243
    Party Soldiers   244
    Independent Operators   246
Representative-Constituent Relationships   249
    Mandate Theory   249
    Independence Theory   249
    American Attitudes toward Congress
    and Members of Congress   251
Changing Roles of Democratic Legislatures   252
    "Transformative" versus "Arena" Legislatures   253
    Growth as Checkers, Revisers, and Overseers   253
For Further Reading   255 / Notes   256

12   **THE EXECUTIVE PROCESS**   258
What Is an Executive?   258
    Executive as the Core of Government   258
    Two Fundamental Executive Roles   259
Executive as Chief of State   259
    Principal Types   259
    Principal Functions   261
    Separation and Mingling of Roles   263
President as Head of Government   264
    Presidents and Prime Ministers   264
    U.S. Presidential Roles   265
    Power and Problems of the U.S. President   273
    Presidency of France   275
    Other Presidencies   277
Prime Minister as Head of Government   278
    Structure of the British Executive   278
    Cabinet Status, Functions, and Powers   279
    Prime Minister and Cabinet   281
    Prime Ministers in Coalition Governments   282
Executive in Nondemocratic Systems   285
For Further Reading   285 / Notes   286

13   **THE ADMINISTRATIVE PROCESS**   288
Distinction Between Executives and Administrators   288
    In Functions   288
    In Selection and Tenure   289
    What About "Bureaucracy"?   289
Formal Status of Administrative Agencies   290
    Size   290

Structure   291
Formal Administrative Functions   293
Regulating   294
Selection and Status of Administrators   297
Politics, Administration, and Policy Making   300
Dichotomy Between Politics and Administration   300
Policy Making by Administrators   303
"Administocracy" in a Democracy: Problem and Solutions   309
The Problem: Making Administrators Responsible   309
Solutions   310
Conclusions   316
For Further Reading   317 / Notes   317

14   **LAW AND THE JUDICIAL PROCESS**   **319**
Rules People Live By   320
Moral Precepts   320
Customs   320
Laws   320
Types of Law   322
Classified by Source   322
Classified by Subject Matter   324
Court Structures in Democratic Nations   325
Special Judicial Functions   325
Two Basic Systems of Justice   327
Hierarchies of Appeal   329
Selection and Tenure of Judges   332
Official Relationships with Legislatures and Executives   335
Role of Judges in Governing   336
Mechanical View   337
Judicial Legislation   340
Judges in the Political Process   343
For Further Reading   347 / Notes   348

Part Four: Public Policies and Their Impacts

15   **HUMAN RIGHTS: PRINCIPLES AND PROBLEMS**   **349**
Philosophical Foundations for Human Rights   349
Basic Terms   349
Evolving Idea of Human Rights   350
Rights Formally Guaranteed by Constitutions   354
Limitations on Government   354
Obligations of Government   355

Choices in the Implementation of Human Rights   356
    Freedom versus Security   359
    The Rights of Some versus Rights of Others   361
Human Rights in the Political Process   364
    Human Rights Conflicts as Political Conflicts   364
    Some Consequences   365
For Further Reading   366 / Notes   366

16   HUMAN RIGHTS: CHALLENGES AND RESPONSES   367
Conflict over Police Powers and Defendants' Rights   368
    Crime and the Police   368
    Rights of Defendants   371
Conflict over the Status of Women   375
    Sexism: Meaning and Manifestations   375
    The Women's Rights Movement   378
Conflict over the Status of African-Americans   382
    Black America, Yesterday and Today   382
    A Brief History of the Civil Rights Movement   383
    African-American Rights in the 1980s:
    Antidiscrimination or Affirmative Action?   392
Apartheid in South Africa   396
    Background   396
    The Policy of Apartheid   397
    "Bantustans"   398
    The Passing of Apartheid   399
For Further Reading   402 / Notes   403

Part Five: The International Political System

17   POLITICS AMONG NATIONS   404
Nature of International Politics   405
    State System   405
    Similarities to Domestic Politics   405
    Differences from Domestic Politics   405
Characteristics of International Conflict   408
    Some Goals of Nations' Foreign Policies   410
Making Foreign Policy   415
    Choosing Goals, Methods, and Capabilities   415
    Agencies and Officials   416
    Some Methods of Foreign Policy   417
For Further Reading   427 / Notes   427

18 **THE QUEST FOR PEACE IN THE THERMONUCLEAR AGE** 428
The New World Order: Good News and Bad News   428
    Good News: The Cold War Is Over   428
    Bad News: Nuclear Weapons Are Proliferating   429
Approaches to Peace within the State System   433
    Balance of Power   434
    Collective Security   435
    Disarmament   438
    International Law   440
Approaches to Peace through the United Nations   444
    Founding   445
    Structure   445
    Maintaining International Peace and Security   448
    Changing United Nations   449
Does Humanity Have a Future?   454
For Further Reading   457 / *Notes*   458

PHOTO CREDITS   459

INDEX   460

Preface

This book is the lineal descendant of two earlier books. The older ancestor was *The Governing of Men*, which was first published in 1958 and revised in 1966, 1971, and 1975. The younger was *Governing: A Brief Introduction to Political Science*, which was first published in 1971 and revised in 1975 and 1982. *Governing* began as a shortened and rearranged version of *The Governing of Men* and consisted of thirteen of its twenty-four chapters. The present book's content and structure differ considerably from that of both of its ancestors—and with good reason. In the years since the earlier books last appeared, political events have marched at a dizzying pace, and many old truths have been replaced with new understandings, new questions, and new doubts.

The world of 1971 was the world of Nixon-Agnew, Heath, Brandt, Pompidou, and Mao Zedong (in those days we spelled it Mao Tse-tung); of detente with the Soviet Union and implacable hostility between the United States and the People's Republic of China; of the war in Vietnam and college campuses racked with protest.

The World of 1975 was a world of Ford-Rockefeller, Wilson, Schmidt, and Giscard d'Estaing; of history's first resignation by a president of the United States; of the slow start of a thaw in Chinese-American relations; of oil shortages and escalating inflation; of quiet campuses, crowded libraries, and worries about getting jobs.

The world of 1980 was a world of Carter-Mondale, Reagan-Bush, Thatcher, Brezhnev, Sadat, Begin, Indira Gandhi, and the Ayatollah Khomeini; of border wars between Vietnam, Cambodia, and China; of Bakke and battles over affirmative action; of the suspension and restoration of democracy in India, and the rise of new democracies after decades of dictatorships in Spain and Portugal.

In 1987 Reagan, Thatcher, and the Ayatollah were still in the headlines, joined by such new stars as Gorbachev, Deng Xiaoping, Mubarak, Shamir, Mulroney, and Rajiv Gandhi. The Reagan and Thatcher "revolutions" had been in place for two terms, and many believed they had permanently transformed their respective countries' politics. New regimes in the Soviet Union and the People's Republic of China seemed to offer great new possibilities. Inevitably, then, much of what concerned us most in the 1950s, 1960s, 1970s, and even the 1980s was forgotten.

In 1990 Prime Minister Thatcher, President Mitterand, and President George Bush were still leading figures. But as the decade opened, the towering figures were Mikhail Gorbachev and Boris Yeltsin. Gorbachev's efforts from 1985 to 1991 to bring *glasnost* (openness) and *perestroika* (restructuring) to the economic practices, political institutions, and foreign policies of his nation made it necessary for me to rewrite most sections of this book that deal with the republics of the former Soviet Union.

In 1992 Bill Clinton was elected as the first Democratic president since Jimmy Carter. But in the midterm congressional elections of 1994, the Republicans won control of the House of Representatives for the first time since 1954 and resumed control of the Senate, which they had held from 1980 to 1986.

The rapid pace of change in world politics has required extensive revisions in each new edition of this book, but the pace has accelerated even more since 1989, and almost every section of this edition has been changed as a result. Consider what has happened just since 1989. The Soviet Union has dissolved and been replaced by fifteen newly independent republics. Mikhail Gorbachev has returned to private life, and the big new names are the presidents of the republics, especially Boris Yeltsin of the Russian republic. The cold war between the United States and the Soviet Union, which dominated world politics from 1945 to 1989, has ended. The Eastern European nations have been freed from Soviet tutelage to go their own ways, and most of them are turning to democratic politics and free-market economies. Many other nations in Africa, Asia, and Latin America are also moving toward democracy, and even South Africa, for many decades the most extreme instance of government-imposed racial segregation and discrimination, has ended apartheid and elected its first black president, Nelson Mandela.

In sum, in the few years since the previous edition of this book, the world has seen political changes that are in many ways more widespread and profound than any considered in the previous editions. Moreover, not only have political events marched a long way, but some of the ways in which political scientists interpret and explain them have changed as well. Consequently, I have made many changes in the topics carried over from the earlier books and have added a large number of new topics. Those changes reflect not only the recent changes in political science, but also the fact that studying how people are governed in the 1990s takes place in an atmosphere very different from that of the 1960s, 1970s, or 1980s.

Politics and government, to be sure, are among the oldest and most universal of human activities and institutions. Many of the greatest minds in history have pondered their nature and possibilities and have enriched us with their reflections. But today the study of governing has acquired a new and terrible urgency. By the calendar, it was not long ago that most people—at least in the "developed" nations of the West and particularly in the United States—were confident that their political systems were the best yet devised. Perhaps they were not perfect, but they were perfectible and were fully capable of achieving humanity's highest goals of personal freedom, social justice, racial and sexual equality, and international peace. Moreover, we assumed that they constituted proper models for new and backward nations. When we spoke of "developing nations," we meant nations in the process of becoming more like ours.

Then, for a decade or more, we were not so sure. Political conflict in the United States and in every Western nation seemed to grow uglier every year. Some blacks said that our most cherished institutions—our courts, our leaders, indeed our whole political system—were nothing more than devices to perpetuate white racism. Some young people saw the Establishment as intent on forcing middle-aged, middle-class materialism and hypocrisy on a new generation seeking a better, more meaningful way of life. Others insisted that the true result of our great material wealth was not a life of richness and satisfaction for all, but a world of foul air, stinking streams, dead lakes, urban blight, and noise. And if all this were not enough, over us all, black and white, men and women, young and middle-aged alike, hovered the shadow of The Bomb and Thermonuclear World War III.

Fortunately, as we reach the mid-1990s, the big war has not happened, although the United States and its allies fought a brief war in the Persian Gulf in 1991, and smaller wars are being fought in the Middle East, Indochina, Central America, Somalia, Bosnia, and elsewhere. Physical scientists and ecologists tell us that humanity now possesses the technical means either to destroy all life on earth or to build a new life of undreamed richness. How to get people to make the right choices to achieve those goals they tell us, is a *political* problem. And so it is. For amid all the doubts and uncertainties about the future one thing is clear: The most crucial choices humanity makes will emerge from political conflict and be implemented by government action.

Most colleges and universities in the United State and an ever-growing number in other nations recognize the crucial role of politics for the human future by giving the study of politics and government a prominent place in their curricula. The study of these matters is primarily, although not exclusively, the province of departments variously called "Political Science," or "Government," or "Politics." Each such department perennially faces the pedagogical problem of introducing students to this vast, complex, and challenging subject. Two approaches are most commonly used: (1) a detailed study of U.S. government; and (2) a "principles-of-political-science" approach that seeks to identify the properties universal to the governing processes in all human societies and to understand the nature and consequences of the major variations of those processes.

I have taught an introductory undergraduate course for a number of years using the second approach. My experiences have alerted me to certain problems arising from its use, and this book, like the successive editions of its predecessors, represents my changing judgments about how best to deal with them.

During the 1950s and early 1960s, the main problem appeared to be giving students some sense of the relevance of politics and government to their own lives, and for some students it remains a problem even now. Students often begin with the belief that politics is a dirty game played by greedy people, and that government is something remote from the really important concerns of their lives. For them

I have tried to take as my point of departure situations that all students have experienced. I have tried to show how those situations affect and are affected by what happens in such apparently remote places as Washington, London, Paris, Moscow, Beijing, and even in the students' own state capitols and city halls. I have drawn illustrations from current political conflicts in an effort to emphasize the concrete activities and interrelations of real human beings that underly such abstract terms as *political culture, political socialization, separation of powers,* and the like.

Many beginning students of political science today will have no doubts that politics is highly relevant to their lives. Some may even feel that what is irrelevant is the way political science treats the subject. "Drop all this scientific pseudo-objectivity," some will say, "and talk about the evils of racism, sexism, poverty, and war, about the power structure that sustains them, and about how we can correct them." However, understanding how and why political systems work as they do to produce the policies they do is necessary for any effective effort to change those policies and make a better world. Political science is best qualified to provide such an understanding; and in a general way, that is what I have tried to do in this book.

There is one other respect in which the seventh edition of this book differs from the previous editions. I have come to agree with many of my students and colleagues that an introduction to political science should recognize that, while the discipline does and should deal with factual descriptions of how modern governments actually govern and the kinds of policies they actually make, it must also consider the great clash of ideas about how governments ideally *should* make policies. Accordingly, I have retained Chapter 4 on Modern Political Ideologies.

Like the author of any textbook, I am indebted to many colleagues and friends. I realize that whatever merit it may have owes much to their help, and I am grateful for the opportunity traditionally provided by a preface to make public my thanks to those to whom I am most deeply in debt. In addition to my general thanks to the authors of the many works cited in the text for the insights and information they have provided, I wish to make the following acknowledgments of help directly received and greatly valued: to my good friend and generous colleague, Jack W. Peltason, president of the University of California; to those colleagues, present and, sadly, departed, who cheerfully read and perceptively criticized particular chapters: Charles B. Hagan, Valentine Jobst III, Benjamin B. Johnston, Philip Monypenny, Charles M. Kneier, and Clyde F. Snider, all at the University of Illinois; to Charles S. Hyneman of Indiana University; Gillian Dean of Vanderbilt University; Joseph G. LaPalombara of Yale University; Warren E. Miller of Arizona State University; James N. Murray of the University of Iowa; Richard L. Park of the University of Michigan; Fred R. von der Mehden of Rice University; to Charles W. Anderson, Bernard C. Cohen, Jack Dennis, Leon D. Epstein, David Fellman, and M. Crawford Young, all at the University of Wisconsin at Madison; to Sigmund Neumann of Wesleyan University; and to Jeane J. Kirkpatrick of Georgetown University and the American Enterprise Institute after her tour of duty as United States Permanent Representative to the United Nations.

I am also grateful to UC Data of the University of California and its former director, Raymond E. Wolfinger, and to Karlyn Keene, managing editor of *The American Enterprise* magazine, for furnishing me with much up-to-date polling information. My cherished and greatly missed friend and mentor, the late Evron M. Kirpatrick, Executive Director Emeritus of the American Political Science Association, guided me in the early stages of the creation of this book's first ancestor and never gave up on my political education. Professor John W. Smith of the Henry Ford Community College has helped me to understand the special needs of today's students. My thanks also go to the reviewers of this edition: M. E. Melody of Barry University and Lois T. Vietri of the University of Maryland. Jennie Katsaros and Serena Hoffman have made Prentice Hall a welcoming home for the book. Finally, my thanks go to Joseph A. Ranney of the law firm of Ross and Stevens, who has given much help at various stages in the preparation of the book and in all of its stages and versions.

Austin Ranney

1

Public life is . . . the crown of a career, and to young men it is the highest ambition. Politics is still the greatest and most honorable adventure.
John Buchan, 1940

Politics are almost as exciting as war, and quite as dangerous. In war you can only be killed once, but in politics many times.
Sir Winston Churchill, 1920

A politician is an arse upon which everyone has sat except a man.
e. e. cummings, 1944

Politics in Human Life

This book is an introduction to political science, so we will begin by saying what political science is about and why people study it. **Political science** is usually defined as *the systematic study of political and governmental institutions and processes.* It is about why in 1992 American voters elected Democrat Bill Clinton over Republican incumbent George Bush president, but gave nearly 20 percent of their votes to independent Ross Perot. It is about the Republicans in 1994 winning control of both houses of Congress for the first time since 1952. It is about the disintegration of the Soviet Union after Mikhail Gorbachev's massive effort to reform its economic and political systems through *perestroika* (new thinking) and *glasnost* (openness). It is about the struggles of President Clinton and Congress to find ways of balancing the budget and providing health care for all Americans without raising taxes. It is about Iraq's invasion of Kuwait in 1990 and the "Desert Storm" war in 1991 in which a U.S.-led coalition of nations drove Iraq out of Kuwait. It is about what, if anything, the United Nations is doing to prevent World War III. Things like that.

They all begin with politics.

What Is Politics?

"POLITICS" IN EVERYDAY CONVERSATION

We all know *something* about "politics." The word and its derivatives pop up again and again in everyday conversation and reading. When a classmate tells us that "X was picked for editor of the school paper because of politics, not because she deserves it," or a university president charges that "politicians are interfering with higher education," or a newspaper columnist declares that a tax increase to balance the budget is "politically impossible," most of us think that we know what such statements mean. Indeed, we are likely to nod sagely and perhaps add a sigh for the imperfections of human nature.

Those statements offer some hints about what politics means to most of us. For one thing, it has something to do with distributing desirable things in scarce supply, with deciding who gets the lion's share and who gets the mouse's. For another, it operates not only in "the government" but in private groups as well (for example, in a school paper as well as in Congress). And it often suggests selfish squabbling for private gain rather than enlightened cooperation for the common good.

There is no doubt that as a group politicians have a poor reputation. Gallup polls have shown that the only kinds of people who are thought to have even lower ethical standards than politicians are insurance salespeople, labor union leaders, advertisers, and car salespeople. Only 22 percent of Americans would like to see their sons go into politics as a life's work.[1] Roget's *Thesaurus* lists such unflattering synonyms for *politician* as *grafter, spoilsmonger, influence peddler, wheeler-dealer, finagler,* and *wire-puller.*[2] When asked what they want to be when they grow up, very few children reply, "a politician."

On the other hand, while most people look down on "politicians," they admire "statesmen." The only trouble is that many can never agree on which public figures deserve which label. To some, for example, Franklin D. Roosevelt was a "great statesman," but to others he was a "lying politician." Similar disagreements have existed about almost every other president from John Adams to Bill Clinton. (Only George Washington seems to have had nearly unanimous approval, and even he lost some ground toward the end of his career.)

Some observers suspect that for most people a statesman is simply a government leader they like and a politician is one they dislike. This suspicion has led some commentators to say that "a statesman is a dead politician"; others declare that "a statesman is a politician held upright by pressures from all sides." It has also inclined most political scientists to use the terms *politics* and *politicians* in the more neutral senses we will use in this book.

POLITICS AS POLICY MAKING

In its broadest sense, politics includes the decision-making and decision-enforcing processes in any group that makes and enforces rules for its members. Several political scientists have studied those processes in nongovernmental groups such as labor unions, business corporations, and medical associations. However, most political scientists have concentrated on the processes of governments rather than on those of private associations. It therefore seems desirable to use the same focus in an introduction to political science.

As the word will be used in this book, accordingly, **politics** is *the process of making government policies.* Let us see just what is involved in this definition.

When government officials are called upon to take some course of action (or inaction) on a particular matter, they are always faced with a number of alternatives they *might* pursue. They cannot, however, pursue all the alternatives simultaneously, if only because some would cancel out others. They have to select from among the alternatives available the few that they intend to put into effect. The courses of action thus chosen become government *policies*. The process by which policy makers choose which actions they will and will not take is, according to our definition, politics.

There are countless illustrations of the point, but let us take just one that has been much in the headlines since the 1970s: U.S. policy toward acid rain. Environmental scientists generally agree that many power plants and industrial factories in the Midwest that depend mainly on burning coal to power their operations emit large amounts of sulphur, which then joins with water vapor in the air to form rain clouds with a high acid content. The prevailing winds carry those clouds over the northeastern states and the southeastern Canadian provinces. When it rains, the acid rain in the rainwater does great damage to forests, fields, rivers, and lakes. Farmers, fishers, and nature lovers in both countries complain that acid rain is ruining their businesses and vacations, and they demand that something be done about it.

The experts on the staffs of Congress and the Environmental Protection Agency (EPA) have suggested several different solutions. One is to require all factories and power plants to install "smoke scrubbers," devices in smokestacks that significantly reduce the amount of sulphur dioxide they discharge. However, the scrubbers are extremely expensive, and many factory owners and unions complain that installing the scrubbers would drive them out of business and thus greatly increase unemployment in the Midwest. Another alternative solution is to require the factories to burn only low-sulphur coal, which is produced mainly in the West. This will increase profits for western mines and jobs for western miners, but it will increase factory costs and also hurt mine profits and jobs in the East. A third alternative solution is to require factories to burn low-sulphur coal, install scrubbers, and pay the increased costs by imposing higher taxes on the utilities. The utilities will pass the cost to the consumer. This solution will please the environmentalists, because it is most likely to control acid rain, but it will not please utility customers. A fourth alternative solution is to encourage the building and use of nuclear power plants, which do not cause acid rain. However, many environmentalists believe that nuclear power generates other highly toxic wastes and creates the ever-present danger of radioactive poisoning from meltdowns.

Clearly, the U.S. government cannot solve the acid rain problem in a way that will satisfy every person and interest involved. If the government requires the factories to install scrubbers and burn only low-sulphur coal, it will end up pleasing the environmentalists, the Canadians, and the western coal miners. However, midwestern factory production costs will significantly increase, making the factories less competitive in international markets where other nations are less concerned with fighting air pollution. Unemployment will rise among midwestern factory workers and eastern miners of high-sulphur coal. If the government eases the burden on the factory owners by increasing their government subsidies, consumers' power bills will increase. If the government encourages nuclear power, the owners and workers in the nuclear industry and Canadian farmers and fishers will be pleased, but American environmentalists and miners in both the West and East will be angered.

In short, the political process by which the United States grapples with the problem of acid rain is like all other political processes. Some legitimate interests clash with other legitimate interests, some people are bound to be hurt if others are helped, and whatever policy is adopted inevitably creates some losers as well as some winners.

Thus, in the United States, as in every country in the world, whether it be a democracy or a dictatorship, every benefit in politics has its costs. Each of the world's countries has its own special ways of conducting politics. Yet, there are some respects in which politics in all countries are essentially the same.

Some Universal Characteristics of Politics —————

POLITICS IS CONFLICT

Politics, as we use the term in this book, is the process of making government policies (or *public policies*, which is another way of saying government policies). But what is the process like? What are its main characteristics? One is that politics everywhere involves **conflict**—that is, *some form of struggle among people trying to achieve different goals and satisfy opposing interests*. A basic, though perhaps painful, first step toward understanding the governing process is thus to face the fact that political conflict is not an unfortunate and temporary aberration from the normal state of perfect cooperation and harmony. Conflict arises from the very nature of human life itself.

Conflict in Human Life

One basic fact of human life is that people live together and not in isolation from one another. Social scientists generally call the largest unit in which people live together a **society**; that is, *a group of people living in a common environment and having common traditions, institutions, activities, and interests*. When we reflect upon our lives and try to understand what has happened to us, we realize that our stories must be told largely in terms of our relationships with other people: parents and teachers, boyfriends and girlfriends, supporters and opponents, bosses and dependents. To be human is to interact with—to affect and to be affected by—other human beings every day of our lives. And to interact with others is, to some extent at least, to be in conflict with them. Why?

Although all people are alike in certain respects, no person is exactly like any other in every respect. One of the most significant ways in which people differ from one another is in the values that each holds. A **value**, as the term is used here, is *an object or situation deemed to be of intrinsic worth, something to be esteemed and sought*. It is something one thinks is important and desirable, whether it be a Mercedes-Benz, passing grades, social prestige, peace of mind, or a brave new world. Social scientists agree that different people have different values and that every person acts in some way to realize some of his or her values. Wherever people come into contact with each other, their values are bound to conflict to some degree. In a world of limited resources, to the extent that some values are satisfied, other values must go unsatisfied. For example, if taxes are increased to support higher welfare payments, some taxpayers will be unhappy. If affirmative action programs give preference for certain jobs to African-Americans and women, some white males will be unhappy. Accordingly, we all find that to some extent we are in competition with our fellow human beings. As we live our daily lives and try to enter the college of our choice, study what interests us, and then find a good job, we discover that others also want those good things and that not everyone has equal success in getting them. That is true of even our most lofty aims: We all want a better, more just world, but we do not all agree on the best way to achieve it. We all strive to achieve our goals in many ways. We work and rest, study and practice, speak and demonstrate, vote and not vote, tell the truth and lie, obey the rules and break them. However, we strive in competition with others who pursue different goals or the same goals in different ways. Conflict, then, is an essential and inescapable consequence of the fact that people live together in societies and not in isolation from one another.

Political Conflict in Society

Wherever people live together in a society, most of them feel that some values can be fully satisfied only by rules that bind everyone in the society. For example, most Americans who believe that racial segregation in public schools must be ended will not be satisfied with the tokenism of entering a few African-American children in unsegregated schools while all others are forced to attend all-black schools. They demand that any African-American child whose parents wish him or her to attend an unsegregated school must be allowed to do so, and they will settle for nothing less, even if it means busing some children to schools distant from their homes. In other words, those people have a **political interest**, which is *something of value to a person or group to be gained or lost by what government does or does not do.*

In most societies, then, most people regard government action as the best way to obtain authoritative and binding rules. Conflict over what the rules should be is thus, according to our definition, *political* conflict. To be sure, many conflicts in any society are fought outside the political arena, in such other areas of life as economics, academics, sports, and marriage. The point is that no society—traditional or modern, more advanced or less advanced, democratic or authoritarian—is entirely without political conflict. And in modern societies most conflicts over values sooner or later, for good or ill, become political conflicts.

GROUP CONFLICT IN POLITICS

Many political scientists emphasize a second universal characteristic of politics: the fact that the antagonists are rarely isolated individuals acting without reference to or support from other people. In most conflicts, a number of people on both sides feel that they have a stake in the outcome and join forces with others who feel the same way. Most political conflict is thus best seen as conflict among groups rather than among individuals. For example, the contest among Jerry Brown, Bill Clinton, Tom Harkin, Bob Kerrey, and Paul Tsongas for the Democratic party's presidential nomination in 1992 was much more than a contest among those five men alone.

DOCTORS VERSUS LAWYERS

Physicians and lawyers are among the best-educated, most-respected, and highest-paid professionals in the United States. It is therefore especially unsettling to learn that in the 1990s physicians and lawyers are locked in a tough political struggle with each other over the issue of medical malpractice lawsuits. Under 1992 malpractice laws of most states, if patients believe that their physician's actions or inactions in treatment have made their physical condition worse rather than better, they can sue the physician for damages in personal injury suits. If the patients' lawyers can use the testimony of expert witnesses and other evidence to convince juries that the physicians' treatments indeed failed to meet accepted standards of sound medical practice, then the juries are likely to award large damages, often amounting to several hundred thousand dollars. Moreover, the patients need not assume all the legal costs. Lawyers usually take such cases on a contingency-fee basis; that is, if the lawyer wins the case, then he or she will be paid an agreed percentage of the jury's award (usually one third and sometimes more). If the lawyer loses the case, there is no charge.

To protect themselves against financial disaster, physicians take out malpractice insurance, with annual premiums now running as high as $100,000 for such high-risk specialists as obstetricians and neurosurgeons.

In recent years the number of malpractice suits has increased, the damages awarded by juries have soared, and the annual premiums for malpractice insurance have nearly doubled. As a result, the American Medical Association has mounted a major campaign to induce state legislatures to put ceilings on the amounts juries can award, reduce attorneys' fees, and set up arbitration procedures for such suits.

The lawyers have not been quiet in the face of the physicians' move. The Association of Trial Lawyers of America (ATLA) has launched a strong countercampaign to block it. ATLA argues that physicians, like lawyers or any other professionals, should be held accountable for the damage they do by slipshod professional behavior. "There is no medical malpractice insurance crisis," ATLA leaders say. "The cause of medical malpractice legislation is medical negligence." And bumper stickers on physicians' cars retort, "Feeling sick? See a lawyer" and "Help support a lawyer. Send your daughter to medical school."

High levels of education, skill, and prestige, it seems, do not keep our top professionals out of political conflict.

Each was supported, opposed, and influenced by certain labor unions, ethnic groups, and business associations and also by majorities of such unorganized but potent groups as African-Americans, whites, women, the middle class, workers, "yuppies" (young urban professionals), and retired people. To describe the contest solely in terms of what the five individuals said and did would present only a partial and misleading picture. For another example, the bitter fights in a number of U.S. metropolitan areas over whether suburban white children should be bused to predominantly African-American inner-city schools and African-American inner-city children bused to predominantly white suburban schools to achieve racial balance have involved not only the children, parents, and school officials directly concerned but also many national pressure groups, both national political parties, and ultimately the president, Congress, and the Supreme Court of the United States.

Defendants in murder trials may appear at first glance to have no group support or interest behind them. Certainly the standard title of such a trial—*The People of the State of New York* versus *John Doe*—seems to suggest that the contest is taking place between Mr. Doe on the one hand and everyone else in New York on the other.

POLITICIANS DEAL WITH PEOPLE IN GROUPS. Senator Dianne Feinstein (D-CA) greets constituents.

If so, it is a highly unequal contest, and Mr. Doe would appear to have absolutely no chance of winning. The fact is, however, that he has considerable support from others. For example, many people in the community believe that every person accused of a crime should be given a fair trial. As a result the state constitution contains such protections as the guarantee of a lawyer paid for by the state if Mr. Doe cannot afford to hire one himself, the power to subpoena witnesses, and the right to prevent persons who are prejudiced against him from serving on his jury. Neither Mr. Doe nor any other person engaged in political or governmental conflict is entirely alone.

Politics, then, is the conflict among individuals and groups over the formation of public policy. Let us now consider the different kinds of groups that participate in politics.

Categoric Groups

A **categoric group** (or social stratum, as some call it), is *a number of individuals sharing one or more common characteristics* (for example, people under twenty-one years of age, people earning more than $5,000 a year, residents of Illinois, tool-and-die makers, blondes, tight ends). The individuals in any particular categoric group may or may not be conscious of their common characteristics and may regard those characteristics as important and direct their behavior accordingly. Few brown-eyed people, for example, feel strong bonds with other brown-eyed people or are acutely aware of a wide gulf between their interests and the interests of blue-eyed people and thus are not likely to unite with other brown-eyed people to advance the cause of brown-eyedness against the blue-eyed peril. Most African-Americans, on the other hand, are well aware of their differences from whites and have formed organizations to improve their condition. Any particular categoric group thus may or may not be socially or politically significant.

Pressure Groups

Political scientists often speak of a person's or a group's *political interest* in a matter, meaning, as we have seen, the stake of that person or group in what government does or fails to do. When people take action to protect or advance a common interest, they become a social force that has to be reckoned with. When one of their main activities is trying to induce government to do something they want or refrain from doing something they do not want, they become the kind of group on which we will concentrate in this book: a **pressure group**; that is, *an organized interest group that acts to achieve some of its goals by influencing government officials and policies.*

TACTICS OF POLITICAL ACTION

Politics, then, is a many-sided conflict among individuals and groups acting to get government to help them or keep government from doing harm. Political action is never easy. The stakes are high, the opposition is tough, and each competitor has to decide what combination of the following main tactics is most likely to bring suc-

POLITICS IS CONFLICT AMONG GROUPS. Confrontation between pro-life and pro-choice activists

cess: lobbying, working inside political parties, mass propaganda, litigation, demonstrations, strikes and boycotts, nonviolent civil disobedience, and violence.

Lobbying

Many legislative chambers have adjoining rooms, called "lobbies," in which legislators and their guests meet and talk. From this practice has emerged the term **lobbying**, which means *direct efforts by representatives of pressure groups to influence public officials to act as the groups wish*. Legislators are the main targets of lobbying, but executives, administrators, and even judges are also frequently approached.

The first prerequisite for successful lobbying is **access**, which is *the ability to get a hearing from government authorities*. Any group that cannot get a serious hearing from even one public official can hardly expect much success. A group's access depends on several things: for instance, its general prestige and social position and the reputation and skill of its lobbyists. For example, a Roman Catholic cardinal is more likely than a representative of the Jehovah's Witnesses to have access to committees of the Massachusetts legislature. A lobbyist whom the legislators have long known as reasonable, knowledgeable, and trustworthy is more likely to get a hearing than is one who is thought to be too aggressive, too careless with the facts, or too likely to talk out of turn.

After lobbyists gain access to one or more government authorities, they can use various techniques of persuasion. They can make a formal presentation of their group's position, marshaling facts, figures, and arguments to show it in the most favorable light; they can threaten an elected official with defeat at the next election and reinforce the threat by stimulating a flood of telegrams, postcards, and letters from the official's constituents; they can offer to trade their group's support of some pet project of the official's for her support of their proposal; and they can even offer bribes, either directly, in the form of cash, or indirectly, in the form of promises of well-paid jobs in private industry after the official has retired from office. In most modern nations, however, bribery has become so generally disapproved, so hard to keep secret, and so dangerous that it is used far less frequently today than it was a century ago. Even in Italy, where for decades bribery of public officials by interest groups had been an accepted way of life, public outrage grew to the point where, in the 1993 general election, the voters threw out hundreds of officeholders and replaced them with newcomers.

In most modern countries campaign contributions to candidates and parties are much better. They are legal, all parties and elected officials have to have them, and elections are held frequently.

Working inside Political Parties

Lobbying is likely to be far more successful with favorably predisposed public officials than with those who are indifferent or hostile. And since political parties nominate most candidates for public office and thereby largely determine what people holding what views occupy the key positions, no major pressure group can afford to ignore the operations of the important parties. In Great Britain and in most

AARP: A LOBBYING POWERHOUSE

One of the hottest U.S. legislative contests in recent years was the 1994 struggle in Congress over various proposals for implementing (or deflecting) President Clinton's ambitious plans for reforming the U.S. health care system. Many commentators on that struggle said that one of its most critical events was the August announcement of the American Association of Retired Persons (AARP) that it would campaign vigorously for the Democratic proposals in both houses.

The AARP is arguably the best-organized interest group and the most powerful lobby in U.S. politics. The organization was founded in 1958, and by 1994 had enrolled more than 33 million dues-paying members, far more than other organizations claiming to speak for the elderly, such as the National Council of Senior Citizens (5 million members).

The AARP provides many services for its members, such as health tips, tax tips, group insurance plans, travel programs, and low-cost pharmacy service. But it is best known for the skilled and successful lobbying by its political arm, AARP/Vote. The organization focuses mainly on government programs benefiting the elderly, such as social security, medicare, funding of research on Alzheimer's disease, and (in 1994) universal health care coverage—and, equally, to blocking efforts to lower the benefits of such government programs. It has won many victories and minimized most losses—a record that has led some political scientists to say that AARP is the most powerful lobbying organization in the United States.

Only a few counterpart organizations purport to speak for the interests of young people, and those few have nothing remotely approaching AARP's numbers or political clout.

European democracies, most pressure groups are closely associated with particular parties and make little effort to influence the policies, candidates, and officeholders of opposing parties. In the United States, however, the relatively loose and undisciplined nature of the Democratic and Republican parties has tended to keep the major interest groups from completely identifying themselves with either party. Rather, they have tried to secure the nomination of sympathetic candidates and the adoption of favorable planks in the platforms of *both* parties.

However, no pressure group can "deliver" the votes of *all* its members to any particular candidate or party. There are many illustrations of this rule, but one of the most striking comes from the late twentieth-century electoral failures of the British Labour party. That party was founded in 1900 as an alliance between labor unions and socialist intellectuals and has always proclaimed itself to be the party of the workers, standing for worker interests against the interests of the landowners and business executives who control the Conservative party. Most of Britain's labor unions are integrated into the Labour party. They are formally affiliated with the party and they provide most of the money that finances the party's operations. Moreover, part of the union dues of every member of the affiliated unions goes directly into the Labour party's treasury unless the member specifically requests otherwise. Surely, then, the overwhelming majority of the union members should always vote for the Labour party and shun the Conservatives. But they do not. Studies of British voters show that in general elections during the 1980s and 1990s only slightly over one-third of union members and their families have voted for

Labour while almost as many have voted for the Conservatives![3] The same can be said of almost every other pressure group that publicly supports particular parties and candidates. They can give the orders and sound the charge, but they can never get all of their troops to fall in line.

Mass Propaganda

Lobbying and working inside political parties are tactics intended mainly to persuade political insiders, such as elected officials, bureaucrats, and party leaders. In the nineteenth century, most pressure groups in most democratic countries concentrated on the inside game and paid little or no attention to mass opinion. In the 1990s, however, the opinions of the general public—whether they are pro, con, or don't know—have a powerful influence on the success of all political groups.

Most modern pressure groups are well aware of this. Consequently, they cultivate mass public opinion through public relations operations and spend millions of dollars every year to create favorable climates of opinion for their political objectives. We are all familiar, for example, with the institutional advertising of organizations such as the Mobil Oil Company, whose full-page newspaper and magazine advertisements are not intended to sell Mobil gasoline and oil products but rather are meant to promote the political ideology of laissez faire (see Chapter 4). Similarly, both unions and employers often use full-page newspaper advertisements to plead their causes during strikes.

The old-fashioned lobbyist and "wire-puller" have thus been joined, and in many instances superseded, by the modern public relations counsel.

NEW TECHNOLOGY MAKES NEW POLITICS. Richard Viguerie, whose organization raises millions for conservative causes by using computerized direct-mail solicitations.

Litigation

Litigation is *the process of conducting a lawsuit*, in which one person or group, called the plaintiff, asks a court of law to order another person or group, called the defendant, to do something or to stop doing something. In the United States far more than in most other nations, filing such suits has long been a favorite tactic for pressure groups, particularly those having little success with the executive, legislative, or administrative agencies and the general public.

One prime example has been the movement for equal rights for African-Americans since World War II. Essentially the story is this: For decades before the 1960s, the National Association for the Advancement of Colored People (NAACP) and other civil rights groups had little success in persuading Congress to pass laws prohibiting racial segregation and discrimination in education, employment, access to public facilities, and other matters. So the NAACP adopted a new tactic of bringing suits against school boards, employers, managers of theaters, and other defendants, charging that the rules against African-Americans' using the same facilities as whites were violations of the provision in the U.S. Constitution guaranteeing every citizen "the equal protection of the laws." The civil rights groups won a tremendous victory when the U.S. Supreme Court, in the 1954 case of *Brown* v. *Board of Education*, ruled that racial segregation in public schools is unconstitutional. They subsequently won many other victories in both Congress and the administrative agencies, but litigation in the courts brought the first great breakthrough.

Many other American interest groups use litigation as a prime tactic. Environmental groups sue electric power companies to prevent the operation of nuclear power plants. Women's groups sue employers for sexual discrimination in hiring and promotion. Gay and lesbian groups sue school boards for dismissing teachers who are homosexuals. Disgruntled state parties sue their national committees for unfairly allocating votes in national nominating conventions. And so on.

Some observers believe that the high volume of political litigation is a serious threat to U.S. democracy and argue that it gives the final word in too many political conflicts to courts and judges, who are appointed for life and are therefore not accountable, as elected legislators and executives are, for their actions. Whatever may be the rights and wrongs of the matter, however, the fact is that in the United States litigation has become—and is likely to remain—one of the most effective and widely used of all the tactics employed by pressure groups.

Demonstrations

For many years some pressure groups, especially those known as "protest groups," have relied heavily upon the tactics of demonstrations, such as picketing, mass marching, chanting slogans, heckling opponents, blocking roads, and occupying public buildings. In the late 1960s and early 1970s, for example, college students protesting the Vietnam War disrupted classes, occupied classrooms and laboratories, staged mass walkouts at graduation ceremonies, and howled down speakers who tried to defend the government's policies. In 1990–1991 protesters

A LITIGIOUS SOCIETY

Several foreign commentators on American politics have been struck by the *litigiousness* of Americans—their tendency to file lawsuits against public officials and other persons for alleged violations of their rights. They note that the United States has far more lawyers per capita than any other country (for example, one lawyer for every 440 Americans as compared with one lawyer for every 10,000 people in Japan). Some note the comments of Arthur Burns, the economist and former chairman of the Federal Reserve Board, that the U.S. economy would be a lot better off if more talented young Americans went into business and fewer went into law. On the other hand, many lawyers say that the basic reason for their large numbers is the predilection of ordinary Americans for using lawsuits to preserve their rights and remedy their grievances.

---

against the war in the Persian Gulf blocked streets, bridges, and government buildings in a number of U.S. cities. Similar methods have been used by groups with quite different political goals: In the United States, civil rights groups have used freedom marches, white-supremacy groups have used "white power" marches, and both pro-life and pro-choice groups have picketed Congress and the Supreme Court. In Great Britain and West Germany, thousands marched in protests against the placement of U.S. nuclear missile bases in their countries. In the United States and many European countries, environmental groups and "green parties" staged sit-downs and blockades to protest the building and operation of nuclear power plants. In the People's Republic of China (PRC), many thousands of students and sympathizers demonstrated for democracy in Beijing's Tiananmen Square until they were ruthlessly crushed by government troops.

Despite the widely different political objectives for which they have been mounted, demonstrations have the same traits as a tactic of political action. First, demonstrations involve direct and active participation by group members, which is quite different from the more indirect and passive participation involved in paying dues and signing petitions. Group members who demonstrate often have emotionally stirring experiences that intensify their devotion to group goals, and the leaders thereby gain a more dedicated and effective group of followers. Second, demonstrations sometimes provoke overreactions from opposing groups and from the police, which may arouse sympathy for the group from outsiders who care little about the group's issues but dislike anything that smacks of repression or brutality. Third, most demonstrations are planned to attract public attention, and many succeed by getting exposure on television. Television broadcasters, to be sure, charge far more than protest groups can afford for broadcasting advertisements presenting the groups' views. However, broadcasters often find in a rousing demonstration just the kind of exciting visual material that gets the attention of their viewers and often give the demonstrators coverage on prime-time newscasts without charging a penny.

Because of their low cost and their power to raise group morale, arouse sympathy, and attract free publicity, demonstrations are widely used, especially by protest groups.

Strikes and Boycotts

The term *strike* usually means a collective work stoppage by industrial workers for economic goals, but strikes can also be used for political purposes. In the United States most strikes are conducted for such nonpolitical objectives as forcing employers to grant higher wages, shorter hours, better working conditions, job security, and union recognition. In many European democracies, on the other hand, strikes are sometimes used for political purposes, such as forcing the government to adopt or reject certain policies or even sparking a revolution. In France, for example, the Communist-dominated CGT labor organization has called a number of strikes since 1945 for the avowed purpose of preventing the French government from participating in such anti-Communist organizations as the Marshall Plan, the European Defense Community, and the North Atlantic Treaty Organization. In some nations—for example, Panama and South Korea in 1988—general strikes have been used in efforts to drive certain public officials, and sometimes whole governments, out of power.

A less familiar variation is the "speedup" strikes that government employees (who are usually prohibited from striking) sometimes conduct. Customs inspectors, for example, enforce to the letter every last law and regulation, carefully inspect every piece of every tourist's luggage, and make tourists so irate that they take their business to other countries. Postal workers, for another example, follow to the letter (so to speak) every rule for inspecting the interior of every mailbag to make sure that it has been emptied of letters, and hand inspect each letter to make sure that it has the proper postage and return address. This can delay mail delivery by many days. In such cases it is ironic but true that paying government workers more money is the only way government leaders can get the workers to stop doing everything the law requires!

A *boycott* is a concerted refusal by a group to deal with another private group or public agency to achieve an economic or political goal. A historic U.S. political boycott began in 1955 in Montgomery, Alabama, when Rosa Parks, in protest against the city's laws requiring racially segregated seating on public transportation, refused to give up her seat on a bus to a white man and move to the back. This refusal touched off a general boycott of the Montgomery bus system by African-Americans, organized and led by Dr. Martin Luther King, Jr. The bus system found that it could not survive without its African-American patrons, and eventually the city repealed its segregated seating laws.

Nonviolent Civil Disobedience

In his leadership of the movement for Indian independence from British rule in the 1930s and 1940s, Mohandas K. ("Mahatma") Gandhi developed a technique for political action that has had a major impact on the Western world. He called it *satyagraha*. Its Western version is **nonviolent civil disobedience**, which is *the refusal to obey certain laws or government orders for the purpose of influencing government policy*. Its leading American theorist and practitioner was Dr. King, and during the early 1960s it provided a philosophy and guided a tactic for much of the U.S. civil rights movement.

Civil disobedience, as Gandhi and King practiced and preached it, requires a protest group first to explore all the possibilities for negotiation and arbitration with its opponents and with the government. If that fails, then the group issues an ultimatum explaining exactly what it will do next and why. The group then employs various tactics to make things inconvenient for its opponents without using violence. The tactics include economic boycotts and noncooperation with government authorities (such as refusal to pay taxes or send children to school) and peaceful disobedience of some laws (for example, traffic regulations or prohibitions against blocking streets). A tactic familiar to television viewers in many nations is what Gandhi called *dharna*, which is sitting down in streets, corridors of public buildings, airport runways, and other public channels of movement. When the authorities enforce the laws by arresting and imprisoning members of the group, they must not resist so that they can, in Dr. King's words, "testify with their bodies" to the justice of their cause. The ultimate objective is not only to win support from neutral outsiders but eventually also to convert the opponents themselves.

The tactics of civil disobedience have scored many impressive victories: for instance, the winning of Indian independence from Great Britain in 1947. And there is no doubt that in the 1960s television's gripping pictures of the contrast between the African-Americans' peaceful demonstrations for their rights and the often brutal measures of repression taken by southern sheriffs and police touched the hearts of many previously apathetic northern whites and won their wholehearted support for the African-American cause.

Violence

Abraham Lincoln, the sixteenth president of the United States, was shot and killed in 1865. Since Lincoln's assassination, serious attempts have been made on the lives of seven presidents—almost one third—and three have succeeded. President James Garfield was killed in 1881. President William McKinley was killed in 1901. Former president Theodore Roosevelt was shot while campaigning for re-election in 1912 but survived. After his election in 1932, president-elect Franklin Roosevelt was shot at and missed, but a bullet intended for Roosevelt killed Mayor Anton Cermak of Chicago. In 1963 President John Kennedy was killed. In 1975 there were two attempts on the life of President Gerald Ford, both unsuccessful. And in 1981 President Ronald Reagan was shot and wounded, but he recovered.

Those presidents constitute only a fraction of the prominent U.S. political figures killed or wounded in the line of duty. For instance, in 1968, Dr. King, Nobel Peace Prize laureate and apostle of nonviolent civil disobedience, was shot and killed. The shock of the assassination touched off a wave of rioting and looting in more than 125 cities in 29 states across the nation. Within a week at least 46 people were killed, more than 2,600 injured, and more than 21,000 arrested. Two months later Senator Robert Kennedy was killed. In 1972, Alabama governor George C. Wallace was shot and crippled for life while campaigning for the Democratic presidential nomination.

The King and Kennedy assassinations led President Lyndon Johnson in 1968 to appoint the National Commission on the Causes and Prevention of Violence. The

POLITICAL ACTION BY CIVIL DISOBEDIENCE. Demonstrators protesting slow progress in research on AIDS.

reports it commissioned constitute the most thorough study yet made of the role of violence in U.S. politics.

The commission stressed two main points that we would do well to heed today. First, violence—the use of physical force to eliminate or terrorize political opposition—is not a new phenomenon in American life, nor is it caused by some national sickness peculiar to our time. It is, as African-American militant H. Rap Brown correctly said, "as American as cherry pie." The United States was born in a violent revolution against Great Britain. Although we have had only one full-scale civil war, it was the bloodiest war in our history; indeed, almost as many Americans were killed in the 1861–1865 war as in all of our foreign wars put together. Much of our continental territory was violently taken from its native inhabitants. Vigilante actions, in which private citizens execute suspected criminals without benefit of legal authority or procedures, first occurred in the 1760s and have recurred many times since. In our own time, the white-supremacy violence of the Ku Klux Klan is countered by the violence of African-American urban rioters, and some opponents of abortion have attacked abortion clinics with fire bombs and even murdered doctors who performed abortions. To all this private political violence we must add the violence, ranging from night sticks to atomic weapons, sometimes used by such government agencies as the police and armed forces to carry out our domestic and foreign policies.

It is quite a record. Yet, the second point stressed by the research is that the United States has no monopoly on either political or nonpolitical violence. For example, in recent years a number of leaders of other countries have been killed, including the presidents of Liberia and Lebanon, Indian Prime Minister Indira Gandhi and her son Rajiv Gandhi, and Swedish Premier Olof Palme. During Peru's election in 1990 three of the five presidential candidates were assassinated. In India's 1991 election campaign a thousand people were killed. In 1994 the leading candidate for the Mexican presidency, Luis Donaldo Colosa Murriata, was assassinated. In 1981 even Pope John Paul II was shot and wounded, but he recovered. As sociologist Charles Tilly puts it, "As comforting as it is for civilized people to think of barbarians as violent and of violence as barbarian, Western civilization and various forms of collective violence have always been close partners."[4] Terrorism, riots, rebellions, coups d'état, violent strikes and strike breaking, sabotage, assassinations, kidnapping, airplane and ship hijacking, massacres of airport patrons, and other forms of violence have been used frequently by many political groups in many parts of the world to try to bring about, or to prevent, social and political change.

Any group's decision of whether or not to use violence involves several questions. Is it right to use violence in *any* circumstance? Pacifists say no, but many political groups say yes. What political price must be paid for using violence? There are many possibilities: little or no price; losing present or potential allies in other groups; alienating the less militant members of one's own group; triggering counterviolence by opposing groups; touching off government repression; and injury and death to innocent people. Will the members regard anything less than violence as knuckling under to the authorities? Finally, are violent tactics more likely than nonviolent ones to achieve the group's goals?

To the extent that a political group's main purpose is to influence government policy—as distinguished from satisfying its members' psychic hungers—this last question seems the most important to be considered in deciding whether or not to use violence. However, it is all too clear that few political groups totally reject violence as a tactic never to be used in any circumstance.

WHO USES WHICH TACTICS?

It is clear, then, that those who want to put pressure on government to do the things they want or to refrain from doing the things they don't want have a wide range of tactics they can use. Which ones are used most? The answer, at least for people in four advanced/industrial democracies as of 1981, is given in Table 1.1.

The figures in Table 1.1 show some interesting differences among the four nations. For example, the British are the least likely and the French are most likely to participate in strikes, and Americans are more likely than the others to try to join

TABLE 1.1   Self-Reported Modes of Political Participation, 1990–1991 (in percentages)

	UNITED STATES	GREAT BRITAIN	GERMANY	FRANCE
Voting				
Voted in last election	53	77	78	69
Campaign Activity				
Tried to persuade someone on vote	38	7	3	8
Attended public meeting	8	1	7	3
Communal Activity				
Signed petition	70	75	55	51
Member of a citizen group	18	11	11	8
Protest Activity				
Engaged in one challenging action	25	25	23	36
Participated in lawful demonstrations	15	13	20	31
Joined in boycott	17	14	9	11
Participated in unofficial strike	4	8	2	9
Occupied building	2	2	1	7

Source: Russell J. Dalton, *Citizen Politics in Western Democracies*, 2d ed. (Chatham, NJ: Chatham House, 1995), Chaps. 3–4.

citizen groups and try to persuade other Americans to vote. However, the principal message of Table 1.1 is that in all four nations the great majority of the people depend mainly on the peaceful and personally undemanding political actions of voting and signing petitions.

Some Characteristics of Political Conflict

Political conflict in every human society displays to some degree the following main characteristics: multiplicity, opposition, overlapping memberships, and imperfect mobilization.

MULTIPLICITY

Every distinction among human beings—whether based on race, gender, religion, age, occupation, educational level, or anything else—generates categoric groups, some of which become political interest groups. The more complex the society, the more distinctions there are among its members, and the more likely the society is to contain large numbers of political interest groups. Each of the highly complex societies on which political scientists focus contains more categoric groups than we can ever count, let alone describe here. But we can at least get some hint of their multiplicity by listing a few of the political cleavages that are most prominent and persistent in all advanced/industrialized nations:

Economic class: rich versus poor; workers versus owners; government employees versus taxpayers.

Occupation: farmers versus industrial workers and owners; some businesses (e.g., buses, newspapers) versus other businesses (e.g., airlines, television); physicians versus lawyers; physicians versus chiropractors and faith healers.

Gender: women versus men.

Ethnicity: blacks versus whites; Hispanics versus Anglos; blacks versus Asians; Flemings versus Walloons (Belgium); Irish versus English (Northern Ireland); Scots and Welsh versus English (United Kingdom); Armenians and Ukrainians versus Russians (Soviet Union); Serbs versus Croats (Yugoslavia); Hutus versus Tutsis (Rwanda).

Religion: Catholics versus Protestants; Baptists versus Congregationalists; Christians versus Jews; Jews versus Muslims; Muslims versus Hindus; Shi'ite Muslims versus Sunni Muslims.

Morality: pro-life versus pro-choice; antipornographers versus libertarians; "straights" versus gays and lesbians.

Ideology: Communists and socialists versus capitalists; Communists versus socialists; liberals versus conservatives; democrats versus authoritarians.

Quality of life: conservationists versus developers; smokers versus nonsmokers; public transportation versus private automobiles.

In addition, of course, there are cleavages in international politics (we will consider them in Chapters 17 and 18) between nation and nation (e.g., the United States versus Iraq, Great Britain versus Argentina, Israel versus Syria), between alliances and blocs (e.g., East versus West, the "Third World" versus the advanced/industrialized nations), and so on.

Hence, if politics is a contest among political interest groups, then every modern industrialized nation has an almost infinite number of active and potential contestants.

OPPOSITION

Every political interest group has opposition; that is, some group or combination of groups seeking conflicting goals. No proposal for public policy therefore ever enlists all the members of society in its support. The closest a nation comes to unanimity is usually in time of war when the overwhelming majority of its citizens unite behind a win-the-war policy. Even then, however, there is opposition from pacifists, who oppose all war measures, opposition from people who oppose the particular war (no one who lived through the war in Vietnam can doubt that), and even opposition from people who want the enemy to win. So, if even wartime does not produce political unanimity in a nation, we can be sure that every political group encounters some opposition in its efforts to induce the government to adopt the policies it wants.

There are many variations in the kind of opposition that particular groups encounter in particular situations. Opposing groups may be organized or unorganized, large or small, powerful or weak, and so on. The degree of hostility between opposing groups ranges all the way from the mild disagreement between groups favoring and opposing free mail service for members of Congress to the bitter and violent disagreements that result in civil war. To be sure, as we noted earlier, not all group conflict is fought out by political means. However, most of the disagreements about which people feel most strongly in modern societies are fought out at least partly in the political arena.

OVERLAPPING MEMBERSHIPS

The more complex a society is, the less likely are its political interest groups to have mutually exclusive memberships; that is, to include people who are members of one particular group and no others (see Figure 1.1a). Political interest groups in complex societies relate to one another as shown in Figure 1.1b, sharing some of their members with other groups. Two groups seldom claim identical membership, however.

This produces the phenomenon of *overlapping membership of political groups*; that is, the fact that members of every political group are also members of several other groups. It is seen in every society that has many distinctions among its members and thus many bases for group formation. Each person belongs to many different groups at the same time, and few individuals belong to exactly the same groups (see Figure 1.1b). Readers can check the validity of these generalizations by comparing their group memberships with those of their close friends. They are likely to find, for example, that friend X is a college student, a Protestant, of Scottish descent, a fraternity member, a Republican, and a member of Young Americans for Freedom; friend Y is a college student, a Protestant, of African-American descent, an independent, and a member of the Young Democrats; and friend Z is a college student, a Catholic, of Hispanic descent, an independent, and a member of the Young Socialists.

IMPERFECT MOBILIZATION

One direct consequence of the overlapping membership of interest groups is the important fact that no group can induce all of its members to support any particular cause. This means that the degree of support any particular group can muster is

FIGURE 1.1   Membership in Political Groups

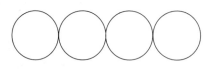

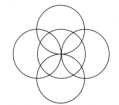

a. Mutually Exclusive Membership   b. Overlapping Membership

likely to vary widely from one issue to another in at least two respects. First, the number of members who support the group changes. Recent studies of voting behavior, for example, show that all the major voting groups studied—older and younger people, Protestants and Roman Catholics, rich and poor, whites and blacks, and so on—are divided among themselves in their voting preferences and activities. Figure 1.2 illustrates the point by showing how some American population groups were split in the 1994 congressional election.

FIGURE 1.2   How Different Population Groups Voted for U.S. House of Representatives, 1994.

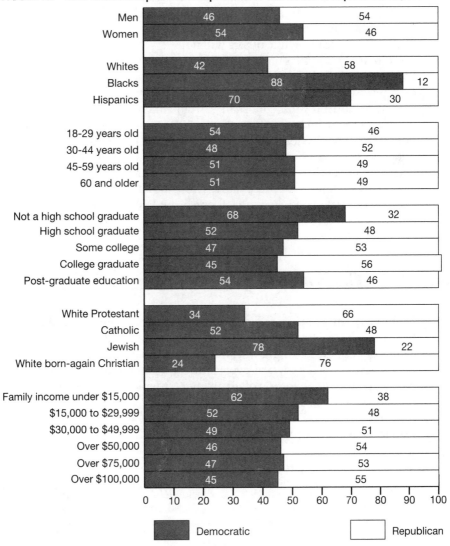

Source: The New York Times exit poll, November 8, 1994.
Note: 5260 respondents; numbers shown are percentages. Reported in *The New York Times National*, November 13, 1994, p. 15. Reprinted by permission.

The point to note about Figure 1.2 is that while some groups voted strongly for one party's candidates (most African-American and low-income people voted for Democrats, and most Asian-Americans, Protestants, and people with the highest incomes voted for Republicans), in every group there was a minority of over 10 percent that voted contrary to the group's majority.

The 1994 election was thus one instance of an important general rule: Labor, farmers, business people, youth, Roman Catholics, and other such groups are far from being disciplined political armies ready to spring into action whenever their leaders give the command. The members of each group also belong to other groups. On any particular issue some—but not all—of each group's members will approve of its political activities; and of those who do approve, some will participate actively and enthusiastically, while others will not.

In certain societies under certain conditions a few political interest groups may have very lopsided majorities for particular parties or causes. In the United States, for example, African-Americans have supported the Democratic party by very wide margins since the 1930s, and almost all African-Americans elected to public office have been Democrats. Even so, although only 12 percent of African-American voters supported Republican George Bush in the 1988 presidential election, President Bush nevertheless chose Dr. Louis W. Sullivan, an African-American, to be Secretary of Health and Human Services. In 1990 Gary Franks, an African-American Republican, was elected to the House of Representatives from the Fifth District of Connecticut. In 1992, Bush was defeated and Sullivan left office, but Franks was reelected. Thus, African-Americans are predominantly—but not unanimously—Democrats.

Politics and Government

Up to this point we have focused upon the fact that political conflict is inescapable in all human societies. But this should not mislead us into viewing politics solely as a kind of permanent jungle warfare, red in tooth and claw, in which every person is implacably hostile toward every other person. To depict politics as unrelieved conflict is no less a distortion of reality than to depict conflict as an unfortunate aberration from normal peace and harmony.

The crucial point was put forcefully by the eighteenth-century philosopher Jean Jacques Rousseau:

> What made the establishment of societies necessary was, if you like, the fact that the interests of individuals clashed. But what made their establishment possible was the fact that these same interests *also* coincided. *In other words*: It is the overlap among different interests that creates the social bond, so that no society can possibly exist save as there is some point at which all the interests concerned are in harmony.[5]

In our time no less than Rousseau's, every society has both politics and government. Politics, as we have seen, consists of *people acting politically*, by organizing political interest groups and trying to induce governments to act in ways that will promote their interests over those of their opponents. Now let us see what governments are and do.

For Further Reading

In this chapter, as in the rest of the book, I have not attempted the impossible task of trying to tell readers everything they may ever want to know about politics and government. I have tried to write an *introduction* to political science, and I hope it will whet the reader's intellectual appetite rather than satisfy or kill it. What follows is a brief annotated list of some leading books on the topics we have covered in this chapter; similar lists will follow each of the chapters to come. Readers eager for more may turn to them with profit. The lists are, of course, far from exhaustive. They are intended only as samplings of the rich literature on politics and government in today's world and as starting points for further exploration. An asterisk before the author's name indicates that the book is available in paperback.

By far the most comprehensive recent coverage of the main approaches, theories, findings, and bibliographies of contemporary political science is Fred I. Greenstein and Nelson W. Polsby, eds., *Handbook of Political Science* (Reading, MA: Addison-Wesley, 1975), eight volumes. Other useful readings on the matters covered in this chapter include the following books.

SCHOLARLY STUDIES OF THE ROLE OF POLITICS IN HUMAN LIFE

*CONWAY, M. MARGARET. *Political Participation in the United States*, 2nd ed. Washington, DC: Congressional Quarterly Press, 1990. A survey of voting and the other ways in which Americans participate in politics.

*DAHL, ROBERT A. *Modern Political Analysis*, 4th ed. Englewood Cliffs, NJ: Prentice Hall, 1984. A short but rich introduction to the nature of politics by a distinguished political scientist.

*EDELMAN, MURRAY. *The Symbolic Uses of Politics*. Urbana, IL: University of Illinois Press, 1964. Stimulating analysis of the role of symbols in political conflict and resolution.

EHRENHALT, ALAN. *The United States of Ambition: Power and the Pursuit of Office*. New York: New York Times Books, 1991. A study of the motivations and tactics of rising politicians in four American cities.

*FINIFTER, ADA W., ed. *The State of the Discipline II*. Washington, DC: American Political Science Association, 1993. Collection of essays on the state of knowledge in each of the main fields of political science.

*HOROWITZ, DONALD L. *Ethnic Groups in Conflict*. Berkeley, CA: University of California Press, 1985. Detailed analysis of ethnic groups in American lobbying and electoral politics.

LASWELL, HAROLD D., and ABRAHAM KAPLAN. *Power and Society*. New Haven, CT: Yale University Press, 1950. Abstract and difficult but important and influential theory of politics based on power as the key concept.

LOOMIS, BURDETT A. *The New American Politician: Ambition, Entrepreneurship, and the Changing Face of Political Life*. New York: Basic Books, 1988. A study of the impact of declining parties and rising new technologies and the kinds of people who enter and succeed in politics.

MASTERS, ROGER. *The Nature of Politics*. New Haven, CT: Yale University Press, 1989. A theoretical analysis, drawing from concepts in other social sciences and the biological sciences.

MERKL, PETER H., JR. *Political Violence and Terror*. Berkeley, CA: University of California Press, 1986. Survey of role of violence and terrorism in modern politics.

POLSBY, NELSON W. *Political Innovation in America: The Politics of Policy Initiation*. New Haven, CT: Yale University Press, 1984. A new look at the policy-making process in the United States, based on eight case studies of recent policy innovations.

*RIKER, WILLIAM H. *The Art of Political Manipulation*. New Haven, CT: Yale University Press, 1976. Distinguished political analyst uses twelve case studies to illustrate how people make political decisions and achieve political goals.

*SCHLOZMAN, KAY LEHMAN, and JOHN T. TIERNEY. *Organized Interests and American Democracy*. New York: Harper & Row, 1986. Detailed survey of organized interest groups in American national politics.

POLITICAL NOVELS

Few of us can personally participate in politics at the highest levels, but we can all acquire a feel of what it is like by reading good novels focused on political conflict. Here is a short list of novels dealing with politics in a variety of settings.

*BURDICK, EUGENE L. *The Ninth Wave*. New York: Dell Books, 1985.

*CAMUS, ALBERT. *The Plague*, trans. by Gilbert Stuart. New York: Modern Library, 1965.

*DOSTOYEVSKY, FYODOR. *The Possessed*, trans. by Constance Garnett. New York: Modern Library, 1936.

*FORSTER, E. M. *A Passage to India*. New York: Harcourt Brace, 1965.

*KOESTLER, ARTHUR. *Darkness at Noon*, trans. by Daphne Hardy. New York: Bantam, 1970.

*O'CONNOR, EDWIN. *The Last Hurrah*. New York: Bantam, 1970.

*ORWELL, GEORGE. *1984*. New York: Signet, 1971.

*PATON, ALAN. *Cry, the Beloved Country*. New York: Charles Scribner's Sons, 1948.

*SAFIRE, WILLIAM. *Full Disclosure*. New York: Ballantine, 1978.

*SCOTT, PAUL. *The Raj Quartet*. New York: Avon, 1979.

*SNOW, C. P. *The Masters*. New York: Macmillan, 1951.

SPRING, HOWARD. *Fame Is the Spur*. New York: Viking Press, 1949.

*TROLLOPE, ANTHONY. *Barchester Towers*. New York: Signet, 1950.

———. *The Palliser Novels*. New York: Oxford University Press, 1975.

*WARREN, ROBERT PENN. *All the King's Men*. New York: Bantam, 1950.

Notes

1. Interestingly, 24 percent would like to see their daughters go into politics: *The Gallup Poll Monthly*, (June 1993), p. 34.

2. Robert L. Chapman, ed., *Roget's International Thesaurus*, 4th ed. (New York: Thomas Y. Crowell, 1977), p. 594.

3. See, for example, Richard Rose and Ian McAllister, *Voters Begin to Choose: From Closed-Class to Open Elections in Britain* (Beverly Hills, CA: Sage, 1986), pp. 58–59.

4. Charles Tilly, "Collective Violence in European Perspective," in *Violence in America: Historical and Comparative Perspectives*, Hugh Davis Graham and Ted Robert Gurr, eds. (New York: Bantam, 1969), p. 4.

5. Jean Jacques Rousseau, *The Social Contract*, trans. by Willmoore Kendall (Chicago: Henry Regnery Co., 1954), Book 2, Chapter 1; italics in the original.

2

I must study politics and war, that my sons may have liberty to study mathematics and philosophy . . . in order to give their children a right to study painting, poetry, music [and] architecture. . . .
John Adams, 1789

Governments and Governing

The television newscasts we watch and the newspapers we read are full of stories and headlines about what various governments, especially our own, are doing or thinking of doing. "Clinton calls for health insurance for everyone." "Congressional Republicans denounce proposal for tax increase." "The Supreme Court upholds the right to abortion." "State legislature increases student fees at State U." "Yeltsin and Russian Parliament deadlocked." "United Nations sends peace-keeping forces to Bosnia." All familiar stuff.

Well, most of us would say, if newspapers and newscasts are full of such things, they must be important. Yet let us admit that many of us really feel that such subjects are pretty remote from the things that truly matter in our lives, such as making friends, getting through school, getting a job, making a living, getting married, raising children, staying healthy, enjoying life.

Yet, however remote government actions may *seem* to us, the joyless first lesson of political science is that those actions are just about the most important forces in our lives. Let us see why.

What Governments Do

IN PRIMITIVE SOCIETIES

For many people in the world today government, as we know it in the United States, hardly exists and plays no role of any importance in their day-to-day lives. Many anthropologists and some political scientists specialize in studying such societies,[1] and they report that most of those societies are run more or less like, for instance, the Inuit (Eskimo) societies of North America.

The political system of the Inuit societies are among the simplest known. Their peoples are scattered from the Bering Straits to Greenland in small communities, each numbering around a hundred inhabitants, with most of the members of each community related by blood or marriage. There are only two specialized roles that are politically significant: those of the shaman and the headman. Both are mixed roles. The shaman is the religious leader, but he (in Inuit society the shaman is never a woman) may also punish those who violate taboos. In the extreme case he may order an offender exiled, which in the Arctic may mean death. The headman is a task leader who is influential in making decisions about hunting or the selection of places for settlement. However, if the other members of the community disagree with his recommendations, then he has no authority or power to impose his choices.

Violations of order are handled mostly through fist fights and "song duels" or, in extreme cases, through family feuds. An individual who threatens the community by repeated acts of violence, murder, or theft may be dealt with by an executioner, who assumes the responsibility for the execution with the approval of the community.[2]

IN "ADVANCED/INDUSTRIALIZED" SOCIETIES

For better or worse, the readers of this book, like its author, do not live in societies like those of the Inuit. We live in nations such as those in North and South America, Western Europe, many in Asia, and some in Africa, societies that political scientists call "industrialized" (because their economies are based on division of labor, mass production, and the heavy use of machines) or even "advanced" (presumably because such societies are farther up some historical ladder of progress, though some political scientists reject both the label and its underlying point of view).

The role of government is very different in such societies. Most of us who live in them are born in government-regulated hospitals and delivered by government-licensed physicians. Government protects us against abuse by our parents. Like it or not, government makes us go to school until we reach the age of 16. We marry and divorce according to rules made by government. We take and leave jobs, set up businesses, engage in professions, buy and sell property, and retire according to rules and regulations laid down by government. Every year we pay a sizable part of the money we earn to government in taxes. We may be ordered by government to serve in the armed forces and even to kill or die at the orders of government officials known as military officers. When we have finally filled out our last government forms and paid our last tax bills, we are buried in government-licensed cemeteries, and our savings and property—minus portions siphoned off by governments in inheritance taxes—are handed on to our heirs by probate courts with the participation of government-licensed lawyers.

There is no escaping it: Governments play a major role in the lives of just about everyone who lives in the United States and the other advanced/industrialized societies. Since an introductory textbook such as this cannot possibly give equal attention to all kinds of societies and governments, we will concentrate mainly on the political and governmental institutions and processes of the society in which we live and others like it.

What Is Government?

GOVERNMENT AND OTHER ORGANIZATIONS

Learning what it means to be a human being is not all fun and games. From birth we become increasingly involved with a growing number of social organizations, and, as we get involved, we learn that each organization claims the right to make and enforce rules governing our behavior. Many of us are born into a family, and our parents tell us that we must drink our milk, brush our teeth, keep our rooms neat, and not draw on the walls or swear. We go to school, and our teachers tell us that we have to attend class, pass examinations, and say no to drugs. We join a religious institution, and our religious leaders tell us that we should attend services, say our prayers, and live according to prescribed moral principles. We get a job, and our bosses tell us that we must get to work on time and do a day's work for a day's pay. And so it goes all the days of our lives.

Furthermore, each organization backs up its rules with **sanctions**, which are *penalties that a group can impose on those who break its rules*. Parents can spank us and "ground" us on weekends, teachers can keep us after school, college professors can fail us, deans and presidents can throw us out of school, religious organizations can expel us from membership, bosses can fire us.

The older we grow, however, the more we become aware of the rules and sanctions of another organization that claims even greater authority over us: "the government." And we learn that its rules have a standing quite different from the rules of all the other organizations in our lives; for if "the government" catches us violating its rules, it can fine us or imprison us or even put us to death.

GOVERNMENT DEFINED

The term *government* is often used in two related but distinct senses. Sometimes it refers to a particular collection of *people*, each with individual idiosyncrasies, faults, and virtues, who are performing certain functions in a particular society at a particular time. Sometimes it refers to a particular set of *institutions*; that is, a series of accepted and regular procedures for performing those functions, procedures that persist over time regardless of who happens to be performing them.

Both senses are incorporated in the definition of government we will use in this book: **Government** is *the body of people and institutions that make and enforce laws for a society.*

Defined thus, government is undoubtedly one of humanity's oldest and most nearly universal institutions. Some political philosophers, to be sure, have speculated about what life would be like in a state of **anarchy**, which is *a society with no government*. Yet, there is no recorded instance of an actual society, past or present, that has operated for long with no government whatever (unless we count "world society"; more on this in Chapter 17). Evidently, people at all times and in all societies have felt that some sort of government is necessary for the way they wish to live their lives.

However, humanity's universal desire for government has by no means led all people at all times and in all societies to establish the same *kind* of government. Indeed, one of the most striking facts about actual governments, past and present, is their enormous variety. Governments have varied in complexity all the way from the simple shaman-headman systems of the Inuit to the highly complex systems of the advanced/industrialized nations. Governments have varied in the treatment of their peoples all the way from the mass executions and brutality of Nazi Germany to the mild and permissive "welfare state" of the Netherlands.

Evidently, then, different societies require different kinds of governments to satisfy their special needs. Yet, no matter how much some governments may differ from others, they all share certain characteristics that make them different from all other forms of human organization.

How Government Differs from Other Social Organizations

In some of the world's more primitive societies—for example, the Inuit in the Arctic and many Indian tribes in the remote Amazon rain forests of Brazil—there is no sharp distinction between the leaders and rules of government and the leaders and rules of families or religions. However, in advanced/industrialized societies, government differs significantly from all other social organizations in a number of respects.

COMPREHENSIVE AUTHORITY

Rules made by any social organization other than government apply, and are intended to apply, only to members of that organization. For example, when the University of California rules that all students must take a course in American cultures, no one expects this rule to apply to students at Yale or Oxford or Slippery Rock. If General Motors decides to split its stock four for one, no one thinks that Ford or Coca Cola must do the same.

On the other hand, the rules of the government of the United States apply, and are intended to apply, to *all* members of U.S. society. When Congress rules that every American with an annual income above a certain amount must pay a portion of that income in taxes, no one imagines that this rule does not apply to those who disapprove of income taxes or to those who cannot afford both to pay the taxes and to buy new cars or to those who let payment slip their minds. When Congress says *every* American, we all understand that it means precisely that because Congress, along with the president and the Supreme Court, have governmental **authority**; that is, *the acknowledged power to make binding decisions and issue obligatory commands.*

INVOLUNTARY MEMBERSHIP

Membership in most social organizations other than government is voluntary; that is, people become members of such an organization and place themselves under its rules only by conscious choice. One does not automatically become a Presbyterian at birth because one's parents are Presbyterian or because one is born in a Presbyterian hospital. One officially joins the church by going through certain formal procedures, such as baptism and confirmation. Membership in a nation, however, is largely involuntary; that is, most people *initially* become citizens of a nation and subject to its rules without any deliberate choice or conscious act. All nations officially regard as citizens either all persons born in their territories or all children born of their citizens, or some combination of both. Most nations also have procedures for noncitizens to acquire citizenship (a process generally called naturalization) and for citizens to renounce it; but initial membership of a nation is involuntary.

AUTHORITATIVE RULES

Rules made by some private (that is, nongovernmental) organizations often conflict with those made by other private organizations. For example, a labor union may order its members to use clubs and fists to keep strikebreakers from crossing picket lines, yet the religious order to which some of the union members belong may teach that physical violence should never be used. In most societies there is no clearly defined and generally accepted hierarchy among organizations and therefore no automatic way to determine which organizations' rules should prevail and which should be overridden in situations of conflict. There is no universal agreement, for example, that a religious denomination is more important than a labor union, and so each union member who is also a member of a particular denomination must decide individually whether to obey the denomination's rules or the union's.

However, the rules of government are quite another matter, for in every nation governmental rules are generally recognized as **authoritative**; that is, they are generally considered to be *more binding upon all members of a society than the rules of all other organizations.* In any conflict between the laws of government and the rules of a private organization, there is general agreement that government laws should prevail. For instance, if a religious sect decrees human sacrifice as part of its ritual but the government forbids the taking of human life by any organization other than itself, most members of the society will regard the government's prohibition as more binding than the religious sect's ritual requirement. If the local building code stipulates that brick walls must be at least twelve inches thick and local engineers think that eight inches is enough, most of the town's citizens—including most of its engineers—will obey the twelve-inch requirement, however misguided they may think it is.

LEGITIMATE MONOPOLY OF OVERWHELMING FORCE

Of course, all government rules are not always obeyed by all the members of any society. After all, every human organization has to deal with people who disobey its rules, and government is no exception. All organizations impose sanctions on rule breakers, but government differs from other organizations in the kind of sanctions it is authorized to impose. Private organizations are generally authorized to withhold certain privileges, impose fines, and require certain penances. Their ultimate legitimate weapon, however, is expulsion. If a member of a labor union or a member of a religious organization refuses to pay the union's dues or worship as the organization prescribes, the most extreme penalty either organization can impose is to expel the delinquent from membership. Government can impose all those sanctions as well, but it can also impose two additional sanctions forbidden to private organizations: It can send lawbreakers to prison, and it can take their lives.

It is important to recognize that governments are not the only organizations that *in fact* impose life-and-death sanctions. Gangsters and drug dealers sometimes kill people who violate their rules, and terrorists sometimes kidnap airline passengers and kill patrons of airports and restaurants. The point is that government alone has the *legitimate* power to execute rule breakers. The concept of **legitimacy** is crucial here, and it means *the general belief of the members of a society that the government's powers to make and enforce rules are proper, lawful, and entitled to obedience.* In every political system most people believe that if any agency may rightfully use the ultimate sanction of execution, government is the only one. Any private organization or person that uses it is committing murder.

All social organizations can muster some physical force to enforce their rules, and some may use it. At the very least they may use the fists of their members, and many also use rocks, bricks, clubs, razors, knives, and perhaps even firebombs, pistols, rifles, and submachine guns. Most Americans do not need to be told that some private organizations sometimes actually use violence to promote their causes: Anyone who reads newspapers knows that some people who oppose abortion have sometimes set fire to abortion clinics and murdered some doctors who perform abortions, and some students who want more women and minority faculty members hired have occupied administration buildings and trashed administrators' offices. But there is nothing peculiarly American about such behavior. No nation, sad to say, conducts its internal political conflicts entirely without violence.

Government differs from other social organizations, not because it occasionally uses force to enforce its rules, but because it can muster maximum force. The rocks and pistols that private organizations can use are feeble indeed compared with the armed police and military forces available to governments.

HIGHEST STAKES

Those special characteristics of government make political stakes the highest for which people contest. Controversies among Roman Catholics about the permissibility of birth control and the ordaining of women as priests are important to Roman

Catholic clergy and laity, but less so to Protestants, Jews, and Muslims. The struggles among ABC, CBS, and NBC for viewers and advertising may dominate the lives of all who work in television, but those struggles are, at most, of merely spectator interest to the United Mine Workers or the American Medical Association. On the other hand, the confrontation in 1990–1991 between Iraq and a U.S.-led coalition of nations over Iraq's invasion of Kuwait led to a short but devastating war killing well over 100,000 Iraqis. And the efforts of the United States and the former Soviet Union to end the "cold war" and limit the spread of nuclear weapons involved no less a stake than the survival of humanity.

As any poker player knows, when the stakes rise, the nature of the game changes. The processes of politics and government have some instructive similarities to their counterparts in private organizations, but governments operate in such a different atmosphere and for such greater stakes that their rule making is profoundly different from rule making by private organizations. It is well to remember this point whenever we are tempted to think of decision making in Washington or Moscow or Paris as just another version of what goes on in our families or faculty meetings or businesses.

Basic Tasks and Tools of Government

Government authorities in most nations believe that the basic duty of any government, whether democratic or authoritarian, is to ensure the nation's survival. That survival involves two fundamental tasks: defending independence against external enemies, and keeping internal conflicts from becoming so bitter that they lead to secession and civil war. To accomplish the second task, the government must satisfy the needs that made the people decide to accept a government in the first place. Government must sift through the many political demands constantly besieging it, blend demands into public policies, and enforce those policies in such a way that no major group of citizens feels compelled to tear the nation apart. National survival is thus the ultimate test of any government.

There is no universal or infallible method for accomplishing this basic task and no sure-fire way to prevent civil wars or win foreign wars. Throughout this book we will review the wide range of policies actually pursued by modern governments. However, we should note that all governments rely upon combinations, varying in emphasis from time to time and from government to government, of a few basic "tools."

INTEREST ARTICULATION

As we saw in Chapter 1, every society's population is divided into many groups distinct from one another in one or more significant respects (for example, in gender, racial, and ethnic identity; education; occupation; and income). Just about every one of those groups and the people who compose them have a **political interest**, a concept that plays a leading role in political analysis. We will define a political interest as *the stake of a person or group in government policy: something of value to be gained or lost by what government does or does not do.* The essence of politics boils down to a great many interest groups making demands that the government do something to help them or refrain from doing something that hurts them. The essence of governing is responding to those demands in one way or another.

If a nation's government simply does not know what demands its people are making, it can hardly deal with the demands effectively. If government is dimly aware of the demands but unaware of their variety or intensity, it is not likely to deal with the demands very well. If government does not cope effectively with the most urgent and widely supported demands, it risks anger, alienation, and perhaps even rebellion from the groups it ignores.

Consequently, governments need effective methods for the articulation of interests. **Interest articulation**, as political scientists use the term, means *the process of forming and expressing demands by political interest groups and transmitting the demands to government authorities.* In later chapters we will consider some of the principal devices by which interests are articulated in modern nations (for example, lobbying, propaganda, protest, mass communications, public opinion polls, and campaigns and elections). Here we note only that every political system needs effective ways for its authorities to know and understand its citizens' strongly felt political demands.

INTEREST AGGREGATION

In Chapter 1 we noted the fact that some political demands inevitably conflict with others and that there is no way a government can fully satisfy each and every demand made on it. Governments can hope to deal with the demands adequately only if the demands are "aggregated" in some way. The term **interest aggregation** means *the process of combining the demands of different interest groups into public policies.* Essentially, the aggregating process consists of adjusting and combining demands so that they do not cancel each other out and so that each major group is reasonably happy with what it gets.

Much aggregation of interests occurs outside formal government, in discussions among individuals and in negotiations and deals within and among pressure groups and political parties. Considerable aggregation also takes place in the legislative, executive, and administrative agencies of government. However interest aggregation is achieved, it is necessary for any political system and is a vital tool of any government.

COERCION AND COMPROMISE

Every government, democratic or authoritarian, perpetually faces the key question of how to achieve acceptance of its policies and compliance with its laws. One obvious and important answer, of course, is government **coercion**, *which is the threat or imposition of force and other sanctions to get compliance.* Governments can apply many kinds of sanctions to lawbreakers: physical, economic, psychological, violent, nonviolent. Governments may deny a license to engage in a business or profession, take away the right to vote and hold public office, withdraw financial aid, revoke citizenship, deport, and exile. Of course, governments can also fine, imprison, "brainwash," torture, and kill. As we noted earlier, government's legitimate monopoly of the death penalty is a prime difference between it and all other social organizations.

Governments generally use coercion to achieve one or both of two main objects: (1) to "make examples" that will convince potential lawbreakers that the consequences of breaking the law will be worse than any likely gains; and (2) to take out of circulation any person who, undeterred by those threats, breaks the law anyway. No doubt an element of revenge often exists as well, but the principal justification for government coercion is deterrence.

Yet no government can rely on coercion alone. It is plainly impossible to execute or imprison massive numbers of citizens. Hence, large-scale and determined resistance to a law simply cannot be overcome by coercion alone. Nor is open defiance the only form of resistance that concerns government. A policy that receives only sullen, foot-dragging, minimal compliance is not likely to be very effective.

THE ULTIMATE GOVERNMENTAL SANCTION.

Accordingly, willing compliance by most people is necessary for any policy to be successful, and enthusiastic popular support can make up for a good many technical deficiencies in any policy. Any government, however brutal and ruthless it is prepared to be, depends upon this kind of voluntary compliance for most of its policies most of the time.

How do governments obtain voluntary compliance? There are many ways, but to some degree all are variations on the basic theme of compromise. Conflicting interests and incompatible demands are inevitable, and so for every political "winner" there is bound to be a "loser." No government can escape this hard fact of life, but it can try to shape the content and impact of each policy so that the "losers" will feel that continuing to live under the existing regime, though perhaps far from ideal, is at least bearable. A government can best keep its competing interest groups satisfied enough not to rebel by giving each group *something* of what it wants. Thus, no group experiences total "defeat" or the despairing feeling that the whole system is rigged against it so that its wishes and needs will never receive serious consideration. To do that, the government must deny total victory to the "winners" by watering down the maximum demands of all clashing interests.

The resulting policies are likely to contain some logically inconsistent provisions and may even appear ridiculous when judged by the rules of logic. However, every government is more concerned with preserving its society than with being logically consistent; and if a policy helps to do the job, no one will care much about its lack of neatness or logical symmetry.

An Illustration: The American Conflict Over Abortion

Since the early 1960s the question of in what circumstances, if any, women should be legally permitted to have abortions has been one of the most bitter and hotly contested domestic issues bedeviling the government of the United States. This issue provides a vivid illustration of the tough choices governments must make in the modern world.

History and anthropology tell us that in just about all societies, ancient and modern, some women have sometimes had abortions (artificially induced terminations of pregnancies) to prevent the birth of unwanted children. In the United States, as in most Western societies, the practice was for centuries generally disapproved, but it was restrained mainly by religious precepts and social customs rather than by laws. In the nineteenth-century United States, however, the new and rising profession of medicine, organized politically by the American Medical Association, took the view that abortion is medically so dangerous that it must be made illegal. Many religious organizations joined forces with the physicians by declaring that abortion is so immoral that the decision to have one must not be left to custom or to the consciences of individual women. Consequently, most states enacted laws making abortion a crime, punishable by imprisonment, although some states made exceptions for abortions prescribed by physicians as necessary to save the mother's life.

Since the early 1960s, however, things have changed radically. The women's rights movement has become one of the most powerful new forces in U.S. life. It has fought for a number of changes in government policy, such as requiring that women have the same access to jobs as do men and that women receive equal pay for equal work. One of the changes for which the movement has fought hardest has been the decriminalization of abortion; that is, the repeal of all laws restricting women's right to have abortions. The well-organized political campaign has been sharply contested by an equally well-organized countercampaign by people who feel that abortion is murder and must be prohibited by law. We will look briefly at the arguments and strategies of both sides.

THE PRO-LIFE SIDE

One side of the struggle, usually called the "anti-abortion" or "pro-life" movement, is a coalition of Roman Catholic Church leaders, such as the National Conference of Catholic Bishops, leaders of evangelical Protestant churches, such as the Reverend Pat Robertson, and leaders of conservative political organizations, such as Paul Weyrich and Phyllis Schlafly. They are conducting an all-out political drive to make abortions permanently and unequivocally illegal except (some say) when necessary to save the mother's life.

The pro-life forces make both secular and religious arguments against abortions. Life, they say, begins at conception. Hence, a fetus at any stage of its development is a human being, with the same right to life as any other human being. Thus, to take the life of a fetus by abortion, they believe, is the same as taking the life of an adult without due process of law. That is, the fetuses are not tried for a crime or sentenced to death as a penalty for a crime. They are simply put to death summarily, and pro-lifers believe that is plain murder.

Moreover, the religious pro-life organizations claim that each fetus has an immortal soul from the moment of its conception and that any soul destroyed before it is baptized is eternally lost to salvation. They believe that human bodies do not belong to the people who occupy them or to the parents who beget them, and they certainly do not belong to society. They believe that bodies belong to God and that God alone has the right to decide what happens to them.

The pro-life groups believe those arguments deeply, and they feel that their efforts to outlaw abortions are dedicated to the most sacred and important cause in politics: the preservation of innocent human beings and their immortal souls from murder and eternal damnation. However, their antagonists, the pro-choice forces, are committed just as passionately to quite a different set of beliefs.

THE PRO-CHOICE SIDE

The pro-choice forces are a coalition of organizations, such as the National Organization for Women, the National Abortion Rights Action League, and Planned Parenthood, and male and female supporters who believe that a woman has the right to seek an abortion or not seek an abortion free of government interference.

SOME POLITICS INVOLVES ORGANIZED GROUP PROTESTS. Pro-life demonstrations in Washington, D.C.

Abortion is the most intensely personal choice that a woman can make, and pro-choicers believe that basic justice demands that she who must bear the consequences should have the right to decide whether or not she will have an abortion. Pro-choicers believe that this most personal of all decisions should never be made for any woman against her will by any organization, profession, or person who is not and cannot be as deeply involved as she; that is, not by physicians, not by biological fathers, and certainly not by politicians and government bureaucrats.

The pro-choice forces also make the pragmatic argument that most pregnant women who want an abortion are going to have abortions whether they are legal or not. Abortions were performed tens of thousands of times when abortions were illegal, and women will continue to have abortions if abortions are made illegal again. The only difference is that when abortions are illegal they are expensive and dangerous, often performed in secret by untrained people under unsafe conditions highly dangerous to the woman's health. Those who do not believe that it is morally wrong to have abortions are not going to obey laws against them any more than the millions of people who did not think it was morally wrong to drink liquor obeyed the law imposed by the Eighteenth Amendment's prohibition of alcoholic beverages in the United States from 1919 to 1933. Prohibition, they say, did not keep people from drinking, but only forced them to drink illegally, and the net effect of clinging to that unenforceable law was to promote disrespect for all laws and a great increase in lawlessness. By the same token, outlawing abortions will not keep women from having them. Like prohibition, it will only give rise to massive violations of the law and increasing general contempt for law.

WHERE THINGS STAND

In the 1960s and early 1970s the pro-choice movement persuaded twelve states and the District of Columbia to repeal their antiabortion laws, but the pro-life forces responded by working to prevent other states from following suit. Neither side was happy about having such a crucial matter decided on a state-by-state basis, and each urged agencies of the federal government, especially the Congress and the courts of law, to make a final and authoritative ruling that would be binding on all the states. That ruling finally came in 1973 in the U.S. Supreme Court's decision in the case of *Roe* v. *Wade* (1973), declaring unconstitutional a Texas law prohibiting all abortions except those necessary to save the life of the mother.[3] The Court did *not*, however, say that no state could ever under any circumstances limit women's right to have abortions. Rather, the Court declared that pregnancies progress by three-month stages, or trimesters, and made a different rule for each: (1) In the first trimester, states may not interfere with a woman's right to obtain an abortion if it is recommended by her physician; (2) in the second trimester, states can make reasonable regulations about where and when abortions can be performed, although they still cannot ban them altogether; and (3) in the third trimester, the state's interest in protecting the unborn child becomes so important that it can constitutionally prohibit all abortions except those necessary to save the mother's life.

The *Roe* v. *Wade* decision remains one of the most controversial decisions the Supreme Court has ever made, and it touched off a political struggle that continues to rage in the 1990s. The pro-life forces have fought to get the decision overridden, either by putting more conservative judges on the Court and getting them to reverse the 1973 decision or by amending the U.S. Constitution so as to outlaw abortions or at least give the states the power to outlaw abortions. The pro-choice forces have taken a mainly defensive position, on the ground that the *Roe* decision, while far less satisfactory than an unequivocal affirmation of a woman's right to have an abortion, is still preferable to the outlawing of all abortions sought by the pro-life forces.

By the early 1990s many observers believed that the conservative justices appointed by presidents Ronald Reagan and George Bush had created a pro-life majority on the Supreme Court, which would soon overrule the Roe decision and throw out the doctrine that the U.S. Constitution guarantees women's abortion rights. They were wrong. By a 5–4 decision, joined in by three Reagan-Bush appointees, the court said:

> After considering the fundamental constitutional questions resolved by *Roe*, principles of institutional integrity, and the role of stare decisis, we are led to conclude this: the essential holding of *Roe* v. *Wade* should be retained and once again reaffirmed.[4]

The decision did not end the battle, but it was a substantial defeat and major disappointment for the pro-life forces.

SOME LESSONS FOR THE STUDY OF GOVERNING

The struggle between the pro-life and pro-choice forces in the United States is surely one of the most bitter and fiercely fought political struggles of our time. It will not be settled definitively one way or the other in the next few years; indeed, it probably will never be settled to the complete satisfaction of one side or the other.

I have not chosen it as an illustration for this chapter because I enjoy writing about it (which I certainly do not). I have chosen it because most readers are likely to feel strongly about the issue and to see it as highly relevant to their personal lives and political ideals, and because thinking about the issue and how the government has handled it up to now teaches us some important lessons about what governing is like in the modern world. What lessons?

The first is one of the most important points to be made in the entire book, and it must be understood by everyone who wants to understand what real-life politics and government are like. One way of putting the point is to say that "in politics there is no free lunch." Another way is to say that every benefit that government gives to some people exacts a cost from other people. To the degree that the Supreme Court, the Congress, or any other government agency allows some women to have abortions under some conditions, the pro-lifers are outraged because, in their view, it is condoning murder. By the same token, to the degree that government prohibits some women who want abortions from having them, it enrages the pro-choicers because, in their view, it deprives women of their right to decide whether to have an abortion or not.

The struggle over abortion, like so many political conflicts, is what some analysts call a "zero-sum game"; that is, a contest, like table-stakes poker, in which the amount the winners win is the same as the amount the losers lose. There is no poker game and no political conflict in which *everyone* wins. The issue in every government decision is not how to give everyone everything they want; it is who will win, who will lose, and how much. Indeed, one of the greatest political scientists of the twentieth century put the point precisely and succinctly when he entitled his book about the basic nature of governing *Politics: Who Gets What, When, How.*[5]

The second lesson from the abortion struggle is that government resolutions of political conflicts—including many that are widely (though never universally) praised—almost always fall far short of being ideal dispensations of justice or models of clarity and logic. Certainly the major premise of the *Roe* decision—that there is some fundamental change in kind, not just in degree, in the nature and rights of a fetus when it passes from one trimester to the next—has no basis in logic or in the science of embryology or in philosophies of religion or ethics. The most that can be said for it is that so far it has enabled the nation to deal with this bitter and divisive issue without resorting to some final Armageddon in which one side wins a total victory and the other suffers total defeat. Perhaps from the standpoint of government that is all the justification it needs. One who understands *why* already understands a good deal about governing.

Nationalism and the Birth and Death of Nations

Every person in the world lives under the authority of governments at several different levels: cities, counties, provinces, states, and the like. But the most important level is the nation. The world's population is divided among independent and sovereign nations, each of which has complete legal authority within its particular territory and none of which acknowledges a government legally superior to its own. We will conclude this chapter by considering what nations are and how they are born and die.

NATURE OF NATIONS

As of January 1, 1995, there were about 185 political units generally accorded the legal status of nationhood (for a list, see Table 15.1 in Chapter 15)—a number that included an increase of at least 19 after 1990 by the breakup of the Soviet Union and Yugoslavia. There are, of course, great differences among those nations on many dimensions: population size, natural resources, economic productivity, military power. But each and every nation has the following common characteristics.

Particular Territory

Each of the world's nations is located on a particular area of the earth's surface and has definite, generally recognized boundaries that do not overlap those of any other nation. To be sure, the exact locations of mutual boundaries are sometimes disputed by adjoining nations, as they are now by some republics of the former Soviet Union; but the *principle* of definite boundaries is accepted by all nations.

Definite Population

Each nation regards certain people as its citizens and all others as aliens. A **citizen** is *a person who has the legal status of being a full member of a particular nation*. This status includes being loyal to that nation above all others, receiving its protection, and enjoying the right to participate in its political processes. By the same token, each nation regards any noncitizen as an **alien**; *that is, a person who is neither a citizen nor a national of the nation in which he or she is present*.

Government: Unitary and Federal

Each nation has an officially designated set of persons and institutions authorized to make and enforce laws for all people within its territory. The governing systems are usually classified as one or another of two types according to how their powers are distributed between national and regional levels (such as states and provinces):

Unitary governments are *those in which the national governments are legally supreme over regional and local governments.* Such powers as the subnational governments may have are granted by the national government, which has the legal authority to take them back any time it wishes. Most of the world's governments are of this type, and such nations as Great Britain, France, Japan, and Sweden are leading examples.

Federal governments are *those in which power is formally divided between the national government and certain regional governments, each of which is legally supreme in its own sphere.* The constitutions of those nations usually specify the matters over which the national governments and the regional governments have authority and stipulate that neither level is subordinate to the other. The United States is the oldest example of a federal government, and Australia, Canada, Germany, and Switzerland also have federal governments. Some scholars contend that other nations—for example, Austria, Mexico, and India—should also be included and predict that the independent but associated nations of the European Community will ultimately form a federal system.

Formal Independence

Each nation has **sovereignty**, which is *the full and exclusive legal power to make and enforce laws for a particular people in a particular territory.* This means that each nation, large or small, strong or weak, has supreme legal authority over its own affairs and in that respect is fully equal to every other nation. Note that this is a purely *legal* principle. It is known in international law as "the principle of the sovereign equality of nations." In actuality, of course, some nations are more subject to influence by foreign nations than others. If India strongly suggests that Sri Lanka adopt a certain policy, Sri Lanka is more likely to accept the suggestion than India would be to act on a similar suggestion put to it by Sri Lanka. *Legally* speaking, however, Sri Lanka has as much right to make decisions for Sri Lanka as India has to make decisions for India.

Nationalism

All nations are rooted in **nationalism**, which is *people's psychological attachment to a particular nation, based upon a common history, common language and literature, common culture, and a desire for political independence.* For many of the world's inhabitants, especially those in the long-established nations, nationalism is the highest allegiance. Many people are more loyal to their nations than to their religions, their social classes, their races, even their families. The most striking evidence of nationalism's power over human thought and behavior is that in modern times wars, the supreme test of people's loyalties, are fought mainly among nations, not among races or religious institutions or social classes, as they once were. When the United States has fought with Germany, U.S. workers, capitalists, Roman Catholics, and Lutherans have killed and been killed by German workers, capitalists, Roman Catholics, and Lutherans.

Some commentators feel that nationalism and national sovereignty are old-fashioned and dangerous principles in a modern, highly interdependent world in which a number of nations have nuclear weapons. Be that as it may, the fact is that nationalism has never been stronger than it is right now. Of the 185 generally recognized nations today, no fewer than 138—nearly three quarters—have achieved their independence since 1945. Indeed, 115—or 62 percent—have come into existence just since 1960. By far the greatest number of new nations has been created in Africa, where 44 of the 48 nations have achieved independence since 1945.

THE BIRTH OF NATIONS

Many nations were originally parts of other nations and then became independent either by winning a war of independence (for example, the United States in 1783 and most of the Latin American nations in the early nineteenth century), by being granted independence by their former colonial masters (for example, most of the new nations established in Africa, Asia, and the Caribbean since 1945), or by declaring themselves to be independent from previous unions (as the constituent republics of the former Soviet Union and Yugoslavia have done since 1989).

THE DEATH OF NATIONS

Nations can start life in several different ways, but they have only two main ways of dying. One is to be conquered and totally absorbed by another nation, as Tibet was by the People's Republic of China in 1951. The other is to break up into a number of new nations. History has seen several instances, such as the dissolution of the Austro-Hungarian and Ottoman empires after World War I, and the disintegration of Yugoslavia in the 1990s. However, the breakup of the Union of Soviet Socialist Republics (USSR) since 1989 is perhaps the greatest national disintegration ever. At the present writing, the development of new political structures in the former USSR is still far from complete, but the story so far is worth outlining.

The USSR was born after the Bolshevik (Communist) revolutionary takeover of the old Russian empire in 1917. A formal union among four constituent Soviet republics was created in 1922, and eleven more republics were added later. The Soviet constitutions of 1936 and 1977 formally provided for a USSR consisting of fifteen republics joined together in a federal union, with some functions assigned to the central government in Moscow and some assigned to the republics. In fact, however, the iron rule of the Moscow-centered Communist Party of the Soviet Union (CPSU) in all of the republics made the USSR a strong unitary government for the control of everything that mattered, including the economy, education, foreign policy, and the military.

Organized thus, the USSR emerged from its victory in World War II as one of the world's two most powerful nations, and from 1945 until the late 1980s world politics was dominated by the cold war between the USSR and the other superpower, the United States.

Then, in 1985, Mikhail Gorbachev became the Soviet leader, and ever since both the Soviet Union and world politics have seen some of the most radical changes in history. They began in 1989 when the three Baltic republics of Estonia, Latvia, and Lithuania declared their independence. At first Gorbachev and the union government used a mixture of military intervention and promises of greater self-rule to keep the republics in the union. The Baltic republics' status remained in doubt, but strong separatist movements also developed in a number of the other Soviet republics. Recognizing the impossibility of treating all the rebellious republics as he had treated the Baltic republics, Gorbachev tried to persuade all of them to sign a "Treaty of Union," which would have transferred most governing powers to the republics but reserved some powers of economic and foreign policy coordination for the central government. Only nine of the fifteen republics were willing to sign away even this much of their sovereignty.

The disintegration was accelerated by the August 1991 coup d'état in which a group of old-line CPSU leaders kidnapped Gorbachev and attempted to take over the union government. Their rebellion was stoutly resisted by the leaders of most of the republics, especially Boris Yeltsin, president of the Russian republic, and the coup collapsed after three days. Gorbachev returned to Moscow, but it was clear that he had been saved by the republics and that they, and not Gorbachev's union, would henceforth be the principal centers of power.

LEADERS OF CHANGE. Boris Yeltsin making a point to Mikhail Gorbachev

After the coup's failure, the USSR moved rapidly to extinction. The Communist party, which had been the union's main centralizing force since 1922, was voted out of existence, its offices were closed, and its central and regional branches were dissolved. All fifteen republics officially proclaimed their independence and thereby stripped Gorbachev's central government of all authority. Estonia, Latvia, and Lithuania were widely recognized as independent nations, and Gorbachev made no further effort to keep them in the union. The leaders of the three largest republics, Russia, Ukraine, and Belorussia, announced that the old union no longer existed and formed a new and much more decentralized association. They called the new association the Commonwealth of Independent States, and moved its capital from Moscow to Minsk. They invited the other republics to join, and eleven of the twelve did so (only Georgia remained outside).

At first, Gorbachev resisted the new commonwealth, but it was hopeless. He rallied little support for saving the old union, even with the radically diminished powers he proposed. Finally, on December 25, 1991, Gorbachev bowed to the inevitable and resigned as president of the defunct union. The hammer-and-sickle flag of the old USSR came down from the Kremlin and was replaced by the flag of the Russian republic. The United States and most other Western nations recognized the republics as independent, sovereign nations.

Thus did the USSR, which for seventy years had been one of the world's two superpowers, die. And though Mikhail Gorbachev was himself divested of power by the tidal wave of forces released by the *glasnost* and *perestroika* he had launched, he could claim a place in history at least as great as Lenin's among those few leaders who have truly changed the nature of world politics.

For Further Reading

BENTLEY, ARTHUR F. *The Process of Government*. Chicago: University of Chicago Press, 1908. Reprinted Evanston, IL: Principia Press, 1935. The classic statement of the group structure of politics and managing group conflict as the essence of the process of government.

DAWISHA, KAREN, AND BRUCE PARROTT. *Russia and the New States of Eurasia*. New York: Simon & Schuster, 1994. Analysis of the status, interrelations, and prospects of the fifteen republics that made up the former Soviet Union.

FINIFTER, ADA W., ed. *Political Science: The State of the Discipline*. Washington, DC: American Political Science Association, 1984. Essays by leading political scientists on the present state and future directions of research and knowledge in the main fields of political science.

FRIEDRICH, CARL J. *Man and His Government: An Empirical Theory of Politics*. New York: McGraw-Hill, 1963. An influential theoretical analysis of the basic nature of government.

HOLMES, LESLIE. *The End of Communist Power*. New York: Oxford University Press, 1993. Ambitious effort to describe and explain the collapse of communism in the Soviet Union and elsewhere.

MASTERS, ROGER D. *The Nature of Politics*. New Haven, CT: Yale University Press, 1990. An analysis of the essential nature of politics and its differences from other aspects of society.

MILIBAND, RALPH. *The State in Capitalist Society*. New York: Basic Books, 1969. A Marxist analysis of the nature of government and its relationship to other social organizations.

NATHAN, RICHARD P. *Social Science in Government: Uses and Misuses*. New York: Basic Books, 1988. Study of how the findings and methods of the social sciences are used and misused in making public policy in the United States.

PLATO. *The Republic* and *The Laws*. Many editions of these works have been published. They and Aristotle's *Politics* were the first systematic studies of the ideal and the actual in politics and government, and they continue to hold far more than historical interest for modern students.

*TRUMAN, DAVID B. *The Governmental Process*, 2nd ed. New York: Albert A. Knopf, 1971. An updating of Arthur Bentley's conception of politics and government, with special attention to the operation of American groups and institutions.

Notes

1. We will often encounter the term *society* in the rest of this book, so let us be clear at the outset that a *society is a broad grouping of people living in a common environment and having common traditions, institutions, activities, and interests.*

2. See Gabriel A. Almond and G. Bingham Powell, Jr., *Comparative Politics: A Developmental Approach* (Boston, MA: Little, Brown, 1966), pp. 42–43.

3. The full citation of the case is *Roe v. Wade*, 410 U.S. 113 (1973). Since there are a number of such citations in this book, readers may find it useful to under-stand what each element of the citation means: The first name is the name of the plaintiff, and the second is the name of the defendant. The numbers tell us that the Court's decision is reprinted in volume 410 of the *United States Reports*, beginning at page 113. And the year in parentheses is the year in which the decision was handed down.

4. *Planned Parenthood of Southeastern Pennsylvania* v. *Casey,* 120 L.Ed.2d 674 (1992).

5. Harold D. Lasswell, *Politics: Who Gets What, When, How* (New York: Meridian Books, 1936).

3

"Oh, well," said Mr. Hennessy, "we are as th' Lord made us." "No," said Mr. Dooley, "lave us be fair. Lave us take some iv th' blame oursilves."
Finley Peter Dunne, *Observations by Mr. Dooley*

We have met the enemy, and they are us.
Walt Kelley, *Pogo*

Political Psychology, Socialization, and Culture

Political Psychology: What Forms People's Political Beliefs and Behavior?

This book is basically about *people*. It is filled with discussion of groups and institutions. But a group, after all, is only some people who have one or more common characteristics, and an institution is only a shorthand expression for a set of well-established ways in which some people usually behave in particular circumstances. Democratic leaders like Bill Clinton and Helmut Kohl are people, and so are the citizens who vote them into office. However diabolical they may sometimes seem, dictators like Saddam Hussein and Muammar al-Qaddafi are also people, and so are the subjects who obey their orders.

So the first step to understanding governing is to learn something about how people think and behave politically. Political scientists have learned a great deal about political attitudes and behavior from psychology, psychiatry, biology, and other disciplines focused on the individual, and we now briefly review some of their findings that help us to understand why people think and behave politically as they do.

BIOLOGICAL NATURE AND NEEDS

Most psychologists agree every human being acquires his or her opinions and determines his or her behavior in part because of the person's own psychological and physical makeup and in part because of the physical and social environment in which the person lives.

Let us look first at the person, then at the environment. One of the most powerful drives shaping people's behavior is their desire to live rather than die, although it is by no means their only desire. To satisfy this desire people must eat, sleep, clothe and shelter themselves, defend themselves against attack by animals and other people, and protect themselves from such onslaughts of nature as floods, fire, hurricanes, and earthquakes. Most people also wish to enjoy sexual relations,

45

reproduce, and protect their mates and children. Furthermore, most want to achieve those goals at levels of some comfort and pleasure. People are thus likely to favor policies they believe will help them to achieve good things for themselves and their families and are likely to oppose policies they believe will prevent or hinder their achievement.

PSYCHOLOGICAL PROCESSES AND COGNITIVE MAPS

In describing and explaining human behavior most psychologists emphasize the *interaction* of the situation and the person. Accordingly, one critical factor in behavior is the individual's neurological-mental apparatus for receiving, ordering, and interpreting the signals received from the outside world and translating them into action. One useful way to picture this apparatus is as a "cognitive map," which is a mental picture of what the physical and social worlds are like and how we relate to them. There is a great deal of variation in the cognitive maps of different individuals and groups, but they all have three main elements: perception, conceptualization, and affect.

Perceptions and "Perceptual Screens"

Psychologists define a **perception** as *an awareness of an aspect of reality derived from sensory processes*. Students of political psychology have found that many people do not perceive the outside world by receiving and recording visual and auditory signals as photographic film receives and records light waves. Rather, those signals must pass through people's "perceptual screens" before they can become part of people's cognitive maps.

For example, suppose that in 1992 voter A supports Bill Clinton for the presidency mainly because he thinks Clinton is a much better bet than Bush to make the country prosperous. Suppose also that A is strongly opposed to imposing special tariffs and import quotas on Japanese cars that will protect the American automobile industry but increase car prices. Then suppose that A hears that Clinton is enthusiastically advocating just such trade barriers. She is likely to be upset when she learns that her candidate is advocating a position she rejects. How does she deal with it?

This is where A's "perceptual screen" comes in. She may, by "selective exposure," simply ignore television and newspaper stories about Clinton's protectionism and instead give her full attention only to stories about Clinton's proposals for tax incentives and about Bush's failed programs. Or she may believe that Clinton does not really believe in protectionism (Clinton is just saying so because he needs labor union votes), but that Clinton has a good economic program even though he speaks as often and as fervently about protection as about tax incentives.

Whatever A may do about her problem, it is clear that most of us have similar problems. As a result, our cognitive maps are not photographically exact reproductions of what is going on in the political world. They are often touched up a bit to make them easier to live with.

Levels of Conceptualization

Perceptual signals of any kind cannot *by themselves* tell us what is going on in the world or serve as a basis for action. We must first give the signals meaning by putting them into what we think are their appropriate categories in our **conceptual frameworks**, which are *the mental categories into which people sort perceptions of the world and give the perceptions meaning.*

Political scientists and psychologists have long been interested in how people conceptualize their political signals. Pioneer work was done in the 1950s by the Center for Political and Social Studies (CPSS) of the University of Michigan. CPSS asked respondents a series of open-ended questions about what they liked and disliked about the parties and presidential candidates in the elections of 1952 and 1956. On the basis of their answers, CPSS concluded that people conceptualized on one or another of four main levels. The first level was *ideology*, where people evaluated the parties and candidates in terms of whether they espoused liberal or conservative policies agreeable to the respondents' own philosophies. Only 12 percent of the respondents were put in this category. The second level was *group benefits*, where people liked or disliked parties and candidates because they thought the parties and candidates were good or bad for a group with which the respondents identified (such as farmers, working people, and middle-class people). Forty-two percent of the respondents conceptualized at this level. The third level was *nature of the times*, where, for instance, the respondents said "times are good, so why change?" or "Republicans cause depressions." Twenty-four percent of the respondents fit this category. The fourth level had *no issue content*, where people said "I like Ike" or "I'm a Democrat." Twenty-two percent conceptualized at this level.[1]

More recent studies show that since the CPSS studies in the 1950s, the proportion of ideological conceptualizers has risen not only in the United States but also in other democratic countries. This is demonstrated by the figures in Table 3.1, which show the proportions of people in eight democratic countries in the 1970s who understood the meaning of the terms *Left* and *Right*,[2] used the ideological categories to sort out political leaders and policies, and were willing to place their own political philosophies on a Left/Right scale.[3]

Table 3.1 shows that in all eight countries over two-thirds of those interviewed were willing to locate their own political outlooks on a Left/Right scale. On the other hand, only in Italy and West Germany were more than half able to give a reasonably clear and accurate explanation of what *Left* and *Right* mean, and only in Italy did over half say that their general preferences for the Left or Right play an important role in their preferences for leaders and policies. On all three counts this kind of ideology was less important for Americans than for the citizens of the other countries.

Affect

The third element of a person's political cognitive map is **affect**, which is *the emotion attached to an idea or object*. It is this quality that makes people support or oppose a particular party, candidate, or policy.

TABLE 3.1   Levels of Ideological Awareness in Eight Democratic Countries, 1974–75 (in percentages)

	RECOGNITION/ UNDERSTANDING LEFT AND RIGHT	ACTIVE USE OF IDEOLOGY	LEFT/RIGHT PLACEMENT
Austria	39	19	75
France	na	na	81
Great Britain	23	21	82
Italy	54	55	74
Netherlands	48	36	90
Switzerland	39	9	79
West Germany	56	34	92
United States	34	21	67

Source: Russell J. Dalton, *Citizen Politics in Western Democracies* (Chatham, NJ: Chatham House, 1988), Table 2.2, p. 25.

In short, our political attitudes and behavior are based upon our particular cognitive maps, and each of our maps consists of our *perceptions* of what is going on in the political world, the *conceptualizations* by which we sort out and give meaning to those perceptions, and the *affective connotation* we give those perceptions that help us decide to act in certain ways rather than in others. We compile our particular maps in part because of our particular biological natures and needs, in part because of our particular psychological processes, and also in part because of our membership in particular social groups.

GROUP MEMBERSHIPS AND PRESSURES TO CONFORM

The Nature of the Process

In Chapter 1 we noted that every person in an advanced/industrial society belongs to many categoric groups, which are groups of people who share at least one characteristic, such as gender, age, race, occupation, or religion. We further noted that some categoric groups are also interest groups; that is, groups whose members are conscious of their shared characteristics, regard themselves as having certain common goals arising from those characteristics, and to some extent direct their behavior accordingly. Finally, some interest groups become pressure groups because they pursue their goals at least partly by seeking to influence government policy.

Several social psychologists have investigated the influence of groups on the attitudes and behavior of their members. Some have focused mainly upon the influence of **primary groups**, which are *groups whose members have regular face-to-face interactions*, such as families, friends, and work associates. Others have studied the broader and more impersonal categoric groups. Those investigators have concluded that primary groups generally have a more direct and powerful influence on the opinions of their members than do larger and more impersonal groups, but that the latter have considerable influence on the opinions of most people.

Perhaps it would be useful to descend for a moment from the dizzying heights of theory to check those generalizations with our own experience. If we think of the people with whom we have the most daily contact—our parents, schoolmates, boyfriends, girlfriends, and work associates—we can ask ourselves, "Are our opinions about most things, including politics, pretty much like their opinions, or do we disagree about a lot of things?" All who honestly answer this question will realize that the social psychologists are talking not only about "other people" but also about us.

Just how does this agreement come about? By what processes do we form pretty much the same opinions as the other members of our primary groups? Research by social psychologists suggests some answers.

In every social group, and particularly in every primary group, certain pressures work for uniformity of opinion among the members. Those pressures arise from several sources. First, membership in particular groups to some extent limits the signals the members receive and therefore affects their ideas of what the world is like. For example, a white male with a high school education applying for a firefighter's job in Memphis is likely to be confronted with somewhat different facts about affirmative action and job qualifications than is a female African-American Ph.D. applying for an assistant professorship of sociology at Berkeley. The white male and the African-American female are thus likely to have different opinions about such matters as the intelligence of African-Americans and for whose benefit the job-getting system is rigged.

Second, most people want to be regarded as normal and part of the group rather than as eccentric and out of step, especially in the eyes of the people and groups that matter to us. Many social psychologists believe that the desire for the approval of one's peers, far more than patriotism or national ideals, accounts for the great courage under fire shown by so many soldiers of so many different nations and ideologies.

Third, if, for instance, people value highly their memberships in particular groups, such as families, sororities, religious organizations, or labor unions, and derive real personal satisfaction from those associations, they may well feel that if they voice opinions sharply different from those of the other members, the groups might shun the dissenters or even break up, thereby depriving the dissenters of the groups' satisfactions and support.

Sometimes those group pressures are exerted by certain members of the group who serve a kind of sergeant-at-arms function. Sometimes pressures are applied through informal communications among members of the group who hold no official position. The strength of the pressures applied to any particular individual depends upon several factors, including the importance of group membership to the individual's own personal satisfactions and the number and strength of the counter pressures exerted by other groups with conflicting goals of which the individual is also a member.

Types of Influential Group Memberships

Social scientists generally agree that primary groups have more influence upon the political opinions of their members than the more impersonal categoric groups. However, most primary groups are segments of particular categoric groups. One useful way to describe the more influential types of group membership is thus to consider pairs of related primary and categoric groups. Table 3.2 illustrates the point by showing the views on some current public issues held by the members of various categoric groups in the United States.

FAMILIES AND ETHNIC GROUPS   The first group of which most of us become aware is our family. We get many of our values, reality perceptions, opinions, and behavior patterns from parents, brothers, and sisters. Indeed, we often hear that most people "inherit" their party affiliations and political attitudes from their parents.

Most families are based largely or exclusively on blood relationships and are therefore parts of particular ethnic groups. Social scientists define an **ethnic group** as *a group of people who share a common ancestry and a common and distinctive culture.* The ethnic groups most often discussed are the presumably genetically based "races" (Caucasoid, Negroid, Mongoloid, and so on), but the term also includes groups associated with particular areas, ancestries, and cultures (Asian-Americans and Hispanic-Americans in the United States; Flemings and Walloons in Belgium; Bretons in France; Scots and Welsh in Great Britain; Basques and Catolonians in Spain; Hutus

TABLE 3.2   Differences in American Groups' Political Opinions (in percentages)

	1992 VOTE			ABORTION			REDUCE DEFICIT BY		
	Clinton	Bush	Perot	Pro-choice	Middle	Pro-life	Cut Defense	Cut Social Progress	Raise Taxes
Men	41	38	21	21	59	20	64	46	25
Women	46	37	17	22	54	24	59	37	21
White	39	41	20	23	57	21	60	45	23
African-American	82	11	7	15	51	34	72	20	23
Protestant	31	50	19	18	58	23	na	na	na
Catholic	44	36	20	16	57	27	na	na	na
Jewish	78	12	10	na	na	na	na	na	na
Some college	42	37	21	27	60	13	68	44	31
High school graduate	43	36	20	17	55	28	55	42	20
High school nongraduate	55	28	17	na	na	na	59	35	15
Age 18–29	44	34	22	21	57	22	56	38	18
Age 30–44	42	38	20	24	56	21	62	40	23
Age 45–59	41	40	19	19	57	24	64	47	13
Age 60+	50	38	12	na	na	na	na	na	na

Source: Figure 1.2 and the Gallup Poll.

and Tutsis in Rwanda and Burundi, Serbs, Croats, and Bosnians in the former Yugoslovia; and, most diverse of all, Armenians, Estonians, Georgians, Latvians, Lithuanians, Russians, Ukrainians, and many others in the former Soviet Union).

Social scientists believe that political opinions are influenced to some extent by membership in particular ethnic groups. Some, indeed believe that ethnic-group passions are rising in many nations, sometimes leading to their breakup (as in the former Soviet Union) and/or civil war (as in the former Yugoslavia and present-day Rwanda). Others feel in most societies the political influence of ethnic groups is weaker than that of families. Ethnic influences appear to be strongest among members of minority groups (for example, African-Americans, Asians, Hispanics, and Jews in the United States, and Tutsis in Rwanda) that feel threatened by larger groups.

FRIENDS AND AGE GROUPS   The second group of which most of us become aware is our circle of friends. Most of us want our friends' approval and we are strongly influenced by their opinions, not only in childhood and adolescence but in adult life as well.

Who are our friends? Many of them are people like ourselves. They live in the same kinds of neighborhoods, attend the same kinds of schools, belong to the religious organizations, come from similar economic levels and social classes, and often work at the same kinds of jobs. Many of our friends are also close to us in age. Moreover, as everyone knows, younger people often see some social and political matters quite differently from older people. Indeed, much of our literature is focused on the conflict between the young and the old ("between callowness and senility," as one cynic has put it). Most social scientists agree that membership in particular age groups has some influence upon most people's opinions, and the data in Table 3.2 support that conclusion.

CONGREGATIONS AND RELIGIOUS GROUPS   Many of us attend Sunday school as young children and later join church or synagogue youth organizations and become members of congregations. Most religions are deeply concerned with values and conceptions of the universe, and most try to educate their members in both. There is no doubt that many people's attitudes on many matters are powerfully influenced by their membership in particular congregations and religious denominations.

Moreover, many organized religions make official pronouncements on some political issues and have some direct influence on the political opinions and behavior of their members. Witness, for example, the role of the Roman Catholic Church in the abortion controversy described in Chapter 2. Nations that encourage particular religions or restrict others—for example, Saudi Arabia (Islam) and Spain (Roman Catholicism)—thereby give the favored religions particularly influential roles in the formation of political opinions and public policy.

However, even in nations such as the United States, which have no officially "established" or favored religion (that is, no particular faith or denomination officially favored by the government), religious leaders have considerable influence upon the political opinions of a great many people. The recent campaigns by certain born-again Protestant groups in favor of prayers in the public schools and by the Roman Catholic Church against abortions are cases in point.

SCHOOLMATES AND EDUCATIONAL GROUPS   Modern nations vary greatly in the amounts of formal education their citizens receive, but in most nations both the proportion of those attending school and the average time spent in school are increasing year by year. The U.S. census estimated that in 1990, 43 percent of the U.S. population aged 18 or older had had at least some college education, 80 percent were high school graduates, and nearly everyone had had some high school education. All three figures were higher than those in the 1980 census reports, and those in the 2000 reports should be higher still. The opinions of most Americans, therefore, are exposed to the influence of both schoolmates and school authorities, and with some impact, as is shown by the numbers in Table 3.2.

The purposes of education in all nations, democratic and authoritarian alike, include instructing the young in some of the skills and techniques needed to perform useful roles in society—for example, reading, writing, counting, and perhaps driving automobiles and operating computers—and also introducing them to the nation's special political values and beliefs. In the United States the schools are committed to educating their pupils in the principles of democracy and capitalism, just as in Iran the schools are committed to educating Iranian youth in the principles of the Shi'ite version of Islam and the late Ayatollah Khomeini's doctrines of the Islamic Republic.

In many nations the schools are considered to be such important shapers of opinion that they are perennial subjects of political controversy. We are all familiar with the frequent clashes in this or that part of our country over whether the schools are teaching our young people the proper values and beliefs. We often hear charges

POLITICAL SOCIALIZATION IN SCHOOLS. A high school social studies class.

from American conservatives that our schools are teaching "sexual immorality," "socialism," and "atheism." We also hear charges from liberals that our schools are "apologists for big business" or "racist." Since most schools in most modern nations, democratic and authoritarian alike, are owned and operated by governments rather than by private organizations, what schools do and how they do it are always political issues. Schools are constantly subject to powerful and often conflicting pressures from public officials, parents, students, teachers, religious groups, and economic pressure groups.

WORK ASSOCIATES AND OCCUPATIONAL GROUPS   Most adults spend half or more of their waking hours at work. In terms of sheer frequency of face-to-face contact, the people we see at work every day constitute one of our most important primary groups, and social scientists have discovered that such groups usually have high degrees of agreement in their political opinions.

Small groups of work associates are also segments of larger and more impersonal occupational groups, such as college professors, retail merchants, carpenters, unskilled laborers, farm managers, business executives, white-collar workers, and the like. However, the evidence suggests that membership in this kind of categoric group has less influence on people's political opinions than does their membership in many of the other kinds of groups we have discussed.

NEIGHBORS, INCOME GROUPS, AND SOCIAL CLASSES   The remaining primary group important to most of us is our neighbors, the people who live in our immediate residential areas. Social scientists have long noted that most neighborhoods are composed largely of people of the same or similar ethnic groups, religious groups, educational levels, and income levels.

They are also likely to be members of the same social class, a concept that requires some definition and explanation. According to Karl Marx, a founder of the theory of communism, a social class is a group of people holding the same position in the production process. In Marx's view, there are only two social classes: the capitalists, who own the instruments of production; and the workers, who operate but do not own the instruments. Marx's doctrine of class struggle holds that there is an inevitable war to the death between capitalists and workers. All politics is simply a manifestation of the war between capitalists and workers.

Non-Marxist social scientists, however, define a **social class** simply as *a group of persons who share the same socioeconomic status*. The non-Marxists view society as being divided into several more than Marx's two classes. Each class, they say, is based upon a number of distinctions (for example, ethnic identity, length of family residence in the nation and in the local community, educational level, income, and occupational prestige). Most of those distinctions are difficult to measure precisely, so the boundaries between one class and another are usually indistinct, and identifying the class memberships of particular persons is often difficult. The criteria of class membership used most often are income and educational level, but few, if any, non-Marxist social scientists consider those criteria to be the *only* factors determining social class. Nevertheless, even though social scientists differ on exactly what characteristics should be used to classify people by class, most believe that class membership has a significant influence upon the political opinions of most people.

Variable Impact of Group Membership

No social group has the same political impact on each and every one of its members. This is made clear by the facts we examined in Chapter 1 about the internal division of every social group in elections. As recent studies of voters in the 1992 election show, 82 percent of African-Americans favored Bill Clinton, but, even so, 11 percent voted for George Bush and 7 percent voted for Ross Perot. Even more striking is the fact that in the 1980 presidential election, despite Jimmy Carter's well-known status as a "born-again" Baptist and Ronald Reagan's divorce and spotty church attendance, Protestants split 56 to 37 for Reagan, while Catholics gave Reagan a smaller but still useful 51 to 40 margin.

Most social scientists believe that the impact of membership in a particular social group upon a person's political views and behavior depends upon several factors.

THE GROUP'S IMPORTANCE FOR THE INDIVIDUAL   Some people regard their status as, for instance, women, African-Americans, Roman Catholics, or union members as the most important thing in their lives, and the particular group membership has a powerful effect on their attitudes and behavior. However, other women, African-Americans, Roman Catholics, and union members do not see those group affiliations as that important, and they develop their political views from a greater variety of sources. Social psychologists tell us that the more strongly a group's members identify themselves with a group, the more likely they are to think and behave in ways that make that group different from other groups. There is also a good deal of evidence that in most cases the strength of a person's identification with a group is closely related to how long the person has been a member of that group. For example, people who have been raised in Democratic families and have always thought of themselves as good Democrats are more likely to be strong partisans than are people who were raised as Republicans but have recently switched parties.

PERCEIVED POLITICAL RELEVANCE OF THE GROUP   Strong identification with a group is not enough by itself to shape a person's politics completely. For example, some union members who strongly identify with their union may nevertheless see it only as an organization that helps them get better wages, hours, and working conditions; and they may not know or care much about its political activities and stands. Their political attitudes and behavior are much less likely to be influenced by their union's politics than are those of unionists who identify strongly with the union in all of its activities, including politics.

TRANSMISSION OF GROUP POLITICAL STANDARDS   The leaders of some social groups make regular efforts to convince their members that the leaders' views on issues and candidates are correct. Leaders of other groups, on the other hand, make weak efforts or no effort at all. Evidence suggests that the organization's importance and political relevance for its members increase as such "transmissions" from the leadership increase.

Political Socialization

CONCEPT

While our memberships in a number of primary and categoric groups have an important impact on our political attitudes and behavior, there is nothing automatic or mindless about it. We know from the studies of childrens' political attitudes that a boy born to upper-middle-class white Republican parents living in an expensive suburb does not say as soon as he begins to talk that he is a conservative or that he favors prayer in the schools or that he admires Newt Gingrich. As an adult he may well say all those things, but he, like the rest of us, was not born with those attitudes. We have all acquired our political outlooks the old-fashioned way: We have *learned* them. Political scientists call this learning process **political socialization**, which is *the developmental process from which people acquire their political orientations and patterns of behavior*. It is the main process by which people's primary and categoric group memberships are translated into their political attitudes and behavior.

PROFILE OF THE DEVELOPING POLITICAL SELF

For most people, political socialization begins early in life and continues until old age or death. There are, of course, many variations in the content and pace of socialization from one person to another, one social group to another, and one nation to another. However, there are enough similarities among people in the United States and in other developed nations that we can outline the socialization cycle in the following general terms.

Beginnings

Political socialization begins as early as the third or fourth year of life, when children first perceive a few basic political objects—such as the president, the police, and "the government"—as somehow different from their families or the people next door. Children also learn at about the same time that they are part of some groups that are larger and more remote than their families (for example, Americans, African-Americans, Jews, females). By the age of seven many children even say unhesitatingly, "We are Democrats" or "We are Republicans" (note the plural form). In those early years the children's identifications have more emotional than cognitive content; that is, they know that they are Democrats or Republicans but they are not very clear about how Democrats differ from Republicans or about why they are one rather than the other. But many of the knowledge gaps are filled in quite soon.

Childhood

From ages six to eighteen, most children live at home and attend public schools through the twelfth grade (legally they must attend until age sixteen). From their parents, teachers, and increasingly from television, they not only acquire such basic skills as reading and arithmetic but also learn a good deal about the political world. Children move from highly personalized conceptions of "the government" as synonymous with "the police officer" and "the president" to more abstract and general notions of institutional character and ideals. Children perceive with increasing clarity the different identities and activities of the president, the police officer, the mayor, the governor, and eventually the legislature and the courts.

Research shows that most children in the fourth grade (average age nine) can name the president of the United States and the mayor of their town. Considerably fewer than half of them, however, can say anything reasonably accurate about the more abstract and general matter of those and other public officials' duties; but higher proportions of eighth graders (average age thirteen) can. This difference illustrates the proposition that political knowledge in children generally develops from the individualized and personalized to the more general and abstract. The process continues, and by age fourteen children's political perceptions are about as sharp and as clear as they will ever be, and their affective responses to many political objects (for example, the political parties) are well established.

Adolescence

Adolescence, according to the dictionary, is "the period of life from puberty to maturity terminating legally at the age of majority": that is, from age thirteen or fourteen (younger for girls) to age eighteen in most nations. Most psychologists believe that adolescence is the most painful and difficult period in personal development. Sexuality emerges, the "silver cord" binding child to parents is frayed or severed, the first independent decisions are made, and so on. The psychic maladjustments often produced by those personal crises sometimes find political outlets, particularly in support for sweeping proposals to clear away the corrupt institutions and hypocritical attitudes of the adult establishment and to replace them with a brave new society cleansed of war, greed, sexism, racism, and all the other evils that most adults seem to accept.

Thus, most investigators of political socialization find that there is a considerable spurt in political learning between the ages of eleven and fifteen, especially in the growth of understanding of the larger political world beyond individuals and their families; and by mid-adolescence most teenagers begin to resemble adults politically.

Studies of adolescent psychology and behavior, however, suggest that only a small minority express their rebellion in active political ways (for example, by becoming members of partisan organizations such as the Young Republicans or the Young Democrats). From the mid-1960s to the early 1970s, to be sure, there was a great wave of active student protest at many colleges and universities not only in the United States but also in Great Britain, Italy, France, Scandinavia, and Japan. Even at its height, however, that protest involved only a minority of students.

Perhaps the clearest evidence of the relatively low level of young people's political involvement is shown by voting turnout figures. All Americans over the age of eighteen were guaranteed the right to vote by the adoption of the Twenty-sixth Amendment to the U.S. Constitution in 1971, but the figures in Table 3.3 show that in presidential elections since then, younger people have voted in far lower proportions than older people.

Adulthood

Table 3.3 shows that the older people become the more likely they are to vote. (They also participate more in other ways.) There are good reasons for this. After reaching the legal age of adulthood, most people begin to acquire an ever-greater stake in society and therefore in what government does or fails to do. They complete their formal educations; take jobs or open businesses; marry; and acquire houses, automobiles, television sets, and debts. As a result of those and other changes in their lives, they become more politicized. That is, they grow more concerned and know more about political affairs; their preferences grow more intense; their group affiliations, such as their party identifications, become stronger; and as a result, older people are more likely to vote and to participate in politics in other ways.

For most of us, politicization in the adult years does not mean switching the party preferences and issue positions we held as children and adolescents; it means intensifying our original preferences and positions. Most adults, for example, do not switch parties. Rather, they move from being "independents" or "weak identifiers" to being more strongly identified Democrats or Republicans, although this tendency has weakened in recent years.

Old Age

When does political old age begin? If changes in the proportions of voters to nonvoters are an indication, then it appears that in the United States political old age begins in the mid-sixties. Some voting studies show a steady increase in voter turnout at each higher age level from eighteen to about sixty-five and a slow decline thereafter. This decline no doubt results partly from increasing physical infirmities, but it also suggests that the decline in general social and economic involvement (especially after retirement) produces some depoliticization that is the opposite of the politicization that takes place from the early twenties to the mid-sixties. Seventy-year-olds still vote substantially more than do twenty-five-year-olds but somewhat less than people between the ages of thirty and sixty.

TABLE 3.3   Voting Turnout by Age Groups, 1980–1992

Age Group	PERCENT VOTING FOR PRESIDENT			
	1980	1984	1988	1992
18–20	35.7	36.7	33.2	38.5
21–24	43.1	43.5	38.3	45.7
25–34	54.6	54.5	48.0	53.2
35–44	64.4	63.5	61.3	63.6
45–64	69.3	69.8	67.9	70.0
65 and older	65.1	67.7	68.8	70.1

Source: Statistical Abstract of the United States 1993 (Washington, DC: Bureau of the Census, 1993), Table 454, p. 283.

AGENTS OF SOCIALIZATION

We noted earlier that people's political orientations and behavior patterns are learned, not fixed at birth. Political socialization, like all forms of learning, is a process of interaction between the learners and certain elements of their environment generally called *socializing agents*. Among the agents political scientists consider most important are families, schools, peer groups, and the mass communications media.

Families

The nuclear family—particularly parents but also to some degree brothers and sisters—is for many people the most powerful socializing agent in their lives. It is the first group of which they become aware. During the crucial formative years from birth to age five or six, people are in far closer contact with the family than with any other group or social influence. One fascinating exception to this general truth is the *kibbutzim* (collective settlements) of Israel, in most of which children are raised in communal centers rather than in their parents' homes. This has political consequences: Several studies have shown that kibbutz children are more "ideological" and more like one another in their attitudes than are children raised in their parents' homes in the rest of Israel. But for most people in most nations, the psychological pressures toward conformity in primary groups, which we considered earlier in this chapter, are strongest of all in the family.

Thus, it is not surprising that there is a widespread tendency for children's political attitudes, preferences, and levels of interest and activity to resemble those of their parents, as is shown by the data about the party identifications of parents and their children in Table 3.4.

Table 3.4 shows that in all three countries, parents' party identifications are a good—but far from perfect—basis for predicting their children's identifications. Parent–child agreements are stronger when both parents have the same identification and weaker when they are divided. They are also stronger when one or both parents often discuss political questions with, or at least in front of, their children and weaker when the parents show little or no political interest or activity.

We should note, however, that parental influence on children's partisanship has weakened noticeably in recent years. Studies conducted since the late 1960s show that people under thirty today are less likely than were people under thirty in the 1960s to have the same party preferences as their parents. Moreover, many of those young people have abandoned their parents' Democratic or Republican affiliations, not to join the other party or even a third party, but to become self-styled "independents."

The strength of those factors, in turn, depends partly upon the society's and the parents' ideas about what kind of conversations, if any, parents should have with (or in the presence of) their children. For example, a comparative study of French and American political attitudes revealed, surprisingly, that the French are generally less involved in politics than Americans. The authors explained that the reason is suggested by the fact that 86 percent of the American respondents, but only 26 percent of the French, could describe their father's party preferences. Why

TABLE 3.4   Party Identifications of Parents and Children in Three Nations (in percentages)

CHILD	PARENT			
United States	*Democrat*	*Independent*	*Republican*	
Democrat	70	40	25	
Independent	20	40	21	
Republican	10	20	54	
	100%	100%	100%	
Great Britain	*Labour*	*Liberal*	*Conservative*	*None*
Labour	51	17	6	29
Liberal	8	39	11	6
Conservative	1	11	50	6
None	40	33	33	59
	100%	100%	100%	100%
West Germany	*SPD*	*FDP*	*CDU/CSU*	*None*
SPD	53	8	14	19
FDP	4	59	1	3
CDU/CSU	9	—	32	12
None	34	33	53	66
	100%	100%	100%	100%

Source: Russell J. Dalton, *Citizen Politics in Western Democracies* (Chatham, NJ: Chatham House, 1988), Table 9.1, p. 182.

this strikingly low figure for the French? Probably because, as the French respondents often said of their fathers, "Il ne disait rien a ses enfants (He doesn't say anything to his children)"; "il n'en parlait jamais (he never talks)."[4] If Papa does not discuss politics with or in front of his children and if his children do not know how he feels about politics, then the socialization process will be more indirect and the family less influential in it.

However, in France as in all advanced/industralized societies the structure of families is changing. Increased rates of divorce have produced many more single-parent families. Increased proportions of wives working have resulted in more children in day care and earlier exposure of children to schools and to a greater variety in the social class and ethnic identities of their schoolmates. The child-rearing responsibilities of wives and husbands have become more equal. All these changes are bound to have a significant impact on the role of families in political socialization, but we do not yet fully understand the nature of that impact.

Schools

All governments try to instill at least some political attitudes and behavior patterns in their citizens. All, for example, try to maximize national patriotism and obedience to law. Some (especially the democratic countries) try to encourage voter turnout and other forms of popular political participation. Others (such as Saudi Arabia) try to encourage the belief that political affairs are best left to the few people who are especially qualified to rule. Still others (like the People's Republic of China) try to encourage popular support of the leaders' policies by training all citizens to perform their assigned duties energetically and enthusiastically.

Whatever their objectives, governments rely heavily on the public schools to instill the desired attitudes. For one thing, it is difficult to monitor and control what parents tell children. Even in the Soviet Union of Stalin and Brezhnev, for example, "the family [acted] as an impediment to full and enthusiastic acceptance of the official system of beliefs, especially of those which stress[ed] militancy, total conformity, and instant adaptation to shifting public demands."[5]

For another thing, the public schools are organized, financed, staffed, and programmed by governmental agencies, and children are required to attend school from ages five or six until middle adolescence. Schools thus provide the government's most effective direct channel for shaping young people's political attitudes and behavior.

Formal education is certainly powerful in children's political socialization. Perhaps the best evidence is the nearly universal tendency for the most educated people to have the strongest sense of *political efficacy* (that is, the feeling that public officials can be influenced by their ideas and wishes), to be the most politically interested and informed, and to take the most active roles in political affairs. Many people regard education as the last and best hope for curing social ills, such as war, sexism, and racism.

However, formal education is certainly not an absolute, irresistible weapon for forming a child's—or an adult's—attitudes. When children hear one thing in the classroom and quite another at home or from their playmates, there is no reason to think that they will believe teachers and textbooks rather than parents and peers. In his classic study of life in a French village, Laurence Wylie tells how the civics textbooks used in the village school had eloquent and lengthy passages on the democratic ideal of trust in others, the high mission of government, the important contributions of political parties, and so on. But, he writes, *outside* school the children

> constantly hear adults referring to Government as a source of evil and to the men who run it as instruments of evil. There is nothing personal in this belief. It does not concern one particular Government composed of one particular group of men. It concerns Government everywhere and at all times—French Governments, American Governments, Russian Governments, all Governments. Some are less bad than others, but all are essentially bad.[6]

In France, as elsewhere, schools and families working together are a good deal more effective than when either is working at cross purposes with the other.

Peer Groups

In addition to parents, siblings, and teachers, most people spend much of their lives in the company of "peer groups" (that is, people who have important characteristics in common, such as age or social status) and derive cues from one another about how to behave. Schoolmates are one important peer group, as are work associates and friendship cliques.

What do we know about the role of such groups in political socialization? In such developed societies as the United States and Sweden the socializing influence of parents and teachers begins to wane in early adolescence, and from then on peer groups become increasingly important in shaping political attitudes and behavior. As people grow older, some peer groups that were highly influential in their adolescence are superseded by others made salient by their new life circumstances, such as work associates, neighbors, and, above all, spouses. One proof is the political homogeneity of various primary groups. Several studies of U.S. voting behavior have shown that the most politically homogeneous of all American groups, primary or secondary, are husband–wife pairs, followed by friendship groups and then by groups of work associates.

In primitive and traditional societies, on the other hand, most people have many fewer contacts and much less involvement with people outside their families; and the peer groups that do exist are much less powerful as socializing agents than in the advanced/industrialized nations. However, one significant effect—and cause—of political modernization in those societies will be a sharp decrease in the family's traditional near monopoly of socialization and a parallel increase in the influence of the schools, peer groups, and the mass communications media.

Mass Communications Media

In Chapter 7 we will consider at some length how mass communications media (mainly television, radio, and newspapers) influence public opinion. Here we note only that in all nations with technologically advanced mass communications, the media play a major role in shaping the cognitive maps as well as the specific opinions of most people.

How could it be otherwise? Most American children begin watching television at the age of three months. By the time they finish high school, they have spent fewer than 12,000 hours in classrooms but more than 22,000 hours in front of television sets. Americans over eighteen spend more time watching television (four hours a day on the average) than doing anything else except sleeping and working. Moreover, most Americans say they get more political information from television—and trust its accuracy more—than from any other source, including their families and friends. The same is true in the other technologically advanced countries.

The media can play an even greater role in the developing nations, for there they provide the government's best tool—far better than the schools—for modernizing citizens' traditional outlooks and behavior. After all, schools affect mainly the young, but political leaders often feel that they must change adult orientations immediately without waiting for the new generation to take over. The mass media can reach the largest number of people—adults *and* children—in the shortest time. Leading illiterate masses out of their ancient ways into new ones is tricky at best, and the communicators must be careful not to attempt too sharp a break too quickly. But socialization through the mass media is the best short-run technique available, and many scholars—and leaders of developing nations—believe that it is crucial to political modernization.

To summarize: Every political system operates as it does largely because of the kind of people, both elites and masses, who make the demands and constitute the targets for the system's policies. The people's basic beliefs about the way things are, their convictions about the way things should be, and their accustomed modes of political behavior all fix very real limits on whether and how government can achieve its goals. People's beliefs and values are not congenital or instinctive. Beliefs are *learned* through the process we call political socialization. Some socializing agents, particularly the schools and the mass media, are directly controlled to some degree by governments to instill the desired attitudes and behavior patterns in their citizens. Other agents, particularly families and peer groups, are much freer from direct government control. Many families and peer groups thus preserve and pass on attitudes that differ significantly from those that governments want their people to absorb.

Whatever their sources, the dominant beliefs and values in any nation constitute what political scientists call political culture; that is, the social-psychological climate that shapes and constrains its political system. We turn now to a closer look at components and consequences of political culture.

Political Culture

COMPONENTS

As we use the term in this book, a nation's **political culture** is *a broadly shared set of ways of thinking about politics and government*, a pattern of orientations to political objects. Political culture provides the psychological environment within which political conflict is conducted and public policy is made, and it has two main components: *cognitive orientations* (knowledge and awareness of political objects) and *affective orientations* (feelings and emotions about the objects).

Cognitive Orientations

Cognitive orientations are what people believe about how things really work in the political world. Scholars of political culture are often struck by the low levels of information many people have about political affairs. Just how low those levels are in the United States is suggested by the scores in Table 3.5.

The numbers in Table 3.5 are intriguing. During the 1992 congressional campaigns Republican challengers of Democratic incumbents in both houses stressed the point that the Democrats had been in control of the House since 1954 and of the Senate since 1986, so a change in party control was long overdue. Yet barely half of those polled knew that the Democrats controlled the House, and less than half knew that the Democrats controlled the Senate. The respondents' knowledge about the American and foreign leaders was spotty. Most knew that Dan Quayle was vice president, but only a handful knew that George Mitchell was majority leader in the Senate, that Tom Foley was speaker of the House, and that William Rehnquist was chief jus-

TABLE 3.5   U.S. Public's Knowledge of Leaders and Institutions, 1992

Question	PERCENT ANSWERING		
	Correctly	Incorrectly	Don't Know
Which party has the most members in the U.S. House of Representatives?	51.7	16.3	32.0
Which party has the most members in the U.S. Senate?	43.4	17.0	39.6
What job or office does this person now hold?			
Dan Quayle	82.3	1.8	15.9
George Mitchell	2.6	13.0	84.4
William Rehnquist	4.3	19.2	76.5
Mikhail Gorbachev	71.3	12.4	16.3
Margaret Thatcher	52.9	27.0	20.1
Nelson Mandela	16.4	48.9	34.7
Tom Foley	10.4	8.6	81.0

Data compiled from the University of Michigan Center for Political and Social Studies, 1992 National Election Study, and made available by the Inter-University Consortium for Political and Social Research.

tice of the United States. On the other hand, more than half correctly identified the positions of Mikhail Gorbachev and Margaret Thatcher but not of Nelson Mandela.

Levels of information can make a difference when evaluating government policies. For example, a study of popular attitudes toward business regulation demonstrated that when people are asked how high business profits are, their answers average between 25 and 30 percent of each dollar of revenue (the correct answer is about 5 percent). Moreover, many more of those whose estimates are high rather than of those whose estimates are low favor strong regulation of business.[7]

Affective Orientations

People, of course, not only believe that certain things are true about politics and government but they also like some things and dislike others. For one thing, people have different values and priorities: Some judge things mainly according to whether they seem to promote "law and order" and "stability" while others place the highest value on "social justice" and "fairness." For another thing, different people can look at the same political objects and have very different likes and dislikes. For example, in the 1992 U.S. presidential election some people saw Ross Perot as a smart, truth-telling non-politician, while to others he was an arrogant rich man trying to buy the presidency. By the same token, some saw Bill Clinton as a smart and resourceful problem solver, while to others he was "slick Willie," a politician willing to say anything to win votes.

It is important to note that the factual beliefs and political preferences that make up a nation's political culture do not have to be logically consistent with one another. Indeed, the evidence suggests that most political cultures, particularly those in the "advanced" nations, fall far short of logical consistency. In the United States, for example, most of us endorse such sentiments as "Love thy neighbor as thyself" and "Help those less fortunate than yourself," but we also hold quite different sentiments, such as "The Lord helps those who help themselves" and "The wheel that squeaks the loudest gets the grease." Most of us believe in "efficient" and "businesslike" government, but we also believe in separation of powers and checks and balances, which inevitably cause a great deal of inefficiency by making it difficult for any one leader or party to take charge. Perhaps of greatest importance, most of us want government to provide good education, social security benefits, a strong defense, good roads and bridges, and many other services, but we strongly oppose raising taxes to pay for them.

Do those inconsistencies in political cultures prove that we are fools and knaves, or do they simply show that we are human beings acting like humans? Without choosing among these labels, we can observe that every nation's political culture contains some incongruities and that, however inconsistent and illogical, every nation's political culture constitutes one of the most powerful influences shaping its political system.

SOME DIFFERENCES AMONG POLITICAL CULTURES

Patriotism: Identification with the Nation

Most political scientists agree that one of the most powerful determinants of a nation's political stability and governmental effectiveness is the extent to which its citizens give their primary political loyalties to their nation, rather than to one of its classes or regions or tribes or religions. For example, many new African and Asian nations have faced crises of identity shortly after achieving independence. Some, such as Botswana, Ghana, and Tunisia, have weathered them well enough, though not without some scars, while others, such as Rwanda, Nigeria, and Pakistan, have had much rougher going.

There are also significant variations in strength of national identity among the developed nations. National identity is very strong, for example, in Japan, Norway, and Sweden. It is strong in the United States, though less so because the United States is a multi-ethnic nation. It is strong in Great Britain, though challenged by Welsh and Scottish nationalism. On the other hand, we learned in Chapter 1 that national identity has recently crumbled completely in at least two Eastern European countries. From 1917 to the late 1980s, the iron rule by the Communist leaders of the USSR kept the lid on the local loyalties and aspirations for independence of the nation's fifteen constituent republics; but when Mikhail Gorbachev eased the pressure after 1986, all fifteen declared their independence and thereby dissolved the USSR. Similarly, for decades after 1945, the Communist leaders of Yugoslavia, notably Marshal Tito, successfully repressed the historically powerful local patriotisms of Croatia, Serbia, and Slovenia, but in the early 1990s Croatia and Slovenia declared their independence and a bloody civil war ensued. Both crises underline the fact that, pure or diluted, strong or weak, the degree of the citizen's identification with the nation powerfully affects the stability and effectiveness of the nation's political system.

Trust in People

A second component of political culture is trust in other people, and it too varies widely from nation to nation. For example, a pioneering comparative study of the United States, Great Britain, Germany, Italy, and Mexico showed, among other things, that most Italians feel that only members of their own immediate families can be trusted and that everyone else is a potential enemy, to be watched and guarded against but never trusted. When people in each nation were asked to agree or disagree with the statement, "Most people can be trusted," only 7 percent of the Italians agreed, compared with 55 percent of the Americans, 49 percent of the British, 30 percent of the Mexicans, and 19 percent of the Germans.[8]

Confidence in Institutions

No government can rely entirely on physical force to ensure obedience to its laws. Realistically speaking, a government can shoot or torture or imprison only a small fraction of its citizens, and when a large number of citizens resolutely refuse to obey, the authorities are authoritative no longer. Thus, every government, authoritarian as well as democratic, has no choice but to rely mainly on most citizens' *voluntary* compliance with its laws. The first prerequisite for such compliance is the prevalence of popular confidence that the authorities have won their posts rightfully, that they make and enforce their decisions by proper procedures, and that their decisions affect matters that are the government's proper business and do not encroach on what is rightfully private and personal. Where such confidence is high, governments need only minimum force to deal with lawbreakers. Where the authorities' legitimacy is widely questioned, however, lawbreaking is a major problem, and even revolution is possible. Table 3.6 shows the levels of confidence in government in five democratic nations.

Table 3.6 offers several interesting international comparisons. The American people have by far the highest average level of confidence in the leaders of their institutions, and the Spanish have by far the lowest in theirs. This probably results in part from the fact that the basic democratic structure of U.S. politics and government has been stable since the end of the Civil War in 1865, while Spain was a dictatorship under Francisco Franco from 1936 to 1975. As recently as 1981 there was an unsuccessful effort by the military to overthrow the fledgling democratic regime, and Spaniards have not yet developed a sense of the strength and permanence of their institutions comparable to the confidence of Americans. Table 3.6 also shows that in most of the five nations public confidence is lowest in labor unions, the business community, and the mass communications media (agencies of competition and conflict), and it is highest in the schools, the military, and the police (agencies of development and law and order). The legislative and judicial agencies of government (agencies of both contention and order) fall in the middle.

However, although confidence in governmental institutions may be higher in the United States than in the European democracies, it is far from complete. For example, a study of the electorate in the 1992 presidential election found that 64 per-

TABLE 3.6   Popular Confidence in Institutions in the United States and Europe

| INSTITUTIONS | PERCENTAGE EXPRESSING "A GREAT DEAL" OR "SOME" CONFIDENCE IN EACH INSTITUTION | | | | | |
	United States	Great Britain	Germany	France	Spain	Average
Police	88	80	80	72	44	73
Schools	82	53	82	82	59	72
Military	86	79	69	59	36	66
Judicial system	77	56	72	62	35	60
Church	85	56	66	53	38	60
Parliament/Congress	83	53	64	55	30	57
Press/radio/TV	69	38	41	48	46	48
Business community	84	55	44	30	26	48
Labor unions	52	29	43	36	26	37
Average	87	61	62	55	38	61

Source: Laurence Parisot, "Attitudes about the Media: A Five Country Comparison," *Public Opinion*, January–February 1988, p. 18.

cent agreed with the statement, "Public officials don't care much about what people like me think." Fifty-three percent agreed that "People like me don't have much say about what the government does." And 64 percent (hopefully, not political science students) agreed that "Sometimes politics and government seem so complicated that a person like me can't really understand what's going on."[9]

Citizens' Obligations

We noted in Chapter 2 that all governments can and sometimes do enforce their laws by *sanctions*, including fines, imprisonment, and even death. We also learned that every government, democratic or authoritarian, depends much more on voluntary compliance than on sanctions.

Accordingly, one of the most important elements in every political culture is the sense of *citizens' obligations*, or what citizens think they owe the government. Most political philosophers have said that the first obligation of a citizen is *loyalty* or *patriotism*, which means putting the security and welfare of their own nation and government above those of all other nations and governments. Closely tied to this is *obeying the law*, which means doing what the authorities have required and not doing what the authorities have forbidden regardless of whether citizens agree with the wisdom or fairness of the authorities' decisions. Not many people enjoy paying taxes and probably even fewer enjoy being drafted into military service, but governments depend upon the willingness of most citizens to do both, voluntarily if not cheerfully. Many democratic theorists argue that citizens also have the obligation to *participate* in the nation's political processes not only by voting but also by signing petitions, writing letters to their elected representatives and newspapers, attending political meetings, joining organizations involved in politics, and the like.

TAX EVASION

Paying taxes is a prime example of a citizen's obligation to government. Governments cannot do anything for very long unless people pay their taxes. Yet governments cannot hire enough tax collectors and auditors to check on more than a small fraction of the millions of people who owe taxes, so they have no choice but to depend on most people's voluntarily filling out the complicated forms and sending in the checks. Withholding some taxes from people's paychecks helps, but government still depends mainly upon voluntary payments.

Consequently, every nation offers great opportunities for people to cheat on taxes. People can fiddle their income tax returns by reporting that they earned less money than they actually did. They can claim exemptions to which they are not legally entitled. They can even bypass the tax system altogether by bartering with others for goods and services with no cash changing hands and no records being kept.

Every nation is concerned with tax evasion and the reasons for it. Although we have no hard evidence on the matter, it is said that in the political cultures of some countries, notably Italy, France, and a number of Latin American countries, the idea that the citizen has the right to evade taxes is at least as widely held as the idea that good citizens should pay what they owe.

In recent years the U.S. government has become more concerned about how much tax evasion there is in the United States and what kind of popular attitudes underlie it. Accordingly, in 1984 the federal government's Internal Revenue Service hired the polling firm of Yankelovich, Skelly, and White to undertake a study of taxpayer attitudes about compliance. They found that about one-third of their respondents believed that under certain circumstances it is okay to pay less in taxes than the government says they owe, and 19 percent admitted that they had on occasion actually cheated on their taxes. Only about half of the respondents said that it was morally wrong to evade taxes under any circumstances![10] What does this say about the state of American political culture and civic virtue?

A nation's political culture, then, provides the general psychological environment within which the political system must work. But governments are much more conscious of and influenced by the day-to-day pressures of public opinion on particular issues. Those pressures are our concern in the next chapter.

For Further Reading

POLITICAL PSYCHOLOGY

*FESTINGER, LEON. *A Theory of Cognitive Dissonance.* Stanford, CA.: Stanford University Press, 1957. A leading study of how people's likes and dislikes affect their factual perceptions and understandings.

*FINIFTER, ADA W., ed. *Alienation and the Political System.* New York: John Wiley, 1972. Collection of essays on aspects of one important dimension of political psychology.

GREENSTEIN, FRED I. "Personality and Politics," in *Handbook of Political Science*, eds. Fred I. Greenstein and Nelson W. Polsby. Reading, MA: Addison-Wesley, 1975, vol. 2, pp. 1–92. Useful survey.

LAU, RICHARD R., AND DAVID O. SEARS, eds. *Political Cognition.* Hillsdale, NJ: Lawrence Erlbaum, 1986. Essays on how people form their views of what the political world is really like.

SNIDERMAN, PAUL M. *Personality and Democratic Politics.* Berkeley, CA: University of California Press, 1975. Use of data to analyze relationship of personality components to "democratic personality."

TAJFEL, HENRI. *Human Groups and Social Categories.* New York: Cambridge University Press, 1981. A study of the impact of membership in social groups on human attitudes and behavior.

POLITICAL SOCIALIZATION

COLEMAN, JAMES S. *The Adolescent Society.* New York: Free Press, 1961. Study of developing political attitudes in teenagers.

*DAWSON, RICHARD E., AND KENNETH PREWITT. *Political Socialization,* 2nd ed. Boston, MA: Little, Brown, 1977. General survey of research findings about the nature of political socialization.

*GREENSTEIN, FRED I. *Children and Politics,* rev. ed. New Haven, CT: Yale University Press, 1967. Early study of political socialization.

*JENNINGS, M. KENT, AND RICHARD G. NIEMI. *The Political Character of Adolescence: The Influence of Families and Schools.* Princeton, NJ: Princeton University Press, 1974. Use of survey data to analyze the role of families and schools in forming adolescents' political attitudes.

*————. *Generations and Politics: A Panel Study of Young Adults and their Parents.* Princeton, NJ: Princeton University Press, 1981. Study of changes in attitudes of parent–child pairs over time.

NIEMI, RICHARD G. *How Family Members Perceive Each Other: Political and Social Attitudes in Two Generations.* New Haven, CT: Yale University Press, 1974. Use of survey data to analyze political conflict and accord within families.

*VERBA, SIDNEY. *Small Groups and Political Behavior.* Princeton, NJ: Princeton University Press, 1961. Examines political influence of primary-group membership.

POLITICAL CULTURE

*ALMOND, GABRIEL A., AND SIDNEY VERBA. *The Civil Culture: Political Attitudes and Democracy in Five Nations.* Princeton, NJ: Princeton University Press, 1963. Comparative sample survey of political attitudes in the United States, Great Britain, West Germany, Italy, and Mexico.

DI PALMA, GIUSEPPE. *Apathy and Participation: Mass Politics in Western Societies.* New York: Free Press, 1970. Comparative study of major aspects of political culture in Western democracies.

ECKSTEIN, HARRY. *Theory of Stable Democracy.* Princeton, NJ: Princeton University Press, 1965. Fullest statement of the concept of political culture and examination of its nature and role in ten nations.

ELLIS, RICHARD J. *American Political Cultures.* New York: Oxford University Press, 1993. Analysis of American political culture and its leading subcultures.

*HUNTINGTON, SAMUEL P. *American Politics: The Promise of Disharmony.* Cambridge, MA: Belknap Press of Harvard University Press, 1981. Exploration of American political culture, emphasizing the clash between liberal-democratic ideals and actual political practices.

INGLEHART, RONALD. *Culture Shift in Advanced Industrial Society.* Princeton, NJ: Princeton University Press, 1990. Survey of recent changes in political culture in several Western nations.

MCCLOSKY, HERBERT, AND JOHN ZALLER. *The American Ethos: Public Attitudes Toward Capitalism and Democracy.* Cambridge, MA: Harvard University Press, 1984. Magisterial study using survey data and historical materials to trace the evolution of important components of American political culture.

MARTIN, CURTIS H., AND BRUCE STRONACH. *Politics East and West: A Comparison of Japanese and British Political Cultures.* Armonk, NY: Sharpe, 1992. An ambitious and stimulating comparison of two very different political cultures.

*PYE, LUCIAN W., AND SIDNEY VERBA, eds. *Political Culture and Political Development.* Princeton, NJ: Princeton University Press, 1965. Examination of the nature and role of political culture in ten nations.

*SMITH, HEDRICK. *The New Russians.* New York: Random House, 1990. Illuminating account of the impact of the Gorbachev regime on the life-styles and attitudes of ordinary Russians, by a former *New York Times* Moscow correspondent.

THOMPSON, MICHAEL, RICHARD ELLIS, AND AARON WILDAVSKY. *Cultural Theory.* Boulder, CO: Westview Press, 1990. An application of cultural theory to the understanding of politics.

*WYLIE, LAURENCE. *Village in the Vaucluse,* 3rd ed. Cambridge, MA: Harvard University Press, 1974. Classic study of the political culture and politics of a small town in the south of France.

Notes

1. Angus Campbell, Philip E. Converse, Warren E. Miller, and Donald E. Stokes, *The American Voter* (New York: John Wiley, 1960), Chapter 10.

2. The terms *Left* and *Right* are widely used all over the world to label the two sides of what many people see as the most important ideological cleavage

in politics. Although neither term has a precise definition on which everyone agrees, *Left* generally means a favorable attitude toward the interests of the working classes and *Right* generally means a favorable attitude toward the interests of the middle and upper classes. For a more extended discussion, see Vernon Bogdanor, ed., *The Blackwell Encyclopaedia of Political Institutions* (London: Basil Blackwell, 1987), pp. 324–25. See also Chapter 4 of this book.

3. A 1989 study of 23,199 respondents drawn from all the member nations of the European Community reported in the *Euro-Barometer, 1989* asked the respondents to place themselves on a Left/Right continuum. There were 4,228 (18 percent) who refused or were unable to do so. Of the 18,971 who placed themselves, 5,918 (31 percent) said they were Left; 7,111 (38 percent) said they were Center; and 5,942 (31 percent) said they were Right.

4. Philip E. Converse and Georges Dupeux, "Politicization of the Electorate in France and the United States," in *Elections and the Political Order*, eds. Angus Campbell, Philip E. Converse, Warren E. Miller, and Donald E. Stokes (New York: John Wiley, 1966), pp. 279–81.

5. Frederick C. Barghoorn, *Politics in the USSR* (Boston: Little, Brown, 1966), p. 109.

6. Laurence Wylie, *Village in the Vaucluse* (New York: Harper & Row, 1964), p. 208.

7. Seymour Martin Lipset and William Schneider, *The Confidence Gap: Business, Labor, and Government in the Popular Mind* (New York: Free Press, 1983), pp. 176–84.

8. Gabriel A. Almond and Sidney Verba, *The Civic Culture: Political Attitudes and Democracy in Five Nations* (Princeton, NJ: Princeton University Press, 1963), Table 4, p. 267.

9. *American National Election Study, 1992* (Ann Arbor: Center for Political and Social Studies, 1993), data made available by the Inter-University Consortium for Political and Social Research.

10. Reported in Madelyn Hochstein, "Tax Ethics: Social Values and Noncompliance," *Public Opinion*, February–March 1985, pp. 11–14.

4

The invasion of armies can be resisted, but not an idea whose time has come.
Victor Hugo, *Histoire d'un Crime* (1852)

Ideas won't keep. Something must be done about them. When the idea is new,
its custodians have fervor, live for it, and, if need be, die for it.
Alfred North Whitehead, *Dialogues* (1953)

It is not the consciousness of men that determines their existence, but on the
contrary it is their social existence that determines their consciousness.
Karl Marx, *Critique of Political Economy* (1859)

Don't watch what we say. Watch what we do.
Edwin Meese, Counselor to President Reagan (1981)

Modern Political Ideologies

In Chapter 3 we observed that what people think, say, and do in politics is shaped by their "cognitive maps," which is a metaphor for the basic mental structures by which people receive and interpret signals from the outside world and form their beliefs and determine their actions or inactions.

There is, however, a much older tradition in the study of politics, one that goes back to some Greek philosophers centuries before the birth of Christ. That tradition (some call it "political philosophy") considers people's political values and behavior in terms of their ideologies. There are similarities between the concepts of cognitive map and ideology, but there are also enough differences to warrant this separate chapter on modern political ideologies. First, we will consider the general nature of ideologies, and then review the main doctrines of the most prominent modern political ideologies.

Nature of Ideologies

WHAT IS AN IDEOLOGY?

The most obvious characteristic of most ideologies is that their labels end in *ism*, as in *liberalism, socialism, and fascism*.[1] But we can do better than that. An **ideology** is not the same as an idea. Rather, it is a *set of ideas that are in some logical way related to one another*. For example, one of the most powerful ideas in economics is the belief (assumption? observation?) that everyone's sole purpose in economic life is to acquire as much material wealth as possible. But that belief is only one part, albeit an important part, of a much larger set of ideas making up the doctrine that the best way to organize an economic system is to base it on the private ownership of the production and distribution of goods and services. That larger set of ideas constitutes the economic ideology called *capitalism*.

Political scientist Roy C. Macridis suggested that there are four main criteria for distinguishing ideologies from ideas:[2]

Comprehensiveness. A full-fledged ideology includes ideas about many great matters, such as the place of human beings in the cosmos, their relationship to God or history or some other superhuman creative force, the highest goals for society and government, the basic nature of human beings, and the best means for achieving the highest social and political goals. Those ideas are more or less consistent with one another logically, and there is often a major organization—a party such as the Communist Party in the former Soviet Union or a movement such as the women's rights movement—that is rooted in those ideas and dedicated to realizing them.

Pervasiveness. The ideology's particular set of ideas has not only been known for a long time but has shaped the political beliefs and actions of many people. For example, people have been talking about democracy, oligarchy, and autocracy since the fifth century before Christ, and great movements mobilizing millions of people have fought about those ideologies for over 2,000 years.

Extensiveness. The set of ideas is held by a large number of people and plays a significant role in the political affairs of one or more nations.

Intensiveness. The set of ideas commands a strong commitment from many of its adherents and significantly influences political beliefs and actions.

INTELLECTUAL COMPONENTS OF AN IDEOLOGY

Every ideology is a set of ideas that fit together logically and also in some respects significantly differ from those of other ideologies. Yet every full-fledged ideology has ideas about at least the following five basic matters.

Values

In Chapter 2 we defined a *value* as an object or situation deemed to be of intrinsic worth and esteem, something to be sought. Every ideology is rooted in the conviction that some values are more important than others, and the highest values provide the criteria by which all other ideas, beliefs, and actions should be judged.

Thus democracy, as we will detail in Chapter 5, rests in part on the conviction that the full realization of each person's human potential is one of the highest goals of society, and it can be realized only in a political system in which each citizen has the same ultimate power over the making of government policies as every other citizen. By contrast, the "national socialist" ideology of Adolf Hitler and his Nazi party rested in part on the conviction that the world would be properly run only when the Aryan (white, non-Jewish, Nordic) race controlled all its affairs, and the greatest good the Third Reich could do for mankind was to exterminate the Jews and place its *gauleiters* in absolute power over all other inferior races.

Vision of the Ideal Polity

Every ideology is inspired by a vision of what a polity[3] would be like if it were organized and managed in the best possible manner. Marxism, for example, foresees a time when there will be no private property, no class distinctions, and no opportunity for one class to exploit another, and where the state will wither away, and human affairs will be conducted entirely by voluntary cooperation among the members of the all-inclusive working class. For another example, Shi'ite Islamic fundamentalism as preached by Iran's Ayatollah Khomeini and his disciples envisions a time in which the world is ruled by devout Shi'ite Muslims, who live their lives according to the rules laid down by the Koran in preparation for eternal life in paradise, and all vestiges of Western materialism and unrighteousness are stamped out forever.

Conception of Human Nature

Every ideology contains beliefs about what makes people, societies, and governments behave as they do. Marxism, for example, holds that capitalists exploit workers, not because capitalists are evil persons but because their position in the economic system as owners of the tools of production forces them to exploit the workers who use the tools. According to Marx, therefore, the only way to get capitalists to treat workers decently is to abolish the institution of private property altogether and thereby destroy the capitalist system that by its very nature compels all owners to exploit all workers.

Classical liberalism,[4] on the other hand, holds that every citizen wants to choose the best possible candidates and policies for the very good reason that all citizens have to bear the consequences of poor leadership and ill-conceived policies. If all the facts and all the arguments for and against every possible leader and policy are put before the people, then people will make the right choice because it is in their interest to do so. The great mistake is to censor or conceal some facts and arguments so that the people will not have all the materials they need to make the right choices.

Strategy of Action

In military terminology, the *strategy* of a nation or an army is its comprehensive basic plan for winning ultimate victory. Similarly, every ideology has a strategy for changing the existing polity into the ideal polity. Thus, Marxism seeks to raise the workers' class consciousness (their awareness that workers will always be exploited under capitalism) to the point where they will overthrow capitalism and replace it with socialism. Libertarianism, as advocated by the American Libertarian party, holds that citizens are best served when government interference in private affairs is kept to an absolute minimum. Libertarians argue that public officials should not try to govern people's business dealings, labor contracts, sexual behavior, smoking, drinking, taking of drugs, or any other aspect of their private lives.

Political Tactics

Tactics, in military terminology, means the maneuvers that a nation or an army uses to carry out its basic strategy. In a similar sense, every ideology chooses and uses certain modes of political action (see Chapter 1).

One of the most striking illustrations is provided by the differences in the tactics advocated and employed by organizations professing different brands of socialism. All socialist ideologies aim to abolish the institution of private property and replace it with a society in which all property is owned in common, and production and distribution are governed by the principle "from each according to [his or her] abilities, to each according to [his or her] needs."

However, ever since the mid-nineteenth century there have been deep schisms among socialists about the best tactics for overthrowing capitalism. Karl Marx wrote that *any* tactics that will do the job are acceptable and appropriate. Many of his followers believed that capitalists will never voluntarily surrender their privileges merely because they have lost a democratic election, so the violent overthrow of capitalism is not only morally permissible but tactically necessary. However, many other socialists—for example, the Social Democrats of Western Europe—reject violence and have faith in the institutions of democracy and in the good sense of ordinary people. Accordingly, those other socialists hold that the only acceptable tactic for ending capitalism is to persuade popular majorities to elect socialist governments that will, by peaceful and constitutional methods, enact laws abolishing private property.

Thus, in ideological politics as in any kind of politics, there are significant disagreements not only about what is the promised land but also about how to get there.

TYPES OF IDEOLOGIES

The modern world contains a large number and a rich variety of political ideologies. Indeed, in canvassing the literature of political science in preparation for writing this chapter, I came across at least fifty-five distinct ideologies, and there are many more. Obviously we cannot discuss them all in this limited space, so we will have to bypass such ideologies as communitarianism, corporatism, guided democracy, Islamic fundamentalism, militarism, pacficism, primitive communism, social Darwinism, syndicalism, Thatcherism, and Trotskyism.

Moreover, it may become confusing if ideologies are discussed one after another as though each were entirely different from all the others. That is because all political ideologies do not address all of the same questions; indeed, they often bypass, cut across, and/or combine with one another. A quick illustration: Most of the British people believe in *monarchism*; that is, they believe that it is right and proper that the official, ceremonial head of their government be a monarch, Elizabeth II, who holds her position because she inherited it from her father, not because she was elected to it. By contrast, most Americans believe in *republicanism*; that is, Americans believe that the official, ceremonial head of the government, like all high officials, should be elected to office, and the counterpart to the British queen is the president who is elected every four years. But do the two people's devotion to those different ideologies make them deadly enemies? Hardly. Almost all British *and* Americans also believe in democracy, the ideology that the ultimate decision-making power of government should be vested in all the people and not in one of them or a small class of them. So political scientists sometimes say that Americans believe in a democratic republic while the British believe in a constitutional monarchy.

Consequently, our purposes in this chapter are best served by arranging the main modern political ideologies into groups that offer different answers to the same questions.

What follows is one way of grouping modern political ideologies: (1) those mainly concerned with the proper limits on the power of government, (2) those mainly concerned with the proper role of government in economic affairs, and (3) those mainly concerned with the proper location of the ultimate power to make political decisions. For most political scientists, the third grouping is the most important, and we will devote Chapter 5 to a detailed exploration of each of its main ideologies. In the remainder of this chapter we will outline the principal doctrines and a bit of the history of the main ideologies in the other two clusters.

Ideologies of Limits on Government

CONSTITUTIONALISM AND CLASSICAL LIBERALISM

Meaning of Constitutionalism

Constitutionalism is *the ideology that government power should be limited so as to protect human rights.* Although the two usually go hand in hand in actual polities, the ideology of constitutionalism is different from the ideology of democracy. Constitutional governments are governments in which constitutional guarantees protect human rights from abridgment by either public officials or private groups. Such governments are called "constitutional" or "free" because of how the *substance* of their policies affects those rights. Model democratic governments, as envisioned in Chapter 5, are governments in which political decisions are made according to the principles of popular sovereignty, political equality, popular consultation, and majority rule. Thus a democratic government is defined by the *processes* by which all its decisions are made, while a constitutional government is defined by how the *contents* of its decisions affect human rights.

It is therefore theoretically possible for a benevolent despot to exercise absolute decision-making power in such a way that all the people have full freedom of speech, press, and religion and are guaranteed all other individual rights. Despots might even promulgate constitutions formalizing those limitations on their activities, while re-serving to themselves the exclusive power to make all other political decisions. Such governments would certainly be free and even constitutional, but they would not, according to the definition used here, be democratic. A democratic government, on the other hand, might have no written constitution and no formal guarantees of civil rights (which is substantially the case in Great Britain) and yet still be a democracy.

However, this distinction between democracy and constitutionalism is more important logically than practically. Most of the nations generally called democratic would certainly also appear on any list of constitutional nations, and none of those generally called authoritarian or dictatorial would win a place on such a list. It therefore appears that most modern democracies have decided that one—though not the only—useful way to maintain their democratic decision-making processes is to have constitutional guarantees protecting the personal freedoms and immunities that make possible genuine political equality and popular consultation.

The Classical-Liberal Foundations of Constitutionalism

Many scholars use the terms *"classical liberalism"* and *"nineteenth-century liberalism"* as more or less equivalent to *"constitutionalism,"* so we should be clear that the word *liberalism* has had two quite different meanings. The word was first used in the late eighteenth century, and until the mid-1930s it meant the ideology advocating maximum freedom for individuals from regulation by governments. However, since the mid-1930s, many people, mostly Americans, have converted the term to mean an ideology that favors not only personal freedom but also strict government regulation of business and government guarantees of minimum standards of living, health, and employment for all.

Perhaps the most famous succinct statement of the classical liberal case for constitutional protections against government is the following:

> We hold these truths to be self-evident, that all men are created equal, that they are endowed by their Creator with certain unalienable Rights, that among these are Life, Liberty and the Pursuit of Happiness—That to secure these rights, Governments are instituted among Men, deriving their just powers from the consent of the governed—That whenever any Form of Government becomes destructive of these ends, it is the Right of the People to alter or abolish it, and to institute new Government, laying its foundation on such principles and organizing its powers in such form, as to them shall seem most likely to effect their Safety and Happiness.

These winged words are, of course, taken from the opening sentences of the U.S. Declaration of Independence, drafted mainly by Thomas Jefferson and adopted by the Congress of the rebel American colonies on July 4, 1776. People who believe in this kind of constitutionalism generally base their stand on one or a combination of two premises: First, human rights are ends in themselves, and their preservation is the justification for the very existence of government and therefore its main function. Second, human rights, though not necessarily ends in themselves, are indispensable means for establishing a good government, a good society, and a good life for its citizens. Let us briefly examine each premise.

RIGHTS AS ENDS   Many who fought for human rights in the seventeenth and eighteenth centuries did so out of a deep commitment to the idea that rights are ends in themselves. Perhaps the most influential exponent of this view was the

English political philosopher John Locke. In his brilliant and widely read *Two Treatises of Civil Government* (1690), Locke raised one of the most basic questions of political philosophy: What is the moral obligation, if any, of citizens to obey the commands of government? The answer, he said, is that people join together in polities and establish governments for only one reason: to secure more firmly the rights to life, liberty, and property that naturally belong equally to all people simply because they are human beings. As Locke put it, "The great and chief end . . . of men uniting into commonwealths, and putting themselves under government, is the preservation of their property [that is, their basic rights]."[5] When a government fails to preserve those rights and thereby ceases to serve the end for which it was created, Locke continued, the citizens have the right—indeed, the duty—to overthrow it:

> Whenever the legislators endeavor to take away and destroy the [rights] of the people . . . they put themselves into a state of war with the people, who are thereupon absolved from any further obedience, and . . . have a right to resume their original liberty, and by the establishment of a new legislative (such as they shall think fit) provide for their own safety and security, which is the end for which they are in society.[6]

Locke's convictions were shared by most of the eighteenth-century American revolutionaries and became the basic rationale for the Declaration of Independence: "Governments are instituted among Men," the Declaration proclaims, "to secure these rights . . . whenever any Form of Government becomes destructive of those ends, it is the Right of the People to alter or to abolish it."

FOUNDERS OF CLASSICAL LIBERALISM. John Locke (left) and Thomas Jefferson (right).

Since 1776 there have been many statements of these Lockean ideals, and one of the most recent is the Universal Declaration of Human Rights adopted by the United Nations in 1948. Articles 1 and 2 of that document proclaim:

> All human beings are born free and equal in dignity and rights. They are endowed with reason and conscience and should act towards one another in a spirit of brotherhood. Everyone is entitled to all the rights and freedoms set forth in this Declaration, without distinction of any kind, such as race, color, sex, language, religion, political or other opinion, national or social origin, property, birth or other status. . . .[7]

RIGHTS AS MEANS   Many modern advocates of human rights base their case on the more pragmatic argument that rights are indispensable means for other, higher ends. They start from their belief in the supreme value of the individual person. Springing from such diverse sources as ancient Greco-Roman Stoicism (c. 300 B.C.) and from more recent developments in Judaism and Christianity, this doctrine holds that all human beings, whatever their individual differences and backgrounds, are equally precious and that each has immense potential for good. A prime goal of all human societies should therefore be to encourage the realization of each person's potential to the fullest possible extent. All institutions, including governments, should be judged by the degree to which they help or hinder achievement of this highest of all social goals. Fully guaranteed human rights are necessary, though not by themselves sufficient, conditions for full human development.

There is another sense in which human rights are a necessary means for the highest social ends. Every nation tries to pursue policies best calculated to achieve the values it holds most dear. Discovering just which of the many policy proposals put forth are the best for those purposes is the greatest problem facing any government. Experience has shown that the most effective way to discover the best policies is to let advocates of each proposal argue their ideas freely and to let the people choose among them; for, in the long run, true ideas and good proposals will win public acceptance over false and bad ones.

This seminal idea was eloquently stated by the English poet and pamphleteer John Milton in his famous pamphlet *Areopagitica* (1644), in which he attacked efforts by the royalist government of England to suppress the printing of writings critical of Charles I and his ministers.

> And though all the winds of doctrine were let loose to play upon the earth, so Truth be in the field, we do injuriously, by licensing and prohibiting, to misdoubt her strength. Let her and Falsehood grapple; who ever knew Truth put to worse, in a free and open encounter? . . . She needs no policies, nor strategems, nor licensings to make her victorious; those are but the shifts and defenses that error uses against her power.[8]

TOTALITARIANISM

A constitutional regime, as we have seen, protects human rights from abridgment by either public officials or private groups. The essence of a totalitarian regime is the government's effort to control all aspects of all citizens' lives so that they will become the kind of people the nation needs (hard workers, fierce fighters, fertile and uncomplaining mothers and totally committed, fanatical patriots). In a totalitarian system the very idea that *any* part of a citizen's life is private and therefore not a proper concern of government is morally outrageous and politically subversive.

This philosophy is carried to an imaginative extreme in the society depicted by George Orwell's frightening novel *1984*. Most political scientists believe that the closest approximations to thoroughgoing totalitarian dictatorships in recent years have included Adolf Hitler's Germany, Joseph Stalin's Soviet Union, Mao Zedong's People's Republic of China, Muammar al-Qaddafi's Libya, Pol Pot's Cambodia, the Ayatollah Khomeini's Iran, and Saddam Hussein's Iraq.

Many observers believe that modern totalitarian dictatorships are twentieth-century inventions quite different from the older forms of authoritarianism, such as the mad despotism of Caligula, the oriental satrapy of Genghis Khan, the renaissance tyranny of Cesare Borgia, and the absolute monarchy of Louis XIV. Each of those premodern autocracies had relatively limited political objectives and made demands only on those aspects of the subjects' lives and thoughts that the dictators calculated were necessary to accomplish their goals. But modern totalitarian regimes set no limits on either their objectives or on the duty of individual citizens to sacrifice friends, religion, family, and privacy to the leaders' demands.

A prominent study has listed the following as essential characteristics of modern totalitarian regimes:

1.   An official ideology covering all aspects of human existence to which every member of the society must adhere, not only by outer form but also by inner conviction.

2.   A single mass party, often led by one person and consisting of a relatively small proportion of the total population, which acts as the official ideology's priesthood.

3.   A system of terroristic police control making full use of modern technology for spying and surveillance.

4.   Complete control by the leader and party of all media of mass communication.

5.   Monopoly of all means of effective armed combat.

6.   Central control of the entire economy through bureaucratic coordination of all previously private business organizations.[9]

In strict logic, dictatorship and totalitarianism are as distinct as democracy and constitutionalism. In theory, there could be a totalitarian democracy. (Indeed, it seems to be what advocates of the limited majority-rule position outlined in Chapter 5 so often fear from unchecked popular majorities.) In fact, however, there is no recorded instance of a government that is both democratic and totalitarian. Although totalitarian governments have been dictatorships of the most ruthless sort, some dictatorships, like their ancient and medieval predecessors, are not very totalitarian. Some, indeed, appear to be well characterized by the description of

Turkey's Ottoman Empire before the 1920s as "despotism tempered by anarchy." But no one would say that of Stalin's Russia, Hitler's Germany, Qaddafi's Libya, Pol Pot's Cambodia, Khomeini's Iran, or Saddam Hussein's Iraq. The continuing clash between the ideologies of constitutionalism and totalitarianism are thus fought for stakes of great importance and their outcomes have great consequences for the people who live under the ideology that triumphs.

Ideologies of Economic Control

Probably the oldest and most frequent ideological clashes in human history have been over the question of who should have the ultimate power to make government policies, and we will devote Chapter 5 to examining the principal ideologies involved in those clashes.

Probably the second most hotly debated ideological issue in modern politics is the question of what role government should play in the ownership and management of the economy. In most modern nations the debate over this issue has revolved around four main ideologies: *laissez faire* (or, as some mistakenly call it, capitalism), *socialism, modern liberalism,* and *modern conservatism.* Let us review each.

CAPITALISM AND LAISSEZ FAIRE

Some Definitions

As we are using the term in this book, *capitalism* is an economic system, not a political ideology. That is, it is a way of making and distributing goods and services based on the private ownership of most enterprises and not a way of making government decisions. There is also, however, a political ideology based on capitalism that is generally called "laissez faire," and that is what we will discuss here.

It is said that Louis XIV's finance minister, Jean Baptiste Colbert (1619–1683), once asked a meeting of French entrepreneurs what the government could do to help them. One answered, "Laissez-nous faire!" ("Leave us alone!") He thus gave a name, **laissez faire**, to *the ideology which holds that there should be minimum government intervention in economic affairs.*

All advocates of laissez faire start from the conviction that capitalism is by far the best economic system, and they believe that a capitalist economy will function best if the government confines itself strictly to providing the basic conditions for free economic competition: maintaining law and order, enforcing contracts, protecting private property, and defending the nation against attack by other nations. Other than that, they believe, government should allow free competition among private persons and businesses so that all decisions will be made by market forces and governed only by natural economic laws. Ideally, then, government should neither hold back the successful nor help the unsuccessful. As Thomas Jefferson put it in his first inaugural address in 1801:

A wise and frugal government, which shall restrain men from injuring one another, which shall leave them otherwise free to regulate their own pursuits of industry and improvement, and shall not take from the mouth of labor the bread it has earned. This is the sum of good government, and this is necessary to close the circle of our felicities.[10]

Laissez faire, then, is an application to economic affairs of the doctrine that "that government is best which governs least," which was first proclaimed in the seventeenth and early eighteenth centuries by John Locke and a group of French economists known as the physiocrats. Its most famous and influential exposition was *The Wealth of Nations*, published in 1776 by the Scottish economist Adam Smith.

The case for laissez faire may be summarized as follows. Society, like the physical universe, is a rationally designed, orderly mechanism governed by natural laws. Those laws of social order can, like the laws of physical order, be discovered by human reason, and some of them—for example, the law that prices in a free market are determined by the interplay of supply and demand—are already well known. A nation that ignores or flouts those laws will encounter economic disaster as surely as a person who ignores and flouts the law of gravity will encounter physical disaster. If government attempts to regulate and restrict economic competition, penalize the efficient and successful, or subsidize the inefficient and unsuccessful, it can only upset the balance of the natural economic system, and the whole nation will be the poorer for it. The best economic policy for government, therefore, is to leave the economy entirely unregulated except by the free market.

Some advocates of laissez faire have carried the doctrine to the logical extreme of anarchy. After all, they believe, if that government is best which governs least, then the best government of all must be one that governs not at all. This position was, indeed, advocated by the nineteenth-century British reformer Thomas Hodgskin. And the modern American Libertarian party comes quite close to this position, although it stops short of advocating total anarchy.

APOSTLES OF LAISSEZ FAIRE. (left to right) Adam Smith, Milton Friedman, Friedrich von Hayek.

On the other hand, Adam Smith, like many other champions of laissez faire, was perfectly willing to accept some deviations from the strict hands-off rule. He believed, for example, that government should not let any citizen, no matter how inefficient, starve. He also believed that government should regulate production and consumption in whatever ways are necessary to ensure adequate defense against foreign attack. He added, however, that such deviations can be justified only on humanitarian and patriotic grounds. From the standpoint of strict economic efficiency, he believed that those deviations are indefensible and should therefore be undertaken only when absolutely necessary to achieve such noneconomic goals as keeping people from starving and defending the nation against foreign enemies.

SOCIALISM

Meaning of the Term

The term *socialism* has been widely used in political discourse since the early nineteenth century. Unfortunately, it is like such terms as *democracy* and *freedom* in that, even in a purely descriptive sense, socialism means different things to different people and for most has a high emotional charge. To many people in many parts of the world, for instance, *socialism* means equality, justice, the end of exploitation of the poor by the rich, and other noble things. To many Americans, on the other hand, *socialism* means government confiscation of property, regimentation of personal life, red tape, inefficiency, and coddling the lazy and incompetent.

In this book, however, **socialism** is used as most political scientists use the term, to denote *an economic system in which the means of production, distribution, and exchange are publicly owned and operated*. So, strictly speaking, the opposite of socialism is **capitalism**, which is *an economic system in which the means of production, distribution, and exchange are privately owned and operated*.

The Case for Socialism

There are several varieties of socialist ideology, and some socialists work harder at denouncing the ideological errors and organizational sins of rival brands of socialism than at attacking laissez-faire capitalism. Despite many, and often bitter, disagreements among themselves, however, socialists have a sufficient number of beliefs in common that we may speak of socialism as one general ideology.

Socialists believe that the main cause of economic suffering and injustice is capitalism's basic institution of **private property**: *the legal ownership of tangible and intangible assets by private persons rather than governments*. Socialists, to a greater or lesser degree, argue that the only cure for the evils of capitalist exploitation and misery is to have most or all of the means of production, distribution, and exchange be owned by society and operated by government. They all propose that the government take over (some say by purchase, others say by confiscation) the "commanding heights" of the economy and distribute economic goods to individuals in accordance with their human needs and not their economic productivity.

Marxism, Leninism, and Communism

During most of the twentieth century, the main schism in modern socialism has been between socialists and communists. The main disagreement between them has been over the question of *how* private property should be abolished and government ownership and operation of the economy should be established and maintained.

Socialists—including adherents of such organizations as the British Labour party, the French and American socialist parties, and the German and Scandinavian Social Democratic parties—place a high value on democracy as well as on socialism. They believe that socialism should be brought about only by such democratic and peaceful means as the organization of socialist political parties, their victory in elections and consequent control of democratic governments, and the peaceful adoption and enforcement of socialist policies. In recent years, indeed, democratic socialists' fervor for the abolition of private property has often yielded to less doctrinaire and more pragmatic programs of piecemeal social reform.

Traditionally, most communists have had quite a different view. From its origins in the writings of Karl Marx and Friedrich Engels in the mid-nineteenth century through its development by V. I. Lenin and Joseph Stalin in the twentieth century to the death of Leonid Brezhnev in 1982, orthodox Soviet communist doctrine (which some people call "Marxism" or "Marxism-Leninism") held, first, that true socialism can be established, as it was in Russia in 1917, only by violent revolution and the liquidation of unrepentant capitalists; second, that it can be maintained only through the "dictatorship of the proletariat" established by the monopoly of all political power by a communist party; and third, that the Soviet Union must be the center, and the Communist Party of the Soviet Union the commander, of the world communist movement, and all communist parties and policies in other nations must unquestioningly follow the Soviet leaders' line. Hence **communism** is usually defined as *a political-economic system in which government, operated by a single authoritarian party, controls the means of production, distribution, and exchange.*

Communist Reform and Reaction in the People's Republic of China

This is one of several places in this book in which we consider in some detail the ideology and practice of communism, especially in the former Union of Soviet Socialist Republics (USSR) and the People's Republic of China (PRC). In the book's various editions since its initial publication in 1958, I have tried to describe the ideology and practice of communism in those countries in such matters as public opinion, mass communications, political parties, and criminal justice because it was important that readers understand something of the principal adversary to the ideologies and institutions operating in the United States and other Western democracies. As one edition succeeded another, there was little need to make substantial changes in the descriptions of communist ideas and practices in either the USSR or the PRC because they changed very little.

That is no longer the case, and it is important to understand that since the mid-1980s major changes have been taking place in communism. It is too early to be cer-

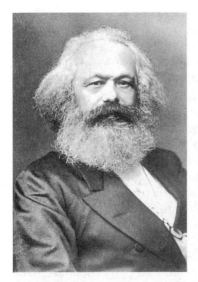

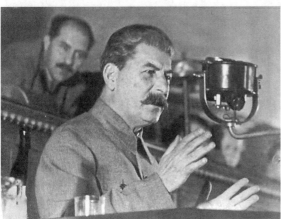

FOUNDERS OF CLASSICAL COMMUNISM. (top) Karl Marx, V.I. Lenin, (bottom) Joseph Stalin, Mao Zedong.

tain just how far those changes will go, but we must take account of what has happened so far.

Change began first in China. Under the iron-handed leadership of Mao Zedong, the Communist party seized control of the country in 1949, and for the next thirty years the PRC adhered rigidly to the doctrines of classical Marxism-Leninism-Stalinism outlined above. After Mao's death in 1976, however, a new group of leaders headed by Deng Xiaoping began to institute a number of sweeping reforms. Most were economic reforms allowing a substantially greater role for private property, individual business enterprise, and economic cooperation with U.S. and other Western business corporations and governments. But there were doctrinal and political changes as well. Public criticism of the content as well as the execution of the

Communist party's policies were allowed more freely than under Mao, many Chinese students were sent to study in Western universities, and Western scholars, students, and tourists were allowed to travel freely in China.

By the late 1980s, most Western political leaders and commentators hoped and believed that the PRC had launched an irreversible movement that would gradually end totalitarian communist dictatorship and replace it with constitutional democracy. They received a rude shock in 1989. An ever-growing number of Chinese, many of them college students, demonstrated by the tens of thousands in Beijing's Tiananmen Square, demanding an end to the Communist party's monopoly of power and calling for the rapid democratization of the PRC's political system. For a time the Communist leaders tolerated the demonstrators, but in late May they decided the time had come to crack down. The army, acting under party orders, drove the demonstrators away and crushed the revolt. In the next two years over a thousand people were sentenced to prison for taking part in the protests, and diplomatic efforts by the United States and other Western nations to persuade the PRC's Communist leaders to go easy on the demonstrators and resume democratization had little success. In the early 1990s the Communist party continued to be the only legal party; only one party-approved candidate was allowed to run for each office; and public criticism of the party and its policies was all but stamped out. No one knows the eventual fate of communism in the PRC, but as the twenty-first century approaches, democracy seems farther off than it did in the mid-1980s.

The Collapse of Communism in the USSR and Eastern Europe

PERESTROIKA AND GLASNOST IN THE SOVIET UNION   The changes in the USSR and the Communist "people's republics" in Eastern Europe began later, but they have gone much further and they continue at a rapid rate. The Communist Party of the Soviet Union (CPSU) took control of the country in 1917, and under the leadership of the charismatic and iron-handed dictators V. I. Lenin (1918–1924) and Joseph Stalin (1924–1953) the Soviet system featured near-total CPSU control of the economy, education, communications, art and literature, and all other aspects of society in a system that was called "Marxism-Leninism" or "Stalinism" or simply "communism."

Stalin had three main successors. Nikita Khrushchev (1958–1964) cracked the ice by publicly condemning some of Stalin's more brutal practices and tried to institute some reforms in the USSR's stagnant economy. He was deposed by Leonid Brezhnev (1964–1982), who rolled back most of Khrushchev's reforms and continued most of the repressive institutions and policies of Lenin and Stalin.

Then, in 1985, Mikhail Gorbachev became the General Secretary of the CPSU and the nation's leader. From the start, Gorbachev vigorously pressed his conviction that the Soviet economy was disastrously inefficient and unable to produce the goods and services the Soviet people needed. He declared that the main causes for its failure were not only the inefficient and obsolete economic ideas and institutions of Stalinism but, more fundamentally, the repressive political institutions and policies of classical Marxism-Leninism.

Gorbachev did not intend to change the USSR into a Western-style capitalist democracy; rather, he hoped to convert its Marxist-Leninist system to a more effective and humane socialism. So he preached from many platforms that the Soviet Union desperately needed two things. One was *perestroika* ("restructuring"), which means reconsidering all Soviet institutions, economic and political, and reforming those that do not work. The other was *glasnost* ("openness"), which means that all aspects of Soviet society should be open to free discussion, for only thus can the nation's leaders and the citizens find out what is wrong and put it right.

Gorbachev dismantled much of the Marxist-Leninist-Stalinist political structure. In 1990 the USSR's first free, multi-candidate election in history elected the members of the National Congress of Deputies, which was the national legislature. The new Congress amended the constitution to abolish the CPSU's official monopoly of power (and eventually outlawed the party entirely), and allowed the formation of new parties. Several new parties were immediately formed, the most noteworthy being the Social Democratic party and the Democratic party. Free and competitive elections were held in many of the other republics, most notably in 1991 when Boris Yeltsin, who had renounced his membership of the CPSU, was elected president of the Russian Republic.

Moreover, Gorbachev instituted a number of new foreign policies that, in effect, ended the cold war between the Eastern European Communist bloc and the Western democracies, which had dominated world politics since 1945. Where the Soviet Union had once sent tanks and troops to crush movements for democracy in

ARCHITECT OF GLASNOST AND PERESTROIKA.
Mikhail Gorbachev.

THE FALL OF COMMUNISM. Muscovite children playing at a pulled-down statue of Lenin.

Hungary (1956) and Czechoslovaia (1968), Gorbachev not only tolerated but encouraged the sudden rise of democratizing movements in the Eastern European countries formerly known as "Soviet satellites." For those initiatives, Gorbachev was awarded the Nobel Peace Prize for 1990, the first time that a Soviet statesman had been so honored.

POLAND   The democratic surge soon followed in the rest of Eastern Europe, starting when Poland ended Communist rule in 1989, when the first free parliamentary election in fifty years gave power to the Solidarity movement/party of Lech Walesa. The Polish Workers (Communist) party not only lost its official monopoly of power, but re-formed itself as the Social Democratic party, renounced Marxism-Leninism, and pledged itself to democratic socialism. In 1990 Lech Walesa was elected president in a free, multi-candidate election.

HUNGARY   In Hungary the Communist party renounced Marxism and changed its name. In 1990 the first free multiparty election since 1945 was held with 54 parties running a total of 1,600 candidates for the parliament's 386 seats. The former Communist party got only 11 percent of the vote, and the new parliament was controlled by a coalition of conservative parties.

CZECHOSLOVAKIA   In 1989 Czechoslovakia ended the Communist party's official monopoly of power, and Vaclav Havel, a playwright and leading advocate of democracy, was elected president. In 1990 the first free parliamentary election since the 1930s elected a coalition government of pro-democracy parties, with the renamed Communists getting only a small minority of the seats.

ROMANIA, BULGARIA, EAST GERMANY   In Romania longtime dictator Nicolae Ceaucescu was overthrown and executed in 1989, and free parliamentary elections were held in 1990. Bulgaria in 1989–1990 threw out its veteran Communist leader Todo Zhivkov, ended the Communist party's official monopoly of power, and installed a new non-communist regime. The German Democratic Republic (East Germany), which had been the great economic success of the Soviet Union's Eastern European satellites, was shaken in 1989 by escalating riots against the communist regime, leading to the overthrow and flight of the longtime dictator, Erich Honecker. In a symbolic gesture televised all over the world, the wall dividing communist East Berlin from democratic West Berlin came down, and in 1990 the first free multiparty election since the 1930s was won by the East German affiliates of the West German conservative Christian Democratic Union party. Finally, in October 1990, East Germany was absorbed as five newly reconstituted *länder* (states) of the democratic Federal Republic of Germany.

By the early 1990s, the old communist system was gone, probably forever. Yet, as we saw in Chapter 2, the new system was not what Gorbachev wanted, and indeed it had no place for his leadership. Despite his personal fall from power, however, Gorbachev's initiatives have made many of the most prominent features of the world's political landscape in the 1990s very different from what they were before 1989. The venerable ideology of Marxist-Leninist-Stalinist Communism, which once governed many nations and many millions of people, now survives mainly in Cuba, North Korea, and the PRC.

Political Ideologies, American Style

Many U.S.-watchers abroad believe that the United States has no doctrinal disagreements worthy of being called "ideological cleavages." They correctly note that public opinion polls show that only tiny fractions of Americans are socialists or communists or fascists. On all the great ideological questions of the twentieth century, they say, Americans are almost unanimous: Americans believe in capitalism rather than socialism, constitutionalism rather than totalitarianism, and democracy rather than oligarchy or autocracy. Some say that Americans believe most of all in **pragmatism**: *the philosophy that judges institutions and policies by their practical consequences.* This philosophy was developed in the early twentieth century by the American philosophers William James and John Dewey, and its essence was succinctly put by James:

> The pragmatic method . . . is to try to interpret each notion by tracing its respective political consequences. What difference would it practically make to anyone if this notion rather than that notion were true? If no practical differences whatever can be traced, then the alternatives mean practically the same thing, and all dispute is idle.[11]

Most Americans, however, would not agree that there is *no* ideological conflict in U.S. politics. Judging from what we read in the newspapers, see on television, and hear in our classrooms and personal conversations, there is a very important cleavage in American politics between an ideology called *liberalism* and an opposing ideology called *conservatism*.

MODERN AMERICAN LIBERALISM

As we noted earlier, one of the confusing things about the word *liberalism* is that in the twentieth-century United States it has come to mean something quite different from what it meant in Europe in the eighteenth and nineteenth centuries. The earlier "classical liberalism" was what some scholars have called "negative liberalism"; that is, it was a philosophy that sought to liberate individual human beings from the economic, political, religious, and moral shackles by which they had been bound through centuries of absolute monarchs, feudal economies, and official religions. As Roger H. Soltau summed it up,

> Originally to be free was not to be a slave, to have legal guaranteed control over one's person, and this is still its essential meaning. To be free is not to be prevented from doing what one wants to do, and not being forced to do what one dislikes doing. Any limitation of this two-fold power is an interference with freedom, however excellent its motives, however necessary its action.[12]

In the 1930s, however, Franklin D. Roosevelt and his New Deal colleagues argued that in the twentieth century, true liberalism must become "positive liberalism." It is meaningless, they declared, to guarantee people's freedom of speech and religion if people cannot feed their families or get a decent education or have good health. Thus, true liberalism, for a New Dealer, not only must prevent government from interfering with people's basic liberties but also must require government to act positively to protect people against life's worst economic and physical hardships so that they can be free to enjoy their intellectual liberties.

New Deal liberals argued that those protections should be guaranteed by converting the old do-nothing state into a **welfare state**, *a system in which the government guarantees to every citizen the minimum conditions of a decent life*. Since the 1930s, liberals have argued that every citizen is entitled to the minimum conditions of a decent life as a matter of basic justice, and no citizens should be denied those minimum conditions because they cannot finance them themselves. Liberals do not all agree, of course, on the exact type and level of benefits that ought to be guaranteed. Some, for example, would include complete medical care "from the womb to the tomb." Others would include only hospitalization insurance. Some would include free public education for qualified students from kindergarten right through the Ph.D. degree. Others would limit the guarantee to the high school diploma. All welfare-state advocates agree, however, that the proper function of government is to provide every citizen with *some* degree of formal education and medical care even if it requires—as it usually does—that the rich be taxed to provide benefits for the poor.

In noneconomic matters, many modern liberals continue the traditions of individual freedom and choice cherished by their nineteenth-century forebears by holding that government intervention in people's moral, religious, and intellectual lives should be kept to an absolute minimum. For example, liberals generally hold that government should maintain an absolute separation between church and state, and that government should not in any way favor one religion over another, or religion-in-general over atheism or agnosticism. Hence, any kind of organized prayer should not be allowed in any public school's curriculum. For another example, most liberals believe that it is every woman's right to decide for herself whether she will have an abortion to prevent the birth of an unwanted child, and that government should not interfere with that right. For yet another example, many liberals contend that government should not decide what people can read in books and magazines and see on television or at the movies; hence there should be no suppression of pornography or any other form of expression. For a fourth example, most liberals hold that people's sexual preferences are entirely their own private business, and government should in no way try to dissuade them from homosexuality or lesbianism; nor should it penalize people who have such preferences.

Finally, modern liberalism has a strong strain of *egalitarianism*; that is, many liberals believe that, while some differences in people's achievements and statuses are probably inevitable, those differences should be kept as small as possible. For example, most liberals believe that government action to prevent white males from discriminating against women or against African-Americans or other disadvantaged groups, while desirable, is not enough. Many liberals believe that the government must make up for the discrimination practiced against minorities and women in the past, and to that end government should impose "affirmative action" rules for employment and "comparable worth" rules for determining salaries. For another example, most liberals believe that taxes should be progressive; that is, persons with higher incomes should pay higher percentages of their incomes than people with lower incomes. Not only is this fairer than taxing everyone at the same rate, they believe, but it helps to redistribute income from the rich to the poor, which is one of the main purposes of taxation. Also, while most liberals do not admire taxes for their own sake, they feel that taxes must be kept high enough to fund welfare-state benefits at decent levels.

In short, modern American liberalism favors considerable government intervention in people's economic affairs and minimum intervention in their moral, religious, and intellectual affairs.

MODERN AMERICAN CONSERVATISM

Modern American conservatism resembles modern American liberalism in that it constitutes a considerable revision of certain European ideas of the eighteenth and nineteenth centuries. Traditional conservatism (in Great Britain it was called *Toryism*) meant conserving society's traditional values and institutions against the radical changes urged by the classical liberals. Nineteenth-century conservatives believed that society should be run, as it had always been run, by royalty and the aristocracy rather than by the newly rising business class. They also held that it was the obligation of the upper classes (called *noblesse oblige*) to make sure that factory workers and farm laborers were secure in their jobs, and that their moral lives were guided by religion and traditional values and not left to the anything-goes permissiveness advocated by such liberals as John Stuart Mill. The good society, they felt, was one in which each person was, by tradition and perhaps even by divine plan, given a particular place in the social hierarchy; everyone "knew one's place"; and aristocrats and peasants alike took pleasure in meeting the obligations, as well as enjoying the benefits, of their particular places.

Conservatism meant substantially the same thing in the United States until the 1930s, when the label came to be applied to all those who, for whatever reasons, opposed the New Deal and its welfare-state philosophy. In the 1990s, American conservatism includes two distinct, sometimes even divergent, themes.

Economic Laissez Faire

Most conservatives follow the lead of such economists as Milton Friedman and Friedrich von Hayek in arguing that government should regulate private business minimally or not at all. Government should enforce the basic rules of free competition, they believe, by enforcing contracts and preserving private property, but government should neither limit the winners' profits nor ease the losers' losses. Because creative entrepreneurs develop and market new and appealing products so that they can make money, conservatives believe that entrepreneurs should be allowed freedom of enterprise, that they will improve old businesses and form new businesses, and that they will create jobs and prosperity for others. But if entrepreneurs are hampered by government regulations and their success is penalized by high taxes, many conservatives believe that investment will dwindle, production will drop, and jobs will vanish. So many conservatives seek to "get the government off people's backs."

Preserving Traditional Moral and Religious Values

Unlike classical liberalism, modern conservatism does not mean minimum government interference in *all* aspects of people's lives. Quite the contrary. Such evangelical Christian conservatives as Pat Robertson believe that government's highest obligation is to make sure that American lives are guided by traditional American values and institutions, such as stable marriages and families, parental authority over children, regular church attendance, monogamous sexual relations and heterosexual practices, and clean and decent magazines, movies, and television. Hence government has not only the right but the duty to require children to pray as part of their regular public school curriculum. They also feel that government has the right and duty to prohibit abortions except, perhaps, where absolutely necessary to save the mother's life. It has the right and duty to make sure that pornographic magazines, movies, and television are prohibited or at least kept from children. Some conservatives say that government also has the right and duty to deny certain jobs, especially in education, to lesbians and homosexuals.

In short, modern American conservatism favors minimum government intervention in people's economic affairs and considerable intervention in their moral, religious, and intellectual affairs.

However, on what many political scientists believe is the most important ideological cleavage of the twentieth century or any other time—the conflict between democracy and other forms of government—almost all Americans, liberals and conservatives alike, are on the same side, as we will see in the next chapter.

For Further Reading

ON IDEOLOGIES IN GENERAL

HAGOPIAN, MARK N. *Ideals and Ideologies of Modern Politics*. New York: Longman, 1985. A short introduction to modern ideologies, with special emphasis on their European intellectual roots.

HOOVER, KENNETH R. *Ideology and Political Life*, 2nd ed. New York: Brooks/Cole, 1987. A survey of modern ideologies and their role in political life.

*MACRIDIS, ROY C. *Contemporary Political Ideologies*, 4th ed. Glenview, IL: Scott, Foresman/Little, Brown, 1989.

A useful introduction to the main ideologies of our time.

MCLELLAN, DAVID. *Ideology*. Minneapolis, MN: University of Minnesota Press, 1986. Analysis of the concept of ideology and its role in modern politics.

RIFF, M. A. *Dictionary of Modern Political Ideologies*. New York: St. Martin's Press, 1988. Brief summaries of leading political ideologies.

CONSTITUTIONALISM AND TOTALITARIANISM

ARENDT, HANNA. *The Origins of Totalitarianism*. New York: Meridian, 1958. Influential philosophical analysis of totalitarianism.

FRIEDRICH, CARL J., AND ZBIGNIEW BRZEZINSKI. *Totalitarian Dictatorship and Autocracy*, 2nd ed. Cambridge, MA: Harvard University Press, 1965. Analysis of ideas and institutions in both Fascist and Communist dictatorships.

*MCILWAIN, CHARLES H. *Constitutionalism, Ancient and Modern*. Ithaca, NY: Cornell University Press, 1958. The classic study of the history of the idea of limited government.

*MILL, JOHN STUART. *On Liberty*. New York: Penguin, 1982. Modern edition of a classic nineteenth-century defense of the idea of limited government.

CAPITALISM, SOCIALISM, AND COMMUNISM

BOWLES, SAMUEL, AND HERBERT GINTLE. *Democracy and Capitalism*. New York: Basic Books, 1986. Analysis of the ideologies of democracy, liberalism, and Marxism.

*FRIEDMAN, MILTON. *Capitalism and Freedom*. Chicago, IL: University of Chicago Press, 1981. Argument by a Nobel Laureate in economics that a free capitalist economy is the basis for civil liberties.

*HARRINGTON, MICHAEL. *The Twilight of Capitalism*. New York: Touchstone, 1977. Case for socialism put by today's leading American socialist theorist.

HOWE, IRVING. *Socialism in America*. New York: Harcourt Brace Jovanovich, 1985. A leading American socialist's presentation of the case for socialism.

MARX, KARL. *Capital*, 3 vols. New York: International Publishers, 1967. A recent edition of the fountainhead of "scientific socialism" and modern communism.

*MILIBAND, RALPH. *The State in Capitalist Society*. New York: Basic Books, 1978. Critique of governing institutions in capitalist democracies by a leading British Marxist.

*VON HAYEK, FRIEDRICH A. *The Road to Serfdom*. Chicago, IL: University of Chicago Press, 1956. Influential statement of the view that economic freedom is the basis for all other freedoms.

AMERICAN LIBERALISM AND CONSERVATISM

*GRAY, JOHN. *Liberalism*. Minneapolis, MN: University of Minnesota Press, 1986. A survey of modern American liberal ideas and policies.

HIMMELSTEIN, JEROME L. *To the Right: The Transformation of American Conservatism*. Berkeley, CA: University of California Press, 1990. An examination of such modern variants of traditional conservatism as the "New Right" and "neoconservatism."

KIRK, RUSSELL. *The Conservative Mind*, 6th ed. Chicago, IL: Henry Regnery, 1986. Survey of the intellectual roots and present doctrines of American conservatism by one of its foremost advocates.

*NISBET, ROBERT. *Conservatism: Dream and Reality*. Minneapolis, MN: University of Minnesota Press, 1986. Survey of the main strands of contemporary conservative ideology by a distinguished social theorist.

NOZICK, ROBERT. *Anarchy, State, and Utopia*. New York: Basic Books, 1977. Influential statement of the minimum-government position.

*RAWLS, JOHN. *Theory of Justice*. Cambridge, MA: Belknap Press of Harvard University Press, 1971. Much-discussed argument for social and economic equality as the proper goal of society and government.

*VAN DYKE, VERNON. *Ideology and Political Choice: The Search for Freedom, Justice, and Virtue*. Chatham, NJ: Chatham House, 1995.

Notes

1. Two experts on American English usage say that "*Ism* is a suffix, forming a noun of action. In addition to this it came to indicate the name of a system, whether in practice or theory.... When the suffix was detached to become a word in itself, denoting some unspecified system or peculiarity, it connoted scorn and disparagement (God knows what ism he's embraced now. I can't keep track of 'em)." Bergen Evans and Cornelia Evans, *A Dictionary of Contemporary American Usage* (New York: Random House, 1957), p. 257.

2. Roy C. Macridis, *Contemporary Political Ideologies*, 4th ed. (Glenview, IL: Scott, Foresman/Little, Brown, 1989), Chapter 1.

3. The reader will often encounter the term *polity* in these pages. I use it, as most political scientists do, to mean *a politically organized society*, a society with some kind of government.

4. For reasons set forth later in this chapter, the ideology of "classical liberalism" or "nineteenth-century liberalism" should be distinguished from the kind of "modern liberalism" that competes with "conservatism" in modern U.S. politics.

5. John Locke, *Two Treatises of Civil Government* (London: J. M. Dent, 1924), p. 180. Regrettably, Locke, like other seventeenth-century philosophers, used the term *men* as synonymous with the term *people*.

6. Ibid., p. 229.

7. From the Universal Declaration of Human Rights, reprinted in the *UNESCO Courier*, December 1963, pp. 16–17.

8. John Milton, *Areopagitica and Other Prose Works* (London: J. M. Dent, 1927), pp. 36–37.

9. Carl J. Friedrich and Zbigniew Brzezinski, *Totalitarian Dictatorship and Autocracy*, 2nd ed. (Cambridge, MA: Harvard University Press, 1965), pp. 9–10.

10. Paul Leicester Ford, ed., *The Works of Thomas Jefferson* (New York: Putnam's, 1905), vol. 9, p. 197. Jefferson, too, used *men* as a synonym for *people*.

11. William James, *Pragmatism* (New York: Meridian, 1959), p. 42.

12. Roger H. Soltau, *An Introduction to Politics* (New York: Longman, 1951), p. 127.

5

For the first time in the history of the world, no doctrines are advanced as antidemocratic. The accusation of antidemocratic action or attitude is frequently directed against others, but practical politicians and political theorists agree in stressing the democratic element in the institutions they defend and the theories they advocate. This acceptance of democracy as the highest form of political or social organization is the sign of a basic agreement in the ultimate aims of modern social and political institutions . . .[1]

Italian Fascism is the realization of true democracy.
Benito Mussolini

Germany under National Socialism is the most ennobled form of a modern democratic state.
Joseph Goebbels

People's democracies are new, higher forms of democracy as compared to the old, bourgeois-parliamentarian democracy.[2]

Democracy and Authoritarianism: Principles and Models

The foregoing statements suggest that just about everyone in the world "believes in" democracy. Fascists believe in it. Communists believe in it. Conservatives believe in it. Liberals believe in it. Only a handful of old-fashioned absolute monarchs like King Fahd of Saudi Arabia and the sultan of Oman scorn to call their regimes democratic.

But what do those statements mean? Nothing more, really, than the fact that the *word* "democracy" arouses strongly positive emotions in most people, who apparently find it psychologically necessary to claim the label for whatever set of political institutions they prefer. Many, indeed, insist that *only* the particular set of institutions they favor are truly "democratic."

Some political observers are not impressed by the near-universal popularity of "democracy." Instead, they are appalled by the fact that democracy seems to be "a kind of conceptual Gladstone bag which, with a little manipulation, can be made to accommodate almost any collection of social facts we may wish to carry about in it."[3]

Most political scientists, however, believe that, whether they like it or not, the word is here to stay and will continue to play an important part in talk about politics. Accordingly, perhaps the best we can do is to identify its principal meanings and specify which one we are using. In this book the term will be used in constructing models of democracy and authoritarianism that will help us to compare and contrast actual governments. We begin by considering some defining principles of democracy.

Principles for a Working Definition of Democracy

Before we explore the principles of democracy, let us acknowledge that neither science nor logic can prove that any particular conception of democracy (including the one set forth here) is the only correct one; that is, the one to which all people must adhere if they are not to be considered irrational or ignorant. The proper meaning of *democracy*, like that of any other word, depends on the degree to which it is generally understood and accepted. Let us further acknowledge that many people do not use *democracy* in exactly the same sense in which it is used here.

Acknowledging these differences does not, however, exempt us from the obligation to adopt a particular definition. The term *democracy* cannot be avoided in discussing certain aspects of governing. Throughout this book we consider the political and governmental agencies and processes of "the democracies"—that is, nations that cluster toward the democratic-model end of a spectrum such as the one shown in Figure 5.1. Our analysis of modern government is likely to be clearer and more useful if we understand from the outset what the model includes and why it has been chosen over others. But it is pointless to insist that this particular conception is the only one that is logically possible or morally permissible.

As the term is used in the book, **democracy** is a *form of government organized in accordance with the principles of popular sovereignty, political equality, popular consultation, and majority rule.* In order to understand the definition, let us briefly examine what is involved in each of its four principles.[4]

POPULAR SOVEREIGNTY

Briefly stated, the principle of **popular sovereignty** requires that *the ultimate power to make political decisions is vested in all the people rather than in some of them or one of them.* This principle, which is the nucleus of the conception of democracy outlined here, has several major aspects.

Sovereignty: Ultimate Decision-Making Power

Political scientists have long argued about the proper meaning and usefulness of the concept of sovereignty. For our purposes it is unnecessary to summarize or take sides in this debate. As we saw in Chapter 2, one characteristic that sets a modern nation apart from all other forms of political organization is that the nation is sovereign; that is, it has the full and exclusive legal power to make and enforce laws for the people within its territory and under its jurisdiction. In every sovereign nation the ultimate power over political decisions is located somewhere in the political-governmental structure. In a democracy power must be vested in all the people and not in one of them or a small group of them.

Vestment in the People

The principle of popular sovereignty does not logically require that all the people directly make all the daily decisions of government. Democracy does not require that every dog license and every parking ticket be issued only when all the citizens specifically and individually consent to it any more than a dictatorship requires that the dictator must personally issue every license and ticket. The people in a democracy, like the dictator in a dictatorship, may lend, or "delegate," part of their decision-making power to legislators, executives, administrators, judges, or anyone else they wish. The people are sovereign as long as they, and not their delegates, have the *ultimate* power—the final word beyond which there is no appeal—to decide which decision-making powers will be kept for themselves and which will be delegated to whom, under what conditions of accountability, and for what periods of time.

"The People": All Adult Citizens

If democracy means government by the people, then we may reasonably ask, who are "the people"? Are the people, for instance, all persons physically present within the nation's borders at a given moment—including infants, aliens, criminals in prison, and so on? The answer is implicit in the previous statement that in a democracy, power rests in all adult citizens rather than in all persons who happen to be around.

The criteria for determining who may share in this power are thus citizenship and adulthood. Every nation distinguishes between the people who are its citizens and the people who are not. Every nation requires its citizens to attain a minimum age (most commonly age eighteen) before they can vote. No one argues that it is undemocratic for, say, Denmark to exclude six-month-old infants or citizens of the United States from voting or holding office in Denmark. Some may feel that the minimum age should be lower (or higher) than eighteen, and it is said that some Europeans feel that they should have a right to vote in U.S. presidential elections, since who is president of the United States is more important for their well-being than who is prime minister of their own countries. But these are quarrels about the applications of the principle, for who would argue that everyone in the world should vote in the elections of every nation?

Sovereignty of All the People

When ultimate power is vested in one person, the government is a dictatorship. When it is vested in a few persons, the government is what political scientists call an oligarchy or aristocracy. Only when it is vested in all the people is the government a democracy.

POLITICAL EQUALITY

The second principle of democratic government, **political equality**, requires that *each adult citizen has the same opportunity as every other adult citizen to participate in the political decision-making process.* This principle clearly means "one person, one vote," but it includes other matters as well. For instance, all citizens of the former Soviet

Union over the age of eighteen were legally guaranteed the right to vote. Until 1989, however, citizens were allowed to vote for only one Communist party-approved candidate for each office and thus had no real choice. Soviet citizens' right to vote, accordingly, carried no real power over political decisions. Thus the former Soviet Union used to embody the principle stated by George Orwell in *Animal Farm*: "All animals are equal, but some animals are more equal than others." Certainly, the Communist party leaders who chose the candidates were "more equal" than ordinary Soviet citizens, who could only rubber-stamp the official candidates or, at some risk, "scratch" their ballots.

The principle of political equality is a logical consequence of the principle of popular sovereignty. If some members of the community have greater opportunities than others—if, for example, their votes are given double or triple weight, or if only they are eligible for public office—then they become a specially favored ruling class, which, according to the principle of popular sovereignty is permissible only in an oligarchy and not in a democracy.

Let us be clear that the principle of political equality means genuinely equal *opportunities* for all adult citizens and not equal actual participation. Democracy guarantees the right to abstain as well as the right to vote. In no known or imaginable democracy does every person actually participate to the same degree as every other person. As long as each adult citizen has a genuinely equal opportunity to participate to the degree that she or he wishes, the requirements of political equality are satisfied.

POPULAR CONSULTATION

The principle of popular consultation has two requirements. First, the polity must have some kind of institutional machinery through which public officials learn what public policies the people wish adopted and enforced. Second, having ascertained the people's preferences, public officials must then put those preferences into effect whether the officials approve or not. This principle, like political equality, is a logical consequence of popular sovereignty. When officeholders do what they, rather than the people, wish and do so without any accounting or danger of losing office, they, and not the people, are sovereign.

This principle holds that the essence of democracy is government *by* the people and that the decisions about which public policies will best promote the people's interests ultimately must be made *by the people themselves*, and not by any self-selected or nonaccountable ruling class of party leaders, scientists, priests, military leaders, business people, or college professors. This means that the claim of a particular policy to the title *democratic* is determined by *how it is made*, rather than by what it contains. A policy's content is relevant only when it directly affects the nature of the decision-making processes themselves.

MAJORITY RULE

When the people in a democracy agree unanimously that a particular policy should be adopted, the principle of popular sovereignty clearly requires that the government must follow that policy. However, in real life such unanimity is almost never achieved. Thus, most political decisions in a democracy eventually become choices among alternative policies, each of which has some supporters among the sovereign people. In every such situation only one group can have its way, and the other group or groups must "lose." So, the problem is, how should a democratic government, which rests on the principle that the basic decision-making power must be vested in *all* the people, determine *which* of the disagreeing groups of people should carry the day?

The principle of **majority rule** requires that *when the people disagree on an issue, the government should act according to the wishes of the larger rather than the smaller number.*[5] Note that this principle does not require that each and every government action be undertaken only after all the people have been consulted and a majority has specifically approved. It is up to popular majorities to decide how they want various kinds of decisions made. A majority may, for example, wish to reserve for itself and future majorities all government decisions, however minor. Or a majority may wish to leave all such decisions to certain elected and appointed public officials and confine itself to deciding in periodic elections whether or not those officials should remain in office. Or it may leave some decisions to public officials and reserve others for direct popular decision by such means as initiatives and referendums (see Chapter 8). As long as the *procedures* used to make government decisions are approved by at least 50-percent-plus-1 of the people, and as long as the same proportion of the people can at any time revise those procedures, the principle of majority rule is satisfied.

Limited Majority Rule?

Some political theorists argue that this kind of "unlimited" majority rule is incompatible with democracy. In a true democracy, they say, popular majorities must not take certain kinds of action. For example, popular majorities must not destroy any of the other principles of democracy by transferring sovereignty from the people to a dictator, must not give certain people extra voting power, must not prohibit certain people from expressing their political views, and must not abolish free elections. Bare popular majorities must also not destroy the liberties and guarantees of due process of law described in Chapters 15 and 16. Any nation in which bare popular majorities do any of those things, those theorists insist, cannot legitimately be called a democracy.

Self-Limited Majority Rule?

Other theorists believe that unlimited majority rule must be a principle of democracy but have no quarrel with the arguments in the preceding paragraph, as far as they go. However, the critical question is, *how* are popular majorities to be prevented from destroying other democratic principles? Some opponents of unlimited majority rule do not answer this question directly but imply two kinds of answers: First, popular majorities in a true democracy must voluntarily restrain themselves from stepping over the line; and, second, when a popular majority in a particular polity fails to restrain itself and destroys essential institutions and guarantees, then that polity is no longer a democracy. Yet both propositions are entirely compatible with the principle of unlimited majority rule presented here, for they assume that in a democracy, popular majorities are *self-limited* only.

Other opponents of unlimited majority rule, however, say that self-limitation is not enough. They insist that bare popular majorities must be limited by some agency beyond their control. They argue that there must be some restraining institution, such as judicial review (see Chapter 14) or requiring extraordinary majorities (that is, majorities of two thirds or three quarters, rather than merely 50-percent-plus-1) for certain kinds of action. In other words, a minority must be able to veto any majority action that the minority considers a threat to the privileged institutions and guarantees.

In this debate, the issue between the advocates of self-limited and externally limited majority rule is most clearly joined. Those who favor self-limited majority rule argue that such external limitations are incompatible with the principles of popular sovereignty and political equality. To give minorities the power to veto, they believe, is to give minorities the power to rule. Why? Because in any decision-making situation there are always a number of possible alternatives, and one of them is always to "do nothing" and thereby continue the status quo. A minority with veto power can, to be sure, choose *only* the status quo, but if it is large enough (if it commands, for example, one third plus one of the votes of the U.S. Congress or a majority of the U.S. Supreme Court), then it can force continuation of the status quo over any alternative policy desired by the majority.

Majoritarian theorists argue that such minority veto power is incompatible with the principles of popular sovereignty and political equality. When a two-thirds vote is required to pass a measure, a person who votes *no* counts for twice as much as one who votes *yes*, and that violates the principle of political equality. Under such a requirement, each person who opposes change and prefers the status quo has more political power than a person who wants change. Thus those who prefer the status quo become a specially favored class, and that violates the principle of popular sovereignty.

For those reasons, then, the conception of democracy outlined here demands that popular majorities have the power to take any government action they wish and insists that that power be subject to no limitations other than those that are imposed—and can be removed—by popular majorities. But what if a popular majority chooses to give all power to a dictator or to abolish freedom of speech or to deprive minorities of the right to vote? The answer is, of course, that in such cases the polities would immediately cease to be democracies. Locating full *power* to take such actions in popular majorities, however, is not in itself inconsistent with democracy; for surely even the power to commit suicide as a democracy must be part of the all-inclusive sovereign power that democracy, as conceived here, vests in the people.

What if a particular majority establishes judicial review or some other device to restrain future majorities? Under the majoritarian conception such a decision is quite compatible with majority rule and the other principles of democracy *provided* that any future majority can at any time abolish judicial review or any other restraining device by the same simple-majority procedures by which the device was initially established. In short, the majority of today cannot bind majorities of to-morrow—unless they want to be bound.

Of course, this conception of democracy is not the only one that is logically possible or morally acceptable. I have described it at such length because, however defined, *democracy* is a concept of great importance in the study of governing, and the reader is entitled to know what I mean by it and why. It should be clear, then, that wherever the term appears in this book, *democracy* means a form of government organized in accordance with the principles of popular sovereignty, political equality, popular consultation, and majority rule.

Models of Democracy

THE NATURE AND USES OF MODELS IN SOCIAL SCIENCE

Modern social scientists use intellectual models as tools to help them understand the complexities of the real world. Among those tools are *semantical models*. As the term is used here, each **semantical model** of democracy and authoritarianism is *an intellectual construct of a government organized in perfect accord with a particular set of principles*. Perhaps the best-known example of a semantical model is one widely used in economic analysis: the model of the free market. The free market is a mental picture of an economic system in which all exchange takes place through free bargaining between sellers and buyers in the marketplace, the only motive influencing human behavior is the universal desire to buy cheap and sell dear, and the price of any commodity or service is determined solely by the interplay of supply and demand.

No actual economic system, of course, has ever operated in perfect accordance with free-market principles. People are in fact influenced by many motives other than their desire to buy cheap and sell dear (for example, their desire to be in fashion). Furthermore, sellers often agree among themselves to set prices at certain levels regardless of supply and demand so that every seller can make a larger profit than would be possible under conditions of unrestricted competition; and every nation's government interferes to some degree with the free interplay of supply and demand.

Uses

Economists talk about the free-market economy when no such thing has ever existed in pure form because they find it useful in isolating certain aspects of actual economies and in studying those aspects apart from all others. To illustrate: Economists want to know if an economy *were* organized as a perfect free market, then what would be the effect on prices of variations in supply and demand? Economists then observe what actually happens in a real economy when supply or demand changes. The difference between the effects the model predicts and the effects actually observed gives economists a rough measure of the actual nature and influence of supply and demand relative to other factors.

Using models is thus one way in which social scientists can achieve something comparable to the results that physical scientists obtain through controlled experiments. Chemists in their laboratories, for example, can hold constant certain variables[6] (such as molecular structure, volume, weight, and density) constant, change another variable (such as temperature), and then observe the outcome. Changes in the results are attributed to changes in the particular variable under inspection, for all the other variables have been held constant. Economists, however, cannot manipulate human economies in this fashion. But they can *imagine* what would happen in a free-market economy when supply is increased, and by comparing the two sets of results increase our understanding of the operation and influence of supply and demand relative to other factors.

Normative and Descriptive Models of Government

In ordinary conversation we often use the word *model* to mean something worthy of imitation, an ideal to live up to. "He is a model boy" or "Her paper is a model of how to write an examination." Social scientists call this the *normative* use of the term, for it equates the model with good and its opposite with bad.

However, in this discussion we are using the term in a purely *descriptive* sense: Model means simply an idea of what a government would be like if it were totally democratic or totally authoritarian. Most of us no doubt believe that governments *should* follow the democratic model. But that moral belief should not cloud the factual observations that some governments *do* follow the authoritarian model rather than the democratic model.

Comparing Political Reality with a Model

Let us see how a model can be used to understand and evaluate some aspect of political reality. One essential principle of the model of democracy outlined later in this chapter is political equality, defined in the model as equal access to political power for every member of the community. The model requires that each adult citizen must have the same right to vote as every other adult citizen, and each vote must count for as much as every other vote.

So much for the model. Now for the reality. In the U.S. states before 1962 most legislatures were elected from districts of widely varying populations. In Vermont, for example, each town, regardless of its population, elected one state representative. The town of Stratton, with twenty-four inhabitants, elected one legislator, and so did the city of Burlington, with 35,531 inhabitants. Thus, each Strattonite's share of the power to determine the legislature's membership was 1,480 times greater than that of each Burlingtonian! In California the smallest state-senatorial district had a population of 14,294 and the largest had 6,038,771; that is, 422 times as many people. Comparable disparities existed in most other states.

In a series of decisions from 1962 to 1992, however, the U.S. Supreme Court has considered the question of whether or not such disparities should be eliminated in obedience to the requirement of the Fourteenth Amendment that "no State shall . . . deny to any person within its jurisdiction the equal protection of the laws" and has decided that the disparities must be abolished. The political equality part of the model, then, has provided both a benchmark for measuring aspects of reality and a goal for political change.

Matters become more complicated, however, when we use models to classify actual governments.

Spectrum Classification of Actual Governments

One more problem remains. If no actual government fully measures up to a particular model, how can we legitimately call any such government democratic or authoritarian? The answer is simple. If we think in terms of two mutually exclusive categories—democracies (all governments that completely correspond to our model in every detail) and nondemocracies (governments that in one or more respects fall short of the model)—then all the governments in the world have to be placed in the nondemocracy category. But if we think in terms of a *spectrum*, we can quite legitimately describe some actual governments as more democratic than others, as pictured in Figure 5.1.

The familiar categories of "rich" and "poor" illustrate the principle of spectrum classification. We all use those categories every day, and nobody thinks that we are talking nonsense when we call this person poor and that person rich. Yet consider for a moment the reasoning underlying those classifications. We could rank each person in the United States in increasing order of net worth. We could agree that those at the top of the list were rich and those at the bottom were poor. But exactly where would we draw the line between rich and poor? At $100,000? If so, would we say that a person worth $99,999.99 was poor and that acquiring one more penny would make that person rich? Clearly not. Yet the lack of an arithmetically precise dividing line between the categories should not prevent us from using the categories at all. They are, to be sure, gross categories, in the sense that they are not as precisely defined as those in mathematics, but most of us find them useful all the

FIGURE 5.1 **Spectrum Classification of Democracies**

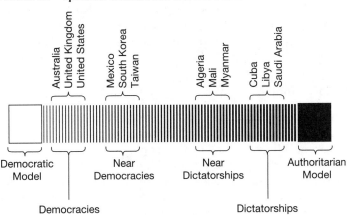

same, particularly in describing people at the two extremes of the spectrum. If someone's net worth is $1,000,000, that person is rich; if it is $1,000, that person is poor; and if it is, say, $50,000, that person is somewhere in between.

This same kind of reasoning, with all its advantages and limitations, underlies the classification and labeling of actual governments in this book. Our spectrum may be shown graphically as in Figure 5.1. Yet, how do we construct such a spectrum and decide which nation belongs where on it? Essentially, we begin by fixing one extreme of the scale with a particular model of democracy, a mental picture of what a government would be like if it were organized in complete and perfect accordance with what we regard as the defining principles of democracy. Some analysts also fix the opposite extreme with a model of authoritarianism, a mental picture of what a government would be like if one person or a small elite had exclusive control of all government machinery and policies. When the spectrum is thus anchored, we ascertain as best we can how each actual government measures up to the principles of our model of democracy or authoritarianism. From those data we can compile a "score" for each government and place that score on the spectrum relative to the scores assigned to other governments.

Several social scientists have ranked the "democratic-ness" of actual governments by such procedures.[7] Despite the fact that those scholars use somewhat different methods and cover only nations with large and medium-sized populations, their lists of democracies are almost identical with one another. The point is that the differences among lists arise from differences in the models used as well as differences in the facts about the countries ranked.

Whether a particular government is called democratic or authoritarian thus depends largely upon the model against which it is assessed.

PARTICIPATORY AND ACCOUNTABLE-ELITES MODELS

As we have seen, most theorists of democracy agree that only governments organized in accordance with *at least* the principles of popular sovereignty, political equality, popular consultation, and majority rule should be called "democracies." Most also agree that those principles have been translated into several different model sets of institutions in the modern world. Those models share significant areas of agreement, but they are sufficiently different to warrant brief separate descriptions of each.

Participatory Model

Most present-day political theorists believe that direct participation by all the millions of citizens in the decisions of government is impossible in modern nations. Some theorists argue, however, that a valid model of democracy must provide for the maximum possible degree of direct popular participation. The basic purpose for which democracy exists is to develop the potential of every person in the community to its fullest. The best way to advance toward this goal, those theorists contend, is to encourage maximum participation by all the people in the making of all the decisions, public and private, that affect their lives. Anything less may demean their humanity and cripple their intellectual and moral growth.

But how can such participation be achieved? For one thing, those theorists declare, a true democracy should encourage greater popular participation in non-governmental decision-making bodies, such as political parties, labor unions, neighborhood associations, small businesses, schools, and religious organizations. In addition, a true democracy should delegate a larger share of public power to government units, such as small municipalities and neighborhoods within big cities, that are small enough to permit effective and meaningful mass participation in decision making.

Other devices are also needed, those theorists say. In large-scale modern nations some theorists especially favor the initiative and referendum (see Chapter 8). However, the first and most important step is to recognize that maximum civic participation develops a person's potentials. When this basic principle is generally understood, we can get on with the lesser technical job of thinking up new and better means for increasing participation.

Accountable-Elites Model

Other democratic theorists point out that, as a matter of observed fact, in almost no human organization do all members participate all the time with equal energy, commitment, and influence. In every organization a few members are more committed, more willing to work, more likely to take initiatives, and as a result more likely to have influence than the more passive majority. Social scientists usually speak of an organization's **elite** as *people who are most interested, active, and influential in making an organization's decisions.*

Does the prevalence of influential elites in human groups mean that democracy is impossible? Not at all, say those theorists. The essence of democracy lies not in the absence of elites but in the popular control of elites. In their model, control is exercised through the *competition* of elites for office and power, popular *selection* of the winners by the people in periodic elections, *limitations* on the power that any elite can exercise while in office, and *removal* of the incumbent elite leaders when-

DIRECT DEMOCRACY. (left) a town meeting in Vermont; (right) a cantonal meeting in Switzerland.

ever they fail to perform to the people's satisfaction; that is, in short, through the *accountability* of governing elites to the people.

For those theorists, government by elected representatives held accountable to the people is in principle every bit as democratic as the participatory kind. Rather than wasting energy on hopeless searches for ways to bring about universal direct popular participation in modern governments, they say, we should focus on the more fruitful quest for ways of establishing effective popular control of such governments. Town-meeting democracy, those theorists add, may be a fine model for the rural cantons of Switzerland or the small towns of New England, but the accountable-elites model is equally democratic and a good deal more appropriate for a modern nation.

PRESIDENTIAL AND PARLIAMENTARY MODELS

Most analysts who prefer the accountable-elites model recognize that modern representative democracies are not all organized in the same way. Some follow the *presidential model*, while others follow the *parliamentary model*.

The essence of the presidential model is *separation of powers*, which is the division of policy-making powers among separate legislative, executive, and judicial branches of government, each of which has a number of checks and balances to keep the other branches from invading its constitutionally assigned sphere. The essence of the parliamentary model is *fusion of powers*, which is the concentration of all policy-making power in the legislature. The legislature not only makes the laws but chooses from among its members a cabinet to exercise the executive powers and direct the administrative agencies.

Of the two models, the parliamentary version is considerably more common. As of 1994 about 125 of the world's nations have regimes that can reasonably be called democratic, and of those only about 15—for example, the United States, Finland, France, and most of the Latin American democracies—have presidential systems; the others have parliamentary systems.

MAJORITARIAN AND CONSENSUAL MODELS

Arend Lijphart, one of the leading scholars of modern representative governments, classifies democracies according to a somewhat different set of models: the majoritarian model and the consensual model.[8]

Majoritarian Model

The majoritarian model is most closely approximated by the political system of Great Britain. It is based upon a plurality electoral system (see Chapter 8) and a two-party system (see Chapter 10), which ensure that almost all of the popular votes and seats in the national parliament (which has only one chamber with significant power) are won by one or the other of two major parties. At each election, one of those parties wins a majority of the seats and thereby acquires control of the *entire* power of the unitary and centralized national government. Its leaders form a cabinet, which controls all the ministries (executive departments) and uses party discipline to make the members of the majority party in parliament support all the measures the cabinet favors and reject all it opposes. The courts have no power to veto any act of the cabinet or the parliament. The party that loses the election (the opposition) speaks against the cabinet's policies and can itself become the governing party if it wins a majority of the seats at the next election; but while it is in the opposition, the out-party has only the power to criticize. In short, the majoritarian model envisions a system in which the popular majority gives full power to a majority party for a specified term, and at the next election holds that party accountable for how it has used its power.

Consensual Model

Lijphart's consensual model is most closely approximated by the governmental systems of Belgium and Switzerland. This model is based upon some form of proportional representation and a multiparty system (see Chapters 8 and 10), which ensure that several more than two parties win seats in parliament and that a single party will hardly ever win a majority. The cabinet is a coalition of the leaders of several parties whose votes sum up to a parliamentary majority. The cabinet stays in power only so long as the parliamentary majority supports it, and when one or more parties leave the coalition and the cabinet loses its majority, that cabinet must resign and be replaced by a cabinet representing another coalition—or a reshuffling of the previous coalition—that will be supported by a parliamentary majority. Thus the legislature has considerably greater power over the executive than in the majoritarian model, and a minority party can do more than merely oppose: By leaving or threatening to leave a coalition cabinet, a minority party can either change a policy or kill it. Thus, while the essence of the *majoritarian* model is to give all power to one majority party with the opposition powerless until it can win a majority, the essence of the *consensual* model is to ensure that policies are made by consensual agreements among several parties.

Lijphart acknowledges that in this analytical scheme the United States, like other presidential democracies, is "frequently a deviant case." However, if we picture a continuum with the majoritarian democracies at one end and the consensual democracies at the other, then the United States falls somewhere in the middle. In short, while modern democracies all rest upon the same basic principles, nations put those principles into practice in several different ways. This is far less true, however, of authoritarian regimes.

Authoritarianism and Dictatorship ━━━━━━━━━

Authoritarianism is *a form of government in which the ruling authority imposes its values and policies on society regardless of the people's wishes.* The authority may be one person, such as Adolf Hitler in Nazi Germany (1933–1945), Joseph Stalin in the

Soviet Union (1922–1953), Muammar al-Qaddafi in Libya (1969–), Fidel Castro in Cuba (1959–), and Saddam Hussein in Iraq (1979–); or authority may be a small ruling clique, often called an *oligarchy*, such as the Soviet Union's Politburo after Stalin's death or the military juntas that have ruled various Latin American nations at various times.

DICTATOR OF THE LEFT. Fidel Castro of Cuba.

DICTATOR OF THE RIGHT. Saddam Hussein of Iraq.

Many today use the term *authoritarianism* as synonymous with *dictatorship*, though some prefer to preserve the older usage in which *dictatorship* meant rule by one person and *oligarchy* meant rule by a small elite. Even the term *dictator* has not always meant arbitrary and unlimited rule by one person, however. The term originated in the republic of ancient Rome. When the city was threatened by foreign invasion or domestic rebellion and the Senate determined that regular governing procedures were inadequate to meet the danger, they appointed a dictator and gave him, for a limited period, absolute power to use all of Rome's resources as he saw fit to save the city. When the danger passed, the dictator's power reverted to the Senate, and he returned, as the great Lucius Quinctius Cincinnatus did, to his former status of ordinary citizen. In the republic's later years, however, ambitious politicians seized the title and power of dictator through armed rebellion or intimidation of the Senate; and for many centuries thereafter a dictator was generally thought to be one who seized and held absolute power illegitimately, in contrast to an autocrat, who also had absolute power but achieved it by such legitimate means as inheriting a throne.

Political scientists have long since dropped those archaic distinctions and most now use the term *authoritarian* to denote all nondemocratic forms of government. Defining the principles of authoritarianism takes less time and argument than defining the principles of democracy. The reason is clear. As we have seen, the word *democracy* kindles such a pleasant emotional glow in most people the world over that they feel compelled to insist that it applies best—perhaps exclusively—to whatever systems or policies they favor. Any effort to claim it for other systems or policies usually encounters resistance and often resentment. The words *authoritarianism* and *dictatorship* carry neither the popularity nor the confusion. For most people those words mean something bad. The much rarer disputes over their usage usually hinge not on what they mean but on whether this or that actual government deserves the insult.

In any event, as political scientist Samuel E. Finer points out, whether an authoritarian government's decisions are made by one dictator or a small clique, all such governments have three main characteristics:[9]

1. The techniques of making decisions by public discussion and voting are largely or wholly supplanted by the decrees of those in authority.
2. The ruler(s) are not restrained by constitutional limitations and can impose whatever policies they choose.
3. The authority the ruler(s) claim does not necessarily nor usually derive from the consent of the governed, but rather from some special quality—some unusual personal charisma or special knowledge—that they alone are thought to possess.

The dictator or ruling oligarchy may acquire power by inheritance, as King Hassan II did in Morocco; by overthrowing an established regime in a civil war, as Fidel Castro did in Cuba and Mao Zedong did in China; or by using the procedures of democracy to gain a foothold and then destroying all opposition, as Adolf Hitler did in Germany.

Authoritarianism is the opposite of democracy. Its essence lies not in the manner in which power is acquired but in who holds power. Its basic principles are sovereignty concentrated in one person or a small group, political inequality, no popular consultation, and minority rule.

Authoritarianism is thus a model in the same sense that there are several models of democracy. Authoritarianism is a full intellectual realization of a particular organizational principle and not a complete and precise description of any actual government. Just as there are degrees of democracy (degrees of approximation to the model), so there are degrees of authoritarianism. In no actual government has one person or a small elite directly controlled *all* decisions. From Tiberius in ancient Rome to Saddam Hussein in modern Iraq all authoritarian rulers have ruled through subordinates who have interpreted and carried out their orders. As we will see in Chapter 13, any interpretation or implementation of an order necessarily creates an area of discretion effectively controlled by subordinates, whatever the organizational charts may say.

Actual dictatorships, like actual democracies, are thus matters of more or less, not of all or none. Dictatorships come in many varieties: the traditional absolute monarchies of Saudi Arabia and Oman, the fundamentalist theocracy of Iran's Ayatollah Khomeini, the military regimes of Iraq and Zaire, and what might be called the "people's dictatorships" of Kim Jong Il in North Korea and Fidel Castro in Cuba.

Classifying Actual Governments

Any classification of actual governments as democratic or authoritarian is likely to be tentative and imperfect. Given the present state of political science, it could hardly be otherwise. Yet in a book such as this, which attempts to describe the main processes of politics and government the world over, we can hardly avoid considering democratic and authoritarian regimes, nor would we wish to do so.

Anyone who examines the form of an actual government must necessarily abstract part of its total reality, and the particular parts on which one chooses to concentrate are determined by one's conception of a model, or perfect example of such a form.

For example, we often hear the governments of the United States and Great Britain called democratic and those of Cuba and Iraq called authoritarian. Let us consider for a moment what the labels of democratic and authoritarian mean and do not mean. They do not mean that the governments of the United States and Great Britain are exactly alike, for we know that certain British public officials (for example, the queen and some members of the House of Lords) inherit their posts, whereas all American public officials are either elected or appointed to their jobs. Nor do the labels mean that the governments of the United States and Great Britain are *completely* different from the governments of Cuba and Iraq, for we know that all four governments make laws, punish those who break the laws, maintain armed forces, collect taxes, and so on.

We know that to some extent the governments of all nations are alike, yet no two governments are *exactly* alike. How, then, can we justify calling some democratic as if they were identical and calling others authoritarian as if they too were identical but completely different from the democracies? The answer is that *in certain respects* the governments of the United States and Great Britain are essentially alike, and *in those same respects* both are significantly different from the governments of Cuba and Iraq. The label of a particular nation's government reflects a form that we discern among certain items *selected* from its unique mixture of laws, customs, and institutions. When we have labeled the government democratic or authoritarian, we have described it only partially, and many other valid statements can also be made about it.

The items we select as the basis for our classifications are derived from our models of both forms of government. My purpose in this chapter has been to make as clear as possible the nature of the models of democracy and dictatorship used and reasons why some actual governments are called democratic and others are called authoritarian.

The Surge of Democracy

Before we leave the subject of democracy, we should note that since the late 1980s the world has seen the most widespread and dramatic surge of democracy in history. In every part of the planet the citizens of many nations with authoritarian regimes have decided that their rulers have failed disastrously to produce the economic well-being and social stability and justice that were claimed to justify the sacrifice of freedom and accountability provided by democracy. In a series of revolts, some bloodless and some violent, people have begun to overthrow their dictatorships and replace them with democracies.

Perhaps the most massive changes from authoritarianism to Democracy have been those in the former USSR and its satellite "people's democracies" in Eastern Europe. But democratic regimes have also replaced authoritarian regimes in other parts of the world. Democracy has also surged in Latin America, replacing both left-wing Soviet-style dictatorships and right-wing military dictatorships with democratic regimes. For example, in **Chile** the military dictatorship of Augusto Pinochet allowed opposition parties to form and in 1988 lost a free referendum on whether Pinochet should receive another eight-year term as president. To the surprise of many, Pinochet abided by the results, and in 1990 opposition leader Patricio Aylwin Azocar was elected president. In **Nicaragua**, communist President Daniel Ortega Saavedra allowed a free election for the presidency to take place in 1990, and, in a major upset, opposition candidate Violeta Barrios de Chamorro defeated him. Ortega's Sandinistas accepted the result, the contra rebels who had tried to overthrow the Sandinista regime disbanded, and democracy returned to Nicaragua. In **Paraguay** in 1989 the longtime military dictator Alfredo Stroessner was overthrown by a military coup, and free parliamentary elections turned power over to a democratic coalition. In **Uruguay** in 1989 the first free elections in twenty years replaced a military dictatorship with a democratic regime.

Some authoritarian regimes in Africa and Asia were also weakened or overthrown by democratic reform movements. Perhaps the most prominent was South Africa's ending of apartheid and holding an election in which, for the first time, all races voted and a black leader, Nelson Mandela, was elected president. Free, multiparty elections were also held, in many instances for the first time, in Benin (1991), Cape Verde (1991), Chad (1990), the Ivory Coast (1990), Gabon (1990), Kenya (1992), Mauritania (1993), Sao Tome and Principe (1990), and Yemen (1993). Several other nations announced that they would soon drop their one-party systems and hold free, multiparty elections: Algeria (1990), the Congo (1990), Guinea-Bissau (1991), Mongolia (1990), Mozambique (1990), Nepal (1990), Niger (1990), Somalia (1990), Togo (1990), Zaire (1990), and Zambia (1990).

On the other hand, there have been several setbacks. For instance, on three different occasions elections were held in Nigeria, but the Nigerian military refused to let the winner take office. Somalia has as yet been unable to establish the stable interim regime needed to permit the holding of a free and peaceful election. Taken together, however, the changes described above constitute the greatest democratic surge in history. Yet, it is too early for democrats to hold a victory celebration. For one thing, there remain many countries in which dictatorships are still well entrenched (for example, China, Cuba, North Korea, Iran, Iraq, Kuwait, Saudi Arabia, Vietnam, and a number of African countries). For another thing, many of the movements toward democracy have just begun, and we do not know how many will succeed. For yet another thing, it remains to be seen whether the new democratic political systems will bring sufficient improvements in such social benefits as economic growth, better education, improved nutrition and health, and longer and more enjoyable lives for most citizens. The people in many formerly authoritarian regimes know only too well that the old dictatorships failed dismally to give them good lives, but the new democratic regimes must prove that they can do better. Some Western democrats may feel that popular sovereignty, free elections, free speech, and due process of law are such good things in themselves that they are all that is needed to justify the triumph of democracy. For good or ill, however, many people barely surviving in many formerly authoritarian countries feel that democracy's success must be measured according to the same standards by which their dictatorial regimes have been found wanting, that democratic political institutions are better only if those institutions produce better economic and social results.

They—and we—will see.

For Further Reading

ABOUT DEMOCRACY

*BACHRACH, PETER. *The Theory of Democratic Elitism.* Boston, MA: Little, Brown, 1967. Short exposition of participatory model.

BARBER, BENJAMIN R. *Strong Democracy: Participatory Politics for a New Age.* Berkeley, CA: University of California Press, 1984. Argument for maximizing participatory grass-roots democracy by devolving power to smaller, local units of government.

BEALEY, FRANK. *Democracy and the Contemporary State.* New York: Oxford University Press, 1988. A reexamination of the concept of democracy and how countries called "democracies" actually operate in the modern world.

*DAHL, ROBERT A. *A Preface to Democratic Theory.* Chicago, IL: University of Chicago Press, 1956. Develops the "polyarchy" model of democracy and analyzes alternative models.

*———. *Polyarchy.* New Haven, CT: Yale University Press, 1982. View of democracy as competition among accountable elites.

*———. *Democracy and Its Critics.* New Haven, CT: Yale University Press, 1989. A reexamination of the nature, underpinnings, and attacks on democracy as a model form of government.

*HELD, DAVID. *Models of Democracy.* Stanford, CA: Stanford University Press, 1987. Analysis of competing models of democracy.

KENDALL, WILLMOORE. *John Locke and the Doctrine of Majority Rule.* Urbana, IL: University of Illinois Press, 1941. Explanation of origins and content of the absolute-majority-rule doctrine.

LIJPHART, AREND. *Democracies: Patterns of Majoritarian and Consensus Government in Twenty-one Countries.* New Haven, CT: Yale University Press, 1984. A broad comparative analysis of the similarities and differences in the basic governing institutions of twenty-one modern democratic countries.

O'DONNEL, GUILLERMO, PHILIPPE C. SCHMITTER, AND LAURENCE WHITEHEAD. *Transitions from Authoritarian Rule.*

Baltimore, MD: Johns Hopkins University Press, 1986. Study of recent transitions from authoritarian to democratic regimes in Spain, Portugal, and several Latin American countries.

PATEMAN, CAROLE. *Participation and Democratic Theory.* New York: Cambridge University Press, 1970. Most thorough defense of participatory model.

*RIKER, WILLIAM H. *Liberalism Against Populism: A Confrontation Between the Theory of Democracy and the Theory of Social Choice.* San Francisco, CA: W. H. Freeman, 1982. Analysis by a leading political theorist of theories of democracy and some of their alternatives.

*SARTORI, GIOVANNI. *The Theory of Democracy Revisited,* 2 vols. Chatham, NJ: Chatham House, 1987. Updated and reconsidered version of the most comprehensive and analytical discussion of the various meanings of democracy.

*SCHUMPETER, JOSEPH. *Capitalism, Socialism, and Democracy,* 3rd ed. New York: Harper Torchbooks, 1950. Influential analysis of democracy as competition among accountable elites.

*SPITZ, ELAINE. *Majority Rule.* Chatham, NJ: Chatham House, 1983. Most recent analysis of argument over status of majority rule in democratic theory.

ABOUT AUTHORITARIANISM

ARENDT, HANNAH. *The Origins of Totalitarianism.* New York: Meridian Books, 1958. Influential philosophical analysis of totalitarianism.

FRIEDRICH, CARL J., AND ZBIGNIEW BRZEZINSKI. *Totalitarian Dictatorship and Autocracy,* 2nd ed. Cambridge, MA: Harvard University Press, 1965. Analysis of ideas and institutions in both fascist and communist dictatorships.

PERLMUTTER, AMOS. *Modern Authoritarianism: A Comparative Institutional Analysis.* New Haven, CT: Yale University Press, 1981. Study of ideas and institutions of modern authoritarian regimes.

Notes

1. Richard McKeon, ed., *Democracy in a World of Tensions: A Symposium,* prepared by UNESCO (Chicago, IL: University of Chicago Press, 1951), pp. 522–23.

2. Soviet journal quoted in Zbigniew R. Brzezinski, *The Soviet Bloc,* rev. ed. (Cambridge, MA: Harvard University Press, 1967), p. 31.

3. Carl L. Becker, *Modern Democracy* (New Haven, CT: Yale University Press, 1941), p. 4.

4. The definition of democracy presented here is a somewhat revised version of that set forth in detail in Austin Ranney and Willmoore Kendall, *Democracy and the American party System* (New York: Harcourt Brace Jovanovich, 1956), Chapter 1–3. I have borrowed heavily from those chapters for the present analysis.

5. In strict arithmetical terms, a popular *majority* is 50-percent-plus-1 of the people voting; hence, when there are only two choices, yes or no, and 51 votes are cast for Yes and 49 votes for No, 51 is a majority and wins. In some situations, however, there are more than two choices, and no one of them may receive a majority. For example, there are three candidates for office, and A gets 40 votes, B gets 35 votes, and C gets 25 votes. Under the principle of majority rule, this can be handled in several ways, but the most common ways are either (1) to drop C and have the majority choose between A and B or (2) to use the derived principle of *plurality rule* and give the win to the alternative that has more votes than the others even though those votes are not a majority of the whole. Under the plurality rule, A would win the election because 40 votes are more than either 35 or 25.

6. *Variable* is a technical term often used in political science as well as in many other disciplines. As we are using the term, a *variable is a characteristic of a social situation or institution that may appear in different degrees or forms in different situations and institutions.*

7. See, for example, Arthur K. Smith, Jr., "Socio-Economic Development and Political Democracy: A Causal Analysis," *Midwest Journal of Political Science,* 13 (1969), 104–5; G. Bingham Powell, Jr., *Contemporary Democracies: Participation, Stability, and Violence* (Cambridge, MA: Harvard University Press, 1982); and Arend Lijphart, *Democracies* (New Haven, CT: Yale University Press, 1984). The nearest thing to a list covering nations of all sizes is the list of the "free" nations published annually by Freedom House: See Table 15.1 in Chapter 15.

8. Arend Lijphart, *Democracies: Patterns of Majoritarian and Consensus Government in Twenty-one Countries* (New Haven, CT: Yale University Press, 1984).

9. Samuel E. Finer, "Authoritarianism," in *The Blackwell Encyclopaedia of Political Institutions,* ed. Vernon Bogdanor (Oxford, England: Basil Blackwell, 1987), p. 34.

6

Governments must concern themselves with the opinions of their citizens, if only to provide a basis for repression of disaffection. The persistent curiosity, and anxiety, of rulers about what their subjects say of them and their actions are chronicled in the histories of secret police. Measures to satisfy each curiosity by soundings of public opinion are often only an aspect of political persecution; they may also guide policies of persuasion calculated to convert discontent into cheerful acquiescence. And even in the least democratic regime opinion may influence the direction or tempo of substantive policy. Although a government may be erected on tyranny, to endure it needs the ungrudging support of substantial numbers of its people.
V. O. Key, Jr.[1]

Public Opinion in Democratic Systems

Although this chapter will focus mainly on public opinion in democratic systems, it is a mistake to believe that public opinion plays a significant role only in the democracies. As the quotation above makes clear, authoritarian regimes also have an important stake in knowing whether their policies are going to receive sullen acquiescence or enthusiastic cooperation.

For those reasons, the cultivation of public opinion is a major preoccupation of most political groups in both democratic and authoritarian systems. In the democracies, political parties, candidates, and pressure groups spend millions of dollars bombarding ordinary citizens with television advertisements, billboard displays, newspaper advertisements, bumper-sticker slogans, and the like, all intended to nudge public opinion in the desired direction. Public relations advisers sit at the elbows of many public figures, advising them on how to cultivate good public images. Commercial polling organizations are hired by newspapers to report on how the public views the parties, candidates, and issues of the moment.

Authoritarian regimes are also vitally concerned with public opinion. Their ministries of propaganda (or "public education" or "public information") employ thousands of workers to whip up enthusiasm for the rulers' policies. Most use a variety of devices—including public opinion polls—to learn how the masses feel about current policies and how they are likely to react to contemplated future policies.

All governments and most political actors thus treat public opinion as a mighty force. But exactly what *is* public opinion? What forces shape it? How can we be sure what public opinion demands, permits, or rejects on this or that matter of public policy? Those questions have long fascinated students of politics, and in this chapter we will review some of their findings.

Nature of Public Opinion ————————————————

As an introduction, let us sketch the opinion processes in an imaginary democracy and then call attention to some of their main characteristics. Let us imagine a New England town with a population of fifteen adults. Citizens A, B, and C have farms on the town's north road and propose that the town pave it; A and B feel very strongly about it, but C is less intense. Citizens D, E, and F, who own farms on the south road, feel discriminated against and oppose the move, although F is less angry about it than the other two. Citizens G, H, and I are merchants who believe that paving the road will mean higher taxes, and they plan to oppose it, unless opposition means the loss of A's, B's, and C's businesses. Citizens J and K are widows living on income from real estate, and they too oppose the proposal because of the higher taxes it will bring, but they consider it unseemly to be too openly political. Citizens L and M, the town's odd-job men, own no farms, pay no property taxes, and could not care less about the issue. Citizens N and O, the town's ministers, have parishioners on both sides, see no moral or religious issue involved, and decide it would be prudent to stay out of the fight.

At the town meeting, A moves that the north road be paved. A, B, and C vote yes; D, E, F, G, H, I, J, and K vote no; L and M have not bothered to attend the meeting; and N and O, though present, do not vote. A's motion is defeated, eight votes to three. Then A has an inspiration. He moves that *both* the north and south roads be paved and that one of them be officially named after the late husband of J. On this second proposal, A, B, and C again vote yes and are joined not only by D, E, and F but also by J and by N (the late Mr. J was one of N's favorite parishioners). Only G, H, I, and K vote against it, and the proposal carries by a vote of eight to four.

What can we say about public opinion in this imaginary democracy? For one thing, on neither issue did *all* the town's members express opinions. For another, not all the members of any side felt equally strongly about the matter. For yet another, when the first issue was replaced by the second there was a reshuffling of the individuals composing the pro and con sides. Although both issues may be said to have been decided in accordance with public opinion, it is misleading to picture "*the* public" as consisting of all fifteen members of the community, all holding views on all issues of public policy. How, then, should we picture public opinion in real-life situations?

DEFINITION

The nineteenth-century British politician Sir Robert Peel doubtless spoke for many political leaders then and since when he referred to "that great compound of folly, weakness, prejudice, wrong feeling, right feeling, obstinacy, and newspaper paragraphs, which is called public opinion."[2]

Most present-day political scientists would reject Sir Robert's unflattering definition and use instead, as we will, V. O. Key's definition: "**Public opinion** consists of *those opinions held by private persons which governments find it prudent to heed*."[3] In other words, public opinion is the sum of all private opinions of which government officials are aware and take into account in making their decisions.

According to this definition, then, public opinion is the cutting edge of a nation's political culture. It is specific to particular political situations and issues and is not a body of ideas on *all* issues held by *all* the members of the community known as *the* public. Each issue produces its particular combination of opinion groups, always including one that expresses no opinion whatever. (Every public opinion poll on a political issue discovers that some responses must be classified as "don't know" or "don't care.") From issue to issue there is always some reshuffling among the individuals composing the various opinion groups, some of the pros and cons on one issue reverse sides or become "don't cares" on the next, and some of the previous "don't cares" take sides.

DIMENSIONS OF PUBLIC OPINION: PREFERENCE AND INTENSITY

Political scientists find it useful to think of public opinions as having two dimensions: *preference* and *intensity*. The preference dimension measures the property of being for or against some party, candidate, or policy; and the intensity dimension measures how strongly people feel about their preferences. In terms of actual political conflict, each dimension is as important as the other. For example, if 60 percent of the electorate prefer Bill Clinton, 40 percent favor George Bush, and all feel strongly enough to vote, Clinton wins by a margin of 3 to 2. But if only half of Clinton's supporters and all of Bush's care enough to vote, then Bush wins by a margin of 4 to 3. History, indeed, records many victories of small but intensely motivated groups over large but more apathetic oppositions.

Political candidates and public officials thus need to know not only what people prefer but how strongly they prefer it. Pollsters often try to measure the intensity of people's preferences by arraying their answers on scales rather than lumping them into pro and con catchalls. For example, in 1992 the National Election Studies poll asked a national sample of Americans this question: "Do you favor or oppose government funding of abortions?" Of the 1,306 respondents who gave a usable reply, 358 (28 percent) strongly favored federal funding; 289 (22 percent) favored it, but not strongly; 171 (13 percent) opposed the laws, but not strongly; and 488 (37 percent) strongly opposed them. Presented graphically, as in Figure 6.1, this distribution of opinion constitutes a classic example of what opinion analysts call a U-shaped curve, which reveals a state of intense disagreement. Most people have opinions, most of those who have opinions hold them strongly, and those who feel strongly are more or less evenly divided between the two extreme positions. Proposals for federal funding of abortions will thus be pressed strongly and opposed strongly, and the capacity of the political system to resolve the dispute will be tested more than if most persons were clustered in the middle categories of preference and intensity.

Some issues, however, produce inverted-U-shaped curves (some call them bell-shaped or normal curves) representing a clustering of opinions at mid-scale, with relatively few persons at either extreme. Some issues produce J-shaped curves, with a majority of the voters on one side and a sizeable minority on the other side.

FIGURE 6.1   U-shaped Curve of Opinion Distribution on the Question: "Do you favor or oppose government funding of abortions?"

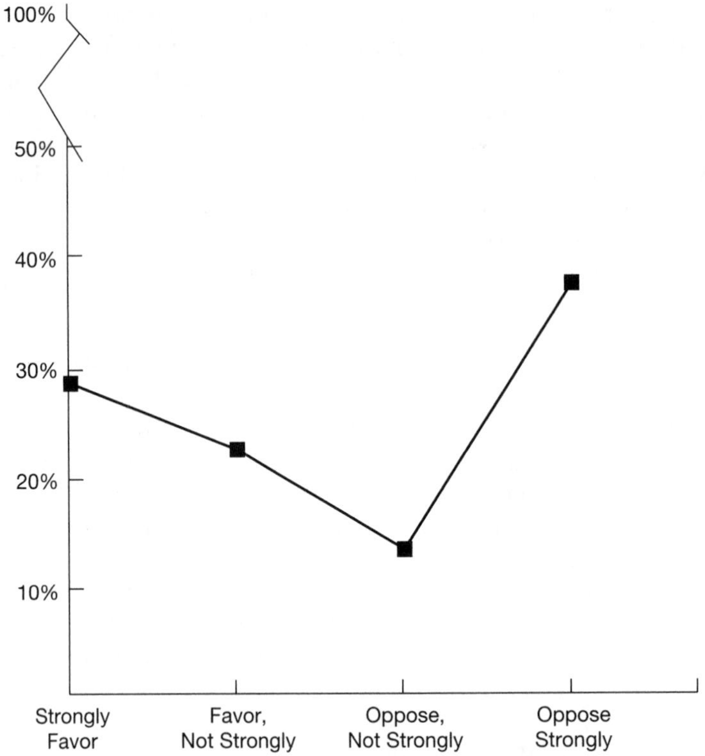

Source: National Election Study, 1992, Inter-University Consortium for Political and Social Research.

For example, in 1992 the National Election Studies poll asked a national sample of American adults this question: "Which do you think: schools should be allowed to start each day with a prayer, or religion does not belong in the schools?" Sixty-five percent of the respondents said that schools should be allowed to start the day with prayers, 26 percent said that religion does not belong in the schools, and 9 percent gave some other response. Shown graphically, as in Figure 6.2, this yields a classical J-shaped curve. Clearly such a distribution of opinion has very different consequences for policy making than the U-shaped curve shown in Figure 6.1.

MEASUREMENT BY PUBLIC OPINION POLLS

Significance

Measuring public opinion is a major concern for every democratic government. Democracy, after all, means government acting in accordance with the desires of popular majorities. If a political system seeks to realize the ideal, then it must

FIGURE 6.2   J-shaped Curve of Public Opinion Distribution on the Question "Which do you think: schools should be allowed to start each day with a prayer, or religion does not belong in the schools?"

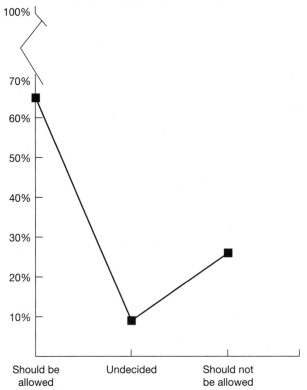

Source: National Election Study, 1992, Inter-University Consortium for Political and Social Research.

have some way of learning how popular majorities feel about political issues; if the government does not and cannot know those feelings, it can hardly act in accordance with them.

Some democratic philosophers, notably Jean Jacques Rousseau, have dreamed of "plebiscitary" democracy, in which the majority's wishes on each and every issue are always clear and, through some kind of continuous popular consultation, control whatever action the government takes. No actual democratic system, including the famed New England town meetings and the Swiss cantonal *landsgemeinden*, has ever been organized along those lines. The principal official devices for ascertaining public opinion in modern democracies have been either indirect and periodic, such as representation and elections, or direct and intermittent, such as the initiative and referendum (see Chapter 8).

Rise of the Polls

Modern social science has developed a device that some think is capable of direct, continuous, and accurate measurement of public opinion. It is the **sample survey**, which is *a study of the opinions of a population conducted by asking questions of a representative sample of the population.* (Such surveys are also, though more loosely, called "public opinion polls.")

No government has yet adopted sample surveys as part of its official policy-making apparatus (although many government agencies conduct polls regularly to learn how people are reacting to government programs). Nevertheless, polls have come to occupy an important position in the analysis and measurement of public opinion all over the democratic world, in part because commercial polling businesses survey public opinion and publish their findings in newspapers. They include such famous American firms as the American Institute of Public Opinion (founded by George Gallup) and Louis Harris and Associates in the United States, Market and Opinion Research International (MORI) in Great Britain, the Société Française pour Études Sondages (SOFRES) in France, and the Allensbach Institut für Demoskopkie in Germany. Some of the most sophisticated work is done by academic organizations, such as the Center for Political and Social Studies of the University of Michigan (CPSS), the National Opinion Research Center of the University of Chicago (NORC), and the Survey Research Center of the University of California, Berkeley (SRC).

Polls have become big business in many democratic nations. In the United States alone, commercial polling organizations together now gross well over $100 million a year, and they are comparably profitable in Great Britain, France, Germany, Japan, and many other advanced/industrial democracies. Commercial polls such as Indemer-Louis Harris and Market Opinion Research International did extensive polling prior to the 1994 presidential election in Mexico, and correctly predicted the election of Ernesto Zedilla Ponce de Léon. In most of these nations, most commercial polling is financed by contracts with manufacturers and concentrates on consumer reactions to their products and advertisements. Some of the pollsters' revenues come from polling opinion on political questions and selling the results to newspapers and television, and it is this aspect of the polls that concerns us here. Polling has also become an important campaigning device for political parties and candidates in every modern democracy, where the major parties regularly use public opinion experts to analyze published polls and to conduct private polls.

How the Polls Work

All national sample surveys work more or less alike. They first draw samples of the adult population, and in the United States those samples number from 3,000 to 6,000 persons. What makes a sample good is not its size but its *representativeness*, that is, how faithfully it reflects the divisions of opinions among all adults. Most pollsters now believe that the best way to get such a sample is to take a "random" or "probability" sample, one in which each member of the population is just as likely to be chosen as any other member. For example, for its final survey for the 1992 presidential election the Gallup organization interviewed by telephone 2,107 adults and sorted out 1,579 of them as likely voters, whose preferences provided the data for their final prediction of the outcome (Gallup predicted that Clinton would receive 43 percent of the votes, and that is exactly what he received.

The next step is to draw up a set of questions that will enable the pollsters to find out how the members of the sample feel about certain topics, and the trick is to avoid biasing the questions in such a way as to elicit particular answers. Then the pollsters' interviewers put the questions to the people in their samples. Nowadays they do so largely by telephone, although a few studies still use personal interviews in the respondents' homes. Finally, the answers are entered into computers and analyzed, and the pollsters make their reports to whatever clients are paying the freight (newspapers, television networks, political parties, and candidates).

Pollsters continue to develop new techniques to make polls faster and more accurate. One wrinkle are the exit polls now widely used by television and radio newscasters in the United States and other democracies. Typically, the pollsters select a small group of representative voting precincts across the nation and station their agents at each precinct. As the voters leave the polls, the agents ask them to mark a secret "ballot," telling how they voted and giving their age, sex, ethnicity, income, and the like. The results are telephoned to the organization's national headquarters, where they are immediately computerized and analyzed. Those polls are especially useful for making quick forecasts of election outcomes and analyses of why the voters voted as they did, because pollsters use interviews with people who have actually voted, and there is no problem in sorting out the likely voters from the likely nonvoters as in preelection polls.

"Tracking polls" are another new technique. In the final weeks of the 1992 U.S. presidential campaign, three different commercial polling firms (Gallup, ABC News, and Battleground '92) interviewed as many as 1,000 voters each night and published a report next day. Some critics said that the tracking polls were too hastily done to be accurate, but their defenders replied that the polls had both correctly predicted the winner and provided valuable information about the impact of various campaign events on people's preferences. Whatever the merits, it seems likely that tracking polls will be as common as exit polls in many democratic countries.

How Accurate Are Polls?

Perhaps the most frequent question asked about polls is whether they accurately report the state of public opinion. So far, no entirely satisfactory method has been developed to check the accuracy of their reports of public opinion on questions of whether the government should follow this or that policy. However, preelection polls on how people intend to vote have the great advantage of being checkable by actual election results, and although such unpredictable factors as the weather on election day may influence the actual voting figures, most public opinion analysts believe that the best method yet developed for checking the accuracy of polls is to examine the polling record in predicting the popular vote in elections.

PREDICTING WHO WILL VOTE

Pollsters know that some of the persons in their samples will vote and some will not. The accuracy of their predictions—and therefore their reputation and ability to attract subscribers— depends on separating the respondents who are likely to vote from those who are not likely to vote; for their task is to predict what the voters will do, not what the entire electorate would have done if everyone had voted. Each polling organization has its own methods for screening the likely voters from the likely nonvoters in their samples, and the likelihood that their predictions will be close to the actual election results depends to a considerable degree on how well their screening procedure works. The Gallup organization's predictions, which, as Table 6.1 shows, usually comes within a point or two of the actual result, are based on the respondents' combined score on these seven questions:

1. If they said they had given "quite a lot" or "some" thought to the coming election.

2. If they said they knew where their neighborhood polling place was located.

3. If they reported having voted previously in the election district where they currently reside.

4. If they said they voted "always" or "nearly always."

5. If they said they planned to vote in the coming election.

6. If they reported having voted in the [preceding] election.

7. If they rated themselves between "7" and "10" on a 10-point scale where "10" represents someone who definitely will vote in the [election to be predicted].

Each respondent gets one point for each "Yes" answer. All respondents who score a "7" on the turnout scale and most of those who score a "6" are included in the "likely voter" base. Gallup reports the distribution of this group's preferences as the predicted distribution of preferences among the voters in the forthcoming election.[4]

By this standard, how accurate are polls? Pollster records in predicting the outcomes of U.S. presidential elections are shown in Table 6.1. The figures in Table 6.1 show that in the period from 1936 to 1992, the major polls made a total of forty-five predictions. Deviations from the actual outcomes ranged from 0.1 points (Gallup in 1964) to 12.7 points (Roper in 1948). The average deviation was 1.6 points for Gallup, 1.5 for Harris, 3.8 for Roper, 4.0 for Crossley, 1.0 for *ABC/Washington Post*, and 3.2 for *CBS/New York Times* (the last two made predictions only in 1980–1992). Thirty-eight of the forty-five predicted winners actually won—an 84.4 percent record of success. Moreover, three of the seven failures came in 1948, when none of the polls correctly forecast President Harry S Truman's reelection, a failure that has had about as much publicity as all the polls' successes put together.

Most observers agree that such evidence shows that the polls have been far more accurate than news commentators or politicians in predicting election results. However, some of the polls' critics argue that success in predicting election results is no sign that polls are equally capable of revealing public opinion on issues. A criticism often heard is that the way in which the questions are asked has a powerful effect on the answers. There is much truth to that charge. There are many examples of this effect, but what follows is typical: In 1968 and again in 1982, the polling firm

TABLE 6.1   Record of the Presidential Polls, 1936–1992 (in percentages)

	ACTUAL	VOTE PREDICTED FOR DEMOCRATIC CANDIDATE BY						
YEAR	DEM. VOTE	Gallup	Roper	Crossley	Harris	ABC/WP	CBS/NYT	NBC/AP, WSJ
1936	60	54	62	54	—	—	—	—
1940	55	55	55	—	—	—	—	—
1944	54	53	54	52	—	—	—	—
1948	49.6	45	37	45	—	—	—	—
1952	44	46	43	47	—	—	—	—
1956	42	41	40	—	—	—	—	—
1960	49.7	49	47	—	—	—	—	—
1964	61	61	—	—	—	—	—	—
1968	43	40	—	—	43	—	—	—
1972	37.5	38	—	—	39	—	—	—
1976	50	49.5	—	—	48	—	—	—
1980	41	45	—	—	43	—	45	41
1984	41	41	43	—	43	40	37	34
1988	46	44	—	—	48	45	45	47
1992	43	43	—	—	44	43	45	44

Sources: The figures for 1936–1960 are reported by permission from James MacGregor Burns and J. W. Peltason, *Government by the People: The Dynamics of American National, State, and Local Government*, 11th ed., p. 217. Reprinted by permission of Prentice Hall, Englewood Cliffs, NJ. Figures for 1964–1992 have been added by the author.

of Yankelovich, Skelly and White asked their respondents this question about government help for each of a number of groups in the population: "[Please tell us] whether you feel the government should do more than it now does, or whether the government should not get involved, or whether you think the government is doing just about enough." Two of the groups asked about were "the poor" and "people on welfare." The respondents' answers in both years are shown in Table 6.2.

The answers in Table 6.2 seem to show that the American people want government to do more for "the poor" but not for "people on welfare," even though most social scientists would say that the two are one and the same. Clearly, then, the results of polls about the desirability of welfare programs depend in part upon which phrase the pollster uses to describe people at the bottom of the economic ladder. Comparable effects can be found in almost any other set of questions. The pollsters are well aware of the problem, and most of them try to phrase questions so that there will be minimum bias in the answers. Even so, the problem is far from solved and perhaps never will be to the satisfaction of all concerned.

How Much Influence Do Polls Have?

Ever since modern pollsters began to achieve their present prominence, people have asked three main questions about the influence of polls on the making of public policy: First, do public officials read poll results and make policy accordingly? There is every reason to believe that most public officials in most democracies do read the results, but it is hard to say just how much what they read influences

TABLE 6.2 Public Opinion on Spending for Lower-Income Groups, 1968, 1982

Question: "For each group described, tell me whether you feel the government should do more than it now does, or whether the government should not get involved, or whether you think the government is doing just about enough." (in percentages)

	SHOULD DO MORE FOR		IS DOING JUST ABOUT ENOUGH FOR		SHOULD NOT GET INVOLVED WITH	
GROUP	1968	1982	1968	1982	1968	1982
The poor	61	59	33	34	6	7
People on welfare	32	26	57	56	11	18

Source: Survey by Yankelovich, Skelly and White for the American Council of Life Insurance. Reported in *Public Opinion*, June–July 1985, p. 28.

the policies they advocate. Most observers believe that for most public officials poll results are one factor among several influencing decisions.

A second question is, do many undecided or weakly committed voters read preelection polls and then decide that they might as well vote for the winner (the "bandwagon effect")? There is no conclusive evidence, but what there is suggests that there is no significant bandwagon effect (voting for the candidate likely to win) or sympathy effect (voting for the candidate likely to lose).

In recent years a third question has received a lot of discussion: Are people on the West Coast of the United States discouraged from voting in presidential elec-

EXIT POLLS FORECAST ELECTION RESULTS. Voters marking cards for a CBS exit poll.

tions by seeing the television networks' forecasts that, based on results in the East, South, and Midwest, a certain candidate has already won? Again, there is no conclusive evidence, but what there is suggests that some weakly-motivated citizens may decide not to bother voting if the polls—or the television networks' election-night "calls" of the probable winners—tell them, in effect, that it is all over and their votes will not make any difference.

Despite those criticisms, however, most political scientists, like most politicians and managers of the news media, believe that public opinion polls are here to stay, not as the key element of democratic government but as a valuable aid in grappling with the problem of one of democracy's most difficult problems: finding out what the people want their government to do so that government can respond to the popular will.

Opinion Distributions in Western Democracies

WHAT CONCERNS PEOPLE?

It seems appropriate to conclude this chapter with a brief survey of the state of public opinion on some leading issues in the United States and other Western democracies at the end of the 1980s, for it should tell us quite a bit about the environment in which candidates are fighting election campaigns and governments are making policies in the 1990s.

The obvious place to begin is to ask these questions: What are people most concerned about? What do they see as the most important values governments should promote? Political scientist Russell J. Dalton has assembled the answers given by American, British, German, and French respondents to these questions, as shown in Table 6.3.

Table 6.3 shows a number of important similarities in public opinion among the four Western democracies. For example, in all four nations, achieving and maintaining economic health, fighting crime, and maintaining law and order are the most important concerns, and aesthetic values, such as more beautiful cities, rank low. The table also shows some intriguing differences. For example, only Americans put a high value on maintaining strong defense forces, and only the French put a high value on making a "friendlier, less impersonal society."

As we would expect, the salience of the various concerns varies not only from one country to another but also from time to time in any particular country. This is well illustrated by Figure 6.3, which shows the changing responses of Americans during the Reagan years to the Gallup poll's standard question, "What do you think is the most important problem facing this country?" As the figure shows, they consistently expressed more concern with economic matters (inflation, unemployment, government spending, taxes) than anything else, but the number doing so declined significantly from 85 percent in 1981 to 35 percent in 1993, no doubt reflecting the fact that in 1993 unemployment was the lowest since World War II and inflation was still well under control.

TABLE 6.3   The Most Important Goals for Government (in percentages)

GOAL	UNITED STATES	GREAT BRITAIN	GERMANY	FRANCE
Fighting crime	43	32	23	22
Maintaining a stable economy	51	23	33	11
Fighting rising prices	29	25	25	33
Economic growth	18	29	26	13
Maintaining order	27	18	23	15
Giving people more say at work and in their community	25	12	8	21
Protecting freedom of speech	14	16	12	18
Maintaining strong defense forces	39	11	5	3
A friendlier, less impersonal society	6	9	11	31
More beautiful cities	4	3	7	6

Source: Russell J. Dalton, *Citizen Politics in Western Democracies* (Chatham, NJ: Chatham House, 1988), Table 5.1, p. 83.

Each respondent could give several answers; the entries are the percentages ranking each goal as the most important or second-most important.

FIGURE 6.3   What Americans Think Are the Most Important Problems Facing the Country.

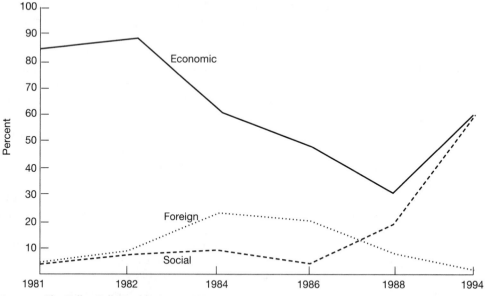

Source: The Gallup Poll Monthly, August 1994, p. 47.

Moreover, foreign-policy concerns (fear of war, arms control, terrorism) declined from a peak of 26 percent in 1984 to 2 percent in 1994, while, in 1993, social concerns (health care, drugs, crime, and AIDS) concerned more people than did foreign-policy issues.

IDEOLOGY

Left and Right in Western Nations

In Chapters 4 and 5 we reviewed the doctrines of the modern world's leading political ideologies, but how much do ideologies really matter in shaping public opinion? Most political scientists have measured the importance of ideology in a country's public opinion by noting how many of its people (1) show some understanding of what the ideologies of Left and Right mean (for my definitions, see Chapter 4), (2) are willing to place themselves in one ideological camp or the other, and (3) use their ideological loyalties as important bases for forming opinions on specific issues and deciding how to vote in elections.

Table 3.1 in Chapter 3 shows how the people in each of eight Western democracies score on each of those questions.

Liberals and Conservatives in the United States

The figures in Table 3.1 (p. 48) showed that ideology is least important to the general public in Austria and Switzerland and most important in Italy and The Netherlands. Americans and Britons rank in the middle, but that does not mean that ideology is of no importance in American thinking about politics. Since the 1970s the Gallup poll has been asking its respondents, "In politics, would you say that you are a liberal, a moderate, a conservative, or what?" Their replies are shown graphically in Figure 6.4.

Figure 6.4 shows that since the 1970s, from 88 to 97 percent of Americans have been willing to place themselves on a scale with "liberal" at one end, "conservative" at the other end, and "moderate" in the middle. Most people have called

FIGURE 6.4 Americans' Self-identification as Conservatives, Liberals, and Moderates

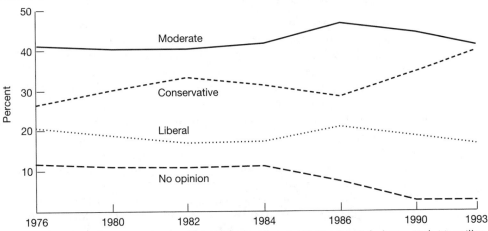

Sources: R. S. Erickson, N. R. Luttbeg, and K. L. Tedin, *American Public Opinion*, 3rd ed. (New York: Macmillan, 1988), p. 69. The data for 1990 are from *The Gallup Poll Monthly*, June 1993, p. 16.

themselves moderates. Other studies have indicated that people in different social categories tend to identify themselves somewhat differently: For example, men are generally more conservative than women; whites are more conservative than African-Americans; older people are more conservative than younger people; Protestants are more conservative than Catholics, both are more conservative than Jews, and all three are more conservative than people who say that they have no religious preference. Least surprisingly, the higher the person's annual income is, the more likely he or she is to be conservative (the proportions of people calling themselves conservatives is about one third among people earning less than $10,000 per year and over half among those earning over $50,000).[5]

But how much do those self-applied labels mean? The answer from dozens of sample survey studies seems to be: something but not everything. For example, when respondents were asked to say what the liberal or conservative position is on particular issues (such as "getting tougher on the subject of crime" and "increasing federal programs to help the poor"), an average of 30 percent said that they did not know, and another 20 percent consistently identified the liberal or conservative position incorrectly (that is, not as the scholars designing the studies identified them). Moreover, only about 20 percent of Americans appear to evaluate parties, candidates, and issues mainly in terms of whether they are liberal or conservative. As a leading study of American public opinion sums it up:

> While the American public displays some familiarity with the terminology of liberalism and conservatism, most people cannot be said to order their political viewpoints by means of a general ideological anchor. . . . [T]he fact that there is little consistency among people's viewpoints—especially when the opinions cut across issue areas—demonstrates that few people use their ideological position as a cueing device to arrange their responses to the political world. The kind of attitudinal constraint that motivates people toward consistently liberal or moderate viewpoints is reserved mainly for a small politically active segment of the American public.[6]

Does College Make a Difference?

Some conservative parents, alumni, and political organizations sometimes say that U.S. colleges and universities are hotbeds of liberalism, where radical faculty members preach left-wing political views in their classes and try to convert their students away from the conservatism they learned from their parents. Some college professors are secretly flattered by this charge, because it assumes that what professors say in class has a major impact on students' outlooks (thereby refuting the old canards that college teaching is "talking in someone else's sleep" or "casting false pearls before real swine"). But is it true?

The answer is complex, but some parts of it are clear. Certainly the faculties of most colleges have higher proportions of liberals than in the general population, although their liberalism varies with the subjects they teach. For example, one study showed that 64 percent of college social science teachers consider themselves liberals, while only 20 percent call themselves conservatives. This is quite different from the general population, which, as Figure 6.4 shows, divides itself into 19 percent liberal, 38 percent conservative, and 44 percent moderate. Teachers of business, engi-

TABLE 6.4 Political Ideologies of College Students and Faculty, 1976–1984 (in percentages)

YEAR	LIBERAL*	MIDDLE OF THE ROAD	CONSERVATIVE†
1976			
Students	38	39	23
Faculty	44	28	28
1984			
Students	25	39	36
Faculty	42	27	31

Source: Ernest L. Boyer, *College: The Undergraduate Experience in America* (New York: Harper & Row, 1987), p. 189. Copyright © 1987 by the Carnegie Foundation for the Advancement of Teaching.
*Comprised of responses to "left" and "liberal."
† Comprised of responses to "moderately conservative" and "strong conservative."

neering, and agriculture are much more likely to be conservative.[7] But one study found that college students in general are substantially more conservative than their teachers, as is shown by the figures in Table 6.4.

Table 6.4 shows that in both 1976 and 1984, college teachers were more liberal than college students. The table also shows that from 1976 to 1984, faculty members became only slightly more conservative, while students became a good deal more conservative. So evidently more powerful forces than indoctrination by their teachers shape the ideologies of college students. It is true that college students, today as in the past, are substantially more liberal than people of college age who do not go to college, but the evidence shows that most young people who go to college are already more liberal in high school than their classmates who do not go to college. In short, there is some evidence that going to college has some effect on making some students more liberal, but there are many other, more powerful forces that make some people more liberal in their twenties than they were in their teens.[8]

Accordingly, perhaps we can get a better understanding of public opinion by looking at people's views on specific issues rather than at their general political ideologies, as in the following discussion.

DOMESTIC POLICY: ECONOMIC AND SOCIAL RESPONSIBILITIES OF GOVERNMENT

For decades now, one of the messages delivered most often and most fervently by former President Ronald Reagan and most American conservatives is that government in the United States is too big, that government is "part of the problem, not part of the solution," and that in order to get a better America we have to "get the government off people's backs." Many polls show that many Americans agree: For example, in 1986, 62 percent agreed with the statement that "the federal government creates more problems than it solves"; and when asked in 1985 whether big government, big business, or big labor is the biggest threat to the country's well-being, 50 percent named big government in comparison with only 22 percent for big business and 19 percent for big labor.

Before we conclude that Americans have become confirmed "Reaganauts," however, let us also note that in 1985–1986, some 85 percent of those polled also said that "there must be substantial government involvement to handle the problem of poverty," while only 15 percent said that "the problem of poverty can be handled mainly by volunteer efforts." Also, 85 percent of the respondents agreed that the federal government should help finance long-term care for the elderly rather than leaving it up to private action; and 87 percent said that "government should make a major effort to help American business become more competitive in foreign markets" rather than leaving it up to businesses to do it by themselves.[9]

Similarly, when people are asked the *general* question of whether the government is spending too much money, three quarters or more say yes; but when they are asked whether government is spending too much or too little on a number of *specific* programs, the answers are quite different, as is shown in Table 6.5. Note that, while some programs were more popular than others, a majority of the respondents called for decreased federal spending in only one (foreign aid) of the eleven programs they were asked about.

It is especially instructive in this regard to compare American public opinion with that in other Western democracies. A number of recent polls have asked respondents in the United States and seven other Western democracies whether they think that government has a responsibility to deal with certain problems. Their answers are shown in Table 6.6.

The figures in Table 6.6 show that, compared with their counterparts in other Western democracies, U.S. respondents are substantially less supportive of the idea that government has a prime obligation to guarantee people's basic incomes, reduce the income differences between rich and poor, and make taxes progressive (require people with higher incomes to pay at higher rates than persons with lower

TABLE 6.5   American Attitudes toward Federal Government Spending in Particular Areas, 1992 (in percentages)

	FEDERAL GOVERNMENT SPENDING SHOULD		
AREA	*Increase*	*Stay the Same*	*Decrease*
Improving and protecting the environment	55	39	6
Foreign aid	4	31	65
Fighting AIDS	65	28	7
Social security	61	36	3
War on drugs	65	27	8
Food stamps	16	50	34
Public schools	64	32	4
Assist homeless	66	29	5
Child care	52	39	9
Assist blacks	28	56	16
Space program	13	43	44

Source: The 1992 National Election Study, furnished through the Inter-University Consortium for Political and Social Research and the University of California, Berkeley Data Archive.

TABLE 6.6. Government Responsibility for Dealing with Problems (percentages agreeing with each statement)

	U.S.	AUS.	SWITZ.	U.K.	NETH.	FRG	AUST.	ITALY
Government should provide everyone with guaranteed basic income	21	38	43	61	50	56	57	67
Government should reduce income differences between high- and low-income people	29	44	43	64	65	61	81	82
Government should provide jobs for all who want one	45	40	52	59	75	77	80	82
Government should provide health care for the sick	89	93	na	99	na	98	98	100
Government should prohibit smoking in public places	46	56	na	51	na	49	58	89
Government should give industry help it needs to grow	63	87	na	95	na	54	75	84
People with high incomes should pay taxes at higher rates	58	65	na	76	na	90	na	86

Source: The American Enterprise, March–April, 1990, pp. 113–15.

incomes). On most of these questions, Italians stand at the opposite end. On the other hand, more Americans than Germans favor government support of private industry, and more Americans than Austrians believe that government should provide jobs for all who want them. In general, Americans are less supportive of the idea that government should manage the economy. There has never been much support in the United States for the socialist ideal of public ownership and operation of major sections of the economy, while much larger portions of European publics support it. Moreover, as we will see in Chapter 10, each of the other democracies has at least one political party pledged to socialism as its basic program while less than 1 percent of Americans support a party advocating socialism.

In all countries, most people think taxes are too high. However, when faced with the choice between cutting taxes and maintaining government services, most people choose the services. How can they be so inconsistent? Some say there is no inconsistency: If governments will just cut out "waste and fraud," they can cut taxes *and* maintain services. The fact that no government seems to manage that very well does not keep people on both sides of the Atlantic from thinking it is a splendid idea.

Until recently questions about equal treatment of the races, sexes, and foreign nationals have been more prominent in American politics and public opinion than in most European democracies. Since the 1960s, however, Great Britain and France have faced mounting problems resulting from the sharply increased flow of immigrants from their former colonies in India, Pakistan, the West Indies, and North Africa, and the native populations have had to face up to problems of equality in jobs, housing, public accommodations, and the like. Even in historically multi-ethnic and tolerant Switzerland, the growing numbers of "guest workers" from other nations have led to deep divisions about whether they should be treated as well as Swiss citizens. The women's movement began earlier and became politically more powerful in the United States and Great Britain than in most countries, but in the 1990s political issues concerning equality of the sexes have become politically hot almost everywhere.

In the United States as in the European democracies, there has been what one scholar calls "a phenomenal growth in racial tolerance" since the 1950s. In the 1940s, many white males believed that women, African-Americans, and other racial and ethnic minorities were not entitled to any government help to improve their positions, but in the late 1980s almost everyone, including white males, believed that sexual and racial discrimination is wrong and that government has an obligation to prevent it. There is still a great deal of disagreement over whether the goal should be equality of opportunity or equality of condition, and over whether programs such as affirmative action and comparable worth are proper means to reach the desired ends. But the ideals of ending racial segregation and providing equal opportunities for all races are now strongly supported by public opinion in all democratic nations.[10]

FOREIGN POLICY

A leading survey of public opinion notes that "because issues of foreign policy are quite removed from everyday experience, 'foreign policy' attitudes are generally held less firmly than opinions on domestic policy."[11] On a few occasions foreign policy has become highly salient because of a war, whether it was an all-out war such as World War II or a limited war, such as that in Vietnam (1962–1973) or the Persian Gulf (1990–1991). But political elites are much more likely than mass publics to have strong and enduring opinions on the more specific foreign-policy questions that fill the newspapers, such as American aid to the contra rebels in Nicaragua or American support of secessionist movements in Yugoslavia. In this respect, American public opinion is very much like that in other democratic countries.

Conclusion

We have reviewed some of the opinions that the governments of the United States and some other democratic polities "find it prudent to heed." In Chapter 7 we will consider some of the ways in which people communicate their political ideologies and policy preferences to each other and to their governments and consider whether the modern revolution in mass communications technology has basically altered the nature of democratic government.

For Further Reading

*ASHER, HERBERT R. *Polling and the Public: What Every Citizen Should Know*. Washington, DC: Congressional Quarterly Press, 1987. Useful brief summary of the techniques, uses, and impact of public opinion polls.

*CANTRIL, ALBERT H. *The Opinion Connection: Polling, Politics and the Press*. Washington, DC: Congressional Quarterly Press, 1990. A study, drawing materials from the 1988 presidential election, of the contemporary role of public opinion polls in the conduct and interpretation of presidential elections.

*DALTON, RUSSELL J. *Citizen Politics in Western Democracies*. Chatham, NJ: Chatham House, 1988. A comparative study, based on survey data, of public opinion in the United States, Great Britain, West Germany, and France.

ERIKSON, ROBERT S., NORMAN R. LUTTBEG, AND KENT L. TEDIN, *American Public Opinion*, 3rd ed. New York: Macmillan, 1988. One of the most recent reviews of American political attitudes based on extensive survey data.

KEY, V. O., JR. *Public Opinion and American Democracy*. New York: Alfred A. Knopf, 1961. A distinguished political scientist's analysis of public opinion.

*LIPPMANN, WALTER. *Public Opinion*. New York: Free Press, 1965. First published in the 1920s, a classic philosophical study of the origins and nature of public opinion.

*NIEBURG, H. L. *Public Opinion*. New York: Praeger, 1984. Survey of the formation, content, and impact of public opinion in the United States.

STIMSON, JAMES A. *Public Opinion in America*. Boulder, CO: Westview Press, 1991. Survey-based study of changing tides in American public opinion.

YANKELOVICH, DANIEL. *Coming to Public Judgment: Making Democracy Work in a Complex World*. Syracuse, NY: Syracuse University Press, 1990. A leading pollster's examination of how public opinion is formed and how it might be improved.

In addition to these books, three magazines are useful in presenting up-to-date information from the polls about the current state of public opinion in the United States and some other countries: *The American Enterprise*, published five times a year by the American Enterprise Institute; *Public Opinion Quarterly*, published four times a year by the American Association for Public Opinion Research; and *The Gallup Report*, published monthly by the American Institute of Public Opinion.

Notes

1. V. O. Key, Jr., *Public Opinion and American Democracy* (New York, Alfred A. Knopf, 1961), p. 3.

2. Quoted in Bernard C. Hennessy, "Public Opinion and Opinion Change," in *Political Science Annual*, ed. James A. Robinson (Indianapolis, IN: Bobbs-Merrill, 1966) vol. 1, p. 245.

3. Key, *Public Opinion*, p. 14.

4. *The Gallup Poll Monthly*, November 1992, p. 3.

5. See the summaries of studies by the Roper organization and the National Opinion Research Center in *Public Opinion* April–May 1985, pp. 37–40.

6. Robert S. Erikson, Norman R. Luttbeg, and Kent L. Tedin, *American Public Opinion*, 3rd ed. (New York: Macmillan, 1988), p. 90.

7. Everett Carll Ladd, Jr., and Seymour Martin Lipset, *The Divided Academy* (New York: McGraw-Hill, 1975), pp. 57–60.

8. See the review of the evidence in Erikson, Luttbeg, and Tedin, *American Public Opinion*, pp. 152–56.

9. The poll results are taken from *Public Opinion*, March–April, 1987, pp. 21–29.

10. For a detailed review of many public opinion polls in the United States and Europe underlying these conclusions, see Russell J. Dalton, *Citizen Politics in Western Democracies* (Chatham, NJ: Chatham House, 1988), Chapter 6.

11. Erikson, Luttbeg, and Tedin, *American Public Opinion*, p. 62.

7

Whatever one or more men can and do talk about, but which is not amenable to direct sensory contact by them, has no reality beyond what can [be] and is said about it.[1]

Political Communication

Let us begin with some facts of American life in the 1990s. Ninety-eight percent of all American households have at least one television set. Sixty-four percent have two or more sets, and 62 percent subscribe to cable television. Seventy-three percent have at least one videocassette recorder. Ninety-nine percent have radios, and the average number of sets per household is 5.4. By the time they reach the age of eighteen, American children on average have spent more time watching television than going to school. The average adult American spends more time watching television than doing anything else except working and sleeping. Most American adults read some part of a newspaper every day, and even more read a Sunday paper.

Much the same can be said about other highly industralized nations. This is demonstrated by the data in Table 7.1, which show that for each 1,000 of population the United States has the most radio sets and the second-most television sets, but ranks well down the list in daily newspaper circulation.

Mass communications play a critical role in the politics of all industrialized nations, democratic or authoritarian. Take an obvious U.S. example: In 1992 about 12 million people, by voting in primaries and caucuses, decided that the Democratic presidential nominee would be Bill Clinton and another 13 million decided that George Bush would run for the Republicans. In November, about 104 million voted in the final election among Clinton, Bush, and Perot. But how many Americans personally knew Clinton or Bush or any of the other hopefuls? How many of us had talked with the candidates or worked with them or seen firsthand how they behave in a crisis? Obviously only a tiny fraction, perhaps one tenth of 1 percent. Where, then, did the rest of us get the information about each candidate's experience, character, and stands on issues that provided the basis for our choices?

Since we could not possibly acquire our information firsthand, we got it the only way we could. We had it *communicated* to us, either in personal conversations or from what we saw on television, heard on the radio, or read in newspapers. Which of those were the most important? When asked in a 1988 national survey, "Where do you usually get most of your news about what's going on in the world?" 65 percent of a sample of American adults said television, 42 percent said newspapers, 14 percent said radio, and 4 percent named other sources.[2] (The figures sum to more than 100 percent because some people gave multiple answers.) Hence, political communication is without question one of the most important aspects of governing in the modern world. Let us begin by seeing what political communication involves.

TABLE 7.1   Television and Radio Receivers in Industrialized Nations

NATION	SETS PER 1,000 OF POPULATION		DAILY NEWSPAPER COPIES PER 1,000 OF POPULATION
	Television	Radio	
Canada	641	1,026	228
Denmark	535	1,030	352
Germany	514	952	338
Japan	620	907	587
Netherlands	906	1,106	311
New Zealand	442	929	324
Norway	425	798	614
Sweden	474	888	533
Switzerland	407	855	463
United States	815	2,123	250

Source: The American Almanac, 1993–1994: Statistical Abstract of the United States (Washington, DC: Bureau of the Census, 1994), Table 1397, p. 856.

The Nature of Political Communication

WHAT IS COMMUNICATION?

In its most general sense **communication** is *the transmission of meaning through the use of symbols*. It is the process by which a person or group tries to make another person or group aware of its ideas about something. In this broad sense communication occurs in many different ways (through pictures, music, mathematical symbols, gestures, facial expressions, even physical blows). The most common form of communication in human society, however, is the system of oral and written symbols that we call language.

It is easy to see that communication is *the* basic social process. A society, let us recall, is a group of people who live in a common environment and have common institutions, activities, and interests. However, if people do not communicate with each other in any way, they cannot even be aware of their common interests let alone take any purposeful common action. So, the conclusion is simple: *no communication, no society.*

Communication plays an especially significant role in politics, for it is the basic process by which political groups are formed and try to influence public policy. For example, the fact that some people are poor and others are rich has no political significance in itself. However, by watching, listening, talking, and reading, poor people can learn that some other members of their society are also poor and some are rich. They can learn that they are members of a particular economic group that is different from and, to some extent, opposed to another economic group. After talking and reading about these matters, some members of each group can decide that they want the government to follow policies favorable to their interests. And through speaking and writing—and perhaps also through cartoons, billboards, protest marches, and other less verbal means—they can try to induce public officials to adopt those policies. Thus communication is the basic process by which political action and political conflict take place.

ELEMENTS OF POLITICAL COMMUNICATION

The nature and role of political communication are best understood if we begin by briefly identifying its main elements.

Communicators

Any person or group that acts to influence government policy is a political communicator. The main types of such communicators in modern democratic polities are political parties and pressure groups, whose organization and activities are described in Chapters 2 and 10. In addition, however, in every democracy many government agencies use "handouts," "backgrounders," and "leaks" to try to influence the opinions of persons in other agencies and the general public. For example, most of the executive departments and other agencies of the U.S. government maintain public relations bureaus that print and distribute pamphlets, send out speakers, produce radio and television programs, and in other ways try to create public support for their programs. Authoritarian regimes have total control of all the mass communications media and use them extensively to get their citizens in

POLITICAL COMMUNICATION BY TALK SHOW. Ross Perot on "Larry King Live," 1992.

the right frame of mind to do what the rulers want them to do. Authoritarian regimes also try to shape the content of all direct personal communications, although that is much more difficult than controlling what their people see on television, read in newspapers, or hear on radio.

Messages

Communicators begin the communication process by sending out messages. Each message consists of the symbols—words, pictures, gestures, and so on—by which the communicators try to convey the ideas in their minds to the minds of their targeted receivers, the people they especially want to receive their messages.

Media

Communicators must use some kind of medium, some way of transmitting their messages so that their targeted receivers can become aware of the messages. There are, of course, many different "media,"[3] such as personal conversations with family, friends, and government officials; television and radio broadcasts; columns and editorials in newspapers and magazines; signs and flags carried in protest marches; and even stones thrown through windows. We will consider the organization and impact of the various media later in this chapter.

Receivers

A receiver is a person who becomes aware of a communicator's message. Some receive the message directly from the original communication, while others receive it indirectly through second-hand reports from other people. In either case the knowledge, level of interest, and cognitive maps (see Chapter 3) of the receivers, as we will see, are among the major factors that determine the message's impact.

Responses

Every political communication is intended to produce some kind of response from its receivers. To illustrate, let us say that a communicator makes a speech advocating the right of women to have an abortion on demand. The speech, like any communication, may not evoke any response at all, or it may even increase the receivers' hostility to the speaker's position. But the speaker, like all communicators, intends it to produce one or another of at least four kinds of favorable response: initiation, conversion, reinforcement, and activation.

Initiation. The receivers have not previously thought much about the issue. Hence the speaker "initiates" their views on the question.

Conversion. Before the speech, the receivers were to some degree pro-life, but the speaker's presentation is so effective that it persuades them to abandon their previous views and support the pro-choice position.

Reinforcement. Before the speech the receivers were mildly pro-choice, but their beliefs were shaken by statements made by pro-life partisans, and some considered switching sides. However, the pro-choice speech refutes the points made in the pro-life statements and gives the audience new pro-choice arguments, and the audience leaves the hall supporting the pro-choice position more strongly than before.

Activation. Before the speech the audience was mildly pro-choice and never seriously considered changing their minds, but they were not excited about the issue and did nothing to advance the pro-choice cause. However, the speaker stirs them up so that they contribute money, volunteer to pass out leaflets, and picket speeches by pro-life advocates.

Many studies have been made on each of the five basic elements of communication, but in the rest of this chapter we will focus mainly on two aspects: the organization and operation of the mass media and the impact of political communication on people's political views and behavior.

Mass Communications Media

Communications media are usually divided into two types. **Interpersonal media** are *media that transmit their messages by direct personal contact between communicators and receivers and include personal conversations, personal letters, and the like.* **Mass media** are *media that "broadcast" messages to large numbers of receivers with whom they have no face-to-face contact.* The most prominent media in this category are television, radio, newspapers, movies, magazines, and books. In all industrialized nations, democratic and authoritarian, television, newspapers, and radio (in that order) have by far the greatest audiences and political impact, so we will concentrate on them in this chapter.

TELEVISION

Ownership, Organization, and Regulation

In the United States, most television broadcasting is privately owned and operated, and most broadcasters receive the bulk of their revenues from the sale of time for broadcasting advertisements. But American broadcasters are very far from having a completely free hand in broadcasting about politics. The political content of their programs is, in fact, much more closely regulated than the political content of newspapers, magazines, and books. Their main regulator is the Federal Communications Commission (FCC), whose main weapon is its licensing power. Every broadcasting station must obtain a license from the FCC before it can operate, and its license comes up for renewal every five years. To qualify for a new or renewed license, each broadcaster must comply with a number of FCC standards and rules, some of which apply to the content of broadcasts about politics. For example, the "equal-opportunities rule" requires that if a station sells or gives time

AMERICAN TELEVISION FACTS, 1993–1994

Number of broadcasting stations		Average hours per week watching television	
Commercial:	1,118	Children 2–5:	28
Public:	364	Children 6–11:	27
Total:	1,482	Teenagers:	22
Number of cable systems: 11,075		Adults 18–34:	29
Annual revenues from advertising: $20.9 billion		Adults 35–54:	30
Percentages of households with television sets		Adults 55 and older:	40
At least one:	98	Men:	30
Two or more:	64	Women:	36
Percentage of television households subscribing to cable:	62		

Sources: *The American Almanac: Statistical Abstract of the United States, 1993–1994* (Washington, DC: Bureau of the Census, 1994), Table 1397, p. 856; and *Nielson Reports on Television* (A. C. Nielson Co., 1984 and 1985).

to a particular political party or candidate, it must make available on the same terms an equal amount of time to any competing party or candidate. The FCC also controls such matters as the operating frequencies and power of broadcasting transmitters, the legal and financial relationships of broadcasting stations with the networks, and the number of stations that can be owned by one person or corporation. The FCC has exercised little if any political censorship, but it has had considerable (not enough, according to some critics; too much, according to others) effect upon the content of programs and upon the financial and legal structure of the broadcasting industry.

There are various patterns of ownership and regulation in other democratic countries. In Belgium, Ireland, and Norway, for example, all radio and television stations are owned and operated by the government. In Sweden, broadcasting is also controlled by a monopoly, but one in which both the government and private interests participate. In most other democracies there is, as in the United States, a mixture of privately owned commercial television and publicly owned noncommercial television. The systems of greatest interest to Americans are probably those of France, Great Britain, and Canada, and we will look at them in a bit more detail.

For many years, all radio and television broadcasting in France was, as in Denmark, a government monopoly. In 1982, however, the system was radically changed. The government retained its monopoly over television transmissions, but all programming was put in the control of seven independent but government-financed companies under the overall supervision of the nine-member Haute Autorité de la Communication Audiovisuelle. Each company has its own budget and administrative council made up of two representatives of the government and one representative each from parliament, the press, and its own staff. All three television channels are financed partly by private advertising but mainly by public funds.

THE ROLE OF THE MEDIA

The mass media in America are business, whether big or little; they are, as George Gerbner has said, "the cultural arm of American industry." That is the primary fact about the mass media in the United States, oriented as they are to marketing. One must understand that fact to grasp the essential meaning of the media and their relationship to the American social order. A similar understanding is necessary for analysis of the [former] Soviet communication system. To grasp the essential meaning of the [former] Soviet mass media and their relationship to Communist society, one must first recognize that the [former] Soviet communication system is an arm of the political order, as it is in any authoritarian society.[4]

Great Britain has a mixture of publicly and privately owned broadcasting. The British Broadcasting Corporation (BBC) was chartered as a "public corporation" by Parliament in 1927 but has never been directly owned or controlled by the government. The BBC's board of governors is appointed by the Queen on the advice of the prime minister, but its members are not political in a partisan sense, and they make policy without supervision by any government agency. Every owner of a radio or television set must purchase a license, and the revenue from the license fees is assigned to the BBC. The rest of BBC revenue comes from the sale of its weekly publication, *Radio Times*, and from the sale of its programs to foreign broadcasters. Most BBC programs are planned and broadcast centrally and relayed over a series of local and regional stations, although some local and regional programs are also broadcast. The BBC now operates two television channels.

The British Parliament has also authorized commercial television (1954) and radio (1972) for private profit. They are supervised by the Independent Broadcasting Authority (IBA). The IBA owns and operates the transmitting stations, but the programs are produced by private companies under contract to the IBA. There are presently (1992) seventeen such companies for television and twenty-one for radio, most of them organized on regional bases. Some are controlled by motion picture interests, others by newspapers, others by general investors. Advertisers do not directly sponsor programs as in the United States but purchase time between programs when a series of advertisements are broadcast—singing commercials and all. IBA also operates two television channels.

The Canadian system is an interesting hybrid of American, British, and continental European practices. The Canadian Broadcasting Corporation (CBC) was created and is periodically renewed by acts of Parliament. The Canadian Parliament directly controls the CBC's finances, whereas the British Parliament has no such control over the BBC's finances. The CBC was once supported entirely by receiver license fees on the British model, but since the 1950s it has been financed by a combination of commercial revenue and annual parliamentary grants and loans. Privately owned broadcasting stations are also licensed and regulated by an entirely separate agency, the Canadian Radio-Television and Telecommunications Commission (CRTC), which is analogous to the American FCC. Those arrangements result in three parallel and separate broadcasting groups: the CBC's national network, the privately owned CTV national network, and a number of independent private stations. Some of the latter are affiliated with the CBC and use some CBC programs at no cost, with the CBC sharing in any commercial revenues raised by the stations in connection with CBC programs. The net result is that although the Canadian system was originally fashioned on the British model, it now more nearly resembles the American model.

Presentation of Political News and Information

In all democratic countries, television broadcasters present political news and information mainly through their regular newscasts, which feature short accounts of the important political events (as selected by their news producers) that have taken place since the previous newscast. Newscasts usually include pictures and words about what political candidates and officeholders have been doing, and they often feature interviews of the political leaders by television correspondents and anchors.

From the politicians' standpoint, this kind of coverage has several advantages and one great disadvantage. On the plus side, the coverage is free and the viewing audience tends to believe that what they are seeing is what has really happened, probably because it comes as news and not as advertisements trying to sell some-

ACCOUNTABILITY BY TELEVISION. President Clinton at a televised press conference.

thing. However, there is also a negative side: The television producers and correspondents control the content of each broadcast. Hence, they, and not the candidates, select the fifteen- or thirty-second segments ("TV bytes" they are called) of the candidates' speeches that will appear on the air, and the newscasters' objective is to make news stories interesting and not to make the candidates look good.

That disadvantage has two consequences. One is a constant drumbeat of complaint by supporters of particular leaders, parties, and ideologies that television's news coverage is biased against them. The other is a demand by politicians for free and unedited access to the airwaves so that they can present their issues and personal characters in *their* way and not the newscasters' way.

The Western democracies meet such demands by some mixture of two devices. One is permitting candidates and parties to purchase air time just like commercial advertisers and use it to present their own political advertisements, usually in thirty-second or one-minute spot advertisements that are shown, like nonpolitical advertisements, during regular entertainment programs. The other is giving the political parties some free air time in which they can present their cases any way they wish without interference by government authorities. These are generally called "party political broadcasts."

Thus in the United States, political parties, candidates, and pressure groups are allowed to buy television time for political advertisements, although in presidential elections there are limits on the total amount of money they can spend on campaigning and therefore on how much they can spend on television. Some public stations provide the equivalent of party political broadcasts, but local commercial stations and national networks will not give the parties free air time in which they, and not the broadcasters, control the contents.

The status of political advertising and party political broadcasts varies considerably among Western democracies. In Great Britain, no party or candidate can purchase time from either the BBC or the IBA for broadcasting political advertising. The only broadcasts whose contents are controlled by the parties are the free party political broadcasts. In the 1959 general election the BBC and the Independent Television Authority (the IBA's predecessor) jointly proposed to the leading parties that the free time made available for party-controlled telecasts be divided into a ratio of four parts for Conservatives, four for Labour, and one for the Liberals (presumably reflecting the parties' respective voting strengths); and the parties were delighted to accept. In subsequent elections from 1964 to 1979, the ratio was changed to 5:5:3, reflecting increased Liberal strength. In the 1983, 1987, and 1992 elections, it was changed again to 5:5:4, with the increased share going to the newly merged Liberal and Social Democratic parties. In each party political broadcast the party decides for itself what to do with its allotted time, and the stations broadcast whatever it has prepared. In addition, the BBC and ITN (Independent Television News, the private news-producing company) produce and broadcast debates, forums, interviews, talk shows, and other political programs and try—not entirely to the satisfaction of the party leaders—to divide the attention given to each party's candidates and programs by the same 5:5:4 formula. This British variation on the American equal-time rule is now well established and likely to persist.

Canada allows political parties to purchase air time for political advertising but limits the total amount the parties can purchase and allocates the time among the parties according to their electoral support and seats in Parliament. In French presidential and parliamentary elections, some free air time is given to each of the presidential candidates and political parties, but no one can purchase air time for political advertising. In Germany, parties are granted free time on television to broadcast a number of 150-second spot broadcasts *(Wahlspots)* corresponding to their shares of the popular votes. Italy also provides free broadcast time to all eligible parties during election campaigns but requires that some of it be used for press conferences.

In summary, then, the United States is one of the few countries in the world (Venezuela is another) in which parties and candidates can purchase as much television time as they can afford for political advertising, and also one of the few in which no air time is given free to the parties or candidates to use as they see fit. In most democracies it is now possible for businesses to purchase air time for broadcasting commercial advertisements, but most of them prohibit parties and candidates from buying air time for broadcasting political advertisements. Of course, in the United States, as in all democratic countries, there are many broadcaster-controlled newscasts, discussion programs, interviews, call-in shows, and the like covering not only election campaigns but many other aspects of public policy and policy making. Most scholars agree that this free television exposure is far more important than paid political advertisements in shaping the way the viewing public feels about candidates, parties, and issues.

Political and Structural Bias in Television News

Ever since television became the preeminent medium of political mass communications, a considerable debate has raged about whether or not the broadcasters' news coverage of political events and issues is biased. The debate has been especially noisy in the United States, where quite a few political partisans have charged that the broadcasters, especially those in the news divisions of the national networks (ABC, CBS, Fox, and NBC), have a strong *political* bias; that is, the networks deliberately slant their coverage so as to help certain candidates and causes and harm others. The most familiar version of this charge is made by a number of conservative organizations and critics, ranging from Reid Irvine and his Accuracy in Media organization and former Vice President Spiro T. Agnew to Pat Buchanan, who was the chief communications aide to President Reagan in his second term and a presidential contender in 1992. They accuse the network newscasts of consistently and deliberately favoring liberals over conservatives, Democrats over Republicans, pro-choice advocates over pro-life advocates, and opponents of prayer in the schools over its proponents.

Less well-known is the mirror-image charge by left-wing critics, such as David Altheide, Robert Cirino, and the organization Fairness and Accuracy in Reporting, that the network newscasters are hired guns for the bosses of big business, and use their broadcasts to glorify the establishment and suppress news of how the power structure is crushing and alienating the masses.

There is a third view: Many scholars of television's coverage of politics—including, among others, Edwin Diamond, Edward Jay Epstein, Doris Graber, Richard Hofstetter, and Michael Robinson—conclude that television's bias is not political but *structural*. Their studies of political programming have convinced them that there is no systematic favoring of liberals over conservatives or Democrats over Republicans. Rather, there is consistently more sympathetic coverage of people who challenge the establishment than of people in power, of "mavericks" than of "party bosses," of candidates running behind than of front-runners, of dark horses than of favorites, of new faces than of old ones, and, perhaps most important of all, of non-politicians than of politicians.

This structural bias, they believe, grows from the very nature of the television medium itself: the legal constraints on how it operates, the fierce competition among the networks, the need to attract and keep huge audiences by featuring vivid pictures instead of boring talking heads, the need to squeeze everything (including commercials) into half-hour broadcasts, and above all the need not to overtax the short attention spans of their viewers, many of whom are quickly bored by political stories.

Broadcasters, of course, heatedly deny that they have *any* kind of bias. One producer for NBC News says, "The news is not a reporter's perception or explanation of what happens; *it is simply what happens.*" A former head of CBS News has described television as an "electric mirror" that simply shows what is going on in the world just as a glass mirror shows what is standing in front of it.[5]

Regulation of Political Broadcasting in the United States

Whatever may be the merits of the charges of bias, we should be clear that the political contents of television broadcasts are regulated far more closely than their counterparts in newspapers, magazines, and books. The First Amendment to the U.S. Constitution declares that "Congress shall make no law . . . abridging the freedom of . . . the press." The U.S. Supreme Court has interpreted this prohibition very strictly. For example, in *New York Times* v. *Sullivan* (1964), the Court held that neither public officials nor public figures can collect damages for defamatory remarks made about them unless they can prove that the remarks were made with malicious intent and with reckless disregard for the truth. Consequently, the print media are free to print just about anything they wish about politics and are constrained very little by libel laws. Print journalists have no *legal* obligation to be fair or balanced in what they say about political issues or personalities, though many try to be unbiased.

Television and radio broadcasters, on the other hand, operate under much tighter legal restraints. The U.S. Supreme Court has repeatedly upheld the constitutionality of these restraints on the basis of the "scarcity doctrine." That doctrine notes that there are only a limited number of frequencies available for broadcasting television and radio signals, and two stations cannot operate in the same area on the same frequency without jamming each other's signal. Hence, the frequencies have to be assigned to particular stations by the FCC, and the Supreme Court has declared that in return for allowing those stations to use such a limited and precious national resource Congress and the FCC have the right to impose certain rules on how the stations operate.[6] And Congress has stipulated that the basic purpose to be served in assigning and renewing broadcasting licenses is "the public interest, convenience, or necessity" and *not* the broadcasters' right to make money or propagandize for their personal political preferences.

In carrying out this mandate, Congress and the FCC have imposed several rules on the broadcasting of political materials. The most important follow.

REQUIREMENT TO BROADCAST PUBLIC AFFAIRS PROGRAMS   The Federal Communications Act (FCA) requires that every station must broadcast a reasonable number of programs on public affairs. The exact ratio of such programs to other programming is never spelled out, but broadcasters understand that it should be at least 15 percent or so. The rule is satisfied mainly by regular broadcasts of national and local news, including political news, although some broadcasters air a few documentaries dealing with public problems and political issues in greater depth than in the short news broadcasts.

THE FAIRNESS DOCTRINE   Until recently the FCC required that whenever a station broadcast material on a controversial issue of public interest, it was required to broadcast—then or later—presentations of contrasting views on that issue. The broadcasters usually discharged this obligation by including in the initial program statements by advocates of both the "pro" and "con" positions on each issue, and occasionally the stations also provided short periods of free time for replies by advocates of opposing views.

At the present writing (1995), the Fairness Doctrine is suspended, perhaps permanently. During most of the Reagan administration Mark Fowler, then chairman of the FCC, contended that broadcasters should be as free as newspapers, books, and magazines to present whatever political news stories and commentaries they wish in any manner they wish. The scarcity-doctrine argument no longer made sense, he argued, because the great expansion of cable television, direct satellite broadcasting, videocassette recorders, and other new technologies have given television viewers even more alternative sources of information than newspaper readers, and it was therefore time to make broadcasting as free as the print media.

Many people—both liberals and conservatives (the issue seems to cut across the usual ideological lines)—do not agree with the Reagan administration's stand. They fear that canceling the Fairness Doctrine will allow broadcasters to slant the news any way they wish to promote their favorite candidates and causes. The fact that television has a much stronger impact than newspapers on people's information and understanding means, they say, that slanted television will distort our democratic system much more than slanted newspapers, books, and magazines do.

In 1987, a federal court of appeals unexpectedly ruled that Congress had not *mandated* the Fairness Doctrine but had merely authorized the FCC to impose it. Fowler and the FCC seized the opportunity and suspended the doctrine. Congress then amended the legislation to *require* the FCC to enforce the rule, but President Reagan vetoed the bill, and the Senate could not muster the necessary two thirds vote to override the veto. In the 1990s it is not yet clear what the president and Congress will do about restoring the Fairness Doctrine, but it continues to be one of the major issues of communications policy.

THE EQUAL-OPPORTUNITIES RULE   As we have seen, the FCC requires that if a station gives free time to a candidate for public office, it must give an equal amount of free time to all other candidates running for that office. If it sells time to a candidate, it must give all other candidates the opportunity to buy equal amounts of time at the same rates. Under recent rulings, however, this does not apply to the coverage of candidates on news programs. Hence there is no need for the stations and networks to give as much news time to minor-party candidates as to major-party candidates, and broadcasters are free to broadcast the debates between the Democratic and Republican presidential candidates without including third-party candidates so long as the broadcasters, and not the candidates, control the debates' formats.

NEWSPAPERS

Since the 1960s, television has replaced newspapers as the preeminent mass communications medium. Nevertheless, it is important to recognize that while people now turn to newspapers less than to television for their political information and trust what they get less than what they get from television, newspapers are still very important elements in the communications systems of most countries, including the United States. As the figures in the box show, the number of American newspapers has declined since 1950. Yet people regard them as their second most important and second most trusted source of political information. Equally important and less obvious, most scholars of communication believe that newspapers—especially the wire services and the top-quality national papers such as *The New York Times, Washington Post, The Wall Street Journal, Los Angeles Times,* and a few others—set the agenda and perform the basic news-gathering function for television news shows. We are told that the first thing TV news producers do every morning is to read carefully the *Times, Post, Journal,* and perhaps one or two other papers. That is how producers find out what is going on in the world and what they need to feature on that night's newscasts. If the top papers give a story big headlines and a lot of space, then the networks will think that the story must be important, and producers will give it a prominent place on newscasts. Broadcasters may go their own way more on lesser news stories and particularly on the weather reports and human-interest stories that are so prominent in their newscasts, but, basically, they rely on the "news consensus" as printed by the major newspapers to tell them what is going on and what is important. Hence newspapers deserve our attention, if not as much attention as we have given to television.

In authoritarian nations, such as Iran and North Korea, all mass media, including newspapers, are government-owned and government-operated monopolies whose mission is to persuade the people to support government policies with

AMERICAN NEWSPAPER FACTS, 1950–1993				
	1950	*1960*	*1970*	*1993*
Number of Newspapers				
Daily	1,894	1,854	1,838	1,735
Semiweekly	337	324	423	584
Weekly	9,794	8,979	8,903	8,218
Total	12,125	11,157	11,164	10,537
Newspaper circulation (in millions)				
Daily	53.8	58.9	62.1	60.7
Sunday	46.6	47.7	49.2	62.1

Source: The figures are taken from *The Statistical Abstract of the United States 1993* (Washington, DC: Government Printing Office, 1993), Table 916, p. 567.

enthusiasm and not to tell the readers what is really going on. In the democracies almost all newspapers are privately owned and operated and are run mainly for the same purpose for which other private businesses are mainly run: to make profits for their owners.

In the United States, newspapers obtain their revenues partly from subscriptions but mainly from advertising, which accounts for 65 to 90 percent of their total income. Increased circulation is therefore a prime goal of all American papers, for it not only brings in more direct revenue but also attracts more advertisers. This goal inclines editors to print material that they think will interest readers and yet not unduly offend present and potential advertisers. No commercial newspaper can afford to print only what its editors think readers ought to read. It must print what editors think readers *want* to read, and this objective plays a great part in determining what is regarded as news. In addition to news, most papers print many features, such as comic strips, recipes, fashion notes, and bridge columns.

Most newspapers also print material explicitly intended to influence the political opinions of their readers, mainly in the form of unsigned editorials and signed columns. The evidence suggests that such material affects the political opinions of readers relatively little. In both the United States and Great Britain, for example, almost every voter regularly reads some part of a newspaper, and the majority of American and British newspapers editorially favor the Republican and Conservative parties, respectively. Yet, the Democratic and Labour parties, despite their usual lack of editorial support, continue to win quite a few elections.

Newspapers have a larger audience than any other mass medium except television. In the United States, for example, approximately 90 percent of all adults regularly read at least some part of a daily newspaper. Elsewhere in the world the largest numbers of newspapers and the largest audiences are found in nations with the highest rates of per capita wealth, industrial development, and literacy. Over 80 percent of the world's total newspaper circulation is in Europe and North America.

RADIO

The advent of the television age has certainly not driven radio broadcasting out of business, even in the United States. In 1950, at the beginning of television's growth, the average American household had 2.1 radio sets; in 1990, thirty years after television had become the leading mass medium, the average household had 5.6 radio sets. The number of commercial radio stations had increased from 5,949 to 9,244, and the number of FM stations had doubled. Much the same growth has taken place in most other nations.

Radio has adapted to the dominance of television, especially in the United States, by changing from "broadcasting" to "narrowcasting." That is, before 1950 most stations and the national networks with which they were affiliated sought, like television broadcasters do today, to attract the largest possible audiences, and so their programs were designed to appeal to everyone. In the 1990s, however, most radio stations cater only to particular segments of the population and broadcast only programs designed to appeal to them. Hence, the radio sections of most big-city newspapers identify each station's specialty—hard rock, soft rock, country and western, classical, "beautiful music," all news, news-and-talk. As Table 7.2 shows, radio is now a distant third to television and newspapers as a source of information for most people.

Radio is probably somewhat more important in the other developed countries than in the United States. It is certainly much more important in the less-developed countries of Africa and Asia, where radio reaches many more people than television and is the principal medium of mass communications.

Political Impact of Mass Communications ─────────

ON MASS PUBLICS

Since the late 1950s, several national polling organizations have been asking respondents where they get their information about what is going on in the world and what sources of information they trust the most. Their answers over a twenty-five year span are shown in Table 7.2. Although the study cited in Table 7.2 has not been repeated, there is little doubt that in the 1990s most people in the advanced/industrialized countries learn most of what they know about politics from watching television and reading newspapers rather from conversations with family and friends, reading books and magazines, or participating directly in politics (for example, 89 percent of the respondents in a 1990 Gallup poll said that television was their main source of information about the Gulf War). There is also no doubt that most of us are voracious consumers of the mass media messages, and even though only a small fraction of those messages have much political content, they are bound to have some impact on our political beliefs and actions. The question is, what kind of impact and how much?

TABLE 7.2   Use of and Trust in News Sources, 1959–1984

"I'd like to ask you where you usually get most of your news about what's going on in the world today— from the newspapers or radio or television or magazines or talking to people or where?" (more than one answer permitted)

SOURCE OF MOST NEWS	1959 (%)	1968 (%)	1974 (%)	1978 (%)	1984 (%)
Television	51	59	65	67	64
Newspapers	57	48	47	49	40
Radio	34	25	21	20	14
Magazines	8	7	4	5	4
People	4	5	4	5	4

"If you got conflicting or different reports of the same news story from radio, television, the magazines and the newspapers, which of the four versions would you be most inclined to believe—the one on radio or television or magazines or newspapers?" (only one answer permitted)

MOST BELIEVABLE	1959 (%)	1968 (%)	1974 (%)	1978 (%)	1984 (%)
Television	29	44	51	47	53
Newspapers	32	21	20	23	24
Radio	12	8	8	9	8
Magazines	10	11	8	9	7
Don't know, no answer	17	16	13	12	9

Source: Burns W. Roper, "Trends in Attitudes Toward the Media: A 26-Year Review," *Public Attitudes Toward Television and Other Media in a Time of Change* (Roper Poll, Television Information Office, 1984), pp. 3, 5.

Some commentators regard modern advertising as an irresistible weapon for making people do what the advertiser wants. They view people as bundles of psychological "knee-jerk" reflexes and are convinced that if a skilled advertiser taps the correct reflexes in the correct ways, then people can be made to do anything, from buying a particular brand of toothpaste to voting for a particular candidate. Thus, for instance, such people believe that Ronald Reagan was elected president in 1980 and reelected in 1984 solely or mainly because he was "the great communicator," an experienced and professional motion picture, radio, and television performer who knew just how to use the mass media to beguile people into seeing things his way.

Let us admit that the great success of the advertising industry and the ability of dictators like Adolf Hitler and the Ayatollah Khomeini to mobilize the masses fanatically behind them lend a certain credibility to this view. Nevertheless, social science research has shown that political communication is not an irresistible weapon. Michael J. Robinson, for example, points out that in the 1984 election, the television networks and major newspapers consistently gave Reagan much more unfavorable treatment than they gave Mondale, and not, he emphasizes, because they were liberal Democrats trying to beat a conservative Republican but because Reagan was both the "establishment candidate" and the front-runner. Yet Reagan won reelection by a large margin, and Robinson's research shows that the more unfavorable the networks' treatment of Reagan became, the larger Reagan's lead grew.

THE NEWS ANCHORS: AMERICA'S MOST POWERFUL MEN? (top) Dan Rather of CBS; Tom Brokaw of NBC; (bottom) Peter Jennings of ABC; Bernard Shaw of CNN.

As Robinson put it, the "good news" that the media reported—the booming economy, the low rates of inflation and unemployment, and the fact that the United States was not at war anywhere—simply overshadowed the "bad press" and the "negative spin" the media consistently gave Reagan by emphasizing his age and his vagueness on the issues.[7]

What, then, *is* the political impact of the mass media? The answer, in my opinion, was best stated by the distinguished political sociologist Bernard Berelson:

> Some kinds of *communication* on some kinds of *issues*, brought to the attention of some kinds of *people* under some kinds of *conditions* have some kinds of *effects*.[8]

Each of the italicized words in Berelson's formulation identifies a significant variable in the process, and each may operate quite differently in different circumstances.

Kind of Communication

A communication may have reportorial or editorial content or both. Reportorial content simply *presents* the known facts about what has happened. Editorial content *evaluates* what has happened and *speculates* about what might happen in the future. Although most attention has been directed to editorializing, the evidence suggests that reportorial content is more effective in influencing opinions. If people are told that "Arab terrorists want to intimidate American leaders," then those people may or may not be impressed. However, if those same people are told that "Arab terrorists have just killed over 200 U.S. Marines in Lebanon with a truck bomb," then they are likely to respond more intensely and actively.

Another aspect of communication that has long interested social scientists is the fact, shown repeatedly by their research, that television clearly has the greatest impact of all the mass media. Why? As I have written elsewhere,

> For most of us an important part of any communication is not only what the communicator says but what kind of human being he or she seems to be. That information is conveyed far more vividly by television's combination of words, voice, and pictures than by the faceless voice of radio or by the faceless and voiceless words of newspapers. Perhaps that explains why most Americans consume more political news from television than from newspapers and why they rely more on the accuracy of what they see on television than on what they read in newspapers.[9]

Kind of Issue

Communication is most effective when it deals with new and unstructured issues on which no strong opinions already exist. Most of us are more likely to accept the judgments, favorable or unfavorable, of people and groups about whom we know little than of those that we know well. For example, if a railroad president is told "All politicians are crooks!" he may well agree. However, if he is told that "X railroad is the most inefficient in the world," he will probably reply that the situation involves too many complex factors to justify such an extreme statement. On the other hand, if both statements are made to politicians, they will probably enter qualifications and reservations about politicians and heartily agree about the railroad.

Communication is likely to be more effective on issues that the receivers regard as relatively unimportant than on those they see as crucial. They may have views on both kinds of issues, but their opinions on what they see as the important ones are likely to be far stronger (and therefore less changeable) than their opinions on issues that seem relatively unimportant.

Kind of Audience

Obviously, communicators can affect the opinions only of those who receive their messages. Thus people who watch a lot of television, read only the comics and sports pages of their newspapers, and never read a book are more likely to be affected politically by what is broadcast on television than by what is printed in newspapers or books. Conversely, people who do a lot of reading as well as viewing are likely to be better informed and less easily influenced by television alone. By the same token, as we have seen, people who already have strong views on a matter are much less likely to be influenced by the mass media, including television, than people with weakly held or no views.

Kind of Conditions

A communicator who controls all the communications media is obviously in a better position to influence opinion than is one who must worry about competing messages. That, of course, explains why the rulers in authoritarian regimes are careful to control the communications media as completely as they possibly can. It also explains why the model of democracy outlined in Chapter 5 requires free access to communications media, and it accounts for the concern that some observers have expressed over the tendencies toward increasing concentration of ownership and control of the mass media in modern democracies. Most observers agree, however, that this tendency has not yet become a full-fledged monopoly. In any case the effectiveness of mass communications is limited by the other factors we are considering here.

Kind of Effects

Berelson argued that the long-range effects of communication are more significant than the short-range effects. Among the long-range effects he included such matters as giving meanings to key political terms, furnishing basic pictures of what the world is like, and emphasizing and perpetuating certain social values.

Communications, especially as they affect political campaigns, appear to have the following kinds of effects on their receivers. The least frequent is *conversion*, which is inducing people to switch preferences from one candidate or policy to another. More frequent is *initiation*, which is establishing attitudes on issues that have previously had little or no visibility for the mass public, and on which most people have no prior opinions. Still more frequent is *reinforcement*, which is bolstering the preferences that receivers already have and providing them with arguments to counter both their own doubts and unsettling propaganda from the other side. The most frequent effect is *activation*, which is making supporters feel that the issue is so important and their side is so right that they will act to advance it by voting, by attending meetings, and by contributing money and services.

Most directors of political campaigns are well aware of those probabilities. As a result, most campaigns are designed not to win people away from the opposition but to keep people already on their side faithful to the cause and to ensure that they go to the polls when it counts.

ON POLITICAL AND GOVERNMENTAL LEADERS

In Election Campaigns[10]

Every democratic election is preceded by a *campaign*, a period ranging from a month or so in most of the parliamentary democracies to six months or more in the United States and other presidential democracies in which the parties and candidates seek to maximize their votes. Thus every campaign targets four types of eligible voters (in increasing order of importance): (1) hostile voters (to be converted; (2) uncommitted voters (to be persuaded); (3) loyal voters (to be reinforced); and (4) all potential supporters (to be energized into casting their votes).

In most democratic nations the nature of campaigning has changed a good deal since the 1950s. In earlier times campaigning was conducted mainly by the parties and to a lesser degree by their candidates. The parties generally used party workers to canvass (i.e., to make direct door-to-door contacts with their known and potential supporters). The campaigners used the mass media mainly to publish newspaper advertisements and to distribute party-printed posters and flyers.

Campaigners in the United States were the first to use new communications technologies in the 1950s, and by the 1990s they have transformed campaigning in many ways. Parties and candidates now depend mainly on paid television advertisements and broadcasters' interviews and appearances on talk shows to sell their candidates and policies to the voters. They hire experts to do frequent polls of voters to check on how well their strategies are working. They canvass voters by telephone rather than by ringing doorbells. Campaign workers and leaders communicate with each other by fax, e-mail, and cellular phones. They store and analyze information about the demographics and past electoral behavior of election districts in computerized databases. And they have taken control of campaigns away from the veteran party politicians and given it to professional campaign consultants.

Political leaders in other democracies have watched U.S. campaigns and pondered whether they should use some or all of these methods in their own campaigns. Many have deplored and some have rejected the "Americanization" (their term) of their campaigns. Others have said that since mass communications play as important a part in their nations as they do in the United States, parties and candidates that want to win have no choice but to use the new technologies in substantially the same way.

POLITICAL COMMUNICATION CAN BE DIRECT. Bill Clinton and Al Gore at a stop on their bus tour campaign in 1992.

The United States held its first nationally televised debates between presidential candidates in 1960, and they have assumed a regular and sometimes decisive role in presidential campaigns. Similar debates among leading parties and candidates are now periodically held also in Brazil, Chile, Denmark, France, Germany, Mexico, Norway, Sweden, and Venezuela.

Political scientist Larry Bartels contends that campaign electioneering, however high tech it may have become, still has little impact on the voters' preferences or decisions to vote or abstain.[11] He may be right, but in most modern democracies today the parties and candidates act as though they believe that the quality of their campaigns is a major factor in winning or losing—and/or that the stakes in winning or losing are so high that they dare not run the risk of conducting old-fashioned, low-tech campaigns or no campaigns at all.

In Government: Handouts, Backgrounders, and Leaks

The mass communications media are at least as important for public officeholders and other policy makers between elections as they are for candidates during elections. Policy makers know that their chances of getting their policies adopted and improving their personal status and power depend mainly on what other policy makers—and ultimately the general public—know and feel about what they are doing.

Consequently, every major elected official and every major administrative agency has some kind of public relations office charged with "getting out its story" through the mass media in the most favorable light. For example, every modern president of the United States has a press secretary and dozens of assistants whose job is to make sure that the 5,000 newspaper and television correspondents assigned to cover the White House publish and air stories that are as favorable as possible. Every cabinet member, every executive department, and every administrative agency has its equivalent, though none draws more than a small fraction of the president's coverage. Every senator and representative has a press secretary with a similar job, and the Senate maintains three and the House six recording studios in which the members can make audiotapes or videotapes for free broadcast by stations in their states and districts.

The main products of press secretaries and public relations bureaus are official handouts and semiofficial "backgrounders." Handouts are prepared documents, often hundreds of pages long, in which the official or agency sets forth in detail defenses of past actions and arguments for proposed actions. Backgrounders are more informal occasions in which press secretaries or perhaps their bosses meet with members of the press and tell them off the record what is really going on so that the correspondents will write the story knowing the "true" facts. It is hoped that this will incline the news writers to portray the policy maker favorably. The correspondents cannot attribute their information to a public official by name, so they attribute information to such sources as "a high White House official" or "an authoritative source in the State Department."

Both handouts and backgrounders are important sources of information for the news media, but perhaps even more important, and certainly more controversial, are the never-ending flow of leaks, one of the most widespread, influential, and deplored processes of modern democratic government. Strictly speaking, a **leak** is an *officially unauthorized transmission of confidential government information to the news media*. There are countless examples, but here are two recent instances prominent in the Reagan administration. In November 1982, the administration was looking for ways to cut the budget deficit, and one possibility under consideration was taxing unemployment benefits on the same basis as regular income. A staff aide to the secretary of the treasury was strongly opposed to the idea, and he secretly told a reporter for *The Washington Post* that it was being considered. The *Post* headlined the story the next day, a storm of protest broke from labor unions, and after a few days the president's press secretary announced that the idea had never been seriously considered and would not be pursued. The leak thus killed the policy, as the leaker intended.

In 1984 there was a struggle inside the administration over how to handle the matter of the former Soviet Union's violations of past arms-control treaties. The hard-liners wanted the president to make a speech about the violations so as to create an atmosphere hostile to any new arms-control treaty with the Soviets, which they feared would weaken America's defenses. The soft-liners wanted the violations to be discussed only with the Soviets and only in secret so that neither side would lose face and a new treaty could be signed. The hard-liners leaked the information about the violations through friendly members of various Senate and House staffs to *The Washington Times*, which then ran a series of stories, complete with maps and charts, reporting the secret information about the violations. As a result, the signing of the treaty was delayed for nearly four years until the administration could satisfy enough members of the Senate that new inspection systems would force the Soviets to live up to the proposed new agreement on limiting intermediate-range ballistic missiles in Europe. In this instance the leaks did not kill the treaty, but they delayed it four years.[12] Perhaps most famous of all leaks are those by a still-unknown official in the Nixon administration, code-named "Deep Throat," to *Washington Post* reporters that provided much of the information about the Watergate scandals that ultimately led to President Nixon's 1974 resignation.[13]

Every president since George Washington has deplored leaks and sought ways of preventing them. In recent administrations, Richard Nixon established a secret "plumbers' unit" to "fix the leaks" by tapping the telephones of persons suspected of passing secret information to reporters. In November 1985, Ronald Reagan signed a secret directive ordering the random use of mandatory lie-detector tests of 182,000 federal employees and defense contractors with access to secret information; but someone who opposed the policy leaked the directive to a reporter for the *Los Angeles Times*. The *Times* immediately published the story, which evoked the comment from Secretary of State George Shultz that "the minute in this government I am told that I'm not trusted is the day that I leave," and the next day Reagan canceled the order.

Not only was this one more of many instances in which a leak has killed a policy, but it confirmed the fact that leaks are a permanent and inescapable part of the mass communications process in modern democratic governments. Why are they so inevitable? One reason is the news media's eagerness to scoop their competitors by publishing exclusive and accurate stories based on leaked information about what is *really* going on behind government's closed doors. Most journalists consider it part of their professional obligation to report all the facts that they can dig up and verify. Moreover, journalists know that most of their viewers and readers enjoy such stories. Perhaps even more important is the fact that all policy makers on occasion find that a leak to the right reporter at the right time can be very helpful in accomplishing their political purposes. Indeed, some of the greatest leakers of all have been cabinet members, agency heads, and even presidents.

So long as that continues to be the case, and so long as the Constitution of the United States stipulates that "Congress shall make no law abridging the freedom of the press," policy makers from the president on down will continue to deplore leaks but use them when they seem likely to help put over a policy they favor or kill a policy they oppose.

In a society where mass communications have become perhaps *the* basic social process, it can hardly be otherwise.

Communications Revolutions, Past and Future ————

What some call "the communications revolution" has already radically transformed just about every aspect of human life, certainly including politics. For example, only the few thousand people who made their way to the towns where they were held heard the famous Lincoln-Douglas debates in 1858. But in 1992, about 100 million people, most of them sitting in their own homes, watched the televised debates between Bill Clinton, George Bush, and Ross Perot. For another example, before the 1950s most political campaigns were planned and conducted by the candidates and their lieutenants, almost all of whom were veteran party politicians. In the 1990s, almost every campaign is planned and conducted not by the "old pols," but by a new breed of professional election consultants—some call them hired guns—who head teams of pollsters, speech writers, television "spot" producers, media analysts, and other high-priced technicians to conduct modern media-dominated, "scientific" campaigns. For yet another example, diplomatic communications were so slow in 1815 that the Battle of New Orleans was fought in the United States several weeks after the peace treaty formally ending the war had been signed in Europe. In the 1990s, every nation's ambassadors can, and are expected to, consult with their superiors back home—it can be done in seconds—before making any commitments.

Thus politics, like almost every other aspect of life, has changed a great deal since the end of World War II because of the communications revolution. However, a number of recent technological advances mean that the revolution still has a long way to go. For instance, cable television can now provide any viewer in any place with eighty or more separate channels, in contrast to the twelve or so provided in most areas by over-the-air stations. Cable news services, especially CNN, C-SPAN, and Court TV, have ended the near-monopoly of televised news and political discussion once enjoyed by ABC, CBS, and NBC. Indeed, the networks' share of the viewing audience has declined from 90 percent in the 1970s to 80 percent in the 1980s and is likely to decline further in the 1990s. In Columbus, Ohio, experiments have been made with the Qube system, a form of interactive or audience-participation television that enables cable viewers to send signals from their receivers back along the cable to the studio and thus to express their opinions on what they are seeing and even to vote electronically on policy questions put to them after televised political discussions, and we have already noted Fishkin's experiments with deliberate samples. Some observers say that there is no technical reason why we cannot extend the Qube system into a national "town meeting" or replace quick polls with deliberative polls.

No one can say with certainty what the impact of those and other new technologies will be on the politics of the future in the United States or anywhere else. But if the communications revolution of 1990–2015 has anything like the impact of the communications revolution of 1945–1980, then a few decades from now much of the political landscape will look very strange indeed to people who were brought up in the 1970s.

A NEW POLLING TECHNIQUE?

Some advocates of the "participatory" model of democracy (see Chapter 5) argue that the answers small samples of people give to pollsters' questions about political issues do not and cannot represent the true preferences of the electorate. They point out that the randomly chosen individuals in the samples are asked to respond off the top of their heads to questions by pollsters who telephone them while they are eating dinner or watching television. There is no discussion, no exchange of ideas, no chance to mull over the many issues and alternatives. Inevitably, their answers are quick and slapdash, and they do not represent the views many would express if they had time to think, read about, and discuss the questions they are asked.

Political scientist James Fishkin agrees with this criticism but believes that the polls can be improved. He proposes that samples of a few hundred people each be chosen, given the opportunity to learn about the issues and discuss them with the other persons in the sample. The opinions that such a sample would give the pollsters would be the product of genuine deliberation rather than the quick-and-impulsive answers people are forced to give in the kind of polls used in democratic nations today.[14]

In 1994 Fishkin was able to try out his ideas in the city of Manchester, England. With support from an English newspaper and a television production company, he first selected a random sample of 400 respondents that was reasonably representative of the city's population. The respondents were first tested on their opinions about the causes of and cures for crime. They then met together over a weekend, discussed the many angles of the issue with one another, and looked up the answers to factual questions that arose in the discussion. At the end of the weekend they were tested again on crime issues, and Fishkin found that, while some of the respondents had not changed their views, many more—especially the better-educated ones, did change. Why? Because, they said, their new information combined with their discussions with the others produced further questions and facts they had not thought of before.[15] Fishkin pronounced the experiment a success, but it remains to be seen whether "deliberative polls" will catch on with pollsters in Great Britain or elsewhere.

For Further Reading

ARTERTON, F. CHRISTOPHER. *Media Politics: The News Strategies of Presidential Campaigns.* Lexington, MA: Lexington Books, 1984. Study of how mass media cover presidential campaigns and how politicians try to use the media for their own ends.

BUTLER, DAVID, AND AUSTIN RANNEY, eds. *Electioneering: A Comparative Study of Continuity and Change.* New York: Oxford University Press, 1992. A comparative study of the "Americanization" of election campaigning in various democratic countries.

*CIRINO, ROBERT. *Don't Blame the People.* Los Angeles, CA: Diversity Press, 1971. An attack on the mass media as apologists for big business and special interests.

DIAMOND, EDWIN. *The Tin Kazoo: Television, Politics, and News.* Cambridge, MA: MIT Press, 1975. Analysis of network news broadcasting by a leading scholar.

*GANS, HERBERT J. *Deciding What's News: A Study of CBS Evening News, NBC Nightly News, Newsweek and Time.* New York: Vintage 1980. Thoughtful analysis of the reporting and editing ideas dominating the mass news media.

GARRY, PATRICK. *Scrambling for Protection: The New Media and the First Amendment.* Pittsburgh, PA: University of Pittsburgh Press, 1994. Argument that the new technologies of mass communications require major changes in regulatory policy.

*GRABER, DORIS A. *Mass Media and American Politics*, 3rd ed. Washington, DC: Congressional Quarterly Press, 1989. A comprehensive introduction to the topic.

IYENGAR, SHANTO. *Is Anyone Responsible? How Television Frames Political Issues.* Chicago: University of Chicago Press, 1994. A study of how television portrays political events in the United States.

IYENGAR, SHANTO, AND DONALD R. KINDER. *News That Matters: Television and American Opinion.* Chicago, IL: University of Chicago Press, 1987. Uses survey data to measure the powerful impact of television's presentation of news on American public opinion.

*KRAUS, SIDNEY, AND DENNIS DAVIS. *The Effects of Mass Communications on Political Behavior*. University Park, PA: Pennsylvania State University Press, 1978. Useful summary of the major empirical studies of the effects of mass communications on political behavior.

*MCLUHAN, MARSHALL. *Understanding Media: The Extensions of Man*. New York: McGraw-Hill, 1966. Still one of the most stimulating sets of ideas about the essential natures of the various mass media and the constraints they impose on who does well or badly with them.

*MARTEL, MYLES. *Political Campaign Debates: Images, Strategies and Tactics*. New York: Longman, 1983. Comprehensive description of candidate debates in presidential and other elections.

*PATTERSON, THOMAS E. *The Mass Media Election*. New York: Praeger, 1980. Informative study, based on sample survey evidence, of the role of newspapers and television in the 1976 presidential election.

*RANNEY, AUSTIN. *Channels of Power: The Impact of Television on American Politics*. New York: Basic Books, 1983. Analysis of impact of television on parties, campaigns, voters, and governing processes.

*RIVERS, WILLIAM L. *The Other Government: Power and the Washington Media*. New York: University Books, 1982. Study of impact of mass media on policy making.

*ROBINSON, MICHAEL J., AND MARGARET A. SHEEHAN. *Over the Wire and on TV*. New York: Basic Books, 1984. Detailed study of content and impact of coverage of the 1980 presidential election by the network news and the wire services.

*TANNENBAUM, PERCY H., AND LESLIE J. KOSTRICH. *Turned-On TV/Turned-Off Voters*. Beverly Hills, CA: Sage, 1983. Analysis of impact of TV election-night projections of winners on West Coast voters.

WEAVER, PAUL H. *News and the Culture of Lying*. New York: Free Press, 1994. Critical analysis of how journalists in newspapers and television portray events.

WESTIN, AV. *Newswatch: How TV Decides the News*. New York: Simon & Schuster, 1983. Description of how network news operates, by a former head of a network news division.

Notes

1. Lee Thayer, "Communication—*Sine Qua Non* of the Behavioral Sciences," in *Vistas in Science*, ed. D. L. Arm (Albuquerque, NM: University of New Mexico Press, 1968), p. 54.

2. The Roper organization for the Television Information Office, reported in *The American Enterprise*, July–August 1990, p. 98.

3. I am well aware that many Americans use the term *media* as the singular form, as in the phrase "the media is biased." However, in this book I will cling to the tradition of centuries and the stipulations of dictionaries that the word *media* is the plural form of the word *medium*.

4. Theodore Peterson, Jay W. Jensen, and William L. Rivers, *The Mass Media and Modern Society* (New York: Holt, Rinehart & Winston, 1965), p. 25.

5. Roan Conrad, "The News and the 1976 Election: A Dialogue," *Wilson Quarterly* (Spring 1977), p. 84; and Sig Mickelson, *The Electric Mirror* (New York: Dodd, Mead, 1972).

6. The leading case upholding the "scarcity doctrine" and the greater regulation of the electronic media is *National Broadcasting Company* v. *United States*, 319 U.S. 190 (1943).

7. Michael J. Robinson, "Where's the Beef? Media and Media Elites in 1984," in *The American Elections of 1984*, ed. Austin Ranney (Durham, NC: Duke University Press, 1985), Chapter 6.

8. Bernard Berelson, "Communications and Public Opinion," in *The Process and Effects of Mass Communications*, ed. Wilber Schramm, (Urbana, IL: University of Illinois Press, 1954), p. 345, italics in the original.

9. Austin Ranney, *Channels of Power: The Impact of Television on American Politics* (New York: Basic Books, 1983), p. 16.

10. This section relies heavily on the descriptions and analyses of election campaigns in different democratic nations in David Butler and Austin Ranney, eds., *Electioneering: A Comparative Study of Continuity and Change*, (New York: Oxford University Press, 1992).

11. Larry M. Bartels, "The Impact of Electioneering in the United States," in *Electioneering*, Butler and Ranney, eds, pp. 244–77.

12. Both examples are drawn from the informative discussion of leaks in Hedrick Smith, *The Power Game* (New York: Random House, 1988), pp. 437–46.

13. The story of "Deep Throat" and (his? her?) leaks is told in rich (and rather self-serving) detail in a book by the two reporters, Carl Bernstein and Bob Woodward, *All the President's Men* (New York: Warner Books, 1976).

14. James S. Fishkin, "The Case for a National Caucus: Taking Democracy Seriously," *Atlantic*, vol. 262 (August 1988), 16–19.

15. Richard Morin, "Political Talk Therapy," *The Washington Post*, June 5, 1994, p. C5.

8

*Elections still remain the primary way of achieving popular goals. . . .
Elections in democracies allow a change of rule in ordinary ways and without
awaiting extraordinary occasions. In such systems, therefore, officials avoid
not only the extremely unpopular action but even the uncomfortable. . . .
[Responsiveness of rulers to the people's wishes] has not been provided by
depending on the good will of rulers, on the presumed identity of interests
between governed or governors, or on institutional controls, such as a federal
structure or supervision by a monopolistic political party. To the ancient
question, "Who will guard the guardians?" there is only one answer: those
who choose the guardians.*[1]

The Electoral Process

Elections in Democratic Systems

Some of Abraham Lincoln's northern political opponents—and he had quite a few—
called him a dictator. Why? Because, in clear defiance of the Constitution, he had
suspended the writ of habeas corpus, clapped some of his political adversaries in
jail, raised an army, spent millions of tax dollars, and authorized military action, all
without even asking Congress for permission.

Lincoln's supporters replied that while he had certainly used the emergency
powers of the presidency to their fullest, he was no dictator. Why not? Because in
the elections of 1862 and 1864, the voters had had a chance to throw first his supporters in Congress and then Lincoln himself out of office. Any public official who
can be turned out of office in a free election, they said, is no dictator. As long as free
elections are held, the people, not the president or any other public official, hold the
ultimate ruling power, as democracy demands.

Just about every theorist of democracy would agree (see Chapter 5). Free elections are certainly not all there is to democracy; but in every modern nation that is
generally called democratic, free elections are, as they always have been, the basic
device that enables the people to control the rulers. In short: *No free elections, no
democracy.*

We should be clear, however, that some nations in the modern world do not
hold elections at all and that many of those that hold elections do not hold *free elections* as we are using the term. For instance, in 1994, over a dozen nations—including
the African countries of Guinea, Mauritania, and Niger; the Middle Eastern countries
of Oman, Qatar, and Saudi Arabia; and the Asian country of Brunei—had not held
elections for many years and had no intention of holding elections in the foreseeable
future. In another instance, for seventy-two years (1917–1989) the former Soviet Union
frequently held elections for a great many offices, and usually well over 90 percent of
the adult population voted. Yet, the elections did not control the nation's leaders, for
the voters had no choice: In each election for each office there was only one candidate
on the ballot, and the voters could either vote for that candidate or not vote at all. Since

the breakup of the USSR in 1991, Russia and a number of the other new nations freed by the breakup have held free several-candidates-for-each-office elections and free referendums, and the same can be said of such other formerly communist Eastern European nations as Bulgaria, the Czech Republic, Hungary, and Poland. Only the few nations that still cling to Soviet-style communism, notably Cuba, North Korea, and Vietnam, still hold one-candidate-per-office elections.

It is appropriate, therefore, to begin our analysis of democratic electoral processes by setting forth the main characteristics that most political scientists think an election must have in order to qualify as a free election.

ESSENTIAL CHARACTERISTICS OF FREE ELECTIONS

Regular Elections

Elections must take place regularly and with reasonable frequency within pre-scribed time limits and may not be postponed indefinitely by public officials when-ever they wish.

Meaningful Choices

To exercise effective control of public officials, voters must have a choice be-tween at least two candidates for each office to be filled. Clearly, this requirement rules out single-candidate elections such as those held in the former Soviet Union. Some commentators say that it also rules out the "Tweedledum versus Tweedledee" contests they say are characteristic of American elections, elections that provide no real choice on such important issues as capitalism versus socialism, militarism ver-sus pacifism, or black power versus white racism. Others reply that although a choice among, say, Bill Clinton, George Bush, and Ross Perot does not provide al-ternatives at the absolute extremes of ideological spectrums, there is a significant choice among three quite different points on each spectrum and, equally impor-tant, among three quite different human beings. However, theorists of democracy agree that a truly free election must furnish the voters meaningful choices, how-ever defined.

Freedom to Put Forth Candidates

All citizens have the opportunity to form political parties and put forth can-didates.

Freedom to Know and Discuss the Choices

If two candidates for an office are allowed to run but only one is permitted to make public speeches or have his or her name on the ballot, then he or she is effec-tively the only candidate. There must be full freedom for all candidates and their sup-porters to publicize their names and policy positions so that the voters can hear what they have to say. Some observers would add that if this requirement is to mean any-thing, then every candidate must be guaranteed at least some financial support and free time on radio and television so that all candidates, rich and poor alike, have at least minimum opportunities to present their views and appeal for popular support.

Universal Adult Suffrage

All adult citizens have the right to vote.

Equal Weighting of Votes

We noted in Chapter 5 that one of the four basic principles of democratic government is *political equality*, which is the principle that each adult citizen must have the same opportunity as every other adult citizen to participate in the political decision-making process. Applied to elections, the principle means not only that all adult citizens must have an equal opportunity to register their choices by voting but also that each citizen's vote will have the same weight as every other citizen's. If some citizens' votes are weighted more heavily than other citizens', then the principle of political equality is violated, and the favored voters constitute a kind of ruling elite.

Free Registration of Choices

Voters must be able to go to the polls without any obstruction or fear of subsequent reprisal. They must be able to vote without coercion or fear of reprisal, which in turn requires that they be able to cast their votes *secretly*.

Accurate Counting of Choices and Reporting of Results

The voting procedures—whether they consist of marking a paper ballot, pulling levers on a voting machine, or punching holes in a card—must permit voters to register their choices accurately and unambiguously. The counting procedures must provide accurate totals of the preferences registered for each alternative. Reporting procedures must guarantee that the totals, which control who wins the contested offices, are honestly published. If any of those principles is ignored, the others are rendered meaningless.

From those eight essential characteristics of free elections we turn to a survey of some of the problems that democratic nations have encountered in trying to satisfy them.

QUALIFICATIONS FOR VOTING

Principle of Universal Suffrage

One of the requirements for a free election is what is often called universal suffrage: that is, the rule that all adults have an equal opportunity to vote. However, this principle has never been interpreted to mean that *everyone* in the community must have the right to vote. No democratic nation has ever permitted ten-year-old children to vote, and no democratic theorist has ever called their exclusion undemocratic. Most democratic nations also exclude aliens, people confined to mental institutions, and criminals in prison, and few people think this violates the principle of universal suffrage.

As a democratic ideal, in other words, the principle of universal suffrage requires that every *member of the community*, rather than every person who happens to be present in the community on election day, has the right to vote. Generally, only adults who have demonstrated their inability (for example, by confinement in a mental institution) or their unwillingness (for example, by conviction for a felony) to assume the obligations of loyalty to the nation and obedience to its laws are considered not to be full-fledged members of the community and therefore are not entitled to vote in its elections.

Qualifications for Voting

The main qualifications for voters in modern democratic polities are the following:

CITIZENSHIP   Most democratic nations permit only their own citizens to vote but make no distinction between native-born and naturalized citizens. This requirement rests upon the conviction that only people loyal to the nation, who prefer that nation to all others, should be permitted to vote in its elections. Citizenship is generally regarded as the best formal indication of such loyalty.

AGE   Just about every society requires its members to attain a certain minimum age before being admitted to full participation in community affairs, on the ground that infants and children are incapable of such participation. Most primitive societies, for example, have special rites for the induction of young people into adulthood and full membership. Every modern democracy requires that its citizens reach a certain minimum age before they can vote.

Every such age limit is, of course, arbitrary in the sense that the limit does not reflect different levels of maturity among different individuals. In all democratic nations, however, the difficulty of conducting individual "maturity examinations" is regarded as greater than the possible injustices resulting from applying one minimum-age requirement to all. As late as the 1960s, the most common minimum age was twenty-one years, but in the 1970s a number of countries—for example, Great Britain, Italy, and the United States—lowered the age to eighteen, and that is now the most common minimum age.

RESIDENCE   Most democratic systems also require voters to live in the nation and in their particular voting districts for certain periods of time before they can vote. For example, in Illinois, voters must live in the state for thirty days before the election in which they wish to vote.

REGISTRATION   To prevent election frauds, most democratic systems supply officials at each election district with a full roster (usually called a "register") of all eligible voters against which the names of those applying for ballots can be checked to make sure the applicants are eligible and have not already voted. Some registration systems are permanent, in that once the roster is compiled it is kept up to date by eliminating ineligible individuals and adding eligible ones. Others are periodic, in that at regular intervals the entire register is scrapped and a new one is drawn up.

The most significant distinction among registration systems lies in who takes responsibility for getting citizens registered. At one end of the scale stand the European democracies, which require public officials to take the initiative by making periodic door-to-door canvasses of each district and registering every eligible person who is not already registered. The United States stands at the other end. Most states require each would-be voter to take the initiative by formally applying by mail or in person. Only a few states permit or encourage door-to-door canvassing and registration in the home. In addition, people who are registered in one state and move to another are not automatically re-registered. Such people must go to the registering officials in the new state and launch the process all over again, and many Americans who move forget to re-register amid the many other strains and demands of moving. Thus in the United States new voters and voters who have moved must take the initiative on two occasions: first, during the registration period and, second, on election day. In other democracies the voters must take the initiative only on election day. Most analysts believe that this explains why there are many more unregistered but otherwise eligible citizens in the United States than in other democracies. Many of those same analysts believe that registration laws are one of the main causes for the low voting turnouts in the United States (see Table 8.1 and the following discussion).

For several decades some reformers urged the U.S. federal government to destroy or remove the states' obstacles to full registration and high turnout. They finally won a notable victory in 1993 when Congress enacted the "motor voter" law. The new law required all states to allow eligible persons to register to vote when applying for a driver's license, to permit mail-in registrations, and to provide voter registration forms at such public assistance agencies as those distributing unemployment compensation payments, welfare checks, or payments to the disabled. This law edges the United States somewhat nearer to the ease of registration enjoyed by citizens of other democratic nations, but U.S. citizens, unlike those of other countries, must still take the initiative to register. It remains to be seen how the new law will affect U.S. registration and turnout figures.

NONVOTING AND COMPULSORY VOTING

John Locke, Jean Jacques Rousseau, Thomas Jefferson, and other early advocates of democracy assumed that once members of a community were given the legal right to vote, they would eagerly exercise that right at every opportunity. The evidence indicates, however, that actual voting participation in modern democratic nations does not measure up to the early democrats' expectations. Table 8.1 shows the average percentage of legally eligible voters actually voting in national elections prior to 1994. The table reveals that a nation's turnout rate depends in part on the counting method used. Most countries figure the turnout rate as the number of persons voting divided by the number of persons on the register (remember that nearly every person of voting age is automatically placed on the register by the authorities). In the United States, on the other hand, voting turnout is customarily calculated by dividing the number of persons voting by the number of

TABLE 8.1   Voting Turnouts in Democratic Nations According to Two Measures*

RANK	TRADITIONAL MEASURE OF TURNOUT	RANK	VOTE AS PERCENTAGE OF REGISTERED VOTERS
1. Australia**	92.4	1. Australia**	92.4
2. Iceland	86.2	2. Iceland	86.2
3. The Netherlands	85.5	3. The Netherlands	85.5
4. Sweden	85.3	4. Sweden	85.3
5. New Zealand	85.2	5. New Zealand	85.2
6. Belgium**	85.0	6. Belgium	85.0
7. Italy**	83.2	7. Italy	83.2
8. Austria	83.0	8. Austria	83.0
9. Denmark	82.8	9. Denmark	82.8
10. Finland	82.1	10. United States	82.4
11. France	82.0	11. Finland	82.1
12. Greece**	81.8	12. France	82.0
13. Germany	78.6	13. Greece	81.8
14. Great Britain	77.7	14. Germany	78.6
15. Israel	77.4	15. Great Britain	77.7
16. Spain**	77.3	16. Israel	77.4
17. Norway	75.8	17. Spain	77.3
18. Canada	71.3	18. Norway	75.8
19. Japan	66.9	19. Canada	71.3
20. Portugal	62.0	20. Japan	66.9
21. United States	55.2	21. Portugal	62.0
22. Switzerland	46.2	22. Switzerland	46.2

Source: Based on David Glass, Peverill Squire, and Raymond Wolfinger, "Voter Turnout: An International Comparison," *Public Opinion*, December–January 1984, pp. 49–55. Turnout figures updated to 1994 by the author.

*Most recent national election prior to 1994.
**Compulsory voting laws.

persons of voting age, which includes aliens, people in prisons and mental institutions, and, most important, persons who are not registered. When turnout rates are figured by those two very different methods, as in the first column of Table 8.1, the United States has the second-lowest turnout rate in the world (only Switzerland's is lower), a fact that is often commented on in the United States and elsewhere. However, when turnouts are compared by using the *same* measure—percent of registered voters who vote, as in the second column of Table 8.1—the United States has one of the higher turnout records in the world (tenth highest among twenty-two democracies). The key to this paradox is simple: In the United States over 80 percent of the registered voters usually vote in presidential elections, but only about 68 percent of those eligible to vote are registered. Thus the problem in increasing U.S. voting turnout is not getting registered voters to the polls. It is, rather, getting eligible people registered. Even so, there was some good news in the 1992 presidential election: Voting turnout increased to 55.2 percent from 52.6 percent in 1988—the first increase in turnout since the presidential election of 1960.

The most thorough recent comparative study of nonvoting in Western democracies was made by political scientist Robert W. Jackman, who used a number of sophisticated analytical techniques to estimate the relative weight of various causes for different turnout rates in nineteen Western democracies. He found that very little can be explained by political culture factors, for although Americans generally score higher than the citizens of the other countries on such measures as belief that voting is a civic duty and confidence that voting makes a difference in who wins elections, the United States still has a lower turnout rate than any other country except Switzerland, where cultural factors also favor voting.

Jackman concluded that, in addition to the differences in registration laws, the main influences on turnout are as follows:

> *Competitiveness.* The closer the elections and the greater the likelihood that the party in power might be defeated, the higher the turnout.
>
> *Proportionality.* The closer the proportion of the offices won by each party is to its share of the popular votes, the higher the turnout.
>
> *Clear winners.* The more likely elections are to produce a clear winning party or candidate with full power, the higher the turnout. Conversely, the more likely elections are to produce coalitions with no clear single winner, the lower the turnout.
>
> *Unicameralism.* Turnouts are higher in countries where the parliament has only one house with real power, and lower in countries, such as the United States, where power is divided between two houses.[2]

Many of democracy's well wishers regard widespread failure to register and vote as both a disgrace and a threat to democratic survival. Many political scientists have therefore sought not only the legal but also the social and motivational causes of nonvoting and have recommended such remedies as European-style registration, reducing the frequency of elections and the number of elective offices, television get-out-the-vote advertisements by civic organizations and advertising councils, and—the great cure for all social ills—more and better civic education.

Table 8.1 shows, however, that some nations have turned to a more radical solution: compulsory voting. In Australia and Belgium, for example, any person on the register who fails to vote in any election is required by law to submit an explanation. If the authorities regard the excuse given as inadequate, the nonvoter is fined. Compulsory-voting laws work very well: They increased turnout from 64 percent to 92 percent in Australia and from 70 percent to 85 percent in Belgium.

Even so, there is no general agreement among political scientists—or, for that matter, among Australians and Belgians—on whether compulsory voting is a good idea. Some commentators argue that the right to abstain is just as precious as the right to vote, and if the right to vote is guaranteed, then the decision about whether to use the right in any particular election should be left entirely to the individual. Others argue that in Australia and Belgium, compulsion has greatly increased the number of irresponsible and "automatic anti" votes. Still others believe that by increasing voting turnout, compulsory voting has increased participation and thus strengthened democracy.

The most we can say here is that in the few democratic nations that have compulsory voting, there is no powerful sentiment to abolish it; but most democracies do not want to go that route and continue to depend upon other agencies, notably political parties and election campaigns (see Chapter 10) to motivate voters to go to the polls.

NOMINATIONS AND CANDIDATE SELECTION

Most free elections involve choices among competing candidates, who are persons legally eligible for the offices contested whose names are printed on official ballots. The first step in the conduct of free elections is thus the process by which a few of the many citizens eligible for office actually get their names on the ballot. This process has two major parts:

> **Nomination** means *the legal procedures by which election authorities certify certain persons as qualified candidates for office and print their names on the official ballot.*
>
> **Candidate selection** is *the mainly extralegal process by which political parties decide which persons will be designated on the ballot and in election communications as their recommended candidates.*

Significance of Candidate Selection

In a democracy, all voters have the legal right to vote for any person eligible for any office. In practice, however, voters do not have any such complete freedom and could not use it if they had. In the United States, for example, about 120 million people presently fulfill all the legal qualifications for the presidency. But if all voters had been required to choose among all 120 million in 1992, to be fair to all, voters would have had to learn the personal qualifications and positions of all 120 million. That is obviously impossible. No human being can have even the dimmest notion of the nature of each of 120 million alternatives, let alone make an intelligent choice among them. But no such impossible task actually confronted the voters in 1992. The various political parties, through their nominating processes, reduced the alternatives from 120 million to the 23 candidates who appeared on the ballots of one or more states. Since most people were accustomed to voting for either the Democratic or Republican candidate, most voters were faced with choosing between only Clinton and Bush, although 19 percent voted for Perot. The major parties' candidate selections thus reduced the alternatives from twenty-three to an even more manageable two, and Perot's followers added a third with their successful petitions to get their man on the ballots of all the states and the District of Columbia.

Most of us can learn quite a bit about the personal qualifications and political opinions of two or three candidates and can make a meaningful choice between them. The reduction process therefore makes meaningful choice possible for us. Surely it is as significant a part of the total election process as is the final election in which the voters reduce the alternatives from two or three to one.

SOME CAMPAIGNING IS PERSONAL. Bill Clinton speaking at a campaign rally, 1992.

Formal Nominating Procedures

The formal nominating procedures of most democratic nations are much simpler than those used in the United States. Three principal methods are now used.

PETITIONS   The formal procedure for becoming a candidate for the British House of Commons is simplicity itself. Any British subject over twenty-one years of age is eligible, with the exception of members of the nobility, judges of the High Court, members of the permanent civil service, convicted felons, and clergy of the Church of England, the Church of Scotland, or the Roman Catholic Church.

Would-be candidates go to the election offices and get an official nomination paper, on which they state their name, address, occupation, and the constituency in which they wish to "stand." The form must also be signed by two voters from that constituency acting as proposer and seconder and by eight other such voters acting as assenters. The completed form must be filed with the authorities, along with a deposit of £500. This deposit will be forfeited to the Treasury if the candidate fails to poll more than 5 percent of the votes cast in the constituency in the ensuing election. (The purpose of this requirement is to discourage frivolous and "nuisance" candidates.) When those minimal requirements have been met, the candidate's name is placed on the ballot, but only since 1969 has Britain allowed the candidates' party labels to be printed by their names. Approximately the same procedure is followed in such other democratic countries as Canada, France, Japan, and New Zealand.

PARTY-LIST DESIGNATIONS   In most nations that use some form of the party-list system of proportional representation (see below), the authorized agent of each recognized political party draws up a list of candidates for each constituency and certifies the list to the election authorities. When the authorities have verified the eligibility of the names on each list, the names are placed on the ballot without further ado. In some countries (for example, Israel) this is the only procedure by which a candidate can be placed on the ballot. In other nations (for example, Denmark and Finland) a hundred or so independent voters can also nominate a single candidate or list of candidates by petition. In general, however, the initiative rests mainly or exclusively with party officials and agencies.

THE UNIQUE AMERICAN DIRECT PRIMARY   Perhaps the sharpest contrast between nominating procedures in the United States and those in other democratic countries is provided by the American direct primary. The **direct primary** is *a procedure in which candidates are selected directly by the voters in government-supervised elections rather than indirectly by party leaders in caucuses and conventions.* This system was first adopted by the state of Wisconsin in 1903, and since then every one of the fifty states has adopted the direct primary for nominations for some offices, and most states require it for nominations for all offices. Note that the direct primary is unique to the United States. No other country in the world uses it.

The direct primary is designed to ensure that nominations are made as nearly as possible in the same way that regular elections are conducted. Any qualified person who wishes to receive a particular party's nomination for public office may file with election officials a petition containing his or her name, address, the nomination desired, and the signatures of a legally designated number of voters registered as members of the party whose nomination he or she seeks. When the filing period has elapsed, the election authorities print ballots for each party including the names of all who have petitioned for each office. On primary-election day, the voters go to the polls and mark their preferences for each office. The person who receives the largest number of votes for each office on each party's ballot is certified as that party's official nominee, and the nominee's name and party designation are then printed on the ballot for the ensuing general election.

The only major differences among the direct primary systems of the various states relate to who is eligible to vote in a particular party's primary: In *closed primaries* (twenty-four states), only persons pre-registered as members of a particular party can vote in its primary; persons registered as independents have no party and thus cannot vote in any party's primary. *Crossover primaries* (fourteen states) are the same as closed primaries, except that on election day all voters, including independents, can vote in the primary of either party after publicly declaring which party they have chosen. In *open primaries* (nine states), there is no party registration or declaration of any kind, and on primary day voters are allowed to vote in either party's primary (but not both) without any public statement of the party they have chosen. In *blanket primaries* (two states), there is no party registration or declaration, and on primary day voters can vote in the primaries of both parties, although they are restricted to voting in only one party's primary for any particular office. Finally, in *nonpartisan primaries* (only Louisiana for state offices but in many states for local offices), there is no party registration or public declaration, and all candidates for each office are put on the same ballot. Each voter votes for one candidate per office, and the candidate who receives a majority of the votes for that office is elected. If no candidate receives a majority, then a later (or run-off) election is held between the two candidates with the largest numbers of votes, and the one who receives a majority in the second election wins the office.

Although some parties in a few nations (for example, Canada, Germany, and Turkey) make their nominations by party-conducted votes of all the enrolled dues-paying party members, the United States is the only country in the world that uses the direct primary in the strict sense: that is, party nominations made by government-conducted elections in which by law all registered voters may participate. Many commentators believe that this is one of the main reasons why. American political parties are so different from the parties in other democracies. We will consider this further in Chapter 10.

Principal Democratic Electoral Systems

In setting up their electoral systems, all democratic countries have tried to satisfy the requirements of free elections outlined at the beginning of the chapter, but they have chosen many different methods for doing so. No nation's system is exactly like any other's in every detail, and the variations are so numerous and often so complicated that we will not try to consider them all here. We will note the main types of systems and the principal differences among them.

SINGLE-MEMBER-DISTRICT SYSTEMS

"First-Past-the-Post" Systems

Most readers are familiar with the "first-past-the-post" system, which is used for elections to the both houses of the U.S. Congress, both houses of most American state legislatures, the British House of Commons, the Canadian House of Commons, and many other legislatures and parliaments, especially in the English-speaking world. The basic principles are simple. The nation is divided into a number of *districts* (the American term) or *constituencies* (the British term) or *ridings* (the Canadian term). Each district elects one member of the legislative assembly at each election, and the voter votes for one candidate. When the votes are counted, the candidate receiving the largest number of votes (a plurality) in each constituency is elected. It is called first-past-the-post because, as in a horse race, the winner is the contestant who leads the others across the finish line, and the margin by which the contestant leads does not matter.

Absolute Majority Systems

A few polities have felt that electing candidates by mere pluralities violates the basic democratic principle of majority rule (see Chapter 5), and so they have installed devices for ensuring that each winner has at least 50 percent plus 1 (a majority) of all the votes.

One such device is the run-off election: If no candidate receives an absolute majority in the first election, a second election is held between the two top candidates, and the one who wins a majority in the second election is the winner.

The most notable use of the absolute-majority system at present is in elections for president of France. For example, in April 1995, the first round of the presidential election was held with nine candidates on the ballot; their vote shares were as follows:

Jospin	23.3%
Chirac	20.8
Balladur	18.6
Le Pen	15.1
Hue	8.6
Laguiller	5.3
de Villiers	4.7
Voynet	3.3
Cheminade	0.3

Two weeks later the second, or run-off ballot was held between the two top finishers, and the results were as follows:

Chirac	52.2%
Jospin	47.8

Another device is the *preferential ballot*, which is now used in elections to the Australian House of Representatives and to four Australian state parliaments. This system requires voters to mark each of the candidates in order of preference by placing numbers beside their names. If no candidate receives a majority of first-place preferences on the first count, the candidate with the fewest first-place preferences is dropped and his or her ballots are redistributed according to the second-place preferences on each ballot. Such redistributions are continued until one candidate's ballots constitute at least 50 percent plus one of all those cast. That candidate is then elected.

FRENCH VOTERS IN THE 1993 ELECTION.

MULTIMEMBER-PROPORTIONAL SYSTEMS

Rationale

Since the mid-nineteenth century, some democratic theorists have argued that first-past-the-post plurality systems make truly democratic representation impossible. They have proposed that all such systems be replaced with some form of proportional representation (PR). Their arguments can be briefly summarized as follows.

A truly democratic representative assembly should be to the nation's political divisions as a map is to its territory. Thus the electoral system should ensure that every political ideology supported by members of the community has a number of advocates in the assembly proportionate to that ideology's adherents in the community.

The first-past-the-post system cannot produce such an assembly. Wherever it operates, the majority party has more assembly seats than its share of the popular vote warrants, and all other parties have fewer seats than their vote shares warrant. Furthermore, the majority system forces a two-party system on the population, for third and fourth parties have little or no chance of electing assembly members. The legislatures that result from this kind of party system cannot accurately express the many shades of public opinion any more than a black-and-white photograph can accurately represent the many colors of reality.

Also, the argument continues, in a truly representative system every citizen should be directly represented in the assembly. That is, each voter should be able

NOT A MAJORITY

There is no denying that first-past-the-post electoral systems can produce complications, especially when three or more candidates share the votes rather evenly. To some degree this was the case in the U.S. presidential election of 1992, when the popular votes were distributed among the three leading candidates thus:

Clinton, Democrat 43%

Bush, Republican 38

Perot, Independent 19

It was even more the case in Venezuela's presidential election in 1993. Each of the three leading parties nominated a candidate, and they were joined by an independent. The popular votes in the December 5 election were distributed as follows:

Rafael Caldera, Independent	30%
Claudio Fermin, AD	24
Oswaldo Alvarez, COPEI	23
Andres Valasquez	11
Others	12

Even so, under the two nations' first-past-the-post systems both Clinton and Caldera were recognized as the constitutional winners and both took office—although some commentators said in each case that the winner's failure to attract a majority of the votes was a significant flaw in his mandate to govern.

to point to at least one member of the assembly and say, "My vote helped to put that member there, so that member represents me." But under the majority systems all those who vote for losing candidates have no such member, and so their votes are wasted.

For those reasons, PR advocates believe that first-past-the-post systems should be replaced with some kind of proportional representation, a system in which no votes are wasted and in which all points of view are represented according to their relative strengths in the electorate. The proportional systems now used in modern democratic nations are variations on two basic types: party-list systems and single-transferable-vote systems.

Party-List Systems

In all party-list systems, political parties are the basic units of representation. The systems all have multimember constituencies, each of which elects from two to twelve or more members (in Israel the entire nation consists of one constituency, which elects all 120 members of the Knesset). The ballots contain lists of candidates nominated by the leaders or executive committees of the various parties, and the voter votes for one or another of those lists. The counting process is designed to distribute seats in the legislative assembly as nearly as possible in accordance with each party's share of the total popular vote.

Party-list systems differ from one another only in the degree to which voters can vote for individual candidates as well as for whole party lists. Some systems, such as in Israel, allow the voters to vote only for one party's entire list, and voters have no way of expressing a preference for any individual candidate on

VOTING IN A FRAGMENTED PARTY SYSTEM. Premier Yitzhak Rabin votes in the 1992 Israeli general election.

that list. Some, such as in Belgium, permit voters to change the order of the candidates on the list of the party they vote for, but those voters cannot vote for candidates on any other party's list. Some, such as in Switzerland, allow the voter to vote for one party's list and also for an individual candidate on that list or on another party's list.

Essentially, however, all party-list systems operate on the assumption that voters are most interested in supporting political parties that best express their political philosophies. Hence, the party, not the individual, is the main unit of representation.

Single-Transferable-Vote Systems

Single-transferable-vote systems operate from the very different premise that voters are more interested in individual candidates than in parties and should be given maximum freedom to indicate their preferences for individuals.

The most notable example of such a system is that used in elections for members of the *Dáil* (parliament) of Ireland. In Ireland, each constituency elects several members to the legislative assembly, and any individual can obtain a place on the ballot by petition, with or without a party designation. Voters indicate their orders of preference among the various candidates by marking numbers in the boxes beside the candidates' names. The ballots are first sorted according to the first-place choices for each candidate. Then the "electoral quota" of total votes needed to be elected is figured according to one of several possible formulas. If a candidate's first-preference votes exceed the quota, the excess votes are distributed to the second-choice candidates marked on the ballots. When no surpluses remain and there are still seats to be filled, the candidate with the fewest first-place choices is dropped, and his or her ballots are redistributed according to the second-place choices on each. Transfers of surpluses of elected candidates and of votes for eliminated candidates are continued until a sufficient number of candidates have satisfied the quota and all the seats are filled.

POLITICAL EFFECTS OF ELECTORAL SYSTEMS

Both the first-past-the-post and proportional systems have strong partisans among modern democratic theorists. We have already surveyed the main arguments for PR, but we should note here that its critics declare that wherever PR has been tried, it has encouraged the development of splinter parties, deepened ideological divisions, and intensified political conflict. PR has also, they say, made governments into weak coalitions of quarreling and mutually suspicious parties, and it has failed to produce popular mandates on immediate and pressing political issues.

A survey of this sort cannot present the full case for each side, let alone declare which is correct. But political science research has provided considerable evidence that can provide the basis—if not the conclusions—for this debate. Political scientist Douglas Rae's systematic study of the political consequences of various electoral systems came to the following conclusions.[3]

First, every electoral system tends to give parties with large shares of the popular votes more than their proportional shares of parliamentary seats. The other side of that coin is that small parties get even smaller shares of the parliamentary seats than their shares of the popular votes. The party with the largest single share of the popular vote profits most from this tendency, but it also helps the number-two party in the sense that it discriminates strongly against third and fourth and even smaller parties. Furthermore, since a party can go from a comfortable majority of seats to a small minority by a smaller decrease in its share of the popular votes over a large number of districts, the system makes possible wild swings in party fortunes. This was certainly the case in the remarkable Canadian general election of October 25, 1993, the results of which are compared to those in the 1989 election in Table 8.2

Table 8.2 details the greatest defeat ever suffered by a governing party in a first-past-the-post general election. After the 1989 election the Progressive Conservative party, led by Brian Mulroney, enjoyed a comfortable majority of 170 seats over a combined 125 seats for the two other parties. In the 1993 election the Progressive Conservatives, now led by Kim Campbell, the first woman prime minister in Canadian history, suffered a vertiginous drop of nearly two thirds in their share of the popular votes, and a catastrophic loss of 168 of their 170 seats. Moreover, not only did they, like the New Democrats, have too few seats to form the Loyal Opposition; that status, important in a parliamentary system, was inherited by the

TABLE 8.2   Votes and Seats in the Canadian General Elections of 1989 and 1993

PARTY	PERCENTAGE OF POPULAR VOTE		NUMBER OF SEATS		PERCENTAGE OF SEATS	
	1989	1993	1989	1993	1989	1993
Progressive Conservative	43.0	16.0	170	2	57.6	0.7
Liberal	31.9	41.3	82	177	27.8	60.0
Reform	—	18.7	—	52	—	17.6
Bloc Quebecois	—	13.5	—	54	—	18.4
New Democratic	20.4	6.9	43	9	14.6	3.0
Others	4.7	3.6	—	1	—	0.3

Source: *Keesing's Record of World Events* (London: Longman's, 1990, 1994).

Bloc Quebecois—a party officially pledged to separating Quebec from Canada! Of course, most of this drastic change was due to the great unpopularity of the Progressive Conservatives' record in government, but the sheer size of it, unprecedented in modern democratic national elections, was due in part to the tendency of first-past-the-post systems to exaggerate the seat gains of winning parties and the seat losses of losing parties.

A more normal illustration of this tendency is provided in Table 8.3, which shows the seats-to-votes ratio produced by the British general election of 1992. Another is the fact that in every one of the twenty-five elections for the U.S. House of Representatives held from 1946 to 1994, the winning party's share of the House seats was larger than its share of the national popular vote. The average "unearned increment" for the winning party was twenty-seven seats.[4]

Second, single-member-district systems tend to produce two-party systems except where third parties are especially strong in particular areas.

Third, proportional systems discriminate against small parties without strong sectional bases less than majority systems do, and, consequently, they tend to produce multiparty rather than two-party systems.

Fourth, to achieve a legislative majority capable of ruling, more parties willing to join coalitions are necessary in proportional than in single-member-district systems.

Finally, the most important single factor affecting the degree of proportionality—that is, the closeness between the shares of the popular vote and the shares of the legislative seats—is the size of the electoral districts. The more members elected from each district, the more proportional are the seat shares to the vote shares. Israel and the Netherlands, both of which elect all the members of their most important legislative house at large from one nationwide constituency rather than from districts, have the highest proportionality of any electoral system. Both nations also have very large numbers of parties with one or more seats in their parliaments.

Those are some of the most notable facts. It may also be mentioned that most of the democratic electoral systems adopted since World War II—for example, in Japan, Italy, Portugal, and Spain—employ some form of PR. On the other hand, most of the English-speaking nations use first-past-the-post systems, and few are seriously

TABLE 8.3   Vote and Seat Shares in the 1992 British General Election

PARTY	POPULAR VOTES	PERCENTAGE OF VOTES	SEATS	PERCENTAGE OF SEATS	DIFFERENCE
Conservative	13,897,730	41.9	336	51.6	+9.7
Labour	11,398,591	34.4	271	41.6	+7.2
Liberal Democrats	5,916,396	17.8	20	3.1	−14.7
Scottish Nationalists	619,813	1.9	3	0.5	−1.4
Plaid Cymru	155,782	0.5	4	0.6	+0.1
Offical Ulster Unionists	268,475	0.8	9	1.4	+0.6
Democratic Unionists	102,750	0.3	3	0.5	+0.2
Ulster Popular Unionists	19,887	0.1	1	0.1	—
Social Democratic and Labour	182,298	0.5	4	0.6	+0.1
Other	583,352	1.8	0	—	−1.8
Totals	33,145,074	100%	651	100%	

Source: *Keesing's Contemporary Archives, 1992* (London: Longman's, 1992), pp. 38868–69.

considering adopting PR. There are two major exceptions. In a 1993 referendum, the voters of New Zealand approved a proposal to replace their first-past-the-post system with a form of proportional representation. Also in 1993, the Italian Parliament, responding to voter demands, voted to abolish the country's forty-five-year-old proportional electoral system and replace it with a mixed system of first-past-the-post and proportional representation somewhat like Germany's (see below). The new system was intended to produce major changes in the Italian political system, and the first general election under the new system, held in 1994, realized the reformers' greatest hopes. A new "Freedom Alliance" coalition of right-wing parties, led by Forza Italia ("Let's go, Italy") won a majority of the seats in the Chamber of Deputies, and the party's leader, wealthy businessman Silvio Berlusconi, formed a new government. The two largest pre-reform parties renamed themselves (the Christian Democrats became the Italian Popular Party and the Communists became the Democratic Party of the Left), but they lost many seats and were entirely out of power for the first time since the end of World War II. As the old saying has it, "Changing the rules changes the game."

THE GERMAN HYBRID

The debate over the respective merits of proportional representation and first-past-the-post systems has been going on since the early nineteenth century, and most democratic polities have chosen one or the other. One of the few major exceptions is the Federal Republic of Germany (FRG). In reconstructing the electoral system in their new, post-Nazi constitution after World War II, the FRG decided to establish a combination of both systems in an effort to maximize the benefits and minimize the drawbacks of each.

The former German Democratic Republic (East Germany) used the old Soviet-style one-candidate-per-office system. However, in 1990 the DDR was absorbed by the Federal Republic of Germany (West Germany) to form a united Germany. The five *länder* (states) of the DDR were added to the eleven states of the FRG, the size of the Bundestag was increased accordingly, and all members of the reconstituted Bundestag were elected by the FRG's hybrid system.

The German hybrid has fascinated many students of electoral systems, and some believe it is the model all democracies should follow. It works thus: For purposes of electing members to the Bundestag (the lower and more powerful house of the nation's parliament), the nation is divided into 328 constituencies. Each constituency elects one member directly to the Bundestag, and 328 additional members are allocated on the basis of the lists of candidates put up in each of the *länder* by the political parties. In 1990 seven additional seats were provided for surplus mandates. Each election has the following main steps:

1. The voters cast two ballots. On the first ballot voters mark their preferences for one of the individual candidates running for the Bundestag in the district. On the second ballot they mark their preferences for the political party they would most like to see in control of the Bundestag.

2. In deciding how many seats each party will get in the Bundestag, the first step is to aggregate all the second votes each party has won everywhere in the nation. The authorities then drop from all further consideration those parties that have won less than 5 percent of the second votes and have elected two or fewer individual candidates in the constituencies. The second-vote totals for the parties thus eliminated are subtracted from the total cast to provide the figure on which the national allocations are made.

3. On the basis of this new figure, a calculation is made of how many of the national total of 663 seats each party deserves based on its share of the national total of second votes.

4. The national allocation for each party is then distributed among each of the parties in each of the sixteen *länder*.

5. In each of the sixteen *länder*, the number of seats won by individual candidates for each party is subtracted from the total number of seats that it has been allocated in step 4. The remaining seats to which it is entitled are awarded to the candidates on each party's list in the order in which they are listed by the parties.[5]

This rather complicated blend of single-member districts and proportional representation has typically produced national allocations of seats that are quite proportional to the parties' shares of the second votes, as is shown by the results of the first election in reunited Germany held in 1990 as summarized in Table 8.4

TABLE 8.4   Vote and Seat Shares in the 1990 German Bundestag Election

PARTY	NUMBER OF SEATS	PERCENTAGE OF SEATS	NATIONAL PERCENTAGE OF SECOND VOTES
CDU	248	37.4	36.7
FDP	57	8.6	11.0
CSU	57	8.6	7.1
SDP	226	34.1	33.5
Greens/Alliance '90	49	7.4	5.1
PDS	24	3.6	2.4
Others	2	0.3	4.2

Source: *Keesing's Record of World Events* (London: Longman's, 1990), pp. 37904–5.

Apportionment of Electoral Districts

As we have seen, every democratic nation except Israel and the Netherlands is divided into a number of geographical subdivisions known as districts or constituencies, each of which elects one or more members of the national legislature. **Apportionment** is *the process of assigning to local areas the number of representatives each will elect to the national legislature.* In political reality apportionment is also the process of allocating political power among the nation's interest groups as well as regions. The problem of achieving fair apportionment is greatest in nations that use single-member districts, but it also exists in those using multimember districts.

PROBLEMS

Fair apportionment is difficult, especially among single-member districts, because a number of competing principles have legitimate claims and it is impossible to satisfy them all. The most obvious and most basic is the principle of "one person, one vote," which, in apportionment terms, means the principle of equal electorates. Any deviation from this standard means a violation of the basic democratic principle of political equality (see Chapter 5). If district A has 500,000 people and district B has only 250,000, but each elects one legislator, then each resident of B has twice as large a share of the nation's electoral power as each resident of A. In the "reapportionment revolution" that it has brought about since 1962, the U.S. Supreme Court has held that the principle of equal electorates must be the primary rule governing the apportionment of both houses of all state legislatures and also of the U.S. House of Representatives. Even minor deviations are constitutionally permissible only when "based on legitimate considerations incident to the effectuation of a rational state policy."[6]

Exactly what qualifies as "legitimate considerations"? The Court has not yet spelled them out, but in most modern democracies there are at least three. First, it is easier and cheaper for local authorities to administer elections if national district lines coincide with the boundaries of local government units. Hence congressional districts and parliamentary constituencies are usually formed by combining counties or metropolitan wards rather than by creating entirely new subdivisions without regard to existing local government boundaries.

Second, because they are drawn up by incumbent legislators, the boundaries are usually drawn so as to minimize the number of incumbents whose districts will be radically changed.

Third, no matter how equal the districts' populations may be, it is always possible for the dominant political party to draw the boundaries in such a way as to make the most effective use of its own votes and to waste those of the opposition. The basic technique is to concentrate large blocs of opposition voters in a few districts and distribute large blocs of favorable voters more broadly. This is generally called **gerrymandering,** which is *the drawing of electoral district boundaries so as to advantage a particular political party or interest group.* Successful gerrymandering may result, for example, in two opposition candidates regularly elected by margins of 10–1 along with five of the dominant party's candidates regularly elected by margins of 3–2. The most faithful application of the other principles will not prevent gerrymandering. The main safeguards against it are the dominant party's sense that it had better show some restraint lest the opposition take revenge at some future time and, above all, the voters' insistence that apportionment not be used to give one party too grossly unfair an advantage over the others.

PROCEDURES

The power to make and revise apportionment rules and to draw and redraw district lines is of considerable importance in any democratic government. The U.S. Constitution stipulates that each state, regardless of population, shall have two members of the Senate and at least one member of the House of Representatives, but leaves it up to Congress to apportion the other seats in the House among the states. Under the present law, after each national census (taken every decade beginning in 1790), Congress determines how many representatives each state will have. Then the legislature of each state establishes the districts from which each of its allotted national representatives will be elected as well as the districts for electing members of the two houses of the state legislature. Thus the key role in apportionment in the United States is played by the state legislatures, not Congress. However, since the case of *Baker* v. *Carr* (1962) the federal and state courts have kept such a close watch on the legislatures' apportionment activities that they no longer have the free hand they once enjoyed.

In Great Britain, Parliament periodically establishes four nonpartisan boundary commissions (one each for England, Scotland, Wales, and Northern Ireland) to review constituency boundaries and recommend revisions. The commissions' recommendations are usually accepted (though sometimes revised) by the ruling political party and enacted by Parliament. The most recent "redistribution" raised the total number of constituencies from 635 to 650 and went into effect for the general election of 1983.

In France *découpage* (districting) is usually accomplished by an ad hoc agreement between the minister of the interior and the prefect of each *département*.

Partisan considerations—for example, minimizing the number of Communist party deputies elected—have sometimes played an important role. In both Switzerland (1962) and Germany (1963), national supreme courts have voided unconstitutional apportionments that strayed too far from the principle of equal electorates. In all democratic nations, apportionment controversies, though seldom as dramatic or as flagrantly partisan as in the United States, are nevertheless frequent and sometimes hotly contested.[7]

Traditionally, gerrymandering in the United States. has been used to maximize the number of offices a particular political party can win. In recent years, however, a new practice has arisen, which some people call "affirmative gerrymandering." Its objective is to maximize the number of offices won by African-Americans and Hispanics. It began when the Department of Justice, acting to implement a 1982 amendment to the Voting Rights Act, required some states with histories of discriminating against African-American and Hispanics (notably Florida, Illinois, Louisiana, New York, North Carolina, and Texas) to redraw their congressional district lines so as to increase the number of African-American and Hispanic candidates elected. This consideration was regarded as more important than such older criteria as geographical compactness and contiguity. Most states complied by piecing together new, strangely shaped districts from predominantly African-American and Hispanic areas to give one or the other group a majority in each district. The new districts worked: There were twenty-six African-American and Hispanic members of the House of Representatives before the 1992 election, and the number jumped to thirty-nine after the election. They also had the unexpected result of reducing the number of districts safe for the Democrats, but most African Americans and Hispanics thought it was well worth the political cost.

Referendum Elections

RATIONALE

Most elections in modern democratic nations are candidate elections, that is, contests between candidates for elective public offices. But there is another class of elections, generally called **referendums**, which are *elections in which questions of public policy are voted upon directly by ordinary citizens*.

The rationale for referendums is rooted in the belief of some democratic theorists that any system of representative government that depends entirely upon the election of public officials is bound to be a poor way of translating the people's will into government action. Rousseau, for example, argued that representation in any form inevitably distorts public opinion to some degree, for when one person's ideas are passed through the mind of a second person, what comes out is always somewhat different from what went in. (Anyone who has ever read a set of examination papers will heartily agree.) For this reason, Rousseau argued, elections to office should not be the sole method of finding out what the people want. At the very least we must supplement it with some device that expresses the popular will directly and without interpretation or alteration by any intervening agency.

Some democratic theorists also contend that referendums help to realize the prime goal of democracy. Democracy is not an end in itself, they say; it is a means for achieving the higher end of the fullest possible development of each and every human being. Since full participation in civic affairs is an important part of human development, that participation will be much more extensive and fulfilling where all the people can make public policy decisions themelves in town meetings and referendums rather than being confined to voting for representatives who will make the policy decisions for them.

Many people believe that the New England town meeting or the Swiss *landsgemeinde* (face-to-face meetings of all the citizens of some rural cantons, government subdivisions roughly comparable to American states) is the ideal device for accomplishing these purposes, and some people believe that public opinion polls can do the job. But town meetings are possible only in small communities, and too many people have too many doubts about the accuracy and meaning of public opinion polls. Consequently, most people who have doubts about representative government believe that representation must be supplemented by some form of the referendum device. Few argue that referendums should replace entirely the election of representatives, but many believe that referendums should be available for use whenever the elected representatives are unable to figure out—or unwilling to do—what the people want.

ORGANIZATION

Approximately 86 nations—by no means all of them democracies—have occasionally used one or another of four basic forms of referendums.[8]

Government-Controlled Referendums

In this form, the government—that is, the leaders of the party or a coalition of parties controlling the legislature and the executive—has sole control over when a referendum will be held, on what issue it will be held, and how the proposition put to the voters will be worded. Most national referendums have been of this type.

Constitutionally Required Referendums

Some countries' constitutions require that certain matters—especially constitutional amendments—be finally adopted only by direct votes of the citizens. The government decides on the wording of the amendment, but it must be approved by the voters before it becomes law.

Referendums by Popular Petitions

A few political systems, notably Italy, Switzerland, and several American states, allow ordinary voters to challenge an act of the legislature by submitting a petition demanding a referendum vote on that act. If the required number of signatures are gathered, a vote must be held; and if a majority vote against the act, it is repealed even though the government wishes to retain it.

Popular Initiatives

In Switzerland and several American states, ordinary voters are allowed to file a petition demanding that a certain measure that the government has not adopted be referred to the voters. The petitioners, not the government, determine the wording of the proposition, and if petitioners secure the required number of signatures, their measure must be set before the voters at the next election. If it receives a majority in the referendum, it becomes law even though the government may think it unwise.

RESULTS AND EVALUATION

Switzerland has been by far the heaviest user of national referendums. From 1866 to 1993, the Swiss held 414 referendums of one type or another, followed by Australia with 44, Italy with 31, France with 21, Ireland with 18, and Denmark with 16.

The United States and the Netherlands are the only democracies that have never held a national referendum, but a number of the American states have held many statewide referendums. As of 1994, every state except Delaware requires popular referendums for the final approval of constitutional amendments; thirty-nine states have some form of referendum on ordinary legislation; fourteen have popular initiatives for constitutional amendments; and twenty-two have some form of popular initiative for adopting ordinary laws. All told, the states have held well over a thousand referendums since 1778, when Massachusetts held the first modern referendum on adopting its new constitution (the voters turned it down).

Dictators have also used referendums. In 1936, for example, Adolf Hitler received 98 percent approval for his policies in a national referendum, and in 1938 he received 99 percent approval for his *anschluss* (uniting) with Austria. More recent examples include the 99 percent approval of the peace treaty with Israel by Egypt in 1979 and the 99 percent approval of the new Islamic Republic constitution in Iran in 1979. Observers in democratic systems may wonder why authoritarian regimes bother with referendums, and the answer seems to be this: The dictators or ruling oligarchies believe that the legitimacy and acceptance of their policies will sometimes be enhanced if they use the forms of democracy even though the substance violates democratic principles of free elections. Our main interest here, however, is with democratic referendums and their impact on other institutions and policies.

Campaigns for and against most referendum measures in the democracies are conducted mainly by organized interest groups rather than by spontaneous citizens' opinion groups. The evidence suggests that, contrary to a belief cherished by editorial writers, newspaper endorsements have little effect upon the outcomes. Occasionally political parties take strong stands on particular measures. When all parties support a measure, it usually passes. When the parties are on opposite sides,

A SAMPLE OF RECENT REFERENDUMS

COUNTRY	DATE	SUBJECT	PERCENTAGE VOTING YES	TURNOUT PERCENTAGE
(California)	1978	Cut property taxes (Prop. 13)	65	55
(Massachusetts)	1986	Prohibit abortions	42	29
(Oregon)	1986	Allow growing and possession of marijuana for personal use	26	50
Brazil	1993	Favor presidential system over parliamentary system	69	na
Canada	1992	Approve special status for Quebec	46	na
Chile	1988	Approve another term for Pinochet	45	99
Denmark	1992	Approve greater monetary and political union within EC	49	83
Denmark	1993	Same	57	86
Hungary	1989	Ban Communist party organizations in the workplace	95	58
Iran	1979	Approve new Islamic constitution	99	65
Ireland	1986	Remove constitutional prohibition of divorce	41	88
Russia	1993	Approve Yeltsin's new constitution	55	58
South Africa	1992	Approve continuing negotiations to end apartheid	69	85
Spain	1986	Remain in NATO	53	59
Switzerland	1971	Allow women to vote	66	58
Switzerland	1986	Approve full Swiss membership in the United Nations	32	48
Switzerland	1989	Abolish Swiss army	36	69

Sources: The national referendum results are taken from David Butler and Austin Ranney, eds., *Referendums Around the World* (Washington, DC: AEI Press, 1994), Appendix A, pp. 265–84; the referendum results for American states are taken from *Public Opinion.*

the voters' party loyalties usually exert strong, but not all-powerful, influences on their voting. Similarly, although measures initiated by governments by no means win all the time, they do considerably better than measures proposed by citizens' groups. Referendum elections usually attract fewer voters than elections for public office, but occasionally the turnout for a hotly contested referendum on a highly controversial measure—for example, the 1971 vote in Switzerland on enfranchising women—will match or even exceed that for candidate elections.

THE VOTING ORDEAL

Entering the polling booth on Tuesday, November 3, 1964, the typical California voter found himself confronted with an immense sheet of finely printed green paper, a dirty black rubber stamp, a tiny ink pad, and thirty decisions to render. A few minutes later (the legal maximum is ten), he emerged and numbly surrendered to a clerk his ballot, now slightly embellished, like the fingers of his decision hand, with black ink stains.

Most of his decisions were made on a lengthy array of [referendum] propositions. In these, questions on an assortment of issues were posed, each couched in language tedious and obscure—as only minds trained in the finest law schools could devise.[9]

But are referendums basically a device for conservative policies or for liberal policies? The evidence from Switzerland and the U.S. states, the heaviest users of referendums, appears to show that the device is neither inherently conservative nor inherently liberal. Rather, referendums are a politically neutral device that generally produces outcomes favored by the current state of public opinion, and public opinion is seldom liberal or conservative on all measures. In the U.S. states in the 1970s and 1980s, for example, referendums generally had liberal outcomes on questions of government spending, conservation of natural resources, and a freeze on nuclear weapons, and generally conservative outcomes on questions of dealing with crime, limiting use of handguns, and taxation (tax-cutting propositions mostly won in the late 1970s but lost after the mid-1980s). Political scientists do not agree on whether referendums are good or bad. Some argue that legislative decision making has two critical advantages over referendums. First, the legislative process encourages competing interest groups to moderate their initial nonnegotiable demands and work out compromises that will give all groups something of what they want and avoid total defeat for any. But a referendum, such as one on outlawing abortions, permits only two choices: Either allow any woman to have an abortion on demand or make all abortions a crime. Referendum results thus often mean near-total victory for one side and near-total defeat for the other, which is dangerous on an issue such as abortion, where the two sides passionately take irreconcilable positions.

Closely related, those critics say, is a second advantage for legislative policy making. Legislatures typically weigh the *intensity* of demands as well as the number of people making them; but in a referendum each voter's preference is equal to any other voter's, and there is no way to register different intensities. Thus a white majority fairly strongly opposed to compulsory open housing for African-Americans can—as it did in California in 1964—defeat an African-American minority passionately convinced that open housing is a basic human right. Such results, the critics conclude, produce neither justice, social peace, nor government stability.

The defenders of referendums reply that all such considerations are less important than the fact that the device enables the voters to express their policy preferences directly, without distortion and dilution by legislative interpretation and compromises. But perhaps the most powerful argument for referendums is that in some circumstances their decisions will be accepted as legitimate where decisions by other means would be rejected as illegitimate decrees imposed by unresponsive elites.

REFERENDUMS AND LEGITIMACY IN EASTERN EUROPE

We noted in Chapter 2 that no structure of government or policy can hope to succeed unless it is generally regarded as *legitimate*—one that has been produced by a proper and lawful process and is therefore morally as well as legally entitled to obedience. The greatest virtue of referendums, some political scientists say, is that they are direct decisions of the people, not indirect and probably distorted expressions of the people's will by intermediaries such as public officials or the mass communications media. As one puts it:

> The citizen is more likely to feel entitled to flout a law promoted by an elite, or procured by blackmail or corruption, than one that is seen to reflect the free and informed consent of the majority of citizens.[10]

That observation explains why referendums have been widely used to make decisions on issues about basic and often disputed questions involving changes of national status and fundamental constitutional forms. Many recent instances occurred in the extensive reconstruction of national entities and constitutions after the collapse of communism in the former Soviet Union and its Eastern European satellite countries in 1989.[11] The highlights of that complex story are as follows:

While still president of the rapidly crumbling USSR in 1991, Mikhail Gorbachev's last effort to restructure and save the Union was a referendum he ordered in all of the fifteen constituent republics for March 17 on the question, "Do you consider necessary the preservation of the Union of Soviet Socialist Republics as a renewed federation of equal sovereign republics, in which the rights and freedoms of an individual of any nationality will be fully guaranteed?" His gambit failed. Six of the fifteen republics boycotted the referendum entirely, and five others changed the question or added questions of their own on independence from the Union. Only four republics put Gorbachev's question unchanged to their voters. After the vote, Gorbachev claimed that 80 percent of the Union's registered voters had voted, and that 76 percent of them had voted Yes, but the claim did not save the Union. By the end of 1991 referendums on sovereign independence carried by large majorities in eleven of the republics. The Ukrainian referendum held on December 1 delivered the final blow when 90.3 percent of the voters approved independence. Gorbachev saw that there was no hope of saving the Union in any form, he resigned as Union President, and the USSR ceased to exist.

Referendums continued to play prominent roles in the newly independent republics' struggles to remake their political systems. In 1992 and 1993 the republics held a total of ten referendums. They played an especially critical part in Russia's conflict between President Boris Yeltsin and the anti-Yeltsin majority in the Supreme Soviet (parliament). Many observers credited the referendum of December 12, 1992, with preventing civil war and establishing and legitimizing the republic's new constitution.

Referendums were also prominent in building post-Communist systems in the former Soviet satellite nations of Eastern Europe. A series of referendums in Hungary in 1989 and 1990 outlawed the Communist Party, established free multi-candidate elections, and created an elected presidency. The two 1987 Polish referendums on economic reform prepared the way for the popular election of anti-Communist leader Lech Walesa as president in 1990.

Many observers believe that a national referendum in Czechoslovakia might have prevented the country's breakup, but none was held and in 1993 the Slovakia parliament voted to secede and establish a separate country, leaving the remainder to what is now called the Czech Republic.

Referendums also played a major part in the breakup of Yugoslavia in 1990–1993. On nineteen occasions during those years referendums on independence and national sovereignty were put to the voters in a number of Yugoslavia's ethnic groups and geographical divisions, such as Serbia, Croatia, Serbs in Croatia, Macedonia, Kosovo, Muslims in Sandzak, Bosnia-Herzegovina, Serbs in Bosnia-Herzegovina, and Albanians in Macedonia. In most instances the referendums inflamed rather than cooled the ethnic loyalties and demands for nationhood that had been repressed by Yugoslavia's former Communist regime.

After reviewing this mixture of beneficial and harmful consequences of referendums in the former USSR and the countries of Eastern Europe, Henry Brady

DEMOCRACY COMES TO PARTS OF THE FORMER USSR. Voters in the former Soviet republic of Georgia voting in its first-ever multiparty election.

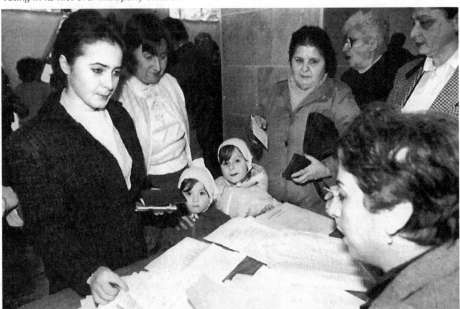

and Cynthia Kaplan offer some conclusions about the special ability of referendums to produce legitimate decisions:

> Referendums can allow public opinion to flower, and during times of transition, these blooms can ease the way to democracy if decision makers decide not to trample them underfoot with force and violence. There are dangers, however. In the giddiness of transitions, referendums can proliferate, creating chaotic gardens as each group jostles for its own space. Elites can prune and shape public opinion in ways that make a mockery of it. And the flower, some might say weed, of nationalism grows more robustly in the referendum garden than the flower of governmental reform. Nevertheless, referendums have been and will continue to be important devices for democratic transitions.[12]

For Further Reading

SUFFRAGE AND CANDIDATE ELECTIONS

BOGDANOR, VERNON, AND DAVID BUTLER, eds. *Democracy and Elections: Electoral Systems and Their Political Consequences* (New York: Cambridge University Press, 1983). Essays on the political impact of various electoral systems.

BUTLER, DAVID, AND BRUCE E. CAIN. *Congressional Districting: Comparative and Theoretical Perspectives.* New York: Macmillan, 1991. A careful examination of the political and technical issues in congressional districting, compared with those involved in drawing constituency boundaries for the British House of Commons.

*BUTLER, DAVID, HOWARD R. PENNIMAN, AND AUSTIN RANNEY, eds., *Democracy at the Polls.* Washington, DC: American Enterprise Institute, 1981. A comparative study of the conduct of elections in twenty-eight selected democratic nations.

CAIN, BRUCE E. *The Reapportionment Puzzle.* Berkeley, CA: University of California Press, 1984. Analysis of political consequences of reapportionment and gerrymandering, with special reference to California.

DUMMET, MICHAEL. *Voting Procedures.* New York: Oxford University Press, 1985. Description of leading electoral systems and their political impacts, with emphasis on strategies of voting.

GINSBERG, BENJAMIN, AND MARTIN SHEFTER. *Politics by Other Means: The Declining Importance of Elections in America.* New York: Basic Books, 1990. Argument that important decisions are no longer made in American elections but rather in such arenas as congressional investigations, media revelations, and litigation.

*GROFMAN, BERNARD, AND AREND LIJPHART, eds. *Electoral Laws and Their Political Consequences.* New York: Agathon Press, 1986. Essays on electoral systems and their political consequences in a number of democratic countries.

*RAE, DOUGLAS W. *The Political Consequences of Electoral Laws,* rev. ed. New Haven, CT: Yale University Press, 1971. A lucid and well-documented analysis of how various electoral systems affect the number and strength of political parties.

RUSH, MARK E. *Does Redistricting Make a Difference? Partisan Representation and Electoral Behavior.* Baltimore, MD: Johns Hopkins University Press, 1993. Empirical study concluding that partisan gerrymandering seldom clearly produces the intended results.

TAAGEPERA, REIN, AND MATTHEW SOBERG SHUGART. *Seats and Votes: The Effects and Determinants of Electoral Systems.* New Haven, CT: Yale University Press, 1989. Comparative survey of how different electoral systems affect the proportions of legislative seats parties receive for their shares of popular votes.

PROPORTIONAL REPRESENTATION

HOAG, CLARENCE G., AND GEORGE H. HALLETT. *Proportional Representation.* New York: Macmillan, 1926. For many years the standard exposition of the case.

LIJPHART, AREND, AND BERNARD GROFMAN, eds. *Choosing an Electoral System: Issues and Alternatives.* New York: Praeger, 1984. Essays on the costs and benefits of proportional and first-past-the-post electoral systems.

NOMINATIONS AND CANDIDATE SELECTION

BARTELS, LARRY M. *Presidential Primaries and the Dynamics of Public Choice*. Princeton, NJ: Princeton University Press, 1988. Analysis of "momentum" in presidential nominations caused by media coverage of sequential primaries.

RANNEY, AUSTIN. *Pathways to Parliament*. Madison, WI: University of Wisconsin Press, 1965. Study of how British parties choose their candidates for Parliament.

GALLAGHER, MICHAEL, AND MICHAEL MARSH, eds. *Candidate Selection in Comparative Perspective*. Beverly Hills, CA: Sage, 1988. Essays on the selection of parliamentary candidates in Belgium, Great Britain, France, West Germany, Ireland, Italy, Japan, the Netherlands, and Norway.

REFERENDUMS

*BUTLER, DAVID, AND AUSTIN RANNEY, eds. *Referendums Around the World*. Washington, DC: AEI Press, 1994. Studies of conduct and impact of referendums in various democratic nations, with appendices listing results of all nationwide referendums held up to the end of l993.

CRONIN, THOMAS E. *Direct Democracy: The Politics of Initiative, Referendum, and Recall*. Cambridge, MA:

Harvard University Press, 1989. Discussion of the uses and potential of initiatives and referendums in the United States.

MAGLEBY, DAVID B. *Direct Legislation*. Baltimore, MD: Johns Hopkins University Press, 1984. Detailed study of the initiative and referendum in the United States, describing their use, financing, and impact on voters.

Notes

1. Gerald M. Pomper, *Elections in America* (New York: Dodd, Mead, 1968), pp. 262–63.

2. Robert W. Jackman, "Political Institutions and Voter Turnout in the Industrial Democracies," *American Political Science Review*, vol. 81 (June 1987), pp. 405–23.

3. Douglas W. Rae, *The Political Consequences of Electoral Laws*, rev. ed. (New Haven, CT: Yale University Press, 1971), especially Chapters 4–10. See also Bernard Grofman and Arend Lijphart, eds., *Electoral Laws and Their Political Consequences* (New York: Agathon Press, 1986).

4. Norman J. Ornstein, Thomas E. Mann, and Michael J. Malbin, eds. *Vital Statistics on Congress, 1991–1992* (Washington, DC: Congressional Quarterly, 1992), Table 2-2, pp. 49–50.

5. The system is described in detail in Max Kaase, "Personalized Proportional Representation: The 'Model' of the West German Electoral System," in *Choosing an Electoral System: Issues and Alternatives*, Arend Lijphart and Bernard Grofman, (New York: Praeger, 1984), pp. 155–164.

6. *Reynolds* v. *Sims*, 377 U.S. 533 (1964).

7. For a comparative analysis of reapportionment in the United States and Great Britain focusing on why

the process is so political and controversial in the United States and so technical and consensual in Britain, see David Butler and Bruce E. Cain, "Reapportionment: A Study in Comparative Government," *Electoral Studies*, vol. 4 (December 1985), 197–213.

8. For a list of all nationwide referendums held from the sixteenth century to the end of 1993 and a survey of their consequences in various parts of the world, see David Butler and Austin Ranney, eds., *Referendums Around the World* (Washington, DC: AEI Press, 1994).

9. John E. Mueller, "Voting on the Propositions," *American Political Science Review*, vol. 63 (December 1969), 1197–212.

10. Geoffrey deQ. Walker, *The People's Law* (Sidney: Center for Independent Studies, 1987), p. 50.

11. This discussion draws heavily from Henry E. Brady and Cynthia S. Kaplan, "Eastern Europe and the Former Soviet Union," in *Referendums Around the World*, Butler and Ranney, eds., pp. 174–217.

12. Ibid., p. 216.

9

The nation blessed above all nations is she in whom the civic genius of the people does the saving day by day, by acts without external picturesqueness; by speaking, writing, voting reasonably; by smiting corruption swiftly; by good temper between parties; by the people knowing true men when they see them, and preferring them as leaders to rabid partisans or empty quacks.
William James, *Memories and Studies*

Voting Behavior

Many of us become upset, frightened, or angry at times about what our government is doing or not doing. Some of us are outraged that violent crime has increased so much that we can no longer safely walk the streets of our cities, and we demand that government do something to protect us. Some of us are concerned about the easy availability of pornography in magazines, movies, and videocassettes, and we demand that government stamp it out. Some of us are concerned about the rapid deterioration of our physical environment and demand drastic antipollution measures before it is too late. And so on.

There comes a time for many of us when we feel that mere talk is no longer enough, that it is time for action—now! But what kind of action? "I'm only one person," we often hear people say. "What can *I* do?"

In a democratic system there are many answers to that question. We can join one of the existing political parties or form a new one and try to elect new public officials. We can join a pressure group to "put the heat" on incumbent officials to do something or stop doing something. We can file lawsuits against the officials. We can demonstrate, boycott, and strike. The physical means are readily at hand even to assassinate the president or start a revolution.

That is what we *can* do, but what do most of us *actually* do to advance our political goals? The answers for the citizens of four Western democracies in 1981 are shown in Table 9.1

The data in Table 9.1 show that most people in all four nations find most forms of political action too demanding, too costly, too dangerous, or morally wrong. Hence, voting for or against particular parties and candidates in periodic elections is for most citizens of democracies the most-used way of trying to influence government policies, and for many of us it is the only way.

Voting may or may not be the most effective way for ordinary citizens to make governments do as they wish, but in every modern democratic system votes are the basic units of political power. When all is said and done, the groups that mobilize the largest numbers of voters in support of the public policies and officials they favor get the largest shares of what they want out of politics. If some people have every quality necessary to be, say, great presidents except the ability to make people vote for them, their other qualities will not make them *any* kind of president. A political party may have the most intelligent and progressive program possible, but if it cannot attract enough voters, its program will never become public policy. A

TABLE 9.1   Levels of Peaceful Political Participation in Four Western Democracies

FORM OF PARTICIPATION	PERCENTAGE REPORTING ACTIVITY, 1981			
	United States	Great Britain	West Germany	France
Voted in last election	68	73	90	81
Sign petitions	61	63	46	na
Contact officials	27	11	11	na
Convince others how to vote	19	9	22	na
Attend meeting or rally	18	9	22	na
Work for party or candidate	14	5	8	na
Participate in demonstrations	12	10	14	26
Join in boycott	14	7	7	11
Participate in unofficial strike	3	7	2	10
Occupy building	2	2	1	7

Source: Russell J. Dalton, *Citizen Politics in Western Democracies* (Chatham, NJ: Chatham House, 1988), Table 3.4, p. 47, and Table 4.1, p. 65.

pressure group may lobby so skillfully that it lines up everyone in the legislature on its side, but if the voters throw those legislators out of office at the next election the group's lobbying efforts will be for naught. Even the power of money, sometimes mistakenly regarded as an irresistible force in politics, ultimately depends upon its ability to produce votes.

So the question of what makes voters vote as they do is of great concern to every party politician and lobbyist. It is of equal concern to every student of democratic politics, and in the past forty years so many excellent studies have been made that voting behavior is now generally considered to be one of the most advanced areas in political science. In this chapter we will review the principal findings of those studies so that we may better understand how and why this basic coin of political power is distributed among parties and candidates.

Intervening Variables in Voting Behavior

In any democratic system the aspect of voting behavior that first concerns both practicing politicians and political scientists is the *result*—how many people vote and which way—because it is at that point that voters have their most direct and powerful impact on the governing process. Hence, most political scientists have taken two dimensions of voting behavior as their main *dependent variables*— that is, the kinds of behavior political scientists are trying to explain.[1] The first dimension is *preferences*, or what makes people prefer one party or candidate over other parties and candidates. The second dimension is *voting and nonvoting*, or what makes people decide to vote or not vote.

The studies of voting behavior typically regard voting behavior as one special form of public opinion, and, as we saw in Chapters 3 and 6, many independent vari-

HIGH TURNOUT IN EUROPEAN ELECTIONS. Miners voting in a German national election.

ables help to shape most political attitudes and behavior, including voting behavior. Those variables include, for instance, voters' biological natures and needs, their psychological makeups, their membership in primary and secondary social groups, and the communications they receive. Should we, then, simply assume that those independent variables explain all public opinion, including voting behavior, and let it go at that?

The authors of the classic study of American voting behavior say no.[2] They point out that when one asks people why they voted as they did in a particular election, few are likely to reply, "Because I have a high socioeconomic status" or "Because I live in a suburb" or "Because my husband told me to." Most people will probably say, "Because I am a Republican" or "Because I don't want my taxes raised" or "Because Bush is a strong leader." In other words, most people think that they vote the way they do because of how they feel about the political parties, the issues, and the candidates. Hence, those feelings *intervene* between the basic independent variables (people's socioeconomic status and primary group memberships) and the dependent variables (voting and nonvoting, voting for Clinton or Bush). In this sense, they are *intervening variables*.

If that is the case, then the first step in understanding how and why people vote is to understand how they feel about the parties, issues, and candidates.

PARTY IDENTIFICATION

Meaning

Party identification is *the sense of attachment a person feels to a political party*. It is thus an inner psychological feeling or attitude, not an outward formal dues-paying attachment to a party such as party *membership* (see Chapter 10). Political scientists usually measure the direction and intensity of people's party identifications by asking a standard question that the Center for Political and Social Studies (CPSS) at the University of Michigan has asked American respondents in its surveys every two years since 1948. The question is: "Generally speaking, do you usually think of yourself as a Republican, a Democrat, an independent, or what?" If respondents answer "independent," they are then asked the follow-up question, "Do you think of yourself as closer to the Republican or Democratic party?" If a respondent answers to the first question "Democrat" or "Republican," then the follow-up question is, "Do you think of yourself as a strong Democrat (Republican) or not so strong?" Their responses are then classified in the eight categories shown in Table 9.2.

Development

Party identification is the first attitude that most people acquire in their political socialization. As we saw in Chapter 3, by age seven or eight most Americans will tell an interviewer, "We [that is, the respondent's family] are Republicans (or Democrats)." Evidently we acquire our initial party identifications as aspects of our identifications with our families. The more united the parents are in their party preferences and the more they talk about them, the more likely their children are to have the same preferences for the rest of their lives. In many people those early preferences are likely to grow stronger through life as a result of the general principle, noted in Chapter 3, that the longer one maintains identification with any group the more

TABLE 9.2   Party Identification in the United States, 1960–1992 (in percentages)

YEAR	DEMOCRATS			Ind.	REPUBLICANS			Other
	Strong	Weak	Ind.		Strong	Weak	Ind.	
1960	21	25	8	8	14	13	7	4
1964	27	25	8	8	11	13	6	2
1968	20	25	9	11	10	14	9	2
1972	15	26	10	13	10	13	11	2
1976	15	25	12	14	9	14	10	1
1980	18	23	11	13	9	14	10	2
1984	17	20	11	11	12	15	12	2
1986	18	22	10	12	15	10	11	2
1988	17	18	12	10	14	14	13	2
1992	20	19	12	9	12	10	9	9

Source: Robert S. Erikson, Norman R. Luttbeg, and Kent L. Tedin, *American Public Opinion* (New York: Macmillan, 1988), Table 1.6, pp. 9–10. Figures for 1992 are taken from the National Election Study, 1992, through the Inter-University Consortium for Political and Social Research.

intense the identification becomes. On the other hand, where, as in France, the usual family relationship does not allow for political discussion by parents with or in the presence of children, fewer people have stable long-term party identifications.

Fluctuation

Another reason for the lower incidence of stable party identifications in France is that the parties themselves have been less stable than in many other democracies. The parties of the Third Republic (1870–1940) disappeared under the Vichy regime (1940–1944), reappeared in somewhat altered form and with some new names under the Fourth Republic (1946–1958), and have undergone more reshuffling in the Fifth Republic (1958–). Furthermore, under the Fourth Republic some parties (the Rassemblement du Peuple Français, Social Republicans, and Poujadists) were purely "flash" parties: They emerged, fought one or two elections, and disbanded. In recent years France and Italy have had fewer durable parties with which the French and Italian people could form lasting identifications than most other democracies have had.

In the United States, on the other hand, the present party alignment has lasted since 1854, in Great Britain and Norway since 1900, in Switzerland since 1919, and in Canada since 1918.

In those countries, party identifications tend to be noticeably stronger and more stable than in France and Italy, but some fluctuations occur nevertheless. According to the CPSS, some Americans switch parties for personal reasons: Maybe a person's spouse has a different party loyalty and he or she switches to keep peace at home or a person achieves a socioeconomic status higher than that of his or her parents or moves to a new neighborhood and switches to the party predominant in the new environment.

Politically, however, the most significant fluctuations are those in which massive numbers of voters switch from one party to another and thus change the balance of electoral power. Such a shift certainly occurred in the United States between 1930 and 1936, when many Republicans became Democrats. Some commentators believe that in the 1990s similar shifts—especially from strong party attachments to weaker attachments to all parties—have been taking place in the United States and other Western democracies: for example, the shift in Great Britain from Labour to the Conservatives from 1979 to 1992, with some signs of a shift back to Labour in the mid-1990s; and the recent radical rejections of one or more major parties in Canada and Italy noted in Chapter 8.

Impact

As we have noted previously, in most modern democracies the most visible contestants in electoral politics today are the same political parties—or at least parties bearing the same names—that have been prominent for periods ranging from sixty years to more than a century. In such nations the parties are about the only political objects that are recognized by almost everyone. Party identification thus serves many people as their main point of reference for making sense of the political events, issues, personalities, charges, and countercharges flooding them from the communications media. Put another way, the one political fact that many of us are sure of is that we are Democrats or Republicans. When in doubt—as we often are—about this issue or that candidate, we can still choose by simply going along with our parties' positions or candidates.

It is therefore not surprising that political scientists have consistently found strong associations between intensity of party identification and most other aspects of voting behavior. For example, the most partisan are also the most interested in, and best informed about, political affairs, the most likely to vote, and the most likely to try to influence others to vote.

The least partisan are quite different. We are all familiar with the inspiring picture of "independents" as ideal citizens, who are deeply concerned with civic affairs, with acquainting themselves with the facts about the issues and candidates, and with making decisions on each according to the merits, and with their thinking unhampered by loyalty to party labels. Without commenting on whether or not good citizens *should* be this way, we must recognize that the voting studies have found only a small fraction of self-styled "pure independents" who fit the ideal. The studies show quite the contrary: Typical pure independents are far less interested in politics than strong partisans, know much less about issues and candidates, care little about how elections come out, and are much less likely to vote. Their independence, in short, results from apathy rather than from a high-minded rejection of partisanship.

Remember, though, that the previous paragraph applies only to the pure independents, people who express no preference of any kind for one party over the other (SPSS calls them "independent independents"). There are also the **independent leaners**—*people who call themselves independents but have some preference for a particular party.* Such people are quite different from the pure independents in several respects: They are much more interested in politics, they know much more about the issues and the candidates, they care much more about how elections come out, and they are far more likely to vote. Indeed, recent studies have shown that independent leaners score higher on all those counts than the "weak Democrats" and "weak Republicans."

In short, in terms of political involvement, knowledge, and activity, the strong party identifiers rank first, the independent leaners are second, the weak party identifiers are third, and the pure independents are a distant last.

Ticket-Splitting and Divided Government in the United States

Voters in most parliamentary democracies cannot split their tickets in national elections because they vote only for the members of parliament from their districts, and the leader of the party that wins a majority of the seats automatically becomes the prime minister (or, if no party wins a majority, the prime minister is selected by a coalition of parties). However, in presidential democracies such as the United States, the chief executive and the members of the legislature are elected separately, and the voters can, if they choose, vote for the presidential candidate of one party and the congressional candidate of the other party.

Table 9.3 shows that in presidential elections from 1968 to 1988, an average of one quarter of American voters have split their tickets by voting for a presidential candidate of one party (mostly Republican candidates) and congressional candidates of the other party (mostly Democrats). We should add that in 1992 split-ticket voters soared to 36 percent of the electorate, no doubt largely due to people who voted for Perot for president and for Democratic or Republican candidates for the House and the Senate.[3]

The recent upsurge in ticket-splitting shown by Table 9.3 has had a major impact on U.S. governments by making divided party control (a chief executive of one party facing a legislature in which one or both houses are controlled by the opposing party) normal rather than exceptional at both the national and state levels. Before 1968 there had been only two relatively brief periods (1841–1858 and 1874–1894) of divided party control in Washington. But the fourteen national elections from 1968 to 1994 have produced only eight years of unified party control (1976–1980, 1992–1994) and at least fourteen years of divided party control, with Republican presidents and Congresses with one or both houses controlled by the Democrats (1968–1976, 1980–1992), and at least two years with a Democratic president and a Republican Congress (1994–).

Moreover, divided party control has been almost as common in the states: From 1946 to 1988, a grand total of 1,052 elections were held in forty-nine of the states (Nebraska, where elections to the one-house legislature are legally nonpartisan, is not counted).[4] Forty percent produced divided party control, and in the non-Southern states just over half produced divided party control. Those facts have led many observers to conclude that divided party control has become normal in the United States and is likely to remain so well into the future.

What difference should that make? Political scientists disagree about whether divided government is good or bad. Some, including James Sundquist and Morris Fiorina, believe that divided party control makes it hard for the voters to decide who is to blame when government policies are not working and whom to reward when policies are working well. Moreover, they add, it contaminates almost every aspect of government with petty partisan politics, and is the main cause for such

TABLE 9.3   Straight- and Split-Ticket American Voters, 1968–1988 (in percentages)

	VOTED FOR				
YEAR	Dem. Pres., Dem. House	Dem. Pres., Rep. House	Rep. Pres., Dem. House	Rep. Pres., Rep. House	Total Splitters
1968	42%	7%	10%	41%	17%
1972	30	5	25	40	30
1976	41	9	16	34	25
1980	34	8	20	38	28
1984	36	5	20	39	25
1988	41	7	18	34	25

Source: National Election Studies data, from the Inter-University Consortium for Political and Social Research through the University of California Data program.

appalling spectacles as the 1991 confirmation hearings on the appointment to the Supreme Court of Clarence Thomas, a conservative African-American Republican nominated by a Republican president, who was reviewed by a Senate controlled by the Democrats.

Why do so many American voters split their tickets when it is obvious that it will often produce divided government and perhaps government gridlock? The answer is that many voters do not think that divided government is bad nor do they believe that members of Congress have an obligation to support the policies of a president of their own party. For example, in 1993 the Gallup poll asked a sample of Americans, "Do you think it is better for the country to have a President who comes from the same political party that controls Congress, or do you think it is better to have a President from one political party and Congress controlled by another?" Forty-eight percent said it is better to have both branches controlled by the same party, 37 percent said it is better to have them controlled by different parties, and the remainder had no opinion. For another example, Gallup also asked, "Do you think the Democrats in Congress who voted *against* President Clinton's budget plan had an obligation to support Clinton, since he is also a Democrat, or don't you think so?" Only 29 percent of all respondents—but 40 percent of the Democratic identifiers—said the congressional Democrats had such an obligation.[5]

Other political scientists, including Gary Jacobson and David Mayhew, contend that divided party control is entirely consistent with the U.S. Constitution's checks and balances and that it has no discernible effect on the quantity and quality of the laws enacted. Whatever the merits of this argument, it is clear that split-ticket voting and the divided government it makes possible is a substantial and continuing feature of the U.S. political system.

Whatever may be the merits of this debate, it is clear that in the United States, as in most democracies, party identifications have never been the only factors influencing people's votes, and in the 1980s and 1990s partisan loyalties seem to be growing steadily weaker.[6]

Even in its heyday before 1968, party identification was obviously never the sole determinant of voting behavior. If it had been, the Republicans would never have won a presidential election, when in fact they have won more than half of the elections since 1948. This record can be explained in part by the countervailing effects of the two other intervening variables, both of which are growing even more important as party identification weakens.

ISSUE ORIENTATION

A **political issue** is *a disputed question about what government should or should not do.* Much of what we hear about politics in our newspapers and on television—especially during election campaigns—describes conflict between (and often within) the parties over issues. Senator A says that the United States should impose import quotas and tariffs to keep the Japanese from selling us so much more than they buy from us, while Senator B says that prices should be kept free from government meddling and find their true economic level. Some people (perhaps even

SPLIT VOTES AND "COHABITATION"

Political scientists usually consider split-ticket voting only in systems where presidents are directly elected in elections independent of those for members of the legislature—not only in the United States but also in other presidential systems, such as France, Finland, and most of the Latin American democracies. Divided government has in fact happened in France on two occasions when the voters, having previously elected socialist François Mitterand as president, gave control of the National Assembly to a conservative coalition; each time the president and the Assembly dealt with each other in an arrangement the French called "cohabitation." It also happened in Venezuela on two occasions, when the elected presidents were members of the COPEI (Social Christian) party, while the Congresses were controlled by the AD (Democratic Action) party. Also, from 1982 to 1986, Colombia's president was Conservative Belisario Betancur Cuartas, while both houses of Congress were controlled by the Liberal party.

It can also happen in the Federal Republic of Germany, which does not directly elect its head of government. In Chapter 8 we observed that in Germany's hybrid electoral system each voter casts one vote for an *individual* member of the Bundestag for his or her particular constituency and a second vote for the *party* she or he prefers at the national level. This makes it possible to vote for, say, a Christian Democrat as the local representative and the Social Democrats as the favored national party. Not only is it possible, but around 10–15 percent of German voters split their votes in this way at each election.[7] This serves to narrow a bit the gaps between the parties' strengths in the Bundestag, but since the government is always formed by a coalition of parties supported by a majority of the Bundestag's members, American-style divided government is not possible in Germany.

---

some readers of this book) who pay considerable attention to discussions of politics in the mass media assume, quite erroneously as we saw in Chapter 3, that everyone else is as interested in politics as they are and knows as much about issues as they do. Consequently, many students of political science, like many political commentators, tend to exaggerate the influence of issues and ideology on the mass electorate.

Why *exaggerate*? The authors of *The American Voter* correctly point out that in order to have a measurable impact on voting behavior, an issue must fulfill three conditions. First, the voters must be aware of its existence and have opinions about it. Second, it must concern voters enough to influence how they vote. Third, voters must perceive that the position of a particular party or candidate on the issue is nearer to their own position than the opposition's. Only when an issue fulfills all three of these conditions for large numbers of voters can it exert significant influence on the outcome of an election.

Studies of voting behavior demonstrate that the more ideological the parties and the more the voters strongly identify with those parties, the more likely are people's stands on issues to be predictable from their party identifications. This association has generally been weaker in the United States than in other Western democracies, mainly because the American major parties have usually advocated less clear and consistent ideologies than the parties in the other democracies. Since the 1950s, issue voting has noticeably increased in all democratic polities including the United States.[8]

Public opinion studies have consistently shown that from the mid-1960s on, increasing numbers of American voters have perceived significant differences between the policy positions of the Democratic and Republican parties and candidates on some issues, and those perceptions have played increasingly influential roles in their voting choices. This has been especially noticeable in the case of at least two issues of overriding importance in the voters' minds. One instance was the role of the Civil Rights Act in the 1964 presidential election, a law that gave the national government great new powers in guaranteeing all races equal access to public accommodations, education, and job opportunities. Most voters knew that Democratic presidential candidate Lyndon Johnson was strongly in favor of the legislation while Republican presidential candidate Barry Goldwater opposed it. A significant number of Democrats who opposed the legislation voted for Goldwater, while an even larger number of Republicans who favored it voted for Johnson.

Another instance occurred in 1972: Most voters were very concerned with the issue of whether or not the United States should immediately withdraw from the war in Vietnam. Most of them also correctly perceived that Democratic presidential candidate George McGovern favored withdrawal and Republican candidate Richard Nixon opposed it. Among strong Democrats, McGovern received nearly two-thirds of the "dove" vote but only a small fraction of the "hawk" vote. There were relatively few Republican doves, but many more of them than the Republican hawks voted for McGovern. In both instances, then, issue considerations clearly overrode party loyalties for many voters, and the same can be said for a growing number of other issues.[9] In 1980 and 1984 impressive popular majorities voted for Ronald Reagan for president, despite the fact that equally impressive majorities opposed Reagan's positions on a number of major issues, and the same was true for George Bush in 1988. All this suggests that issue voting, while on the rise, is still far from being the only factor that determines American election outcomes.

CANDIDATE ORIENTATION

Candidate orientation means *voters' opinions of candidates' personal qualities considered apart from their party affiliations or stands on issues*. For example, when one votes for Bill Clinton mainly because he is the Democratic candidate, party identification is the prime factor; when one votes for Clinton mainly because he favors women's abortion rights, issue orientation is most prominent; and when one votes for Clinton because of a conviction that he is intelligent and forward-looking, then candidate orientation is the prime factor.

Contrary to what we sometimes read or hear, candidate orientation is never the only consideration in voting and often not even the most important one. Its power varies with several circumstances: the conspicuousness of the office, the type of election, whether things are going well or badly. It is strongest when voters vote directly for the occupant of the office, when voters choose between well-publicized candidates, and when the incumbent is so often in the news that the office is prominent in most voters' minds. It is thus probably at its strongest in elections for the chief executives of the presidential democracies.

This is clearly demonstrated in the case of the United States by the comparison, shown in Figure 9.1, of three different measures of the Democratic party's voting strength in the period from 1952 to 1992. In those 40 years the Democrats' share of voters' party identifications varied between a low of 47 percent in 1984 and a high of 61 percent in 1964, a difference of 14 points. Their share of the total national vote for U.S. representatives varied even less, from a low of 49 percent in 1994 to a high of 57.5 percent in 1964—a difference of 8.5 points. But in presidential voting their share fell as low as 37.5 percent for George McGovern in 1972 and rose as high as 61 percent for Lyndon B. Johnson in 1964—a difference of 23.5 percentage points. Clearly, then, many voters' choices in presidential elections are strongly affected by how they feel about the personal qualities of the candidates.

The great electoral success of Ronald Reagan illustrates the importance of candidate orientation. Reagan is arguably one of the great vote getters in American history: In 1980 he defeated incumbent president Jimmy Carter by the impressive margin of 51 percent of the popular votes to Carter's 41 percent, and in 1984 he was re-elected by the landslide margin of 59 percent to Democrat Walter Mondale's 41 percent. What accounts for his great success? Clearly party identifications played a lesser role, because in both elections Reagan ran as the candidate of the less popular party. What about issue orientation? Certainly, as we saw in Chapter 6, American public opinion was turning more conservative in the 1980s, and perhaps Reagan merely rode the crest of the wave. Yet a good deal of the evidence shows that substantial majorities of the public consistently opposed many of Reagan's most cherished policies, so issue orientation is certainly not the whole explanation.

FIGURE 9.1   Democratic Share of Party Identification and Votes

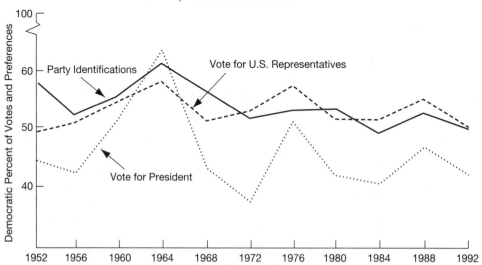

Source: Norman J. Ornstein, Thomas E. Mann, and Michael J. Malbin, *Vital Statistics on Congress, 1993–1994* (Washington, DC: Congressional Quarterly, Inc., 1993), Table 2–2.

Thus candidate orientation—the fact that a lot of Americans liked Reagan the man, as distinct from his Republican affiliation or his conservative policies—had a lot to do with it. Just how much is suggested by the results of an interesting ABC News/Washington Post poll taken in May 1984 just before Reagan started his re-election campaign. They asked their respondents two questions: Do you like Reagan personally? Do you approve of his policies? Thirty-nine percent said they liked *both* Reagan and his policies; 18 percent said they disliked both Reagan and his policies; 11 percent said they disliked Reagan personally but approved of his policies; and 28 percent—the second-largest group—said they liked Reagan personally but disapproved of his policies. Added together, only 50 percent of the respondents approved of his policies, while 67 percent liked him personally.[10] Clearly, then, a good many people who voted for Reagan did so because they liked him personally (candidate orientation) and not because they liked his Republican affiliation (party identification) or because they agreed with all his conservative policies (issue orientation).

Candidate orientation is said to be less significant in the parliamentary democracies, where the prime ministers are not directly elected but achieve office as a result of their parties' winning majorities of the seats in parliament. In some of those nations, however, the personalities of party leaders appear to be growing more and more prominent in election campaigns (the "Americanization of politics" some call it). For example, many analysts believe that the British Conservative party won the general elections of 1979, 1983, and 1987 in part because its leader, Margaret Thatcher, was widely thought to be a much stronger and more determined leader than the leaders of the Labour party. (On the other hand, the Conservatives also won the 1992 general election despite the fact that their new leader, John Major, was regarded more as a nice man than a strong leader.) Other indirectly elected prime ministers whose personalities have notably attracted voters to (or repelled them from) their parties have included Pierre Elliott Trudeau and Brian Mulroney in Canada, Menachem Begin in Israel, Helmut Schmidt in West Germany, and Indira Gandhi in India. Although candidate orientation probably remains more powerful in the presidential than in the parliamentary democracies, it appears to be growing steadily more important in many of the latter.

However, direct election does not in itself guarantee high candidate orientation, for the less prominent the office, the less important are the candidates' personal qualities in affecting the outcome. In many American states, for example, the voters first choose—usually with some confidence—among candidates for president, Congress, governors, and state legislatures. Usually voters are also called upon to choose among candidates for state secretary of state, treasurer, comptroller of public accounts, attorney general, and superintendent of public instruction. When voters have made those choices they still are not finished: They have to vote for county supervisor, clerk, treasurer, sheriff, auditor, clerk of the circuit court, coroner, superintendent of schools, justices of the peace, sanitary commissioners, park commissioners, and recorder of deeds.

By the time voters get down to the contest for recorder of deeds, even the most conscientious are likely to say to themselves, "I don't know either of these candi-

"REVOLUTIONS" SOMETIMES HAPPEN AT THE POLLS. Canadian voters in the 1992 election reduced the number of Conservative MPs from 170 to 2.

dates, I don't know what the recorder of deeds does, I can't imagine that it makes much difference which candidate gets the job, and I'm tired!" So, they either leave that part of the ballot unmarked or, more likely, simply vote for the candidate of their party. Direct elections for such minor offices, we can say with confidence, seldom feature high candidate orientation for anyone except the candidates' relatives. In such situations, party identification remains the most powerful psychological variable intervening between the voters' behavior at elections and the wider context of political events, institutions, and communications.

For Further Reading

*BERELSON, BERNARD, PAUL F. LAZARSFELD, AND WILLIAM N. MCPHEE. *Voting.* Chicago, IL: University of Chicago Press, 1954. Pioneer sample survey study of the 1948 presidential election in Elmira, New York, and summary of findings from other studies of determinants of voting behavior.

*BUTLER, DAVID, AND DONALD STOKES. *Political Change in Britain,* 2nd ed. New York: St. Martin's Press, 1974. The authoritative study of British voting behavior.

CAMPBELL, ANGUS, PHILIP E. CONVERSE, WARREN E. MILLER, AND DONALD E. STOKES. *The American Voter.* New York: John Wiley, l960. Still generally regarded as the leading work on American voting behavior, based on sample surveys for the 1952 and l956 presidential elections.

*DALTON, RUSSELL J., SCOTT C. FLANAGAN, AND PAUL ALLEN BECK, eds. *Electoral Change in Advanced Industrial Democracies.* Princeton, NJ: Princeton University Press, 1984. Analysis of recent changes in voting patterns in a number of Western democratic nations.

*FLANIGAN, WILLIAM H., AND NANCY ZINGALE. *Political Behavior of the American Electorate,* 7th ed. Boston: Allyn & Bacon, 1991. Useful analysis of current patterns in U.S. voting behavior.

JACOBSON, GARY C. *The Electoral Origins of Divided Government, 1946–1988*. Boulder, CO: Westview Press, 1990. Analysis of where and why American voters have so often voted for Republican presidents and Democratic congresses.

JENNINGS, M. KENT, AND THOMAS E. MANN, eds. *Elections at Home and Abroad*. Ann Arbor, MI: University of Michigan Press, 1994. Essays on research on voting behavior in a number of Western democracies.

KEITH, BRUCE E., DAVID B. MAGLEBY, CANDICE J. NELSON, ELIZABETH A. ORR, MARK C. WESTLYE, AND RAYMOND E. WOLFINGER. *The Myth of the Independent Voter*. Berkeley, CA: University of California Press, 1992. Analysis of U.S. voters showing that independent-leaners are more partisan than weak party identifiers.

KEY, V. O., JR. *The Responsible Electorate*. Cambridge, MA: Harvard University Press, 1966. Early emphasis on importance of issue voting.

*LIPSET, SEYMOUR MARTIN. *Political Man*. Baltimore, MD: Johns Hopkins University Press, 1981. Reprint of a comparative survey of preference and participation patterns in many democratic countries.

MAYHEW, DAVID R. *Divided We Govern: Party Control, Lawmaking, and Investigations, 1946–1988*. New Haven, CT: Yale University Press, 1991. Careful examination of legislative outputs in periods of unified and divided party control, concluding that there is little difference between them.

MILLER, WARREN E. *Without Consent: Mass-Elite Linkages in Presidential Politics*. Lexington, KY: University Press of Kentucky, 1988. Analysis of the movement of voters during the Reagan administration, concluding that the major changes in attitudes took place among Republican elites rather than the mass electorate.

*NIE, NORMAN H., SIDNEY VERBA, AND JOHN R. PETROCIK. *The Changing American Voter*. Cambridge, MA: Harvard University Press, 1976. Uses survey data to update *The American Voter*, with emphasis on the rise of issue voting since the 1950s.

*ORNSTEIN, NORMAN, ANDREW KOHUT, AND LARRY MCCARTHY. *The People, the Press, and Politics*. Reading, MA: Addison-Wesley, 1988. A new look at the structure of the American electorate based on a massive public opinion survey sponsored by the Times Mirror Company.

ROSENSTONE, STEVEN J., AND JOHN MARK HANSEN. *Mobilization, Participation, and Democracy in America*. New York: Macmillan, 1993. Survey-based analysis of political participation in the United States.

SUNDQUIST, JAMES L. "The New Era of Coalition Government in the United States," *Political Science Quarterly*, 103: 613–635 (1988–1989). Leading exposition of the view that divided party control damages America's ability to make effective public policies.

Notes

1. The reader should understand the meanings of the following technical terms often used by political scientists:

   Variable: See Chapter 5, footnote 6.

   Dependent variable: A variable whose characteristics are thought to be affected by other variables; roughly equivalent to an effect in a cause-and-effect relationship.

   Independent variable: A variable whose characteristics are thought to affect the status of a dependent variable; roughly equivalent to a cause in a cause-and-effect relationship.

   Intervening variable: A variable whose characteristics are thought to be the channel through which an independent variable affects a dependent variable; see the discussion in the text.

2. Angus Campbell, Philip E. Converse, Warren E. Miller, and Donald E. Stokes, *The American Voter* (New York: John Wiley, 1960), Chapter 2.

3. The figure for 1992 comes from the National Election Study, 1992, made available through the Inter-university Consortium for Political and Social Research.

4. Nebraska elects its state legislators without party labels and so cannot be counted for these purposes.

5. *The Gallup Poll Monthly*, August 1993, p. 45.

6. For evidence of the weakening of party loyalties in European democracies, see the articles in Ivor Crewe and D. T. Denver, eds., *Electoral Change in Western Democracies* (New York: St. Martin's Press, 1985). For the United States, see Martin P. Wattenberg, *The Decline of American Political Parties, 1952–1984* (Cambridge, MA: Harvard University Press, 1986).

7. Eckhard Jesse, "Split-Voting in the FRG," *Electoral Studies*, 7 (April 1988), p. 109–24.

8. For the rise of issue voting in European as well as American elections, see Russell J. Dalton, *Citizen Politics in Western Democracies* (Chatham, NJ: Chatham House, 1988), pp. 192–200.

9. For a detailed survey of the evidence on the rise of issue voting in the United States since the 1950s, see Robert S. Erikson, Norman R. Luttbeg, and Kent L. Tedin, *American Public Opinion* (New York: Macmillan, 1988), pp. 252–71.

10. ABC News/Washington Post poll quoted in Austin Ranney, ed., *The American Elections of 1984* (Durham, NC: Duke University Press, 1985), Table 1.4, p. 34.

10

[P]olitical parties created democracy and . . . modern democracy is unthinkable save in terms of the parties. . . . The most important distinction in modern political philosophy, the distinction between democracy and dictatorship, can be made best in terms of party politics. The parties are not therefore merely appendages of modern government; they are in the center of it and play a determinative and creative role in it.[1]

Political Parties and Party Systems

Political Parties in Democratic Systems

WHAT IS A POLITICAL PARTY?

Political parties are a special kind of political organization. In both democratic and authoritarian regimes they differ from other political associations, such as presssure groups, in that only parties have all of the following fundamental characteristics:

1. They are groups of people to whom *labels*—"Republican," "Communist," "Liberal," and so on—are generally applied by themselves and others.

2. Some of the people are *organized*—that is, they deliberately act together to achieve common goals.

3. The larger society recognizes as *legitimate* the right of parties to organize and promote their causes.

4. In some of their goal-promoting activities, parties work through the *mechanisms of representative government, such as elections and legislatures*.

5. A key activity of parties is thus *selecting candidates* for elective public office.

By those criteria, then, a political party differs from a group like consumers because it is organized. It differs from a group like the American Medical Association because it nominates candidates and puts them forth in elections with its own label. Pressure groups, as we learned in Chapter 1, resemble political parties in many respects. They often take part in elections by endorsing candidates, raising money, issuing campaign propaganda, and ringing doorbells. But most pressure groups are concerned mainly with what government *does* while parties are equally or more concerned with who holds office. The "who" and "what" of government are not completely separate, of course, but parties generally put greater emphasis on the "who" aspect, as demonstrated by the fact that candidates run for office with official party labels. Pressure groups do not provide this kind of sponsorship and are more concerned with the "what" aspect of government.

PARTY IDENTIFICATION AND MEMBERSHIP

Identifiers, Supporters, and Members

In Chapter 9 we saw that most citizens in most modern democratic nations have some party identification; that is, some degree of preference for a particular political party over other parties. We also noted that most people acquire their party identifications early in life; that the identifications tend to grow stronger as people grow older; and that, although in recent years party identifications have weakened in many Western democracies, they are still a major influence on voting behavior and constitute one of the most stable and powerful factors affecting the outcomes of free elections.

However, being a *member* of an organization usually means something different from being an identifier or a supporter. The loyal Green Bay Packers fan who attends all the games, cheers the team, jeers the opposition, and offers free (though unheeded) advice to the coach is a team identifier and supporter, but no one would call the fan a team *member*. Membership implies that one assumes obligations to the organization and at the same time has access to the organization's decision-making processes. Accordingly, a person who tells a Gallup poll interviewer "I am a Democrat" but never contributes money, attends rallies, hands out leaflets, or makes any contribution to the party other than occasionally voting for its candidates is, like our Packers fan, an identifier and occasional supporter but not a member. Hence, **party membership** means *formal attachment to a political party, usually involving the assumption of obligations to the party and receiving privileges from the party.*

Party Membership Rules

In most democracies other than the United States, political parties are purely private organizations, like bowling leagues or garden clubs. Few if any laws regulate how they manage their affairs. All matters—including membership requirements and admission procedures—are controlled by the rules each party makes and enforces for itself.

Most parties in most countries other than the United States have at least mildly demanding requirements. They usually require a person to apply formally for membership, and party officials can accept or reject the application (though in fact they are almost always accepted). To continue as a party member in good standing, the person must at least pay annual dues (usually the equivalent of only $5 or $10 per year) and sometimes also take an oath to support the party's principles and candidates. Moreover, the party can expel a member for nonpayment of dues, deserting the party's principles, supporting the candidates of opposition parties, and the like (although such expulsions are very rare). The number of people willing to make this kind of commitment varies substantially from one party to another and from one nation to another: For example, the parties of Great Britain taken together have only about 1,500,000 dues-paying members, while in Sweden one party alone (the Social Democrats) has 1 million members out of an adult population of about 8 million. In general, however, only 1 to 3 percent of the adults in most democracies are formal party members, and the numbers are declining in many countries.[2]

Political parties in the United States operate quite differently. In most states, party membership requirements are fixed by law in order to control who can vote in a particular party's direct primary elections (see Chapter 8). To qualify as a Republican in a closed-primary or crossover-primary state, for example, a voter must publicly state a preference for the Republican party to registration officials before the voter can vote in Republican primaries. The law usually permits a party representative to challenge a voter's declared party choice, but voters need only make sworn statements of their sincerity and there the matter ends. Such challenges are extremely rare, so a simple self-declaration is in fact the only test any American has to pass in order to become a Democrat or a Republican. In open-primary states, citizens may vote in the primary of either party without even having to state their choices publicly. Accordingly, the American Democratic and Republican parties are unique among the world's parties in that the party leaders do not control admissions to party membership, and there is no formal difference between members and participants.

Many political scientists believe that those wide-open membership rules are a major cause of the weakness of American parties and their lack of clear and consistent programs. Whether this is true or not, in several states (California, New York, and Wisconsin are leading examples) some party activists have tried to overcome the effects of loose legal membership by imitating parties in other democracies. They have established dues-paying party "clubs," which operate outside the legal machinery, support particular candidates in primaries, and take on the main burden of raising funds and campaigning. However, in most states, party members are simply people who designate themselves as such prior to voting in party primaries.

Members and Activists

Although party membership in most democratic systems involves more than simple self-designation, all the members of any party are never equally active or influential in party affairs. As in any human organization, some members—whom we will call *activists* (in some countries the term is *militants*)—feel especially strongly about their party's goals, devote much time and energy to its affairs, and consequently have the most to say about what the party does.

To give just one illustration, membership in the British Conservative party is open to anyone who declares his or her support of the party's "objects," and pays dues equivalent to about two dollars a year to the local Conservative constituency association. The average membership of those associations is around 5,000, but only a few—estimated at 1 to 3 percent of those enrolled—are consistently active in association affairs. Most of the time those few dominate the only important business of the local associations, which is selecting parliamentary candidates for their constituencies.

Almost every democratic party's activists differ from its identifiers and members in several significant respects. The most important is the fact that the activists' political philosophies and policy preferences are generally more extreme than those of the party's identifiers in the electorate. This is true not only of the "missionary" parties but also of the "broker" parties (those terms will be discussed later), such as the American Democrats and Republicans. A recent illustration of this was provided by *The New York Times* in 1988. The *Times* asked a sample of the delegates to the Democratic and Republican national party conventions—most of whom fit our activists category—a series of questions about their personal political ideologies and views on the leading issues in the campaign, and then compared their answers with answers to the same questions given by a sample of each party's identifiers and by a sample of all adults. The answers given by each group are presented in Table 10.1.

The figures in Table 10.1 show that Democratic party activists are substantially more liberal than ordinary Democratic identifiers, Republican party activists are substantially more conservative than ordinary Republican identifiers, and partisans on both sides are ideologically more extreme than the general adult population.

This situation is normal for democratic political parties, and it poses a real dilemma for party leaders. On the one hand, the leaders have to satisfy the ideological activists in order to win leadership posts; on the other hand, the leaders also have to satisfy the more moderate party identifiers and the still more moderate general public if they hope to win elections. Perhaps that is why it is so difficult to become—and remain—a popular and successful party leader.

TABLE 10.1   Convention Delegates, Party Identifiers, and General Public on Issues, 1988 (in percentages)

	DEMOCRATIC DELEGATES	DEMOCRATIC VOTERS	TOTAL ADULTS	REPUBLICAN VOTERS	REPUBLICAN DELEGATES
Call themselves conservatives	5	22	30	43	60
Call themselves liberals	39	25	20	12	1
Prefer smaller government giving fewer services	16	33	43	59	87
Prefer larger government giving more services	58	56	44	30	3
Favor increased federal spending on education	90	76	71	67	41
Favor increased federal spending on day care and after-school care for children	87	56	52	44	36
Say abortion should be legal, as it is now	72	43	40	39	29
Say government is paying too little attention to needs of blacks	68	45	34	19	14
Favor defense spending at least at current level	32	59	66	73	84
More worried about Communist takeover in Central America than about U.S. involvement in a war there	12	25	37	55	80

Source: *The New York Times*, August 14, 1988, p. 14.

PRINCIPAL ACTIVITIES OF PARTIES

Selecting Candidates

From the standpoint of democratic government, selecting candidates is the most important activity of a political party. The nominating process, as we saw in Chapter 8, plays a crucial role in the selection of public officials. In all democratic countries parties virtually monopolize nominations, which gives them tremendous power to shape governments and policies. Parties also accomplish a task that must be accomplished if the voters are to have manageable and meaningful choices.

The process of candidate selection is also important for success at the polls and for internal control of the parties themselves. For one thing, the ability to make *binding* nominations—nominations that are regularly accepted and supported by most of the party's workers and members—is vital to winning elections. For another, control of the party's nominations is the principal source of power in any political party. Those who control candidate selection control most matters vital to the party: the image it presents to the electorate; the choice and phrasing of its official policies; and the distribution of the patronage and power it acquires by winning elections. Accordingly, most party leaders and activists believe that winning struggles with opposing factions inside the parties over nominations is at least as important as winning contests with the opposition parties for elective office.

On the basis of the studies of candidate selection in a number of democratic countries, we can say that selection processes vary substantially from one nation to another on several dimensions.

CENTRALIZATION   At one extreme, all power over the selection of party candidates for all elective offices is centralized in a national party agency. At the other extreme, power is dispersed among regional and local party organizations. A good example of highly centralized selection processes are those of the Israeli parties. In Israel the entire nation is a single parliamentary constituency. Each party submits one national list of up to 120 candidates for the Knesset (the one-house national legislature). Each list is prepared by the party's national executive committee or comparable inner circle, and, although the selectors usually try to achieve reasonable geographic balance in their list, the choice of particular names and of their order on the list is entirely in the hands of the leaders. The order of the names is important because the party is sure to receive well less than half of all the popular votes cast and can elect only the percentage of its candidates that corresponds to its percentage of the popular votes. Those successful candidates are taken from the top of the party's list one at a time until the party has filled all the seats to which it is entitled. Thus if a party wins 36 percent of the popular votes it is entitled to forty-three seats filled by the top forty-three names on the party list. Hence, the party leaders can place candidates they like at the top of the list and, in effect, veto candidates they dislike by keeping them off the list entirely or by putting them so far down on it that they have no chance of election. It is a considerable power.

At the opposite extreme are the Democratic and Republican parties of the United States. To be sure, each party's presidential candidate is selected at a national convention, but the convention is made up mainly of delegates already pledged to particular candidates and chosen by state direct primaries and conventions. Furthermore, each party's 100 senatorial and 435 congressional candidates are selected in *local* (state or district) direct primaries or (rarely) conventions, and neither the national committee, the national chairperson, nor any other party agency has the power to veto any candidate locally selected.

Somewhere between the Israeli and U.S. extremes are the nominating systems of most other democratic parties. In Great Britain, for example, national agencies of both the Conservative and Labour parties have the power to veto any locally chosen candidate and also have limited opportunities to place candidates in constituencies they are likely to win. However, both parties have rarely used their veto powers, and more often than not their efforts at placing particular candidates in particular constituencies have been blocked by local constituency organizations who indignantly refused to submit to national orders. In Norway, on the other hand, each party's list in each of the twenty parliamentary constituencies is chosen by a provincial nominating convention made up of delegates from the party organizations in the cities, towns, and rural communes of the constituency. The decisions they make are final, and the national party agencies have no power to participate in the nominations or veto the results.

PARTICIPATION   Another important dimension of candidate selection is participation, that is, the degree to which rank-and-file party members are guaranteed the opportunity to participate in selecting the candidates. At one extreme the selection process is controlled by a small party elite operating behind closed doors with no opportunity for other party members to influence the selection. At the other extreme the process is open to all party members, and the candidate is selected publicly on the basis of receiving a larger number of all the members' votes than any of the rivals.

No actual selection system falls entirely at either extreme. The Israeli system is probably the most nearly closed, and the U.S. system is the most nearly open. But even in the United States the wide-open selection processes called for by direct-primary laws in many states and localities are sometimes dominated by small groups of party "slate makers," who choose candidates in secret and then push them in the primaries. In most situations, however, it is dangerous to make such a move, for few things can devastate a candidate's chances of winning a primary more than being seen as "the candidate of the party bosses." Thus, where the formal procedures appear to provide an entirely open process in U.S. parties, the political facts may sometimes, but not often, make it closed.

Election Campaigning

Once their nominees have been selected, most democratic parties play major roles in conducting and financing the campaigns to get them elected. In this area, as in many others, U.S. party organizations are less active and important than their counterparts in other democracies, and their role in financing and managing presidential and congressional campaigns has all but vanished. U.S. party organizations have been largely replaced by a new breed of "political consultants," whose leaders include Roger Ailes, David Garth, Robert Squier, and Robert Teeter. Those professionals, hired by the candidates for substantial fees, organize high-tech campaigns that feature such up-to-date (and costly) techniques as raising money by computerized direct-mail solicitations, preparing and buying choice air time for spot advertisements on television, and conducting and analyzing polls to determine how the candidate's "packaging" is affecting his or her popularity with the voters. The "old pols," the national, state, and county party chairpersons and committee members who used to direct campaigns, are now out of the picture almost entirely.

Such high-tech electioneering is increasingly prominent in all democratic nations (where it is sometimes deplored as the "Americanization of politics"). Even so, in most democracies parties continue to play major roles in political campaigns, and party campaigning is still the principal organized activity that arouses popular interest in elections and stimulates citizens to vote. This is less true in the United States, but even there party labels if not party organizations play noteworthy roles. As we learned in Chapter 9, the more Americans identify with a party, the more likely they are to vote and to participate in politics in other ways. Americans with the weakest party identifications are the least active. If maximum participation in the election of public officials is as desirable as most students of democracy think, then political parties deserve a large measure of praise—which they do not always receive—for encouraging participation more effectively than any other social organization.

Organizing Government

Every modern democratic government requires a great deal of organization. If all government officials acted entirely on their own without any mutual consultation or cooperation, chaos would surely result. In Chapters 11 through 14 we will consider some of the main agencies that conduct modern democratic governments. We should recognize here, however, that official agencies do not do the job alone. In every modern democratic country the successful candidates of each political party form some kind of party organization within the government. For example, the legislators belonging to a particular party usually join together in a caucus or group; they select policy committees and floor leaders; they determine who will serve on what legislative committees; and they consult on matters of legislative policy and strategy. The parties thus backstop the formal organization of the legislature with informal party organizations and thereby give some order and direction to the legislature's activities. More on this in Chapter 11.

Differences Among Parties in Democratic Systems ——————

IN THE NATURE AND ROLE OF IDEOLOGY

Every democratic party adopts some sort of platform or program, some set of published statements about how its candidates will use government power if elected. The platforms of some parties in some countries are mainly restatements and elab-

A DEMOCRATIC TRANSFER OF POWER. In January 1995 House Democratic minority leader Richard Gephardt handed the gavel to Speaker Newt Gingrich, leader of the new Republican majority.

orations of one or another of the ideologies we reviewed in Chapter 4. The platforms of other parties say relatively little about ideologies and focus mainly on the parties' proposed solutions to specific problems that especially concern voters at the time of the election. Political scientists have found it useful to classify most political parties as belonging to one or another of the following two main types according to the nature of their ideologies and the role those ideologies play in shaping party attitudes, programs, and operations.

Missionary Parties

At one extreme on this dimension are **missionary parties**, which are *parties whose principal aim is to win converts for their ideologies, not to maximize their votes so as to win elections.* As an example, let us consider the Socialist Workers party (SWP) of the United States. This party is dedicated to "non-communist Marxism." That is, its members believe that true Marxism (as opposed to what they think is its corrupted form in, say, Cuba and the People's Republic of China) is the key not only to understanding what society is now but also to fixing goals for the society and the party.

As Marxists, they believe that the core of history and society is the conflict between those who control wealth (the bourgeoisie) and the workers (the proletariat). History's final destination is victory for the proletariat, followed by the establishment of a classless society. The SWP is convinced that history and truth are on its side. The party's electioneering activities seek not votes but converts. Although the vast majority of Americans share few, if any, of its beliefs, the SWP will not change its ideology to become more popular. The SWP believes that if the party's ideology is rejected by the voters, then it is the voters who must change and not the ideology. The ideology is believed to be *true*, and no part of it may be changed or softened in an effort to gain popularity. The SWP's strategy for winning power (if indeed it has such a goal) is to convert the masses gradually, over many decades or even centuries if need be. In the 1992 presidential election the SWP's party's presidential candidate, James Warren, polled only 23,096 votes of the national total of 104,425,014 (two one-hundredths of 1 percent), but none of the party faithful thought this was any sign whatever that the party was not doing what it should be doing. In this sense, then, the SWP is a missionary party, as are many European parties and some other American parties, such as the Prohibition party and the Libertarian party. Some European Social Democratic and Christian Democratic parties are not above occasionally altering their ideologies a bit to make themselves more attractive to the voters, but even so they are much closer to the missionary type than are the major parties in the English-speaking countries.

Broker Parties

At the other extreme stand the **broker parties**, which are *parties whose main goal is to win elections, and who therefore appeal to as broad a spectrum of interests and ideologies as possible*. Leading examples of such parties are the Democratic and Republican parties of the United States. Neither has a full-fledged ideology, comparable to Marxism or even American-style liberalism or conservatism, that is shared by all its members and activists. The Republican party includes more conservatives and the Democratic party includes more liberals (see Chapter 4); but the Democrats also have a significant number of conservatives, and the Republicans also have some liberals (though nowadays they are generally called "moderates"). In the Democratic party, neither the liberals nor the conservatives can accurately claim to be "the *real* Democrats" if for no other reason than the fact that the law stipulates that anyone who wins a Democratic primary, no matter what his or her philosophy, is every bit as much a Democrat as anyone else who wins a Democratic primary. The same is true for the conservatives and moderates in the Republican party.

Each of the parties appeals to and draws voters from every major interest group in the nation. Rather than trying to convert people to the one true ideology, as the SWP does, Democrats and Republicans try to put together a program that will attract support from the greatest number of voters. The Democratic and Republican parties measure their success not by whether their programs, leaders, and supporters rigidly follow a particular ideology but by how many candidates they elect.

Some critics, especially those who are dedicated Marxists or devotees of laissez faire, are contemptuous of the Democrats and Republicans and all other broker parties. They do not stand for anything (as one critic put it, "They are two bottles with different labels, but both are empty"); they paper over the vital political conflicts between rich and poor, African-American and white, male and female; and they provide the voters not with real alternatives but with meaningless choices between the Tweedledees and the Tweedledums.

These criticisms have merit if—and only if—we concede that only a choice between, say, a Communist party and a Fascist party is a real choice. There is strong evidence, however, that many Americans think that there are a number of important differences between the Democratic and Republican parties, more than enough to justify choosing one over the other. A recent illustration of this fact is provided by Figure 10.1, which arrays the answers given by Americans in 1994 to the question of which party is best able to deal with a range of national problems.

FIGURE 10.1   Do You Think the Republican Party or the Democratic Party Would Do a Better Job Dealing with These Problems?

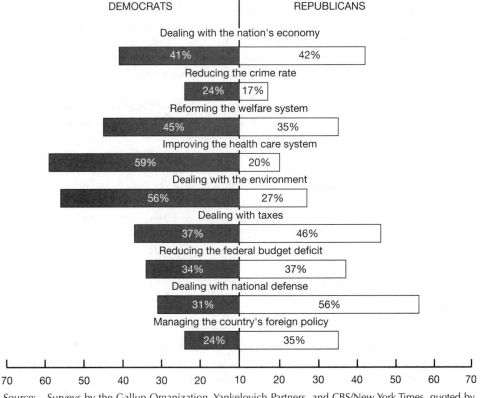

Source: Surveys by the Gallup Organization, Yankelovich Partners, and CBS/New York Times, quoted by *The American Enterprise*, March/April, 1994, pp. 79–80.

The other democratic parties of the world can be ranged between the mission-ary and broker extremes. The Liberal and Progressive Conservative parties of Canada, for example, are almost as much broker parties as the major U.S, parties. The British, Australian, and New Zealand Conservative and Labour parties have somewhat more clearly defined ideologies, but they too are more broker than missionary parties. The left-wing (Communist, Socialist) and right-wing (Conservative, Monarchist) parties of most European democracies fall nearer the missionary extreme.

IN CENTRALIZATION

Most parties in the democracies maintain organizations at the national, regional, and local election-district levels. They differ sharply, however, in the way in which they distribute power among the various levels. Those differences can be most clearly seen by noting the various methods by which the parties select their candidates.

From this standpoint, the U.S. Democratic and Republican parties are the most decentralized in the world. Their national conventions nominate only candidates for president and vice president. Moreover, today even those conventions are domi-nated by the organizations developed by particular presidential aspirants and by in-traparty pressure groups such as the women's caucus, the African-American caucus, and the pro-life and pro-choice caucuses. Candidates for the U.S. Senate are nomi-nated in state primary elections, and candidates for the House of Representatives are nominated in district primaries. If the national leaders of either party object to a par-ticular person running in a state or district primary because he or she is not a "true Democrat" or a "real Republican," they are helpless to block the nomination if the unwanted candidate wins the primary.

On a few occasions in the past, a popular national party leader has intervened in local primaries trying to prevent unacceptable local candidates from being nom-inated, but all have failed. A notable example was President Franklin D. Roosevelt's attempt in 1938 to defeat in the primaries twelve Democratic members of Congress who had opposed his New Deal programs. Popular as FDR was, eleven of the twelve were renominated. Roosevelt failed, as all such efforts in U.S. parties have failed, because the national leaders have been unable to win the help of local organizations and because many voters and party leaders have resented such interventions as out-rageous violations of their rights and prerogatives.

Thus, in the Democratic and Republican parties, power over nominations—the main objective of the leaders of any major democratic party—is highly decen-tralized. Instead of being controlled at the national level, candidate selection is in the hands of state, county, and district party organizations as well as pressure groups and temporary candidate organizations.

The United States is not the only democratic country with decentralized par-ties. Many European conservative parties are little more than loose federations of local associations and leading parliamentary personalities. In Switzerland, all the major parties, with the possible exception of the Social Democrats, are organized mainly in the cantons (governing regions below the national level, similar to but more powerful than American states). The Swiss national parties are even looser federations of local parties than those in the United States. There are no outstanding national party leaders, but only leading local figures who are generally unknown to most people outside their own areas. In the Scandinavian countries, candidates for the national parliaments are generally selected by district committees or conventions, and national party leaders can only advise on who should and should not be selected.

Most democratic parties are more centralized in their nominating procedures and other activities. In Great Britain, for example, the local Conservative and Labour constituency associations select candidates for Parliament, but national party agencies have the power to veto candidates. The Conservatives have used this power very seldom and Labour somewhat more often. Still, both are considerably more centralized than most parties in Switzerland and Scandinavia. Canadian parties, despite their federal organizations, nominate candidates much as British parties do. In most European nations, which use the party-list form of proportional representation (see Chapter 8), national party agencies select the candidates for their lists and determine the order in which they will appear on the ballot.

IN DISCIPLINE

In any human organization, **discipline** means *the leaders' control of the members obtained by dispensing rewards and imposing sanctions.*

The leaders of every democratic political party possess disciplinary weapons, but some weapons are more effective than others. For example, presidents of the United States can, if they wish, give patronage jobs to a few obedient members of their parties and withhold jobs from party rebels and mavericks. Presidents can also make their public support of their parties' other candidates dependent on those candidates' support of presidential policies. Presidents can even try to defeat in party primaries candidates who oppose presidential programs. None of those weapons is very effective, however. Presidents have little patronage to hand out. In addition, most candidates for Congress do not need presidential support to be elected. They know it and presidents know it. Finally, as we have seen, presidents have never been successful in "purging" unwanted candidates by intervening in congressional and senatorial primaries. Presidential discipline in both American parties thus involves little more than persuasion and coaxing. All presidents, as even Franklin Roosevelt and Bill Clinton learned, must expect considerable opposition to some policies from members of their own parties.

The leader of a British major party is in a much stronger position. All the members of the party in Parliament know that when "the whip is laid on" (that is, when the party leader tells the members how to vote on a particular bill), the members risk their political careers if they disobey. The prime minister controls who gets the ministerial offices, and the leader of the opposition party controls who will get them when it wins power. Since the ordinary member of Parliament (MP) cannot, as in the United States, rise to power and influence through seniority, the only road to political success is through the good will of the party leaders. Also, as we have seen, the national party organization, which the leader controls, can veto the renomination of MPs who get out of line and thus deny them their parliamentary seats (though the veto is seldom used). But the leader's greatest power comes from the fact that in the British parliamentary system, control of the government is in the hands of the majority-party "team." When that team can no longer muster majority support in Parliament, a new election must be held. Therefore, any MP's vote against his or her party is, in effect, a vote to put or keep the other party in power. It is not surprising, then, that party discipline in Britain is widely (though not universally) regarded as a vital underpinning for the nation's version of parliamentary democracy.

Most of the missionary parties of Europe and Scandinavia give their national leaders the power to expel from the party members of the national parliament who refuse to vote the party line. While expulsion from the party is less likely than in Britain to result in the loss of the individual's seat in the parliament, he or she may no longer take a part in the party's decision making. As a disciplinary weapon, therefore, this is somewhat less powerful than the British party leaders' vetoes, but it is much more powerful than any weapon available to American party leaders.

IN COHESION

The differences in centralization and discipline are reflected in different degrees of cohesion within various democratic parties. As the term is normally used, a party's **cohesion** is *the extent to which party members holding public office act together on policy issues*. If a party's legislative members vote alike on every issue, it is said to have perfect legislative cohesion. If a party's legislative members split fifty-fifty on every issue, it is said to have zero legislative cohesion.

Democratic parties vary widely in cohesion. The major British parties are among the most cohesive, for on almost every issue each party can count upon all of its members in the House of Commons to vote as the party leaders direct. On the few occasions in which some members have not supported the leaders' policies, the dissenters have been more likely not to vote at all than to vote against the leaders' wishes. Since the mid-1970s there has been some increase in the number of such occasions. Even so, the parties can count on the support of all their members over 90 percent of the time.

At the other extreme, some small parliamentary parties in France split on almost every public issue and therefore have little or no legislative cohesion. The other democratic parties fall somewhere between those two extremes. The larger French, Scandinavian, and German parties, for example, are almost—but not quite—as cohesive as the British parties. The American parties in Congress, though relatively uncohesive, are more cohesive than the smaller French parties. In the various American state legislatures, the parties cover almost the entire range of cohesion, from very high to very low. In Italy until recently, party cohesion could not be measured because votes in parliament were cast by secret ballot and it was impossible to say whether the members of a particular party stuck together or not.

The variations in ideologies, centralization, discipline, and cohesion of each nation's parties have a considerable impact on the way in which the parties interact with one another in the nation's party *system*. Hence, there are also a number of differences among the types of party systems that operate in modern democracies.

Fractionalization of Democratic Party Systems

In analyzing and comparing political parties in modern democratic nations, political scientists often speak of *party systems*. The term refers to certain general characteristics of party conflict in particular political environments that can be classified according to various criteria. On the basis of the factors described in the preceding section, for example, we can speak of missionary and broker party systems or of centralized and decentralized party systems. However, many political scientists are especially interested in the degree of **party fractionalization**, which is *the degree to which a nation's votes and offices are evenly divided among a large number of parties*. By this standard, the least fractionalized system would be one in which only one political party exists and wins all the votes and offices all the time. At the other extreme, there is no theoretical limit to how high fractionalization can go, but a highly fractionalized system would be one in which a great many parties more or less evenly share both the votes and the public offices. We will consider both levels of fractionalization in the rest of this chapter.

MEASUREMENT: RAE'S INDEX OF FRACTIONALIZATION

Until recently, political scientists generally classified all party systems as either one-party, two-party, or multiparty. However, their techniques for measuring degrees of fractionalization were developed mainly for the analysis and comparison of the party systems of the American states. Those techniques were thus of little use in analyzing the many variations among the European party systems, which were usually lumped together as multiparty systems. To fill this void, Douglas W. Rae devised

CHOICES IN A HIGHLY FRACTIONALIZED PARTY SYSTEM. An Israeli voter contemplates the election posters of over twenty competing parties.

an ingenious index of party fractionalization that can be applied to any party system. Rae's measure taps two dimensions: the *number of parties* receiving shares of the popular vote and seats in the national legislature and the *relative equality* of their shares. At one end of the scale is a model one-party system, in which one party receives all the votes and seats for an index score of 0.00. As we will see, the one-party system of the former Soviet Union fulfilled all those requirements. As the number of parties and the relative equality of their shares of the votes and seats increase, the index score rises. In a theoretically perfect two-party system, two parties would split the votes and seats evenly, for a score of 0.50. If ten parties split the votes and seats evenly, the system would have a score of 0.90.[3]

Table 10.2 presents the fractionalization scores for twenty-five democratic nations, calculated from the results in three recent general elections for members of the lower house of their national legislatures.

For most of the twenty-five nations ranked in Table 10.2, the score for legislative fractionalization was a bit lower than the score for electoral fractionalization. Those data support Rae's conclusion that all electoral systems—even those using proportional representation—discriminate to some degree in favor of the larger parties.

Figure 10.2 makes the general picture more concrete by showing the vote shares and fractionalization scores in recent elections in each of five party systems, covering a wide range of fractionalization, from a score of .4998 for the U.S. system (close to a perfect two-party system score) to one of .7532 for Norway's system.

CHARACTERISTICS OF THE MORE FRACTIONALIZED SYSTEMS

What differences does fractionalization make? The party systems of Western European democratic nations generally rank on the high side of the fractionalization scale. In each of those nations, at least three, and often as many as five or six, parties regularly win enough votes and legislative seats to be called "major" parties. A single party hardly ever wins a majority of the seats, and the cabinets and ministries are composed of coalitions of several parties rather than members of one majority party.

As we saw in Chapter 8, the debate over proportional representation turns partly on whether one believes that a high degree of party fractionalization is a good thing. The critics of highly fractionalized party politics say that it produces unstable and constantly changing governments, splits the nations into hostile camps, and fails to mobilize popular majorities either for or against government programs. This, they say, seriously weakens democracy's ability to survive. They often point to the party systems of Germany's Weimar Republic (1919–1933) and France's Third (1871–1939) and Fourth (1945–1958) republics as examples of the damage that highly fractionalized party systems can do.

The defenders of proportional representation claim that the wide range of party ideologies in the more fractionalized systems accurately reflects the shades of public opinion in their countries and thereby gives the voters truly meaningful choices. Consequently, they contend, such systems come much closer to the ideals of representative democracy than do the kaleidoscopic, all-things-to-all-people parties in the less fractionalized systems.

TABLE 10.2   Party Fractionalization in 25 Democracies, 1977–1988

COUNTRY	AVERAGE FRACTIONALIZATION SCORE	INDEX OF FRACTIONALIZATION*
Belgium	.8464	.3464
Finland	.8340	.3340
Denmark	.8138	.3138
Switzerland	.8041	.3041
Italy	.7357	.2357
Netherlands	.7302	.2302
Israel	.7299	.2299
Portugal	.7191	.2191
Norway	.7175	.2175
Sweden	.6984	.1984
West Germany	.6862	.1862
France	.6527	.1527
Japan	.6447	.1447
Venezuela	.6408	.1408
Ireland	.6152	.1152
Spain	.6152	.1152
India	.5845	.0845
Australia	.5812	.0812
Austria	.5760	.0760
Colombia	.5436	.0436
Greece	.5435	.0435
United Kingdom	.5348	.0348
United States	.4796	.0204
Canada	.4839	.0161
New Zealand	.4931	.0069

Source: Calculated by the author from election returns published in *Keesing's Record of World Events*.

*The difference between the average fractionalization score and .5000. A perfect two-party system would have an index-of-fractionalization score of .0000.

We cannot decide the merits of this debate here, but some things seem clear. First, since a single party almost never wins a majority of all the seats in the national legislature, the countries are typically ruled by **coalition governments**, which are *arrangements in which the government is managed by an alliance of two or more separate parties, each of which has members in the top ministerial posts.*

Second, government instability does not necessarily result from more fractionalized party systems and coalition governments. For example, the party systems of Finland, Denmark, Switzerland, and the Netherlands usually produce coalition governments, but they are just as stable as the governments in nations with less fractionalized systems.

Third, the fractionalization of the party systems does not appear to be a prime *cause* of the deep ideological and social divisions in nations like Italy and Belgium. Most students of Israeli politics believe that the large number of parties in that coun-

FIGURE 10.2   Fractionalization in Five Democratic Elections

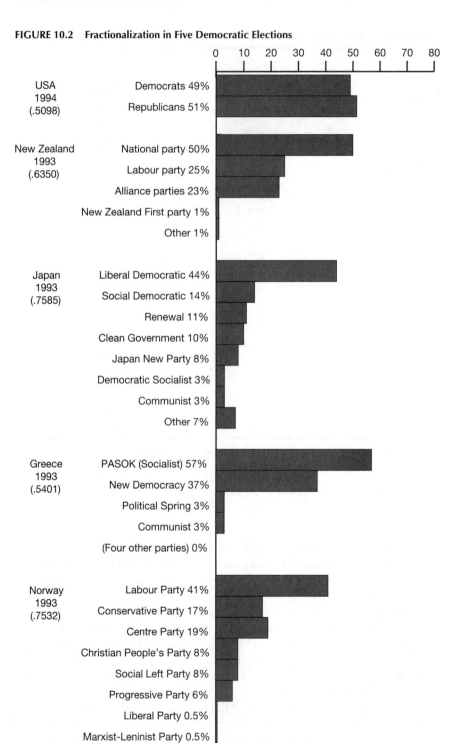

try has resulted from deep ethnic and religious divisions that are far more basic and complex than the particular kind of party system. This is not to say that more fractionalized systems are "better" than less fractionalized ones, but that a nation's party system is only one factor—and in many instances not the most important factor—that determines the nature of its basic political conflict.

CHARACTERISTICS OF THE LESS FRACTIONALIZED SYSTEMS

The party systems of the English-speaking democracies, including those of the United States, Great Britain, New Zealand, Australia, and Canada, are generally less fractionalized than those of Western Europe (see Table 10.2). The major parties of the English-speaking nations differ from one another in various ways, but they are also very similar in certain important respects. Among their leading similarities, four are especially noteworthy.

Broker Parties

The major parties tend to be broker rather than missionary parties. Some, like the various labor and socialist parties, have somewhat more distinct ideologies than the others, but all are more concerned with winning elections here and now than with eventually making permanent converts.

General Appeals

The major parties direct their appeals for votes at all major population groups. The U.S. Republicans and the British Conservatives, for example, never say to labor union members, "We stand for business first, last, and always, and if we get power, we intend to destroy the unions!" Rather they say, "We stand for the welfare of *both* labor and business. If you want fair and decent treatment for labor and management alike, vote for us instead of them." Their programs and platforms are not as clear and logically consistent as those of the missionary parties, because those statements are intended to win as many votes as possible from many, often incompatible interests.

Moderate Parties

The major parties are moderate and try to offer programs that will not seriously upset any major interest group. Major parties also try to avoid or postpone taking clear and uncompromising stands on any issues on which the society is sharply divided. Furthermore, extremists in the ranks of either major party must moderate their views as the price of retaining their positions in the party's inner circles.

Narrow Differences between the Parties

The major parties tend to be a lot alike in their basic philosophies and specific programs and agree generally on the basic form of government and the general direction of public policy. When one party replaces the other in power, there is seldom a drastic shift in government policy. For example, in the 1994 elections, the Republicans won control of both houses of Congress for the first time since 1952. Many observers hoped (or feared) that the new majority, led by Speaker Newt Gingrich, would throw out many Democratic programs. However, while the Republican majority (often with the help of some Democrats) did reduce the funding of some programs, they totally abolished very few.

Yet the major parties are not identical, so the voters have real choices. Usually interparty disagreements concern the details of policies and the *pace* at which certain policies should be adopted or abandoned. Consequently, most voters believe that the parties are sufficiently different to justify a preference for one over the other (for a U.S. illustration, see Figure 10.1).

The major American parties, as we have seen, are considerably more decentralized than those in the other English-speaking nations, but otherwise the major parties in all the less fractionalized systems are essentially alike.

Authoritarian One-Party Systems

Authoritarianism is as old as government itself, but authoritarian rule by means of a single all-powerful political party is an invention of the twentieth century. In fact, one clear difference between the governments of Stalin's Soviet Union, Mao's China, Hitler's Germany, and Mussolini's Italy and older authoritarian regimes was the key role played by the single omnipotent party in each of the modern despotisms. In each case the party had many of the trappings of parties in more democratic systems, but none of their competition.

Yet there are different degrees of authoritarianism, as there are of democracy. Hence it is not surprising that there are significant differences among the party systems of modern authoritarian regimes. Western political scientists have paid some attention to those differences, especially in studies of party systems in the new nations of Africa and Asia. But a Polish political scientist, Jerzy J. Wiatr, suggested that it is useful to distinguish among three different subtypes of one-party systems. In order of increasing fractionalization they are (1) **monoparty systems**, in which *only one party is legally permitted to exist*; (2) **hegemonic systems**, in which *several parties are permitted to exist but they run candidates only when allowed to do so by an officially superior party, and no competition between the parties is permitted*; and (3) **dominant systems**, in which *any party may organize and run candidates, but one party wins almost all of the votes and offices because of its hold on the voters' loyalties.*[4]

MONOPARTY SYSTEMS

All democratic parties value democratic government as much as they value their particular social and economic aims. Thus, democratic parties tolerate the existence of opposing parties, use only peaceful and democratic methods to pursue their goals, and peacefully accept the verdicts of the voters in elections. Essential to all democratic party systems is the general acceptance of the principle of *loyal opposition*. This is the principle that a party that opposes a nation's governing party or coalition does so only by constitutionally permitted means, remains—and is recognized as remaining—loyal to the nation and its political system, seeks to overthrow the party in power only by winning elections, and thereby has the right to participate freely in the nation's politics.

The single parties that monopolize the field in communist and fascist regimes resemble democratic parties only on the surface. They are more like armies in combat, and many of them use military terms *(vanguard, phalanx, spearhead)* to describe themselves and their operations. An even better comparison is that between a totalitarian party and a militant religious order. Every totalitarian party arises from and is committed to a kind of secular religion, each with its sacred texts *(Das Kapital, Mein Kampf)*, its prophets (Marx, Lenin, Hitler), its total explanation of the nature of society (dialectical materialism, the genetic superiority of the Aryan race), and its ethical system (the end justifies the means). The party has its "priesthood" and its "missionaries," and no doubt also its less-than-fanatical members and supporters.

Many in the democratic world are puzzled over why communist and fascist regimes bother with the democratic trappings of political parties at all. When we look a little more closely at the authoritarian monoparty systems, however, we can see that the ruling party performs several roles that the rulers need performed.

In the nations in which there is a single legal political party, such as Cuba and the People's Republic of China, those pseudodemocratic trappings make it possible for tightly knit, well-organized, and devoted oligarchies (small groups of all-powerful leaders) to operate the formal governing structures more efficiently. Second, they provide useful psychological and organizational bridges between the nations' masses and their rulers, bridges that older, more aristocratic oligarchies lacked, with the result that they were more vulnerable to revolts by the masses.

In those and other respects, then, communist and fascist parties are essentially alike. To see how they differ, let us briefly examine each type of monoparty system.

Communist Monoparty Systems

THE LENINIST-STALINIST PROTOTYPE   From 1917 to 1989 the single-party system of the Soviet Union was the oldest and most powerful of the communist monoparty systems, and served as the model not only for all other communist systems but also for many aspects of the fascist systems. Briefly stated, its main features were the following: The Communist Party of the Soviet Union (CPSU) was the only legal party, and any attempt to form a rival party was punished as treason. The party was intended to be not a massive organization of all Soviet citizens but an elite cadre of the people best educated in and dedicated to the principles of communism. Accordingly, a person could be admitted to the CPSU only after years of training and screening in party youth organizations, and less than 10 percent of Soviet citizens were CPSU members. The party's decisions were made by the principle of "democratic centralism," according to which free discussion of policy choices was permitted within party ranks (not, of course, outside the party) before a decision was made. However, after the decision was made all party members had to sup-

*LEADERS OF A MONOPARTY GOVERNMENT.
A meeting of the Chinese Communist party's
leaders.*

port it enthusiastically. Finally, the CPSU acted as "the government of the government"; that is, every executive, legislative, administrative, and judicial agency of the formal government at all levels had a parallel CPSU organization, which staffed its major posts and in fact made all its decisions.

All that is gone now. As we observed in Chapter 4, in 1990 the USSR held its first free, multi-candidate election for the national legislature, and the new legislature amended the constitution to abolish the CPSU's legal monopoly of power. In most of the constituent republics the CPSU received very little support in the free elections, and in many of the republics the CPSU went out of business altogether. After the aborted coup of 1991, the CPSU was banned. Much the same happened in the Eastern European "people's republics," whose Communist parties also lost their longstanding monopolies of office and power. However, while the old Communist parties have been outlawed in the Eastern bloc countries and in the new republics that formerly constituted the Soviet Union, some of the leaders and supporters of those parties have formed new parties with new names and (partly) new programs, and in some places they have fared well in the new multi-candidate elections.

THE LEFTOVERS   By the early 1990s the only remaining examples of old-style communist monoparty regimes were the People's Republic of China, Cuba (where all power belongs to Fidel Castro's Partido Communista de Cuba), and North Korea where the Korean Workers Party (for several decades commanded by "the great leader," Kim Il Sung, and later by his son, Kim Jong Il) continues to monopolize power. Since it is by far the largest and most important leftover, the Chinese system deserves a brief description.

The Chinese Communist Party (CCP) is similar to the old CPSU in many respects. It is the only legal party, and, as the world learned from the ruthless suppression of democratic dissent in Tiananmen Square in 1989, efforts to form rival movements to challenge its power are prosecuted as treason. Like the CPSU, the CCP is not a mass organization, but an elite of Communist leaders; only about 40 million persons in China's population of over 1 billion are members. Only persons approved by the CCP can be elected to public office, and there is only one candidate for each office in elections. The CCP also lays great stress on "democratic centralism" in making its decisions, but in practice this means that the party's national Politburo not only makes all the decisions but decides what can and cannot be openly discussed by other party members and ordinary citizens. The CCP is also the "government of the government," in that each agency of the formal government at all levels has a parallel party organization, which holds the top posts and controls the actions of the formal agency.[5]

Fascist Monoparty Systems

In its pre-1945 Italian and German versions, fascism, like communism, was a kind of secular religion at war with all other ideologies. It had its sacred texts and prophets, its total explanation of society, and its ethical system. It too regarded its single chosen party as a priesthood of true believers dedicated to spreading the doctrine and converting or eliminating unbelievers. Even though fascism glorified the nation and the race, while communism glorified the Soviet Union and the international working class, the two ideologies organized their parties and governments in similar ways.

The Fascist party in Mussolini's Italy from 1922 to 1943 and the National Socialist German Workers' (Nazi) party in Hitler's Germany from 1933 to 1945 were the only legal parties in their respective nations. The structure of each party paralleled the structure of the formal government and became the government of the government. As in Communist one-party systems, the Fascist parties acted both as ruling bodies and as agencies for whipping up mass support for the leaders' policies.

In the organization of Fascist parties the *Führerprinzip* (leadership principle) was officially more important than it was in Leninist-Stalinist Communist party organizations, although in practice neither Hitler nor Mussolini dominated his party or nation more completely than Lenin and Stalin dominated theirs. Both the Fascist and Nazi parties were organized like armies. The Duce and the Führer were absolute commanders in chief, and the black-shirted Fasci di Combattimento, the brown-shirted storm troopers, and the black-uniformed elite guard (SS) were the "shock troops."

People became members of the Fascist parties mainly through prior service in their youth organizations, the Italian Balilla and Avenguardia and the German Hitler Youth for people from the ages of six to twenty-one. Both parties conducted periodic purges (including the murderous Nazi "blood purge" of 1934) to eliminate all but the most fanatical members. Like the communist parties, both were intended to be elites rather than unselective mass organizations.

DOMINANT PARTY SYSTEMS

In Democratic Systems

From 1854 to the late 1970s, no Republican candidate was elected to any state office in Louisiana. In most elections no Republican even bothered to run, and the few who did rarely received more than 5 percent of the votes. During the same period the Democrats did only a little better in Vermont. After the Republican party was founded in 1854, the Democrats did not win any Vermont state office until 1958 and they have never held more than a small fraction of the seats in the state legislature. In Great Britain, the Welsh coal-mining constituency of Ebbw Vale has for decades given Labour candidates majorities of 75 percent or more. In France many working-class districts in Paris, Lyons, and Lille regularly give comparable majorities to the Communist party.

In short, every democratic nation has areas with "dominant party systems." But those systems differ from the monoparty systems of the dictatorial regimes in one vital respect: Rival parties are not outlawed, nor are their ideologies and programs suppressed. Rival parties have the same opportunities to win votes and offices as the dominant parties, and over the years rival parties may even gradually increase their support, as the Democrats have in Vermont and the Republicans have in Louisiana and most of the South.

In Developing Nations

A few developing nations—Oman and Saudi Arabia, for example—do not pretend to have government by popular election of public officials, so they do not permit political parties of any kind. But most developing nations go through the motions of popular elections, and some honor their substance as well.

About a quarter of the developing nations have monoparty systems based more or less on communist or fascist models. Only one party is legally permitted, and efforts to form opposition parties are considered treason. The official party is usually a version of the political movement that originally won the nation's independence or overthrew its previous regime and is usually dominated by one individual (for example the Arab Socialist Union in Libya by Muammar al-Qaddafi and the Ba'ath Party in Iraq by Saddam Hussein). The dictator generally uses the party much as fascist parties and communist parties do: to tighten national unity by stamping out opposition, to mobilize popular enthusiasm behind the dictator's program, to give the people a sense of participation in government, and to keep the ruler informed on how far a program can be pushed before popular resistance makes it unworkable.

When outsiders criticize those systems, the dictators and their party lieutenants usually reply with the classical fascist and communist party arguments. The official party, they say, represents the whole nation, and opposition to it is opposition to the whole nation: in a word, treason. Quarreling parties and contested elections would only divide the people and make the nation easy prey for its colonialist enemies. They conclude that even if party competition might conceivably be tolerated in times of peace, plenty, and security, that time is not now.

In some other developing nations, party competition is legally tolerated. Parties other than the "National Liberation" party organize, nominate some candidates, contest some elections, and win a few seats in the national legislature. But the National Liberation party regularly wins most of the votes and offices and government power. Most conflicts over public policy are thus fought out within the dominant party rather than in contests between it and opposition parties.

Perhaps the leading example of such a party system has been that of Mexico. The Mexican Revolution of 1910 was followed by two decades of political confusion and instability that were finally ended in 1929 with the establishment of a national party that united most of Mexico's major groups and interests. That party underwent several reorganizations and changes of name, but in 1946 it adopted its present name, the Party of Revolutionary Institutions (PRI). From 1929 to the mid-1980s the PRI was opposed by the Conservative (PAN), Marxist (PPS), and dissident PRI (PARM) parties, but the PRI won all presidential elections by overwhelming margins and held more than 80 percent of the seats in Congress.

In recent years Mexico's increasing economic difficulties and charges of widespread corruption in the government have resulted in increasing discontent with PRI's dominance and have presented a growing challenge, especially by PAN. In the presidential election of 1988 the PRI candidate, Carlos Salinas de Gortari, was challenged as never before not only by the PAN candidate, Manuel Clouthier, but also by Cuanthemoc Cardenas of the National Democratic Front (FDN). For nearly a week after the votes were cast, no results were announced, and there were widespread charges of fraud. In the end, the official election commission declared the PRI candidate the winner, but with only 47 percent of the vote to 27 percent for Cardenas and 21 percent for Clouthier, the first time since the PRI's founding in 1929 that the PRI candidate received less than half of the votes. In the 1994 presidential election the PRI candidate, Ernesto Zedilla, won over two other major candidates, attracting just over half of the popular votes against; and most foreign observers testified that there was little or no fraud. Thus, whatever the future might bring, most in Mexico agreed with Salinas de Gortari's declaration that the day of one-party dominance by the PRI has passed in Mexico.

Nevertheless, a number of commentators continue to believe that, despite its recent failures, the Mexican dominant-party system and others like it in Gabon, Malaysia, and elsewhere provide an important third alternative to the full competition of two-party and multiparty democracies on the one hand and the iron monopolies of power in the authoritarian one-party systems on the other. Those commentators feel that the dominant-party system offers new and struggling nations a way out of what some people see as an impossible choice between too much party competition and none at all. For this reason, if for no other, the dominant-party system deserves to be studied as carefully as the other types of party systems.

Thus political parties and party systems come in many different forms and constitute an important—but not universal—device for organizing modern political systems. As we have seen, democratic and dictatorial regimes alike depend upon parties to perform important tasks. In formulating policies, selecting leaders, and arousing popular support, political parties enable governments to operate in densely populated modern nations. The differences among the kinds of party systems that perform those tasks account for many of the differences between democratic and authoritarian systems.

Some analysts have suggested that modern mass communications, and especially the manner in which television permeates every aspect of modern life, have rendered political parties obsolete. That may or may not be so; but, if it is, then it is far from clear what agencies will replace parties in performing the many functions that have made them vital forces in most modern governments.

For Further Reading

DEMOCRATIC POLITICAL PARTIES

BLACK, GORDON S. AND BENJAMIN D. BLACK. *The Politics of American Discontent*. New York: John Wiley, 1993. Argument that the United States needs a new third party to deal effectively with the nation's problems.

*DUVERGER, MAURICE. *Political Parties*. New York: John Wiley, 1954. Influential work by a French political scientist outlining a general theory of political parties applying to many nations.

ELDERSVELD, SAMUEL J. *Political Parties in American Society*. New York: Basic Books, 1982. Comprehensive and sophisticated description of the American party system.

*EPSTEIN, LEON D. *Political Parties in Western Democracies*. New Brunswick, NJ: Transaction Press, 1980. Covers much the same ground as Duverger's book but in a more empirical and pragmatic manner.

———. *Political Parties in the American Mold*. Madison, WI: University of Wisconsin Press, 1986. An in-depth analysis of the unique character of American political parties and the historical, legal, and political reasons for their peculiar evolution.

*HERRING, PENDLETON. *The Politics of Democracy*. New York: Holt, Rinehart & Winston, 1940. Classic defense of the decentralized American party system.

*LAVER, MICHAEL, AND NORMAN SCHOFIELD. *Multiparty Government: The Politics of Coalition in Europe*. New York: Oxford University Press, 1991. Survey of the formation and operation of multiparty coalition governments in selected European nations.

*MICHELS, ROBERT. *Political Parties*. New York: Free Press, 1949. First published in 1915. Exposition of the much-discussed "iron law of oligarchy," based on a study of European Socialist parties in the early twentieth century.

*OSTROGORSKI, M. I. *Democracy and the Organization of Political Parties*, 2 vols. New York: Macmillan, 1902. Classic study of the history and organization of British and American parties up to 1900 and an attack on "permanent parties." Also available in an abridged paperback edition.

*POLSBY, NELSON W. *Consequences of Party Reform*. New York: Oxford University Press, 1983. Thoughtful analysis of the purposes, methods, and impact of extensive party reforms adopted in the United States since 1969.

*RANNEY, AUSTIN. *The Doctrine of Responsible Party Government*. Urbana, IL: University of Illinois Press, 1954. Description of the origins of the idea that

American parties should be centralized and disciplined on the British model.

*————. *Curing the Mischiefs of Faction: Party Reform in America*. Berkeley, CA: University of California Press, 1975. Analysis of theory, practice, and consequences of party reform from the 1820s to the present.

*SARTORI, GIOVANNI. *Parties and Party Systems: A Framework for Analysis*. New York: Cambridge University Press, 1976. Broad theoretical analysis of party systems, with special attention to interparty competition, drawing upon experience of many nations.

SCHATTSCHNEIDER, E. E. *Party Government*. New York: Holt, Rinehart & Winston, 1942. Influential exposition of the responsible-parties model and criticism of American parties.

*WATTENBERG, MARTIN P. *The Decline of American Political Parties, 1952–1980*. Cambridge, MA: Harvard University Press, 1984. Describes the decline of American parties in voter loyalty and organizational strength and functions.

SEMI- AND NON-DEMOCRATIC PARTIES

GEHLEN, MICHAEL P. *The Communist Party of the Soviet Union*. Bloomington, IN: Indiana University Press, 1969. General description.

HUNTINGTON, SAMUEL P., AND CLEMENT H. MOORE, eds. *Authoritarian Politics in Modern Society*. New York: Basic Books, 1970. Essays on the nature and problems of leading contemporary one-party systems.

*LAPALOMBARA, JOSEPH, AND MYRON WEINER, eds. *Political Parties and Political Development*. Princeton, NJ: Princeton University Press, 1966. Comprehensive survey of the role of parties in developing nations.

MCINNES, NEIL. *The Communist Parties of Western Europe*. New York: Oxford University Press, 1975. Comparative description of their organization, operations, and relations with Moscow.

PEMPEL, T. J., ed. *Uncommon Democracies: The One-Party Dominant Regimes*. Ithaca, NY: Cornell University Press, 1990. Essays on various dominant-party systems and their differences from monoparty systems.

WALLER, MICHAEL. *Democratic Centralism: An Historical Commentary*. New York: St. Martin's Press, 1981. Examination of origins and present meaning of a key principle of Communist government.

Notes

1. E. E. Shcattschneider, *Party Government* (New York: Holt, Rinehart & Winston, 1942), p. 1.
2. See Leon D. Epstein, *Political Parties in Western Democracies* (New Brunswick, NJ: Transaction Pres, 1980), pp. 98–129, 233–60, 369–77.
3. Douglas W. Rae, *The Political Consequences of Electoral Laws* (New Haven, CT: Yale University Press, 1967), pp. 53–58. For mathematically inclined readers who may want to make their own index scores, Rae's formula for calculating the index (F_e) follows:

$$F_e = 1 - \left(\sum_{i=1}^{N} \tau_i^2 \right)$$

where T1 = any party's share of the legislative seats, expressed as a decimal fraction.

4. Jerzy J. Wiatr, "One-Party Systems: The Concept and Issues for Comparative Studies," in *Cleavages, Ideologies, and Party Systems*, Erik Allardt and Yrjo Littunen, eds. (Turku, Finland: Westermarck Society, 1964), vol. 10, pp. 281–90.
5. Lucian W. Pye, *China: An Introduction*, 3rd ed. (Boston, MA: Little, Brown, 1984), Chapter 10.

11

No political truth is certainly of greater intrinsic value, or is stamped with the authority of more enlightened patrons of liberty than that . . . the accumulation of all powers, legislative, executive, and judiciary, in the same hands, whether of one, a few or many, and whether hereditary, self-appointed, or elective, may justly be pronounced the very definition of tyranny.
James Madison, *The Federalist*, Number 47

The Legislative Process

In this and the next three chapters we will consider the principal official policy-making institutions of modern governments—"official" because those institutions are formally established by constitutions and laws and generally regarded as parts of the government—in contrast to unofficial agencies outside the government, such as political parties and pressure groups.

In the course of this survey we will see that the legislatures, executives, administrative agencies, and courts of the Western democratic nations are substantially alike in many ways. But we will also see that some democratic systems differ significantly from others in certain respects, particularly those relating to the official status and interrelationships of legislative and executive agencies. Those differences are so important that we begin our survey of official institutions by briefly describing and contrasting the two major forms of modern democratic governments: presidential democracies and parliamentary democracies.

Presidential and Parliamentary Democracies

Presidential democracies differ from parliamentary democracies mainly in that presidential democracies are organized according to the principle of **separation of powers**, which is the principle of *the division of government power among coequal legislative, executive, and judicial branches*. **Parliamentary systems**, by contrast, are *governments organized according to the principle of fusion of powers*.

There are many more parliamentary democracies than presidential democracies in the modern world. Presently about 110 nations have democratic systems of some sort, and only about fifteen have presidential systems. The government of the United States is the oldest government based on separation of powers, and a number of Latin American countries, including Argentina, Brazil, Colombia, Costa Rica, and Mexico, have systems fashioned more or less closely on the U.S. model. (In 1993 Brazil held a nationwide referendum on a proposal to convert their presidential system to a parliamentary system; only 39 percent of the voters approved, and Brazil kept its presidential system.) Finland and France also have presidential systems, although they differ from the U.S. system in several respects. Switzerland is hard to classify. Unlike other democracies, it has a *plural* executive—a seven-person Federal Council whose members are elected by a joint meeting of the two houses of the national parliament. The joint meeting also picks one of the seven as president of the Confederation for one year, and thereafter the position passes yearly from one council member to another in order of seniority. Switzerland also has separation of powers: once elected, the members of the Federal Council remain in office for seven-year terms, and the parliament has no power to remove them. Also, when the parliament rejects a policy proposed by the Federal Council, the Council has no power to dissolve parliament and hold an unscheduled parliamentary election.

The numerous remaining established democracies all have parliamentary systems, including Great Britain, the British Commonwealth nations, the nations of Western Europe and Scandinavia, and such non-European countries as India and Japan.

Most of the republics of the former Soviet Union are still working out their new forms of government, and it is too soon to make confident predictions about which ones will become stable democracies and which forms of democratic government they will adopt. By the mid-1990s most appeared to be working toward versions of presidential democracy closer to the French than the U.S. model.

Why, then, have some democracies, including the United States, deviated from the norm by basing their systems on the principle of separation of powers?

DOCTRINE OF SEPARATION OF POWERS

James Madison's statement, which opens this chapter, forcefully declares a view of government and human rights held by almost all of the fifty-five men who drafted the Constitution of the United States in the summer of 1787. They believed that in constructing a government that is truly just and free, people must steer between two very different but equally great dangers. On the one hand, government, with its great legal powers and physical force, is a permanent threat to people's liberties, and the people must always be vigilant against government's inherent tendencies to tyranny. On the other hand, the lawlessness and anarchy that result when government is too weak are equally dangerous to human rights. The great objective of statecraft is therefore to establish a government that is strong enough to maintain law and order but sufficiently restrained to keep from becoming tyrannical. But how?

The answer, Madison and the other framers believed, is to vest each of the government's three basic powers in a separate and independent branch of government. When all three branches act in concert, government can do what it must, but no executive, legislature, or court will ever be able to use the whole power of government to work its way heedless of restraint. *Any* concentration of powers in a single branch is tyrannical, no matter whether that agency is an elected and responsible representative assembly or an irresponsible hereditary monarch. Only true separation of powers protects the liberties of the people against the aggressions of government.

SEPARATION OF POWERS IN PRESIDENTIAL DEMOCRACIES

The U.S. version of presidential democracy separates governmental powers by separation of personnel and checks and balances.

Separation of Personnel

The Constitution of the United States specifically prohibits any person from holding office in more than one of the three branches of government at a time. Article I, Section 6, declares that "no Person holding any Office under the United States, shall be a Member of either House during his Continuance in Office." Thus, if the attorney general wishes to be a senator from New York, he or she must resign the executive position, as Robert Kennedy did in 1964. If a senator from Texas wishes to be secretary of the treasury, he or she must resign the Senate seat, as Lloyd Bentsen did in 1993. If the assistant attorney general wishes to become a justice of the Supreme Court, he or she must resign the executive post, as Byron White did in 1961. If a justice of the Supreme Court wishes to become U.S. ambassador to the United Nations, he or she must resign the seat on the bench, as Arthur Goldberg did in 1965.

Checks and Balances

The U.S. Constitution does not try to isolate the three branches of government from one another completely. Rather, each branch is given a number of checks with which it can keep the others in proper balance. Thus Congress is empowered to check the president by refusing to pass bills the president requests, withholding appropriations for executive and administrative agencies, denying approval of presidential appointments to other top executive posts, and even by impeachment. Congress is empowered to check the Supreme Court by limiting its appellate jurisdiction and by withholding approval of the appointments of new judges. The president is empowered to check Congress by vetoing its acts and to check the Supreme Court by the initial appointment of its judges. The Supreme Court can check both Congress and the president by using its power of judicial review (see Chapter 14).

FUSION OF POWERS IN PARLIAMENTARY DEMOCRACIES

The essential principle of all parliamentary democratic systems is what some analysts call the **fusion of powers**, which is *the concentration of all powers in the parliament*. The powers are fused by two devices, each of which is the direct opposite of its counterpart in the presidential democracies: overlapping of personnel and formal supremacy of parliament.

Overlap of Personnel

With rare exceptions, the constitutions of the parliamentary democracies require that everyone who holds a top executive position—a minister or a subminister (see Chapter 12)—*must* be a member of the parliament. Thus the top levels of the executive branch, such as the cabinet and the ministry, are in effect committees of the parliament that preside over the executive agencies.

Formal Supremacy of Parliament

The ministers' authority to direct the executive agencies in a parliamentary system is granted to them by the parliament. Any time the parliament decides to remove a particular cabinet or ministry it needs only to pass a vote of "no confidence" in them. When that happens, either the ministry must resign and be replaced by another acceptable to the parliamentary majority or a general election must be held to elect a new parliament, which may then reappoint the old ministry or replace it with a new one. In short, disagreement and deadlock between the legislature and executive, which are so common in presidential systems, cannot be tolerated in a parliamentary system and must be resolved by changing the membership and behavior of either or both branches of government so that agreement between them can be restored.[1]

CROSSING BOUNDARIES

Most present-day political scientists believe that the traditional three-way classification of government powers is inadequate and misleading. They recognize that in all modern democratic systems no agency sticks exclusively to the job formally assigned to it. Legislative bodies often engage in executive activities (for example, their investigations of wrongdoing in government, schools, and labor unions). Courts often "make" laws (as in their interpretations of constitutions and laws). Executive and administrative agencies often make and interpret laws (for example, making administrative regulations, determining whether particular persons have violated them, and imposing penalties on those who have).

PARLIAMENTARY DEMOCRACY AT WORK. The opening session of a new German parliament.

A few political scientists have attempted to preserve the traditional conception by calling the judicial activities and powers of executive agencies "quasi-judicial." Most, however, have concluded that the adjectives *legislative, executive,* and *judicial* should be used only as convenient tags for identifying particular government agencies and do not constitute complete and accurate descriptions of what the agencies actually do.

In this chapter, accordingly, we will focus on those agencies generally called *legislatures.* According to Nelson W. Polsby, legislatures can be distinguished from executives and courts by their special combination of six characteristics: (1) Legislatures, like executives and courts, are *official* government agencies, in the sense we discussed in Chapter 2; (2) like juries and appellate courts, they are *multimembered;* (3) their members, like some executives and judges, are *directly elected* by the citizens; (4) their *members are formally equal* (that is, the vote of each legislator is counted the same as the vote of every other legislator); (5) they arrive at their decisions by *deliberating on alternatives;* and (6) they register decisions by *counting the votes* of their members.[2]

In examining the legislative process we will deal with the principle activities of those bodies, but we will not be concerned with the question of whether or not their activities are truly legislative in the eighteenth-century sense of the term. For our purposes, *any* function performed by a body called a legislature is a legislative function. We will proceed from similar premises in subsequent chapters on the executive, administrative, and judicial processes.

Functions of Legislatures

STATUTE MAKING

The first function of legislatures in modern democratic systems is making statutes. I use the term *statute making* rather than *law making* because the former more accurately describes what legislatures actually do. *Law* means a rule of behavior that officially emanates from any authorized government agency, while a statute is *a law formally enacted by a legislature.* Statutes constitute an important segment of any democratic system's total body of law, but that body of law also includes such elements as common law and rules of equity made by the courts as well as the more significant executive and administrative decrees and regulations. Legislatures thus monopolize the making of statutes but not the making of laws.

CONSTITUTION MAKING AND AMENDING

The legislatures in most democratic systems have certain powers over the establishment and amendment of their national constitutions. Many constitutions are originally drawn up by legislatures, and every legislature is authorized to play some role in making formal amendments. In some democratic countries, such as Great

Britain and New Zealand, the national legislature is the sole agency authorized to amend the constitution. In many others, such as Australia, Switzerland, and France (and most American states), the legislature normally proposes amendments and the voters ratify or defeat those proposals in referendums. In still others, such as the United States, amendments are proposed by the national legislature and ratified by state legislatures or conventions.

Most democratic legislatures have also added to their constitutions by enacting certain kinds of statutes. In the United States, for example, Congress has adopted statutes establishing the executive departments, the regulatory commissions, and the federal courts below the Supreme Court. (The Supreme Court is explicitly established by the Constitution.)

ELECTORAL FUNCTIONS

Most democratic legislatures play an important role in selecting some or all of the top executives. The outstanding instances are the indirect "elections" of prime ministers by the legislatures of the parliamentary democracies. Those legislatures do not always directly cast ballots for various candidates for this office, of course. Yet, every time a legislature votes on a motion of no confidence (see Chapter 12) it is, in effect, reelecting or defeating the incumbent prime minister.

Even in the presidential democracies the legislatures have some electoral powers. The U.S. Constitution, for example, provides that if no candidate for president or vice president receives a majority of the votes in the Electoral College, the House of Representatives will choose the president from among the top two or three candidates, and the Senate will choose the vice president in a somewhat different way. No president or vice president has been selected by those procedures since 1824, but Congress retains its electoral powers against the day when they may be needed again.

FINANCIAL FUNCTIONS

In every modern democracy the legislature holds the basic "power of the purse" and determines the nature and amount of taxes and appropriations. Governments can legally spend only funds appropriated by the legislature. Like many other legislative functions, the main initiatives in government finance have passed from the legislatures to the executives in most democratic systems. Most legislatures now merely revise budgets proposed by executives, rather than drawing up their own from scratch. How much revision particular legislatures make depends upon how much control the executives have, a matter we will consider later in this chapter.

QUASI-EXECUTIVE FUNCTIONS

In addition to acting upon executive budgets, most democratic legislatures also pass upon some other kinds of executive proposals. In most democratic countries, for example, international treaties are negotiated by the executives but must be approved by the legislatures before they become effective. In the United States the president appoints various officials (federal judges, cabinet members, heads of administrative agencies, and ambassadors) "by and with the Advice and Consent of the Senate" (Article II) (that is, the appointments are only "interim" until approved by a majority of the Senate). Anyone who watched the Senate hearings on the nominations of Robert H. Bork (1988) and Clarence Thomas (1991) for membership on the Supreme Court knows that the performance of this legislative function occasionally becomes front-page news, and the Senate sometimes rejects presidential nominees.

QUASI-JUDICIAL FUNCTIONS

Some legislatures also perform quasi-judicial functions. The U.S. Constitution, for instance, provides that the House of Representatives may impeach any civil officer of the national government (including the president, the vice president, cabinet members, and judges). An impeachment, remember, is not a conviction. Rather, it is a formal accusation of crime, comparable to a grand jury's indictment in an ordinary criminal case. Any officer so impeached must be tried by the Senate, where a two-thirds vote is necessary for conviction. The House has impeached a total of fifteen officers since 1789: thirteen judges, one president, and one cabinet member. Only seven, all judges, have been convicted and removed from office. President

CONGRESS WORKS IN COMMITTEES. Clarence Thomas testifies at the Senate Judiciary Committee hearings on his nomination to the Supreme Court.

Andrew Johnson escaped conviction in 1868 by the bare margin of one vote and in 1974 President Richard Nixon resigned when it became clear that the House was going to impeach him. A similar incident took place in Brazil in 1992. The Chamber of Deputies voted to impeach President Fernando Collor de Mello for accepting bribes, but Collor resigned before the Senate could try him, and he was succeeded in office by Vice President Itamar Franco.

Similarly, the French national assembly can indict the president of the republic and the ministers for treason and other crimes, although indicted officials are tried by the high court rather than by a legislative body. The British House of Lords has lost most of its other powers but continues to be the nation's highest court of law. Most of the Lords' judicial work, and all of its work as a court of appeals, is performed in the name of the whole chamber by a small group of ten to fifteen legal experts, including the lord chancellor, the nine lords of appeal in ordinary (the "law lords"), and other members of the Lords who have held high judicial office (for example, former lord chancellors).

INVESTIGATIVE FUNCTIONS

Legislative investigations often receive considerable publicity, especially in the United States. Congressional probes, such as those by the Ervin Select Committee on Presidential Campaign Activities in 1973 (on the Watergate scandals) and by the 1988 joint House-Senate committee on the secret efforts of National Security Adviser John Poindexter and his aide Oliver North to sell arms to Iran and use the proceeds to finance aid to the Nicaraguan contras are the best-known recent examples. U.S. legislatures have no monopoly on this kind of activity, however. The British House of Commons establishes a number of "select committees" for the purpose of digging up information it desires on matters not covered by its standing committees. The select committees hold hearings, subpoena witnesses and records, and then submit reports that sometimes stimulate changes in existing legislation, administrative practices, or both. Although the British, unlike the Americans, conduct many of their government investigations through royal commissions (bodies composed of both legislators and outsiders), the select committees nevertheless have a significant role in the development of legislative and administrative policy.

INFORMATIONAL FUNCTIONS

Some legislative investigations are conducted mainly to collect information necessary for new legislation. Many, however, are intended mainly to inform other government agencies and the general public about what is going on. For example, the Ervin committee's investigation of the Watergate scandals in 1973 was intended only in part to provide the basis for new legislation regulating campaign finance and practices. The probe was also designed to determine whether or not the legislation already on the books had been violated by President Nixon or members of his administration and campaign organization. For other examples, in the late 1970s both houses of Congress created committees to investigate the assassinations of

President John F. Kennedy in 1963 and Martin Luther King, Jr. in 1968 to see whether they were the acts of individual assassins, as earlier investigations had concluded, or were the results of conspiracies.

Legislative investigations are one way of informing the public, and legislative debates are another. In many legislatures, party lines are so strong that legislative debate hardly ever changes a member's vote. Even so, debate provides the main forum in which the pros and cons of issues are aired. It thus serves much the same function of informing and activating public opinion that election campaigns are supposed to perform. Debates in the British House of Commons, although they almost never change legislative votes, sometimes change the opinions of voters, and some observers describe parliamentary debates as a continuing election campaign. If an informed and enlightened citizenry is indeed a prime requisite for healthy democracy, then informing the public is far from the least significant of the legislature's functions.

Structure and Procedures of Legislatures

NUMBER OF HOUSES

Approximately two-thirds of all modern democratic nations have bicameral (two-house) legislatures, and one-third have unicameral (one-house) legislatures. Although there are several variations in the structure of the bicameral legislatures, most are organized in similar ways. One of the two houses (or chambers), generally called the lower house, has the larger membership and the shorter terms of office and is elected (under one of the electoral systems described in Chapter 8) by the widest franchise. Examples of such chambers are the U.S. House of Representatives, the British House of Commons, the French Assemblée Nationale, and the Swiss Nationalrat. The other chamber, generally called the upper house, has the smaller membership and the longer terms of office and is selected in various ways. The members of the U.S. Senate, for example, are elected by the voters in statewide constituencies for six-year terms; some members of the British House of Lords inherit their positions, and others are appointed for life on the advice of the prime minister (none are elected); the members of the Canadian Senate are appointed for life by the governor-general on the advice of the prime minister; and the members of the Austrian Bundesrat are elected by the legislatures of the various *länder* (provinces).

Why should a nation establish two legislative chambers rather than one? Historically there have been two main reasons. First, some federal democracies have thought it necessary to give their subnational units (states, provinces, *länder*) equal representation in the national legislature (for example, the U.S. Senate has two members from each state, regardless of its population or wealth). Perhaps even more important has been the desire to provide an internal check on legislative action. The lower houses have been thought to be more closely in tune with popular appetites and passions and have, therefore, been regarded as more dangerous to national stability and welfare. Many nations, accordingly, have at one time or another established higher property and age qualifications for people who elect members of the upper houses than for those who elect members of the lower houses, and a few nations still retain those special franchise requirements.

In recent years a number of democratic nations have formally or informally abandoned bicameralism, mainly on the ground that it dilutes the power of the chamber most representative of the people. A few nations, such as Denmark, New Zealand, and Sweden, have officially abolished one of their chambers. Other nations have reduced the powers of one chamber so drastically that those chambers are now little more than advisory bodies, and the other houses have become, for all practical purposes, unicameral legislatures. For example, until the nineteenth century the British House of Lords was in most respects as powerful as the House of Commons. After the democratization of the Commons in 1832, however, the powers of the Lords began to slip away. The Parliament Act of 1911 stripped the chamber of all but a few delaying powers, and an act of 1949 reduced the Lords' powers still further. Accordingly, today the House of Lords is merely an advisory and delaying body, with little or no legislative power. It rarely uses its delaying power, although in 1990 it did reject a bill passed by the House of Commons allowing trials of suspected World War II criminals, and thereby delayed the bill's enactment by a year. Most observers believe that the House of Lords performs useful advising and revising functions, but Parliament has become a de facto unicameral legislature. The same thing has happened to a greater or lesser degree in almost all the unitary (non-federal; see Chapter 2) democracies. Only in four democracies—Belgium, Italy, Switzerland, and the United States—do the upper houses retain powers formally equal to those of the lower houses.

MAIN STEPS IN HANDLING BILLS

Despite differences in procedural details, the legislatures of most democratic regimes put bills through similar steps before they become law.

Introduction

In most legislatures, any member may introduce a bill either by giving it a "first reading" on the floor and moving its adoption or, as in both houses of the U.S. Congress, merely by dropping the bill in the "hopper" at the clerk's or secretary's desk. This formal equality in the right to introduce bills is misleading, however. Many democratic legislatures, such as the British House of Commons, make a formal distinction between government bills (those introduced by ministers on behalf of the cabinet) and private members' bills (those introduced by ordinary members on their own initiative). Only government bills are likely to be passed. The government introduces about 85 percent of all bills in Great Britain, and over three quarters of the bills passed are government bills. No such formal distinction is made in the U.S. Congress, but a bill generally known to be an administration bill (one backed by the president and pushed by presidential partisans in Congress) has a much better chance of passing than one that lacks administration backing.

Consideration by Committee

Later in this chapter we will examine the structure, activities, and role of committees in the legislative process. Here the point to note is that in most democratic legislatures, bills are referred to and considered by committees *before* they undergo general consideration and debate by the whole chamber. Committees therefore have a great deal to say not only about the contents of bills but also about which bills have a realistic chance of becoming laws. In the British House of Commons, however, bills are referred to committees *after* general debate and *after* most details have been established by the whole house (which means by the cabinet). Thus British committees, unlike those in most other democratic legislatures, are charged with cleaning up details, and with very little else. British Commonwealth nations, such as Canada and Australia, generally follow British practice in this regard, but the United States and most European democracies assign their legislative committees far more decisive roles.

General Debate

The few bills that survive the screening process in committees are then reported back to the whole house in original or altered form and are given "second readings" (which usually means only that the presiding officer or the clerk announces the number and title of each bill about to be considered, not that anyone literally reads its contents aloud). At this point all legislators have a chance to express views on the basic policy questions involved in the bill and also to offer amendments to it. If the bill survives this stage, then its chances of final passage are excellent.

Final Passage

After general debate and after all proposed amendments have been accepted, rejected, or revised, the bill is given its third and final "reading," and the question is put as to whether the whole bill, as amended, should be passed. An affirmative vote means that as far as the particular chamber is concerned, the bill should be law.

Consideration by Conference Committees

In many nominal two-house legislatures, as we have seen, the upper houses have the power only to suggest amendments and to delay bills passed by the lower houses. After the delaying period has elapsed and after the lower house has accepted or rejected the upper house's amendments, the bill moves on to the next and final stage, regardless of further objections by the upper house. But in the United States and in a few other nations, each bill must pass both houses in identical form before it can move on to the final stage. When the two houses disagree on the final wording of a bill, whether on a minor detail or on a major policy question, and neither is willing to accept the other's version, the differences must be ironed out and the bill worded in a manner that will be approved by majorities in both houses. This problem arises with 30 to 50 percent of all the bills that pass both houses of the U.S. Congress, including almost every major bill.

SECRET BALLOTS IN ITALY'S CHAMBER OF DEPUTIES

In most democratic legislatures, the members' votes on every major issue are cast publicly, recorded, and printed. The purpose is to ensure that each member's constituents and the pressure groups concerned will know how the member has voted on each issue so that the member can be held accountable for his or her votes. Until recently, however, the Italian Chamber of Deputies was a notable exception. All its votes were taken by secret ballot, and there was no effective way anyone could learn how a particular member had voted on any issue. This practice had a number of consequences. It obscured the members' accountability. It made party discipline difficult to enforce, and lowered party cohesion. It enabled disgruntled members (called "snipers") of the parties forming a coalition cabinet to vote against the cabinet and bring it down without being publicly branded as traitors to their parties.

In 1988, the leaders of the two leading parties in the coalition cabinet of the moment—Bettino Craxi of the Socialists and Ciriaco de Mito of the Christian Democrats—succeeded in persuading the Chamber to end parliamentary voting by secret ballot. But the deputies agreed to do so only if they could retain secret voting on issues affecting civil rights, linguistic minorities, and changes in parliamentary rules and electoral laws. On those issues, accountability and party discipline remain as difficult—and "sniping" as prevalent—as ever.

In a genuinely bicameral legislature, the necessary ironing-out activities are conducted by some version of the U.S. conference committees, which operate as follows. In each case in which the two houses have passed somewhat different bills on a similar subject, the presiding officer of each house appoints from three to nine members to represent the house as conferees. The two sets of conferees constitute a conference committee, which tries to work out a version of the bill on which all or most of the conferees can agree. Conference committees generally produce compromises between the versions of the two houses, but they sometimes write substantially new bills. When the conferees have reached agreement, they report to their respective houses. Their reports cannot be amended by either house but must be accepted or rejected in their entirety. The reports are usually accepted, for the very good reason that most members of both houses know that if a conference committee's version is not accepted, there will probably be no bill at all.

Conference committees, accordingly, have considerable power over the final content of legislation, so much that some observers call them "the third house of Congress." However, some such institution is indispensable in any genuinely bicameral legislature.

Final Action by the Executive

After the legislature has enacted a bill, it is submitted to the executive for official approval and inclusion in the collection of statutes in force. In the parliamentary systems, the chiefs of state—monarchs or presidents—have no choice but to approve the bills and declare them law. In the presidential systems, however, the presidents can veto bills. If the president of the United States vetoes a bill, it can become law only if repassed by both houses with a two-thirds majority in each.

LEGISLATIVE COMMITTEES

Organization

Every democratic legislature establishes committees of its members to perform various functions. Committees appear to be a universal response to two main needs. First, the sheer size of most legislatures prevents them from effectively handling questions of detail and wording. Most legislatures have several hundred members, and hundreds of people can deal effectively only with dozens of broad questions of policy and not with thousands of questions of detail. Second, the sheer number of bills introduced requires some way of weeding out the few that will get serious consideration. In an average session of the U.S. Congress, for instance, 10,000 to 12,000 bills are introduced, obviously far too many to consider seriously. In fact only about 500 to 1,000 survive to final passage.

In the United States and most European democracies, most of the weeding out is accomplished by legislative committees. Each house of the U.S. Congress maintains a number of *standing committees* (those considered permanent) established according to subject matter: agriculture, appropriations, armed services, foreign affairs, education and labor, and so on. The standing committees range in size from nine to fifty members and include legislators of the majority and minority parties in approximately the same proportions as the two parties' shares of the seats in the whole house. Nominally the members of each committee are elected by the whole house, but actually the leaders of each party (assembled in its "committee on committees") determine which of their members will sit on which committees. In making those selections the leaders are bound by a series of informal but nonetheless powerful rules. For example, all the previous members of a committee must be reappointed if they so desire, and every major area and interest must have a spokesperson on a committee that deals with matters affecting it.

The *commissions* of the French national assembly are in some respects similar to American legislative committees. The principal French variation is the institution of the *rapporteur* (reporter). As each bill is received by a particular *commission*, it appoints one member to be the *rapporteur* for that bill. The *rapporteur* then takes the lead in studying the bill, in preparing the *commission's* report on it, and in defending the *commission's* position in the debate before the whole assembly.

The British House of Commons, in contrast to the U.S. and French legislatures, maintains only eight "alphabet" standing committees (so called because they are officially designated committee A, committee B, committee C, and so on rather than "armed forces" or "agriculture" and the like). The British and French committees are not specialized by subject matter and are far less powerful than their counterparts in many other legislatures.

Besides standing committees, democratic legislatures from time to time establish *select committees*, which make special inquiries into, and recommendations on, particular questions. The bicameral legislatures sometimes establish *joint committees*, composed of members from each house, to supervise certain matters (for example, the U.S. Congress's Joint Committee on Atomic Energy, created to oversee the Department of Energy's administration of nuclear energy matters).

Activities and Power

Most legislatures' standing committees have two main activities. The first is disposing of bills referred to them by their chambers. A powerful committee has a wide range of choice in deciding how to dispose of a particular bill. The committee may simply shelve it—which is what happens to most bills—or it may immediately report the bill in its original form back to the whole house with a recommendation "that it do pass." The committee may also decide to work the bill over before making any recommendation, in which case it may hold hearings at which representatives of various interested groups are invited to testify. When the hearings are over, the committee may then go into a "mark-up session" and rewrite the bill as little or as much as it sees fit, up to and including deleting everything but the title and substituting an entirely new bill!

Committees are not restricted to acting only on bills referred to them. They may decide to draw up and have members introduce new bills of their own. They may decide to investigate possible wrongdoing in the executive, administrative, or judicial agencies (or, for that matter, in schools, labor unions, athletic competition, and the like).

The power of legislative committees over the general legislative process varies considerably among modern democracies. At one extreme stand the committees of the U.S. Congress and state legislatures, which are the most powerful in the world. Not only do those committees receive bills before general debate and before basic policy decisions have been made but they also can, and often do, make major decisions on basic policy as well as on matters of detail and wording. "Little legislatures," Woodrow Wilson called those committees, and the phrase is as apt today as it was when he wrote it in 1885.[3]

At the other extreme stand the committees of the British House of Commons. They do not receive a bill until after its second reading, when the basic policy decisions have already been made. They are authorized to make alterations and amendments only on minor details. They do not specialize in particular subject-matter areas, so they develop no special expertise in any area. Their members are subject to strong party discipline both inside and outside the committees. The committees therefore play a relatively unimportant role in the British legislative process.

Under the Third and Fourth Republics of France, the powers of the French *commissions* were more like those of American committees. However, the Constitution of the Fifth Republic (1958) reduced the *commissions'* powers and thereby reduced the fragmentation of policy making that had tied up the legislatures under the earlier regimes. The number of *commissions générales permanentes* (standing committees) was reduced from nineteen specialized committees on the U.S. model to six unspecialized committees on the British model. It is now the government's bills—not the committees' amendments and counterproposals, as in the old days—that come before the whole assembly for debate and final action.

The power of legislative committees in the other democracies falls between those extremes. On the one hand, committee reports usually serve as the basis for debate and action in the whole legislature, and a committee has considerable power to redraft and amend the bills referred to it. On the other hand, in most parliamentary democracies the cabinet's control of the legislative agenda and the political parties' control of their members' votes are so strong that the committees rarely do anything against the cabinet's wishes.

PARTY ORGANIZATION

Principal Agencies

Almost every member of every democratic legislature is elected as the candidate of a political party. In every legislature the members of each party form some kind of organization to consult on matters of policy and strategy in order to advance their common cause most effectively. Although those legislative party organizations vary in detail from nation to nation and from party to party within some nations, most include some version of each of the following agencies.

CAUCUS   In its most general sense, the term **caucus** refers to *a meeting, usually secret, of the members of a political party or interest group to agree on strategy or to select candidates, or both.* A legislative party caucus is an assembly of all the party's members in the particular house. The U.S. versions are called conferences or caucuses; the British versions are called parliamentary parties; the French versions are called *groupes,* and so on. Their main function is to select their parties' legislative leaders, although occasionally some also decide what stands their members should take on particular legislative issues.

EXECUTIVE COMMITTEES   The caucus usually selects a few of its members as some kind of executive committee and authorizes those members to take the lead in setting the party's strategy and tactics. The U.S. versions are called steering committees or policy committees, the British versions are called the leadership or the cabinet (see Chapter 12), the French versions are called the party executive, and so on.

FLOOR LEADERS   Each caucus also selects one of its members as its official leader and main spokesperson. The U.S. versions are called the majority leader and the minority leader (depending on whether the party has a majority or a minority of the seats in the chamber), and the British equivalents are the prime minister and the leader of Her Majesty's loyal opposition.

WHIPS   The caucus or leader selects a few members to act as assistant leaders, generally known as whips.[4] Their functions are to inform the rank and file of the leadership's decisions about policy and strategy, to keep the rank and file from straying from the leaders' line on key legislative issues, and to inform the leaders about any dissatisfactions and resentments the members may have.

Power and Role

We noted in Chapter 10 that the discipline and cohesion of legislative parties vary widely among democratic nations. At the high end of the scale stand the British parliamentary parties. The majority party picks its leader, who automatically becomes prime minister. The prime minister, in turn, chooses the members of the cabinet and ministry; and together they constitute the British executive. Led by the prime minister, the cabinet controls the proceedings and decisions of the House of Commons. Organized opposition is dominated by the second-largest party's leader and "shadow cabinet," which not only criticize the majority party's policies but also expound the alternative policies the opposition proposes to adopt when the voters make them the majority party. As a result, British government is essentially *party* government, in the sense that party organizations and operations are the very core of its legislative and executive processes.

Near the low end of the party-cohesion scale stand a few of the smaller center and right-wing parties in democratic nations with high degrees of fractionalization (see Chapter 10). Their members ordinarily feel little obligation and no compulsion to act or vote together and are thus little more than aggregations of independent legislators who happen to bear the same formal party labels.

The Democratic and Republican parties in the U.S. Congress stand between those two extremes. On matters of personnel (for example, electing the presiding officers and allocating committee positions), U.S. parties are as cohesive as British parties. On most issues of public policy U.S. parties are less cohesive than British parties but more cohesive than some French parties. To illustrate: Since the late 1940s a number of pressure groups have kept scores on how every senator and representative has voted on issues of particular concern to them. Records show that around 70 percent of the votes cast by Democrats in both houses supported labor and liberal positions, whereas only about 25 percent of the Republicans' votes did so. They also show that some Democrats (for example, Senators David Boren of Oklahoma and Howell Heflin of Alabama) were as conservative as most Republicans and that some Republicans (for example, Senators Robert Packwood and Mark Hatfield of Oregon) were as liberal as most Democrats. On most key issues in Congress, then, majorities of Democrats oppose majorities of Republicans. However, each party has some mavericks who often vote with the opposition party. Rarely do *all* Democrats vote one way and *all* Republicans vote the other way, as is shown by the sample of congressional votes on key issues shown in the box.

We also noted in Chapter 10 that in centralization, discipline, and cohesion, the dominant parties in most democracies fall somewhere between the British and U.S. major parties. However, in every democratic nation the parties' power over their legislators' votes and actions determines the role of parties in the nation's legislative process and also sets the conditions for the individual legislator's public life.

Legislative Ways of Life

For our present purposes, legislators in modern democracies may usefully be divided into two general types. The first type is the "party soldier," exemplified by the ordinary members of the British House of Commons (MPs), who are subject to such strict party discipline that except under the most unusual circumstances they

MAJORITY PARTY LEADERS IN CONGRESS. House Speaker Newt Gingrich (Georgia) and Senate Majority (Republican) Leader Bob Dole (Kansas).

feel compelled to vote as their party leaders direct. The second type is the "independent operator," exemplified by ordinary members of the U.S. Senate or House of Representatives, who are subject to such weak party discipline that they can, if they wish, freely vote contrary to their leaders' requests.

PARTY SOLDIERS[5]

Life on the Back Benches

Most of the members of the British House of Commons are **backbenchers**, who are *MPs who hold no ministerial office*. As we saw in Chapter 10, while the number of occasions on which MPs have voted against their party leaders' orders have increased in recent years, it is still the case that almost all MPs almost always vote as their party leaders direct, and practically speaking they have no independent power. Accordingly, the only way backbenchers can achieve personal success is to be appointed to ministerial office by party leaders. If MPs are ambitious—and not all of them are—whatever they do as backbenchers must convince their leaders that they are of ministerial caliber. Even if the backbenchers have no hope of reaching ministerial rank, they have little freedom to use their votes to gain other goals.

What, then, can backbenchers do? For one thing, they can speak in parliamentary debates. If they are good at it, then they may win the attention and approval necessary for advancement to ministerial office. Even if they do not, backbenchers may still enjoy the applause of their colleagues and favorable notices in the newspapers. For another thing, they can keep the ministers on their toes by asking sharp questions during "question time." For still another, they can rise to eminence in their parties' committees of backbenchers and through those commit-

SAMPLE OF CONGRESSIONAL VOTES, 1993–1994

House and Issue	DEMOCRATS			REPUBLICANS		
	Yes	No	Cohesion Index*	Yes	No	Cohesion Index
HOUSE						
"Brady bill" for handgun control	184	69	46	54	119	38
"Motor voter" registration	237	14	88	21	146	74
Lift ban, leave gays-in-military issue to Clinton	157	101	22	11	163	88
Balanced budget amendment to Constitution	99	151	60	172	1	99
SENATE						
"Brady bill" for handgun control	47	8	78	16	28	32
Reject House ban on funding abortions for poor women	34	21	24	6	38	72
"Motor voter" registration	56	0	100	6	36	71
Lift ban, leave gays-in-military issue to Clinton	30	25	10	3	38	86
Omnibus crime bill	54	2	96	7	36	83

Source: Congressional Quarterly Reports, 1993 and 1994.

*See pp. 214–215 for the definition of cohesion.

tees exert substantial influence on the leaders. They can introduce motions that may cause some public stir. They can introduce private bills, a few of which may pass. There is always the possibility, however remote, that by abstaining or threatening to abstain from voting in a major crisis they may help to bring down an unwanted government (as in the unseating of Neville Chamberlain's government in 1940) or reverse a disastrous government policy (as in the crisis over the seizing of the Suez Canal by Britain and France in 1956).

By U.S. standards, the British backbenchers' position is not impressive. Their votes are not their own; they have little independent power to put pressure on administrators; they are paid very little, the equivalent of about $50,000 a year plus modest secretarial, living, and travel allowances; and most have to share offices with three or four other MPs. Yet backbenchers are by no means nobodies. They belong to one of Great Britain's most exclusive clubs (about the only club in London that guarantees parking space for its members), they are insiders in the nation's most fascinating game, and their positions as MPs may be highly useful in their careers in journalism, law, or business. Relatively few MPs retire voluntarily, and many who are defeated in general elections try to win their way back. Evidently, then, even the party soldiers who never rise to ministerial rank find considerable satisfaction in being backbenchers.

Relations with Constituents

Because ordinary backbenchers do not control their own parliamentary votes, they have no meaningful individual voting records for their opponents to attack or their supporters to praise. But in their constituencies they are much more than mere names with party labels. They are expected to provide certain local services, and if they manage affairs well they can have significant voices in constituency affairs. Although the institution of ministerial responsibility (see Chapter 12) prevents them from exerting direct pressure on civil servants as members of Congress do, they can explain local problems and dramatize local needs through speeches in the House of Commons and private talks with ministers.

Most MPs hold regular "surgeries" in their constituencies; that is, they have office hours during which they are available to all constituents who care to call on them, express their views, and make requests about such matters as ill treatment by the ministry of pensions or difficulty with the ministry of local government and planning. If the MPs find merit in their constituents' claims, they can at least make sure that the relevant ministries pay attention. Conscientious MPs also grace local festivals, celebrations, and ceremonies with their presence. At their constituents' request they can provide tickets of admission to the Strangers' Gallery (from which they can watch the House of Commons in session, usually a good show) and frequently also invite them to tea on the handsome terrace overlooking the river Thames.

MPs who shirk their local duties are more likely to find themselves in trouble with their constituency party organizations than with the voters, but recent research shows that there is some electoral payoff as well. Other things being equal, Labour voters are more likely to vote for an incumbent Labour MP (who presumably has been tending to his or her constituents' needs) than for a nonincumbent Labour candidate standing in the same constituency and that a higher proportion are likely to vote for an incumbent Conservative MP than a nonincumbent Conservative candidate.[6] Thus the local obligations of British MPs are an important—and often wearying—part of their public life. In some respects, then, the party soldiers have many of the independent operators' burdens but few of their powers.

INDEPENDENT OPERATORS

Life in the U.S. Senate and House of Representatives

Members of the U.S. Congress operate in quite a different setting from British MPs. U.S. legislators owe their nominations to the people who vote in the direct primaries in their districts, and the national leaders of their parties cannot keep them from being renominated. In some instances the members' chances of reelection may be marginally affected by the success and support of their national party leaders, but their political fortunes depend mainly upon what the local voters think of them. Not only do the national leaders have little effective power to punish members of Congress for voting against their parties' policies, but also a member's reputation for independence and "refusal to submit to the party bosses" may well be worth thousands of votes in many districts. Then too, voting against a party policy is in no sense a vote to put the other party in control of Congress or the presidency. Fixed

AN MP's LETTER TO HIS CONSTITUENTS

In 1714 a British member of Parliament, Antony Henry, received a communication from his constituents asking him to vote against an excise (tax) bill. He is said to have replied:

"Gentlemen: I have received your letter about the excise, and I am surprised at your insolence in writing to me at all.

You know, and I know, that I bought this constituency. You know, and I know, that I am now determined to sell it, and you know what you think I don't know that you are now looking out for another buyer, and I know, what you certainly don't know, that I have now found another constituency to buy.

About what you said about the excise: may God's curse light upon you all, and may it make your homes as open and as free to the excise officers as your wives and daughters have always been to me while I have represented your rascally constituency."[7]

---

terms and separation of powers take care of that. The vote of every member of Congress therefore belongs to the member alone. Members may voluntarily decide to go along with their parties on most issues. A majority, as we have seen, do just that. But the fact that their parties cannot effectively *make* them to vote this way or that makes their positions very different from those of British MPs.

How do U.S. legislators use this heady independence? Most political scientists have answered this question by identifying the different roles that various legislators choose (or are forced) to play. James David Barber's study of Connecticut first-term state legislators, for example, distinguished among "spectators," "advertisers," "reluctants," and "lawmakers." The pioneering study by John C. Wahlke, Heinz Eulau, William Buchanan, and LeRoy C. Ferguson of state legislators in California, New Jersey, Ohio, and Tennessee identified several sets of roles. In their representational functions, legislators were classified as "trustees," "politicos," and "delegates." In their dealings with pressure groups legislators were "facilitators," "neutrals," or "resisters." Several studies distinguish between members of Congress who are "members of the inner club" and "outsiders." The common theme of all those studies is that legislators are impelled to choose certain roles by their own psychological makeups, their perceptions of the legislative process in the capital and of the electoral process in their states and districts, and their goals and ambitions. The roles they choose have much to do with both their activities and their effectiveness.

Several recent studies of Congress have concluded that more and more members of Congress are choosing to follow an "outside" rather than an "inside" strategy. As Norman Ornstein points out, prior to the advent of the television age in the 1960s, the ambitious young member of Congress had no choice but to play the "inside" game of conforming to the norms of behavior prescribed by the old hands. In the famous words of Sam Rayburn, the Speaker of the House from 1940 to 1961, "to get along you have to go along." But in 1960 John F. Kennedy, a relatively minor member of the Senate, used his popular appeal on television to win the presidency, and since then, local and national television newscasters have found that individual members of Congress—especially *colorful* ones—make good copy. So more and more members appear in the interview slots on the networks' national news programs, and the result has meant a significant change in the way members of Congress conduct themselves. As Ornstein sums it up:

> As media coverage expanded, the number of members of Congress who were brought to public attention mushroomed, and more and more of the publicized members came from the rank and file. . . . This trend toward personal publicity provided, in contrast to the Rayburn era, a range of tangible and possible outside incentives. No longer did a member have to play by inside rules to receive inside rewards or avoid inside setbacks. One could "go public" and be rewarded by national attention; national attention in turn could provide ego gratification, social success in Washington, the opportunity to run for higher office, or, by highlighting an issue, policy success.[8]

Relations with Constituents

Most members of Congress, like most British MPs, cannot concentrate solely on their dealings with their fellow legislators, for the voters back home have the ultimate power over their political careers. Hence, members of Congress, like MPs, must perform a number of services for their constituents. Furthermore, constituency services are even more important to members of Congress than they are to MPs, for the congress members' electoral fortunes are much less tied to those of their parties, and, unlike MPs, they *can* exert some pressure on executives and administrators.

Thus, failure to provide good constituency services is much more likely to count against members of Congress than against MPs at election time. Success is much more likely to keep members of Congress in office regardless of how well or badly their parties are doing in national elections. The most striking proof of this is the fact that during most congressional elections since 1946 over 90 percent of all incumbents running for reelection to the House of Representatives have been reelected (Democrats as well as Republicans, and liberals as well as conservatives). For example, even in 1984, when Republican Ronald Reagan won 59 percent of the votes and carried 49 of the 50 states, 255 Democratic members of the House of Representatives ran for reelection and 242—95 percent—were re-elected.

In 1994, however, Democratic incumbents did not do so well. Of the 225 Democrats who ran for reelection, 35 (16 percent) were defeated. In most elections incumbent Senate members have been more vulnerable than House members; however, in the 1994 election, 6 Democratic incumbents voluntarily retired, some no doubt because they were facing defeat. Of the 16 Democratic incumbents running for reelection 2 (12.5 percent) were defeated, while no Republican incumbent lost to a Democratic challenger.[9]

The perceived difficulty of defeating incumbent legislators led some Americans to believe that the best way to ensure that U.S. legislatures get fresh blood and new ideas is to impose limits on the number of terms legislators can serve, and several states adopted such limits. However, in May 1995 the Supreme Court declared such term limits unconstitutional.

There are even greater differences between members of Congress and British MPs. The votes of the British legislators are in most instances controlled by their parties, but the votes of U.S. legislators are almost entirely their own, to be cast as they see fit and not according to orders from the president or their parties' floor leaders in the House or Senate. In deciding how to cast those votes, members of Congress often have to face very difficult issues about whether they should vote as they think best or vote as their constituents want them to vote.

Representative-Constituent Relationships

One of the oldest and most debated issues about democracy concerns the proper relationship between representatives and their constituents. Two distinct positions were first fully stated in the eighteenth century, and most subsequent pronouncements on the issue have been restatements of them.

MANDATE THEORY

Some early democratic theorists, notably John Lilburne and Jean Jacques Rousseau, argued that the proper function of the representative assembly in a true democracy is not to initiate policies on its own but only to register the policy preferences of the popular majority it represents. Thus the ideal method of popular consultation is a face-to-face assembly of all the people. However, this is impossible in a large and densely populated nation, so the next best thing is for the people to express their will through their elected representatives. As a member of the American Constitutional Convention of 1787 put it:

> What is the principle of representation? It is an expedience by which an assembly of certain individuals chosen by the people is substituted in place of the inconvenient meetings of the people themselves.[10]

In this view, as long as the representative assembly confines itself to registering its constituents' views, representation involves no significant deviation from democratic principles. But when the assembly begins to make policy on its own, in either ignorance or defiance of its constituents' desires, it becomes a kind of oligarchy.

Those theorists concluded that individual representatives may rightfully act only on the basis of *mandates* from their constituents (that is, instructions by their constituents to support in the assembly whatever positions would be supported by the constituents if they could be there). If the constituents order the representatives to support proposals that the representatives believe are wrong, then the representatives must either swallow their objections and vote as they are mandated or resign in favor of representatives who will vote as they are told. Under no circumstances should representatives vote contrary to their mandates. If they do not know their constituents' desires on any issue, they should go home and find out before they vote in the assembly.

INDEPENDENCE THEORY

Other theorists have argued that the kind of representative system advocated by Lilburne and Rousseau is neither possible nor desirable in a modern nation. They say that the problems of modern government are so complex and difficult that they can be understood and handled effectively only by people who make governing a full-time job. Constituents have to spend most of their time and energy on earning a living and cannot possibly acquire the necessary information and understanding as effectively as their representatives can. The representative assembly must therefore initiate—and not merely register—policies if the nation is to prosper. This way of doing things will not convert democracy into some kind of legislative oligarchy, for the power to decide who sits in the legislature is still the basic power to rule, and that power is retained by the constituents. The classical statement of this view was made by the eighteenth-century British politician and philosopher Edmund Burke:

> [The constituents'] wishes ought to have great weight with [the representative]; their opinions high respect; their business unremitted attention. . . . But his unbiased opinion, his mature judgment, his enlightened conscience, he ought not to sacrifice to you, to any man, or to any set of men living. . . . If government were a matter of will upon any side, yours, without question, ought to be superior. But government and legislation are matters of reason and judgment, and not of inclination; and what sort of reason is that in which the determination precedes the discussion, in which one set of men deliberate and another decide, and where those who form the conclusions are perhaps three hundred miles distant from those who hear the arguments?[11]

A logical corollary of Burke's position is the proposition that representatives should exercise their judgment on public affairs independently and without surrendering the final decisions to their constituents. When representatives' terms end, their constituents should certainly ask whether the representatives have used their powers of independent judgment wisely. If the constituents' conclusion is negative, the voters can and should throw the representatives out. So long as the representatives are in office, however, they should use their own best judgments, not orders from their constituents, in deciding how to vote on legislative issues.

Political theorist Hanna Pitkin has pointed out that the long-standing dispute between the mandate theory and the independence theory arises from their quite different conceptions of true representation. The mandate theorists say that government in which representatives can do the opposite of what their constituents want is not truly representative. The independence theorists reply that representatives who never act on their own and serve merely as conduits for their constituents' preferences are not truly representing. It is hard to disagree with Pitkin's comment that

> Confronted by two such arguments, one wants to say that both are somehow right. The man is not a representative if his actions bear no relationship to anything about his constituents, and he is not a representative if he does not act at all. Of course, in either case he may still be formally the representative of a certain group, but the substance is missing.[12]

Pitkin concludes that we should not view representation as a single precise standard that, if rightly understood, will settle the controversy between the mandate and independence theories once and for all. We should view it rather as a set of limits "beyond which we will no longer accept what is going on as an instance of representation." Complete independence, whatever its desirability might be on other grounds, is certainly inconsistent with the conception of democracy set forth in this book, which requires government response to the citizens' desires (see Chapter 5). On the other hand, complete mandating is simply not possible, because constituents have no clear or strong views on many issues that come before legislators, and the legislators have no effective way of finding out what their constituents want. We should therefore be willing to accept a mixture of both theories, with the proportion of each adjusted by each legislator according to his or her best judgment of what is needed in particular circumstances.

Indeed, it appears that this is the position that most legislators in modern democracies actually live by, regardless of what they say. In those rare instances in which their constituents hold strong views, the legislators are well advised to go along if they wish to be reelected. Legislators also need the cooperation of other legislators if they are to accomplish anything. They have supporters in certain pressure groups whose help they need to continue in office. Even in the United States, legislators belong to parties to which they feel some loyalty and obligation, though party leaders cannot "purge" them. Moreover, legislators themselves are not mere puppets jerked about by external pressures. They are human beings with values, perceptions, and convictions about right and wrong. Lacking the confining but simplifying all-powerful party constraints of MPs, U.S. legislators have the freedom—and the necessity—to balance the many forces bearing on them. It is seldom easy.

AMERICAN ATTITUDES TOWARD CONGRESS AND MEMBERS OF CONGRESS

How do Americans feel about Congress and its members? The answer is a paradox. Most of them all of the time have low esteem for Congress as a whole, and most of them some of the time have much higher esteem for the representative from their own districts, as is shown by the data in Table 11.1.

TABLE 11.1   Popular Approval of Congress and Own Representative, 1992

"Do you approve or disapprove of the way Congress has been handling its job?"
"In general, do you approve or disapprove the way [your particular U.S. Representative] has been handling (his/her) job?"

	PERCENT REPLYING	
	Congress	Own Representative
Approve strongly	11	42
Approve, not strongly	28	42
Disapprove, not strongly	22	9
Disapprove strongly	39	7
	100%	100%

Source: National Election Study, 1992, Data provided by the Inter-University Consortium for Political and Social Research.

The replies on Congress as a whole confirm the findings of other studies. For instance, since 1966 the Harris poll has asked its respondents annually, "As far as people running various institutions are concerned, would you say that you have a great deal of confidence, only some confidence, or hardly any confidence at all in them?" In almost every year the respondents have expressed less confidence in the leaders of Congress than in the leaders of the executive branch and the Supreme Court. Over the entire period 1966–1994 Congress has averaged 19 percent saying "a great deal of confidence," compared with 23 percent for the executive branch and 33 percent for the Supreme Court.[13]

These feelings explain the growing popularity in the American states in recent years of constitutional limitations on the number of terms members of state legislatures can serve: From 1990 to 1995, twenty-two states held referendums on proposals to limit legislators' terms, and all twenty-two were approved by substantial majorities of the voters. A number of proposals for similar limitations on the terms of U.S. representatives and senators have been discussed, but many analysts believe that such proposals violate the U.S. Constitution's provision that "Each House shall be the Judge of the Elections, Returns, and Qualifications of its own Members (Article I, Section 5).

On the other hand, the replies in Table 11.1 on approval of the U.S. representatives from the respondents' own districts (84 percent approve, while only 16 percent disapprove) also confirm previous findings that many of the people who detest Congress as a whole approve of their particular member. Perhaps that helps to explain the fact that even in elections, such as that of 1994, in which the disgust with Congress is unusually high, most incumbents running for reelection still manage to win. In 1995 a constitutional amendment limiting members of both houses of Congress to twelve years was introduced, but it failed to get the necessary two-thirds majority in the House of Representatives.

Changing Roles of Democratic Legislatures

In the spring of 1988 a select joint committee of the U.S. Senate and House of Representatives held a series of dramatic, nationally televised hearings on what some called the "Irangate affair," which concerned the role of National Security Adviser Admiral John Poindexter and his aide, Marine Lieutenant-Colonel Oliver North, in using the proceeds of secret sales of arms to Iran for support of the contra rebels against the Marxist Sandinista regime in Nicaragua. The main argument made by Poindexter, North, and their supporters was that Congress, by repeatedly changing its mind on how much and what kind of aid should be given to the contras, had made it impossible for the United States to conduct an effective policy in Central America. Accordingly, they said, it was not only the right but also the duty of Poindexter and North, as assistants to the president, to do what had to be done to counter the grave threat the Sandinistas posed for other Central American countries and for the security of the United States itself.

This dispute stirred up hard feelings and harsh words on both sides, but in the larger perspective it was only the most recent renewal of one of the oldest, most fundamental, and most difficult issues about the proper extent and limits of the legislature's power in a presidential democracy.

"TRANSFORMATIVE" VERSUS "ARENA" LEGISLATURES

How much power do modern democratic legislatures have relative to other government agencies? How much power *should* they have? As a baseline for answering those questions, political scientist Nelson W. Polsby suggests that we place actual legislatures along a continuum anchored at each end by a model of the sort discussed in Chapter 5. One model is the "transformative" legislature, which possesses "the independent capacity, frequently exercised, to mold and transform proposals from whatever source into laws." The other model is the "arena" legislature, which serves as a "formalized setting for the interplay of significant political forces in the life of a political system," forces such as the executive, the bureaucracy, political parties, and pressure groups.[14]

The authors of the original conception of separation of powers believed that the legislature should be the main policy-making agency in any properly organized government. After all, they reasoned, statutes and public policy are the same thing. The legislature originates, amends, and adopts all statutes, so it necessarily monopolizes the making of public policy. Thus in the debates on the proposed new Constitution of the United States in 1787–1789, most of the framers agreed that the most powerful—and potentially the most dangerous—part of the new government would be the House of Representatives. Not only would the House be a legislative body, which automatically made it very powerful, but it would also be the only body directly elected by the people and thus subject to the passions of popular majorities little restrained by consideration for minority rights and interests.

However, political scientists today agree that, setting aside the question of whether or not democratic legislatures *should* be transformative, the fact is that most of them are much nearer the arena model. In almost every modern democratic nation during the past century, the legislature has increasingly lost the initiative in policy making to the executive and administrative agencies. The loss has perhaps been most dramatic in France, where the national assembly dominated the executive and controlled policy making in the Fourth Republic (1945–1958) but has played only a minor role in the Fifth Republic (1958–). In almost all parliamentary democracies the prime ministers, cabinets, and ministries not only originate almost all major bills but also control the timing, the agendas, and in most instances majorities of the legislatures' votes.

GROWTH AS CHECKERS, REVISERS, AND OVERSEERS

It would be a great mistake to conclude from the foregoing that the legislature plays *no* significant role in modern democratic government. It certainly does play a role, but a different one from that envisioned in traditional ideas of separation of powers.

Although democratic legislatures have lost their power as initiators of policy to the executive and administrative agencies, they have greatly increased their power and activities as checkers, revisers, and overseers of policies initiated by others. After all, legislatures still retain their formal powers to make statutes, which means that for a great many of the policies most desired by executive agencies (for example, those relating to taxes, appropriations, treaties, and statutes of all types), the legislature's consent must be won. Where, as in Great Britain, the cabinet's control of the legislature through the majority party is at maximum strength, the executive appears able to ram through whatever policies it wishes. Yet a rebellion within the majority party is always possible (in the 1980s Margaret Thatcher in Great Britain and Bob Hawke in Australia were driven from their positions as prime minister because of rebellions by their parties' backbenchers), and defeat by the voters at the next election is always possible. No British cabinet can or does totally ignore resentments and discontent among its backbenchers or sharp criticisms by the opposition party, especially those that appear to represent the feelings of substantial portions of the electorate or powerful pressure groups. In Great Britain, although the objections and misgivings of legislators cannot force the executive to change its policies, they can and often do persuade the executive that a certain amount of sail trimming and course changing will make for much smoother passages for the policies they favor.

In countries like the United States and the democratic nations of Europe, where the executives' control over the legislatures is weaker than in Great Britain, the legislatures' functions of revision and criticism are even more prominent. The president of the United States may initiate most major pieces of legislation, but must expect some to lose and most to emerge from Congress in somewhat altered form. Furthermore, a congressional investigation may draw public attention to the mistakes of executive officers and administrators, object to various contracts and appointments, and in general confute the notion that the president alone has a mandate to run the government.

If there were ever any doubts that the U.S. Congress is still important, those doubts have been removed by the events since 1973. Richard Nixon was reelected president in 1972 by a landslide, but in less than two years Congress enacted legislation severely limiting presidential power to make war and substantially increasing its own budgetary powers. Then came the Watergate crisis in 1973–1974, when the certainty of impeachment by the House of Representatives and probable conviction by the Senate forced Nixon to become the first president in the nation's history to resign his office. The personal integrity and adherence to the law of Nixon's successors, Gerald Ford and Jimmy Carter, were never in question, yet neither had much more success than Nixon in getting Congress to adopt presidential programs without major alterations. Even Ronald Reagan, who is widely regarded as one of the most powerful and successful presidents of recent times, was balked by Congress on many occasions (for example, when the House of Representatives refused to vote the money Reagan requested to support the Nicaraguan contras, and when Congress rejected his proposal for a constitutional amendment outlawing abortion). His successor, George Bush, was even more popular in the polls, but in 1991 that did not prevent the Democrat-controlled Congress from rejecting much of Republican

DIVIDED GOVERNMENT WORKS BOTH WAYS. President Clinton meets with Senator Dole and Speaker Gingrich, the new leaders of the Republican-controlled Congress, 1995

Bush's proposed legislation. For that matter, in 1993–1994 the Democrat-controlled Congress changed some of Democrat Bill Clinton's proposals and rejected others, notably those for health care reform.

U.S. presidents, no less than British prime ministers and European premiers, are always aware that they have to deal with the legislature. Who, after all, is to say that the modern legislature's role of criticizing, revising, and overseeing the executive and the administration does not constitute as valuable a contribution to the health of democracy as the monopoly of policy making originally assigned to it?

For Further Reading

LEGISLATURES

*DAVIDSON, ROGER H., and WALTER J. OLESZEK. *Congress and Its Members,* 2nd ed. Washington, DC: Congressional Quarterly Press, 1985. Knowledgeable description of how members of Congress do their jobs.

*FENNO, RICHARD F., JR. *Congressmen in Committees.* Boston, MA: Little, Brown, 1973. Perceptive analysis of the nature and role of congressional committees.

HUITT, RALPH K. *Working Within the System.* Berkeley, CA: Institute of Governmental Studies, 1990. Collection of essays on the inner workings of Congress by a pioneering scholar.

JUDGE, DAVID. *Backbench Specialization in the House of Commons.* Exeter, NJ: Heinemann Education Books, 1982. Study of changing role of nonministerial members of the House of Commons.

KING, ANTHONY, and ANNE SLOMAN. *Westminster and Beyond.* New York: Macmillan, 1973. Survey of the life of MPs based on extensive interviews.

LONGLEY, LAWRENCE D., and WALTER J. OLESZEK. *Bicameral Politics: Conference Committees in Congress.* New Haven, CT: Yale University Press, 1989. Detailed examination of how conference committees have settled legislative differences between the U.S. Senate and House of Representatives.

MALBIN, MICHAEL J. *Unelected Representatives: Congressional Staff and the Future of Representative Government.* New York: Basic Books, 1980. Analysis of enormous growth in size and influence of congressional staffs.

POLSBY, NELSON W. "Legislatures," in *Handbook of Political Science*, Fred I. Greenstein and Nelson W. Polsby, eds., Reading, MA: Addison-Wesley, 1975, vol. 5, pp. 257–319. Broad survey of main types of legislatures.

*SCHICK, ALLEN. *Making Economic Policy in Congress.* Washington, DC: American Enterprise Institute, 1983. Authoritative analysis of new congressional

budget process with description of how it was used by the Reagan administration.

SCHWARZ, JOHN E., and L. EARL SHAW. *The United States Congress in Comparative Perspective.* Hinsdale, IL: Dryden, 1976. Comparative study of legislatures.

SMITH, STEVEN S., and CHRISTOPHER J. DEERING. *Committees in Congress.* Washington, DC: Congressional Quarterly Press, 1984. Detailed description of the organization and operation of congressional committees.

WAHLKE, JOHN C., HEINZ EULAU, WILLIAM BUCHANAN, and LEROY C. FERGUSON. *The Legislative System.* New York: John Wiley, 1962. Pioneering study of legislative roles and attitudes in four states, based on extensive interviews.

REPRESENTATIVE-CONSTITUENT RELATIONS

BURKE, EDMUND. "Address to the Electors of Bristol," in *The Works of Edmund Burke.* Boston, MA: Little Brown, Vol. 2. Classic statement of the "independence" theory of representative-constituent relationships.

CAIN, BRUCE, JOHN FEREJOHN, and MORRIS FIORINA. *The Personal Vote: Constituency Service and Electoral Independence.* Cambridge, MA: Harvard University Press, 1987. Comparative study of legislators' services to constituents in Great Britain and the United States, and the consequences for their support by voters.

*FENNO, RICHARD F., JR. *Home Style: House Members in Their Districts.* Boston, MA: Little, Brown, 1978. American styles of representation based on direct observation by a leading political scientist.

MAYHEW, DAVID R. *Congress: The Electoral Connection.* New Haven, CT: Yale University Press, 1974. Study of impact of districts on behavior of congressmen.

PITKIN, HANNA FENICHEL. *The Concept of Representation.* Berkeley, CA: University of California Press, 1966. The most comprehensive and influential analysis of the leading theories of representation, including the mandate and independence theories.

———, ed. *Representation.* New York: Atherton Press, 1969. Collection of essays on theories of representation, with a useful introductory paper by the editor.

ROUSSEAU, JEAN JACQUES. *Considerations on the Government of Poland.* Several editions have been published. Classic statement of the mandate theory of representative-constituent relationships.

SEARING, DONALD. *Westminster's World: Understanding Political Roles.* Cambridge, MA: Harvard University Press, 1994. An interview-based study of how British MPs behave in Parliament and in their constituencies.

Notes

1. Political scientist Arend Lijphart proposes a different typology of democratic governments. He says there are two basic models. One, exemplified by Great Britain, is the *majoritarian model*, maximizing principles of fusion of powers and cabinet dominance, concentration of executive power in the single majority party of a two-party system, unitary and centralized government, and parliamentary sovereignty. The other, exemplified by such European countries as the Netherlands and Switzerland, is the *consensus model*, maximizing principles of executive power sharing through coalition cabinets, formal or informal separation of powers, proportional representation, multiparty systems, and decentralized power. Since the U.S. system has elements of both models, Lijphart calls it an "intermediate" form, and

places it in the middle of a continuum between the two models: *Democracies: Patterns of Majoritarian and Consensus Government in Twenty-one Countries* (New Haven, CT: Yale University Press, 1984).

2. Nelson W. Polsby, "Legislatures," in *Handbook of Political Science*, Fred I. Greenstein and Nelson W. Polsby, eds., (Reading, MA: Addison-Wesley, 1975), vol. 5, pp. 257–319.

3. Woodrow Wilson, *Congressional Government* (Boston: Houghton Mifflin, 1885), p. 57.

4. The title is said to be derived from the "whippers-in," who, in British fox hunting, have the job of keeping the hunting dogs from straying from the pursuit of the fox to seek their own prey.

5. For a recent interview-based account of how British

MPs view and perform their jobs, see Donald D. Searing, *Westminster's World: Understanding Political Roles* (Cambridge, MA: Harvard University Press, 1994).

6. Bruce Cain, John Ferejohn, and Morris Fiorina, *The Personal Vote: Constituency Service and Electoral Independence* (Cambridge, MA: Harvard University Press, 1987).

7. Quoted in Peter G. Richards, *Honourable Members* (London: Faber & Faber, 1959), p. 157.

8. Norman J. Ornstein, "The Open Congress Meets the President," in *Both Ends of the Avenue*, Anthony King, ed. (Washington, DC: American Enterprise Institute, 1983), p. 202.

9. The 1984 results are taken from Norman J. Ornstein, Thomas E. Mann, and Michael J. Malbin, eds., *Vital Statistics on Congress, 1993–1994* (Washington, DC: Congressional Quarterly, 1994), Table 2-7, p. 58, and Table 2-8, p. 59. The 1994 results are taken from *Congressional Quarterly*, November 12, 1994, pp. 3232–46.

10. William Paterson at the U.S. Constitutional Convention of 1787, quoted in *Records of the Federal Convention of 1787*, Max Farrand, ed., (New Haven, CT: Yale University Press, 1937), vol. 1, p. 561.

11. Edmund Burke, "Address to the Electors of Bristol," in Burke, *Works*, (Boston, MA: Little, Brown, 1871), vol. 2, pp. 95–96.

12. Hanna Fenichel Pitkin, "The Concept of Representation," in *Representation*, ed. Atkin (New York: Atherton Press, 1969), p. 19.

13. In 1994 the Times Mirror Center for the People and the Press in the United States coordinated polls in seven democratic countries asking if respondents thought their national legislatures were "having mainly a good influence on the way things are going in this country or mainly a bad influence on the way things are going in this country." In Canada, Spain, Mexico, and France substantially more respondents said their legislatures were having a good influence than a bad one; but in the United States 39 percent said "good" and 44 percent said "bad," in the United Kingdom 27 percent said "good" to 43 percent "bad," and in Italy it was 13 percent "good" and 55 percent "bad." Reported in *The American Enterprise*, July–August 1994, p. 87.

14. Polsby, "Legislatures," pp. 277–302.

12

. . . with the passage of time legislative and judicial institutions broke off, so to speak, from the central core of government. . . . Executives did not emerge; being the core of government, they were already there. The executive alone, on this account, does not need to be explained: it is neither more nor less than what is left of government (the greater part, as it happens) when legislatures and courts are removed. If this view is accepted, it follows that there is little point empirically in trying to identify other functions or procedures that are uniquely the executive's: the executive is simply whatever the legislature and the judicature are not.[1]

The Executive Process

Most Americans can name the president of the United States, and many can also name the governor of their state and perhaps one or both of the state's U.S. senators. But the handful who can name their U.S. House member or their representatives in the state legislature are exceptionally well informed.

The fact that most of us know more about top executives than top legislators does not mean that we are poor citizens. It means that for most Americans, as for most citizens of other democratic nations, executives are the "stars" of government. Those who edit our newspapers and produce our television shows pay more attention to executives than to legislators (with rare exceptions, such as Senator Edward Kennedy and Speaker Newt Gingrich) because they think that executives are more newsworthy. That is, editors and producers think that ordinary people are more interested in executives than in legislators or judges.

The fact that executives in most democratic systems normally receive more public attention than other officials is both a result and a cause of the changing roles and positions of legislatures and executives. We noted in Chapter 11 that in most democratic countries today, legislatures have lost their traditional policy-initiating roles and have become mainly checkers, revisers, and overseers of policies initiated by executives. In this chapter we will take up the other side of the story: the general expansion of executive power and prestige that has occurred in just about every democratic nation.

What Is an Executive?

EXECUTIVE AS THE CORE OF GOVERNMENT

It is harder to define an executive than a legislature or a court. There are two reasons for this. One is that historically the executive has always been the core of government, and what we today call legislatures and courts are, so to speak, branches that have grown out from the original executive trunk.

Political scientist Anthony King points out that in the early years of most polities, all government power was exercised by a monarch or a ruling oligarchy. As other centers of economic and social power emerged, the new elites wanted to limit, but not abolish, the power of government and they calculated that the best way to do this was to establish new institutions or adapt old ones, make those institutions independent of the sovereign, and give them the power to check and limit the sovereign's powers.

THE TWO FUNDAMENTAL EXECUTIVE FUNCTIONS

For the forgoing reasons it is tempting to define "executive" officers and agencies simply as those officers and agencies that are clearly not part of either the legislature or the courts, but it may be a bit neater to define **executives** as *the heads of nonlegislative and non-judicial agencies who are elected or appointed for limited terms to supervise the making and execution of government policies.* In this chapter we will not try to describe the almost countless activities and functions of the almost numberless officials and agencies that fit this definition. Instead, we will focus on the top executives in modern governments—the presidents, prime ministers, monarchs, dictators, and juntas—that receive so much attention from political scientists and the news media.

We begin our survey by noting that in modern governments those top executive officials play one or another—and in a few instances both—of two quite distinct roles. Every government has an official who serves as its **chief of state**, which is *the official who acts as the government's formal head and spokesperson.* Every government also has an official who serves as its **head of government**, which is *the official who leads and supervises the officers and agencies that initiate and enforce the government's policies.*

The head-of-government role has much the greater impact on the making of public policy in modern governments, and so we will devote most of our attention to it in this chapter. The other role is by no means insignificant, however, and so we will briefly review what the chief-of-state role involves, how it is performed, and who performs it.

Executive as Chief of State

PRINCIPAL TYPES

Since the executive has always been the core of government and the formal head of every government has been an executive, it is not surprising that several different types of chiefs of state have developed. Four are most common: hereditary monarchs, elected "monarchs," elected heads of government, and collegial executives.

Hereditary Monarchs

In forty-three nations today the chiefs of state are **hereditary monarchs**, who are *persons who inherit their positions as chiefs of state*. They perform their functions either directly (for example, the British queen, the Belgian and Scandinavian kings, and the Japanese emperor) or indirectly through official representatives known as governor-generals (for example, in such nations of the British Commonwealth as Australia, Canada, and New Zealand).

As recently as the nineteenth century, many hereditary monarchs not only served as their nations' chiefs of state but also played prominent roles in policy making, and some were close to being absolute dictators. Even today government in many constitutional monarchies is formally conducted in the monarchs' names. The British queen, for example, opens and dissolves Parliament, gives her assent to all acts of Parliament before they become law, appoints all ministers and judges, and awards all titles of nobility and other honors. Yet the queen, like her fellow sovereigns in Belgium, Denmark, Japan, Norway, Spain, Sweden, and the other constitutional monarchies, does those things only on the advice of her ministers, who are selected by and responsible to Parliament. Only in a few monarchical dictatorships, such as Saudi Arabia and Oman, do present-day monarchs play policy-making roles approaching those of such absolute monarchs of history as Philip V of Spain or Louis XIV of France. Constitutional monarchs, then, are chiefs of state *only*; and in this capacity they perform functions we will consider in a moment.

Elected "Monarchs"

In the twentieth century most absolute monarchs have been toppled from their thrones, and many have been replaced with more democratic regimes. In the constitutional monarchies this change has been accomplished by stripping the monarchs of all policy-making powers and leaving them only the ceremonial functions of a chief of state. Other nations have entirely abolished their monarchies and replaced them with regimes formally headed by officials, usually known as presidents, who are selected by the national legislatures or by special electoral colleges and who perform the chief-of-state functions but have no power over policy making. The presidents of Austria, Germany, Iceland, India, Italy, and Turkey are examples of such "elected monarchs."

Directly Elected Heads of Government

A few democratic countries vest the functions of chief of state in directly elected presidents who also act as heads of government. The outstanding instance of such an official is, of course, the president of the United States, but similar dual roles are performed by the presidents of Argentina, Brazil, Colombia, Costa Rica, Cyprus, Ecuador, Finland, France, and Venezuela. In every such nation the performance of those two very different roles by a single official generates complications, some of which we will examine later.

EX-KING FOR A DAY

The occasions on which constitutional monarchs refuse to follow the advice of their ministers are so rare that they fall in the "man bites dog" class of news events. But they do happen. In 1990, for a recent example, the parliament of Belgium enacted a law legalizing abortion, but, as in all constitutional monarchies, King Baudoin had to sign the act to make it a law. However, Baudoin, a devout Roman Catholic, said he could not in good conscience sign the bill but that he "would not block the proper functioning of democratic government." What to do? After a good deal of hand wringing, the cabinet of Premier Wilfried Martens invoked an article of the constitution that allows the king's responsibilities to be taken over by the cabinet if he cannot perform his duties. So Baudoin abdicated for one day, and the cabinet assumed his responsibilities and signed the bill into law. The next day the cabinet voted to restore Baudoin to the throne, and the brief constitutional crisis was over.

Swiss Collegial Executive

In only one modern democratic nation are the executive powers and functions neither divided between two officials, as in the parliamentary systems, nor concentrated in one official, as in the presidential systems. In Switzerland they are performed by a seven-member Federal Council, selected every four years by the two houses of the national parliament meeting in joint session. The parliament also selects a member of the council to serve for one year as president of the Confederation, and the office rotates annually among the members of the council in order of seniority. Ceremonial functions are performed by the member who happens to be president at the moment, but the policy-directing functions are performed by the whole council.

The Swiss council has as much independent power as any chief executive in a presidential system. The constitution prohibits the legislature from holding a vote of no confidence, and if the legislature defeats a proposal made by the council, no law or custom requires the council to resign. Thus, Switzerland has a de facto separation of executive and legislative powers, and most scholars classify the Swiss system as a hybrid form closer to presidential democracy than to parliamentary democracy.

PRINCIPAL FUNCTIONS

Symbolic and Ceremonial

In Chapters 1 and 2 we noted that one of the greatest problems facing the people of every modern democratic nation is maintaining a society and government in which interest groups can freely pursue their conflicting objectives yet continue to live together as one nation under one government. We observed that every such nation faces the ever-present possibility of civil war and disintegration and that it also contains certain social forces and institutions that encourage national unity and consensus. In the final analysis, we concluded, the citizens of the United States, like those of any democratic nation, will continue to live together peacefully as one nation only so long as they think of themselves as *Americans* as well as African-Americans, Catholics, workers, or whatever.

Every nation has symbols and ceremonies that help to remind its citizens of their common national identity, achievements, and aspirations. No American needs to be told of the significance of the Stars and Stripes, the Pledge of Allegiance, or the Fourth of July; and other nations have their equivalents. Most citizens of every democratic nation evidently feel the need to include among those symbols a special person who officially embodies their national identity and on great occasions speaks for the whole nation both to the outside world and to the nation itself.

This need is the main reason that every nation, democratic or authoritarian, has an official chief of state (almost always a single official), and the chief of state's functions are intended to meet the need. When, for example, a member of the armed forces receives the nation's highest decoration—for instance, the Congressional Medal of Honor or the Victoria Cross—the president or the queen pins it on. When the nation pays tribute to its war dead, the president or the queen lays a wreath on the unknown soldier's tomb. When the Red Cross, the Boy Scouts, or some other worthy enterprise needs a boost, the president or the queen speaks on its behalf and is photographed with its leaders. In those and many other ways the president and the queen personalize and humanize that sometimes grim abstraction "the government" and remind the citizens of their common heritage and hopes.

Reigning

Constitutional monarchs and elected "monarchs" perform mainly ceremonial and symbolic functions, but they also reign; that is, they provide the formal channel through which power is passed in a peaceful and orderly way from one head of government to another.

In the parliamentary democracies, for example, when the prime minister leaves office and must be replaced by another, the chief of state officially accomplishes the transfer by summoning the new leader and giving him or her the responsibility of forming a new government. On the great majority of such occasions in Great Britain and other parliamentary democracies, the chief of state has no option but to summon the leader of the party with the most seats in the national legislature.

Yet British monarchs occasionally make real choices. The clearest instance was in 1957, when the Conservative party leader and prime minister Sir Anthony Eden suddenly resigned. Because the Conservatives held a majority in the House of Commons, Queen Elizabeth II had to replace Eden with another Conservative, but the party had never decided whether it wanted Eden's successor to be Harold Macmillan or R. A. Butler. After private consultations with her personal advisers, the queen summoned Macmillan, and he became the new prime minister. She is widely believed to have played a similar role in the choice of Sir Alec Douglas-Home over Butler in 1963. Since then, however, the Conservatives (and all other British parties) have adopted procedures that enable them to choose new leaders in a few days, and so it is unlikely that any future British monarch will have as much freedom of choice as Elizabeth II had in 1957 and 1963.

SEPARATION AND MINGLING OF ROLES

During the Korean War (1950–1953), President Harry S Truman was scheduled to award a posthumous Congressional Medal of Honor to an American serviceman through his father, but the father refused to accept it, saying, "Harry Truman isn't fit to honor my son." This episode dramatized the disadvantages of combining in one executive officer the two separate roles of chief of state and head of government. The serviceman's father was not saying that the United States itself was unfit to honor his son, but only that the individual Harry Truman—who was not only president of the United States but also the feisty head of the Democratic party, "the man who got us into the war," a Fair Dealer, and many other political things— was objectionable. In other words, the father objected to the head of government, not to the chief of state, but both officials came wrapped in the same Missouri package.

Television and radio networks face a related problem. When a U.S. president speaks free of charge in a national broadcast and the opposition party demands equal free time to reply, the networks must decide whether the president was speaking as chief of state or as head of government. If he was speaking as chief of state, the opposition's demand should be denied, but if he was speaking as a *political* leader, fair play requires that the opposition be given equal time.

It is illuminating to recall in this regard that when the English kings Charles I (1625–1649) and George III (1760–1820) played active parts in policy making and strove to become the heads of their governments, they were widely and openly criticized (indeed Charles I was executed). Now that such monarchs as Harald V of Norway and Elizabeth II of Great Britain are chiefs of state *only*, they are largely beyond public criticism and certainly are in no danger of losing their heads. Occasionally British monarchs and their heirs have been criticized for making political speeches (that is, speeches favoring certain policies), but such criticism means only that particular individuals may have stepped outside their proper roles and not that the roles themselves have become intermingled and confused, as in the United States. Herman Finer has summed up the advantages of assigning the two roles to different officials:

> As a father-image, or an impersonation of the romantic, says the psychoanalyst, king or queen stands scatheless, the noble father or mother, while the politicians may be vilified and scourged. This duality is politically comfortable. On the one hand, politics might be red in tooth and claw; on the other, royalty reminds the nation of its brotherhood and their conflicts. The silk gloves are something to be thankful for.[2]

Conversely, being chief of state is useful to the president of the United States in his role as head of government. Like his counterparts in other democracies, the president in his capacity as head of government has come to play *the* central role in the making and enforcement of public policy.

President as Head of Government

PRESIDENTS AND PRIME MINISTERS

Every modern democratic nation except Switzerland has a single executive officer who assumes the demanding and key role of head of government. However, the manner in which the head of government performs this role is greatly affected by whether he or she operates in a presidential or a parliamentary democracy (see Chapter 11).

Most modern democracies, as we have seen, have parliamentary systems. In each of those systems the role of head of government is performed by a leader formally designated by the chief of state for the post but actually selected by a majority of the legislature. In some countries the leader's official title is premier or chancellor, but the most common title is prime minister. In most cases the prime minister has no fixed term of office but depends upon his or her ability to get and keep the support of a legislative majority. When that majority turns down a major bill proposed by a prime minister, or when it passes a motion of no confidence, the prime minister must resign, and the chief of state must either call a new election or appoint a new prime minister whom the legislature will support. In Great Britain, Australia, Canada, New Zealand, and the other parliamentary democracies with strong national two-party systems, the prime ministers are normally the leaders of the parties holding majorities in the main legislative chamber.

As we observed in Chapter 10, however, a number of democratic countries have highly fractionalized party systems, and therefore no legislator can hope to lead a party that commands a majority in the legislature, as the British prime minister usually does. In those multiparty democracies the heads of government are chosen because they can put together coalition governments, each consisting of the leaders of several parties and supported by their members in the parliament. When one or two of the participating parties decide to withdraw their support, the prime minister's government falls and is replaced by a new coalition put together by a new prime minister, who may, of course, be the same person as the old prime minister. Prime ministers in the more fractionalized party systems vary widely in their security of tenure, their power, and their constitutional ability to direct public policy. Near one extreme we can place the Italian prime ministers, whose tenures of office have averaged less than one year and who are widely regarded as much weaker than the prime ministers in the two-party nations. Near the other extreme we can place not only the British prime ministers but also the prime ministers of several stable though highly fractionalized systems, such as those of the Scandinavian countries, the Netherlands, and Israel.

A few democracies, however, vest the powers of the head of government in a chief executive called the president ("the one who presides"). Those officials cannot be members of the legislatures and are elected to office either directly by the voters (for example, in Argentina, Brazil, Colombia, Costa Rica, Ecuador, Finland, France, Mexico, and Venezuela) or indirectly by an Electoral College (for example, in the United States). The presidents hold office for legally fixed terms whether or not they command the "confidence" of the legislatures. As we noted in Chapter 11, the presidency of the United States is the oldest and best-known office of this type and is in many respects the prototype for the others. We turn now to a more detailed examination of its powers and problems.

U.S. PRESIDENTIAL ROLES

Chief of State

The first role of the president of the United States is that of chief of state, in which capacity he performs symbolic and ceremonial functions similar to those of all chiefs of state. Although the combination of roles of chief of state and head of government in the presidency generates a certain amount of confusion (see above), it also lends U.S. presidents a kind of majesty that assists them considerably in their policy-making role. When the leader of the Republican party walks into a room, there is no reason for any Democrats or even most Republicans to pay him or her more than ordinary courtesy. However, when the president of the United States walks into a room, every American should stand up out of respect for the nation and the office that symbolizes the nation. Therefore, being president of the United States is bound to help the leader of any party in political campaigns and transactions with Congress. By far the greatest single asset any candidate for the presidency can have is to be the incumbent president, even though, as Gerald Ford, Jimmy Carter, and George Bush can testify, it does not guarantee reelection.

Chief Executive

The president formally heads most of the agencies charged with enforcing and administering acts of Congress and decisions of the national courts. In the mid-1990s President Bill Clinton was responsible in one way or another for the work of 14 major departments, more than 100 bureaus, 500 offices, 600 divisions, and a host of other agencies. Together they employed a total of about 3 million people, not counting members of the armed forces. This figure included approximately one out of every 65 civilians in the nation, in contrast to the ratio of one out of every 2,000 in George Washington's time.

For many years the president's principal assistants in supervising administrative agencies were the heads of the executive departments. There are now fourteen such departments: Agriculture, Commerce, Defense, Education, Energy, Health and Human Services, Housing and Urban Development, Interior, Justice, Labor, State, Transportation, the Treasury, and Veterans Affairs. Since the early 1790s, the secretaries of the executive departments have regularly met with the president and advised him not only on matters of administration but on matters of policy as well. In their collective advisory capacity they are known as the cabinet. Some presidents have been strongly influenced by their cabinets, whereas others have given theirs only a secondary role. Abraham Lincoln, for example, used his cabinet as little more than a sounding board for his own ideas, while Dwight Eisenhower and Ronald Reagan regarded their cabinets as among their most important advisory bodies.

FIRST AMONG UNEQUALS. President Clinton and his cabinet, 1994.

Over the years the cabinet has increasingly become an advisory body on policy rather than an administrative or supervisory agency, and recent presidents have turned more and more to other agencies to assist them in their mammoth task of overseeing the 3 million civil servants. In 1939 Congress established the Executive Office of the President for this purpose. That office now has more than 1,700 full-time employees and includes such agencies as the White House Office, the Office of Management and Budget, the Council of Economic Advisers, the Council on Environmental Quality, and the National Security Council.

Probably even more important than these official aides is the president's "kitchen cabinet," the small group of his most trusted advisers with whom he can talk most comfortably and those upon whose candid advice he counts, whether they hold official positions or not. Any list of the people most influential in shaping recent presidents' views on policy would include several who have held minor posts or none at all: Clark Clifford and Bill Moyers (Lyndon B. Johnson); H. R. Haldeman and John Ehrlichman (Richard M. Nixon); Dick Cheney and Donald Rumsfeld (Gerald R. Ford); Hamilton Jordan, Jody Powell; Charles Kirbo, and Rosalynn Carter (Jimmy Carter); Justin Dart, Holmes Tuttle, Joseph Coors, and Nancy Reagan (Ronald W. Reagan); Jonathan and Barbara Bush (George Bush); and Hillary Rodham Clinton (Bill Clinton).

Thus the presidency is no longer—if it ever was—something that the president carries around under his hat. It has become a large, complex network of public officials and private advisers performing in the president's name a wide variety of tasks only a small fraction of which he can supervise personally.

THE JOB OF PRESIDENT

A President has a great chance; his position is almost that of a king and a prime minister rolled into one.

Theodore Roosevelt

Measured against the opportunities, the responsibilities, and the resources of others in our political system and in other nations, the powers of the presidency are enormous. It is only when we measure these same powers against the problems of our age that they seem puny and inadequate.

Nelson W. Polsby[3]

I sit here all day trying to persuade people to do the things they ought to have sense enough to do without my persuading them. . . . That's all the powers of the president amount to.

Harry S Truman

Before he reached the White House, Woodrow Wilson once remarked: "Men of ordinary physique and discretion cannot be Presidents and live, if the strain be not somehow relieved. We shall be obliged always to be picking our chief magistrates from among wise and prudent athletes—a small class." . . . This formula needs some revision. The strain is vastly greater now, with no relief in sight. If we want Presidents alive and fully useful, we shall have to pick them from among experienced politicians of extraordinary temperament—an even smaller class.

Richard E. Neustadt[4]

Chief Diplomat

The president has always dominated the formation and conduct of U.S. foreign policy. He is the sole official channel of communication with foreign nations, and by receiving or refusing to receive official emissaries from foreign nations, he alone determines whether or not the United States formally recognizes their governments. He and his representatives negotiate all international treaties and agreements. The U.S. Constitution requires that all treaties be approved by two thirds of the Senate, but recent presidents have concluded a great many "executive agreements" (international agreements made by the president on his own authority and not referred to the Senate for ratification). The importance of such agreements is shown by the Supreme Court's refusal to decide whether or not they are just as binding as treaties ratified by the Senate.

Commander in Chief

The U.S. Constitution designates the president as commander in chief of all armed forces. The framers of the Constitution wrote this clause mainly to establish the cherished principle of civilian supremacy and control over the military, and some wartime presidents (such as Abraham Lincoln and Franklin D. Roosevelt) have been very active in planning strategy and even directing troop movements, whereas others (such as James Madison, Woodrow Wilson, and George Bush) have left such matters entirely to professional soldiers. The main significance of the president's position as commander in chief is this: The Constitution gives Congress, not the president, the power to *declare* war. However, as commander in chief the president can order the armed forces to go wherever he wants them to go and do whatever he wants them to do, including making armed attacks on other nations.

Since the mid-nineteenth century a number of presidents have done just that. To mention only some recent instances, in 1950 President Truman ordered U.S. armed forces to resist the North Korean attack on South Korea. For two years the United States fought a "police action" in Korea that was not a war only because Congress did not formally declare it. A series of executive decisions by Presidents Eisenhower, Kennedy, and particularly Johnson escalated U.S. involvement in Vietnam from the supplying of advice and material to a full-scale war involving more than 500,000 American troops. Only Congress's Tonkin Gulf Resolution of 1964 (repealed in 1970) served as a broad after-the-fact authorization. In 1983 President Reagan, at the request of some neighboring countries and in order to rescue U.S. students from possibly being held hostage, ordered an armed invasion of the Caribbean country of Grenada. In 1986 Reagan ordered U.S. warplanes to bomb targets in Libya to deter the government of Muammar al-Qaddafi from continuing to train and finance terrorists for attacks on U.S. and European civilians. In 1989 President Bush ordered U.S. forces to capture Panama City, arrest Panamanian dictator Manuel Noriega, and bring him to trial for helping to smuggle illegal drugs into the United States. When Iraq invaded Kuwait in 1990, Bush immediately ordered 200,000 U.S. troops to defend Saudi Arabia against invasion. In 1991, the army of an international coalition led by the United States recaptured Kuwait and invaded part of Iraq. In 1994 President Clinton sent military forces to Haiti to help reinstate President Jean-Bertrand Aristide, who had been overthrown by a military coup in 1991.

Until the 1970s, the U.S. Supreme Court consistently held that all these presidents were acting properly under their powers as commander in chief. In 1973, however, Congress took the first major step in over a century to limit the president's war-making powers. It passed a law setting a sixty-day limit on the president's power to commit troops abroad without a prior congressional declaration of war or specific authorization for the commitment of troops. The law also provides that Congress can at any time pass a concurrent resolution (a congressional act that does not require a presidential signature to take effect) ending any unauthorized presidential commitment of combat troops. President Nixon vetoed the bill, arguing that it would endanger the nation's security by preventing him and future presidents from acting swiftly in emergencies. But Congress was more concerned with recovering its constitutional power over war and peace, and both houses overrode the veto, with consequences first experienced by President Ford (see his boxed comments) and strong objections by Ford and every president since. Nevertheless, when President Bush in 1991 determined that economic sanctions would not be enough to drive Iraq out of Kuwait, he took military action only after asking Congress for authorization to do so. By relatively small majorities both houses voted the authorization, and only then did the military operation "Desert Storm" begin. However, in 1994 President Clinton did not ask for congressional authorization to send troops to Haiti, but, like many of his predecessors, he believed his authority stemmed from his constitutional position as commander in chief of the armed forces.

Former President Gerald R. Ford writes of the difficulties of taking action under the restrictions of the War Powers Act of 1973:

Once the consultation process began, the inherent weakness of the War Powers Resolution from a practical standpoint was conclusively demonstrated. When the evacuation of Da Nang was forced upon us during Congress's Easter recess, not one of the key bipartisan leaders of the Congress was in Washington. Without mentioning names, here is where we found the leaders of Congress: two were in Mexico, three were in Greece, one was in the Middle East, one was in Europe, and two were in the People's Republic of China. The rest we found in twelve widely scattered states of the Union. . . .

On June 17, 1976, we began the first evacuation of American citizens from the civil war in Lebanon. The Congress was not in recess, but it had adjourned for the day. As telephone calls were made, we discovered, among other things, that one member of Congress had an unlisted number which his press secretary refused to divulge. After trying and failing to reach another member of Congress, we were told by his assistant that the congressman did not need to be reached. We tried so hard to reach a third member of Congress that our resourceful White House operators had the local police leave a note on the congressman's beach cottage door: "Please call the White House."[5]

Emergency Leader

In the spring of 1861, faced with the secession of a number of Southern states and the imminent collapse of the Union, Abraham Lincoln ordered Fort Sumter to be provisioned and reinforced, knowing full well that his action would start a civil war. After Fort Sumter had been fired on, Lincoln—on his own authority and without prior authorization by Congress—proclaimed a naval blockade of Southern ports, called for volunteers to build up the Union army, spent government money on war supplies, suspended the writ of habeas corpus, and generally ignored constitutional restraints on his power. Lincoln knew that he had violated the Constitution by those acts, but in a letter to one of his critics he explained why he had done so:

I felt that measures otherwise unconstitutional might become lawful by becoming indispensable to the preservation of the Constitution through the preservation of the nation. Right or wrong, I assumed this ground, and now avow it. I could not feel that, to the best of my ability, I had even tried to preserve the Constitution if, to save slavery or any minor matter, I should permit the wreck of the government, country, and Constitution all together.[6]

Lincoln believed that any government must have an emergency power, a power to do whatever is necessary to save the nation in a crisis. Because the president can act more swiftly than Congress, this power must necessarily be his. Lincoln's reelection in 1864 and his subsequent elevation to something approaching national sainthood suggest that the American people in his time and since have not only approved his actions in this crisis but have also expected his successors to take over in other crises. Subsequent presidents have at various times intervened in strikes, closed the banks, suspended stock market operations, and ordered troops to take military action abroad or suppress disorder at home. There is no doubt that in any future crisis—a great depression, a nuclear war, major domestic violence—most Americans will look to the president rather than Congress to lead them.

Party Leader

The president is also either the chief Democrat or the chief Republican. The U.S. national parties, as we observed in Chapter 10, are mainly devices for nominating and electing presidents, to a smaller degree agencies for staffing the top political positions in the administrative agencies, and to a still smaller degree agencies for making policy in Congress. In all those operations the president is the leader of one of the two major parties. He names the chair of its national committee, and if he is a candidate for reelection, usually dominates its national convention. Through his appeals to party loyalty and his promises to help reelect his party's members of Congress, the president can exert some modest influence over Congress. In none of those capacities is the president as powerful as national party leaders in most other democratic nations, but he certainly comes much nearer to being the national leader of his party than anyone else. No matter how strongly the president may wish to be "above parties" and "the president of all the people," he will sooner or later be forced to act as a partisan. For example, President Dwight D. Eisenhower (1953–1961) at first wished to avoid partisan campaigning in the 1954 congressional elections, but the pleas of his fellow Republicans for help became so strong that he not only issued a public blanket endorsement of all Republican candidates but also personally campaigned more actively than any president had ever done in an off-year election, at least until President Reagan's efforts in 1982 and 1986.

The party that has *lost* the presidency, however, has no equivalent leader. Its defeated presidential candidate—like the Democrats' Jimmy Carter in 1981, Walter Mondale in 1985, and Michael Dukakis in 1989—may or may not still be liked by the party, but with rare exceptions he is regarded as a political has-been. Even when the "out-party" controlled one house of Congress, as the Democrats did after the defeats of Carter, Mondale, and Dukakis, their chief leaders (House speakers Thomas P. O'Neill, Jim Wright, and Tom Foley) made no claim to be the head of the whole party and would have been ridiculed if they had. The fact is that the out-party has *no* single recognized leader and does not get one until it nominates its next presidential candidate.

This is in sharp contrast with British practice. After each general election the leader of the largest party in the House of Commons becomes prime minister, and the leader of the second largest party is automatically named to a salaried official position that has no U.S. counterpart: the Leader of Her Majesty's Loyal Opposition (a position held in 1994 by Tony Blair, the leader of the Labour party). This makes a major difference: If Americans want an authoritative statement from the "out-party" (that is, the party other than the one led by the president) about what it would do about, for instance, tax reform or health care, that party simply has no single leader who is authorized to speak for it and will not have one until it nominates its next presidential candidate. However, when the British want to know the official opposition's position on any issue, the leader of the opposition is clearly authorized—indeed, paid by public funds—to state it.

Chief Legislator

In the capacity of chief executive the president can make a great deal of law, as the term *law* is defined in this book. The president can issue proclamations, directives, regulations, and orders, all of which are legally binding on those to whom they apply and enforceable by the courts. For example, two days after he took office in January 1993, President Bill Clinton issued two executive orders canceling orders made by his Republican predecessors: (1) he lifted the "gag rule" that had prohibited anyone except doctors at federally funded family-planning clinics from discussing abortions with patients; and (2) he lifted the ban imposed by Reagan and Bush on medical research using tissue from fetuses derived from elective abortions.

The president is generally also regarded as our chief legislator mainly because he now takes most of the initiative in the nation's statute-making process (see Chapter 11). Most of the major public bills passed by Congress are conceived and drafted by the president's advisers in the cabinet and the administrative agencies and steered through Congress by the president's supporters in both chambers.

Congress does not, of course, meekly obey the president's every order. Far from it. Congress almost always revises his requests, sometimes drastically, and not infrequently rejects them entirely. However, to the extent that the U.S. system has a single source and supervisor of an overall legislative program, the president is it.

Legislative relations between the president and Congress are more often a contest than an effort at cooperation. Congress retains the formal power to enact statutes and make appropriations, so it is far from helpless in this perennial contest. Over the years, however, various presidents have fashioned weapons to overcome Congress's constitutional advantages. They include the following.

CONVINCING CONGRESS   During his service as floor leader of the Senate Democrats (1953–1960), Lyndon Johnson won a reputation as one of the most skilled legislative leaders in history. In his first years as president (1963–1966) he matched— many think excelled—Franklin Roosevelt's record of inducing Congress to adopt his programs, including such major and controversial measures as the Civil Rights Act of 1964, the Voting Rights Act of 1965, and the War on Poverty. Most observers believe that his basic method was to convince members of Congress that it was in the nation's interest *and* in the members' interest to vote for his programs. He used direct conversation (the White House phone was in constant use), favors and reminders of past favors, and detailed knowledge of the politics and needs of the congressional districts and the states, which permitted him to know whom to press when, how, how hard, and how often. His phenomenal success suggests that the best way to win the legislative contest with Congress is to make his initiatives appear to be accommodations of mutual interests rather than tests of strength.

On the other hand, when Ronald Reagan took office in 1981 he not only had never served in Congress but had never held any federal office. Nevertheless, he performed what many observers regarded as a legislative miracle in his first months in office. He proposed abrupt slowdowns in many long-established federal programs, a massive increase in defense spending, and a substantial reduction in personal income taxes. Despite the fact that the opposition Democrats held a substantial majority in the House of Representatives, Reagan got his program through, mainly by winning the support of nearly all the Republicans and adding to them enough defecting Democrats to construct a legislative majority. By contrast, although his fellow Democrats had majorities in both houses of Congress during his first two years in office (1993–1994), Bill Clinton had a great deal of difficulty in getting his measures enacted, especially his proposal for health care reform.

Thus skill, not experience, is what gets the job done. But even when Congress refuses to be persuaded, the president still has some other shots in the locker.

THE VETO AND THREAT OF VETO   The U.S. Constitution provides that if the president vetoes (refuses to approve) an act of Congress, it can become law only if re-passed by a two-thirds vote in each house. Such majorities are usually very difficult to muster. From 1789 to 1993 a total of 2,903 bills were vetoed, and only 103 (3 percent) were overridden by Congress. The veto is thus a powerful negative weapon. It has also become a positive weapon, for many a president has let it be known through his congressional co-partisans that if a particular provision is retained in a particular bill he will veto it and has thus often induced Congress to eliminate an objectionable provision.

The effectiveness of the veto is limited, however, by the fact that it is not an item veto such as those enjoyed by the governors of many U.S. states. The president must either approve or veto a bill in its entirety and cannot veto only some items while approving others. Like many of their predecessors, presidents George Bush and Bill Clinton repeatedly urged Congress to give them the power to veto particular items in bills, especially appropriations bills. In 1995, each house of Congress passed a bill giving the president the item veto. The two bills were very different, however, and a conference committee was unable to reconcile them.

The absence of such a power makes possible the practice of attaching "riders": Congress includes items that the president opposes in a bill (especially an appropriations bill) that he cannot afford to veto. No doubt that handy way of getting certain items past the president accounts in part for the longstanding reluctance of Congress to give the president the item veto. But even without it his veto power is a strong weapon of legislative leadership.

PARTY LEADERSHIP   To some extent every president since William McKinley (1847–1901) has used his position as party leader to influence Congress to follow his wishes. Some, notably Woodrow Wilson, Franklin Roosevelt, Lyndon Johnson, Ronald Reagan, George Bush, and Bill Clinton have used party leadership with some success. As we noted in Chapter 10, however, a president can remove a rebellious member of Congress belonging to his party only by defeating the member in a state or district primary election. Only a few presidents have tried to do so, and they succeeded only on the rare occasions when they were able to gain the support of the local party organization. Thus, the president's party leadership is one of his weaker weapons.

TALKING BACK TO THE PRESIDENT

The personal touch with members of Congress does not always work for presidents. A classic case in point was the effort by President Eisenhower in 1957 to persuade Congressman Otto Passman (Democrat, Louisiana) to drop his opposition to the 1957 foreign aid bill. Rowland Evans describes what happened:

"It was kind of embarrassing, you understand," he told me in his musical southern voice. "I refer to it as the Passman trial. They sent for me in a long black Cadillac, I guess the first time I had ever been in one. I felt real important, which is not my usual way of feeling. When I got to the President's study at the White House, all the big shots were there. Admiral Radford and Secretary Dulles and the leaders of Congress. We had tea and little cakes and they sat me right across from the President. They went around the room asking for comments, one minute each. When they got to me, I said I would need more than one minute, maybe six or seven minutes, to tell what was wrong with their program. . . ."

Passman's lecture was complete with footnotes and fine print. Figures down to the last thin dime, unobligated balances in the various foreign aid accounts, carryover funds, re-obligated, de-obligated obligations, supplies in the pipe-line, uncommitted balances, and so on— in that mysterious verbal shorthand that only a man who lives and breathes foreign aid could comprehend. . . . After . . . everyone left, the President turned to his staff and said, "Remind me never to invite that fellow down here again."

Source: Rowland Evans, Jr., "Louisiana's Passman: The Scourge of Foreign Aid," Harper's Monthly, January 1962, pp. 78–83. Used with permission.

APPEAL TO PUBLIC OPINION   Wisely used, the president's most powerful weapon against balky legislators is a direct appeal to the people to pressure their representatives to support the administration's program. Most presidents have considered it a weapon of last resort, to be used only when all others have failed. If the president is more nearly in tune with the state of public opinion than Congress, and if his appeal to the people is skillful, Congress can hardly resist him, for such an appeal hits legislators where they are most vulnerable: in the ballot box. However, if Congress has gauged the popular temper more accurately than the president, if the president's appeal is inept, or if he makes too many appeals on too many issues, he loses his credibility. The trick is knowing when, how, and on what issues to make such appeals. Most observers believe that Ronald Reagan's professional skills and experience as a movie actor and television host—unique in the history of the presidency—enabled him to use this weapon more effectively than any president since Franklin Roosevelt. But even Reagan often failed to get the results he hoped for with his appeals on national television.

POWER AND PROBLEMS OF THE U.S. PRESIDENT

In trying to be an effective head of government, the typical U.S. president has several advantages over the typical prime minister. For one, presidents are not elected by, or responsible to, the Congress (except for the impeachment device, which has been used against a president only twice in over 200 years). For another, presidents have a number of independent constitutional powers (as chief executive, sole channel of communications with foreign nations, and commander in chief) that enable them to make and enforce many policies on their own without even consulting Congress, let alone winning its approval. Perhaps most important, the president's many roles reinforce one another and strengthen his domination of the policy-making process. As Rossiter sums it up:

> He is a more exalted Chief of State because he is also the Voice of the People, a more forceful Chief Diplomat because he commands the armed forces personally, a more effective Chief Legislator because the political system forces him to be a Chief of Party, a more artful Manager of Prosperity because he is Chief Executive.[7]

Yet there are many limitations on the president's power. As Richard Nixon learned the hard way in 1974, the constitutional process of impeachment is still more than a quaint historical anachronism. The U.S. Constitution limits the president to two elected terms in office, and because of this, his legislative and party leadership are inevitably weakened to some degree, especially in his second term. Dwight Eisenhower learned this in his second term (1957–1961), Richard Nixon was forced to resign partway through his second term (1973–1974), and Ronald Reagan learned the same hard lesson in his second term (1985–1989), particularly in the last two years. And Gerald Ford (1976), Jimmy Carter (1980), and George Bush (1992) lost the elections in which they sought second terms.

The U.S. Constitution also assigns large independent powers to Congress and the Supreme Court, which means that the president cannot command them; at best, he can only persuade them. When Congress denies the president the legislation and appropriations he seeks, he cannot, as a prime minister can, dissolve Congress, force a new election, and get another Congress more to his liking. The Supreme Court can declare some of the president's acts unconstitutional (as it declared President Truman's seizure of the steel mills in 1952 unconstitutional), and though the president may threaten to "pack" the Supreme Court as Franklin Roosevelt did in 1937, the widespread belief in an independent judiciary will frustrate him. The president can never count upon either solid or energetic support for all his policies from all the members of his party in Congress or in the country. Despite the president's formal position as chief executive, he cannot even be sure that his orders to his administrative subordinates will be carried out just as he wishes.

The presidency remains the key institution of American government, but although the system allows the president many opportunities to persuade, it offers him little power to command. Here is testimony from one who knew:

> In the early summer of 1952, before the end of the campaign, President Truman used to contemplate the problems of the General-become-President should Eisenhower win the forthcoming election. "He'll sit here," Truman would remark (tapping his desk for emphasis), "and he'll say, 'Do this! Do that!' *And nothing will happen*. Poor Ike—it won't be a bit like the Army. He'll find it very frustrating."[8]

PRESIDENCY OF FRANCE

Before 1958 the president of France was an indirectly elected "monarch" of the type described earlier in this chapter. But the Constitution of the Fifth Republic, adopted in 1958 and still in force, converted the French presidency into a very different kind of office, and it has changed further in the years since.

The 1958 constitution provided France with a form of government that does not fit easily into either the "presidential" or "parliamentary" category we have been using. President Valery Giscard d'Estaing (1974–1981) called it "presidentialist," and most observers think it has become much more presidential than parliamentary.

The French president is directly elected by the voters for a seven-year term, and there is no limit on how many terms he can serve. The president appoints the premier, theoretically with a view to the preference of the members of his party in the National Assembly but actually as his personal choice. In 1958 President Charles de Gaulle chose as his first premier Michel Debre, a member of the Assembly and second in command of the new Gaullist party, the *Union pour la Nouvelle Republique* (UNR). In 1962 the two men disagreed about calling a national election, and Debre resigned—not, be it noted, because the National Assembly voted against him but because *le grand Charles* dismissed him. De Gaulle replaced Debre with Georges Pompidou, a businessman and longtime loyal supporter, who had never been elected to public office. This choice made it clear that the premier does not hold the position because he or she is the number-two leader of the largest party in the assembly. The premier is premier because the president personally chose him or her. The premier, so to speak, is the national commander's chief of staff. When Pompidou succeeded de Gaulle as president in 1969, he in turn selected his own man, Jacques Chaban-Delmas, rather than accepting someone picked for him by his party.

The French president has many other broad powers. He can dissolve the National Assembly and call a general election whether the premier requests it or not. Article 16 of the constitution stipulates that when the nation's independence or institutions are threatened, the president is authorized to suspend regular government procedures and take whatever measures he sees fit (as de Gaulle actually did during the 1961 revolt by the French colonists in Algiers). The president can submit constitutional amendments directly to the voters for popular referendums without prior authorization by the National Assembly (as de Gaulle did in the referendum of 1962, in which his constitutional amendment providing for direct popular election of the president was approved).

Some observers thought that the Fifth Republic and its presidency were the personal creations of de Gaulle and that when he left the scene both would change radically. Their expectations were put to the test in 1969. De Gaulle resigned after the voters in a referendum rejected his proposals for constitutional reform. A special election to replace him was held, Pompidou was elected, and Pompidou's presidency differed some in style and policy but very little in executive power from de Gaulle's. The same has been true of the presidencies of Giscard d'Estaing, Francois Mitterand, and Jacques Chirac.

What kind of government, then, *is* the Fifth Republic? The best way to answer this question is to ask what would happen if the president and a majority of the National Assembly had an irreconcilable difference on an important policy matter. In a pure presidential democracy there would be a deadlock but each branch would nevertheless serve out its term in office. In a pure parliamentary democracy either the prime minister would resign, or a new election would be called and the new legislative majority would either reappoint the old prime minister or select a new one. What about France?

Events in 1986–1988 have suggested something of an answer. Francois Mitterand, the leader of France's Socialist party, was elected president in 1981, his party won a majority in the legislative elections a month later, and for the next five years he named a succession of Socialist leaders to be premier. In the legislative elections of 1986, however, a coalition of conservative opposition parties won a small majority in the National Assembly. Socialist premier Laurent Fabius immediately resigned, and Mitterand asked Jacques Chirac, the principal leader of the newly dominant conservative coalition, to become the new premier.

In doing so, Mitterand acted just as the chief of state in a parliamentary democracy would act, but his term as president still had two years to run, he still had many constitutional powers independent of the assembly, and the question of whether France's system is parliamentary or presidential could not be answered finally until either the assembly or the president flatly refused to take an action demanded by the other. Such a situation had never arisen before, so no one could say with certainty what the outcome would be.

Though many expected it, the final confrontation did not take place. Both Mitterand and Chirac stopped short of forcing a showdown, and they continued as president and premier in an arrangement the French called *cohabitation* (a delightful French word for an informal political truce). In 1988 Mitterand ran for another seven-year term as president against Chirac and won. Chirac resigned as premier, and Mitterand appointed a member of the Socialist party, Michel Rocard, as the new premier. In the parliamentary elections a few weeks later, however, the Socialists won only 48 percent of the seats in the National Assembly, so a new form of *cohabitation* began.

Under the new situation Rocard could cobble together majorities to support his legislative proposals only by getting some support from the Communists or the conservatives. There were two ways in which Rocard could be removed as premier. One was for Mitterand to do it himself without regard to what the National Assembly wanted, and he did just that in 1991 when Rocard resigned and Mitterand replaced him with Edith Cresson, the first woman to serve as premier in France. The other way was for an absolute majority of all the members of the National Assembly to vote for a censure motion, which would require total cooperation between the Communists and the conservatives. So both Rocard and Cresson had to negotiate a new legislative majority for each of their proposals, but remained in office as long as Mitterand wanted them there (Cresson was forced to resign in 1992, and Mitterand appointed another Socialist, Pierre Beregevoy, to the post).

In 1993 the conservative coalition again won a majority of seats in the National Assembly, Socialist premier Beregevoy immediately resigned, and Mitterand appointed another conservative, Edouard Balladur, as premier. In 1995 Mitterand retired and Chirac was elected to replace him.

Thus cohabitation (the French equivalent of divided government in the United States, discussed in Chapter 10) has become a part of the French constitutional system, and the question of whether the French system is closer to the American model or the British model remains unanswered.

OTHER PRESIDENCIES

Although the presidencies of other presidential systems, unlike that of France, have been modeled on the office of president of the United States, most have become even more powerful than their Washington prototype. Most have all the U.S. president's formal powers: position as chief of state, power of appointment, direction of administration, dominance over foreign policy, command of the armed forces, a veto over legislation, and so on. Many also have some additional formal powers, notably the right to introduce bills directly in the legislature.

Those other presidents are generally free of some of the U.S. president's handicaps. For example, some have the power to make most or all administrative appointments without having to secure legislative approval. Moreover, in none of those nations does a merit system cover as many offices as in the United States, and the presidents' appointment powers thus go far beyond those of their Washington counterpart. Furthermore, the legislatures of Argentina, Brazil, Chile, Colombia, Mexico, Venezuela, and the rest generally pass legislation couched in much more general and permissive language than is used by the U.S. Congress. As a result, their presidents have powers to issue *decretos con fuerza de ley* (decrees having the force of law) to carry out general legislative instructions, powers that are far broader than any comparable power of the U.S. president. In some nations, indeed, the president's *potestad reglamentaria* (regulatory power) applies to substantially more of the total policy-making process than does the legislature's statute-making power.

One striking recognition of the executive power in the other presidential democracies is their longstanding limitations on presidential tenure. The United States has had such a limitation only since 1951, and France has none at all. The most common rule in the other presidential democracies is a requirement that the president cannot be reelected until a specified period has elapsed after leaving office (four years in Colombia, ten years in Venezuela, forever in Mexico).

The great formal powers of those other presidents are in every case equaled or exceeded by their informal powers. The presidents are considerably stronger leaders of their national parties than the occupant of the White House, and their control of extensive patronage enables them to keep potential rebels in line far more effectively than the U.S. president can. They are no more dictators than he is, for with all their advantages they must still persuade their legislatures to go along, and in some nations some of the time they are not very successful. Like the U.S. president, they have limited tenure in office and little or no influence over the choice of their successors. However, while they are in office the presidents of the Latin American democracies enjoy more political weapons and fewer political handicaps than the U.S. president.

Prime Minister as Head of Government

STRUCTURE OF THE BRITISH EXECUTIVE

The British executive, or "the Government" as it is often called,[9] is composed of three interrelated but distinct sets of officials: the prime minister, the ministry, and the cabinet.

Prime Minister

The first stage in the formation of a British executive (or Government) occurs when the reigning monarch summons one of her subjects and asks him or her to become prime minister and form a government. In most instances the monarch has no option but must pick the leader of the party holding the largest number of seats in the House of Commons (though, as we noted earlier, on a few occasions when the leading party has not designated a leader the monarch has exercised some choice). The prime minister must be not only a member of Parliament but also, since 1902, a member of the House of Commons. Note the difference between the two systems: In the presidential democracies the chief executive *cannot* be a member of the legislature, whereas in the parliamentary democracies the chief executive *must* be a member of the legislature.

Ministry

The prime minister automatically becomes First Lord of the Treasury (a paid office with no administrative duties). He fills the other top and secondary executive posts by making recommendations to the monarch, which are invariably accepted. Those posts include the top ministers, the heads of the twenty ministries (which are equivalent to U.S. executive departments): for example, the Foreign Office, the Home Office, and the Ministry of Defense. They also include some additional ministers without specific departmental duties, such as the lord privy seal and the chancellor of the Duchy of Lancaster; and some with duties, such as the economic secretary to the treasury and the minister of state in the Foreign Office. In addition to those top officials there are also the parliamentary secretaries, who serve as deputies to the ministers of the various departments; several law officers (such as the attorney general and the solicitor general); and the whips (see Chapter 11). Those top executives (amounting to about one hundred officials in all) plus the prime minister constitute the ministry, or the Government.

In making recommendations to the monarch, however, the prime minister does not have an absolutely free hand. In the first place, with rare exceptions, every member of the ministry must be a member of Parliament, and most important

---

REPLACING A FORMIDABLE PRIME MINISTER

The prime ministers of Great Britain acquire their positions because they are the leaders of the majority party. When their parties reject them, they can no longer be prime minister. Case in point: Margaret Thatcher. In 1975, the members of the Conservative party in the House of Commons decided they had had enough of their leader, Edward Heath, who had led them to two straight election defeats. By secret ballot they chose Margaret Thatcher to replace him. She thereby became the first woman in history to lead a major British party, and when the Conservatives won a majority of the seats in the House of Commons in the 1979 general election, she became the first woman prime minister in British history. She proved to be one of the most formidable, controversial, and successful prime ministers ever. She turned British government sharply away from the welfare-state policies

it had followed since 1945. She led the Conservatives to victory in the general elections of 1983 and 1987. She held office for a record eleven years.

In 1990, however, many Conservatives in Parliament had become fed up with her imperious manner, her uncompromising right-wing ideology, and especially the likelihood, suggested by public opinion polls, that her leadership would cause them to lose the next election. So they held another secret-ballot leadership election. After the first ballot showed that she would probably lose, she withdrew from the contest, and the party elected John Major as her successor. Because the majority party had rejected her as its leader, she could no longer serve as prime minister. She immediately resigned, Queen Elizabeth II called on Major to replace her, and Thatcher became a backbencher and, later, a member of the House of Lords.

---

ministers must be members of the House of Commons. In the second place, most members of the ministry and all the important members must be leaders of the majority party, except in coalition or national (all-party) governments such as those established during times of crisis (for example, from 1915 to 1922 and from 1940 to 1945). In the third place, the prime minister must find posts for the other top leaders of the parliamentary party regardless of how he or she feels about them personally, and must also make sure that no major faction of the party feels left out.

Cabinet

The ministry never meets or deliberates as a body. Such meetings are left to the cabinet, which consists of those members of the ministry whom the prime minister regularly invites to consult with him or her as a group. Its size and composition change from time to time, in accordance with the prime minister's wishes, but normally it has between eighteen and twenty-three members. (John Major's new cabinet in 1992 had twenty-one members.) It includes all the top ministers both with and without departmental duties. It has thus been called "a select committee of Parliament," but it is better described as "a committee of the top leaders of the majority party."

CABINET STATUS, FUNCTIONS, AND POWERS

Some commentators on the British system emphasize the convention according to which the cabinet, like the ministry and the prime minister, remains in power only as long as it "commands the confidence of the House of Commons"; that is, as long as the House does not vote down any measure that the cabinet regards as impor-

FIRST AMONG EQUALS. British Prime Minister John Major and his cabinet, 1992.

tant and does not pass a motion of no confidence in the whole cabinet or any of its members.

This emphasis is misleading. Since 1894 only four prime ministers and cabinets have resigned because of adverse votes in the Commons (Lord Rosebery in 1895, Stanley Baldwin in 1924, Neville Chamberlain in 1940, and James Callaghan in 1979), and the discipline and cohesion of British parties are so strong that such episodes are highly unusual. The cabinet cannot and does not totally ignore the feelings of the Commons, of course, but it can usually count on as much of its full statutory five-year tenure of office as it wishes.

Although a number of its members have administrative and supervisory duties, the cabinet is primarily a policy-making body. Its members and their advisers conceive, draft, and introduce most of the major public bills in Parliament. They defend government policies in parliamentary debate, guide government legislation through the various parliamentary stages, decide which amendments to accept and reject, and generally control what Parliament does.

The dominance of the cabinet over Parliament is thus far greater than that of the U.S. president over Congress. There are many reasons for this, some of which, such as the great cohesion and discipline of British parties, we have already noted. We should add one more: the prime minister's power to dissolve Parliament and force a general election. According to British law, a general election for all members of the House of Commons *must* be held every five years, but it *may* be held at any time earlier than that chosen by the prime minister. Thus in Great Britain the dates of elections are not fixed by law and known in advance, as they are in the United States. Indeed, one of the favorite games for British politics buffs is guessing when the prime minister is going to call the next general election. When the prime minister asks the monarch to dissolve Parliament, the monarch must do so, and a general election for a new House of Commons must be held forthwith. This requirement means, of course, that should the Commons kick over the traces and deny the prime minister and cabinet some important piece of legislation, the prime minister need not meekly resign or carry on in office even though he or she cannot get policies adopted. The prime minister can call a new election. From the standpoint of the rebel MPs in the governing party, the trouble with a new election is that the opposition party might win. So a vote against one's party can amount to a vote to put the other party in power. Most MPs are unwilling to go quite that far in their occasional rebellions. Most analysts believe that the power of the prime minister to withhold the party label from rebellious MPs and, even more, the power to dissolve Parliament whenever he or she wishes are the cabinet's basic and nearly irresistible weapons in getting the House of Commons to follow the prime minister's leadership.

PRIME MINISTER AND CABINET

Not so long ago it was fashionable to say that the position of the prime minister in the cabinet is that of *primus inter pares* ("first among equals"), much like that of the chair of a corporation's board of directors. However, most present-day commentators believe that the modern prime minister has become the dominant figure within the cabinet and therefore within the whole British system of government. The prime minister, not the cabinet, has the power to ask the monarch to dissolve Parliament and to appoint and dismiss ministers, judges, and diplomats. The prime minister, not the cabinet, represents Britain at international summit conferences of heads of government. The prime minister determines who sits in the cabinet; the cabinet does not determine who is prime minister.

The present dominance of the prime minister is the result of three main factors. First, the increasing centralization, discipline, and cohesion of British political parties have given their leaders increasing control not only over the parties' rank and file but also over the second-echelon leaders who make up the cabinet and the ministry. The majority party's top leader is always the prime minister.

Second, the combination of universal suffrage and modern mass communications has increased the salience of the party leaders and decreased the salience of their parties in general elections. The campaigns are centered mainly on the personalities and qualifications of the major parties' leaders, who do most of the campaigning for their respective parties. Most people still vote mainly for the party they prefer or against the party they cannot stand. However, British voters today are less devoted to parties than they used to be, and so the personal popularity or unpopularity of each party's leader is increasingly important in British voters' decisions about which party to vote for in particular elections.

The prime minister's position is well summed up by Lord Robert Cecil:

> I should say that if you really looked into the real principal of our constitution now, it is purely plebiscital, that you have really a plebiscite by which a particular man is selected as Prime Minister, he then selects the Ministry himself, and it is pretty much what he likes, subject to what affects the rule that he has to consider—namely, that he must not do anything that is very unpopular.[10]

Third, the same kinds of economic and military crises that have, as we have noted, taken power away from the collegial body of the U.S. Congress and given it to the U.S. president as "emergency leader" have also taken power away from the collegial body of the British cabinet and given it to the prime minister as "emergency leader."

The prime minister is thus in some respects even more powerful than the president, particularly in the ability to lead the party and the legislature. But such power is certainly not enjoyed by the heads of government in *all* parliamentary systems.

PRIME MINISTERS IN COALITION GOVERNMENTS

The British prime minister's power is firmly rooted in leadership of a disciplined and cohesive political party that holds a majority of the seats in the House of Commons. As long as the prime minister commands its loyalty, he or she need not worry about how the opposition votes: It will usually vote against his or her proposals but will not have enough votes to defeat them. The prime minister's main political concerns are that the voters will approve the Government's policies and performance, that they will renew its mandate to govern at the next general election, and that his or her party will want the same leadership in its new term.

However, in the democratic nations with more fractionalized party systems (see Chapter 10), one party rarely if ever wins a majority of the legislative seats, and so the governments are necessarily coalitions of several parties. The prime minister (or premier) of such a coalition cannot rely solely upon his or her own party's backing, for the coalition needs the votes of all its members' parties to stay in office. So the prime minister's first concern must be what the coalition partners, rather than the voters, think of his or her actions and proposals.

How does this concern affect the first prerequisite for effective leadership, which is the ability to stay in office? The answer evidently depends upon the nature of the other parties in the coalition rather than upon the degree of fractionalization in the party system as a whole. Evidence for this conclusion is presented in Table 12.1, which shows that executive tenure in modern democratic countries is far from a simple reflection of party fractionalization.

For the most part, the figures in Table 12.1 show what we would expect: The most fractionalized party systems (Belgium, Denmark, and Italy) had the most changes in heads of government, and the least fractionalized systems (New Zealand, Canada, the United States, Great Britain) had far fewer. On the other hand, Israel, which ranks fourth in fractionalization, has had fewer changes than Great Britain;

TABLE 12.1   Party Fractionalization and Executive Tenure, 1945–87

NATION	FRACTION-ALIZATION RANKING	MEAN LEGISLATIVE PARTY FRACTION-ALIZATION, 1945–87*	CHANGES IN HEAD OF GOVERNMENT 1945–87**
Belgium	1	.3464	24
Denmark	2	.3138	15
Italy	3	.2357	30
Israel	4	.2299	6
Norway	5	.2175	8
West Germany	6	.1862	2
France	7	.1527	5
Ireland	8	.1152	12
Australia	9	.0812	4
Austria	10	.0760	4
Great Britain	11	.0348	7
United States	12	.0204	5
Canada	13	.0161	5
New Zealand	14	.0069	5

Source: Keesing's Record of World Events.

*Difference between mean party-fractionalization score and .5000 (see Chapter 10).
**Changes from one party to another or, in Belgium and Italy, from one faction of a coalition leading party to another; changes within the same party caused by death or resignation rather than by political developments are not counted.

and Ireland, which has a lower fractionalization score than Norway or France, has changed its head of government much more frequently. The fewest changes of all took place in West Germany prior to reunification, which ranked in the middle of the fractionalization scores.

Italy had the dubious honor of having the shortest executive tenures. All postwar Italian premiers except two have been members of the Christian Democratic party, but that party was organizationally weak and internally divided by strong ideological disagreements among its various factions. The result, at least until 1994 (see the box on page 284), was Byzantine maze of factional struggles within and between parties in the ruling coalition resulting in a rapid-fire succession of premiers and cabinets.

The position of the prime minister in a coalition government seems to depend upon several factors. If the legislative seats are divided among many little parties instead of a few big ones (as is usually the case in Belgium, Israel, and the Netherlands), then the prime minister will have that many more party leaders to find ministerial offices for and keep happy. If there are deep ideological divisions among the principal parties—and, even worse, among the factions of the prime minister's own party, the prime minister will have to construct his or her program very carefully. If the party and factional leaders dislike one another personally, the prime minister will have to handle them with special tact. Being prime minister of such a government is not the most desirable executive position in the world, though no nation seems to suffer any shortage of politicians trying to fill it.

A STABLE GOVERNMENT FOR ITALY?

Previous editions of this book used Italy as an extreme example of rapid changes of premiers and governments in parliamentary systems. A box listed each change of government in the period after 1979, and the final score for the fifteen years from 1979 to 1994 was:

Heads of government resigning: 15
Persons asked to form new governments: 21
Persons unable to form new governments: 8
Persons forming new governments: 14
General elections: 3

However, some observers predicted that radical changes in Italian electoral politics since 1993 would produce a new, more durable kind of premier and government. The changes stemmed from the Italian people's rage over the corruption pervading the old system, sparked by the revelations that many leaders of Parliament, including two former premiers, had taken bribes. In a referendum held in April 1993, 82 percent of the voters approved ending the 45-year-old system of proportional representation which had permitted so much corruption. In August 1993 Parliament voted to end the old system and replace it with a mixed system somewhat like Germany's (Chapter 8). Three-quarters of the members of the Chamber of Deputies were to be chosen by plurality votes in single-member constituencies, and the other seats were to be allocated proportionally to ensure that minor parties would have at least a few.

The first general election under the new system was held in March 1994. Remarkably, all of the principal old-line parties (the Christian Democrats, Communists, Socialists, Italian Social Movement, Social Democrats, Republicans, and Liberals) either changed their names or were absorbed by the new parties. The principal new party was the Forza Italia ("Let's go, Italy"), which advocated free-market policies and a flat-rate tax system. It was led by Silvio Berlusconi, the business tycoon who headed the country's private mass communications industry. Some observers said that Berlusconi was "Italy's Ross Perot," in that both men were business leaders who used their private fortunes to enter politics and found new organizations challenging politics-as-usual by establishment politicians.

The other parties were: the National Alliance (descended from the old neofascist Italian Social Movement; the Northern League, a regional party dedicated to breaking the power of the central government in Rome so that the prosperous North would no longer have to pay high taxes to support the less productive South; the Italian Popular party, which contained the remnants of the old Christian Democrats; the Democratic Party of the Left, composed mainly of the moderate wing of the now-defunct Communist party; and the Refounded Communist party, the successor to the hard-line wing of the old Communist party.

The election gave Forza Italia the most seats, and President Oscar Luigi Scalfaro asked Berlusconi to form a new government. After some delay, Berlusconi put together a coalition with the Northern League and the National Alliance, and the other new parties went into opposition. Berlusconi thus became the fifteenth premier in the fifteen years from 1979 to 1994.

Many Italians hoped that the combination of a new electoral system, a new set of political parties, a new coalition, and new leadership from a business tycoon rather than a politician would at last bring to Italy the stable government that many other multiparty countries enjoyed. But it was not to be.

From the beginning there were sharp frictions within Berlusconi's coalition, and in December 1994—only eight months after he took office—a major coalition partner, the Northern League, left the coalition and proposed a no-confidence vote. Berlusconi urged President Scalfaro to hold an immediate general election. Scalfaro refused and Berlusconi resigned.

In January 1995 Lamberto Dini, a "technocrat" with as little experience in politics as Berlusconi, became the premier in the new government—the fifty-fourth since 1947. Few observers expected the new coalition to hold together very long, and some concluded that, while the reforms had certainly given the system a new look, they evidently had not changed the basic structure of Italian government and politics.

Executives in Nondemocratic Systems

We need not linger long over the similarities and differences between executive roles in democratic systems and those in nondemocratic systems. In almost every Western-style democracy, as we have seen, the executive has become the single most powerful agency for making public policy. But we have also seen that the executive is far from being all-powerful. Even the most powerful democratic chief executives (the president of the United States? of France? of Finland? of Venezuela?) must operate within very real limits set by legislatures, courts, opposition parties, factions in their own parties, pressure groups, and ultimately the electorate.

The nondemocratic political systems have at least one trait in common, whether they be the Communist systems of China and Cuba or the one-party regimes or military dictatorships of Africa and Asia. In each the executive agency *is* the government. Indeed, in 1994, twenty nations had no legislature whatever. In this sense, then, the core agency of *all* governments is the executive, not the legislature, for, while a number of nondemocratic regimes operate with no legislatures, *no* regime, democratic or nondemocratic, operates without an executive. To be sure, the constitutional chief executives of some nondemocratic regimes may be only the chief lackeys of the all-powerful parties or ruling cliques. But the point is that their legislatures are essentially sounding boards and cheering sections for the dictators, party leaders, or ruling juntas. Their courts of law operate as arms of the executives and not as checks upon them. Accordingly, Western political scientists do not bother much with questions of the power of executives relative to the legislatures and courts in the nondemocratic nations.

Perhaps the most interesting comparative observation is that in many modern governments, democratic and authoritarian alike, a great deal of government policy is made in the *name* of the executive or legislature, but, in fact many policies are made by "nonpolitical" public employees presumably hired to carry out the wishes of the "political" executives and legislatures. Those employees have a number of labels: civil servants, bureaucrats, *apparatchiks*, and the like. But whatever they are called, those employees play powerful—though often obscure—roles in determining what rules their governments actually impose on the people under their jurisdiction. We will examine their roles in the next chapter.

For Further Reading

PRESIDENTS

*ANDREWS, WILLIAM G. *Presidential Government in Gaullist France*. Albany, NY: State University of New York Press, 1982. Study of the formative years of the unique French presidency under the Fifth Republic.

BRODY, RICHARD A. *Assessing the President: The Media, Elite Opinion, and Public Support*. Stanford, CA: Stanford University Press, 1991. Explains the rise and fall of American presidents' popularity as a factor of public response to elite opinions as filtered through the mass communications media.

*EDWARDS, GEORGE C., III. *At the Margins: Presidential Leadership in Congress*. New Haven, CT: Yale University Press, 1989. Analysis of how presidents use party leadership, personal contacts, appeals to the public, and other devices to persuade Congress to adopt their programs.

*HARGROVE, ERWIN C., AND MICHAEL NELSON. *Presidents, Politics, and Policy*. New York: Random House, 1984. Survey of current operation of the presidency and its role in policy making, with special emphasis on changes under the Reagan administration.

HERRING, E. PENDLETON. *Presidential Leadership*. New York: Holt, Rinehart & Winston, 1940. Classic study, based mainly on observation of Franklin Roosevelt's presidency.

JONES, CHARLES O. *The Presidency in a Separated System*. Washington, DC: The Brookings Institution, 1994. Analysis of how presidents operate when Congress is controlled by the opposition party.

KELLERMAN, BARBARA. *The Political Presidency*. New York: Oxford University Press, 1986. Study of recent presidents' strategies for getting their policies adopted.

KERNELL, SAMUEL. *Going Public: New Strategies of Presidential Leadership*. Washington, DC: Congressional Quarterly Press, 1986. Study of presidential appeals to public opinion, with special emphasis on the Reagan administration.

*KING, ANTHONY, ed. *Both Ends of the Avenue*. Washington, DC: American Enterprise Institute, 1984. Essays focusing on the changing relationships between the president and Congress.

LIGHT, PAUL C. *Vice-Presidential Power*. Baltimore, MD: Johns Hopkins University Press, 1982. Exploration of the increasing importance of the vice presidency in governing and as a steppingstone to the presidency.

LOWI, THEODORE J. *The Personal President: Power Invested, Promise Unfulfilled*. Ithaca, NY: Cornell University Press, 1984. Stimulating discussion of the conversion

PRIME MINISTERS

JONES, G. W., ed. *West European Prime Ministers*. London: Frank Cass, 1991. Comparative study of the powers and roles of prime ministers in Germany, France, Italy, Spain, the Netherlands, and Ireland.

*KING, ANTHONY, ed. *The British Prime Minister*, 2nd ed. Durham, NC: Duke University Press, 1985. Collection of essays on the British executive.

——, "Executives," in *Handbook of Political Science*, eds., Fred I. Greenstein and Nelson W. Polsby. Reading, MA: Addison-Wesley, 1975, vol. 5, pp. 173–256. Best broadly comparative analysis available, with a useful bibliography.

of the presidency into a direct relationship with the people, with adverse consequences for the governing system.

NEUSTADT, RICHARD E. *Presidential Power and the Modern Presidents: The Politics of Leadership from Roosevelt to Reagan*. New York: Free Press, 1990. An updated version of one of the most influential studies of the presidency, analyzing the performances of presidents from Franklin Roosevelt to Ronald Reagan.

*PAGE, BENJAMIN I., AND MARK P. PETRACCA. *The American Presidency*. New York: McGraw-Hill, 1983. Comprehensive description of the modern presidency, set in a theoretical framework explaining the powers and limitations of the office apart from the persons who occupy it.

PATTERSON, BRADLEY H., JR. *The White House Staff and Its Expanding Role in Government*. New York: Basic Books, 1988. Detailed study of the growing importance of the American president's personal staff in exercising presidential powers.

*POLSBY, NELSON W. *Congress and the Presidency*, 4th ed. Englewood Cliffs, NJ: Prentice Hall, 1986. The best short discussion of the relationship between the president and Congress.

*REEDY, GEORGE R. *The Twilight of the Presidency*, rev. ed. New York: New American Library, 1987. Lyndon Johnson's press secretary analyzes changes in the presidency from the Vietnam War era to the Reagan administration.

*ROCKMAN, BERT A. *The Leadership Question: The Presidency and the American System*. New York: Praeger, 1985. Analysis of presidential leadership in the fragmented American political system of the 1980s.

*MACKINTOSH, JOHN P. *The British Cabinet*, 2nd ed. New York: Barnes and Noble, 1968. Analysis stressing the "presidentialization" of the prime minister's position and the weakening of the cabinet's powers.

*ROSE, RICHARD, AND EZRA N. SULEIMAN, eds. *Presidents and Prime Ministers*. Washington, DC: American Enterprise Institute, 1980. A comparative study of heads of government in Great Britain, Canada, France, West Germany, Italy, Norway, Spain, and the United States.

Notes

1. Anthony King, "Executives," in *Handbook of Political Science*, eds., Fred I. Greenstein and Nelson W. Polsby (Reading, MA: Addison-Wesley, 1975), vol. 5, pp. 181–82.

2. Herman Finer, *Governments of Greater European Powers* (New York: Holt, Rinehart & Winston, 1956), pp. 189–90.

3. Nelson W. Polsby, *Congress and the Presidency*, 4th ed. (Englewood Cliffs, NJ: Prentice Hall, 1986), p. 84

4. Richard E. Neustadt, *Presidential Power and the Modern Presidents: The Politics of Leadership from Roosevelt to Reagan* (New York: Free Press, 1990), p. 163.

5. Gerald R. Ford, *The War Powers Resolution: Striking a Balance between the Executive and Legislative Branches*

(Washington, DC: American Enterprise Institute reprint no. 69, 1977). Copyright American Enterprise Institute.

6. Abraham Lincoln, letter to A. G. Hodges, April 4, 1864, quoted in Louis Brownlow, *The President and the Presidency* (Chicago, IL: Public Administration Service, 1949), p. 58.

7. Clinton Rossiter, *The American Presidency* (New York: Harcourt Brace Jovanovich, 1956), p. 25.

8. Neustadt, *Presidential Power*, p. 10, emphasis in the original.

9. British political commentators customarily use the term *the Government* to denote the entire body of politicians who for the moment control the administrative agencies and take the lead in making public policy. The Government includes twenty or so senior ministers who are members of the cabinet, thirty or so senior ministers who are not members of the cabinet, and fifty or so junior ministers. There is no exact U.S. equivalent to the term, but "the Administration" comes close. Just about everything said in the text about the structure and operation of the British executive also applies to the executives of Australia, Canada, and New Zealand.

10. Quoted in Herman Finer, *Theory and Practice of Modern Government*, rev. ed. (New York: Holt, Rinehart & Winston, 1949), p. 363. If Lord Cecil were writing today, of course, his pronouns would have to take account of the fact that the person who has served as prime minister in Great Britain longer than anyone else was a woman.

13

For forms of government, let fools contest;
Whate'er is best administered is best.
Alexander Pope, *An Essay on Man*

The Administrative Process

For all but a handful of citizens in any advanced industrial society, the *real* government consists of what political scientists call *administrators* or *bureaucrats*, not the top-level legislators, executives, and party leaders we have considered up to now. For one thing, 99 percent of all the people who work for the government fall in this class. For another thing, many of us think that members of Congress, members of Parliament, presidents, and prime ministers are not real people; rather, they are media figures, like movie stars and television anchors, in the sense that we never meet them face to face or deal with them directly. We know them only from what we see on television or read in the newspapers.

On the other hand, almost all of us have bought stamps at a post office or taken a test for a driver's license, and so we know firsthand what post office clerks and driving examiners are like and how they do their jobs. Governmentally speaking, they, and not most of the loftier public officials discussed in this book, are "where the rubber meets the road."

Accordingly, in this chapter we ask the following questions: What kind of people work in government jobs? How are they hired and fired? How good are they? Are they merely flunkies who carry out the orders of superiors, or do they make a lot of decisions on their own?

Political scientists usually begin their answers to those questions by making some important distinctions.

Distinction Between Executives and Administrators ————

IN FUNCTIONS

During the formative period of the U.S. Constitution, most Americans believed in the traditional conception that the governing process is divided into three distinct kinds of activity: law making, law enforcement, and law adjudication. They also believed that power over law enforcement should be assigned exclusively to the executive, and that the executive agencies should confine themselves largely to enforcing policies adopted by the legislature.

In Chapter 12 we observed that since the nineteenth century the executives of most democratic nations have acquired ever-increasing influence over policy. Toward the end of that century a number of political scientists, notably Woodrow Wilson and Frank J. Goodnow, recognized that the traditional description of the executive as an enforcer rather than an initiator of policy no longer fit the facts. Yet they wished to make some kind of distinction between policy-making and policy-enforcing officials, and they also wished to reconcile the ideal of a permanent, professional civil service with the ideal of a responsive democratic government. Consequently, they proposed a distinction between "political" (that is, policy-making) officials, including the president and other top executives, and "administrative" (that is, policy-enforcing) officials.

We will return to the Wilson-Goodnow formula in a moment, but we should note here that it underlies the distinction many political scientists continue to make between executives and administrators. **Executives** are *political heads of executive agencies who are elected or appointed for limited terms to initiate policies and direct the work of administrators.* **Administrators** are *persons appointed to executive agencies to enforce laws and carry out policies and whose tenure and promotion depend on professional merit rather than political affiliation.* We will learn that those distinctions become blurred in real life, but they will do as a place to start.

IN SELECTION AND TENURE

Although some political scientists continue to distinguish between executives and administrators (or civil servants, as administrators are often called) in the foregoing manner, most today believe that because many administrators play major roles in policy making, the politics-administration distinction is meaningless. However, few go on to argue that *all* public officials should be replaced whenever a majority of the voters transfer their support from one political party to another. Most continue to believe, with Wilson and Goodnow, in a permanent, professional civil service loyally doing the bidding of "political" legislators and executives, whose employees should be hired, promoted, or fired, not because of their party affiliations or political philosophies but rather because of their technical **merit**—their *praiseworthy qualifications for and/or performance of the tasks assigned to their positions.*

WHAT ABOUT "BUREAUCRACY"?

Some political scientists and sociologists use the term *bureaucracy* as a neutral synonym for civil service. They follow the German social theorist Max Weber in thinking of bureaucracy as a large and complex organization with fixed and official areas of jurisdiction, a hierarchical system of centralized authority, and a body of officials with special professional skills who follow systematic general rules and procedures.

However, that is not what many people mean by *bureaucracy*. To them, bureaucracy is a kind of congenital government disease, the leading symptoms of which are the addiction of public officials to labyrinthine procedures, buck-passing, senseless and rigid rules, rudeness to citizens, and operating at glacial speed:

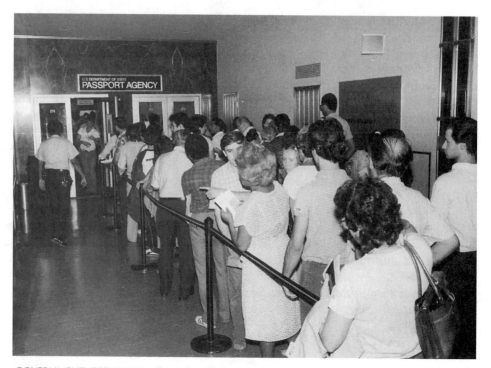

GOVERNMENT "RED TAPE." A line of passport applicants.

in short, everything summed up in the term *red tape*. We will therefore stick to the more neutral terms *administration* and *civil service* to denote the parts of government with which we are concerned in this chapter.

Formal Status of Administrative Agencies

SIZE

In terms of the number of people employed, the administrative agencies constitute by far the largest element of any modern government. Table 13.1 shows the number of civilians (persons serving in the armed forces are excluded) employed in the various branches and agencies of the U.S. federal government in 1991.

The figures in Table 13.1 show that the overwhelming majority of all federal employees work for the executive branch and that well over half work for just two huge agencies: the Department of Defense and the U.S. Postal Service. The grand total of 3,111,912 federal employees constitutes only 3 percent of all gainfully employed civilians, but when the 15,452,000 state and local government employees[1] are included the proportion is 16 percent. Some countries with less elaborate struc-

TABLE 13.1   Civilian Employment in the U.S. Federal Government, 1991

BRANCH OR AGENCY	NUMBER	PERCENTAGE OF TOTAL
Legislative branch	38,504	1.2
Judicial branch	25,805	0.8
Executive branch	3,047,603	98.0
Total	3,111,912	100.0
Executive departments		
Defense	1,012,716	33.2
Veterans Affairs	256,145	8.4
Treasury	166,433	5.5
Health and Human Services	129,483	4.2
Agriculture	125,640	4.1
Other departments	365,435	12.0
Independent agencies		
U.S. Postal Service	804,338	26.5
Other agencies	187,413	6.1
Total executive employees	3,047,603	100.0

Source: The American Almanac 1993–1994 (Washington, D.C.: Bureau of the Census, 1994), Table 531, p. 343.

tures of regional and local government than the United States employ smaller proportions of their labor forces in civil service jobs; in the early 1980s, for example, government employees constituted only about 6 percent of the gainfully employed in Great Britain and 15 percent in France.

STRUCTURE

A few decades ago most students of public administration believed in certain principles of organization, certain correct ways of "interrelating the subdivisions of work by allotting them to people who are placed in a structure of authority, so that the work may be coordinated by orders of superiors to subordinates, reaching from the top to the bottom of the entire enterprise."[2] Today most political scientists are dubious about the scientific validity or practical applicability of those principles, but many continue to believe that most administrative agencies should be organized in accordance with two principles: the principle of hierarchy and the principle of separating staff and line functions.

Principle of Hierarchy

According to the principle of hierarchy, the people in any administrative agency should be formally related to one another in a clear chain of command reaching from top to bottom and a line of responsibility from bottom to top. All employees should know just who are their superiors, equals, and inferiors and therefore to whom orders may be given and from whom orders must be taken. Often mentioned as models are the organization of any modern army and the clerical hierarchy of the Roman Catholic Church. The principle is illustrated by the organization of the U.S. Department of the Interior shown in Figure 13.1.

Principle of Separating Staff and Line Functions

This principle is based on the idea that every agency performs two basic types of functions. The U.S. Department of the Interior, for example, supervises the care of over 500 million acres of federally owned land; monitors health and safety procedures in the nation's mines; promotes the development, conservation, and use of fish and wildlife resources; preserves the nation's scenic and historic areas; and supervises the relations with our former trust territories in Micronesia. Those are Interior's "line" functions. In addition, the department, if it is to operate efficiently, must also perform a number of "staff" or "housekeeping" functions such as hiring and firing, determining promotions and pay increases, and budgeting. Many scholars of public administration believe that the two types of functions should be performed by different subagencies, each reporting to the agency's head but each independent of the other.

The point—and its complications—are also illustrated by the official organization chart of the Department of the Interior in Figure 13.1, which shows that the Department of the Interior's organization sticks closely to the two principles. The hierarchy is clear. The secretary is the head, the deputy secretary is the secretary's chief subordinate, and the staff agency heads, such as the executive secretary, solicitor, and inspector general, all report directly to the deputy secretary, who reports

FIGURE 13.1   Organization Chart of the U.S. Department of the Interior

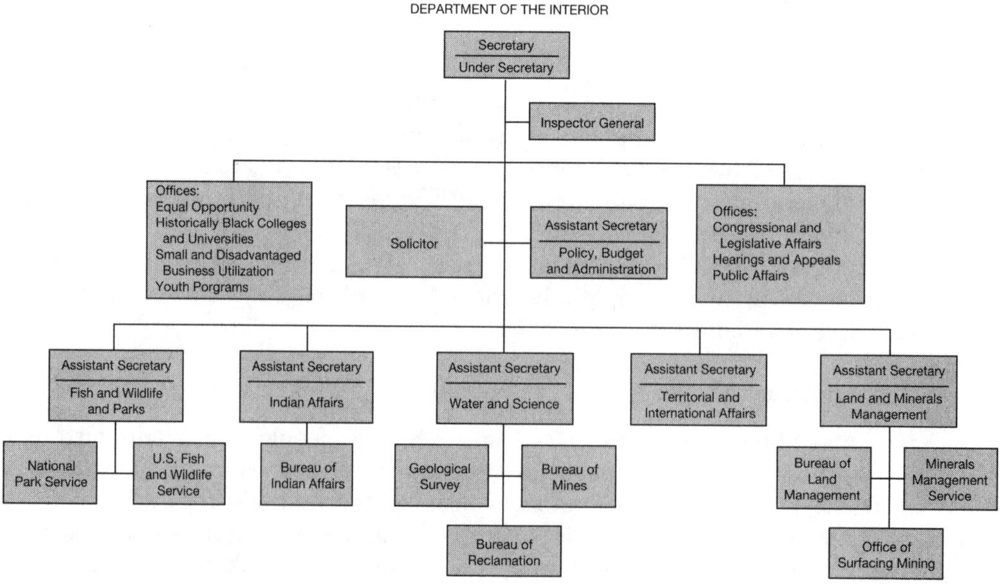

Source: *The United States Government Manual.*

to the secretary. Each of the line agencies reports to an assistant secretary, who in turn reports to the deputy secretary. For example, the heads of the U.S. Fish and Wildlife Service, the National Park Service, and the National Biological Survey all report to the assistant secretary for fish and wildlife and parks.

But a glance at almost any of the other organization charts in the *United States Government Manual* will show that the lines between staff and line agencies are often blurred, and many agencies bypass the assistant secretaries to report directly to the secretaries and undersecretaries.

Most modern students of public administration recognize that the practical problems of real-life agencies usually force deviations from the principle of hierarchy and the principle of separating staff functions from line functions. They say that what really matters is the informal organization and not the formal organization.

An agency's formal organization is the organization publicly prescribed by written acts of Congress and written rules adopted by the agency (for example, the formal organization of the Department of the Interior shown in Figure 13.1). On the other hand, anyone who closely observes an actual administrative agency soon learns that the *real* relationships among the various subdivisions, assistant secretaries, and bureau chiefs do not correspond exactly to those shown in the official organization chart. Thus the chart in Figure 13.1 shows that assistant secretary A and assistant secretary B are equal in power. However, in reality the secretary may think that A is lazy and see A as little as possible, and may think that B is shrewd and works hard and may see B every day and often take B's advice. Hence, while A and B are completely equal in the formal organization, B is clearly A's superior in the informal or actual organization.

Accordingly, an agency's formal organization chart is at best a rough guide to its actual organization, and it is the actual organization that gets things done. As this point has become more clearly understood, a growing number of political scientists have chosen to study administrative agencies as part of the larger subject of behavior in all human organizations. Thus political scientists, while aware of the prescribed legal powers and responsibilities, focus mainly on the networks of communication and influence among the people who are actually doing the work, for that is where decisions are really made and administrative functions are actually performed.

FORMAL ADMINISTRATIVE FUNCTIONS

Every administrative agency performs one or two, but rarely all, of the following basic functions.

Providing Services

Some agencies provide services for all who wish to use them. For example, the Agricultural Research Service of the U.S. Department of Agriculture conducts an elaborate program of research on such matters as pest control, fertilizers, and breeding and raising livestock. It makes the results available at low cost to farmers who wish to improve their operations. The British National Health Service, for another example, provides government-subsidized medical care and hospitalization for all who wish them. But in the United States, as in all advanced industrial nations, the largest services are defense and education, as described in the box.

REGULATING

Some agencies regulate the operations of private individuals and businesses to keep them from doing certain harmful things and to make sure that they do certain helpful things. The best-known example of regulation, of course, is the enforcement of criminal laws by the police, but there are many others, as is shown by the following list.

Regulating Economic Competition

Enforcement of contracts and granting and protecting copyrights and patents

Control of the issuance and sale of stocks and bonds

Prohibition of unfair competitive practices, such as false and deceptive advertising

Prohibition of unfair labor practices by employers or unions

Enforcement of antimonopoly laws, corporation income taxes, excess-profits taxes, and the like, in an effort to prevent excessive concentration of economic power

Control of banking procedures, reserve funds, and accounting practices

Control of the volume of currency and credit, control of prices, initiation of public works, and other measures to prevent extreme fluctuations in the business cycle

Regulation of contributions to, and expenditures by, political candidates, parties, and political action committees

Regulation of rates charged by power companies, telephone companies, and other public utilities

Prevention of signal interference and maintenance of programming standards by licensing television and radio broadcasting stations

Regulating Safety, Welfare, and Morals

Detection, capture, trial, punishment, and rehabilitation of persons committing crimes

Preventing and putting out fires

Enforcement of safety standards in the construction and operation of buildings, roads, bridges, harbors, airports, nuclear power plants, automobiles, aircraft, lawnmowers, and so on

GOVERNMENT SERVICES: AN EXAMPLE

Of all the services modern governments provide, defense and education cost the most, and education affects by far the most people. Every modern government has laws requiring all citizens to attend accredited schools, usually for ten years beginning at age six and ending at age sixteen. The main purposes of the required education everywhere are to teach young people skills they will need to play productive roles in the economy and to instill the attitudes that will make them good citizens. Every government also provides opportunities for some students to continue their studies in colleges and universities.

In many democratic nations some people fulfill the education requirements by attending accredited private schools, but most people attend schools that are owned and operated by governments and staffed by government employees (in the United States in 1991, 39 million students were enrolled in public schools at all levels, and 7.2 million were enrolled in private schools). In some democracies, such as Great Britain and the United States, private schools are more important at the college and university level, but even those schools depend heavily on government financial support.

How does the U.S. educational system compare with the systems in other democratic nations? The U.S. Bureau of the Census reports that in the 1980s the United States ranked sixth among seventeen leading democratic countries in the percent of the population enrolled in elementary and secondary schools (Ireland, New Zealand, France, the Netherlands, and Norway had higher percentages) and first in the percent of the population enrolled in colleges and universities.

What percent of their gross domestic products do nations spend on education? The U.S. Bureau of the Census reports that the United States ranks second in educational expenditures at all levels (only Canada spends a higher percentage), and first in expenditures on higher education.[3]

Thus, the United States spends more on education at all levels than most other countries and spends more

on higher education than any. Moreover, the percentage of Americans enrolled in colleges and universities is several times higher than that in other countries. Many democracies abroad believe that only a few, extremely well-qualified students should be admitted to college-level institutions, and stiff requirements are set for high scores in national examinations to select the few who get in. On the other hand, the United States has long proceeded on the conviction that all citizens who can profit from a college education should have a chance at it, even if their test scores and secondary-school grades are not at the top.

However, the U.S. educational system differs from those in other nations mainly in its *decentralization*. Although there has been a national Department of Education since 1979, the 50 states and the 14,556 local school districts provide most of the money and make most of the policies for the elementary and secondary schools and for the public colleges and universities as well.

But how does the *quality* of U.S. education compare with that in other nations? Many students, educators, parents, and politicians in many countries have long and inconclusively debated that question. While there are no universally agreed answers, many commentators, both in the United States and abroad, have concluded that pupils in primary and secondary schools (K-12) in the United States score worse on cross-national standardized tests and are less well-educated in such basic skills as reading and writing, foreign languages, mathematics, and science than are their counterparts in Western Europe, Scandinavia, and Japan. Those commentators also conclude that U.S. education looks better at the higher levels. Undergraduate students in American colleges and universities come closer to matching the skills and performance of their counterparts in other countries, and, at the top, the quality of graduate and professional programs in law, medicine, and engineering are at least as good as any in the world. Certainly, many more foreign students come to the United States for such advanced training than Americans go abroad for it.

GOVERNMENT REGULATION. A scientist in the Food and Drug Agency tests a new drug for possible licensing.

Enforcement of health and sanitation standards in the production, labeling, and distribution of food and drugs

Enforcement of professional qualifications through the examination and licensing of doctors, nurses, pharmacists, lawyers, architects, teachers, pilots, and so on

Enforcement of rules governing private exploitation of mineral, forest, wildlife, wilderness, and other natural resources

Prevention and cleaning up of pollution of air, water, and other aspects of the environment

Enforcement of moral standards in the production and distribution of liquor, drugs, gambling, movies, books, magazines, and television and radio programming

Encouragement of employment of minorities by affirmative action programs

Minimum-wage and maximum-hours laws

Limitation of aliens' access to professions and employment

Control of the spread of infectious and epidemic diseases by such means as quarantines

Zoning and anti-billboard regulations to preserve the aesthetic qualities of parts of the environment

Licensing

In most democratic nations, a private person or corporation can legally conduct certain kinds of business only after obtaining a license from an administrative agency. Thus licensing involves not only the performance of a service but also a considerable measure of regulation. This point is illustrated by the description in Chapter 7 of how the U.S. Federal Communications Commission uses its power to grant and renew licenses for radio and television stations as a device to control the way broadcasters present political issues and candidates. Similar regulatory power is involved in any agency's power to grant or withhold licenses.

Adjudicating Disputes

The job of settling disputes by applying the law to particular situations is assigned exclusively to the courts in the traditional allocation of government powers and functions.

Yet in many democratic nations in recent decades, administrative agencies have undertaken a number of quasi-judicial functions ("quasi" only because the functions are performed by administrators instead of judges). When, for example, a U.S. worker or employer complains to the National Labor Relations Board (NLRB) that an employer or a union is engaging in an unfair labor practice in violation of the law, the NLRB is empowered to hold hearings, render a decision, and dismiss the complaint or order the challenged practice stopped. For another example, in Great Britain, complaints by workers about the orders of their superiors in the nationalized coal industry are brought before the National Coal Board, which then decides what action, if any, should be taken. This type of administrative activity has drawn increasing attention to issues concerning the regular courts' powers to review and reverse administrative decisions, and we will return to the problem later in this chapter.

SELECTION AND STATUS OF ADMINISTRATORS

Selection

At some period in its history, every modern democratic nation has selected its civil servants for reasons other than merit.[4] For example, in Great Britain before the nineteenth century, most government posts were filled by *patronage*, which was an arrangement whereby members of the nobility and landed gentry literally owned certain government jobs and, as "patrons," filled those jobs with relatives, friends, and retainers, many of whom were too incompetent to hold any other kind of job. In France's *ancien régime* before the revolution of 1789, all but the few highest offices were regarded as a kind of private property, to be sold, bequeathed, or given away by their owners to whomever they pleased. In the United States before the late nineteenth century, most civil-service posts were filled by the **spoils system**, *awarding government jobs to supporters of the party in power*.

Prussia (and later united Germany) was the first modern nation to select its civil servants by the **merit system**, which is *the selection, retention, and promotion of government employees on the basis of demonstrated technical merit*.

Beginning in the late eighteenth century, civil service reform movements emerged in most democratic nations, aimed at abolishing patronage and spoils and replacing them with merit systems on the Prussian model. The movement succeeded earliest in France in the 1790s, when Napoleon Bonaparte installed a professionalized civil service. In Great Britain the reform began in the 1830s when the administrators of British India established a merit system for selecting members of the Indian civil service. It was extended to the whole British civil service after the adoption in 1853 of the Northcote-Trevelyan Commission's report on the organization of the permanent civil service. In the United States national reform began in 1883 with the passage of the Pendleton Act, which established the Civil Service Commission and provided merit-system rules for the selection and promotion of members of some administrative agencies.

In most democratic countries today all or nearly all civil-service employees are selected by some kind of competitive examination, and tenure is largely or entirely independent of party affiliations. The U.S. national civil service has been somewhat slower in this respect than most, but, as Figure 13.2 shows, it has come a long way since 1883. By 1993 about 97 percent of all the federal government's civilian employees were under the merit system, and in most other democratic nations the proportion was as high or higher.

At present about 58 percent of all U.S. federal civil servants are under what is officially called the *competitive service*. Employees in this classification are appointed after they have passed written examinations drawn up and administered by the Office of Personnel Management (OPM), established in 1978 to succeed the old Civil Service Commission. The remaining 42 percent are under what is called the *excepted service*, in that they do not come under the jurisdiction of OPM. However, all but a handful in the excepted service are also selected on merit-system principles because they have special qualifications and skills needed for the jobs they fill, and the agencies that hire them run their own merit systems. This is the case, for example, with all Postal Service employees, all foreign-service officers in the State Department, and all agents of the Federal Bureau of Investigation. Only between 1 and 3 percent of the employees can be appointed by the president or his subordinates without any kind of special examination. Those include a variety of appointees, such as executive assistants, confidential secretaries, and ambassadors, whose first and most important qualification is that they be loyal to the president and his policy views.

FIGURE 13.2   Growth of the American Merit System

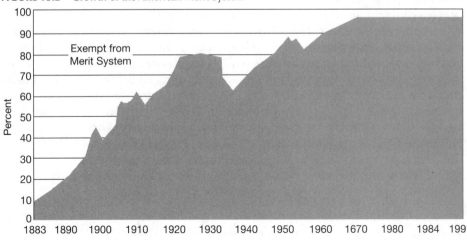

Source: Statistical Abstract of the United States, 1993 (Washington, D.C.: Bureau of the Census, 1994), Table 512.

Aside from this handful, almost all civil servants in the United States and in every other modern democracy are permanent in the sense that their tenure in office is not limited and they are not directly subject to the approval or disapproval of the voters through ordinary electoral processes.

Political Activity

Most modern democratic systems try to "keep politics out of administration"; that is, they try to insulate civil servants from interference by political parties so that civil servants may serve with equal faithfulness and efficiency the leaders of *any* political party that currently controls the legislative and executive policy-making agencies. The most common means for achieving this end is to protect civil servants from losing their jobs when one party replaces another in power. A number of democracies have added another means: restricting civil servants' participation in partisan political activities. In the United States, for example, members of the national "competitive" civil service and state and local employees of programs financed wholly or partly by the national government are forbidden by law from taking an active part in partisan politics. Those civil servants may vote, privately voice their political opinions, and even attend party rallies as spectators. However, they may not solicit funds for a party or candidate, make partisan public speeches, hold party office, or work for a party in any other way.

In Great Britain the rules prohibit "policy-making" civil servants from engaging in partisan activities, such as canvassing, making partisan public speeches, or standing as candidates, that might conflict with their roles as impartial servants of all parties. In recent years, however, British civil servants with "routine" posts have been permitted more freedom of partisan activity. France is among the few modern democracies that place no restrictions upon such activities, but even in France the ministers and top administrators can and often do use administrative regulations to prevent civil servants from supporting extreme antigovernment parties.

Administrative and political career lines are far more blurred in Japan than in most other democracies. Not only are civil servants allowed to engage freely in party and pressure politics, but movement from the civil service into political leadership—very rare elsewhere—is quite common in Japan. Career administrators tend to retire early and go on to a second career. Many retirees go into positions in private business, but many stand as candidates for the Diet (parliament). Indeed, "in recent years, roughly a third of the [ruling Liberal Democratic party] Dietmen and nearly half of the Cabinet ministers with portfolio have been ex-bureaucrats."[5]

Unions and Strikes

The traditional weapons used by workers in private businesses to protect and advance their interests are organizing unions and striking. What about government workers? Most modern democratic systems permit their civil servants to form unions but limit or deny altogether their right to strike. For example, employees such as police officers, fire fighters, and postal workers are generally prohibited from striking on the grounds that the continuous operation of their services is necessary to avoid national calamity.

However, those laws are sometimes difficult to enforce: It is impossible, for example, to jail hundreds of thousands of postal workers and school teachers, as U.S. governments at all levels have learned from time to time; and strikes or large-scale "sick-outs" by firefighters, police officers, sanitation workers, and others are by no means unknown. Public employees can also evade the prohibition of strikes in less risky ways. To illustrate, on several occasions British postal employees have sought higher wages through "work-to-rule" campaigns, in which they rigidly enforce every last postal regulation, with the result that mail delivery is so delayed that the government feels compelled to make concessions. Employees of nationalized railways and coal mines, on the other hand, generally have the right to strike, although every effort is made to avoid such strikes by prior arbitration. Even so, the year-long strike by British coal miners in 1984–1985 was one of the longest, costliest, and most bitter strikes by public employees in a long time. The net effect of those rules in most democracies is that a civil servant's right to organize in a union is almost as well-protected as that of a worker in private industry, but the civil servant's right to strike is much more restricted.

Politics, Administration, and Policy Making ━━━━━

DICHOTOMY BETWEEN POLITICS AND ADMINISTRATION

Many nineteenth-century U.S. reformers placed high value on the ideal of government efficiency and believed that a Prussian-style permanent, professionalized civil service would help to achieve efficiency in the United States. Most also valued the

STRIKES BY PUBLIC EMPLOYEES: THE CASE OF THE AIR TRAFFIC CONTROLLERS

The heavy traffic by commercial airliners and private planes into and out of most airports has made necessary the services of air traffic controllers (people on the ground who tell airplane pilots when they can land and take off and what routes they must fly). In the United States the controllers are federal employees working for the Federal Aviation Administration (FAA). For many years until 1981 they were allowed to form a union, the Professional Air Traffic Controllers Organization (PATCO), which served as their official bargaining agent with the government. However, the law prohibited air traffic controllers from striking.

In 1981 PATCO demanded a new contract for its members providing for $740 million in wage increases, but the FAA was willing to offer only $40 million. PATCO's president, Robert Poli, put the government's proposal to his members for a vote, and they turned it down by 13,495 to 616. So on August 3 the union went on strike. Federal judge Thomas Platt immediately issued an injunction against the strike and imposed fines of $2.4 million a day on the union for ignoring a back-to-work order, saying that such strikes "are substantially more than merely unfair labor practices—they are crimes."

President Ronald Reagan and Secretary of Transportation Drew Lewis took the same line. They gave the strikers forty-eight hours to return to work and said that any who failed to do so would be fired and banned from ever again working for the federal government in any capacity. The FAA staffed the control towers with military controllers and speeded up the training and certification of nonmilitary controllers, and air traffic continued, although at a reduced rate. Poli said that PATCO was willing to return to the bargaining table, but Reagan and Lewis said the time for that had passed. The strikers had broken the law and thereby forfeited the right to negotiate.

Other unions, including the American Federation of Labor and Congress of Industrial Organizations, showed some sympathy for PATCO, but many unions did not. Poli took the line that the air traffic control system had become badly understaffed and very unsafe, but John O'Donnell, the president of the airline pilots' union, said that the system was quite safe.

Secretary Lewis then instituted action in the courts to "decertify" PATCO (that is, revoke its certification as the officially recognized bargaining agent for federal air traffic controllers), and in August the courts made the decertification. This was the first time any U.S. union of public employees had ever been decertified.

On December 31, 1981, Poli resigned as PATCO's president. The air traffic control system was gradually restaffed, the strikers went into other lines of work, and the strike was completely crushed. The final irony of the episode was the fact that in the 1980 election, PATCO had been one of the few labor unions to endorse and give money to candidate Ronald Reagan.

The jobs embargo against former PATCO strikers ended in 1993 when President Bill Clinton declared that the embargo had lasted long enough, and announced that they would again be considered by the FAA for jobs as air traffic controllers.

---

ideal of democracy and had no wish to see the entire governmental process "Prussianized." They were reluctant to choose between the two ideals, and therefore for many the most urgent question was, How can a permanent, professional civil service be reconciled with the ideals and institutions of democracy?

Toward the end of the century, some political scientists advanced a doctrine that appeared to harmonize the two ideals, and for several decades thereafter many analysts of administration believed that this doctrine had settled once and for all the problem of the proper place of permanent administrators in a democratic government.

Origins and Content

Most students of U.S. public administration credit the first statement of the doctrine to an article published in 1887 by a young political scientist at Princeton named Woodrow Wilson. Briefly summarized, Wilson's argument ran as follows: The old classification of governmental powers and functions into legislative, executive, and judicial categories does not fit the facts of modern government. All governments perform only two basic functions: politics, which is the making of general policies and laws; and administration, which is the application of policies and laws to particular individuals and situations. Because administration is so different from politics, Wilson contended, it must be kept nonpolitical; for, in his words, "administrative questions are not political questions. Although politics sets the tasks for administration it should not be suffered to manipulate its offices. The field of administration is a field of business."[6] A quarter-century later Wilson became the twenty-eighth president of the United States and found that political reality is even more difficult than scholarly theory.

Wilson's dichotomy between politics and administration was taken up by another eminent political scientist, Frank J. Goodnow, and was elaborated into a broad doctrine of the proper place of administrators in a democracy, which he advanced in his influential book *Politics and Administration* (1900). Like Wilson, Goodnow argued that all government activities are either politics ("operations necessary to the expression of [the government's] will") or administration ("operations necessary to the execution of that will"). Unlike many of his advocates, Goodnow believed that those two functions could not be completely separated or exclusively assigned to entirely separate parts of government. He recommended, however, that as much as possible some agencies should be mainly political and others mainly administrative. He concluded that in a democracy the mainly administrative agencies must be subordinate to, and controlled by, the mainly political agencies. As he put it, "popular government requires that . . . the executive authority . . . shall be subordinate to the expressing authority, since the latter in the nature of things can be made much more representative of the people than can the executing authority."[7]

Consequences

For forty years after 1900, the politics/administration dichotomy was almost universally accepted by political scientists and shaped their thinking about the proper role of administrators in democratic government. This had three main consequences. First, for most scholars and reformers the doctrine provided a satisfactory theoretical justification for the presence of a permanent, professional civil service in the United States or any other democracy. If administrators only carry out policies assigned to them by political agencies, they reasoned, then there is no need to make civil servants directly responsible to the voters.

Second, the doctrine provided the theoretical foundations for a new "science of public administration," which first emerged in the United States in the decade after the publication of Goodnow's book. This new branch of political science concentrated on such problems as how to organize administrative agencies and how to recruit and train administrators so that administration can be conducted with maximum efficiency and economy. Those problems were similar to those taken up by the new and rising "scientific management" movement in private industry, headed by Frederick W. Taylor, the first of the modern "efficiency experts." The new specialists in public administration did not think that by concentrating on the values of efficiency and economy they were slighting the values of democracy. Democratic values, they felt, were the concern of politics, not administration; and civil servants should concentrate on how to maximize efficiency and leave to others the problems of maximizing democracy.

Third, the doctrine provided a clear and sensible set of principles for organizing governments. All policy-making officials were to be elected or appointed by elected officials for short terms, and all administrators were to be selected by the merit system and were to hold office as long as they remained technically competent and efficient.

Present Eclipse

Since the late 1930s, a growing number of political scientists, led by such scholars of public administration as Luther Gulick, Robert A. Dahl, Charles S. Hyneman, Carl J. Friedrich, and Francis Rourke, have rejected both the politics–administration dichotomy and the revised version of separation of powers based on it. They have abandoned the dichotomy because they believe it is an inaccurate description of the governing process. The exercise of discretion, they argue, is the essence of policy making; and all public employees, whether they are called politicians or administrators, exercise discretion. If politics means policy making and not merely partisanship, they conclude, it cannot be "taken out of administration" as long as administrators exercise the discretion to interpret the laws they administer and to decide when, how, and how much to enforce them. There is no way to prevent the exercise of this discretion even if it were desirable to do so.

Those scholars have come to this conclusion mainly through observing what administrative agencies actually do. They have found that no matter how professionalized and formally non-political administrative agencies are supposed to be, those agencies have a great deal to say about what policy is, and in the very nature of things administrators cannot be confined merely to carrying out policies laid down by legislatures and executives. Those scholars are convinced, furthermore, that the policy-making powers of administrators do not result from their hunger for power or contempt for democracy, but are inevitable products of modern government. Let us briefly survey the evidence on which they base those conclusions.

POLICY MAKING BY ADMINISTRATORS

Administrative Influence on Legislative and Executive Policies

In almost every human decision-making organization, experts—people who know the organization's problems inside out and have detailed technical knowledge about the possibilities and practicality of the various proposed solutions—

have an enormous advantage over nonexperts, who at best have only a general, partial, and probably shaky technical knowledge. The more complex and difficult the problems, moreover, the greater the experts' advantage. Since the problems of modern government are the most difficult faced by any human organization, expert administrators in a democracy have a very great advantage indeed.

For many reasons, administrators have a much better chance than legislators or executives to become experts on particular subjects. For one thing, administrators' careers tend to make them specialists on *one* subject, whether it be writing military procurement contracts, issuing passports, or regulating airline fares. Legislators and executives, on the other hand, necessarily deal with all those matters and many more besides and cannot afford to specialize. What is more, legislators and executives are often getting ready for the next election and must therefore spend considerable time raising money, planning strategy, and campaigning. Administrators, however, are forbidden to engage in such activities and can therefore spend their full time and energy on the policy questions before their agencies.

Finally, most legislators and executives are considerably less permanent than merit-system civil servants: It is said that the average U.S. assistant secretary of an executive department stays in office for only two years, while the average civil servant of comparable age and skill in the same department stays in office for decades. Thus legislators and executives do not have nearly such long periods in office during which to acquire the detailed knowledge and "feel" that constitute expertise.

In all modern democracies, accordingly, short-term, part-time, and unspecialized political officials often ask advice from long-career, full-time, and specialized administrative experts on the relative merits of policies, and far more often than not they follow the advice. Administrators' own policy preferences inevitably enter into and affect their advice. How could it be otherwise? Most of them are intelligent, well-meaning, conscientious people. They spend years pondering full-time the complexities of a few policy questions. As their knowledge and involvement grow, they are bound to develop strong preferences for some policies over others. Also they understandably feel that it is their patriotic duty as well as their professional obligation to express their conclusions and to do their best to see that the government follows wise rather than foolish policies.

Thus when administrators are asked for advice, they can hardly avoid making their views known, and when, as often happens, "political" officials and their constituents have no strong views of their own, civil servants' preferences are likely to become policy.[8]

Occasionally, of course, "political" officials have strong views of their own that run sharply counter to those of the civil servants formally subordinate to them. The Goodnow doctrine requires that the administrators in such situations set aside their own preferences and loyally carry out those of their political superiors. But government by no means always works this way, as is vividly illustrated by the "Irangate affair" in the United States in the late 1980s, which is sketched in the box.

ADMINISTRATIVE POLICY MAKING: THE "IRANGATE AFFAIR"

The "Irangate affair," which began in the early 1980s and had repercussions into the 1990s, involved complex questions about making and carrying out three major foreign policies of the Reagan administration. The first and highest on the administration's agenda was the effort to supply military and nonmilitary aid to help the contra rebels overthrow the hard-left Sandinista government of Nicaragua. The second was the effort to secure the release of a number of Americans kidnapped in Lebanon and held hostage by Shi'ite Muslim terrorists thought to be controlled by Iran's Shi'ite leader, the Ayatollah Khomeini. The third was the effort to develop contacts with presumed "moderate forces" in Iran as the basis for improving relations with that country after the Ayatollah left power.

From the day of his first inauguration, President Ronald Reagan repeatedly urged the Congress to supply aid to the contras. On some occasions Congress (in which the House of Representatives was controlled by the Democrats) voted both military and nonmilitary aid, on other occasions it approved only nonmilitary aid, and on some occasions it refused to provide any kind of aid. Moreover, in 1982 and 1984, Congress adopted the Boland Amendment (named after its author, Representative Edward P. Boland (D-Mass.), which prohibited the Defense Department and the Central Intelligence Agency from channeling any aid to the contras.

Congress's stop-go actions posed major difficulties for the administration's Central American policy, but Reagan and his national security adviser, Robert McFarlane, were also concerned about the kidnapping and possible torture of the hostages in Lebanon and about the possibility that Iran might win its war with Iraq and, because of its hatred for the United States ("the great Satan" in Khomeini's words), would destroy the U.S. strategic position in the Persian Gulf area.

In 1985, McFarlane proposed that secret approaches be made to the Iranian "moderates" so as to build a basis for better relations after the Ayatollah died. With Reagan's approval, and in close association with his chief aide, Marine Lieutenant Colonel Oliver North, McFarlane made a secret trip to Teheran, during which he worked out a deal to show good will toward Iran by selling arms to its leaders in return for Iran's showing good will toward the United States by securing the release of the hostages. In 1986 Reagan directed McFarlane's successor, Admiral John Poindexter, to continue the policy, the arms were sold, and the proceeds were placed in a secret Swiss bank account.

One hostage was released (while three more were captured), and nothing much came of the opening to the "moderates." However, fearing that Congress's denial of aid to the contras would destroy resistance to the Sandinistas, North and Poindexter used some of the funds in the Swiss account to purchase military supplies for the contras, and added funds they had secretly solicited from private donors and from some foreign governments. In late 1986, however, a Beirut newspaper published a story describing the arms sales, and Attorney General Edwin Meese investigated and discovered the diversion of the funds to the contras. Reagan announced that North was relieved of his post, and Poindexter resigned.

That did not end the matter. In 1987, both the House and the Senate appointed committees to investigate the arms sales and the diversion of the funds, and an independent counsel, Lawrence E. Walsh, was appointed to gather the facts and recommend indictments if the transactions had violated the law. In dramatic, nationally televised committee hearings during much of the summer of 1987, North, Poindexter, and a number of other people involved in what North called "the enterprise" testified about what they had done and why they had done it.

The testimony was far too lengthy and complex to be detailed here, but some highlights are worth noting. For our purposes, the key issue was this: Were North and Poindexter carrying out President Reagan's orders, or were they acting on their own? Both men testified that Reagan did not specifically direct the diversion of the funds and did not know about it, but they nevertheless felt that they were doing what was needed to carry out his general policy of aiding the contras. As Admiral Poindexter said, "I felt it was within my authority because it was an implementation of a policy that was well understood, that the President felt very strong about. . . . So it wasn't a matter of going out and making a secret foreign policy. The policy was clear. This was a way of going about, of carrying out that policy." He also said that he was careful *not* to tell the president what was going on "because I knew very well it would be controversial, and I wanted the President to have some deniability so that he would be protected and at the same time we would be able to carry out this policy and provide the opposition to the Sandinista government."[9] (North later changed his story and said that Reagan knew about and approved what North and Poindexter were doing, but Reagan continued to deny it.)

Two other statements are worth noting. In a nationally televised speech after the hearings concluded, President Reagan said, "Let me put this in capital letters: I did not know about the diversion of the funds. . . . Yet the buck does not stop with Admiral Poindexter, as he stated in his testimony;

it stops with me. I am the one who is ultimately accountable to the American people. . . . I have the right, the obligation to make my own decision."

And at the conclusion of North's testimony, Representative Lee Hamilton (D-Indiana) said to North: "I don't have any doubt at all, Colonel North, that you are a patriot. . . . For you, perhaps patriotism rested in the conduct of deeds, some requiring great personal courage, to free hostages and fight communism. . . . But there's another form of patriotism which is unique to a democracy. It resides in those who have a deep respect for the rule of law and faith in America's democratic traditions. To uphold our Constitution requires not the exceptional efforts of the few but the confidence and the trust and the work of the many."[10]

Administrative Rules

One of the many issues raised in the "Irangate" hearings was whether the Boland Amendment prohibited only the Pentagon and the Central Intelligence Agency (CIA) from giving aid to the contras not authorized by Congress, or whether, by not mentioning the National Security Council (NSC), the amendment allowed NSC officials like North and Poindexter to do what they did. North, Poindexter, and some members of Congress said it did. Most members said it did not. But this was just one more instance of an inescapable problem in governing modern nations.

Every statute, amendment, and executive order is necessarily written in general terms, in that its language cannot possibly describe in detail every conceivable situation that might arise. Legislatures and executives try to make their intentions clear and set forth general principles to guide administrative agencies in implementing those intentions. However, those agencies have to ascertain the facts in future situations and then decide whether those facts are what the legislatures and the executives had in mind when they laid down their general rules. Consequently, no administrative agency can avoid exercising discretion, and most develop their own bodies of **administrative rules**, which are *rules drawn up by administrative agencies to implement general guidelines laid down by legislatures and executives*. Most students of government are convinced that it is absolutely necessary for administrative agencies to make such rules, and that making those rules necessarily involves administrators in policy making. The broader and more general the directives handed to administrators, the more important administrative rules become in shaping public policies as they actually affect people.

One of countless illustrations of the point is provided by the "equal access" rule of the U.S. Federal Communications Commission. The Federal Communications Act stipulates that "if any [television or radio broadcasting station] shall permit any person who is a legally qualified candidate for any public office to use a broadcasting station, [the station] shall afford equal opportunities to all other such candidates for

"LOOSE CANNON" BUREAUCRATIC POLICYMAKER OR FAITHFUL SERVANT OF ELECTED POLICYMAKERS? Lt. Col. Oliver P. North testifying before the congressional committee investigating the "Irangate" affair, 1987.

that office in the use of such broadcasting station." Fair enough, but does that mean that if a caller on a talk show urges the listeners to vote for the Democrat, then the station must give equal time to the Republican to reply? The FCC's rules say no: The Commission interprets Congress's language to require equal access only when a candidate appears in person and does not apply to programs or advertisements in which other people express support for the candidate. Clearly, then, if the Democrat appears in person, the Republican must be given equal opportunity. But what about the Socialist, Libertarian, and Socialist Workers candidates? The FCC says no: Its rules allow a station to exclude minor-party candidates and other "fringe" candidates the station feels have no chance of winning. What if the station in an editorial urges viewers to vote for a particular candidate or a particular side in a referendum? Must it give equal opportunity to the other main party or side? The FCC rules say yes in the case of candidates and no in the case of referendums. In short, access to radio and television by candidates and issue advocacy groups is controlled at least as much by the FCC's rules as by the original act of Congress.[11]

Pressure groups in broadcasting, like those trying to influence government in other areas, have long known this political fact of life. The most successful and powerful among them, accordingly, have never regarded their work as finished when the legislature has passed a bill or the executive has issued an order. They have shifted their attention to the appropriate administrative agencies to ensure that those agencies carry out the statute or directive as the pressure groups wish. For example, in the United States the Sierra Club and other environmentalist groups keep a close eye on the Environmental Protection Agency to make sure that it is working vigorously to stop manufacturers from polluting air and water with toxic wastes. The National Association for the Advancement of Colored People and other civil rights groups vigilantly watch the Equal Employment Opportunities Commission to ensure that it faithfully enforces affirmative action policies. Indeed, recent studies of pressure politics in various democratic nations have shown that administrative agencies are becoming targets of increasing importance for pressure groups.

Administrative Discretion

Administrators also acquire a good deal of policy-making power from the discretion they *must* have in the enforcement of their own rules as well as the legislative acts, executive decrees, and court orders of their legal superiors.

Police enforcement of automobile speed limits provides an illustration. Let us say that the law sets top limits of fifty-five miles per hour for intercity highways, forty for suburban arterial boulevards, twenty-five for residential streets, and fifteen for streets in business districts. The police know that there are plenty of people who think those limits are too low and will ignore them whenever they can. The police also know that the state legislature and the city council will never give them enough officers and cars to patrol every inch of every road every minute of every day. No one expects them to do that, so we know that they have to have some discretion about where to patrol and when, and we expect them to use it wisely. So the police use their discretionary power, as they must, to *select* patrolling areas and times. They may even develop their own rules of thumb. For example, police will stop everyone going over sixty-five on the highway, but no one going under sixty, thereby making the official limit of fifty-five into an actual limit of sixty.

The point is not that some police officers do not enforce the letter of every law all the time and are therefore derelict in their duty. The point is that no officer can possibly enforce all of the laws everywhere all of the time, and thus all officers have no choice but to use discretion in deciding which laws to enforce, when, where, and against whom. If this is true for the police, it is also true for, say, the Federal Reserve Board when it considers whether to raise the discount rate, or the Food and Drug

Administration when it considers whether to allow doctors to prescribe a certain drug, or the Federal Trade Commission when it considers whether to ban advertisements for tooth-decaying candy on children's television programs.

For all those reasons, there is no escaping the conclusion that, whatever their *formal* status and powers may be, administrative agencies make a lot of public policies in every modern democratic nation. Until recently, most democratic countries have emphasized, and to a large degree have succeeded in, getting politics (partisan politics, that is) out of administration; but they have given less attention to the significant fact that administration has gotten into politics (that is, making policy) in a big way. This fact not only makes the politics/administration dichotomy of Wilson and Goodnow obsolete but also poses a grave problem for those nations that wish their governments to be *both* democratic *and* efficient. We will conclude this chapter by analyzing the problem and reviewing some of the efforts that have been made to solve it.

"Administocracy" In a Democracy: Problem and Solutions

THE PROBLEM: MAKING ADMINISTRATORS RESPONSIBLE

The term **administocracy** was coined by Guy S. Claire to denote an *"aristocracy of administrators—a government effectively run by career civil servants."*[12] The problem of administocracy is this: Citizens of most democratic polities want their governments to be efficient, and they are convinced that a permanent, professionalized civil service recruited and promoted according to standards of technical merit is the most likely to be efficient. They have no wish to return to the bad old days of the patronage and spoils systems. Yet most of them also wish their governments to be democratic (that is, to do what the people want and not what some bureaucratic elite thinks is good for them). Most of us want *both* efficiency and democracy, and we do not wish to sacrifice one ideal to promote the other.

But are the two ideals compatible? Can we pursue them both? Those questions have long concerned political theorists. For several generations, as we have seen, most scholars believed that the politics/administration dichotomy solved the problem. But most present-day political scientists believe that this dichotomy is based upon a misconception of what administrators actually do and offers no solution at all.

Accordingly, most political scientists today believe that the solution to the problem of administocracy lies not in any futile attempt to prevent administrators from making policy, but rather in ensuring that administrators are *responsible* in their policy-making activities. When we examine their ideas closely, however, we discover that they use the key word *responsibility* in two distinct senses, and their proposals for making administrators responsible reflect different emphases on the two meanings of the word.

Responsibility as Conforming to Professional Standards

A number of political scientists, notably Carl J. Friedrich, have argued that the political responsibility of administrators can never be enforced completely by formal accountability to elected officials. Friedrich argues that we must place heavy reliance on developing functional or objective responsibility; that is, we should select and train our administrators so that they will operate according to built-in professional standards and adhere to a professional code of ethics. Ideally, according to Friedrich, administrators should be responsible in the same sense and for similar reasons that judges are responsible:

> Judicial decisions are relatively responsible because judges have to account for their action in terms of a somewhat rationalized and previously established set of rules. Any deviation from these rules on the part of a judge will be subjected to extensive scrutiny by his colleagues and what is known as the "legal profession." Similarly, administrative officials seeking to apply scientific "standards" have to account for their action in terms of a somewhat rationalized and previously established set of hypotheses. Any deviation from these hypotheses will be subjected to thorough scrutiny by their colleagues in what is known as the "fellowship of science."[13]

Responsibility as Accountability to Elected Officials

Other political scientists, notably Charles S. Hyneman, have argued that, although administrative responsibility in Friedrich's sense is a fine thing, a democratic government must make its administrators responsible mainly by making them accountable to and controlled by elected public officials. Only thus, Hyneman insists, can we establish the popular control of administrative policy making that democratic government demands. As Hyneman put it:

> Government has enormous power over us, and most of the acts of government are put into effect by the men and women who constitute the bureaucracy. It is in the power of these men and women to do us great injury, as it is in their power to advance our well-being. It is essential that they do what we want done, the way we want it done. Our concept of democratic government requires that these men and women be subject to direction and control that compel them to conform to the wishes of the people as a whole whether they wish to do so or not.[14]

Both Friedrich and Hyneman thus believe that some kind of external control of administrative policy making is necessary to solve the problem of administocracy, although they do not agree about how important such control is. We will conclude our discussion by examining briefly some of the principal methods of external control currently employed by democratic nations.

SOLUTIONS

Making Administrators Representative

Some political scientists have suggested that one of the best ways to prevent administocracy is to have a "representative bureaucracy"—one whose employees are drawn from all the nation's social, racial, religious, sexual, and economic groups—

though not necessarily in exactly the same proportions that exist in the whole society. Such a bureaucracy, they argue, is likely to be responsive to the people's desires because it *is* the people, or at least a cross section of them. Indeed, the bureaucracy may be in some ways more representative than elected officials, for it will include members of some minority groups slighted by electoral majorities but appointed under affirmative action policies (see Chapter 16).

Perhaps so, but James Q. Wilson, a leading scholar of the way administrators behave, has concluded that there is little evidence that administrators' social backgrounds affect how they behave in their jobs. He is much more impressed with the impact of their professional training and values—for example, as lawyers or economists—and he illustrates his point with examples from the Federal Trade Commission (FTC):

> Because of their training and attitudes, lawyers in the FTC prefer to bring cases against a business firm that does something clearly and demonstrably illegal, such as attending secret meetings with competitors to rig the prices that will be charged to a purchaser. These cases appeal to lawyers because there is usually a victim (the purchaser or a rival company) who complains to the government, the illegal behavior can be proved in a court of law, and the case can be completed rather quickly. Economists, on the other hand, are trained to measure the value of a case, not by how easily or quickly it can be proved in court, but by whether the illegal practice imposes large or small costs on the consumer. FTC economists often dislike the cases that appeal to the lawyers. The economists feel that the amount of money such cases save the consumer is often small and the cases are a distraction from the big issues—such as whether IBM unfairly dominates the office-machine business or whether General Motors is too large to be efficient. Lawyers, in turn, are leery of big cases because the facts are hard to prove and take forever to decide (one big case can drag through the courts for ten years). In many federal agencies, professional values such as these help explain how power is used.[15]

Control by Elected Officials

UNITED STATES   Political control of administrative agencies in the United States is exercised by the president and Congress, both jointly and separately. Jointly they enact the legislation that creates the administrative agencies, defines the agencies' objectives and powers, and establishes standards of performance. They also provide the money that administrative agencies spend; collaborate on appointments to top administrative posts; establish the procedures by which lesser appointments are made; and review, criticize, and sometimes stop the actions of administrators.

In addition, the president, as chief executive, formally controls most civil servants. He appoints the heads and chief subordinates of most executive agencies, and they are responsible to him. They, in turn, formally control the employees of their agencies. *Formally*, the president, like any commander in chief, can send orders down the administrative hierarchy, count on having them obeyed, and expect his subordinates to keep him informed about what is going on. But organization charts are one thing and reality is another. Not only are the number of civil servants and the number and variety of their activities far too vast for any one person to keep an eye on, but the more dedicated the administrators are, as we have seen, the more likely they are to develop strong feelings about what policies ought to be followed, feelings that do not always coincide with those of the president. Most Americans, civil servants or civilians, feel that their highest duty is to work for what they believe is in the nation's best interests, and losing a presidential order in the bureaucratic maze is not difficult. As Jonathan Daniels, a former presidential aide, wrote of cabinet officers:

> Half of a President's suggestions, which theoretically carry the weight of orders, can safely be forgotten by a Cabinet member. And if the President asks about a suggestion a second time, he can be told that it is being investigated. If he asks a third time, a wise Cabinet officer will give him at least part of what he suggests. But only occasionally, except about the most important matters, do Presidents ever get around to asking three times.[16]

Richard Neustadt, a perceptive modern student of the presidency, concludes that the president's power over his subordinates is not so much the power to command as the power to persuade, an opportunity "to induce them to believe that what he wants of them is what their own appraisal of their own responsibilities require them to do in their own interest, not his."[17] Presidential control of administrators is thus not enough to keep them strictly obedient to the will of elected policy makers.

Congress, on the other hand, relies mainly on *oversight*—that is, reviewing and checking the activities of administrators. Most appropriations run for only a year or two, and when the agencies' requests for new funds come before Congress, the various subcommittees of the appropriations committees in each house use the occasion—when administrators are understandably very cooperative—to review the agencies' past conduct and future plans, and to make whatever criticisms committee members think appropriate. Investigating committees provide another useful means of making administrators toe the line. Congress frequently grants powers to administrative agencies for limited periods of time and uses the occasions of renewing the grants to review not only policies but also the way they have been carried out.

Those examples are but a few of the many means used by elected officials in the United States to direct and control administrative agencies. If Congress and the president use those means vigorously and intelligently, with a clear understanding of what they are about, then administocracy can be kept well within acceptable bounds. Hyneman argued, however, that control of administration in the United States is made more difficult by the constitutional independence of Congress and the president from each other. Because they are elected by different constituencies for different terms of office, more often than not the president and Congress have conflicting views about what policies administrators should pursue. Other students of public administration are skeptical about Hyneman's proposed solution: a joint executive-legislative council to formulate policy and direct administration. But most agree with his judgment that until the problem is solved, the overall control of administrative agencies by elected officials in the United States will continue to be less effective than it should be.

PARLIAMENTARY SYSTEMS   At first glance the control of administrators by elected officials in parliamentary systems appears to be better organized and more effective than in the United States. In most of them, as we observed in Chapter 11, the legislatures and executives usually speak with one voice, at least formally. The administrators in each executive department are directly responsible to the minister, the minister is responsible to the cabinet, and the cabinet and the parliament are always in formal agreement about both policy ends and administrative means.

When we look closer, however, we learn that matters are not quite that simple or neat. For one thing, many parliamentary democracies have established government corporations that, like the British Broadcasting Corporation, are not subject to direct ministerial control. For another, members of the parliaments in many of those nations apparently think that ministerial control by itself is not sufficient to prevent administocracy. Consequently, many parliamentary democracies have created such institutions as the British "question time" and the French *interpellation*.

On each of the first four days of every legislative week, any member of the British House of Commons may, after having given one or two days' notice, ask a question of any member of the Government. The questions are put in both oral and written form. They may be simple requests for information or they may require the ministers to explain and justify actions taken by their departments. Furthermore, the questioner and other MPs may ask supplementary questions arising from the ministers' oral answers to the initial questions. Questions are asked not only by the opposition to embarrass the Government, but also by backbenchers of the majority party.

Question time thus not only offers an arena for conflict between the majority party and the opposition party; it often also provides an opportunity for contests between legislators and administrators without regard to party. Asking questions, indeed, is the principal method by which rank-and-file MPs can review and criticize the actions of the civil service and one of the few areas in which they can participate in the governing process free of the shackles of party discipline and cabinet control. An average of 70 to 100 oral questions are asked each day, a total of about 11,000 each year. Some observers believe that they have proved to be at least as effective as ministerial control in keeping civil servants in line.

The British have adopted another device that has to some extent been copied by the United States. Most acts of Parliament set general objectives and standards and leave the writing of detailed regulations to the appropriate administrative agencies. When an agency has drawn up a set of regulations, the regulations are published in a collection known as a *statutory instrument*, which is then placed before Parliament for a period of forty days. If no MP objects, then the instrument becomes law. But if an MP moves a "prayer for annulment," then a vote must be taken; and if a majority of the House of Commons agrees, then the whole set of regulations are voided and another must be drawn up. To be sure, the cabinet usually imposes party discipline to preserve the regulations, but having them challenged can be embarrassing, and the procedure makes the administrators try hard to avoid promulgating rules that might antagonize an unduly large number of MPs.

In the Third and Fourth Republics of France (1871–1946, 1946–1958), members of the National Assembly also asked questions in a procedure similar to question time in the House of Commons, though the questions were designed mainly to elicit information. Far more formidable was the practice of *interpellations* (requesting ministers to explain and justify the actions of their departments). After a minister had replied to a particular *interpellation*, a general debate was held, ending in a motion either censuring or approving the minister's reply and the department's action. These practices constituted a powerful weapon for legislative control of administrators.

In the Fifth Republic (1958–), however, *interpellations* have been severely limited. Question time is now restricted to one day a week, and the greater power of the executive makes it extremely unlikely that a minister or the whole cabinet will be turned out because of unsatisfactory answers to legislators' questions.

AUTHORITARIAN SYSTEMS   Whatever may be the *theory* of authoritarianism (see Chapter 5), the *fact* is that no such system is a perfect hierarchy rigidly controlled by all-knowing and all-powerful leaders who closely scrutinize the lowliest bureaucrats' every move. Even such "absolute" dictators as Adolf Hitler and Saddam Hussein cannot personally know and oversee all the actions of all their administrative subordinates, and we know that in all authoritarian regimes the orders from the top are often watered down or slowed up by low-level bureaucrats.

In the few remaining Communist nations, most enterprises are owned and operated by the state, and so public employees constitute much greater proportions of their work forces than their counterparts in the Western democracies. Judging from what their own commentators say, one of the Communists' most difficult and recurring problems is controlling bureaucracy, establishing and maintaining an *apparat* (civil service) that is efficient, incorruptible, and quickly responsive to the wishes of the rulers.

Under Lenin, Stalin, and Brezhnev, the Soviet Union attacked the problem mainly by using the Communist party as the watchdog of the state administrative apparatus right down to the level of village governments and individual factories and collective farms. The central ministries customarily issued detailed instructions to regional and local units and enterprises, allowing them only small areas of discretion. Each unit and enterprise had some party members on its staff or overseeing it from local party headquarters, an updated version of the ancient Russian institution of "the inspector."

Furthermore, the party encouraged ordinary nonparty citizens to report and criticize lapses in zeal or performance by local *apparatchiks* (administrators), factory managers, and collective-farm managers. Even so, the managers of the state factories and farms developed a number of tricks for protecting themselves. Knowing that they would be in serious trouble if they did not fulfill their assigned production quotas, they sought to have low quotas assigned, underreported plant capacity and current output, or maintained inventories of finished products or raw materials unknown to the central planners. In this way they could be confident of meeting their assigned quotas and even be praised for exceeding them.

Many of the reforms proposed after 1985 by Mikhail Gorbachev as part of his program of *perestroika* (restructuring) were aimed at promoting local and personal initiative by decreasing Moscow's centralized control of economic enterprise and by reducing the party's role as everyone's watchdog. It is significant, ironic—and probably inevitable—that some of the strongest opposition to *perestroika* came from the local party *apparatchiks*, who had such a good thing under the old regime.

The People's Republic of China has tried several different control systems. Before the Communist takeover in 1949, China had one of the world's oldest traditions of professional bureaucracy and a distinct administrative class with great prestige. To Mao Zedong and his followers, those administrators epitomized all that was wrong with the old regime, and as a result, under Mao's regime (1949–1976) there was great hostility to traditional bureaucracy. At first the Mao regime followed the old Soviet model of parallel party and management structures, with the party keeping a close eye on the bureaucrats. In the early 1950s it turned to "one-man management" of local enterprises. After that the Communist party leaders sought to eliminate the evils of bureaucracy by weakening or eliminating all centralized structures and encouraging local enterprises and local party groups to carry out central directives without bureaucratic intermediaries. After Mao's death in 1976, however, the new regime of Deng Xiaoping stressed industrial modernization and returned to more traditional bureaucratic ways to achieve their goals.

Control by Courts

In addition to legislative and executive methods of ensuring that administrative agencies adopt and enforce policies in accordance with popular desires, all democratic nations also provide various judicial restraints to prevent them from violating the rights of individuals. If private citizens believe that an administrative agency has used its power unreasonably to harm them or their property, or stepped outside its jurisdiction in giving them an order, or exceeded its regulatory powers, or unfairly denied them a license, they can take their complaint to a court. The remedy may take the form of money paid in damages, a writ of mandamus (that is, a court order to a public official ordering him or her to do the duty as the law requires), or a writ of injunction (that is, a court order prohibiting an administrative official from performing a specified action).

Several democratic countries, including the United States and Great Britain, assign all judicial review of illegal administrative actions to their ordinary courts, whereas others, including France, Italy, and Sweden, have established special administrative courts to adjudicate such disputes. The main purpose of judicial control of administration in most nations, whether exercised by regular or special courts, is not to prevent administocracy as the term is used here but rather to protect the personal and property rights of individuals against violations by administrators.

Intervention by Ombudsmen

For many private citizens, suing an administrative agency in the courts is not feasible. It is time-consuming, costly, and unpleasant, and there is no guarantee of winning. Judicial control, which leaves the initiative to the aggrieved, is thus more a last resort than a device often used for keeping administrators in line.

Recognizing this difficulty as long ago as 1809, the government of Sweden established the special office of **ombudsman** (the term means "parliamentary commissioner"), *an official appointed by a legislature to hear and investigate complaints by private individuals against administrators.* The ombudsman is appointed by the Riksdag (parliament) to investigate and publicize instances in which administrators have used their powers wrongly or failed to act when they should. Any citizen may register a complaint with the ombudsman. He or she investigates each complaint and, on the basis of the findings, publicly either exonerates or censures the administrators involved. In most instances public censure by an ombudsman is enough to make erring administrators mend their ways in a hurry, but if they remain adamant, then the ombudsman is authorized to direct the public prosecutor to take the matter to court.

In this way most of the initiative and bother and all of the expense of obtaining a remedy are born by the office of the ombudsman rather than by private citizens, and many observers believe that the ombudsman is one of the most effective devices democracies have for keeping administrators in line. Most democratic nations have now established ombudsmen for investigating complaints about national administrators. The United States, which still has no national ombudsman, is one of the few exceptions, but a number of U.S. states have instituted such positions. No country believes that having an ombudsman solves all the problems of administocracy, but most believe that it helps.

Conclusion

It is clear that the great numbers and power of career civil servants have elevated them to positions of enormous influence in all modern political systems, democratic and authoritarian, and their professionalization has given rise to problems of administocracy. Some modern Cassandras, indeed, have cried that all is lost and that administocracy and "the new despotism" are already upon us. However, the evidence presented in this chapter strongly suggests that such lamentations are, to say the least, premature. The fact that career administrators have great influence in the making of public policy does not mean that they have taken over the whole process and become absolute and unchecked despots. The democratic systems' various legislative, executive, and judicial controls can fix firm limits upon what civil servants can and cannot do. As long as those who exercise those controls do so with the confidence that they are doing what their constituents want them to do, administrators will continue to be valuable servants—but not masters—of democratic regimes.

For Further Reading

ABERBACH, JOEL D. *Keeping a Watchful Eye: The Politics of Congressional Oversight.* Washington, DC: The Brookings Institution, 1990. A study of how Congress attempts to revise and control administrative policy making.

BURKE, JOHN P. *Bureaucratic Responsibility.* Baltimore, MD: Johns Hopkins University Press, 1986. A new statement of the view that bureaucrats' internalized professional standards are the best safeguards for keeping them responsible.

CAMPBELL, COLIN. *Governments Under Stress: Political Executives and Key Bureaucrats in Washington, London, and Ottawa.* Toronto, Ontario: University of Toronto Press, 1983. Study of relationships between political executives and top bureaucrats in three democratic countries.

EDLEY, CHRISTOPHER, JR. *Administrative Law: Rethinking Judicial Control of Bureaucracy.* New Haven, CT: Yale University Press, 1990. A critical examination of the oversight of bureaucrats by courts.

FESLER, JAMES W., AND DONALD E. KETTL. *The Politics of the Administrative Process.* Chatham, NJ: Chatham House, 1990. Survey of the organization of administrative agencies and their role in policy making.

GOODNOW, FRANK J. *Politics and Administration.* New York: Macmillan, 1900. Classic statement of the politics-administration dichotomy.

GOODSELL, CHARLES T. *The Case for Bureaucracy,* 3rd ed. Chatham, NJ: Chatham House, 1994. A spirited defense of the goals and accomplishments of the civil service, mainly in the United States.

GORMLEY, WILLIAM T., JR. *Taming the Bureaucracy: Muscles, Prayers, and Other Strategies.* Princeton, NJ: Princeton University Press, 1989. Descriptions and prescriptions of various ways of controlling "administocracy."

GRUBER, JUDITH E. *Controlling Bureaucracies: Dilemmas in Democratic Government.* Berkeley, CA: University of California Press, 1987. Analysis of problems and possibilities for controlling "administocracy" in the United States.

HENNESSY, PETER. *Whitehall.* New York: Free Press, 1989. In-depth description and analysis of the relations between elected politicians and career bureaucrats in Great Britain.

HYNEMAN, CHARLES S. *Bureaucracy in a Democracy.* New York: Harper & Row, 1950. Influential discussion of the problem and methods of democratic control over permanent civil servants.

KOH, B. C. *Japan's Administrative Elite.* Berkeley, CA: University of California Press, 1989. A study of one of the most powerful bureaucracies in the world's democratic nations.

PAGE, EDWARD C. *Political Authority and Bureaucratic Power.* Knoxville, TN: University of Tennessee Press, 1984. Analysis of bureaucracies of France, Germany, Great Britain, and the United States, with emphasis on the problem of control by elected officials.

ROSEN, BERNARD. *Holding Government Bureaucrats Accountable.* New York: Praeger, 1982. Analysis of problems and possibilities of holding civil servants accountable for policy-making activities.

*ROURKE, FRANCIS E. *Bureaucracy, Politics and Public Policy,* 3rd ed. Boston, MA: Little, Brown, 1984. Survey of the role of permanent civil servants in the making of public policy in the United States.

SILBERMAN, BERNARD S. *The Rise of the Rational State in France, Japan, the United States, and Great Britain.* Chicago: University of Chicago Press, 1993. Historical account of how and why professionalized civil services developed in four nations.

SIMON, HERBERT A. *Administrative Behavior,* 2nd ed. New York: Macmillan, 1957. Nobel laureate's influential study of administrative decision making from the point of view of organization theory and social psychology.

TUMMALA, KRISHNA K., ed. *Administrative Systems Abroad.* Washington, DC: University Press of America, 1982. Collection of case studies of administrative agencies in Third World countries, especially in Asia.

WILDAVSKY, AARON. *The Politics of the Budgetary Process.* Boston, MA: Little, Brown, 1964. Analysis of a key administrative activity, emphasizing that change takes place in small incremental steps, not great leaps.

WILSON, JAMES Q. *Bureaucracy: What Government Agencies Do and Why They Do It.* New York: Basic Books, 1989. A leading scholar of administrative behavior develops some new theories by reflecting on a number of routines and conflicts in federal agencies.

Notes

1. *The American Almanac 1993–1994* (Washington, DC: Bureau of the Census, 1994), Table 499, p. 317.

2. Luther Gulick, "Notes on the Theory of Organization," in *Papers on the Science of Administration,* L. Gulick and L. Urwik, eds. (New York: Institute of Public Administration, 1937), p. 6.

3. *The American Almanac 1993–1994* (Washington, DC: Bureau of the Census, 1993), Table 1384, p. 850.

4. In the civil service context, *merit* means above-average qualifications for and/or performance of the tasks assigned to an administrative position.

5. Bradley M. Richardson and Scott C. Flanagan, *Politics in Japan* (Boston, MA: Little, Brown, 1984), p. 51.

6. Woodrow Wilson, "The Study of Administration," *Political Science Quarterly*, 2 (1887), pp. 197–222.

7. Frank J. Goodnow, *Politics and Administration* (New York: Macmillan, 1900), p. 24.

8. Those points are well and truly made with many real-life illustrations in the books listed at the end of this chapter. I confess, however, that I find them made as accurately and much more entertainingly in two long-running British television series, *Yes, Minister* and *Yes, Prime Minister*, which feature the repeated and usually successful schemes of Sir Humphrey Appleby, a senior civil servant, to maneuver his presumed political "master," cabinet and later prime minister Jim Hacker, into adopting Sir Humphrey's policies as his own. Readers who have a chance to see the series should not miss them.

9. *Congressional Quarterly Weekly Report*, July 18, 1987, p. 610.

10. *Congressional Quarterly Weekly Report*, July 18, 1987, p. 605.

11. Harvey L. Zuckman and Martin J. Gaynes, *Mass Communications Law in a Nutshell* (St. Paul, MN: West, 1983), Chapters 9–11.

12. Guy S. Claire, *Administocracy* (New York: Macmillan, 1934).

13. Carl J. Friedrich, "Responsible Government Service under the American Constitution," in *Problems of the American Public Service* (New York: McGraw-Hill, 1935), pp. 36–37. Used with permission of McGraw-Hill Book Company.

14. Charles S. Hyneman, *Bureaucracy in a Democracy* (New York: Harper & Row, 1950), p. 38.

15. James Q. Wilson, *American Government: Institutions and Policies*, 4th ed. (Lexington, MA: D. C. Heath, 1989), pp. 373–74.

16. Jonathan Daniels, *Frontier on the Potomac* (New York: Macmillan, 1946), pp. 31–32.

17. Richard E. Neustadt, *Presidential Power and the Modern Presidents* (New York: Free Press, 1990), p. 40.

14

This I know, my lords, that where laws end, tyranny begins.
William Pitt, the Elder

The law is a sort of hocus-pocus science, that smiles in your face while it picks your pocket, and the glorious uncertainty of it is more use to the professors than the justice of it.
Charles Macklin

The law is the last result of human wisdom acting upon human experience for the benefit of the public.
Dr. Samuel Johnson

Law is a system of social relationships which serves the interests of the ruling classes and hence is supported by their organized power, the state.
Penal Code of the former Soviet Union

The prophecies of what the courts will do in fact, and nothing more pretentious, are what I mean by the law.
Justice Oliver Wendell Holmes, Jr.

Law and the Judicial Process

No person acts completely randomly without rhyme, reason, or pattern. To be sure, our behavior patterns may be hard to figure out and may change as we grow older, move, acquire new friends, enter new occupations, and so on. But there is always *some* pattern at every stage of our lives.

Every society, moreover, has certain "normal" behavior patterns—that is, particular ways in which most members behave in particular situations. Most Americans, for example, wear *some* clothes, even on hot summer days when we might be more comfortable without them. Most wear "modern" clothes, not togas, loincloths, or sarongs. Most eat with knives and forks rather than chopsticks or fingers, pay money for what we buy, drive on the right-hand side of the road, and do not eat human flesh or kill rambunctious children. Some of what we do is governed by habit, and it never occurs to us to do otherwise. Much, however, is governed by *rules*; that is, most Americans consciously believe that we ought to act in certain ways, and we also know that if we break the rules, our associates will disapprove and we will be punished. There are three main types: moral precepts, customs, and laws.

Rules People Live By

MORAL PRECEPTS

Every person's behavior is guided to some extent by **moral precepts**—*rules of behavior based on ideas of right and wrong*. We may try to obey such Judeo-Christian commandments as "thou shalt not kill," "honor thy father and mother," and "do unto others as you would have them do unto you." Or we may adhere to such commandments as "never give a sucker an even break" and "let's do it to them before they do it to us."

Some or all of a person's moral precepts may come from religious sources. The commandments may be laid down by a religious institution and have behind them some sort of supernatural sanction, such as a priest's warning that sin offends God and may condemn the sinner to the eternal fires of hell. Part or all of a person's moral precepts may also come from nonreligious sources. The commandments may emanate from the person's philosophy of right and wrong and have behind them such nonsupernatural sanctions as the inner conviction that "virtue is its own reward" and that living immorally will make it hard to face yourself in a mirror.

Whatever their sources, moral precepts differ from other kinds of social rules in that people obey them because they believe it is good to do so, not because they fear some kind of earthly retribution from other people.

CUSTOMS

Human behavior is also guided to some extent by what we think others expect of us. For example, neither religious institutions nor our private moral philosophies require us to wear business suits instead of togas or monks' habits to the office, to leave tips for waiters at restaurants, or to begin our letters "Dear ____" and close them "Sincerely yours." Yet most of us regularly follow these rules because we know that if we do not, then most of our associates will regard us as peculiar—and few of us want to be pointed out or stared at as peculiar.

Customs are *rules of behavior based on long-established and widespread ways in which most people actually behave*. They are powerful regulators of behavior in all societies. According to anthropologists, in most primitive societies customs are the most powerful regulators of all, and even in industrialized nations they play an important role.

Different groups have different customs, of course. Nevertheless, customs in general are powerful shapers of human behavior. For example, many college students grow their hair long, wear blue jeans, and regard themselves as rebels against conformity. Many insurance executives have short haircuts, wear pin-striped suits, and regard themselves as upholding the sartorial decencies. But how many insurance executives have long hair and wear blue jeans regardless of what their friends and associates think, because it expresses *their* individuality? By the same token, how many college students have short haircuts and wear pin-striped suits, regardless of what their friends and associates think, because that expresses *their* individuality? Look around and see. The fact is that all of us, however we feel we are doing our own thing, conform more or less faithfully to *some* group's customs.

LAWS

Law is *the body of rules emanating from government and enforceable by the courts.* Law differs from customs in that it emanates from a specific source, the government. It differs from moral precepts in that it is enforceable by the courts. Above all, legal rules are made and enforced by governments.

Some of us may sometimes be tempted to agree with the more cynical views of what law is all about, especially when we have just received a parking ticket or paid a lawyer's bill. But most of us believe, with Dr. Samuel Johnson, that law is one of the great achievements of human civilization, and that people's chances of living together peacefully in society depend largely on their willingness to live according to the law.

The writers of the first constitution of Massachusetts in 1778 declared that their purpose was to establish "a government of laws, and not of men." That hope surely still lives in the hearts of most of us, who want our lives, our fortunes, and our sacred honor to be governed, not by the passing whims of a dictator or the prejudices of a ruling class or even the enthusiasms of a momentary popular majority, but by fundamental principles of right and reason. The actual laws that govern us at the moment may not measure up to this ideal, to be sure, but in most of us the hope is strong.

Perhaps that is why many Americans admire judges more than executives or legislators. The evidence from the public opinion polls on this point is quite clear. Since 1966 the Harris poll has regularly asked its respondents, "As far as the people running various institutions are concerned, would you say you have a great deal of confidence, only some confidence, or hardly any confidence at all in them?" Their changing responses are presented in Table 14.1.

The percentages in Table 14.1 show that, with the exception of 1984, when Ronald Reagan's popularity was at its highest, the Supreme Court has been consistently held in higher esteem than the Congress or the presidency, and, indeed, the Court challenges the military and higher education for the highest esteem of all the institutions listed.

TABLE 14.1   Popular Confidence in Leaders of Institutions, 1984–1992

	PERCENTAGE EXPRESSING "A GREAT DEAL OF CONFIDENCE"				
	1984	*1986*	*1988*	*1992*	*Average*
Congress	28%	21%	15%	10%	19%
Executive branch	42	18	16	13	22
The Supreme Court	35	32	32	30	32
The military	45	36	33	50	41
Colleges and universities	40	34	34	25	33
TV news	24	27	28	22	25
Major companies	19	16	19	11	16

Source: The Harris Poll, March 22, 1992.

To some extent, of course, those ratings reflect how the respondents felt about the particular judges, presidents, and members of Congress in office at the moment. Beyond this, however, most of us have a mental picture of "the judge" that is close to reverential, even though no actual judge may quite live up to our ideal.

For our ideal judge sits on the bench, listening attentively and impartially to the plaintiff and the defendant, seeing to it that each side receives its full rights under the law and handing down the decision, not to please this political party or that pressure group but to declare what the law says regarding the just settlement of such disputes.

There is little doubt that the law, and the judges and courts that interpret and apply it, occupy a place of high prestige in our attitudes toward government. To what extent do actual judges and courts live up to their ideal models? Perhaps we can discover some answers in this chapter, in which we survey the structure and role of law and courts as they currently operate in the democratic nations.

Types of Law

The courts in modern industrialized societies make and apply several types of laws, and the differences among them are important enough for us to review the principal ways in which laws are classified and the main kinds of laws in each classification.

CLASSIFIED BY SOURCE

One way of classifying types of laws is according to the agency that promulgates them. There are six main types: constitutional law, statutory law, administrative law, common law, equity law, and Roman (and civil[1]) law.

Constitutional Law

Every nation has a **constitution,** *a body of fundamental rules, written and unwritten, by which its government operates.* Though some of the rules consist of unwritten customs, most are, strictly speaking, constitutional law, which includes a basic written constitution, a number of organic laws, and the interpretations made by the courts. Examples include the constitutions of the United States, France, Germany, and just about every industrial nation (Great Britain is said to have an "unwritten constitution"). Constitutional law also includes legislative acts establishing basic agencies of government, such as the U.S. Judiciary Act of 1789 establishing the lower federal courts and the British Parliament Act of 1911 abolishing the lawmaking power of the House of Lords. Constitutional law also comprehends the decisions of supreme courts that authoritatively hand down declaring how the various constitutional rules apply to particular cases. (One well-known example is the U.S. Supreme Court's 1954 decision in *Brown* v. *Board of Education* (1954) declaring that the equal–protection clause of the Fourteenth Amendment prohibits the states from racially segregating the public schools. Constitutional law is everywhere regarded as the most fundamental of all types of law, in the sense that any law that contravenes a constitutional rule is superseded by the constitutional rule. Maintaining constitutional supremacy is the special prerogative of the courts in some nations. In other nations the job is done by the legislatures. We will consider this later.

Statutory Law

Statutory law consists of all the rules *enacted by the legislature* that command or prohibit some form of behavior. An example is the U.S. Voting Rights Act of 1965 (see Chapter 16) or the French law prohibiting the publication of poll results within two weeks prior to an election. In most nations statutes are collected and published in "codes" or books of "statutes in force."

Administrative Law

In Chapter 13 we noted that in all modern democratic systems, many executive and administrative agencies are authorized by the constitutions and the legislatures to make rules and regulations within certain specified limits. Examples include the U.S. Environmental Protection Agency's rule requiring all cotton textile mills to install adequate ventilating systems and the Federal Communication Commission's rules regarding election candidates' equal access to television and radio. The total body of such rules is generally called administrative law, and in most Western nations it has grown to considerable size.

Common Law

In twelfth-century England, judges acting on behalf of the king began to travel around the country to settle various local disputes according to their understanding of the prevailing "customs of the realm." During the ensuing centuries, generations of judges generally followed the principle of *stare decisis* ("let the decision stand"), according to which judges are obligated to follow precedent. That is, when judges decide a case to which a rule made in an earlier case applies, they must decide according to the old rule rather than make up a new one each time a new case comes along. As a consequence of their general adherence to *stare decisis*, the English judges over the centuries built up an elaborate body of legal rules that came to be known as "the common law" (to distinguish it from the law created by acts of Parliament). Examples include the rule that a person must perform in good faith the obligations of a contract, and the rule that a jury must be composed of twelve persons (recently modified by statutes in some jurisdictions reducing the number to six).

The common law was also applied by courts in the English colonies around the world. When some of those colonies—such as Australia, Canada, India, New Zealand, and the United States—became independent, their courts continued to apply English common law, although in all those nations English principles have been adapted to local circumstances. If a common-law rule contravenes a constitutional or statutory rule, the common-law rule gives way. But in the nations mentioned, common law continues to govern many matters on which their constitutions and statutes are silent.

Equity Law

During the long evolution of the common law in medieval England, an increasing number of English subjects demanded relief from injustices that they claimed resulted from the judges' rulings. The kings turned over such complaints to their chief legal officers, the chancellors, who in turn handed them on to assistants known as "masters in chancery." Eventually the masters in chancery came to constitute a regular court, the Court of Chancery. The rules developed by this court outside the common law have come to be known as equity law, and equity law too was exported to the English colonies and revised after those colonies won independence. An example is the "clean hands" rule, which stipulates that if relief is sought in a court of equity, the plaintiff must have behaved properly in the matter. Equity law, like common law, is superseded by constitutional and statutory law where there is conflict, but it still governs such matters as the administration of trusts, mortgages, and other financial obligations on which the statutes and common law are silent.

Roman Law and Civil Law

Every modern nation has constitutional law, statutory law, and administrative law, but common law and equity law operate mainly in the English-speaking nations. The nations of Western Europe and Latin America (as well as the U.S. state of Louisiana and the Canadian province of Quebec) supplement their constitutional, statutory, and administrative law with a system of jurisprudence commonly called the civil law. The civil law consists of a body of rules and procedures that, though differing somewhat from nation to nation, is based upon the *jus civile* of ancient Rome, which was rediscovered and adopted by European judges in the early Middle Ages (hence, it is sometimes called Roman law). Its best-known and most influential codification is that made in France by the order of Napoleon I in 1804, which came to be known as the Code Napoleon or *Code civil*. Modern civil law differs from common law and equity law not only in specific rules and procedures but also in its general tone and manner of growth. Common law and equity law are largely made by judges and remain pragmatic in tone, whereas civil law consists to a considerable degree of rules expounded by theorists of jurisprudence and has a more rationalistic and deductive tone than the common law.

Various other kinds of law (for example, admiralty and maritime law, and international law) are applied by modern courts, but the types outlined here are the principal elements of modern democratic legal systems.

CLASSIFIED BY SUBJECT MATTER

One other classification of law significant for our purposes is that which distinguishes between criminal and civil law.

Criminal Law

Criminal law, of course, deals with crimes. A crime is a wrong committed against the whole community, "an act done in violation of those duties which an individual owes to the community, and for the breach of which the law has provided that the offender shall make satisfaction to the public."[2] Crimes are usually classified as either felonies (more serious) or misdemeanors (less serious) and are punishable by death, imprisonment, fines, compulsory social service, and other penalties.

Civil Law

Civil law deals with wrongs committed by one private individual against another but not considered to be damaging to the whole community; hence, the community's only stake is making sure that the issue is settled fairly. (Note the difference between this use of the term and the European system of "the civil law" previously noted.) For example, if A spreads malicious stories about B in the hope of ruining B's reputation, A is considered to have slandered B but not to have harmed the whole community. B's remedy is to sue A for damages. But if A maliciously shoots and kills B, then A is considered to have threatened the basic safety and security of the entire community, and the government will prosecute A for murder. If found guilty, A will be imprisoned or executed.

Our next concern is the way in which the courts that apply those types of law in modern democratic nations are structured.

Court Structures in Democratic Nations ————————

SPECIAL JUDICIAL FUNCTIONS

For many centuries, organized societies did not make theoretical or organizational distinctions between lawmaking and law enforcing, nor did they establish government agencies specializing in one kind of operation over the other. Kings, as well as their ministers and courts (a "court," after all, was simply a king's retinue) made *and* enforced laws. In the late Middle Ages, however, the idea began to grow that justice is best served by having one kind of agency—which came to be called the executive—specializing in watching over the behavior of the king's subjects and prosecuting those subjects who violated the law, and another kind of agency specializing in trying the people thus accused. The agencies that tried the cases retained the ancient title of "courts," and by the eighteenth century in most nations courts were at least somewhat distinct in both theory and organization from executive agencies and had largely taken over the function of interpreting and applying law to a broad range of disputes. Thus the courts came to perform what are today regarded as the two distinctively judicial functions: law enforcement and dispute settlement.

Law Enforcement

Every law is a general rule made by a government agency either commanding or prohibiting a specified kind of behavior. Every government from time immemorial has established certain official agencies to enforce the law; that is, to detect instances in which "persons" (including both flesh-and-blood individuals and corporations, which are considered to be legal persons) have violated those general rules and then to punish the offenders. Every agency performing this function must conduct a number of basic operations, which may be illustrated by the following hypothetical example:

A nation has a law against murder, which is defined as the taking of another's life by deliberate intent and "with malice aforethought." One of its citizens, A, is found dead, and some of the people in the neighborhood tell the government (the police and the prosecutor) that they think that B shot A. The first thing the government does is *ascertain the facts*: Is A really dead? Did A die from a gunshot wound? Did B fire the shot that killed A? Did B fire the shot with deliberate intent to kill A, and had B thought about it well in advance of the shooting? Second, the government must *interpret and apply the law*. It must decide whether or not what B did is an instance of the behavior prohibited by the law against murder. Third, if B is found to have committed murder, the government must *punish the offender*. It must decide how severe a penalty is warranted by the facts and the law, pass sentence on B accordingly, and make sure the sentence is carried out.

Dispute Settlement

Every case that comes before a court involves a dispute between two parties. One party, the *plaintiff*, makes a complaint against the other party, the *defendant*. Either or both of the parties may be private individuals, business corporations, labor unions, pressure groups, public officials, or government agencies. But the essence of any case at law is a dispute over the merits of the plaintiff's complaint against the defendant. The two parties could, of course, settle their disputes with fists or guns, but the damage done to either or both—to say nothing of innocent bystanders—might well be greater than any benefit to the winner. And certainly the community has a stake in having the dispute settled peacefully and justly. So there are three distinct sets of interests in every law case: the plaintiff's, the defendant's, and the community's. The community's interest in the peaceful and just settlement of disputes is protected by having its representatives, a judge and (in some cases) a jury, hear the plaintiff's and defendant's arguments and evidence and decide which should win and how much.

Courts, to be sure, are not the only government agencies that settle disputes. Legislatures, executives, and administrators also settle a good many. But settling disputes is only one among many functions they perform, whereas it is essential to the role played by the courts in democratic countries. In that sense, then, settling disputes is especially, but not exclusively, a judicial function.

Judicial Review

Judicial review is *the power of a court to render a legislative or executive act null and void on grounds of unconstitutionality.* Although some English judges in the seventeenth century claimed this power, judicial review first became generally established in some of the U.S. states during the late eighteenth century and was made part of the national constitutional system by Chief Justice John Marshall's decision and opinion in *Marbury* v. *Madison* (1803). During the nineteenth and twentieth centuries the institution of judicial review gradually spread to other nations, and the period since World War I has seen its widest adoption. At present about thirty nations expressly assign this power to their courts, and in two other nations the constitutions have been construed by the courts—as in the United States—as giving courts this power. In several nations—Syria is an example—judicial review exists only on paper, for both the courts and the legislatures do whatever the ruling executive authorities order. In other nations (for example, Canada, France, Italy, Japan, Germany, and the United States), the courts can—and on occasion do—render legislative and executive acts null and void on grounds of unconstitutionality, and their decisions are accepted as authoritative (though people who object to particular decisions sometimes try to get them reversed: *Roe* v. *Wade* (1973) is an example; see Chapter 2). In Chapters 15 and 16 we will consider a number of instances in which the U.S. Supreme Court has used its power of judicial review to make rules governing political speech and the status of women, African-Americans, and other minorities.

TWO BASIC SYSTEMS OF JUSTICE

Adversarial

Most court proceedings in the United States, Great Britain, and the former British colonies in various parts of the world are based on the premise that justice is best achieved by the **adversarial system of justice**, which is *a system in which a neutral court hears the arguments and evidence presented by the plaintiff and the defendant and makes its decision on the basis of what it has heard.* These are the fundamental ideas underlying the adversarial system: The task of the courts is to settle legal disputes. A legal dispute results from a plaintiff's charge that a defendant has in some way damaged the plaintiff illegally. In a criminal case, the government, through its official prosecutor, accuses the defendant of breaking the law. In a civil case, one private party accuses another of illegally harming his or her person or property. The trial itself is a contest between the two adversaries. Each side presents its arguments, supports them with testimony from witnesses and other evidence, and tries to discredit the other side's case by cross-examining its witnesses, challenging its evidence, and refuting its arguments. The court's function is to umpire the contest and to declare the winner. The court makes sure that each side, in presenting its case and attacking its adversary's case, stays within the established rules of the contest (rules of proper evidence, argument, demeanor, and so on). The court hands down

CRIMINAL TRIALS SOMETIMES TAKE A LONG TIME. O.J. Simpson and two of his lawyers, 1994–1995.

the decision according to its determination of the true facts and relevant law that emerge in the contest between plaintiff and defendant.

The criminal-law version of this pattern is the Anglo-American accusatorial system for determining the guilt or innocence of suspects. The police investigate the facts and report to the prosecutor. The prosecutor goes before a grand jury to convince them that there is enough evidence to justify *indicting* (formally accusing) a particular person in order that a full trial may take place. The person thus indicted is the defendant in the ensuing trial, and the government is the plaintiff. The court (a judge, either acting alone or with a trial jury) listens to the arguments and evidence presented by the prosecution and the defense, and decides whether or not the defendant is guilty as charged. If the verdict is "innocent," then the defendant goes free. If the verdict is "guilty," then the court fixes the penalty, within limits laid down by the law. But the court itself has little or no power to produce evidence, cross-examine witnesses, or act as anything other than a neutral umpire of the contest between the prosecution and the defense; hence, the label "adversarial system of justice."

Inquisitorial

France and a number of continental European countries use the quite different **inquisitorial system of justice**; that is, *a system in which the court takes an active role in obtaining evidence and questioning witnesses as the basis for its decisions.*

To illustrate, the French criminal procedure begins when the police notify the public prosecutor (*procureur*) that they believe that a designated person probably committed a particular crime. If the prosecutor agrees, he or she notifies an examining magistrate (*juge d'instruction*), who proceeds to conduct the important preliminary investigation (*enquête*). This *enquête* goes a great deal further than a hearing before a grand jury in an adversarial system. The magistrate examines the accused and the witnesses in private. The magistrate is empowered to open mail, tap telephones, commission reports by experts, and take other steps to learn the facts. When faced with conflicting testimony by two or more witnesses, the magistrate can question them until satisfied that there is no perjury and that discrepancies in testimony have been reduced to a minimum. When the *enquête* is completed, the *juge d'instruction* decides whether or not to send the case to trial and does so only if convinced that the accused is guilty. The subsequent trial is usually little more than public verification of the record accumulated in the *enquête*. (The award-winning French film Z provides a dramatic description of an *enquête* in which the original accusers end up as the defendants.)

The inquisitorial system of France differs from the adversarial system of the Anglo-American democracies in three main respects. First, the decision of whether or not to try a person accused of a crime is made by a professional judge representing the Ministry of Justice and not by a lay grand jury. Second, the body of evidence and arguments by which the fate of the accused is determined is controlled by the judges (both in the *enquête* and the later trial, if any, rather than by the adversaries; and the judges can take the initiative to get any evidence they need to make a just decision. Third, the result is less affected than in the adversarial system by the skills of the lawyers representing the plaintiffs and defendants.

On the available evidence, however, we cannot say that either the adversarial or the inquisitorial system is clearly more effective in punishing the guilty or protecting the innocent. But it is important to note that those two quite different systems are used by various democracies to achieve the goals of fair procedures and just results they all seek.

HIERARCHIES OF APPEAL

Principle of Hierarchy in the Process of Appeal

In Chapter 13 we observed how important to many administrative systems is the principle of "hierarchy" that every agency should be clearly either the superior, the equal, or the inferior of every other agency. The same principle is basic to every court system, especially in the process of appeal.

THE INQUISITORIAL SYSTEM OF CRIMINAL JUSTICE. A French court trying Klaus Barbie for war crimes, 1987.

The court systems of all modern democracies provide a process of appeal; that is, a process whereby the loser of a case can ask a higher court to review the manner in which the trial was conducted. If the higher court conducts such a review and finds that the first trial was improperly conducted in some important respect, it can throw out the first trial and order that a new trial be held. This appellate process is possible only if all the courts are related to each other in a clear hierarchy of appeal. The hierarchy of appeal among the main courts in the United States is shown in Figure 14.1.

Some hierarchy of courts such as the one shown in Figure 14.1 is essential to any process of appeal, for if it were possible for the loser in *any* case to appeal the decision to any other court, then the process of appeal could go on forever, no final decisions could ever be made, and plaintiffs and defendants would grow poorer while lawyers grew richer.

As it is, however, every court system provides a process of appeal from lower to higher courts up to but not beyond a supreme court. When the supreme court has handed down a decision, the only further judicial appeal possible is a request to the supreme court to reconsider and reverse its own decision, a request rarely granted.

General Structure of Hierarchies of Appeal

Although the details of the courts' names and the cases they are authorized to hear vary considerably from one country to another, most hierarchies of judicial appeal have four main levels, listed in order of increasing power:

FIGURE 14.1   Heirarchy of Appeals in the American Court System

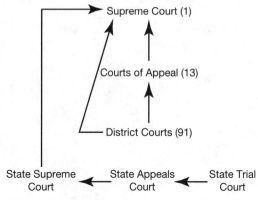

Source: *United States Government Manual.*

PRELIMINARY COURTS   In many systems the lowest courts on the judicial ladder are what may be called preliminary courts, such as justices of the peace (in Great Britain, Switzerland, and France), *conciliatores* and *praetors* (Italy), *Amtsgerichte* (Germany), and so on. Those tribunals have the power to try only small civil cases and misdemeanors, and most refer major cases to the next level of courts.

GENERAL TRIAL COURTS   Every system has as the first major rung of its judicial ladder a number of courts authorized to try most civil and criminal cases. In the U.S. national system, for instance, they are called federal district courts; in Great Britain, county courts for civil cases and crown courts for criminal cases; in France, *tribunaux de première instance*; and in Germany, *Landsgerichte*.

INTERMEDIATE COURTS OF APPEAL   Most systems provide a level of intermediate courts that mainly hear appeals from the trial courts and rarely or never act as trial courts. For instance, in the U.S. system there are regional federal courts of appeal and one for the District of Columbia; in Great Britain there is the national Court of Appeal; in France there are a number of regional courts of appeal; and in Germany there are several *Oberlandesgerichte*.

SUPREME COURTS   Every system has a national supreme court. In each nation this tribunal acts as the final court of appeal, and in some nations the tribunal also acts as a trial court in a few special cases. Those bodies include the Supreme Court of the United States, the British House of Lords, the French and Italian Courts of Cassation, the German *Bundesgerichtshof*, and the Swiss Federal Tribunal.

A few democracies have established special national tribunals (like Italy's *Corte Constituzionale*) in addition to their regular supreme courts to pass upon the constitutionality of legislative and executive acts in the process known as judicial review. However, most of the systems using judicial review vest final reviewing power in their regular supreme courts.

THE UNITED STATES SUPREME COURT, 1995.

SELECTION AND TENURE OF JUDGES

Lawyers and Judges

Every modern democratic nation has a distinctive legal profession whose members are specially trained in its legal principles and procedures by law schools or as apprentices to established lawyers. Most are required to pass government-administered examinations to become certified as full-fledged members of the legal profession. In the United States all such professionals are called lawyers, and no formal distinctions are made among them because of their specializations within the profession. Great Britain, on the other hand, separates its lawyers into two categories: solicitors, the "office lawyers" who give advice and prepare documents but can appear only in certain lower courts; and barristers, the "trial lawyers" who can appear before all courts, who do the actual pleading before the higher courts, and from whose ranks all higher court judges are appointed.[3] The French have three classes of lawyers: *avouéts*, who are comparable to British solicitors; *avocats*, who are analogous to barristers; and *notaires*, who specialize in drafting and registering legal documents.

The main difference between the Anglo-American and French systems is that in the Anglo-American system the legal profession is regarded as the source not only for legal advisers and advocates but also for all but minor judicial positions.

JUDGES DIFFER IN MORE WAYS THAN ONE.
British judges, bewigged and ready for court.

All judges of the higher courts are former lawyers, all have had the same kind of legal training and experience as practicing lawyers, and lawyers and judges alike are regarded as members of one profession pursuing different aspects of a legal career.

In France, however, a sharp distinction is made between the legal and judicial professions. Young French citizens interested in the law decide early in their training whether they want to be lawyers or judges. If they decide to be lawyers, they take the appropriate training, pass examinations, and become *avouéts, avocats,* or *notaires.* If they choose judicial careers, then, after finishing legal training, they go to the *Centre National d'Études Judiciaires* for four years. The successful graduates become, in effect, civil servants under the Ministry of Justice and are assigned to courts of first instance and work their way up to the higher judicial posts much as junior civil servants rise in other ministries.

Appointment and Removal of Judges

With a few exceptions, which we will consider later, most modern democratic nations select all their judges, from the lowest justice of the peace to the presiding judge of the highest court, by appointment. The appointing officials vary somewhat from nation to nation, but in many nations all judges are appointed by the chief executive or by the minister of justice or the equivalent. In a few nations, judges of some lower courts are appointed by judges of higher courts. Generally speaking, all appointed judges hold office "during good behavior," which means that they can be removed only by a special act of the legislature, called an address of Parliament in Great Britain and impeachment in the United States. This removal power is rarely exercised, however, and most judges in most democratic nations hold their offices for life.

Election and Recall of Judges

Appointment for life tenure is the general rule for judges, but a handful of systems follow different paths. In Switzerland, some cantons choose some or all of their judges by popular election for limited terms of office, and the twenty-six members of the Federal Tribunal, the Swiss national supreme court, are elected by the national legislature for six-year terms.

However, the major exception to the appointment-for-life pattern is to be found in the U.S. states. As of 1992, sixteen states elected all their judges, in seven states most judges were elected and a few minor ones appointed, in seventeen states higher judges were appointed initially but later had to win reelection by popular vote, in six states all judges were appointed for life, and in four states most judges were appointed and a few were elected.

In four states, furthermore, judges were subject to "recall." Under this procedure, if a specified number of voters sign a petition asking for the removal of a certain judge, then a special election is held to determine whether or not the judge will remain in office. If a majority of the voters vote to recall the judge, then he or she immediately leaves office, and the post is filled either by appointment or by a special election. (This is exactly what happened in 1986 to Rose Bird, chief justice of the California supreme court.)

Thus, in the states there is far more direct popular control over the selection and tenure of judges than in any democratic polity except possibly Switzerland. On the other hand, all *federal* judges in the United States are appointed by the president with the approval of a majority of the Senate and remain in office until they die, resign, or are impeached and convicted by Congress (which has happened only fifteen times, but twice in 1989).

Does the way judges are selected make any difference? Many political scientists, jurists, and lawyers argue that the popular election of judges in the U.S. states is a serious weakness in those states' judicial systems, and they have urged the replacement of elective systems with some version of appointment and permanent tenure. They argue that a judge who must worry about reelection is more a politician than a judge and cannot develop the calm, detached judicial temperament that every judge should have. They further argue that popular elections produce frequent turnover among judges and that few stay in office long enough to acquire the experience necessary to be a good judge. They also contend that when judges who face reelection are considering the decisions in their cases they are likely to pay at least as much attention to what will be popular with the voters as to what are the correct decisions under the law.

How valid are those arguments? No one can say with certainty, mainly because there is no universal agreement about just who are the good judges and who are the bad ones. In recent years, however, an increasing number of U.S. states (twenty-three in 1994) have established nonpartisan judicial selection commissions, usually composed of leading lawyers, law school professors, and retired judges, to consider the qualifications of potential new judges and present short lists of the best qualified to the governors, who can make their judicial appointments only from persons on those lists.

OFFICIAL RELATIONSHIPS WITH LEGISLATURES AND EXECUTIVES

Separation of Judges from Prosecutors

Many people and nations that reject the doctrine of separation of powers (see Chapter 11) nevertheless strongly support the ideal of an independent judiciary. This ideal calls for organizing the judiciary in accordance with two main principles. The first principle is that the prosecutor and the judge should never be one and the same person or agency; for, if they are, then the court loses all semblance of impartiality and becomes merely an arm of the prosecution, a "star chamber" travesty of justice (the Star Chamber was a body established by the English monarchs in the sixteenth century to administer summary "justice" in secret to their political opponents). This evil can be avoided only by making the courts independent of the executive.

This principle is most clearly and firmly established in the English-speaking democracies. At both the national and state levels in the United States, for example, the prosecuting function is vested in an executive agency headed by an attorney general. The U.S. attorney general is appointed by the president with the approval of the Senate, and supervises the work of a number of local U.S. attorneys. Each state has an attorney general (some are directly elected and others appointed), and in each state a number of state's attorneys and district attorneys act for the state and county governments). In Great Britain the prosecuting function is vested mainly in the director of public prosecutions, who, under the direction of the attorney general, prepares the cases against persons accused of crime and engages lawyers to prosecute the cases in court.

The Western European nations, on the other hand, treat judges and prosecutors as different sections of the same public service. In France, for example, there is a single profession—*la magistrature*—which includes three kinds of offices: the "sitting judges," who preside over the courts much as British and U.S. judges do; the *parquets*, who form a kind of public prosecutor's office attached to each court; and the administrative staff of the Ministry of Justice. All are regarded as civil servants under the same ministry, and any member of the *magistrature* may serve in any of these three offices. It is not uncommon, in fact, for a particular *magistrat* to move from work on the bench in one court to work in the *parquet* of another, from there to a position in the ministry, and perhaps back again to a high judicial post. In any regular French court, both the judge and the prosecutor are officers of the Ministry of Justice, and the two functions are much less clearly separated than in the Anglo-American democracies.

Insulation of Judges from Political Pressure

The second principle of the independent judiciary is that the judicial process should operate in an atmosphere of calmness, deliberation, and, above all, insulation from pressures by parties and pressure groups with axes to grind. Thus the courts should be independent of the legislature as well as the executive. In accordance with this principle, the insulation of judges from political pressure is generally sought by securing their tenure from partisan interference. The U.S. Constitution, for instance, provides that all federal judges shall hold office "during good behavior" (that is, until removed by impeachment for "high crimes and misdemeanors") and that their salaries shall not be reduced during their tenure in office. Judges can be removed from office only through impeachment by a majority of the House of Representatives and conviction by a two-thirds majority of the Senate. In Great Britain and other English-speaking democracies, judges can be removed from office only by "an address of Parliament" (that is, by resolutions of parliamentary majorities calling for the removal of particular judges).

In France and most Western European countries before World War II, the tenure, salary, and promotion of judges depended mainly on the decisions of the various ministries of justice. Since 1945, however, some nations have followed France's lead by establishing special bodies to ensure that the status of judges will be somewhat better protected than by ordinary ministerial procedures. France has established a special judicial supervisory body, the *Conseil Supérieur de la Magistrature*, chosen partly by the national assembly and partly by the judicial profession itself, to supervise the status of judges separately from that of the *parquets* and other civil servants. However, the ministry retains the power of veto over the council's recommendations for the appointment and promotion of judges.

On the basis of those facts, then, it seems that the English-speaking nations come nearer to realizing the ideal of an independent judiciary than most Western European nations do, but the Europeans appear to be moving in that direction. However *formally* independent they may be, the *actual* separation of judges from "politics" is a different matter, as we will see next.

Role of Judges in Governing

Since the 1970s U.S. courts have been attacked more than at any time since President Franklin Roosevelt tried to "pack" the Supreme Court with judges sympathetic to his policies in 1937. Those attacks, moreover, have come from both the Right and the Left. Right-wing critics have been outraged by the Supreme Court's decisions in the school-segregation cases in the 1950s; in the cases on school prayer, legislative apportionment, and rights of defendants in the 1960s; and in the cases on capital punishment, abortion, busing of schoolchildren, and affirmative action in the 1970s and 1980s. The conservative critics have charged that the Supreme Court, especially under Chief Justices Earl Warren (1953–1969) and Warren Burger (1969–1986), acted like liberal politicians rather than learned jurists and, worst of all, conservatives charge, the justices "legislated": that is, they wrote their own ideas of policy into the U.S. constitution rather than applying the ideas written by the constitution's framers.

The courts, of course, have not lacked their defenders. In a rather ironic switching of sides, liberals in the 1980s and 1990s made essentially the same arguments that conservatives had made in the 1930s to defend the conservative Supreme Court that was throwing out New Deal programs as unconstitutional. In the 1980s Presidents Reagan and Bush appointed a number of new Supreme Court justices who share their conservative political philosophies. In the 1990s, Bill Clinton nominated two moderate liberals. The net result is that on most issues the Court became more moderate than either strongly conservative or strongly liberal.

This repeated switching of sides has led some observers to conclude that the debate over the role of the courts is really a fight between liberals and conservatives over the *content* of the courts' decisions and not about the *procedures* by which the decisions are made. After all, when conservative judges controlled the Supreme Court in the 1930s, liberal critics wanted to reduce its powers while conservatives praised the Court as the bastion of American liberty. When liberal judges came to control the court, conservatives wanted to reduce its powers while liberals praised its independence. Now that moderates are in control, neither strong conservatives nor strong liberals are satisfied with the Court's role.

For our purposes, the most interesting aspect of all those debates about the courts is that the leading advocates on both sides have a "mechanical" conception of the judicial process, which may be summarized as follows.

MECHANICAL VIEW

Judges as Technicians

We noted earlier in this chapter that, according to the traditional conception of the proper distribution of governmental powers, the function of the courts is to interpret and apply, in particular cases, the general rules formulated by lawmaking bodies. Judges do not *make* the law. They *discover* and *apply* it.

This view of the judicial function stems mainly from the views expressed in perhaps the most widely read and influential of all books among lawyers in the English-speaking world for two centuries: the *Commentaries on the Laws of England* by the eminent eighteenth-century English jurist Sir William Blackstone. To Blackstone (and, apparently, to many of his readers) judges are "the living oracles . . . who are bound by an oath according to the law of the land." Even when judges reverse earlier rulings on points of law, he wrote, "it is declared not that such a sentence was *bad law*, but that it was *not law*."[4]

A CONSTITUTIONAL CONVENTION?

In the 1980s the conservative attack on the Supreme Court increasingly took the form of calling for a new constitutional convention to launch such amendments as forcing the president and Congress to adopt balanced budgets, outlawing abortion, and reinstituting prayers in the public schools. (In fact, economist Herbert Stein suggested that all those proposals be consolidated into one omnibus amendment that would require schoolchildren to pray for a balanced budget!) Article V of the U.S. Constitution provides that "the Congress . . . on the application of the Legislatures of two thirds of the several states shall call a Convention for proposing Amendments. . . ." No such convention had ever been called in the nation's history, but by 1992, a total of thirty-three state legislatures—just one short of the necessary thirty-four—had adopted resolutions calling for a convention to consider a balanced-budget amendment. Constitutional experts were widely divided on a number of questions about such a conven-

tion: Do the state resolutions have to be in identical form? How would the members of such a convention be selected? Would the convention be required to consider *only* a balanced-budget amendment, or could it take up any matter and propose any amendments it wished? There were no definitive answers because there were no precedents.

Some members of Congress feared that such a convention would "run amok," and they urged Congress to come up with its own balanced-budget amendment. Such an amendment was voted on by the House of Representatives in 1992 and by both chambers in 1995, but it failed to get the two-thirds majority support in both required by the Consitution.

No constitutional convention has yet been called, but it remains a live option with a large number of potential complications and consequences.

Blackstone's picture of judges as skilled technicians "declaring" rather than making law is well summarized in the following statement by the nineteenth-century American jurist James C. Carter:

> That judges *declare*, and do not *make*, the law is not a fiction or a pretense, but a profound truth. If courts really made the law, they would have and feel the freedoms of legislators. They could and would make it in accordance with their own views of justice and expedience. . . . I need not say that the case is precisely contrary. . . . They must decide it consistently with established rules. . . . Any judge who assumed to possess that measure of *arbitrary* power which a legislator really enjoys would clearly subject himself to impeachment.[5]

Ideal of a Nonpolitical Judiciary

According to the mechanical conception, then, judges should "declare" law that others have made. Judges should not make laws themselves. Thus, in interpreting the U.S. Constitution, the justices of the Supreme Court should ask only what was the original intent of the framers of the constitution and follow that intent rather than imposing their own ideas of justice. Finding out what the law *is* is thus a task for legal technicians, not politicians. It demands a high order of legal skill and training and a "judicial temperament." Therefore, adherents of the mechanical conception insist that the courts should be organized so that those difficult technical tasks are performed effectively and the judges consider each case strictly on its legal merits without being influenced by political considerations.

Four conditions must exist for that ideal to be realized: First, the judiciary must be independent of both the legislature and the executive, which are necessarily political agencies. Second, the judiciary must be insulated from the selfish and noisy demands of political parties and pressure groups. Third, judges should be selected for their legal skill and judicial temperament rather than for their political preferences. Fourth, judges should refrain from public statements of their policy preferences and should be careful to use only the technical language of the law in writing their decisions.

Judges, in short, should remain completely aloof from politics, and politics should not contaminate their deliberations. The strength of this ideal is suggested by the fact that until 1941, U.S. state and national judges were allowed to punish for contempt of court any person who sought to influence a judge while a case was in process. Even the Supreme Court decision that struck down this rule was made by a bare majority. In Great Britain even today a newspaper can be fined heavily for discussing a case in any but the vaguest terms while it is *sub judice* ("under judicial consideration").

Description or Ideal?

Many people who uphold this view of the judicial process believe that some judges *do* behave in this fashion, although they usually disagree on *which* judges do. As we have seen, conservatives in the 1930s generally believed that the U.S. Supreme Court was only doing its constitutional duty in throwing out New Deal legislation,

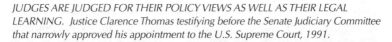

JUDGES ARE JUDGED FOR THEIR POLICY VIEWS AS WELL AS THEIR LEGAL LEARNING. Justice Clarence Thomas testifying before the Senate Judiciary Committee that narrowly approved his appointment to the U.S. Supreme Court, 1991.

whereas the liberals accused the judges of writing their own social and economic views into the Constitution. In the 1960s and 1970s, the tables were turned. Liberals praised the Court for protecting constitutional liberties and conservatives attacked it for trying to pervert the Constitution with the justices' "left-wing political ideas," and radicals scorned it as a "front for the establishment." In the 1980s liberals were again attacking the Court and conservatives were praising it.

The point is that today, just as in the 1930s, a great many of *both* the Court's critics and its defenders adhere to the traditional mechanical conception in the sense that they believe that it is the correct standard to apply to actual judges, and that it is not only morally right but also an attainable ideal if we have the right kind of judges on the bench. In this sense, then, the traditional conception has had a powerful influence upon people's thinking about the role of judges in governing.

JUDICIAL LEGISLATION

An Avoidable Deviation?

The abiding controversy over whether the U.S. Supreme Court is "legislating" its social and economic views or merely "declaring" the Constitution is not unique to the 1930s or our time. Such controversies have flared up over and over again ever since the birth of the Republic. The Jeffersonians, for example, accused John Marshall's Supreme Court and the rest of the Federalist-packed judiciary of trying to write Federalist party policies into the Constitution. Andrew Jackson and his chief justice, Roger B. Taney, were attacked by the Whigs on similar grounds, and the Taney Court's decision in the Dred Scott case in 1857 was condemned perhaps more bitterly than any other in history. The conservative justices of the late nineteenth and early twentieth centuries were often charged with trying to write their laissez-faire preferences into the Constitution. We have already noted the controversies over the Court in 1937 and since 1954.

Complaints about "judicial legislation" have thus been frequent in the United States and are probably a permanent feature of U.S. politics. The scattered evidence available suggests that similar, though perhaps less frequent and noisy, complaints are perennial in every nation with a well-established tradition of an independent judiciary. When we examine the political views of those who attack and those who defend the courts on this issue, we find that with very few exceptions people who approve the political effects of a particular line of decisions defend the courts for "enforcing the Constitution," whereas those who dislike those effects claim that the courts are improperly "engaging in judicial legislation." It depends, it seems, on whose ox is being gored.

The point is, however, that most of those who have charged the U.S. Supreme Court with engaging in judicial legislation seem to believe that it is an *avoidable* deviation from the Court's true function of declaring the law and that the right kind of justices—that is, jurists who are skilled technicians and who accept and adhere to the proper mechanical function of declaring the law—can restore the Court to its proper role in the governmental process.

Inherent in the Judicial Process?

By no means all analysts of the judicial process regard judicial legislation as something that could and would be eliminated if all judges had the right attitudes toward their jobs. A growing number of legal scholars, judges, and political scientists believe that judicial policy making is an inherent and inescapable consequence of the very nature of the judicial process itself. Many start from a premise stated by the eighteenth-century jurist and Anglican bishop Benjamin Hoadly: "Whoever hath an *absolute authority to interpret* any written or spoken laws, it is *he* who is truly the *Law-Giver* to all interests and purposes, and not the person who first spoke or wrote them. . . ."[6] They contend that all constitutions, statutes, executive and administrative rules, and other laws are necessarily general to some degree and must therefore be somewhat vague. Laws have to be interpreted in specific cases, but usually there is no single interpretation that is agreed upon by all people with legal training and skills. Lawyers and judges often disagree among themselves about what the law means in particular situations. Previous court decisions rarely settle the question, for some precedent can be found for just about every possible interpretation. Indeed, it is the duty of the lawyers for both sides to bring before the court lists of such precedents, each list calling for interpretations different from those presented by the other side. Every judge is thus continually faced with different—but, judged by any reasonable standard, equally logical—interpretations.

Each interpretation necessarily favors the interests of some groups and damages those of others. The judge cannot help choosing one of the interpretations and therefore cannot avoid promoting the interests of some and hurting those of others. When we look behind the legal jargon, we have to recognize that the process by which judges choose one interpretation over the others and make their decisions is, by our definition, *political*. Why? Because whatever decisions courts make necessarily satisfy some values and frustrate others.

This observation is true, those commentators argue, of *every* court, because every court has the power to interpret, if not to strike down, laws. It will continue to be true until jurists perfect a machine like a cash register on which the judge can punch keys labeled "the facts," pull down a lever called "the law," and read "the decision" that pops out.

To illustrate this characterization of the policy-making functions of the judiciary, let us consider the role that the U.S. Supreme Court has played in the conflict over racial segregation in the schools.

An Illustration: "Equal Protection" and the Schools

The Fourteenth Amendment to the U.S. Constitution declares that "no State shall . . . deny to any person within its jurisdiction the equal protection of the laws." Beginning in the late nineteenth century, the southern and border states enacted a series of "Jim Crow" laws prohibiting African-Americans from attending the same schools, riding in the same train cars, using the same public swimming pools and golf courses, and eating in the same restaurants as whites. A number of antisegregationists thought that those laws violated the equal-protection clause. On the other

SOME RECENT JUDICIAL LEGISLATION IN THE UNITED STATES

Since the early 1950s, the U.S. Supreme Court has not merely waited for Congress and the president to take the lead in all important policy areas and then followed their leads. The court has itself *initiated* a number of major public policies. Among the most important are the following:

School desegregation: voiding all laws requiring white and African-American children to attend separate schools.

School integration: requiring all public schools to have a reasonable mixture of African-American and white children even if that requires busing some white children to predominantly African-American schools and vice versa.

Legislative reapportionment: requiring all congressional and state legislative districts to have approximately equal populations, so as to maximize the principle of "one person, one vote."

Criminal justice system: guaranteeing a lawyer to every accused person and strengthening limitations on police conduct of questioning and searches.

State and local antipornography laws: weakening them to the point where it is now legal to publish and sell just about any kind of book, magazine, or movie that explicitly portrays any and all variations on the sex act.

Birth control and abortion: removing restrictions on the sale of birth control devices and on the legal right of pregnant women to choose whether or not to have abortions.

---

hand, many whites were segregationists, and they had no doubt that such laws were perfectly in accord with the equal-protection clause. Certainly the wording of the clause is vague enough so that reasonable people—and even specialists in constitutional law—could and did disagree about whether it prohibits or permits segregation laws.

In the case of *Plessy* v. *Ferguson* (1896), the Supreme Court was called upon to decide whether or not a state law requiring racial segregation on trains was constitutional. The Court found that under the equal-protection clause, segregation *in itself* is not unconstitutional as long as the accommodations provided for each race are substantially equal to those provided for the other. This ruling came to be known as the separate-but-equal formula.

From then until the late 1930s the Court, following the Plessy formula, upheld all state segregation laws and, indeed, was easily satisfied with what constituted equality of accommodations. In the 1930s, however, the Court began to take a different line. It insisted, for example, that states that would not admit African-Americans to their public universities must provide *really* equal facilities for them. In *Sweatt* v. *Painter* (1950), the Court ordered Texas to either admit an African-American applicant to the University of Texas law school or establish a separate law school for African-Americans that would be its equivalent in every respect, a multimillion-dollar project.

Next came the landmark case of *Brown* v. *Board of Education* (1954), in which the Court explicitly overruled the Plessy decision and held that, no matter what accommodations are provided, racial segregation in public schools is *in itself* a denial of equal protection for African-Americans, and that therefore all state laws requiring such segregation are in violation of the Fourteenth Amendment.

There matters stood until the late 1960s and early 1970s, when the Court decided that equal protection does not mean merely no forced segregation; equal protection means full integration. The Court took the position that the ultimate goal is to have both African-American and white children in every school, and while every school does not have to reflect the proportions of the races in the whole community and some one-race schools may be permissible in special circumstances, any school system that has ever deliberately practiced racial segregation can be forced to meet racial quotas and to use mandatory busing of children of both races to achieve a proper racial mixture.

Many commentators have sharply attacked the Court for its role in the school-segregation and busing controversies, and some of the present argument about the proper role of the Court arises from it. The Court's critics charge it with making policy. So it has, beyond a doubt. However, some of those critics seem to imply that *all* judicial policy making is highly irregular and wrong, regardless of the content of the policies made. What those critics forget, or at least may not wish to remember, is that the phrase "equal protection of the laws" is so vague that no single interpretation is clearly preferred by all persons of good will and legal expertise. The point is that the 1896 Court, which declared the separate-but-equal formula, was *also* making policy. In throwing out that formula in 1954 and in developing its later desegregation-requires-integration position, the Court was not making policy for the first time; rather, it was reversing policies made earlier.

If present critics of the Court, liberals or conservatives, were given complete freedom to amend the U.S. Constitution and put on the Court justices whose policy preferences were exactly like their own, they could very likely force the Court to make the kind of policy they prefer. However, there is no conceivable way, short of abolishing it altogether, to prevent the Court from making *some* kind of policy. Policy making is inherent in the nature of the judicial process itself.

JUDGES IN THE POLITICAL PROCESS

In recent years a number of political scientists, whose approach was pioneered by Jack W. Peltason in his monograph *Federal Courts in the Political Process* (1955), have viewed the judicial process as simply one aspect of the total political-governmental process and have used many of the same techniques used to study the legislative, executive, and administrative processes. Peltason suggested a number of generalizations, most of which have been confirmed by subsequent research.[7]

Peltason contended that courts are as much involved in political conflict (as the term is used in this book) as any other government agency, for every case that comes before a court involves a conflict of interest between a plaintiff and a defendant, and many cases involve the interests of groups far broader than just the parties themselves. In deciding each case—for example, ordering this person to go to jail for rioting or that corporation to pay damages to someone its products have in-

THE ROLE OF THE LAW CLERKS

Every justice of the Supreme Court has from one to three law clerks to help him or her with the work. Although some effort is made to draw them from various parts of the country, most law clerks are recent graduates of the nation's most prestigious law schools. It is a high honor to be chosen as a clerk and a great start for a lawyer's career. The competition is fierce for the few posts available each year; the law graduates chosen rank at the very top of their classes, and most have been editors of their schools' law reviews.

The clerks do a good deal of the justices' routine but necessary work. They screen thousands of petitions every year by people who want the Court to review their cases, and they recommend to the justices which few should be reviewed. They research the facts and legal precedents relevant to the cases before the Court. They often write memoranda for their justices on points of law that have to be decided in the cases. They often try to persuade their justices to vote a particular way on a particular case and to follow certain lines of reasoning in their written opinions. One of the less praiseworthy indications of their importance is the fact that interviews with current and recent clerks about how the justices really behave behind the scenes were the main sources of information used by Bob Woodward and Scott Armstrong in their sensational popular exposé *The Brethren* (1980).

However, the most striking testimony to their importance is made by Martin Shapiro, a distinguished scholar of judicial behavior:

It is a long-time open secret, although rarely discussed in print, that most of the words in most of the opinions are written by clerks. At one extreme, a justice may tell his clerks which party he wants to win in a given case and then let them do the whole job, merely reading the clerk's finished product and signing it. At the other, a justice may write the entire opinion, asking his clerks only for research assistance on particular points. Some of the justices fall near the first extreme in the handling of nearly every case. Others choose to do a good deal of original writing in certain select cases. There may be a few justices who actually write a majority of the words they sign as their own each year.[8]

jured or that school board to bus African-American children to white schools—the courts make policies in precisely the same sense that other government agencies do. Policies made by courts differ from those made by legislatures, executives, and administrators only in form and not in substance.

This has become even more clear in recent years with the increase in the number of "class-action" suits heard and decided by the courts. A **class-action suit** is *a case brought by a plaintiff on behalf not only of the plaintiff but of all other persons similarly situated*. The original school desegregation case in 1954 is a famous example. The suit was brought on behalf of Linda Brown, an African-American who was required by the rules of the Board of Education of Topeka, Kansas, to attend an exclusively African-American school. But in bringing the suit, the National Association for the Advancement of Colored People (NAACP) asked the court to outlaw forced segregation not only in Topeka but also everywhere else, and to allow not only Linda Brown but also every other African-American child similarly situated to attend schools with white children. The Court agreed, and the effect of the decision was to outlaw legally required racial segregation in the schools everywhere.

Peltason further suggested that for all the lip service paid to judicial independence, the interests most powerfully affected by court decisions have never refrained from trying to influence their outcomes. Perhaps the main difference between political conflict centered on the courts and conflict centered on the other government agencies is that legal conflict must be conducted in an atmosphere generated by the general acceptance and respectability of the mechanical conception of the judicial process. If a pressure group announces quite openly, "We intend to put pressure on Congress, the president, and the bureaucracy to get our policies adopted," few will think that is improper. However, let that group announce with equal frankness that "We intend to put pressure on the judges to make their decisions in our favor," and some potential allies will become enemies because they disapprove such efforts to "tamper with the integrity of the courts." Thus while a great many political interest groups in fact try to influence judicial decisions, they rarely *talk* as though that is what they are doing. Rather they talk of "defending the integrity of the courts," "defending the law against political judges," "making sure that people with sound views of the Constitution become judges," and the like.

This kind of talk does not alter the *fact* of political conflict in the judicial process, but it does mean that such conflict is conducted in a rather special way. Peltason pointed to three main areas of political conflict in the judicial process.

Selection of Judges

When selecting federal judges in the United States, most presidents and senators have *talked* as if they have been selecting only technicians of jurisprudence but have *acted* as if they have been selecting policy makers whose views agree with their own. "Since 1885 over 90 percent of all federal judges have been filled by members—in most cases active members—of the same party as the President who chose them and most have been supporters of the Senator who nominated them."[9] The only president in recent years to fall below this average was Republican Gerald Ford, whose judicial appointments included only 81 percent Republicans. Democrats Jimmy Carter and Bill Clinton appointed over 90 percent Democrats, and Republicans Ronald Reagan and George Bush appointed over 90 percent Republicans.

The American Bar Association (ABA), the national professional organization of lawyers, has asked for a greater voice in the selection of judges (after all, the ABA argues, lawyers know the technical competence of potential judges better than anyone else), but the many other interests involved have been reluctant to turn over so much power to what is, in many situations, a rival interest. On the other side, many judges have clung to their posts long after age and failing health have made their retirement advisable. Why? Because they have so strongly opposed the political views of the incumbent president that they have not wished that president to name their successors. Thus in the mid-1980s there were persistent rumors that liberal Supreme Court justices William Brennan and Thurgood Marshall, though old and in poor health, were determined to stay on the Court as long as possible to keep conservative Presidents Ronald Reagan and George Bush from naming their successors. Brennan ultimately retired in 1990 and Marshall in 1991, and both were replaced by conservatives. However, the resignations of Byron White (1993) and Harry Blackmun (1994) enabled President Clinton to name as their replacements two new justices (Ruth Bader Ginsburg and Stephen G. Breyer) whose moderate-liberal political philosophies were close to his own.

Decision Making

Interest groups try to influence the selection of judges whenever they can, but judges' long tenure means that for the most part the groups have to work with and through the judges who are in office. An interest group takes a terrible risk if it tries to influence a judge in the same manner in which it might try to influence a member of Congress or an administrator. Most groups therefore exert direct influence only through such accepted channels as employing skilled and expensive lawyers, presenting well-written briefs, and so on. It is interesting to note that in recent decades it has become increasingly common for interest groups to submit *amicus curiae* ("friend of the court") briefs and to offer other legal help to plaintiffs and defendants who represent legal principles that they want established or upheld. Many such briefs were submitted on both sides, for example, in the school-segregation cases of 1954 (see the earlier discussion) and the Bakke case on affirmative action in 1979. The ablest lawyers and the best-writtem briefs by no means always ensure victory, of course, but they help.

Implementation of Decisions

In Chapter 13 we noted that just because a law has been enacted by the legislature and approved by the executive does not necessarily mean that it will be applied by the administrative agencies exactly, or in some instances even approximately, as its authors intended. The administrative process can be as significant a determinant of the policies that government actually follows as the legislative and executive processes.

Much the same can be said of the judicial process. Just because the Supreme Court or any other judicial body has declared what the law is on a particular point does not necessarily mean that every other court and government agency will act accordingly. For one thing, the Court's decision is technically binding only on the specific parties in the particular case, and if interest groups similar to those represented by the losing party choose to ignore the decision, they can often get away with it. In 1947, for example, the Supreme Court declared that the Board of Education of Champaign County, Illinois, had violated the constitutional separation of church and state in its "released-time" program by allowing teachers to hold classes in religion in the public schools and requiring pupils either to attend the classes or to remain in study hall. After the decision the Champaign school board discontinued its program, but similar released-time programs were continued in many thousands of other school districts throughout the land as if nothing had happened. An even more dramatic illustration occurred in 1955, when the Supreme Court ordered the desegregation of all public schools "with all deliberate speed." Yet, for over a decade the schools in many southern states remained almost as segregated as they had been before the 1955 order.

Furthermore, the formal hierarchical structure of court systems is no guarantee that the lower courts will invariably interpret the law exactly as the higher courts wish. As Peltason pointed out,

The subordinate judge's task of applying the Supreme Court's mandates is no more mechanical than is the Supreme Court's task of applying the Constitution's mandates. The high court decisions which are supposed to guide and control the subordinates are frequently just as ambiguous as is the Constitution or statute which is supposed to guide the Supreme Court, and they admit of many interpretations. Hence, just as it is said that the Constitution is what the judges say it is, so it can be said that a Supreme Court decision is what the subordinate judges who apply it say it is.[10]

Finally, groups whose interests are damaged by an adverse Court decision do not have to accept their defeat as final, and they rarely do. Such groups can, for example, try to have the Constitution amended to prevent such rulings in the future (the Eleventh and Sixteenth Amendments were adopted for just such purposes); to persuade the Court to reverse itself (as it did, for example, in the *Brown* case); to induce the lower courts to ignore the decisions; or to pack or threaten to pack the Court. Judicial decisions thus do not necessarily settle once and for all the political conflicts with which they deal, any more than legislative acts or executive orders do. But because of the high prestige and officially nonpolitical atmosphere of the judicial process, a favorable court decision is an important political victory for any interest group.

For Further Reading

LAW AND COURT STRUCTURES

*ABRAHAM, HENRY J. *The Judicial Process*, 6th ed. New York: Oxford University Press, 1993. Clear and informative description of court structures and procedures in the United States, France, and Great Britain.

DANASKA, MIRJAN R. *The Faces of Justice and State Authority*. New Haven, CT: Yale University Press, 1986. Comparative study of the administration of justice in modern nations.

*JACOB, HERBERT. *Justice in America*, 4th ed. Boston, MA: Little, Brown, 1984. Survey of court structures and legal systems in the United States.

MARSHALL, THOMAS R. *Public Opinion and the Supreme Court*. Boston, MA: Unwin Hyman, 1989. Makes extensive use of public opinion polls to measure popular attiudes toward the Supreme Court's major decisions and the institution of judicial review.

SHAPIRO, MARTIN. *Courts: A Comparative and Political Analysis*. Chicago, IL: University of Chicago Press, 1986. Comparative study of the structure and role of courts in Western democracies.

SOPER, PHILIP. *A Theory of Law*. Cambridge, MA: Harvard University Press, 1984. Discussion of nature of law compared with other types of social rules.

THE JUDICIAL PROCESS

*AGRESTO, JOHN. *The Supreme Court and Constitutional Democracy*. Ithaca, NY: Cornell University Press, 1984. An argument for judicial restraint as the best solution to the perennial problem of reconciling judicial review with democracy.

BERGER, RAOUL. *Government by Judiciary*. Cambridge, MA: Harvard University Press, 1977. Attack on excessive power exercised by courts in American policy making.

BLAIR, PHILIP M. *Federalism and Judicial Review in West Germany*. New York: Oxford University Press, 1981. Useful comparative study of operation of judicial review in a European federal democracy.

*CHOPER, JESSE H. *Judicial Review and the National Political Process*. Chicago, IL: University of Chicago Press, 1982. Analysis by a leading legal theorist of the role of courts and judicial review in the American political system.

FRANK, JEROME. *Law and the Modern Mind*. New York: Brentano's, 1930. Leading exposition of "legal realist" view.

*JOHNSON, CHARLES A., and BRADLEY C. CANON. *Judicial Policies: Implementation and Impact*. Washington, DC: Congressional Quarterly Press, 1984. Analysis of what happens to court decisions after they are handed down.

*PELTASON, JACK W. *Federal Courts in the Political Process*. New York: Random House, 1955. Seminal exposition of the conception of the judicial process as part of the political process.

PERRY, MICHAEL J. *The Constitution, the Courts, and Human Rights: An Inquiry into the Legitimacy of Constitutional Policymaking by the Judiciary*. New Haven, CT: Yale University Press, 1982. Analysis of role of courts in civil liberties decisions as an approach to evaluation of judicial review.

STUMPF, HARRY P. *American Judicial Politics*. New York: Harcourt Brace Jovanovich, 1988. Survey of research on how political and legal interpretations interact in the making of U.S. judicial decisions.

Notes

1. In American and British jurisprudence, the term *civil law* has two quite different meanings. One is used interchangeably with *Roman law* to denote the body of laws that prevailed in ancient Rome and that today underlies the systems of law in continental European countries. The other usage denotes noncriminal laws, in the manner used later in this chapter. See *Black's Law Dictionary*, 4th ed. (St. Paul, MN: West, 1968), pp. 312, 1494.

2. *Black's Law Dictionary*, 4th ed., p. 445.

3. In 1989, Great Britain's chief legal officer, the Lord Chancellor, suggested some major revisions in the legal profession. He proposed that the distinction between solicitors and barristers be abolished, that all lawyers be licensed to appear before all courts, and that judges be chosen from the ranks of all lawyers rather than from barristers alone. Some modest changes were made in solicitors' access to courts, but Britain continued to have a two-tier legal profession.

4. William Blackstone, *Commentaries on the Laws of England*, ed. Thomas M. Cooley (Chicago, IL: Callaghan and Cockroft, 1871), vol. 1, p. 69, italics added.

5. James C. Carter, "The Province of the Written and Unwritten Law," (1890), quoted in Fred V. Cahill, Jr., *Judicial Legislation* (New York: Ronald Press, 1952), p. 17, n. 26, italics added.

6. Quoted in Cahill, *Judicial Legislation*, p. 99.

7. Jack W. Peltason, *Federal Courts in the Political Process* (New York: Random House, 1955).

8. Martin Shapiro, "The Supreme Court," in *The New American Political System*, ed. Anthony King (Washington, DC: American Enterprise Institute, 1978), p. 199.

9. Peltason, *Federal Courts*, p. 21.

10. Ibid., p. 14.

15

And though all the winds of doctrine were let loose to play upon the earth, so Truth be in the field, we do injuriously, by licensing and prohibiting, to misdoubt her strength. Let her and Falsehood grapple; who ever knew Truth put to worse, in a free and open encounter? . . . . She needs no policies, nor strategems, nor licensings to make her victorious; those are but the shifts and defenses that error uses against her power.
John Milton, *Areopagitica* (1644)

[A student may be disciplined] for racist or discriminatory comments, epithets or other expressive behavior . . . directed at an individual . . . if such comments, epithets or other expressive behavior . . . demean the race, sex, religion, color, creed, disability, sexual orientation, national origin, ancestry or age of the individual. . . .
Rule of the University of Wisconsin (1989)

. . . the best test of truth is the power of the thought to get itself accepted in the competition of the market, and . . . truth is the only ground upon which their wishes can safely be carried out. That, at any rate, is the theory of our Constitution. It is an experiment as all life is an experiment.
Justice Oliver Wendell Holmes, Jr., *Abrams v. U.S.* (1919)

Human Rights: Principles and Problems

Philosophical Foundations for Human Rights

BASIC TERMS

In this and the next chapter, we consider some of the philosophical issues and practical problems involved in one of the most important of all the areas in which governments relate to people: the area variously called *human rights, civil liberties*, and *civil rights*. As we will see, the philosophical issues are complex, and resolving those issues almost always involves choosing between one good thing and another good thing and not between something wholly good and something wholly bad.

Let us begin by making clear what some of the terms mean. The most basic concept is that of **human rights**, which are *protections to which all human beings are entitled because of their humanity and not because of their social status or individual merit*. Some of those rights are claimed and enjoyed without regard to the political order, but since this book is concerned with politics and government, we will focus on the two types of human rights that are most closely involved with the actions of governments: civil liberties and civil rights.

As we use the term in this book, **civil liberties** are *constitutional protections of persons, opinions, and property against arbitrary interference by government*. They in-

349

clude such protections as freedom of speech, freedom of the press, freedom of religious belief, and freedom from arbitrary arrest and punishment.

Civil rights are *legally guaranteed benefits provided by positive actions of government.* They include such guarantees as education, protection against illness and starvation, and financial support in unemployment and old age.

EVOLVING IDEA OF HUMAN RIGHTS

Government as the Enemy

The basic idea of human rights is rooted in the ideologies of constitutionalism and classical liberalism we considered in Chapter 4. For our present purposes we need to recall the beliefs of such seventeenth- and eighteenth-century philosophers as John Locke and Thomas Jefferson that the most precious value in human society is the individual human being, and the great goal of governments—indeed, the only moral justification for any government's existence—is to liberate individuals from the economic, political, religious, and moral shackles by which they had been bound through centuries of subjection to absolute monarchs, feudal economies, and official religions. And the best way to do this is by instituting *constitutional* governments, governments whose powers are limited in such ways that those powers cannot and will not be used to abridge individual liberties (see Chapters 4 and 5).

According to classical liberalism, then, government was the principal enemy of human rights, and constitutionalism was the answer. Thus the constitutions of liberal democratic nations written before World War I guarantee only rights of persons *against* government. Their "bills of rights" contain only lists of actions that government is prohibited from taking against individuals, such as abridging freedom of speech and religion, conducting unreasonable searches and seizures, and coercing confessions. The classical meaning of a *civil liberty*, in short, was something that a government may not do to a person.

This conception of human rights was rooted in the conviction of the constitution makers of the eighteenth and nineteenth centuries (following the ideas of John Locke) that human beings are naturally free and that government is an artificial creation of people rather than a universal creation of nature. As such, government is inherently hostile to human freedom and must be watched vigilantly and restrained resolutely.

Locke and his followers also recognized, however, that people's rights are unsafe in a state of anarchy, for when human aggressions are entirely unrestrained, there is grave danger that the strong will ride roughshod over the rights of the weak. Some kind of government, they believed, is indispensable to the protection of the rights of *all* humans, weak and strong alike.

Thus, they faced a dilemma: Human rights cannot be preserved without government, but government itself is inherently hostile to those rights. The only way Locke and the other philosophers could see out of the dilemma was to organize government so that it would maintain law and order without abridging people's rights. The only way to do that, they were convinced, was to organize government according to their version of the ancient doctrine of constitutionalism. All rightful governments, they held, must operate within strict limits specified by constitutions. Each constitution, in turn, must firmly restrain government power by listing what government may not do (as in a bill of rights), carefully defining what it may do (as in a list of enumerated powers), and establishing separation of powers; that is, distributing government power among three separate and independent branches of government, the legislative, executive, and judicial (see Chapter 11). In this way, they believed, the power of government could be restrained so as to minimize its inherent danger to human rights.

It is not surprising that Locke and his followers regarded government as the principal enemy of human rights. After all, the governments under which they lived acted according to such principles as the divine right of kings and the privileges of royalty and nobility over peasants and yeomen. The violations of human rights of which they were aware—the suppression of antimonarchy speeches and writings, the secret jailing and torture of the monarch's opponents and dissenters from the official religion—were all committed by agents of authoritarian governments in the name of royal prerogatives and "reasons of state." The only serious and visible threat to human rights in Locke's time was government. As a result, Locke's belief in those rights led him logically to the antigovernment doctrine of constitutionalism, the doctrine that government power should be limited so as to protect human rights.

In modern times, however, the liberal democratic nations have instituted governments whose decisions are made not by autocratic monarchs and their lackeys but by popular majorities and their elected representatives. Even so, many citizens of modern democracies fear that popular majorities may sometimes try to override the rights of minorities. They believe that constitutional government is just as necessary to the preservation of human rights against popular majorities as it ever was to their preservation against the authoritarian governments condemned by Locke and Jefferson centuries earlier.

The constitutions of the U.S. states and the national government written after 1776 were the first in modern times to attempt to put the ideal of constitutionalism into practice. It soon became apparent that the new systems needed "watchdogs"; that is, agencies whose special duty and power are to determine whether or not any branch of government is exceeding its constitutional limits. In the United States the courts, rather than the legislatures or the executives, took over this role in 1803 by assuming the power of judicial review, which is the power of courts to annul legislative and executive acts by declaring those acts unconstitutional (see Chapter 14). Some nations with constitutional governments have assigned the watchdog function to their legislatures rather than to their courts (and some nations whose constitutions formally establish judicial review have no watchdogs and thus in reality have governments that are neither free nor constitutional).

Whether or not they have the power of judicial review, the courts in all free nations have a special role in the protection of human rights, because a great many (though not all) of the conflicts over rights are fought out in cases at law. When a person is tried for a crime, for example, the court must not only determine the defendant's guilt or innocence but must also decide whether or not the defendant's rights to a fair trial and due process of law are respected in the framing of the charges, selection of the jury, admission of evidence, and provision of counsel. When a court decides a libel suit brought by plaintiff A against defendant B, it must determine whether or not in the particular circumstances A's right to a good reputation has been unduly damaged by what B has written about A and whether or not punishing B would abridge B's freedom of speech and press. Only some free nations give their courts the power to void laws as unconstitutional, but the courts of all free nations necessarily have the power to interpret and apply in specific cases the laws and constitutional provisions guaranteeing civil liberties. Court decisions and judicial interpretations thus constitute a significant body of data in discovering the actual status of civil liberties in any free nation, whether or not its courts have the power of judicial review. In Chapter 16 we will review a number of such decisions and interpretations.

The Modern View: Government as Both Enemy and Ally

Most citizens of modern free nations agree with their eighteenth- and nineteenth-century ancestors that human rights must be protected against repressive government actions. Unlike their forebears, however, they do not regard government as the *only* serious threat to those rights. They believe that there are at least three additional threats, each of which is as dangerous as government repression and each of which can be countered only by enlisting the power and authority of government to protect the individual.

NATIONAL GOVERNMENT VERSUS SUBNATIONAL GOVERNMENTS   The first threat is aggression against the rights of national citizens by subnational governments. A good deal of the conflict over human rights in the United States since the Civil War (1861–1865) has arisen from efforts by certain state and local governments to impose racial segregation and white supremacy on African-Americans. The Fourteenth Amendment to the U.S. Constitution makes African-Americans citizens of the United States first and citizens of the states in which they reside second. Furthermore, the amendment stipulates that "no State shall make or enforce any law which shall abridge the privileges or immunities of citizens of the United States. . . ."

To secure their constitutional privileges and immunities, African-Americans, particularly in the southern states, have often turned to the national government as their principal ally against oppression by state and local governments. In Chapter 16 we will examine this conflict in detail, but this brief mention should serve to illustrate the point that many Americans, and certainly most African-Americans, no longer view *all* governments, in pure Lockean terms, as threats to their rights. Many Americans have come to see that government has different levels and agencies, some of which may well be the only instruments powerful enough to protect human rights against infringements by other governments and by private persons and groups.

GOVERNMENT VERSUS MOBS   The second threat is aggression against the rights of private individuals by other private individuals. For example, the right to a fair trial is sometimes threatened by lynch mobs. The most effective protection of that right in such situations lies in the ability and determination of law-enforcement officers to save the accused from the mobs and thereby guarantee their right to fair trials by the courts. The rights of some African-Americans and Jews to live in the neighborhoods of their choice have been violated by "restrictive covenants," which are private agreements among property owners to sell only to white gentiles; and the right of minorities to decent housing can often be protected best by the passage and enforcement of open-occupancy laws prohibiting such agreements. The rights of members of any sexual, racial, or ethnic group to equal opportunities for job training, jobs, and promotions according to ability and achievement have often been abridged by private employers' discriminatory practices; and such employment rights can sometimes be secured only by the enforcement of fair-employment-practices laws forbidding such discrimination (problems posed by affirmative action plans will be discussed in Chapter 16.) The rights of African-American children to attend unsegregated schools may be violated by white mobs trying to overturn school buses, and only the intervention of the police can secure the children's rights and perhaps even save their lives. In all those situations, government is far from being the enemy of human rights. It is, in fact, their chief defender.

GOVERNMENT VERSUS LIFE'S ADVERSITIES   In Chapter 4 we noted the nearly universal acceptance in modern nations of the ideal of the welfare state, founded on the conviction that all people have a right to at least the minimum conditions of a decent life for themselves and their families. The third kind of threat includes such adversities as unemployment, poverty, old age, illness, and, above all, ignorance. Here, too, most modern citizens look to government not as their enemy but as their main hope for overcoming those adversities.

Whether or not government's obligations to help people have been formally enshrined in their constitutions, all modern democracies have clearly accepted the principle and from time to time have brought new rights under government protection. Indeed, the principle of the welfare state and some of its guarantees, such as universal free public education and protection against starvation, are so firmly established in all industrialized modern nations that any effort to remove those guarantees would be considered as drastic an attack on human rights as a proposal to repeal the constitutional guarantees of freedom of speech and fair trial.

Similar developments have occurred in the first two categories as well. In the United States as early as 1866, for example, Congress enacted laws penalizing anyone who "willfully subjects any person to a deprivation of any rights or privileges secured by the Constitution or laws of the United States." For many years the enforcement of those laws was left in the hands of U.S. attorneys in various localities, and few people were prosecuted for violating them. In 1939, however, U.S. Attorney General Frank Murphy established the Civil Rights Section in the Criminal Division of the Department of Justice and charged the section with undertaking more vigorous enforcement of the 1866 and 1870 laws. Since then the national government has played a far more active part in protecting human rights. The greatest single advance came when Congress passed the Civil Rights Act of 1964, which commits the national government to positive action to secure for all citizens full equality in their rights to be served by private businesses offering public accommodations, to use public facilities, and to enjoy equal job opportunities.

We will examine the act and its impact further in Chapter 16, but it should be marked here as the greatest legislative triumph for modern-style liberalism in the United States since the ratification of the Thirteenth, Fourteenth, and Fifteenth Amendments to the Constitution.

Rights Formally Guaranteed by Constitutions

Every modern constitution contains at least some formal guarantees of human rights. Needless to say, not every formal guarantee in every nation's constitution represents a genuinely protected right of the people living in that nation. However, the presence of formally guaranteed rights in any nation's constitution means that the framers, for whatever reasons, deemed it desirable to pay at least lip service—and perhaps more—to the idea of human rights. Therefore the main guarantees found in modern constitutions are listed here.

LIMITATIONS ON GOVERNMENT

Rights followed by an asterisk are expressly protected by the U.S. Constitution.

Protections of Belief and Expression

Religious worship*
Speech*
Press*
Secrecy of correspondence
Preservation of distinct subnational languages and cultures

Protections of Action

Assembly*
Petition*
Suffrage*
Secrecy of votes
Prohibition of slavery*
Practice of chosen profession
Privacy of domicile*
Movement within and to and from the nation
Organization of labor unions and trade associations
Strikes
Collective bargaining

Protections for Persons Accused of Crime

Prohibition of bills of attainder*
Prohibition of ex post facto laws*
No guilt by association
Prohibition of unreasonable searches and seizures*
No trial without indictment*
No double jeopardy for the same offense*
No coerced confessions*
No excessive bail or fines*
No cruel and unusual punishments*
No extradition for political crimes
No capital punishment
No imprisonment for debt
Guarantee of the writ of habeas corpus*
General guarantee of due process of law*
Guarantee of a speedy and public trial*
Trial by an impartial jury*
Ability to confront hostile witnesses*
Subpoena power for the defendant*
Assistance of counsel*
Equality before the law or equal protection of the laws*

Protection of Property

Just compensation for private property taken for public use*
Patents and copyrights*
No impairment of the obligation of contracts*

OBLIGATIONS OF GOVERNMENT

To Provide Economic Assistance

Work
Equal pay for equal work regardless of sex, age, nationality, or caste
Minimum wages
Maximum hours
Unemployment assistance
Social security

To Provide Social Assistance

Education

Prohibition of child labor

Protection of families, children, and motherhood

Preservation of historical monuments

Recreation and culture

Choices in the Implementation of Human Rights

Each year for a number of years, Freedom House, an organization based in New York City, has surveyed the status of civil liberties around the world and has rated each nation according to three criteria: (1) the freedom of its press, radio, and television to criticize the government; (2) the freedom of its citizens to speak and write what they wish; and (3) the citizens' ability to sue the government and win in court. Their ratings for 1995 are shown in Table 15.1.

If the Freedom House ratings are even approximately correct, then the cause of human rights, like that of democracy, has made great gains in recent years, as shown in Table 15.2, which compares the Freedom House classification of nations in 1995 with those made in 1988 and 1991.

Table 15.2 shows that since 1984 there has been a steady increase in the proportion of nations Freedom House has rated Free and a decrease in the proportion rated Not Free. Of course, in each year's ratings some nations moved toward freedom and others moved away. For example, in the period 1988 to 1995, four nations (Antigua and Barbuda, Brazil, the Dominican Republic, and Honduras) moved from Free to Partly Free, six (Bahrein, Bhutan, Egypt, the Ivory Coast, Nigeria, and Swaziland) moved from Partly Free to Not Free. On the other hand, eleven nations moved from Not Free to Partly Free, and three (Benin, Cape Verde Islands, and Guyana) moved from Partly Free to Free.

What has happened to the nations that have overturned their communist authoritarian regimes since 1988? Of the five former Soviet satellite nations in Eastern Europe, two (Bulgaria and the Czech Republic)[1] have moved from Not Free to Free, two (Hungary and Poland) have moved from Partly Free to Free, and East Germany has been absorbed by the Federal Republic of Germany, which has always been on the Free list.

Of the fifteen constituent republics of the former Soviet Union, in 1995 three (Estonia, Latvia, and Lithuania) were rated Free; seven (Armenia, Belarus, Georgia, Kirghizia, Moldova, Russia, and Ukraine) were rated Partly Free; only five (Azerbaijan, Kazakhstan, Tadjhikistan, Turkmenistan, and Uzbekistan) were rated Not Free.

Fifty-four nations—including the People's Republic of China, Cuba, Iran, Iraq, Kenya, North Korea, Saudi Arabia, and Syria— are Not Free. Even so, the period

TABLE 15.1   Freedom in Modern Nations, 1995

FREE	PARTLY FREE	NOT FREE
Andorra	Albania	Afghanistan
Argentina	Antigua & Barbuda	Algeria
Australia	Armenia	Angola
Austria	Bangladesh	Azerbaijan
Bahamas	Belarus	Bahrein
Barbados	Brazil	Bhutan
Belgium	Burkina Faso	Bosnia-Herzegovina
Belize	Cambodia	Brunei
Benin	Central African Repub.	Burundi
Bolivia	China (Taiwan)	Cameroon
Botswana	Colombia	Chad
Bulgaria	Comoros	China (PRC)
Canada	Congo	Cuba
Cape Verde Islands	Croatia	Djibouti
Chile	Dominican Republic	Egypt
Costa Rica	El Salvador	Equatorial Guinea
Cyprus (G)	Fiji	Eritrea
Czech Republic	Gabon	Ethiopia
Denmark	Georgia	Gambia
Dominica	Ghana	Guinea
Ecuador	Guatemala	Indonesia
Estonia	Guinea-Bissau	Iran
Finland	Haiti	Iraq
France	Honduras	Ivory Coast
Germany	India	Kazakhstan
Greece	Jordan	Kenya
Grenada	Kirghizia	Korea, North
Guyana	Kuwait	Laos
Hungary	Lebanon	Liberia
Iceland	Lesotho	Libya
Ireland	Macedonia	Maldives
Israel	Madagascar	Mauritania
Italy	Malaysia	Myanmar (Burma)
Jamaica	Mali	Nigeria
Japan	Mexico	Oman
Kiribati	Moldova	Qatar
Korea, South	Morocco	Rwanda
Latvia	Mozambique	Saudi Arabia
Liechtenstein	Nepal	Sierra Leone
Lithuania	Nicaragua	Somalia
Luxembourg	Niger	Sudan
Malawi	Pakistan	Swaziland
Malta	Papua New Guinea	Syria
Marshall Islands	Paraguay	Tadzhikistan
Mauritius	Peru	Tanzania
Micronesia	Philippines	Togo
Monaco	Romania	Tunisia
Mongolia	Russia	Turkmenistan
Namibia	Senegal	United Arab Emirates
Nauru	Seychelles	Uzbekistan

TABLE 15.1   *(Continued)*

FREE	*PARTLY FREE*	*NOT FREE*
Netherlands	Singapore	Vietnam
New Zealand	Sri Lanka	Yemen
Norway	Suriname	Yugoslavia
Palau	Thailand	Zaire
Panama	Tonga	
Poland	Turkey	
Portugal	Uganda	
St. Kitts & St. Nevis	Ukraine	
St. Lucia	Venezuela	
St. Vincent	Zambia	
San Marino	Zimbabwe	
Sao Tome & Principe		
Slovakia		
Slovenia		
Solomon Islands		
South Africa		
Spain		
Sweden		
Switzerland		
Trinidad & Tobago		
Tuvalu		
United Kingdom		
United States		
Uruguay		
Vanuatu		
Western Samoa		

Source: *Freedom Review*, January–February 1995, p. 39. Copyright 1995 by Freedom House, Inc.

TABLE 15.2   Growth of Freedom, 1984–1995

	NATIONS CLASSIFIED AS					
	Free		Partly Free		Not Free	
YEAR	*Number*	*Percent*	*Number*	*Percent*	*Number*	*Percent*
1984	53	31.7	59	35.3	55	33.0
1988	58	34.7	59	35.3	50	30.0
1995	76	39.4	63	32.6	54	28.0

Sources: For 1984, *Freedom at Issue*, January–February 1985, p. 30; for 1988, *Freedom at Issue*, January–February 1991, p. 23; for 1995, *Freedom Review*, January–February, 1995, p. 39.

from 1984 to 1995 has seen one of the greatest advances for human rights in history. For the first time since Freedom House began its surveys, more people live in Free (19.9 percent of the world's population) and Partly Free (40 percent) regimes than in Not Free (40.1 percent) ones.

Threats from authoritarian ideas of the Left and Right are by no means the only problems faced by human rights today. Even if every fascist, communist, and fundamentalist Muslim were to become an avowed liberal, liberal regimes would still face enormously complex problems in preserving their peoples' rights. We cannot begin to understand these problems until we recognize that they all involve making painful choices among cherished—but competing—values.

The point may be clarified by considering the two main choices that any constitutional government must make when dealing with human rights.

FREEDOM VERSUS SECURITY

Problem

One dilemma government faces in a free society arises from two facts: First, most citizens value *both* freedom and security. They value freedom for the reasons outlined earlier in this chapter; and they value security—government preservation of law and order—for the reasons outlined in Chapter 1. Second, freedom and security are always in conflict, and whatever government does to advance one may well injure the other.

To illustrate, consider the conflicting claims of freedom and security in a hypothetical example. A child is kidnapped and later found brutally tortured and murdered. The outraged townspeople demand that the murderer be arrested and punished immediately. The police turn up enough evidence to convince them that a drifter named John Doe is the murderer—but they cannot gather enough evidence to guarantee his conviction under the stringent rules used in U.S. courts. So they arrest Doe "on suspicion" and grill him in an effort to make him confess, knowing that a confession added to the evidence they already have will be sufficient to convict him. But Doe refuses to confess and repeatedly claims that he is innocent. The police are convinced that he is lying, and so they give him the "third degree," beating him with a rubber truncheon, keeping him without sleep for days, and shining bright lights in his eyes while questioning him. Finally the pressure is too much, and Doe breaks down and confesses. The townspeople, meanwhile, are angry about the delay, and they fear that Doe will go free on some legal technicality and the hideous crime will go unpunished. Someone suggests dragging Doe out of jail and hanging him from the nearest lamppost.

Consider what is involved. If security—which means punishing the guilty and deterring potential criminals—were the *only* value held by the townspeople and the police, then the question of what to do would be easily answered. They should beat a confession out of Doe or just string him up without a trial.

This course of action is, sad to say, no mere theoretical extreme dreamed up to make a point. In Brazil and Argentina, for example, capital punishment was not legal until recently, and no convicted criminal ever served more than 30 years in jail. Some police in both countries felt that this practice amounted to unendurable coddling of the guilty, so they formed small secret "death squads" that tracked down, tortured, and executed criminals who they thought had cheated the law. In parts of the southern United States not long ago lynching was the accepted form of instant trial and punishment for African-Americans accused of major crimes against whites. In the North there have been all too many cases in which prosecutors—despite their sworn duty to protect the innocent as well as to prosecute the accused—have concealed and distorted evidence to build up their conviction scores.

In a nation with liberal traditions and values, however, punishing the guilty is only one of the values that people hold. Most Americans, for instance, also believe that no innocent person should be jailed or executed. The townspeople and police in our example have no wish to hang Doe if he is innocent. They must therefore choose which they value more: punishing the guilty or protecting the innocent. If they choose the former and torture or lynch Doe, then they run the risk of punishing an innocent man; and if they choose the latter and give Doe all his constitutional rights to a fair trial, then they run the risk of letting a murderer go unpunished. They cannot have it both ways. They have to take one risk or the other.

Most citizens of liberal nations, then, are not willing to sacrifice all security for absolute freedom or to abandon all freedom for absolute security. In such nations, accordingly, there is always the problem of determining in each situation just where the line should be drawn between the conflicting claims of freedom and security—for conflicting they will always be.

Some U.S. Standards for Drawing the Line

If we recognize that this kind of decision must be made in every case in which government restraint of human activity is involved, then most of us would agree that it should be made according to the most just and sensible general standards we can devise. We certainly do not want to leave it entirely to the whims of whatever law-enforcement officer happens to be around or whatever judge happens to be assigned to the case.

Yet we should recognize that such decisions are not and cannot be made in social vacuums in which the decision makers operate entirely free from all political and psychological pressures for particular decisions. They are made by fallible human beings, often operating under strong cross-pressures. That being the case, we can learn a good deal about how civil liberties decisions are made—and with what consequences—by focusing on some of the leading decisions made and issues pending in the United States in recent years.

We may begin by noting that the U.S. Supreme Court has developed several general standards for drawing the line between freedom and security. The best known have been developed in cases involving the question of when, if ever, speech and writing may be suppressed without violating the First Amendment's command that "Congress shall make no law . . . abridging the freedom of speech or of the press." Three leading standards may be briefly summarized as follows.

CLEAR AND PRESENT DANGER   The decision in *Schenck* v. *United States* (1919) first ruled that speech and writing can be constitutionally suppressed, but only when "the words are used in circumstances and are of such a nature as to create a clear and present danger that they will bring about the substantive evils that Congress has a right to prevent."[2] This **clear-and-present-danger test** holds that *speech can be constitutionally suppressed only when the words said and the circumstances in which they are said are such that the words create an unmistakable and imminent danger for the com-*

munity's safety. The presumption is clearly against suppressing speech, and the burden of proof rests on those who would suppress it. This test, with occasional departures, has been generally followed by the Court in free-speech and free-press cases since 1919.

GRAVITY OF EVIL   In its opinion in *Dennis* v. *U.S.* (1951) upholding the conviction of eleven Communist party leaders for conspiring to advocate violent overthrow of the government, the Court took a somewhat different tack. It held that freedom of speech can be restricted whenever "the gravity of evil, discounted by its improbability, justifies such invasion . . . as is necessary to avoid the danger."[3] Under this "gravity-of-evil" test, the presumption is substantially more in favor of suppressing speech than it is under the clear-and-present-danger test. The Dennis standard has been used by the courts in some post–World War II cases involving the advocacy of communist doctrines. In cases involving speech by those people other than Communist party members, the Court has sometimes followed one standard and sometimes another.

FIGHTING WORDS   In 1942 the Supreme Court added an additional standard for laws limiting free speech:

> There are certain well-defined and narrowly limited classes of speech, the prevention and punishment of which has never been thought to raise any Constitutional problem. These include the lewd and obscene, the profane, the libelous, and the insulting or "fighting" words—those which by their very utterance inflict injury or tend to incite an immediate breach of the peace.[4]

This became known as the "fighting words" standard, and in subsequent cases the Court narrowed the definition so as to include only words that "have a direct tendency to cause acts of violence by the person to whom, individually, the remarks are addressed." The mere fact that words are abusive, harsh, or insulting is not enough.[5] For example, if a city government refuses to issue a permit to the Ku Klux Klan to march through an African-American section of town with banners displaying racial epithets and slurs, the city must prove, on the basis of similar episodes in the past, that the march is likely to provoke a violent reaction from the African-American residents and thus trigger a riot in which people could be injured. If the city does not or cannot offer convincing proof of such a likelihood, then the refusal to permit the march will be overruled as an unconstitutional violation of the Klan members' freedom of speech. This standard has recently become important in determining the constitutionality of universities' rules against students making sexist, racist, and homophobic expressions about women and minorities.

RIGHTS OF SOME VERSUS RIGHTS OF OTHERS

Some people try to escape the hard choices demanded by the conflict between liberty and security by declaring that "We should all be free to exercise our rights so long as we do not interfere with the rights of others." This platitude has a comfortingly plausible air of sweet reasonableness about it, and its popularity is not sur-

FREE SPEECH OR FIGHTING WORDS?

In recent years a number of universities have sought to fight sexism, racism, and other forms of discrimination against women and minorities on their campuses by adopting rules prohibiting students from expressing views demeaning to women or minority groups. One of the most prominent of those rules was adopted by the University of Wisconsin (UW) in 1989. The rule provided that a student could be disciplined "for racist or discriminatory comments, epithets or other expressive behavior" directed at other individuals that "demean the race, sex, religion, color, creed, disability, sexual orientation, national origin, ancestry or age of the . . . individuals; and create an intimidating, hostile or demeaning environment for education . . . or other university-authorized activity."

Several students were disciplined for violating the rule. One was disciplined for calling a residence hall staff member "a piece of shit nigger." Another was disciplined for putting on the university computer system the message, "Death to all Arabs! Die Islamic scumbags!" Yet another was disciplined for yelling at a female student in public, "You've got nice tits."

In 1991 a student newspaper and ten UW students brought a suit in a federal district court charging that the university's rule was a violation of UW students' constitutional right to free speech. Judge Robert W. Warren agreed and enjoined the university from enforcing the rule. He declared that such a rule would be constitutionally permissible only if it satisfied the fighting words standard, and so the university had an obligation to prove that the prohibited expressions would probably lead to violent reactions by the persons demeaned. The university, he said, had offered no such proof but had merely declared that the prohibited words were offensive and created a hostile environment for the persons demeaned. Accordingly, he concluded, the rule did not satisfy the stringent requirements of the Supreme Court for permitting people to be punished for the content of their speech and writing.

In response to this decision, some universities rewrote their rules to discipline students for making racist and sexist expressions when such expressions created a clear and present danger of violent reactions. At the present writing (1995) it is not clear whether the rewritten rules will be upheld by the courts.

---

prising. The only thing wrong with it is that it seldom works, because, in most real-life situations, protecting the rights of some citizens inevitably abridges the rights of others.

Consider, for example, one of the most difficult and bitterly disputed civil liberties issues of the 1980s and 1990s, discussed in Chapter 2: the clash between the right of a woman to choose whether to have an abortion and the right to life of the fetus. Until the early 1970s most states had laws prohibiting abortions except when deemed necessary by physicians to save mothers' lives. In the 1960s and 1970s, however, one wing of the women's rights movement (see Chapter 16) challenged the constitutionality of those laws with increasing vigor. They argued that every woman has a fundamental right to the control of what affects her own body, and that right entitles her to terminate an unwanted pregnancy just as much as it entitles her to refuse unwanted sexual intercourse. Their opponents argued, with equal moral fervor, that every human being has just as much right to life between conception and birth as after birth, and that legalized abortion therefore amounts to legalized murder.

As we saw in Chapter 2, it is a tough and painful issue, but one aspect of it, at least, is quite clear: It cannot be resolved by any pat formula that a pregnant woman's rights leave off where her fetus's begin, or vice versa. If we protect the fetus's right to birth, then we cannot avoid abridging the woman's right to control what affects her own body; and if we protect the woman's right, then we cannot avoid abridging the fetus's right to live. We cannot, sad to say, have it both ways.

Whatever may be the merits of the issue, the Supreme Court ruled in *Roe* v. *Wade* (1973) that the decision to have an abortion in the first three months of pregnancy is strictly up to the woman and her physician, and their freedom to make that decision may not be restricted by any state or national law. The Court added that governments may exercise some limited control over abortions in the second three months of pregnancy, and they may constitutionally prohibit abortions altogether only in the final three months. And, as we noted in Chapter 2, in 1992 the Court reaffirmed the *Roe* decision.

Some Americans hailed the Court's decisions as great victories for women's rights, and others denounced them as grievous blows to unborn babies' right to life. The issue is still far from settled, however. The pro-life forces have pressed hard for the Court to reverse the *Roe* decision or for a constitutional amendment to override

COURT DECISIONS HAVE POLITICAL CONSEQUENCES. Pro-life activists protesting the Supreme Court's decision in Roe *versus* Wade *(1973).*

it so as to allow states to outlaw abortions, and some of the more zealous members of the movement have even set fire to legal abortion clinics. The pro-choice forces have battled hard to preserve the decisions and block the proposed amendment, and the bitterness on both sides has escalated alarmingly.

It is no business of a book like this to say who is right on the issue. But it is necessary to point out that there is no way that *either* right can be fully protected and freely exercised without to some extent abridging the other. The Supreme Court—like the state legislatures whose laws it overrode—had to choose in 1973 and 1992, and choose it did. We may agree or disagree with their choices, we may believe that its reasoning was sound or muddled, we may even question the Court's power to have the final word, but we cannot escape the fact that a choice has to be made. And so it is with all questions of human rights.

Human Rights in the Political Process

HUMAN RIGHTS CONFLICTS AS POLITICAL CONFLICTS

We are likely to understand better what is involved in conflicts over human rights if we remember that those conflicts are fundamentally political in nature. To be sure, disputes over human rights are often fought out largely (though never entirely) in courts of law, and some people mistakenly regard the judicial process as somehow not political in the same sense that legislative and executive processes are political. This may obscure the political nature of litigation over human rights issues. Yet, according to the analytical framework used in this book, such litigation cannot be other than political. Disputes over human rights issues in the courts, just as those in legislatures and executives, involve questions of government policy. The immediate question in all such disputes is: Should government restrict this person's or that group's freedom of action? As we saw in Chapters 1 and 2, every government action promotes some people's interests and damages the interests of others.

This is equally true of government actions on human rights. If, for example, government promotes affirmative action programs for allocating places in medical schools, it improves the chances of African-Americans and other minorities to become doctors, but it also means that some whites with higher grades and test scores will be rejected in favor of some African-Americans with lower grades and test scores. When government prohibits the police from tapping the telephones of suspected criminals without prior authorization by a court, it makes it harder to catch and punish criminals, but it also makes it less likely that innocent persons will be wrongly convicted.

Government decisions on what to do in those and similar situations are thus, in our sense of the term, *political*. We should therefore expect that they will be made as all other political decisions are made: as the result of conflict among competing political actors. Most of those actors will, of course, publicly defend their positions in terms of constitutional rights rather than self-interest; and most will sincerely believe that freedom of speech, due process of law, racial justice, and other lofty ideals demand decisions favorable to their positions. This rhetoric should not, however, obscure the fact that in matters of human rights, as in all other matters of government policy, some people stand to gain and others stand to lose. Students of politics and government will better understand the conflicts over human rights if they explore, in addition to the ideological and legal aspects of the conflict, the question of who stands to win what and who stands to lose what.

SOME CONSEQUENCES

Viewing human rights conflicts as political conflicts may suggest that the processes by which those conflicts are conducted and the government decisions affecting human rights are essentially the same as the processes by which all other political conflicts are conducted and all other government decisions are made. This approach to human rights conflicts may well provide an understanding otherwise absent. Some people, for example, think that government policies (including court decisions) on questions of human rights should always be made in conformity with a set of clear and mutually consistent logical principles, and they are disturbed that such decisions often seem to shift logical grounds according to time and circumstances. Perhaps they would be less disturbed if they recognized the political nature of human rights conflicts, for then they would start with the assumption that particular decisions are the products, not of ill will or temporary aberrations from sanity by judges and legislators but rather of the decision makers' estimates of the variations in the nature and fluctuations in the strength of the competing interests involved.

Another consequence of this view is awareness that in any political system the process by which conflicts are conducted and by which the rights of individuals are determined are shaped by the same forces that shape the system's other political conflicts and decisions. The condition of human rights in a particular system depends largely on such matters as the number and variety of its competing interests, the issues that separate those interests and bring them into conflict, the degree of overlapping membership among competing forces, the degree to which the competing groups are mobilized, the number and strength of common interests and other unifying forces, the general level of material well-being and its distribution, the degree of security from foreign attack, and all those other factors affecting politics and government that we have previously examined.

Like everything else in politics (and human life), then, human rights have considerable costs as well as great benefits. What costs are the free nations and their competing groups willing to bear? We will find some of the answers in the next chapter, in which we consider some of the principal challenges to human rights in modern times and some of the ways in which democratic nations have responded to those challenges.

For Further Reading

*BRIGHAM, JOHN. *Civil Liberties and American Democracy.* Washington, DC: Congressional Quarterly Press, 1984. Description of current conflicts in civil liberties.

DONNELLY, JACK. *Universal Human Rights in Theory and Practice.* Ithaca, NY: Cornell University Press, 1989. Study of international efforts to establish basic human rights for all nations, with special attention to the Universal Declaration of Human Rights and the Helsinki accords.

*DWORKIN, RONALD. *Taking Rights Seriously.* Cambridge, MA: Harvard University Press, 1977. Strong civil-libertarian view of present controversies over rights.

ETZIONI, AMITAI. *Rights and the Common Good.* New York: St. Martin's Press, 1994. Argument that excessive emphasis on individual and group rights has harmed democracy in the United States, and proposal of a new "communitarian" emphasis on the common good.

*KRAMER, DANIEL D. *Comparative Civil Rights and Liberties.* Washington, DC: University Press of America, 1982. Study of status of human rights in various parts of the world, especially the United States, the Soviet Union, and France.

MCCLOSKY, HERBERT, and ALIDA BRILL. *Dimensions of Tolerance: What Americans Believe about Civil Liberties.* New York: Basic Books, 1984. Magisterial study of popular attitudes toward civil liberties, based on massive survey studies.

*MILL, JOHN STUART. *On Liberty* (1859). Many editions have been published of this classic defense of free speech and press.

MILTON, JOHN. *Areopagitica* (1644). Many editions have been published of this early and still influential argument for free speech and free press.

*SCHAUER, FREDERICK. *Free Speech: A Philosophical Inquiry.* New York: Cambridge University Press, 1982. In-depth analysis of the philosophical pros, cons, and limits of free speech.

*SHAPIRO, IAN. *The Evolution of Rights in Liberal Theory.* New York: Cambridge University Press, 1985. Account of the development of theories of individuals' rights from the seventeenth century to the present.

*WOLFF, ROBERT PAUL, BARRINGTON MOORE, JR., and HERBERT MARCUSE, eds. *A Critique of Pure Tolerance.* Boston, MA: Beacon Press, 1969. New Left attack on liberal ideas of free speech, especially interesting for Marcuse's ideas on "repressive tolerance."

Notes

1. In 1992 Czechoslovakia was divided into two nations: the Czech Republic (rated "Free" by Freedom House), and Slovakia (rated Partly Free).
2. *Schenck* v. *United States*, 249 U.S. 47 (1919).
3. *Dennis* v. *United States*, 341 U.S. 494 (1961).
4. *Chaplinsky* v. *New Hampshire*, 315 U.S. 568 (1942).
5. *Cohen* v. *California*, 403 U.S. 15 (1971).

16

In all criminal prosecutions, the accused shall enjoy the right to a speedy and public trial, by an impartial jury of the State and district wherein the crime shall have been committed . . . and to be informed of the nature and cause of the accusation, to be confronted with the witnesses against him; to have compulsory process for obtaining witnesses in his favor, and to have the Assistance of Counsel for his defense.
Sixth Amendment to the U.S. Constitution

No State shall make or enforce any law which shall abridge the privileges or immunities of citizens of the United States; nor shall any State deprive any person of life, liberty, or property without due process of law; nor deny to any person within its jurisdiction the equal protection of the laws.
Fourteenth Amendment to the U.S. Constitution

The history of liberty has largely been the history of the observance of procedural safeguards.
Felix Frankfurter, *McNabb* v. *U.S.* (1943)

Marriage, to women as to men, must be a luxury, not a necessity; an incident of life, not all of it. And the only possible way to accomplish this great change is to accord to women equal power in the making, shaping and controlling of the circumstances of life.
Susan B. Anthony

I have a dream that my four little children will one day live in a nation where they will be not be judged by the color of their skin, but by the content of their character.
Martin Luther King, Jr.

Human Rights: Challenges and Responses

In every nation that values liberty the problem of preserving human rights in a society racked with clashes among groups and interests is both persistent and enormously difficult. In the United States and most other such nations, the problem has, in recent years, broken out of the quiet of the scholar's study and the judge's chambers into the forefront of political struggle.

"Moral Majority Denounces Supreme Court's Ban on School Prayer." "Police Claim They Are Handcuffed in Arresting Criminals." "School Bus Wrecked in Protest over School Race Balancing." "Abortion Clinic Bombed by Right-to-Lifers." "Affirmative Action Plan Clashes with Union Seniority Rule." Such headlines have been prominent in U.S. newspapers since the end of World War II, and current disputes over civil rights are among the most hotly disputed in U.S. politics.

The dilemma confronted by free nations in preserving human rights, as we saw in Chapter 15, cannot be solved by the simplistic formula that we should all be free to do what we wish so long as we do not interfere with the rights of others. Every government action makes some people do something or prevents some people from doing something. Unavoidably, every such action restricts *someone's* freedom to some extent. Guaranteeing a pregnant woman's right to an abortion abridges her fetus's right to life. Protecting Jehovah's Witnesses' right to seek converts by door-to-door canvassing abridges the residents' right to privacy. Protecting a suspected criminal's privacy by prohibiting the tapping of his or her telephone handicaps police efforts to protect other people's rights to security of life and property. Affirmative action plans to increase the hiring of African-Americans and women makes it harder for whites and men to get jobs. Preserving human rights forces all free nations to make choices, often hard choices, always *political* choices.

Accordingly, this chapter details some of the situations that pose in their most acute form the great problems—and possibilities—of governing in the last quarter of the twentieth century. It is, of course, impossible in the space of one chapter to describe all the challenges to human rights and all the government responses to those challenges in all modern free nations. So our discussion will be limited to a survey of three areas of political conflict over civil rights that, especially in the United States, get the most attention today: police powers and defendants' rights, the status of women, and the status of African-Americans.

Conflict over Police Powers and Defendants' Rights

CRIME AND THE POLICE

In the United States as in all constitutional democracies, the critical problems in criminal justice arise from the inescapable conflict between the need to catch, convict, and punish criminals and the need to protect the rights of persons accused of crime. We begin by sketching the extent of crime and the tasks and problems of the police.

Crime: Organized and Unorganized

We noted in Chapter 2 that government differs from all other human organizations mainly in that it makes authoritative rules that bind all people living in the society and that take precedence over the rules of all other organizations. Because people are people and not angels, no government's rules are obeyed by all of the people all of the time. The most serious kind of violation is called a crime—that is, "any act done in violation of those duties which an individual owes to the community, and for the breach of which the law has provided that the offender shall make satisfaction to the public."[1] Crimes are usually subdivided into felonies (the more serious) and misdemeanors (the less serious) and are punishable by fines, imprisonment, or death.

Crimes are different from *torts*, which are offenses committed against private individuals but not considered damaging to the whole community. For example, if A spreads malicious stories intended to ruin B's reputation, A is considered to have slandered B but not to have injured the whole community. Hence B's remedy is to sue A for damages, and the community's interest lies solely in ensuring that the dispute is conducted fairly and settled equitably. But if A shoots and kills B, then A is considered to have damaged not only B but also the basic security of the whole community. Therefore, the government will prosecute A for the crime of murder, not the tort of slander, and if A is found guilty A will be imprisoned or executed.

No one knows precisely how many crimes are committed in each year in any modern nation, for some are always undetected and others are unreported. However, reasonable estimates suggest that crime rates have fluctuated in many Western democracies in recent years. The most authoritative annual estimates of U.S. crime rates are made by the Federal Bureau of Investigation (FBI), and its figures are summarized in Table 16.1.

A majority of the crimes reported in Table 16.1 were "unorganized"; that is, they were committed by individuals acting alone or in small groups, as in the muggings that have made the streets and parks of so many U.S. cities unsafe. However, a good many offenses were committed by "organized crime," including large and well-organized criminal "corporations" like the Mafia "families" that operate for profit both illegal enterprises (narcotics, loan sharking, extortion, "protection," and so on) and legal businesses (gambling casinos, real estate, restaurants, bars and taverns, vending machines, and the like).

Crime ranges from crimes of passion in families to adolescent joy riding in stolen automobiles to such highly organized and profitable businesses as selling narcotics and running the numbers game. Organized or unorganized, crime continues to present a serious threat to everyone living in the United States as well as a massive challenge to the police forces, which bear the main government responsibility for preventing crime and capturing criminals.

TABLE 16.1   Crime Rates in the United States, 1982–1991 (number per 100,000 population)

YEAR	VIOLENT CRIME*	PROPERTY CRIME†	TOTAL CRIME
1982	571	5,033	5,604
1984	539	4,492	5,031
1986	617	4,863	5,480
1989	663	5,078	5,741
1991	758	5,140	5,898

Source: The American Almanac, 1993–1994 (Washington, DC: Bureau of the Census, 1994), Table 300, p. 192.

*Includes murder, forcible rape, robbery, aggravated assault.
†Includes burglary, larceny-theft, motor vehicle theft.

Job of the Police

To ensure that its laws are obeyed, every political system must rely mainly on the willingness of its citizens to obey the law voluntarily, even when some citizens do not believe that a particular law is just. After all, it is simply not possible to put half or three quarters of the population in jail or to shoot them or to exile them. Consequently, as we noted in Chapter 2, any political community in which a substantial part of the people rejects the legitimacy of the government's powers and refuses to obey its laws is no longer a community but a battlefield for civil war.

Yet no political system depends *entirely* upon voluntary obedience to the law by all its citizens. Every system has some kind of organized police to deal with lawbreakers. There is wide variation among (and within) modern nations in the organization, specialization, training, methods, and effectiveness of police, but in all nations police are charged with detecting and arresting lawbreakers and delivering those suspects to the executive and judicial agencies for determination of their guilt or innocence. Many authoritarian systems have also relied heavily upon special secret police concerned with such "crimes against the state" as speaking and working against the regime. The best-known examples in recent years have been the Nazi Gestapo, the Savak of the former Shah of Iran, and the former Soviet agency known successively as the Cheka, GPU, NKVD, MGB, MVD, and KGB.

We are concerned here only with tasks generally assigned to nonsecret "regular" police. Those tasks include preventing violations of law from taking place (patroling streets and checking stores to discourage muggers and burglars), stopping law violations that do take place (removing political protesters who are blocking public highways), determining who has committed crimes, arresting suspects and delivering them to the prosecuting authorities, and providing evidence at the suspects' trials. In a free nation the police have at least one additional major duty: to protect the legal and constitutional rights of all persons, whether those persons are lawbreakers or innocent bystanders.

Lot of the Police

The police officer's job, then, is to enforce the law, but only by the means and within the limits allowed by the law. A character in a Gilbert and Sullivan operetta sings that "The policeman's lot is not a happy one," and it seems that in many modern nations, including the United States, that is indeed the case. The duties of the police are always demanding, and police officers often risk physical injury and even death. All too often police are underpaid, undereducated, and overworked. Furthermore, they frequently must work among people who distrust and hate them, particularly in urban slum and ghetto areas, where crime rates are high. The most common epithets applied to the police—"pig," "flatfoot," "cossack," "the fuzz"—do not encourage them to feel that they serve in a proud profession respected by all. Even the occasional "Support Your Local Police" bumper sticker or a sympathetic television program like *Law and Order* does not help their morale very much.

At bottom, however, the lot of the police is unhappy because, more than most public officials, they operate on the front lines of the conflict between society's widely held but conflicting values of security and freedom. We can sit in our classrooms and righteously endorse *both* law and order and civil liberties without having to adjust one to the other more than verbally. However, the police are charged with fighting crime *and* with protecting the rights of everyone, including lawbreakers. Depending upon the kind of trouble the police may have in resolving this conflict, they may be charged with brutality, incompetence, laxity, or corruption.

To understand the police's dilemma better, let us briefly survey some of the rights police officers are charged with protecting while fighting crime.

RIGHTS OF DEFENDANTS

Law

Although there are many variations in detail from one nation to another, the main rights of defendants most commonly guaranteed by law in the Western democratic systems include the following.

PRETRIAL RIGHTS   The law guarantees every person *immunity from arbitrary arrest*: A suspect may be arrested only in pursuance of a warrant issued by a judge or upon a police officer's belief, supported by some valid evidence, that the suspect may have committed a crime. If the suspect's arrest satisfies neither requirement, he or she can collect damages by suing the arresting officer for false arrest. Shortly after detention, the suspect has the right to the *assistance of counsel*, and if he or she cannot afford a lawyer, then the government is obligated to provide one. During interrogation by the police, the suspect has the *right to remain silent* and that silence cannot be used as evidence against the suspect. The *prohibition of coerced confessions* means that the suspect cannot in any way be forced to give testimony that might help to convict him or her. Perhaps most important of all, the suspect has the right to a *writ of habeas corpus*. If the police arrest and jail the suspect but refuse to formally charge him or her before a court, the suspect or the suspect's lawyer can petition a judge for a court order commanding the jailer to produce the prisoner and show cause for the detention. If the judge decides that the detention is unlawful—that the charges are too vague or the evidence is insufficient—then the judge orders the prisoner's immediate release. More than any other legal device, the writ of habeas corpus is a safeguard against "preventive detention" and imprisonment without trial, devices that are commonplace in authoritarian methods of law enforcement.

RIGHTS DURING TRIAL   The law guarantees a fair trial to every person accused of crime and requires that *advance knowledge of the specific charges* be given to the accused so that the accused may prepare his or her best defense. The accused's right to the *assistance of counsel* means that if the accused cannot afford a lawyer to conduct his or her defense, the court must appoint and pay for a defense lawyer. There must be an *impartial judge*, an *impartial jury*, or both to decide the case on the basis of law and evidence and without prejudice against the defendant.

The accused, who now becomes the defendant, can obtain a *change of venue* if the judge can be convinced that the climate of opinion at the trial site is prejudicial to the accused's defense. The defense has the same power as the prosecution to *subpoena witnesses*. The defendant (or the defense lawyer) has the right to *confront and cross-examine hostile witnesses*. The defendant's *immunity from double jeopardy* means that if in a valid trial he or she is found innocent of a particular crime, then the defendant can never again be tried on that same charge in the same jurisdiction. *No ex post facto law* can be applied to the defendant; that is, the defendant cannot be convicted of a crime that was not a crime when the events in question occurred. If convicted, the defendant has the *right of appeal* to a higher court, and if the defense can convince the appellate court that the defendant has not been allowed full exercise of his or her rights, the conviction will be set aside. (Note that the prosecution cannot appeal a verdict of not guilty.) If the conviction stands, *no cruel and unusual punishment* can be inflicted on the convicted person.

In sum, the law in most constitutional systems presumes the defendant's innocence and places the burden of proof on the prosecution. Insufficient or inconclusive evidence and reasonable doubt are supposed to be resolved in the defendant's favor. This legal premise reflects the conviction that it is important to make sure that no innocent person is punished even if the price is that some guilty persons escape punishment.

Issues in the Conflict

Each of the defendant's rights just listed makes it harder for police to detect and arrest suspected criminals and harder for prosecutors to convict persons accused of crimes. In every democratic system, accordingly, there is always some pressure to attack crime more effectively by giving police and prosecutors more freedom of action. There is also countervailing pressure to make defendants' rights more secure by tightening the restraints on law-enforcement officers. In the United States this perennial conflict between the claims of law and order and the claims of civil liberties has grown more intense in recent years. It has involved mainly the following issues.

ELECTRONIC SURVEILLANCE   Modern electronics has developed a wide variety of easily hidden "bugging" devices capable of eavesdropping on private telephone conversations and even on unwired conversations in offices and homes. Police find those devices very useful in gathering information about the activities, associations, and plans of suspected criminals, and the width of police electronic nets was dramatized by the revelation in the 1973 Watergate hearings that the private telephones of many high officials in the Department of State had been tapped on the orders of President Nixon. Many citizens strongly object to the use of those devices, arguing that bugging allows government to invade every area of private life, just as totalitarian governments do. Many law-enforcement officials argue with equal vehemence that depriving the police of this tool would make it much harder for investigating officers to detect, catch, and convict criminals.

The legal phase of the conflict centers upon the Fourth Amendment's prohibition of "unreasonable searches and seizures" and the amendment's requirement that investigating officers obtain in advance search warrants "particularly describing the place to be searched, and the persons or things to be seized."

A generation ago, the Supreme Court ruled that wiretapping in itself does not violate those rules. However, several recent Court decisions have greatly restricted the circumstances in which police may constitutionally use electronic surveillance devices, mainly by requiring that in most circumstances investigators must first get a warrant from a judge, thus satisfying the requirement that the places to be searched and the things to be seized must be specified in advance.

After intense pressure to sidestep—and counterpressure to support—the Court's restrictions, Congress included in the Omnibus Crime Control and Safe Streets Act of 1968 an authorization of police wiretapping and bugging in investigations of a wide variety of specified crimes. In most instances the police are required to obtain warrants first, but in investigations of organized crime or national-security cases if police find that an emergency exists, then police officers can intercept private communications for forty-eight hours without a warrant.

This law was a major victory for the police-powers side, but it did not end the fight. Most observers believe that many more rounds will be fought in the courts.

VOLUNTARY CONFESSIONS   A defendant's confession, unsupported or contradicted by other evidence, is not sufficient to convict him or her. On the other hand, if the prosecution has some evidence pointing to the suspect's guilt but not enough to convince the judge or jury beyond a reasonable doubt, the suspect's confession usually provides the clincher. It is therefore not surprising that police and prosecutors try hard to make defendants confess and that defendants, both guilty and innocent, resist.

As in most constitutional democracies, courts in the United States will admit confessions as evidence only if confessions are voluntarily given, for, in the well-known phrase of the Fifth Amendment, "no person . . . shall be compelled in any criminal case to be a witness against himself." "Taking the Fifth" refers to a defendant's exercise of the constitutional right to refuse to answer any question put to a defendant by public authorities if he or she can convince a court that the answers "may tend to incriminate"; that is, be used to convict the defendant in the present or some future criminal trial. The defendant has a right to remain silent, and the courts have ruled that silence may not be used by the prosecution as an indication that the defendant is hiding something. However, there is no way of keeping a jury from drawing its own conclusions, and if the defendant voluntarily takes the witness stand, then there is no immunity from cross-examination by the prosecution.

In other controversial opinions in the 1960s the Supreme Court went far to ensure that confessions used as evidence in criminal cases are truly voluntary. The culmination was the decision in *Miranda* v. *Arizona* (1966), which stipulated that any evidence, including material obtained by the police in pretrial "custodial interrogation," will be admissible as evidence only if the police have told the defendant that he or she has the right to remain silent; that anything the accused says can be used against him or her, that the accused has a right to have an attorney present during the questioning; that if the accused cannot afford an attorney one will be provided; and that the accused has the right to terminate the police interrogation at any time.

The Miranda decision evoked a storm of protest from many law-enforcement officials, who stated that about 90 percent of all criminal convictions result from guilty pleas, which, they argued, means that pretrial interrogation and investigation are critical stages in law enforcement. The Court's restrictions, they said, would make convicting criminals much more difficult and thus seriously cripple the police in their war against crime. The 1968 Crime Control Act authorized the trial judge to investigate the circumstances in which a confession is made, determine whether or not it is voluntary, and instruct the jury to decide what weight should be given to it. In making this determination, the judge need not be bound by any single factor of those stipulated in the Miranda decision but can take the whole situation into account.

This law was also a major victory for the police-powers side, but in the United States, as in other constitutional democracies, the courts, and especially the Supreme Court, have the last word about whether any particular defendant has been coerced into confessing and unjustly convicted as a result.

Sometimes investigators and prosecutors determine that they would rather have a witness reveal his knowledge about a large body of crimes than convict him or her for relatively minor criminal acts, a strategy that received much publicity in 1987 when the congressional committees investigating the "Irangate" scandals agreed to give Oliver North and John Poindexter immunity from having anything they said in their testimony to the committees used against them in any future criminal prosecutions. After immunity has been granted, the witness has no further constitutional right to refuse to testify.

EXCLUSIONARY RULE   As we have seen, the courts have specified a considerable number of actions that the police may not take in the course of arresting, questioning, and gathering evidence on crime suspects. For example, police may not tap a suspect's telephone without a warrant, torture the suspect to force a confession, question the suspect without an attorney present if one is requested, or fail to inform the suspect of the right to remain silent. But what if the police cut some corners on those restrictions and, as a result, get evidence that proves the suspect's guilt and use it in court to convict? Or, to put it another way, what can the courts do to ensure that the police obey constitutional rules in gathering evidence for prosecutors?

The answer is that in trying cases against persons accused of crime the courts use the **exclusionary rule** first laid down in *Mapp* v. *Ohio* (1961). This rule stipulates that *evidence obtained in violation of a defendant's constitutional rights must be excluded from the trial*. Under this rule the appellate courts will overturn any conviction resulting from a trial in which illegally obtained evidence has been used. The defendant may be tried again and be convicted in a trial in which such evidence is not used, but the defendant can never be convicted in any trial in which it is used.

Some critics say that it makes no sense to let criminals go free because the police misbehave. Why not let a court examine all the evidence, including the misbehavior of the police, and make a decision after weighing all the relevant facts? For that matter, why not punish the police—not the general public—if the police misbehave?

In recent decisions the Supreme Court has relaxed the exclusionary rule to some degree. Some people have urged that when the police believe "in objective good faith" that they have obtained evidence in a constitutional manner, the evidence should be admitted even if the police have slipped up on a point or two. The Court has not yet gone quite that far; but in two 1984 cases the Court ruled that where a police officer has obtained a search warrant from a magistrate, the evidence obtained thereby is admissible even if the magistrate lacked probable cause to issue the warrant (*U.S.* v. *Leon*) or the warrant was technically defective (*Massachusetts* v. *Sheppard*). Even so, the Court has yet to hold that evidence gained entirely without a search warrant can be used if the police were acting "in objective good faith." Until the Court so holds, the exclusionary rule—which clearly tips the scales in favor of defendants' rights over the suppression of crime—remains a prime guiding principle in U.S. criminal justice.

Conflict over the Status of Women

SEXISM: MEANING AND MANIFESTATIONS

With the dubious exception of the legendary Amazons, in almost all societies in almost all periods of history, women have been treated in many ways as men's inferiors. Historically, women have been barred from owning property, from holding any but menial service jobs, from holding public office, even from voting. This discrimination has often been embodied in laws and even more often in social customs and it has been rooted in many men's—and women's—views about the appropriate social and legal consequences of women's unique biological function of bearing and nursing children and of men's generally greater physical size and strength. The child-bearing trait has inclined societies to impose on women—and women to accept—the prime obligation of caring for children from birth to adulthood. Women's relative physical, social, and economic weakness has helped men to keep in their inferior roles even those few women who have rebelled against those rules.

Sex discrimination has been particularly prominent in politics. History tells of a few powerful queens: Elizabeth I, Anne, and Victoria of England; Catherine the Great of Russia; and Christina of Sweden. But in most nations of the old order, the Salic law excluded women from succeeding to the throne, and so they could play political roles only as wives and mothers (Catherine de Medici, Anne of Austria) or mistresses of kings (Diane de Poitiers, Nell Gwyn).

The twentieth century has seen more improvement in the status of women, at least in the developed nations, than in all previous history. Most Western nations, including the United States, gave women the right to vote around the time of World War I (1914–1918). In the 1920s the new Soviet regime placed women in many jobs they had never held before (for example, bus drivers, airline pilots, even combat soldiers), and in the 1950s the new communist regime in China followed suit. In the communist systems, however, women have been and are far from achieving political or economic equality: For example, in the former Soviet Union and in present-day China only about 10 to 20 percent of the members of the all-powerful Communist parties have been women, no woman has yet been the head of government or held one of its top positions, and, as in Western nations, women have been disproportionately employed in lower-paying jobs and have been paid less than men who have done the same jobs. In the non-communist nations of the West, this century's modest social and political gains for women seem to many to highlight not so much how far women have come as how far they still have to go. We will therefore examine women's present economic and political status in the United States, where the movement for women's rights is one of the most powerful in the world.

In Employment and Pay

In 1994 women constituted 51.2 percent of the population of the United States, but 38.3 percent of its full-time workers and 70 percent of its part-time workers. Even so, the proportion of full-time workers had increased markedly from 28.1 percent in 1947. Over 60 million new jobs were added to the labor force from 1960 to 1990, and 61 percent of those jobs went to women (for example, 75 percent of the new bus drivers and over 50 percent of the new newspaper reporters were women). However, women's continuing underrepresentation in the labor force doubtless reflects in part their responsibilities for rearing children. In 1970, only 30 percent of all women with children under the age of six (when most children start attending school full time) were employed, compared with nearly half of the women with older children or no children. In 1992 the figures were 60.5 percent for women with children under six and 61 percent for women with older children or no children. Thus, not only have the two figures risen rapidly in recent years but the gap between the figures has closed. More women are working today than ever before in U.S. history, and the proportion is bound to rise even more.

However, the proportion of women with jobs of some kind tells only part of the story. Another part is the inferior status of women in the types of jobs they hold and in their rates of pay. In 1992 the median weekly pay for all women working full time was $400, compared with $539 for men working full time.

For many years my own field of political science was no exception, but women have recently drawn even. In college and university departments of political science in 1972, 82 percent of the men held "tenure track" appointments, compared to 63 percent of the women. In 1993 the figures were 93 percent for men and 90 percent for women. The median salary of full professors in 1993 was $54,000 for both men and women; for associate professors it was $41,500 for men and $40,500 for women; and for assistant professors it was $33,500 for men and $34,500 for women.[2] In many jobs, however, men are still paid more than women for the same work, so it is not surprising that the women's rights movement continues to put a high priority on the goals of equal job opportunities and equal pay for equal work.

In Politics and Government

In 1992, women constituted 52.6 percent of the voting-age population of the United States, but a far smaller proportion of the political elite. Neither major party has ever nominated a woman for the presidency (although several minor parties have), and in 1984 Democratic Representative Geraldine Ferraro became the first (and so far the only) woman ever nominated by a major party for the vice presidency.

Equally striking is the small number of women candidates for Congress. In 1994, for example, there were sixty-eight major-party candidates for the U.S. Senate, of whom four were women (compared with nine in 1986); two were reelected, two were defeated, and in 1995 there were a total of seven women senators. In 1994 there were 846 major-party candidates for the House of Representatives, of whom 101 (12 percent) were women. Forty-two were elected, so in 1995 women constituted 7 percent of the members of the Senate and 9.6 percent of the members of the House. In 1994 only one woman governor (Ann Richards, Democrat of Texas) ran for reelection, and she was defeated, leaving Christine Todd Whitman (Republican of New Jersey) as the only woman governor in 1995. Perhaps most striking of all, in 1981 Sandra Day O'Connor became the first woman ever appointed to the U.S. Supreme Court, and in 1994 Ruth Bader Ginsburg became the second.

Women in other democratic nations have fared little or no better. For example, in the 1992 British general election, 568 women were candidates for Parliament, and the 60 who were elected comprised 9 percent of the total of 650 MPs, not very many but the highest proportion in British history. Western European parliaments vary widely in the proportion of women members:[3]

France: 6 percent

Italy: 8 percent

Spain: 16 percent

Germany: 22 percent

Netherlands: 27 percent

Sweden: 33 percent

Denmark: 34 percent

Norway: 38 percent

On the other hand, while no woman has yet been president of the United States, several other nations have chosen women as their heads of government: Bangladesh (Khaleda Zia), Canada (Kim Campbell), Dominica (Mary Eugenia Charles), France (Edith Cresson), India (Indira Gandhi), Israel (Golda Meir), Nicaragua (Violeta Barrios de Chamorro), Norway (Gro Harlem Brundtland), Pakistan (Benazir Bhutto), the Philippines (Corazon Aquino), and the United Kingdom (Margaret Thatcher).

U.S. women have made somewhat greater progress in getting elected to state and local offices. In 1975, for example, only 8 percent of the members of all state legislatures were women, but in 1992 the figure had more than doubled to 20 percent. In 1975, 456 women were members of county governing bodies, and in 1988 the number had increased over threefold to 1,653.[4]

The main political advance for American women in recent years has resulted from the efforts of both major parties, but especially the Democrats, to increase the

WOMEN LEAD SOME NATIONS.
Nicaraguan President Violeta Chamorro
celebrating her election, 1990.

proportions of women among the delegates to their national nominating conventions. In 1972 the Democrats used a semi-quota system; in 1976 they changed it to an affirmative action policy; and in 1978 the Democratic National Committee adopted a rule that henceforth at least half of every delegation to the convention must be composed of women, an explicit mandatory quota system. The results are shown in Table 16.2.

It could be argued that the increased proportion of women delegates in both parties shown in Table 16.2 represented no great victory for women's interests, since the powers of the national conventions have in recent years been reduced to registering the decisions made by the voters in presidential primary elections. Even so, it is clear that for some time to come women will continue to hold a higher proportion of official positions in the major parties' national conventions than in any other level of U.S. politics and government.

WOMEN'S RIGHTS MOVEMENT

Ever since the eighteenth century occasional feminist movements have mobilized in several countries to improve the status of women by political action. Among the most successful were the women's suffrage movements of the late nineteenth and early twentieth centuries, which played major roles in securing women's rights to vote in a number of Western nations. New Zealand in 1893 was the first to establish women's suffrage, followed by Norway in 1913, Great Britain in 1918, and the United States in 1920. France and Italy did not give women the right to vote until 1946, and Switzerland—often said to be a model democracy—did not do so until 1971.

TABLE 16.2   **Women Delegates in National Nominating Conventions, 1968–1992**

	PERCENTAGE OF WOMEN AMONG ALL DELEGATES						
PARTY	1968	1972	1976	1980	1984	1988	1992
Democratic	13	40	33	49	51	52	51
Republican	16	29	31	29	46	37	42

Source: Barbara G. Farah, "Delegate Polls, 1944 to 1984," *Public Opinion*, August–September 1984, Table 1, p. 44. Copyright American Enterprise Institute. The figures for 1988 were taken from *The New York Times*, July 17, 1988, p. 11; and August 14, 1988, p. 14. The figures for 1992 were furnished by the Democratic and Republican national committees.

Organization and Objectives

The American women's rights (or women's liberation) movement has been in high gear since the 1970s, and it has surpassed the suffragette movement of the early 1900s as one of the most active and powerful feminist movements the world has yet seen. Like most protest movements (for example, the African-American civil rights movement, discussed later), the women's rights movement has no universally agreed-upon list of demands or beliefs. It has its radicals (who say that men are incurably hostile and oppressive to women, and women should always deal with men as potential or active enemies), its moderates (who say that women should have the same basic rights and opportunities as men, and right-thinking men can and will help women achieve those rights), and its conservatives (who say that women will and should always be primarily wives and mothers, though perhaps women deserve a somewhat better break politically and economically than they have had).

The women's movement also has no one dominant organization. Among its leading pressure groups are the National Organization for Women (NOW), the Women's Equity Action League, the National Abortion Rights Action League (NARAL), and the Women's Political Caucus. The prime objectives sought by these and other women's organizations include the elimination of all gender-based discrimination in employment opportunities, pay, and advancement; affirmative action to maximize women's employment and promotion; laws against sexual harassment of women employees; liberalized birth control and abortion laws; expanded children's day-care programs; liberalized tax deductions for child-care expenses; more women candidates and public officeholders; and the repeal of all laws that in any way give women a legal status inferior to men's.

The women's organizations, with help from male allies, have used most of the broad range of pressure-group tactics to persuade or force the national and state governments and political parties to adopt policies and platforms promoting these goals. Like other protest movements, the women's movement has won a few and lost a few; but compared with most such movements, it has done well and is likely to do even better, as is evident from some recent developments.

THE NATIONAL ORGANIZATION FOR WOMEN (NOW) IN ACTION.

Equal Rights Amendment

Many leaders of the women's movement believe that their cause must rest on firmer ground than the vagaries of administrators' plans and judges' interpretations, and for decades their central strategy was to amend the U.S. Constitution so as to prohibit all forms of gender-based discrimination once and for all. The first of several such amendments was introduced in Congress as early as 1923, but none got anywhere until 1971, when Congress approved and sent to the states for ratification the equal rights amendment (ERA), which read as follows:

> Equality of rights under the law shall not be denied or abridged by the United States or by any state on account of sex.

The U.S. Constitution requires that all amendments be ratified by at least three quarters of the states (thirty-eight of fifty), and the ERA got off to a fast start. Twenty-two states ratified it in 1972, eight more followed suit in 1973, and it looked as though the remaining eight would ratify in 1974. However, a militant opposition movement was formed by noted conservative activist Phyllis Schlafly. The opposition argued that the ERA would deprive women of the legal protections they now enjoy, force women to be drafted for military combat service, outlaw separate sanitary facilities, deprive divorced women of alimony, and so on. Schlafly and her supporters added that women are by nature primarily wives and mothers, that women should be protected as such, and that the price for such protection is to preserve the special role of men as husbands, fathers, breadwinners, and soldiers. The amendment's supporters, especially NOW, retorted that those alleged protections have helped women very little, that the protections have served mainly as masks and justifications for discrimination, and that reasonable gender-based legal distinctions—as opposed to the sexist discrimination that now prevails—could still be made.

The battle between the two sides was joined with increasing heat in the unratifying states, and the ERA's progress slowed sharply: In 1974 only three states ratified, in 1975 only one, in 1976 none, and in 1977 only one more. The amendment's terms required that it be ratified by 1979; and as that fateful year approached, the total of ratifying states was stuck at thirty-five, and the prospects for getting three more by 1979 looked bleak. However, effective lobbying by the women's movement induced Congress to allow thirty-nine additional months for ratification, so the deadline was moved back to June 30, 1982. The extra time did not help, however: No additional states ratified the ERA, and it finally died on the appointed day in 1982.

Undaunted by this failure, a coalition of pro-ERA members of Congress introduced an identical new amendment in February 1983; but in November 1983 it failed by six votes to get the necessary two-thirds approval in the House of Representatives, and many advocates of women's rights concluded that the ERA was dead and that a new strategy had to be adopted.

After ERA

Since the ERA's 1983 failure, the women's rights movement has advocated a number of specific policy changes and has pursued those changes by the classical tactics of lobbying, electioneering, and litigation. They have pressed for such measures as federal funding of abortions for poor women, expanded publicly funded day-care programs to make it easier for women to work, liberalized leaves of absence from work for women to bear and care for babies, and the barring of all discrimination in life insurance premiums and benefits based on the fact that on the average women live longer than men (seventy-nine years for women, seventy-three years for men). Since the late 1980s, the growing strength of pro-life forces and the increasingly conservative tendency of the Supreme Court have forced women's organizations, especially NOW and NARAL, to devote considerable resources to resisting efforts to overturn the Court's 1973 *Roe* v. *Wade* decision barring the states from restricting a woman's right to an abortion in the first three months of pregnancy (see Chapter 2).

In the 1990s, the women's movement has also vigorously advocated the idea of "comparable worth," the proposition that workers in jobs of comparable social value should be paid the same regardless of whether they are held mainly by women or men.

But how is a job's social worth to be determined? No procedure has been approved in every detail, but many advocates of comparable worth suggest that a representative committee in each industry and government agency should identify *and weight* all the major variables that should be involved in determining rates of pay—for example, education, experience, manual and intellectual skills, and physical strength. The committee would then assign to each job a number representing the sum of all the job's scores on all the weighted variables, and the law would require that jobs with similar numbers receive similar wages regardless of who held them.

Comparable worth has met considerable opposition. Its opponents say that any "job-worth" number is bound to be highly arbitrary, that determining it will become a political test of strength rather than a scientific or economic judgment, that the cost of leveling wage rates up (no one expects them to be leveled down) will be staggering, and that in the end wage rates will continue to be determined, as they always have been, by the relative needs of employers for certain kinds of skills and by how much employers are willing to pay to get such skills in competition with other employers in the labor market.

U.S. public opinion on comparable worth is mixed. On the one hand, an overwhelming 97 percent of those polled, men and women alike, agree with the statement that "Men and women should be paid equally for jobs of comparable worth." But when asked, "Do you think it is possible to compare jobs that are quite different—such as a secretary and an electrician—using some kind of rating or evaluation system, and then set fair salaries or pay rates as a result?" 65 percent agree with the statement that "such comparisons would be too difficult to do and, therefore, not fair." When asked, "To the extent that comparable worth is a good idea, who do you think should decide if two jobs really are of comparable worth and thus merit the same pay?" 19 percent say that the government should decide, 18 percent say that the courts should decide, and 41 percent say that private employers should decide.[5]

It is too early to tell whether comparable worth will fare better than the ERA, but it and the issue of abortion rights are likely to be among the main battlegrounds for the women's rights movement in the 1990s.

Conflict over the Status of African-Americans ───────────

BLACK AMERICA, YESTERDAY AND TODAY

Racial discrimination *imposes handicaps on all members of a particular race solely because of their race and without regard to their individual merits.* For example, barring any African-American, no matter how intelligent or well prepared, from attending a particular school is a form of racial discrimination. Prohibiting a Vietnamese refugee, no matter how pleasant and neighborly, from buying a house in a particular neighborhood is another form.

Racial discrimination is one of the oldest and most often encountered aspects of man's inhumanity to man. Wherever people of different races (and sometimes ethnic groups) have been thrown together in the same society, at least some members of the dominant group have attempted to discriminate against members of another group or groups: gentiles against Jews, whites against blacks, Africans against Indians, Anglos against Latinos, Occidentals against Asians, Japanese against Koreans, Serbs against Croats, and so on. In most societies conflicts over discrimination sooner or later become political. Groups favoring discrimination try to have their views enforced by laws, and antidiscrimination groups try to get the discriminations outlawed.

The United States, as we will see, certainly has no monopoly on racial discrimination, public or private. However, discrimination against African-Americans in this country has, justly or not, received more attention and comment both here and abroad than has discrimination in any other nation, with the possible exception of the policy of *apartheid* (racial separation and white supremacy) in the Republic of South Africa.

The problem of the status of African-Americans has plagued U.S. society and government for more than three centuries. By the 1780s enough African slaves had been imported so that questions of what to do about slavery and how to count slaves for purposes of congressional representation sharply divided the Constitutional Convention of 1787. The question of whether slavery should be extended, maintained, or abolished was a main cause of the Civil War (1861–1865), the bloodiest war in U.S. history. The war resulted in the legal emancipation of the slaves, but for a century after Appomattox, African-Americans remained second-class citizens.

Since 1945 the struggle over the status of African-Americans has greatly intensified. It has become one of the most divisive domestic political issues of our time, and there is still no end in sight. It involves the status of only 12.6 percent of the U.S. population—but that means nearly 33 million human beings. African-Americans are not only the most numerous and visible of our nation's economically depressed minorities, but they are also politically the most significant. African-Americans differ sharply from the white majority in appearance, history, culture, and other respects, some of which are shown in Table 16.3.

Table 16.3 makes it clear that, compared with whites, African-Americans today have a higher proportion of families headed by mothers, have lower life expectancies, have less formal education, work disproportionately in the lower-status and lower-paid occupations, make less money, have more unemployment and more persons below the poverty line, and vote in smaller proportions. Indeed, many of the toughest problems U.S. governments face—the "urban problem," poverty, undereducation, unemployment, and so on—are largely manifestations of the underlying problem of the status of African-Americans. Let us begin our examination of that problem by reviewing the history of the issues and the contending forces in this longstanding conflict.

A BRIEF HISTORY OF THE CIVIL RIGHTS MOVEMENT

White Supremacy and Legally Forced Segregation

Until the 1950s the status of African-Americans in the United States was determined largely by a powerful group of whites who believed in racial segregation and white supremacy. Their belief in racial segregation was based on the doctrine

TABLE 16.3 African-Americans and Whites in the United States, 1992

CHARACTERISTICS	AFRICAN-AMERICANS	WHITES
Householder		
Married couple	47%	82%
Male householder	7	4
Female householder	46	14
	100%	100%
Life Expectancy in Years at Birth		
Male	68.1	79.0
Female	76.2	79.7
Education		
Not a high school graduate	32%	19%
High school graduates	36	36
Some college, no degree	15	16
College graduate	13	21
Advanced degree	4	8
	100%	100%
Employment Status		
Percent employed	86%	94%
Percent unemployed	12	6
	100%	100%
Occupation		
Managerial and professional	19%	30%
Technical, sales, and admin. support	26	31
Service	22	11
Precision production, craft, and repair	9	12
Operators, fabricators, and laborers	22	13
Farming, forestry, and fishing	2	3
	100%	100%
Median family income	$21,548	$37,783
Percent of persons below poverty line	33	11
Voting Turnout Percent		
1984 election	56	60
1986 election	43	47
1988 election	52	59
1990 election	39	47
1992 election	54	64

Source: The American Almanac, 1993–1994 (Washington, DC: Bureau of the Census, 1994).

that whites and blacks should conduct most of their activities in all-white and all-black situations and that there should be racially segregated schools, housing, transportation, athletic contests, public accommodations, recreation facilities, religious

CHANGING TIMES, CHANGING NAMES

The people whom we call "African-Americans" in this book have been know by a variety of names. After their emancipation from slavery in 1865, they were widely called "colored people" (as is illustrated by the fact that the first major organization, formed in 1909, to advance their interests called itself the National Association for the Advancement of Colored People). They were also widely called "Negroes."

However, this changed after World War II. Many members of the new civil rights movement made a point of using the term *blacks*, for reasons given by the authors of a book prominent in the movement: "There is growing resentment of the word 'Negro' . . . because the term is an invention of our oppressor; it is his image of us that he describes. Many blacks are now calling themselves African-Americans, Afro-Americans, or black people because that is *our* image of ourselves."[6] Since most of those who were most active politically used the term "blacks," that is the usage we employed in early editions of this book.

However, the Reverend Jesse Jackson and many other leaders have recently said that they prefer to be called African-Americans. As Rev. Jackson said in 1988, "To be called African-Americans has cultural integrity. It puts us in our proper historical context. Every ethnic group in this country has a reference to some land base, some historical cultural base. African-Americans have hit that level of cultural maturity."[7]

Accordingly, in the current edition we have adopted the new usage wherever appropriate.

---

organizations, jobs, and so on. Their belief in white supremacy meant that whites should dominate both parts of the segregated society by deciding which areas of life would be segregated and the conditions in which each race would live and work. The people who believed in racial segregation and white supremacy declared that both should be enforced by the kind of "Jim Crow" compulsory segregation laws that were so common before the 1950s. The most prominent advocates of racial segregation and white supremacy were whites living in the South, probably because that is where most African-Americans lived. Many whites in the North, Midwest, and West felt the same way, but few African-Americans lived in their areas and the issues of race relations were less prominent.

Struggle Against Discrimination: Organizations and Leaders

What history has come to call the civil rights movement began to emerge and gather strength in the 1930s. It was led by a number of organizations, most of them multiracial in membership but predominantly African-American in leadership. The most influential follow.

THE NATIONAL ASSOCIATION FOR THE ADVANCEMENT OF COLORED PEOPLE (NAACP)   The oldest of the organizations in the civil rights movement, the NAACP, founded in 1909, has consistently emphasized pressure on Congress and constitutional challenges to discrimination in the federal courts and has won many notable legislative and judicial victories. Its emphasis on acting within the system, its occasional acceptance of whites in positions of leadership, and its strong resistance to the hatred of all whites expressed by some African-Americans have won the NAACP the reputation of being the conservative wing of the civil rights movement.

LEADERS OF THE AFRICAN-AMERICAN CIVIL RIGHTS MOVEMENT. (top) Roy Wilkins, Joseph Lowery; (bottom) Jesse Jackson, Martin Luther King, Jr.

THE NATIONAL URBAN LEAGUE   Founded in 1910, this organization has stressed interracial educational programs in local communities aimed at ending segregation and discrimination, particularly in housing and employment. It has operated as actively in the North as in the South. Its first directors, Whitney M. Young, Jr., and then Vernon Jordan, have been generally regarded as among the leading moderates in the African-American rights movement.

THE SOUTHERN CHRISTIAN LEADERSHIP CONFERENCE (SCLC)   The SCLC was founded in 1957 by the greatest moderate leader of the civil rights movement, Dr. Martin Luther King, Jr. He headed the organization until his murder in 1968, and he is the only African-American leader who, in addition to his Nobel Peace Prize, has had the nation honor him by making his birthday a national holiday. Under his leadership the SCLC pioneered the use of Gandhian nonviolent resistance (see Chapter 1) and won major victories over discrimination against African-Americans in the 1960s. In recent years, under the leadership first of Ralph Abernathy and then of Joseph Lowery, the SCLC has joined with impoverished whites and Hispanic

Americans to press for greater government efforts to end poverty, but it has been troubled by internal conflict between those who want to put more emphasis on protest activities and those, including Lowery, who prefer to emphasize the funding of social welfare projects and lobbying Congress and the administration for larger appropriations for jobs for African-Americans.

THE CONGRESS OF RACIAL EQUALITY (CORE)   CORE was at one time the most militant of the civil rights organizations. It was founded in 1941 by James Farmer. It pioneered the use of such direct-action techniques as picketing, demonstrations, sit-ins, and boycotts. In 1969, Farmer, to the consternation of some of his colleagues, accepted an appointment in the Nixon administration as assistant secretary for administration of the Department of Health, Education and Welfare. In 1976 the organization split between a group that recruited African-American Vietnam War veterans to fight in the Angolan civil war in Africa and an older group who felt that this was going too far outside the organization's basic purposes. CORE's internal divisions, like those of the SCLC, weakened its position in the civil rights movement.

PEOPLE UNITED TO SAVE HUMANITY (PUSH)   Since the mid-1970s, one of the most dynamic and visible leaders of the African-American rights movement has been the Reverend Jesse Jackson. He founded PUSH mainly to encourage African-American parents and African-American children to work hard in school and equip themselves to compete successfully with whites in the business and educational worlds. In 1984 Jackson entered the contest for the Democratic party's presidential nomination. His participation in the contest stimulated a record number of African-Americans to register and vote. He won over 3 million votes in the primaries (18.6 percent of all the votes cast) and finished a solid third behind the winner, Walter Mondale, and Mondale's chief challenger, Gary Hart.

In 1988 Jackson did even better: He again sought the Democratic presidential nomination and not only attracted over 90 percent of all African-American votes but substantially increased his support among white voters. He won a total of over 6.5 million votes (29 percent of all the votes cast), and finished second to the eventual winner, Michael Dukakis. Although he did not run in 1992, most observers felt that Jackson's two campaigns had established him not only as the first serious African-American contender for the presidency but also as the most prominent and powerful leader of African-Americans in the 1990s.

From those brief sketches it is clear that there have been some disagreements both among and within the African-American rights organizations. Far more important is the fact that for decades those organizations fought side by side in many battles and won many victories in the struggle to end the many forms of legal and extralegal discrimination against African-Americans.

Struggle against Discrimination: Areas and Issues

From the 1930s to the 1970s, the main goal of most people in the civil rights movement was to end all forms of segregation and discrimination against African-Americans, and most of them looked forward to the day when the United States

AFRICAN-AMERICANS IN MAINSTREAM POLITICS. Jesse Jackson campaigning for the Democratic presidential nomination in 1984.

would become truly "color blind," a society in which people's educations, jobs, incomes, residences, and social statuses would be determined solely by their abilities and achievements and not by the color of their skin. The main struggles took place in the following policy areas.

VOTING   After the post–Civil War Reconstruction period ended in the late 1870s, southern whites tried to keep the newly emancipated African-Americans from exercising the voting rights granted to them by the Fifteenth Amendment to the U.S. Constitution. Among the devices used were poll taxes, selectively administered literacy tests, "white primaries," and physical violence and intimidation. The impact of those devices is shown by the fact that as late as the 1940s, only 12 percent of southern African-Americans of voting age were registered to vote, and well less than half of even that handful bothered—or dared—to go to the polls.

By the 1980s this form of discrimination was almost entirely abolished. The Twenty-Fourth Amendment, ratified in 1964, outlawed all state requirements for the payment of poll taxes as a precondition for voting. Even more important was the Voting Rights Act of 1965, which requires the U.S. attorney general to determine whether or not an unusually low voting turnout in any of the nation's counties results from racial discrimination. If the attorney general determines that it does, then the federal Department of Justice is empowered to send federal registrars into any such county with authority to register all qualified voters, regardless of what the local officials may or may not do. Furthermore, the federal registrars must ignore any local laws that discriminate against African-Americans and must supervise the conduct of elections to make sure that no registered voter is in any way inhibited from voting.

Federal registrars have been sent into a number of southern counties, and in other areas local registrars have voluntarily given up trying to keep African-Americans from voting. As a result, the percentage of voting-age African-Americans registered to vote in the eleven southern (ex-Confederate) states rose from 12 percent in 1947 to 63.9 percent in 1992. The Bureau of the Census estimates that in the 1992 presidential election, 51 percent of voting-age African-Americans in the South actually voted, compared with 44 percent in 1964 and 28 percent in 1960, and 55 percent of all eligible whites in the nation.

EDUCATION   For many years people in both North and South who believed in maintaining racial segregation and white supremacy insisted that under no circumstances should African-Americans be permitted to attend the same schools as whites, arguing that African-Americans' supposed genetic mental inferiority would be a drag on the educational development of white children. Immediately after the Civil War, most states adopted constitutional or statutory prohibitions of racial integration in public schools. In the succeeding decades, however, most states outside the South repealed those laws, and twenty-two states adopted provisions specifically prohibiting racial segregation.

The great turning point came in 1954. In that year a total of nineteen states (four of them outside the South) and the District of Columbia legally required racial segregation in their public schools. On several occasions those laws had been challenged in the Supreme Court as violations of the clause in the Fourteenth Amendment that stipulates, "No State shall . . . deny to any person within its jurisdiction the equal protection of the laws." However, the Court consistently upheld the segregation laws, following the separate-but-equal rule first laid down in the case of *Plessy* v. *Ferguson* (1896). According to this rule, segregation in itself is not a denial of equal protection as long as equal facilities are provided for both races.

In the early 1950s, however, the NAACP, under the leadership of its chief constitutional lawyer, Thurgood Marshall (who later became the first African-American justice of the Supreme Court),[8] again challenged the constitutionality of state school-segregation laws. This time, in a unanimous opinion written by Chief Justice Earl Warren in *Brown* v. *Board of Education* (1954), the Court reversed the *Plessy* decision and ruled that racial segregation *in itself* is a denial of equal protection, regardless of the facilities provided; and in 1955 the Court ordered the federal district courts to proceed "with all deliberate speed" to ensure that local school boards complied with the ruling.

For the next ten years desegregation proceeded very slowly in some areas, especially in the states of Alabama, Georgia, Louisiana, Mississippi, and South Carolina. In 1964, however, Congress—under the leadership of Senator Hubert Humphrey and the relentless prodding of President Lyndon Johnson of Texas (the first southerner to be president since the Civil War)—passed the most far-reaching federal civil rights legislation since Reconstruction. We will observe the impact of this legislation in other areas, but we note here that Title VI authorizes the Office (now Department) of Education to cut off federal financial aid to any school district that refuses to pursue an acceptable program of desegregation. That speeded up desegregation considerably, but in the 1970s and 1980s the conflict over desegregation became overshadowed by the conflict over integration by busing; and it became clear that desegregation and integration are not the same thing.

As it was originally conceived by the civil rights movement, desegregation meant an end to all laws and practices forcing African-American children to attend exclusively African-American schools. As we have just seen, the first mortal blow to legally forced segregation was delivered by the decision in *Brown v. Board of Education*, and the final blow was given by the enforcement procedures in Title VI of the Civil Rights Act of 1964. But in the early 1970s the issue became *integration*— that is, ensuring that all public schools are racially mixed.

The problem of converting desegregation into integration arises from the fact that in most cities in all parts of the country, most neighborhoods are in fact racially segregated; that is, many African-Americans live in exclusively African-American areas, many whites live in exclusively white areas, and relatively few neighborhoods are racially mixed. Moreover, one of the oldest and most widely admired traditions is the belief that schools should be located in particular neighborhoods and attended by children living in those neighborhoods. Clearly, then, if residential neighborhoods are racially segregated, schools are bound to be racially segregated as well.

Many people in the civil rights movement who believe that the goal should be not mere desegregation but full integration of the schools have proposed a number of plans to overcome the difficulty. The method most often used and most controversial is busing, which is assigning African-American children living in African-American neighborhoods to schools in white neighborhoods, assigning white children living in white neighborhoods to schools in African-American neighborhoods, and carrying out the assignments by requiring children to travel in buses to schools miles from their homes.

The controversy over this policy first became a major issue in the early 1970s, when a number of federal district judges decided that desegregation really means integration, that all public schools must have certain minimum percentages of both African-American and white children (for example, a judge in Richmond, Virginia, ruled that every school must have from 20 to 40 percent African-American pupils), and that busing black children to mainly white schools and white children to mainly black schools is an appropriate way to fill the racial quotas.

School integration and busing turned what was mainly a southern controversy into a national controversy. Busing aroused intense opposition by large numbers of white parents in Boston, Denver, Louisville, Detroit, Indianapolis, and many other non-southern cities. Some opponents expressed their opposition by obstructing the movement of school buses, and others by taking their children out of public schools and putting them into mostly white private schools. Congress has adopted a number of resolutions intended to prohibit busing for racial integration, but the Supreme Court has approved busing as a tool that judges can constitutionally use in certain circumstances. The Court's general rule is this: If the Court finds that the schools in a school district are segregated as the result of the school board's deliberate policy to keep schools segregated, then it will uphold a lower court's order to require bus-ing to integrate the schools. On the other hand, if the Court finds that the absence of racial integration in a school district results from racial housing patterns and not from a deliberate policy to keep the schools segregated, then it will not uphold lower-court orders to bus children across school district lines.

HOUSING   For many years African-Americans (and, to a lesser extent, Asian-Americans and Jews) have been denied equal opportunities for housing by means of "restrictive covenants"; that is, by agreements among white and gentile property owners not to sell their houses to African-American or Jewish buyers, thus pre-serving all-white and all-gentile neighborhoods. These covenants used to be inserted in formal contracts among property owners. An owner who violated such a covenant by selling to an African-American or a Jew could be sued in the courts for breach of contract. In 1948, however, the Supreme Court struck a powerful (though not mortal) blow at restrictive covenants by ruling that though those covenants are not in themselves unlawful, they cannot be enforced by any court, state or federal; for such enforcement would make the courts parties to the covenants, in violation of the Fourteenth Amendment.

However, this decision was at best a negative sanction, and many restrictive covenants continued to be made and effectively enforced as unwritten "gentlemen's agreements." Finally, in 1968, after years of battle over the issue, Congress passed a major open-housing law that prohibits racial discrimination in the sale or rental of most of the nation's housing. The law applies to all public housing and urban-renewal projects, all private multiple-unit dwellings except those of no more than four units that are occupied by their owners, all single-family houses not owned by private individuals, and all privately owned single-family houses that are sold or rented by real-estate agents or brokers. About the only exceptions are privately owned homes whose owners sell or rent them without the services of real-estate brokers or agents. The act is thus estimated to apply to about 80 percent of all the nation's housing units.

PUBLIC ACCOMMODATIONS   Segregationists long sought to keep African-Americans from using the same public services and accommodations as whites: rid-ing in the same parts of trains and buses; sitting in the same parts of theaters; and using the same restaurants, golf courses, swimming pools, barbershops, restrooms, and drinking fountains. In 1954, more than twenty states had Jim Crow laws re-quiring such segregation, but they were deemed unconstitutional after the *Brown* decision threw out the old separate-but-equal formula. Another twenty states adopted laws prohibiting racial discrimination by private businesses offering pub-lic accommodations or by any publicly owned and operated facility. Many of those laws were enforced little or not at all, however, and African-Americans were com-monly refused service. Civil rights leaders came to believe that only strong action by the federal government would guarantee truly equal rights in this area.

Their goal was achieved in the Civil Rights Act of 1964. Title II forbids racial discrimination in all publicly owned or operated facilities. It also prohibits racial discrimination in serving customers by all private businesses providing public accommodations (hotels, motels, restaurants, gasoline stations, theaters, sports arenas, and the like). As a result, racial discrimination in those areas has almost entirely disappeared, even in the small towns and rural areas of the deep South.

EMPLOYMENT   African-Americans have long been the most economically depressed ethnic group in the United States, although some African-Americans are better off today than they were twenty years ago. The figures in Table 16.3 show that the median income of African-American families in 1992 was only 57 percent as high as the median income of white families, and not by chance. For many decades after the end of slavery, many white employers and white-dominated labor unions made sure that the only jobs open to most African-Americans were the lowest paying, and most African-Americans worked as unskilled industrial and farm laborers and domestic servants. Even in 1992, as Table 16.3 shows, 46 percent of all working African-Americans were employed in the lower-paying service, manual labor, and farm labor jobs, compared with only 27 percent of all working whites.

Accordingly, most African-Americans, whatever their differences may be on other issues, give top priority to ensuring that they get better jobs and more pay. One of the top demands of the civil rights movement up to the 1970s was that qualified African-Americans must have as good a chance at desirable jobs as qualified whites. African-Americans also urged the government to provide massive programs for training African-Americans in the knowledge and skills that will enable them to perform well in the more demanding and better-paying jobs.

Before 1964, some states had adopted fair-employment-practice laws, but many had not. Here again the federal Civil Rights Act was a major turning point. Title VII forbids private employers to practice racial discrimination in hiring or promotion and also prohibits labor unions from excluding any applicant for membership because of his or her race. The rules are enforced by a five-person Equal Employment Opportunity Commission (EEOC), which is empowered to hear and investigate charges of discrimination against employers and unions and to ask the U.S. attorney general to force compliance when efforts at persuasion fail.

As a result, there has been considerable progress not only toward equal employment rights for African-Americans but also toward all of the other objectives of the original civil rights movement as well. In the 1970s, however, some deep fissures began to appear in the movement, and conflict over the status of African-Americans in the 1990s has become a good deal more complicated than it was from the 1930s to the 1970s. The deepest of those fissures has been the increasingly bitter disagreement among different parts of the old civil rights movement over the issue of affirmative action. Let us examine that dispute in some detail.

AFRICAN-AMERICAN RIGHTS IN THE 1980s: ANTIDISCRIMINATION OR AFFIRMATIVE ACTION?

Antidiscrimination

The civil rights movement's thirty-year fight against racial discrimination had sought to achieve a society in which the competition for the good things of life, such as well-paying jobs, decent houses in decent neighborhoods, and good educations, is truly open and fair. In such a society African-Americans would in no way be hand-icapped in the competition because of the color of their skins, and whites would in no way be advantaged because of the color of theirs. The competition's results would thus be determined by the individual merits of the competing persons and not by their color. Able and hard-working African-Americans would get every bit as much, but no more, of life's good things as equally able and hard-working whites. To be sure, the competition, like all free competitions, would produce unequal results: Some African-Americans and whites would win more of the good things than other African-Americans and whites. But African-Americans would have just as good a chance as whites to be winners.

In short, the old civil rights movement wanted a truly "color-blind" society, one in which persons would be judged, in Martin Luther King's famous words, "not by the color of their skin, but by the content of their character." To achieve this noble goal, the movement sought to eradicate every kind of handicap imposed on African-Americans by government or private agencies so as to achieve truly fair color-blind competition. Most who fought for that goal also believed that if poor education in underfunded ghetto schools kept African-American children from taking advantage of the new opportunities for fair competition, that handicap too should be re-moved by special remedial education and training programs such as the preschool Head Start program begun by the federal government in 1965. But the ultimate goal of those who believe in nondiscrimination is equality of *opportunity* and not equal-ity of *result*.

Affirmative Action

Some successors of the old civil rights movement have come to believe that while ending discrimination against African-Americans is certainly desirable, the goal of fair competition is not enough. For three centuries, they point out, white America has either made African-Americans into slaves or allowed them only a few crumbs from its table even after the legal end of slavery. This monstrous injustice, they say, cannot be remedied today merely by dumping modern African-Americans into a competition in which, because of those centuries of slavery and discrimina-tion, they have no fair chance to win. Jesse Jackson puts the argument in terms of a much-used analogy:

> Two world-class distance runners begin the grueling human test of trying to run a sub-four-minute mile. Two minutes into the race, officials observe that one runner, falling far behind, still has running weights on his ankles. They stop the race and hold both runners in their tracks. The weights are removed from the runner far behind, the offi-cials re-fire the starting gun, and both runners continue from the points where they were when the race was stopped. Not surprisingly, the runner who ran the entire race without the ankle weights comes in with a sizable lead.[9]

Clearly, such a competition would be unfair. What is the best way to make it fair? Start the race over with both runners unshackled at the starting line? That might be the way for future generations, Jackson says, but it will not do for this one. Give the previously shackled runner some kind of special advantage to compensate for his previous unfair treatment? If so, what kind of advantage, and how much? Fix the races so that the previously shackled competitors win 12.6 percent of the time? Fifty percent of the time? Over 50 percent of the time? At what point does "fairness" to the previously shackled runner become "unfairness" to another runner who was never shackled but did not personally participate in any shackling of any competitors?

One widely proposed remedy is what some people call "compensatory racial preferences," others call "reverse discrimination," and Jesse Jackson calls "racial reparations." This remedy requires that since the proportion of African-Americans in the general population is 12.6 percent, then it should be guaranteed that at least 12.6 percent of the students entering colleges, law schools, and medical schools should be African-Americans; 12.6 percent of the persons holding the high-paying skilled craft jobs should be African-Americans; 12.6 percent of top-level government workers should be African-Americans; and so on. Only when all traces *and consequences* of past discrimination against African-Americans have been wiped out, these proponents contend, can the nation justly return to "fair competition" as the prime objective in dealing with the status of African-Americans.

People who, like Jesse Jackson, want racial reparations for African-Americans through guaranteed results rather than nondiscriminatory fair competition believe that the best way to get the reparations is to establish **affirmative action programs**, which are *programs designed to remedy the effects of past discrimination by increasing the proportions of women and African-Americans and other ethnic minorities in desirable social and economic positions.*

Many women's groups insist that affirmative action programs should also guarantee proper proportions of such benefits for women. For both African-Americans and women, proper proportions and appropriate shares mean proportions close to their proportions in the general population: 12.6 percent for African-Americans and 51.2 percent for women.

The two watchwords for those who favor affirmative action are *goals* and *timetables*. The ultimate goal of each program is full proportional equality in the numbers of African-Americans and women both in initial hirings and in promotion to higher positions. A timetable is a firm commitment to achieve the goal by a stipulated time in the not-too-distant future.

The great trouble with affirmative action, say its opponents, is that such goals are in fact nothing more than *quotas*—that is, minimum numbers of places that must be reserved for African-Americans because they are African-American and for women because they are women, without regard to whether the qualifications of the favored individuals equal or exceed the qualifications of the white males seeking the same places. Reserving some of the limited number of places available for African-Americans and women will inevitably mean that some whites and some males will be denied places for which they are better qualified than the African-Americans and women who get the reserved places. Hence, the opponents say, affirmative action amounts to reverse discrimination, which replaces the old sin of discrimination against African-Americans and women with the new sin of discrimination against whites and males.

AFFIRMATIVE ACTION OR REVERSE DISCRIMINATION?

The first great test of whether affirmative action programs are constitutional came in one of the most-discussed Supreme Court cases in recent years: *University of California Regents v. Bakke*, 438 U.S. 265 (1978). The Medical School of the University of California at Davis (UCDMS) admitted only 100 applicants each year, but instituted an affirmative action program setting aside sixteen of those places to be filled exclusively by African-Americans, Hispanics, and members of other minority groups. In August 1973 a total of 3,737 persons applied for admission to UCDMS, including Allan Bakke, a thirty-two-year-old white man. Bakke's undergraduate grades were above the average of those of the persons admitted, and his aptitude test scores were well above the average. Nevertheless, he was denied admission. In June 1974 he sued UCDMS for admission, claiming that some of the persons admitted under the affirmative action program had lower scores than he and that the program had therefore racially discriminated against him and other qualified whites in violation of both the Civil Rights Act of 1964 and the Fourteenth Amendment to the U.S. Constitution.

The case eventually went to the Supreme Court. The basic issue was whether it is constitutionally permissible for a tax-supported institution, the UCDMS, to compensate African-Americans and other minority groups for past discrimination against them by guaranteeing a certain number of places for them but not for white males. This issue was highly important not only to Allan Bakke but to many other people and groups not directly parties to the case. A total of fifty-seven organizations filed *amicus curiae* briefs supporting one side or

the other: For example, UCDMS was supported by the NAACP, the National Association of Minority Contractors, the Association of American Medical Colleges, and a number of labor unions. Bakke was supported by a number of Jewish organizations, the American Federation of Teachers, and the U.S. Chamber of Commerce.

The Court handed down its decision in June 1978. It was extremely complicated, with no fewer than six of the nine justices writing separate opinions. Their disagreements boiled down to a three-way split: Four justices (Warren Burger, William Rehnquist, John Paul Stevens, and Potter Stewart) held that the UCDMS special admissions program and all programs like it constitute racial discrimination against whites and are therefore unconstitutional. Four other justices (Harry Blackmun, William Brennan, Thurgood Marshall, and Byron White) held that the UCDMS program and all like it are constitutionally permissible ways of compensating minority groups whose forebears were victims of discrimination in the past. The swing vote was cast by Justice Lewis Powell, who held that while the UCDMS program was unconstitutional because it used a specific numerical quota, other programs that take race into account (without quotas) along with other factors in admitting applicants to universities or jobs are constitutional.

The upshot was that nobody won a total victory or suffered a total defeat. Bakke was admitted to UCDMS (he later graduated and received his medical degree); numerical racial quotas were outlawed; but affirmative action programs giving special help to minority applicants continue to operate under Powell's interpretation.

This difficult and hotly disputed issue has deeply divided the old civil rights movement. Since the Supreme Court first gave its complex ruling in the 1978 Bakke case (see the box), many subsequent decisions have still not definitively settled the fate of affirmative action programs. Many observers conclude that the Court has clearly accepted a certain amount of tilting the scales in favor of women and African-Americans and other minorities in order to remedy the damage done by past tilting of the scales against them. Perhaps the clearest stand taken by the Court is that *goals*—setting ultimate objectives for hiring and promoting women and minorities in proportions corresponding to their proportions of the general population—are constitutionally acceptable, but *quotas*—requiring employers to hire and promote specified percentages of women and minorities—are not. Even so, many people still believe that any kind of "reverse discrimination" that *guarantees* more good things for African-Americans and women than their individual merits justify is just as wrong as the original discrimination that denied them the good things that their merits deserved. Consequently, affirmative action programs that guarantee preferential treatment are likely to be as controversial in the 1990s as they were in the 1970s and 1980s.

Apartheid in South Africa

The United States is by no means the only modern nation in which powerful political groups have pressed for a government policy of segregation and white supremacy. Most Australians, for example, long regarded their nation as "a white island in an Asiatic sea"; and for many years after its independence from Great Britain in 1900, Australia followed the "white Australia" policy of prohibiting all but a trickle of nonwhite immigration and giving the native aborigine population less-than-equal status. Even Great Britain, long considered a model of racial equality, has had its troubles. The great influx of Pakistanis and West Indians in the 1950s and 1960s led to the creation of racial ghettos and even race riots in several big cities. It also led to the passage in 1961 of the Commonwealth Immigrants Act, which ended the free entry of West Indians and Pakistanis but did not end the tensions between whites and nonwhites and angry complaints by nonwhites about discrimination and poor treatment.

However, governmentally enforced segregation and white supremacy went furthest in the Republic of South Africa's policy of "apartheid" (separation), which controlled race relations from the 1940s to the early 1990s.

BACKGROUND

The Republic of South Africa presently has a population of over 42 million, of whom 17 percent are of pure European descent, 10 percent are "colored" (of mixed native and European descent), 3 percent are Asian (mainly Indian), and 70 percent are of pure native descent (some whites call them *Bantus*, the Zulu word for men, but the blacks consider the label demeaning). Most of the whites have been highly conscious of their status as a small minority surrounded by a large black majority, and their consciousness has been reinforced by the knowledge that on the whole continent of Africa there are only about 8 million whites compared with over 400 million blacks.

From the time of the earliest white settlements, most whites in South Africa—the Afrikaners (settlers of Dutch descent) and the British-descended settlers alike—have been apprehensive about what many Afrikaners called the *swart gevaar* ("black menace" in Afrikaans, the language of the Dutch-descended Boers) and have resolved to maintain the *baaskap* (literally "boss-ship") of whites over blacks.

THE POLICY OF APARTHEID

For a half-century the white rulers of South Africa pursued the policy of *apartheid*. The long-range goal of the policy was the complete separation of blacks from whites, with each living in its own special areas but with ultimate government power over all areas and people held exclusively by whites. However, many white South Africans regarded the achievement of this goal as centuries away. So as a short-range policy, apartheid meant segregation of the races in most activities, especially residence and work, and white supremacy in all aspects of life, especially political participation and power. Among its leading legal implementations were the following.

Separation

The Population Registration Act of 1950 provided for the classification and registration of the entire South African population into three categories: European (white), native (black), and colored (mixed). Each person had to carry an identification card showing to which of the three races he or she belonged. The Group Areas Act of 1950 empowered the government to designate particular areas for exclusive occupancy by particular races, and the Native Resettlement Act authorized the forcible relocation of blacks to all-black "reserves." All blacks had to carry identification cards, and if they wished to travel or work outside their reserves they had to show passes authorizing them to do so. After 1950 the government moved several hundred thousand blacks to reserves in accordance with this legislation, but fewer than half of the blacks lived in reserves. Those who did were required by the government to follow their ancient forms of tribal government and chieftainship, even though many blacks believed that those forms were outmoded and wished to adopt more modern systems.

Political Participation

In only one of South Africa's five provinces, Cape Province, were blacks and coloreds allowed to vote for members of the national Parliament. The Representation of Natives Act of 1936 confined the blacks to voting for only seven members of Parliament, all of whom had to be white. In 1960 the blacks and coloreds in Cape Province were deprived of even those rights, and the black representatives were abolished. In 1983 South Africa adopted a new three-chamber Parliament: the House of Assembly for whites, the House of Representatives for Coloreds, and the House of Delegates for Asians. The blacks had no chamber and no representation, and the House of Assembly continued to have the final say on everything. In the elections of 1984 and 1989 the turnout by coloreds and Asians was just over 10 percent of the registered voters, and though the representatives elected took their seats in the two new chambers they had no power.

Occupations

Blacks in South Africa had long been informally barred from engaging in any occupation higher or better paid than domestic service and unskilled labor. The Industrial Conciliation Act of 1954 placed the power of the government behind this

REFERENDUMS AS TURNING POINTS. A black South African watches a white South African go to the polls in the 1992 all-white referendum on apartheid negotiations.

discrimination by authorizing the Minister of Labor to determine at his or her own discretion which occupations would be open to members of the various races. On occasion the minister used it to admit blacks to some new occupations, such as druggists and clerks in certain kinds of stores, but no black had any chance at a managerial or professional position.

Public Accommodations

Complete racial segregation in such areas as transportation, hospitals, cemeteries, restaurants, and theaters was long practiced by the private individuals who managed them. The Separate Amenities Act of 1953 made such segregation legally compulsory. After 1978 the government moderated the policy a bit by allowing all people to use the same public transportation, to attend the same religious institutions, to participate in the same sports, and to attend a total of twenty-six integrated theaters. However, most of the essentials of the longstanding policies of racial segregation and white supremacy remained in full force after 1978.

"BANTUSTANS"

In 1959 the Nationalist government enacted the Promotion of Bantu Self-Government Act, which proposed to establish four exclusively native areas, use those areas for the massive relocation of blacks from the Republic itself, and eventually give the areas the power of self-government under South African supervision. In 1963 the government announced that self-government had been granted to Transkei, in 1977 the government made a similar announcement about Bophuthatswana, in 1979 one concerning Venda, and in 1981 one concerning Ciskei. However, no nation other than South Africa recognized any of the four as independent nations. In 1959 the South African government announced that any funds spent on the development of the "Bantustans" would have to come from the blacks themselves. Since there was no possibility that the blacks could ever provide from their own resources anything remotely approaching what was needed for true development and independence, all four areas remained parts of South Africa, and apartheid continued to mean governmentally enforced racial segregation and white supremacy rather than the complete separation of the races.

THE PASSING OF APARTHEID

Some South African liberal whites opposed apartheid all along, but until 1989 they were a small and powerless minority. The main internal opposition came from the disfranchised blacks, who formed several organizations dedicated to the abolition of apartheid and the creation of a democratic government based on universal suffrage and rule by the black majority. The most prominent was (and remains) the African National Congress (ANC), headed by Nelson Mandela. Despite the fact that for decades the ANC was illegal and forced to operate underground, it instigated demonstrations, strikes, and appeals to foreign nations to impose sanctions to force the white government in Pretoria to end apartheid. The ANC sometimes clashed with Inkatha, a Zulu organization headed by Chief Mangosutha Gatsha Buthelezi, which was willing to accept a slower pace for reform (and which was shown to have been secretly financed by the South African government).

For decades most of the rest of the world treated South Africa as an outlaw nation. The United Nations suspended South Africa's membership in 1974 and subsequently adopted a series of resolutions calling on member nations to impose diplomatic pressure and economic sanctions until South Africa abolished apartheid. The United States and the United Kingdom were slower than most other nations to comply, but in 1986 both countries joined the sanctions movement.

Real change began in 1989. Frederik Willem de Klerk became president of South Africa, and, to the great surprise of many, announced that he would work to end apartheid. In 1990, de Klerk released Nelson Mandela from the prison where he had been confined since 1963 and persuaded parliament to legalize the ANC and other anti-apartheid organizations. De Klerk stated that the time had come to repeal all apartheid legislation, and the parliament began the process by repealing the Population Registration Act, the Group Areas Act, and all laws requiring racial segregation in public accommodations.

Soon after de Klerk launched his initiatives a number of militant Afrikaners declared that since de Klerk had not disclosed his plans to end apartheid in his 1989 election campaign he had no legal or popular mandate to pursue them. After a pro-apartheid candidate won a parliamentary by-election in early 1992, de Klerk de-

SOUTH AFRICAN LEADERS AGAINST APARTHEID. The former president of South Africa, F.W. de Klerk, and his successor, President Nelson Mandela.

cided that he needed an indisputable mandate to continue the negotiations. He called a referendum on the question, "Do you support continuation of the reform process which the State President began on February 2, 1990, and which is aimed at a new constitution through negotiation?" He also announced that he would resign if a majority voted no.

Under the existing constitution, only whites could vote in the referendum, which led some observers to predict that de Klerk's opponents and apartheid would win. They were wrong. Eighty-five percent of the eligible voters voted in the referendum, and 1,924,186 (69 percent) voted yes, while 875,619 (31 percent) voted no.

After the referendum, the de Klerk government and the Mandela-led ANC agreed to hold a multiracial convention to draw up a new constitution. But several difficult problems remained: for example, the dispute between the ANC and Inkatha about who spoke for which blacks, and the dispute between the ANC and the de Klerk government about whether the new constitution should provide for unlimited black-majority rule or should have special protections for the white minority.

In recognition of the progress thus far, the United Nations General Assembly, in December 1991, unanimously adopted a resolution calling on all nations to start restoring cultural, scientific, and academic ties with South Africa. In 1993 Mandela and de Klerk shared the Nobel Peace Prize for their efforts.

In 1992, representatives of seventeen political parties, including the ANC, Inkatha, and de Klerk's ruling National party, convened a Convention for a Democratic South Africa in Johannesburg to draw up amendments to the constitution that would establish universal suffrage and a new multiracial government.

In early 1993 the convention agreed on procedures for holding an all-races election in 1994 to choose a new parliament that would write a new constitution to come in effect in 1999. The election was held in April 1994 with an electorate composed as never before: 74 percent blacks, 14 percent whites, 9 percent colored, and 3 percent (East) Indians.[10]

The ANC won a sweeping victory, with 63 percent of the popular votes and 252 seats; de Klerk's National party finished a distant second with 14 percent of the votes and 82 seats; Inkhatha won 10.5 percent of the votes and 43 seats.

The new parliament met and chose Mandela as the new president. Many whites feared that Mandela and the ANC would use their new power to take revenge for the long reign of apartheid by shutting whites out of power altogether and seizing white property to distribute among blacks. It did not happen. Beginning with his inaugural address, President Mandela rejected racial revenge and proclaimed a policy of fair treatment and reconciliation of all of the nation's races. As part of implementing his policy, Mandela honored his campaign pledge to have a multiracial cabinet and appointed de Klerk to the cabinet as second deputy president. Many economic and social problems remained to be solved, but *apartheid*— and the spectre of racial civil war—were gone.

THE END OF APARTHEID. Black and white South Africans celebrate Nelson Mandela's election as president, 1994.

For Further Reading ———————————————————————

POLICE POWERS AND DEFENDANTS' RIGHTS

ABRAHAM, HENRY, and BARBARA PERRY. *Freedom and the Court*, 6th ed. New York: Oxford University Press, 1994. Updated edition of a survey of Supreme Court's interpretations of the U.S. Constitution's Bill of Rights.

*LEWIS, ANTHONY. *Gideon's Trumpet*. New York: Random House, 1964. Dramatic account of a famous Supreme Court decision on defendants' right to counsel.

PRITCHETT, C. HERMAN. *Constitutional Civil Liberties*. Englewood Cliffs, NJ: Prentice Hall, 1984. Authorita-

tive account of current civil liberties issues, with emphasis on Supreme Court interpretations.

*WILSON, JAMES Q. *Varieties of Police Behavior*. New York: Atheneum, 1970. Study of police behavior in selected communities.

*———. *Thinking about Crime*, rev. ed. New York: Basic Books, 1982. Thoughtful analysis of causes, detection, and punishment of crime in a free society.

THE STATUS OF WOMEN

*AARON, HENRY J., and CAMERON LOUGY. *The Comparative Worth Controversy*. Washington, DC: The Brookings Institution, 1986. Analysis of what has become one of the leading issues in the conflict over women's rights.

CONOVER, PAMELA JOHNSTON, and VIRGINIA GRAY. *Feminism and the New Right: Conflict over the American Family*. New York: Praeger, 1983. Account of conflict over ERA and the abortion issue.

EVANS, SARAH F., and BARBARA J. NELSON. *Wage Justice: Comparable Worth and the Paradox of Technocratic Reform*. Chicago, IL: University of Chicago Press, 1989. A favorable discussion of the premises and implementation of the policy of comparable worth, with special attention to its application in Minnesota.

*FRIEDAN, BETTY. *The Feminine Mystique*. New York: W. W. Norton, 1968. The book that, more than any other, helped to launch the contemporary women's rights movement.

GELB, JOYCE. *Feminism and Politics: A Comparative Perspective*. Berkeley, CA: University of California Press, 1989. A study of types of feminist theories and

forms of political action in Great Britain, Sweden, and the United States.

KIRKPATRICK, JEANE J. *Political Woman*. New York: Basic Books, 1974. Instructive study of prominent women state legislators as examples of women who, like its author, have been successful in politics.

KLEIN, ETHEL. *Gender Politics*. Cambridge, MA: Harvard University Press, 1984. Account of the rise and impact of feminist political movements from the late 1960s to the 1980s.

LOVENDUSKI, JONI. *Women in European Politics*. Amherst, MA: University of Massachusetts Press, 1987. Survey of the role of women and women's political movements in Western European nations.

MANSBRIDGE, JANE J. *Why We Lost the ERA*. Chicago, IL: University of Chicago Press, 1986. Account of the politics of the women's movement in the context of the struggle over the ERA.

NELSON, BARBARA J., and NAJMA CHOWDHURY. *Women and Politics Worldwide*. New Haven, CT: Yale University Press, 1993. Comparative study of the role of women in politics in forty-three nations.

THE STATUS OF AFRICAN-AMERICANS

BURSTEIN, PAUL. *Discrimination, Jobs, and Politics*. Chicago, IL: University of Chicago Press, 1985. Study of efforts to mandate equal employment opportunities for African-Americans since 1945.

GOLDMAN, ALAN H. *Justice and Reverse Discrimination*. Princeton, NJ: Princeton University Press, 1979. Scholarly argument against affirmative action programs.

GRAHAM, HUGH DAVIS. *The Civil Rights Era: Origins and Development of National Policy, 1960–72*. New York: Oxford University Press, 1990. Description of the

civil rights movement when the main goal was nondiscrimination rather than affirmative action.

GREENE, KATHANNE. *Affirmative Action and Principles of Justice*. New York: Greenwood, 1989. A careful review of the legal, ethical, and political issues involved in the controversy over affirmative action, ultimately making the case for it.

*HOCHSCHILD, JENNIFER L. *The New American Dilemma: Liberal Democracy and School Desegregation*. New Haven, CT: Yale University Press, 1984. Analysis of current state of racial desegregation and integration of schools, with discussion of busing and other methods and their impact on the quality of education.

KING, RICHARD H. *Civil Rights and the Idea of Freedom*. New York: Oxford University Press, 1992. An account of the dominant ideas and organizations in the U.S. civil rights movement of the 1960s.

KIRP, DAVID L. *Just Schools: The Idea of Racial Equality in American Education*. Berkeley, CA: University of California Press, 1982. Study of problems and conflicts in school desegregation and integration.

O'NEIL, ROBERT M. *Discrimination Against Discrimination*. Bloomington, IN: Indiana University Press, 1975. Scholarly defense of affirmative action.

*SINDLER, ALLAN P. *Bakke, DeFunis, and Minority Admissions: The Quest for Equal Opportunity*. New York: Longman, 1978. Thoughtful analysis of the issues involved in affirmative action programs for admission to graduate and professional schools.

WALTERS, RONALD W. *Black Presidential Politics in America: A Strategic Approach*. Albany, NY: State University of New York Press, 1988. Analysis of how African-Americans can use presidential politics to improve their positions in government and society.

Notes

1. *Black's Law Dictionary*, rev. 4th ed. (St. Paul, MN: West, 1968), p. 445.

2. *APSA Survey of Departments 1992–93* (Washington, DC: American Political Science Association, 1993), pp. 2, 7.

3. Alan Riding, "Frenchwomen Say It's Time to Be 'a Bit Utopian,'" *The New York Times*, December 31, 1993, p. A5.

4. *The American Almanac, 1993–1994* (Washington, DC: Bureau of the Census, 1994), Table 451, p. 281.

5. *Public Opinion*, September–October 1986, pp. 34–35.

6. Stokely Carmichael and Charles V. Hamilton, *Black Power: The Politics of Liberation in America* (New York: Vintage Books, 1967), p. 37. Copyright Random House Inc.

7. *The New York Times*, December 21, 1988. However, in 1991 a poll sponsored by the Joint Center for Political and Economic Studies asked a national sample of black Americans what they preferred to be called; the answers of those polled: black, 72 percent; African-American, 15 percent; Afro-American, 3 percent; Negro, 2 percent; no opinion, 8 percent (*The New York Times*, January 29, 1991).

8. In 1991, Clarence Thomas became the second.

9. Jesse Jackson, "Reparations Are Justified for Blacks," *Regulation*, September–October 1978, pp. 17–28. Copyright American Enterprise Institute.

10. *Facts on File*, May 12, 1994, p. 337.

17

Politics Among Nations

After World War I the German novelist Erich Maria Remarque wrote a scene in his war novel *All Quiet on the Western Front* that must strike a responsive chord in anyone who has ever crouched in a slit trench, peered out of a bomber at bursting flak, or huddled in a bomb shelter during a raid, and in all who think that one day they may have to do so. In this scene a group of German soldiers are in a rest area behind the lines, and the following conversation takes place after one of them, Tjaden, has asked what causes wars. His comrade, Albert Kropp, replies:

> "Mostly by one country badly offending another," . . .
>
> Then Tjaden pretends to be obtuse. "A country? I don't follow. A mountain in Germany cannot offend a mountain in France. Or a river, or a wood, or a field of wheat."
>
> "Are you really as stupid as that, or are you just pulling my leg?" growls Kropp. "I don't mean that at all. One people offends the other—"
>
> "Then I haven't any business here at all," replies Tjaden. "I don't feel myself offended."
>
> "Ach, man! he means the people as a whole, the State —" exclaims Muller.
>
> "State, State—" Tjaden snaps his fingers contemptuously. "Gendarmes, police, taxes, that's your State;—if that's what you are talking about, no thank you."
>
> "That's right," says Kat, "you've said something for once, Tjaden. State and home-country, there's a big difference."
>
> "But they go together," insists Kropp, "without the State there wouldn't be any home-country."
>
> "True, but just you consider, almost all of us are simple folk. And in France, too, the majority of men are labourers, workmen, or poor clerks. Now just why would a French blacksmith or a French shoemaker want to attack us? No, it is merely the rulers. I had never seen a Frenchman before I came here, and it will be just the same with the majority of Frenchmen as regards us. They weren't asked about it any more than we were."

One of the soldiers then proposes a solution that would surely be endorsed by a great many GIs, Tommies, *poilus*, and Ivans:

> Kropp on the other hand is a thinker. He proposes that a declaration of war should be a kind of popular festival with entrance-tickets and bands, like a bull fight. Then in the arena the ministers and generals of the two countries, dressed in bathing-drawers and

armed with clubs, can have it out among themselves. Whoever survives, his country wins. That would be much simpler and more just than this arrangement, where the wrong people do the fighting.[1]

The questions these fictional soldiers—and so many real soldiers and their sweethearts, parents, and friends—have asked are among the most difficult and urgent facing anyone concerned with the impact of politics on modern life: What causes wars? How can wars be prevented? One way to start answering those questions is to understand how international politics is conducted in the modern world.

Nature of International Politics

STATE SYSTEM

The first thing to understand is that in the 1990s, as for centuries past, politics among nations is conducted within a basic framework that political scientists call the **state system**, which is *the division of the world' population into nations, each of which has complete legal authority within its particular territory and none of which recognizes a government legally superior to its own.*

In Chapter 2 we considered the legal characteristics and popular mind sets that make different parts of the world's population form, maintain, and be recognized as separate sovereign nations and noted that nations are the main players in international politics. Despite the fact that politics within nations differs in many ways from politics between nations, what we have learned about domestic politics can tell us a lot about international politics. Hence we begin by noting the principal similarities and differences between them.

SIMILARITIES TO DOMESTIC POLITICS

International politics resembles domestic politics in several respects. First, international politics consists of conflict among people, acting mainly in groups, whose values and interests differ and are to some extent incompatible. If some values are satisfied then other values must go unsatisfied, and it is impossible to satisfy *all* groups equally.

Second, each group to some extent and in some manner *acts* to achieve its values as fully as possible, which inevitably brings each group into conflict with other groups taking different actions. In international politics as in domestic politics, *conflict* among individuals and groups is thus not an unfortunate but avoidable aberration from what is normal; it is the very essence of politics and human life itself. International politics no less than domestic politics is a perpetual struggle over "who gets what, when, and how."

Third, international conflict is not much more cumulative than domestic conflict. We observed in Chapter 1 that conflict in domestic politics tends to be noncumulative in the sense that when one issue replaces another in the center of the political stage there is always some reshuffling of the conflicting individuals and groups.

Some pros and cons on issue A remain associated on issue B, but some former allies find themselves on opposite sides, some old partisans are indifferent to the new issue, and some who were indifferent on issue A become partisans on issue B. The hostilities generated by one issue are thus not fully reinforced on each new issue but are to some extent redirected and moderated by the succession of new issues.

International conflict is also relatively noncumulative, for the shuffling and reshuffling of allies and enemies is as frequent as it is in domestic politics. From 1941 to 1945, for example, Great Britain and the United States were allied with the Soviet Union and China in a gigantic war against Germany and Japan. From 1945 to the late 1980s, Great Britain and the United States relied heavily in the support of their former enemies, West Germany and Japan, in their "cold war" with their former allies, the Soviet Union and China. From 1949 to the late 1950s the Soviet Union and the People's Republic of China (PRC) stood shoulder to shoulder in a worldwide struggle against the Western powers. Then the two communist giants had their own cold war with each other, and the relations of both with the United States and other nations have warmed (considerably with the republics of the former Soviet Union and less so with the PRC).

Some onlookers may regard this kind of shifting about as evidence of the mendacity and hypocrisy of the great powers, but others may find it merely an indication that politics is politics whatever the arena. In fact, unless we long for an Armageddon in which the good nations wipe out the bad ones once and for all, perhaps we should view this international reshuffling as fortunate.

Finally, in both international and domestic politics competing groups sometimes use violence to achieve their goals. The horrors of international war sometimes make us forget that more people have been killed in civil wars than in international wars.[2] Americans should know this very well, because more Americans were killed in the Civil War (1861–1865) than in nearly all U.S. international wars put together, including the undeclared wars in Korea in the 1950s, Vietnam in the 1960s, and the Persian Gulf in the 1990s. Yet domestic violence is very different from international war. Internal political conflict is often nasty, expensive, and sometimes violent; but unlike international conflict, there is no possibility that domestic violence will escalate into full-scale thermonuclear war and the extermination of large parts of the human race. Domestic conflicts such as those between the pro-life and pro-choice factions in the United States or the Catholics and Protestants in Northern Ireland, bitter and sometimes violent though they may be, are not likely to be settled by one side dropping hydrogen bombs on the other. However, no one can predict with confidence that the disagreements between, say, Israel and the Arab nations or India and Pakistan, will not be settled that way. The differences between international and domestic politics, therefore, are at least as significant as the similarities.

DIFFERENCES FROM DOMESTIC POLITICS

International politics differs from domestic politics mainly in the nature of competing groups and the legal, social, and political framework in which the competition is fought out.

FRIENDS OR ENEMIES?

In international politics as in domestic politics, yesterday's allies can become today's enemies, and vice versa. One of the most dramatic examples is the changing attitudes of Americans toward the former Soviet Union: In 1983, 1987, and 1991 a national sample of Americans were asked, "Do you feel that the Soviet Union is a close ally of the United States, is friendly but not an ally, is not friendly but not an enemy, or is unfriendly and an enemy of the United States?" Those polled replied as follows.

	1983	1987	1991
Close ally	1%	2%	14%
Friendly	4	11	49
Not friendly, not enemy	30	37	27
Enemy	63	39	7
Not ascertained	2	11	3
	100%	100%	100%

Source: World Opinion Update, 15 (March 1991), 27.

Little Overlapping Membership

The main contestants in domestic politics are individuals and interest groups. The main contestants in international politics are nations. Nations differ from the domestic political interest groups we have discussed in previous chapters mainly in that there is far less overlapping membership among nations. Within any nation, as we noted in Chapter 1, each person is a member, formal or informal, of many different groups. Among nations, however, the situation is different. Although a few people have dual citizenship (two or more nations claim them as citizens) and a few others are stateless (no nation recognizes them as citizens), nearly every one of the world's 5.5 billion inhabitants (as of 1991) is legally a citizen of one nation only. Moreover, very few people think of themselves as equally Americans and Russians or Israelis and Egyptians, or, for that matter, as "citizens of the world."

Absence of a Government

In domestic politics, as we have seen many times, political interest groups try to achieve their ends solely or mainly by inducing their nation's government to make and enforce policies the groups favor. Every government makes authoritative and binding rules, and domestic politics is a contest among the nation's groups to shape those rules.

There is, however, no world government with the power to make and enforce policies binding upon all peoples and all nations. (We will see in detail in Chapter 18 how the United Nations falls short of being a world government.) Each nation therefore seeks to achieve its goals by inducing other nations, both allies and antagonists, to act as it wishes. A nation's power is thus measured by its success in this effort and not by its success in influencing the policy decisions of a nonexistent world government.

Accordingly, international politics is like domestic politics in that the essence of both is conflict among human groups to determine who gets what, when, and how. International politics differs from domestic politics mainly in that its contestants are nations with little or no overlapping membership and in the lack of a government with effective authority over all nations. Those differences arise from the fact that international politics is conducted within the state system and not within some system of world government.

The fact is that the international political system constitutes the nearest thing the world knows to true anarchy (a political system in which there is no government with the legal right or physical power to force people to do what they do not wish to do). Some political theorists argue that anarchy is the ideal form of political organization. Under anarchy, they say, people would participate in cooperative activities only by the free and independent consent of each and never by orders from a popular majority or a ruling class or a monarch. We noted in Chapter 2 that no human society has ever deliberately adopted anarchy as its organizing principle, although governments have from time to time broken down and lost their power to make authoritative rules (witness the disintegration of the former Soviet Union in 1991) albeit usually only for brief periods of time.

Yet the state system, in both legal principle and political reality, comes close to being true anarchy. Its basic legal principle is "the sovereign equality of nations," which means that every nation has the legal right to make and enforce laws without interference from outside. That in turn, means that no international law that a nation has not accepted voluntarily is binding upon it. Nations may and sometimes do cooperate with other nations, but they do so because their policy makers think it is in the nations' interest and not because of some moral commitment to cooperation for its own sake.

There is no world legislature to make laws binding upon all nations, no world executive and police force to make sure that world laws are obeyed, and no world judiciary to adjudicate violations of the law and punish the violators. The United Nations General Assembly is, to be sure, a pseudo-legislature, the United Nations Security Council is a pseudo-executive, and the International Court of Justice is a pseudo-supreme court. But none of those institutions has any real power beyond what the individual member nations allow at any given time.

The state system, in short, means that international politics is conducted within a framework that approaches both legal and political anarchy. That is the basic fact shaping the nature of international conflict.

Characteristics of International Conflict

For many years after 1945 a good number of Americans thought that the only international conflict that mattered was the cold war between the constitutional democracies led by the United States and the communist nations led by the Soviet Union. However, as we were sometimes pained to learn, many other nations rarely saw things that way. India and Pakistan, for example, were much more concerned with the status of Bengal and went to war over the independence of Bangladesh.

The Arab nations of the Middle East and Israel had (and continue to have) no doubt that their hot-and-cold war is the crucial contest. Iran and Iraq fought a bloody war from 1981 to 1988. In 1990 the Soviet Union supported the United Nations resolutions, urged by the United States, authorizing the use of military force to make Iraq abandon its conquest of Kuwait.

Today, the cold war is over, as we will detail in Chapter 18. We do not yet know what kind of new world order will succeed the cold war, but it is clear that there is no longer a *single* international conflict dividing the whole world into two great camps. Instead, there are many divisions cutting across one another. The United States is currently involved in no shooting war with any nation, but there are many other international conflicts: Arabs versus Israel, India versus Pakistan, Vietnam versus the People's Republic of China, North Korea versus South Korea, and Serbia versus Croatia, to name a few. Each of those conflicts has its own constellation of issues and contestants, and each is in some respects different from all other international conflicts. Yet most political scientists believe that all past and present international conflicts under the state system are alike to some degree. Hence, identifying what those conflicts have in common will help us to understand what is involved in any particular conflict, including those in which the United States is most involved.

NEW NATIONS, NEW ALLIANCES. The "Unified team," composed of athletes from five former Soviet republics, enters the 1992 Winter Olympic Games.

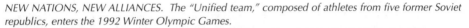

In this section, accordingly, we will examine what political scientists generally believe to be the enduring characteristics of all international conflict under the state system.

SOME GOALS OF NATIONS' FOREIGN POLICIES

Every nation's foreign policy stems from its policy makers' answers to these questions: What should be our national goals? Since some are bound to be incompatible with others, which goals are the most important? What are our *vital* interests? Of what kinds of international actions are we capable? Which are best calculated to achieve our most important national goals?

National foreign policies thus originate in national goals. Although those goals vary considerably from one nation to another, the most common goals can be classified under five headings: security, markets and prosperity, territorial expansion, defending and spreading ideology, and peace.

Security

The first goal of every nation—the one to which all other goals are usually sacrificed if necessary—is security. Security has two main aspects. The first is the preservation of the nation's legal right and practical power to rule its own affairs. The second is the creation and maintenance of a state of affairs in which the nation can be relatively free of fear for its survival and independence. There is no such thing as absolute security or complete freedom from fear, of course. Consequently, each nation strives for the degree of security its leaders think can reasonably be attained. Even this minimum level of security is by no means the nation's only goal, however, and sometimes conflicts with some other goals.

Markets and Prosperity

Every nation wishes to maintain and improve its citizens' standard of living. In foreign policy this goal affects a wide variety of matters, including tariffs and trade agreements, currency exchange rates, giving or receiving economic aid, and so on. One illustration known only too well by most Americans is our continuing (and increasingly urgent) efforts to improve our international balance of payments; that is, to get other nations, especially Japan, to buy as many or more of U.S. products as the United States buys of theirs.

Some Marxist analysts (see Chapter 4) declare that aggression, imperialism, and war are entirely the products of capitalism and thus can be eliminated only by overthrowing capitalism and establishing socialism the world over. Capitalism, according to them, produces surplus capital and goods. Domestic markets cannot absorb the surpluses, and so the capitalists direct the government (which, of course, they "own") to plunge into imperialist ventures for the purpose of gaining control of new markets. Those ventures involve nations in wars with natives of the areas to be conquered and with other capitalist-imperialist nations trying to conquer the same areas for the same reasons. For instance, the United States is thus said to have precipitated World War II, the Korean War in the 1950s, the Vietnam War in the 1960s, and the Gulf War in 1991 to protect old markets and to gain new ones; and Israel, for another instance, is said to have invaded Egypt in 1956 and 1967 for the same reason; and so on.

This analysis is appealing in its simplicity and its clear identification of heroes and villains, but most political scientists believe that it has little scientific validity. Among other deficiencies, it does not explain aggressive behavior by socialist nations, of which there has been plenty: for example, the former Soviet Union's conquest and annexation of Estonia, Latvia, and Lithuania in the 1930s and its invasion of Hungary in 1956, Czechoslovakia in 1968, and Afghanistan in 1979; the invasion of Communist Vietnam by the Communist People's Republic of China in 1976; the invasion of Communist Kampuchea by Communist Vietnam in 1978. Since some socialist nations war with other socialist nations, evidently the capitalist drive for markets is not the *only* force that drives nations to make war. Most political scientists therefore continue to believe that expanding markets and promoting economic prosperity are only two of several goals of foreign policy.

Territorial Expansion

Few diplomats brazenly proclaim that their nations want more territory, but just about every nation has at one time or another tried to get more. Nations have followed expansionist—or, as they are sometimes called, imperialist—policies for various reasons: to obtain economic advantages expected from controlling new resources and opening up new markets; to provide more living space for their people; and to realize their "manifest destiny" to rule (which characterized U.S. westward expansion in the nineteenth century).

Defending and Spreading Ideology

Political scientists have long argued about the proper role of political and economic interests on the one hand and moral ideals on the other in the formation of foreign policy. Some analysts, such as Hans J. Morgenthau and George F. Kennan, have contended that the real goal of any nation's foreign policy is to defend and promote its national interest, conceived mainly as its most advantageous power position for preserving and improving its political, military, and economic security and well-being. All the palaver about political ideals and moral values, they say, is at most a way of disguising and promoting the nation's underlying *real* interests. However, if the policy makers forget the true nature and purpose of such talk and begin to take the talk seriously, their naiveté may plunge the nation into serious trouble. The opposing position, advanced by such scholars as Frank Tannenbaum and Malcolm Moos, holds that one of the main purposes of a democratic nation's foreign policy is—or should be—to promote such moral values as freedom, democracy, and human rights for all people everywhere. Otherwise, they say, foreign policy and international politics become merely a global chess game, hideous because it is played with human lives and meaningless because it lacks any higher purpose.

EUROPEAN COMMUNITY

Nations, like interest groups in domestic politics, often pursue their goals by forming associations with other nations for certain specified purposes, providing for voluntary cooperation by the associating nations, which nevertheless remain independent and sovereign. The oldest and most common form of international associations are *alliances*, which are agreements of two or more nations to further their common interests (usually, but not always, by adopting a common military strategy and perhaps even a unified command). Alliances can be long term, like the North Atlantic Treaty Organization (NATO), established in 1948 and still in operation; or they can be short term, like the twenty-nine-nation coalition whose forces, under the command of General H. Norman Schwarzkopf, drove Iraq out of Kuwait in 1990–1991.

Another form of international association is a *customs union*, an agreement of two or more nations agreeing to reduce tariffs, limit production subsidies, and take other actions calculated to increase trade between and prosperity within the associating nations.

By far the largest and most successful customs union in history is the European Community (EC). After some preliminary agreements on the production and sale of coal and steel, the EC began in 1957 when six nations (Belgium, France, Germany, Italy, Luxembourg, and the Netherlands) signed the Treaty of Rome (the EC has since been joined by six additional nations—Denmark, Greece, Ireland, Portugal, Spain, and the United Kingdom). The treaty's first goal was to create a "common market," in which the member nations could trade goods and exchange workers unfettered by traditional national trade barriers. A Council of Ministers was established that meets periodically to pass on proposals for changing EC rules and regulations. The European Commission, an international body of civil servants based in Brussels, was established that enforces the regulations and proposes new ones to the Council.

Potentially most important of all, a European Parliament was established and meets in the French city of Strasbourg. Its 518 seats are allocated among the twelve nations according to their population and economic strength (France, Germany, Italy, and the United Kingdom each has eighty-one seats, while the others have from six to sixty seats). Since 1979, the members have been directly elected for five-year terms by the voters in their respective nations (the most recent election was held in 1989). The members of the European Parliament group themselves not by nations but in nine distinct parliamentary parties that more or less correspond to the partisan divisions in the member countries (the largest parties are the Socialists and Christian Democrats). There is also a European Court of Justice, based in Luxembourg, that adjudicates disputes between the Commission and member states.

Many associated with the EC have worked to change it from a customs union to a "United States of Europe," a true federal government with a common set of social and economic laws, a common judicial system, a common foreign policy, and a common defense force. Others, particularly in Denmark and the United Kingdom, have resisted the surrender of that much national sovereignty. However, in 1991 the European "federalists" scored a major triumph over the "anti-federalists" when the member nations' leaders met in Maastricht, the Netherlands, and agreed that by 1999 a common European currency (the "ecu") administered by a central EC bank would replace all national currencies. They also agreed that the EC would immediately establish mechanisms to work for a common foreign policy and a common defense force.

To soothe British fears, the other member nations allowed the UK to opt out of the new agreements. In 1992 voters in a Danish referendum voted not to ratify the Maastricht accord, but another Danish referendum in 1993 approved ratification. Many observers believe that by the early twenty-first century there will be a true United States of Europe. If and when that happens, the European Community will have a population and an economy greater than that of either the United States or Japan, and the whole structure of international politics will be profoundly altered.

In my opinion this debate is about a false issue, that of ideology *versus* other national interests, as though the two were incompatible and one had to be totally sacrificed to the other. There is every reason to believe that *both* ideology *and* other national interests are goals of every nation's foreign policy. We have already noted some of the other goals. Let us examine ideology for a moment.

Most Americans wish to preserve the independence and security of the United States and to defend and promote its national interests. However, let us ask ourselves *why* is preserving the United States important enough to justify risking thermonuclear war. Some people will reply, "It isn't!" Many more will insist that it is necessary to guarantee the independence and preserve the U.S. way of life. That way of life includes not only a high standard of physical wealth and comfort but also some cherished ideals, such as freedom of speech and religion, democracy, and due process of law.

The same is true of other peoples in other nations. After 1933, for example, many Germans left Germany because they could not bear to live under the totalitarian regime of Adolf Hitler. Many of them later fought with the Allies in the 1939–1945 war against Germany. To many Germans, therefore, the Germany of Hitler was not worth preserving. How many of us would feel the same about the United States if it came to be ruled by a fascist or communist dictator?

Such attitudes among ordinary people—who, let us remember, make up the nation—help to account for some, though by no means all, of the foreign policies pursued by nations. In 1939, for example, a strong argument could have been made that the clash of U.S. and British interests in the Western Hemisphere made Great Britain more dangerous to the United States than Germany was. Yet, the United States lined up with and ultimately fought beside Great Britain against Germany. Why? Surely, one powerful reason was that the British, like the Americans, were committed to democratic ideals and were therefore defending values that Americans also held dear, whereas aggressively Fascist Germany was seeking to destroy those ideals.

I am not arguing here that a democratic nation does or should always support all other democratic nations and oppose all dictatorial regimes in all circumstances. After all, from 1941 to 1945 the United States and Great Britain gladly allied with the Soviet Union against their common enemy, Germany. Later, both nations also accepted help from authoritarian regimes of both Left (the PRC) and Right (Pakistan), in the cold war with the Soviet Union; and both nations allied with such authoritarian regimes as Saudi Arabia and Syria in the Gulf War of 1990–1991 against the authoritarian regime of Iraq. Furthermore, the United States did little to help democratic rebellions in Hungary in 1956, Czechoslovakia in 1968, or Poland in the 1980s. In the latter instances the United States held off because three presidents, one moderate Democrat (Carter) and two conservative Republicans (Nixon and Reagan), thought that no U.S. interest involved was vital enough to risk World War III.

The point is that defending and spreading its ideology constitute *one* of the goals of every nation, including the United States. Like every goal of foreign policy, it is sometimes in conflict with other goals and must compete with those goals for priority in the process of making foreign policy. To overlook or slight the significance of ideology as a factor in foreign policy and international politics is therefore just as unrealistic as to give ideology the leading role.

Peace

Judging by public opinion polls and by what national leaders say, almost all nations and almost all peoples of the world cherish peace, regard war as the greatest of evils, and condemn those who cause wars as the worst of villains. The Charter of the United Nations declares that the organization's first purpose is "to maintain international peace and security," requires its members to "settle their international disputes by peaceful means," and opens membership to "all other peace-loving states." In most international conflicts all sides strive constantly to portray themselves—and perhaps even think of themselves—as the true lovers and defenders of peace and their enemies as aggressors and warmongers.

Ordinary people feel the same. If we take a poll among our friends on the question, "Do you want America to go to war with Iraq again to get rid of Saddam Hussein once and for all?" only a handful will say yes. A comparable poll taken in Baghdad would undoubtedly produce the same results. So just about every person and every nation sincerely wants peace.

Thus the accusation, often heard at the United Nations and elsewhere, that this or that nation "wants war" (because it loves war for its own sake?) is nonsense. However, despite this universal love for peace, it is difficult to find a single year in world history in which no wars were fought anywhere. Today even though just about every person and nation in the world abhors the prospect of thermonuclear World War III, most people believe it is possible. So we are faced with this great paradox: Everyone wants peace, and yet wars are more normal than peace and have been for centuries. How can this be?

Perhaps the following line of reasoning provides the answer: Peace is the absence of war, and it takes at least two nations to make a war. If the United States (or Iraq or Israel or any other nation) *really* wants peace, then let it announce to all the world today that under no conditions whatever will it fight and that it is dumping all its weapons into the ocean immediately. This policy is absolutely guaranteed to bring peace, and anyone who *really* wants peace at any price should urge immediate unilateral disarmament on the leaders of all nations, beginning with their own.

However, many would say that that is ridiculous. If the United States unilaterally disarmed, then the communists or whatever world power would simply move in and take over. Others would say that unilateral disarmament would render the United States helpless to support allies and contribute to United Nations peacekeeping forces. Either or both opinions may be true, but does the United States want peace or not? The answer, perhaps, is that the United States does, but not at any price.

The solution to the paradox is that people and nations genuinely want peace, but peace is only one of the things they want. Sometimes the desire for peace conflicts with other things they want, such as winning independence from colonial masters, preserving independence already won, or advancing the cause of social justice or democracy or human rights. When that happens, people and nations must choose which goals they want most and be prepared to sacrifice those that they want less. Such choices are the very essence of making foreign policy.

Making Foreign Policy

CHOOSING GOALS, METHODS, AND CAPABILITIES

Making foreign policy in any nation involves making at least three kinds of choices. First is the choice of goals, deciding what should be the nation's general objectives in international politics and its particular objectives in particular situations. As we have noted, this choice often involves sacrificing or risking some goals in order to pursue other, more cherished goals.

Second, once the goals and their order of priority are set, the next step is to select and put into operation the methods most likely to achieve the goals. We will survey the most commonly used methods later.

Third, capabilities must be assessed. Both of the first two choices must necessarily be influenced by the policy makers' judgment of what the nation can and cannot do relative to the capabilities of the other nations involved. For example, Cuba is a small nation, militarily more powerful than most other nations in the Western Hemisphere but not as powerful as the United States. If Fidel Castro dreamed of dominating the whole hemisphere he would be well advised not to pursue his goal by launching a military attack on the United States. Like any other nation, Cuba can successfully pursue only the goals and employ only the methods within its powers and capabilities. If it ventures beyond them, then it is likely to end up worse off than it began. Even the world's "superpowers," the United States and the former Soviet Union, learned—for example, in Vietnam and Afghanistan—that being "global police" was beyond their capabilities.

We should not, however, picture the making of any nation's foreign policy as a process in which steel-nerved and far-seeing diplomats coolly survey an infinite range of possibilities and unerringly choose those best calculated to promote the national interest. Many people who have actually engaged in making foreign policy have testified that the decisions are made by all-too-fallible human beings subject to a variety of pressures from other government agencies, pressure groups, public opinion, and the mass communications media. In a democracy foreign policy can never be made in complete isolation from the demands of domestic policy. Moreover, the makers of foreign policy are subject to internal doubts and hesitations, for they are hemmed in by real-life circumstances in which the possibilities do not seem nearly as numerous as they may appear to critics in college seminars and opposition parties. The policy makers have to make the best choices possible within limits imposed by their individual abilities and the circumstances in which they find themselves. The eminent British diplomat and historian Sir Harold Nicolson, who knew firsthand what it is like to make foreign policy, has given us something of the feel in this illuminating passage:

Nobody who has not watched "policy" expressing itself in day-to-day action can realize how seldom is the course of events determined by deliberately planned purpose, or how often what in retrospect appears to have been a fully conscious intention was at the same time governed and directed by that most potent of all factors—"the chain of circumstance." Few indeed are the occasions on which any statesman sees his objective clearly before him and marches towards it with undeviating stride; numerous indeed are the occasions when a decision or an event, which at one time seemed wholly unimportant, leads almost fortuitously to another decision which is no less incidental, until, link by link, the chain of circumstance is forged.[3]

AGENCIES AND OFFICIALS

In almost every modern nation the government agencies most directly and exclusively concerned with making and conducting foreign policy are directed by the head of government, although in none of the democracies does the executive have a total monopoly over foreign policy (see Chapter 12). The principal agency working under his or her direction is a department specializing in foreign affairs, called variously the Department of State (United States), the Foreign Office (Great Britain), the Ministry of Foreign Affairs (France, Germany, and Japan), and so on. The head of this department—the secretary of state or the foreign minister—is generally regarded as the number-two person in the executive and often succeeds to the top position.

The top career civil servants under the foreign minister's direction are generally known as the foreign service, which in most nations was one of the first administrative agencies to be put under the merit system (see Chapter 13). Foreign service officers perform one of two types of activities: consular and diplomatic. The consular activities are the older but today the less important. Consuls in various foreign cities concentrate mainly on reporting economic information about their host countries and promoting the sale of the home country's products. They also perform some services for the home country's citizens traveling abroad.

Diplomatic officials, whether stationed in the foreign-affairs office at home or in the nation's various embassies abroad (most nations rotate their foreign service officers from home duty to foreign duty and back to home duty), have four main functions:

1. *Communications and negotiations*: Transmission and reception of all official communications with foreign nations and negotiations of international treaties and agreements.

2. *Intelligence*: The study of current and probable future events in foreign nations likely to affect their foreign policies and reporting conclusions to the home office. In many nations military services also conduct intelligence operations, and in the United States, an additional body, the Central Intelligence Agency, performs this function.

3. *Policy recommendations*: Athough the authority to make foreign-policy decisions belongs to the foreign secretary, the chief executive, and the legislature,

subordinate officers and some employees of the foreign affairs department are expected to make recommendations in their particular areas of concern. For reasons discussed in Chapter 13, thoe recommendations often become policy.

4. *Services*: Issuing passports and visas, assisting citizens who have encountered legal trouble in foreign nations, and so on.

SOME METHODS OF FOREIGN POLICY

Diplomacy and Recognition

Diplomacy is *the conduct of international relations by negotiations among nations' official representatives*. Basic formal relations between any two nations are established through the exchange of official diplomatic missions, which are composed of a top envoy known as an ambassador, minister, or chargé d'affaires, and a number of subordinate aides, secretaries, attachés, and so on. In deciding whether to receive officially some particular foreign diplomatic mission, each nation determines whether it formally "recognizes" the authorities who send the envoys as the foreign nation's legitimate rulers. A nation or a set of rulers whose envoys are not recognized by any other nation is in great trouble, for it cannot conclude formal international treaties or agreements, provide legal protection for its citizens traveling abroad, or engage in any of the legal relations that are basic to being recognized as an established part of the state system.

The decision on whether or not to recognize a particular foreign regime can thus become a major issue in any nation's foreign policy. The basic question is whether to recognize all governments that are in fact in full control of their particular nations or only those governments that pass certain minimum standards of moral and political respectability. Some nations have attempted to answer these questions by extending de jure recognition to governments of which they approve and de facto[4] recognition to those of which they disapprove. The United States, however, has occasionally refused formal recognition to regimes that were in full control. Notable instances include the communist governments of China (from 1949 to 1978), Cuba (since 1961), and Vietnam (since 1975).

Short of going to war, perhaps the most extreme way a nation can show its displeasure with a foreign nation is to sever diplomatic relations by withdrawing its diplomats and ordering the other nation's diplomats to leave, as most Arab nations did to Egypt after the signing of the Egypt-Israel peace treaty in 1979, and as the United States did to Iran after the seizure of the U.S. hostages in 1979. On the other hand, the quick recognition of Israel by the United States in 1948 shortly after Israel had proclaimed itself to be an independent sovereign nation helped considerably in establishing its independence, though the Arab nations (except Egypt and Jordan) have never recognized Israel.

From the beginning of the state system until the outbreak of World War I in 1914, professional diplomats in foreign missions played significant parts in the formation and conduct of foreign policy. Their official titles as ambassadors and min-

PERSONAL DIPLOMACY AT THE SUMMIT.   U.S. President Bill Clinton and Russian President Boris Yeltsin sign a trade agreement, 1994.

isters plenipotentiary (meaning "with full power") were accurate descriptions of their powers, for the long time it took to communicate with officials at home necessarily gave diplomats wide discretion in negotiating and concluding agreements with their host nations. Since World War I, however, professional diplomats have lost much of their power of independent negotiation and agreement and have become mainly cultivators of good will, reporters of developments in their host nations, and advisers to the top policy makers back home. Most important negotiations are conducted by foreign secretaries, special envoys, or even heads of government in "summit" meetings.

Whoever may conduct it, diplomacy can be used for different purposes. First, diplomacy can be used to seek genuine agreements, as in 1987 when the United States and the Soviet Union negotiated an agreement to limit the number of intermediate ballistic missiles in Europe (after the breakup of the Soviet Union in 1991 similar agreements had to be negotiated with the newly independent republics of Russia, Belarus, Ukraine, and Azerbaijan).

Second, it can be used as a propaganda device to embarrass the nation's antagonists. For example, if nation A has twice as many intercontinental ballistic missiles as nation B and nation A proposes an immediate freeze on the testing, manufacture, and deployment of such weapons, then it puts nation B in an awkward diplomatic position. If nation B accepts the proposal, then that guarantees permanent military superiority for nation A. If nation B rejects the proposal, then nation B is denounced as a "warmonger" intent on "escalating the arms race," while nation A preempts the desirable label of "peace-loving nation."

Finally, diplomacy can be used to play for time while awaiting improvement in the military situation. An example is the lengthy peace talks between the Chinese Communists and United Nations representatives in Korea in 1952 and 1953, in which the Chinese threw up one negotiating roadblock after another for more than a year while continuing intermittent military offensives. Only when the Chinese became convinced that their military situation would not markedly improve did they begin to negotiate seriously; and once they did, a truce was concluded in a mere two months.

Trade Policies and Foreign Aid

Most nations use trade restrictions such as tariffs, import quotas and licenses, export controls, regulation of rates and conditions of international currency exchange, and even barter to control their economic relations with other nations. Many have also entered into agreements, such as the U.S. reciprocal trade agreements and the European Community, to give one another preferential treatment under such controls. The most inclusive of such agreements is the General Agreement on Tariffs and Trade (GATT). Founded in 1948, in 1994 GATT had 123 nations as members, and 29 more accepted its rules.

In 1994 most of GATT's member nations signed a revised treaty establishing a new World Trade Organization (WTO) to monitor international trade and resolve disputes over tariffs and import quotas. The treaty was ratified by 104 of the members, but several major trading powers (notably Australia, India, Japan, South Korea, and the United States) delayed ratification because of strong opposition from several of their most powerful pressure groups.

In all the delaying nations some prominent political leaders argued that the new organization would abridge their nations' sovereignty to make their own trade policies. U.S. environmentalist groups feared that the proposed organization would favor economic development over protection of the environment. Some human rights groups were afraid that some nations would use the WTO to protect their profits from labor by children and convicts. And some labor unions argued that the WTO would countenance some nations' anti-union policies and low wages, and thereby disadvantage nations with strong unions and high wages.

On the other hand, American proponents of the new treaty and organization argued that the changes would not infringe on U.S. sovereignty and that it would open new markets for American markets. In the end the proponents won. In December 1994 the treaty was ratified by both houses of Congress, and the WTO began operations in 1995. Thus, over 90 percent of the world's international trade is now conducted according to GATT and WTO rules on such matters as import and export quotas, customs regulations, and, above all, tariff rates on imported goods.

For a long time the main purpose of trade policies was to promote the economic prosperity of the nation pursuing them, but since World War I increasing numbers of nations have used trade policies for political purposes as well. For instance, trade policies have been used to promote the economic health of friendly

RELIABLE ALLIES?

In 1994 a Gallup poll asked random samples of adults in four Western nations this question: "I'd like you to rate some countries in terms of how reliable an ally each one would be to [respondent's country] in case of a serious crisis today. First, how would you rate [one of the five foreign countries] as an ally—very reliable, somewhat reliable, not very reliable, or not at all reliable?"

NATION RATED	RESPONDENTS FROM			
	France	Germany	Great Britain	United States
FRANCE				
Very reliable	—	15%	12%	19%
Somewhat reliable	—	53	42	52
Not very reliable	—	21	27	17
Not reliable at all	—	4	13	8
No opinion	—	7	6	4
		100%	100%	100%
GERMANY				
Very reliable	16%	—	11%	15%
Somewhat reliable	49	—	46	54
Not very reliable	23	—	25	17
Not reliable at all	10	—	10	9
No opinion	2	—	8	5
	100%		100%	100%
GREAT BRITAIN				
Very reliable	16%	9%	—	54%
Somewhat reliable	49	41	—	33
Not very reliable	24	34	—	5
Not reliable at all	9	8	—	3
No opinion	2	8	—	5
	100%	100%		100%
JAPAN				
Very reliable	3%	7%	6%	9%
Somewhat reliable	18	33	34	45
Not very reliable	42	34	33	27
Not reliable at all	28	12	17	15
No opinion	9	14	10	4
	100%	100%	100%	100%
RUSSIA				
Very reliable	2%	3%	3%	5%
Somewhat reliable	11	17	26	35
Not very reliable	43	43	42	34
Not reliable at all	40	28	19	22
No opinion	4	9	10	4
	100%	100%	100%	100%
UNITED STATES				
Very reliable	22%	27%	49%	—
Somewhat reliable	48	48	39	—
Not very reliable	20	14	6	—

	RESPONDENTS FROM			
Nation Rated	France	Germany	Great Britain	United States
UNITED STATES				
Not reliable at all	8	4	3	—
No opinion	2	7	3	—
	100%	100%	100%	

Source: *The Gallup Poll Monthly*, June 1994, p. 3.

These answers show several interesting patterns: In rating each of the six nations, the U.S. "reliability score" of 78 (average ratings of "very reliable" plus "somewhat reliable" for the five nations rated) was substantially higher than that received by the other nations—67 for Great Britain, 64 for France and Germany, 52 for Japan, and 34 for Russia. American respondents also gave somewhat higher reliability scores than did the respondents in the other three rating nations, averaging 64 percent "very reliable" and "somewhat reliable" to 63 percent for German respondents, 55 percent for British respondents, and 54 percent for French respondents.

American, British, and German respondents regarded Russia as the least reliable ally (an average of 62.7 percent rated Russia as "not very reliable" or "not reliable at all," and only the French respondents regarded Japan as the least reliable.

nations or to damage that of unfriendly nations. In many nations, indeed, the economic and political purposes of trade policies often conflict. For example, since the 1980s the balance of trade between Japan and the United States has tilted sharply in favor of Japan. In 1992 Japan sold $97 billion worth of its goods to the United States but bought only $48 billion worth of U.S. goods. The imbalance was particularly great in electronics, automobiles, and steel. This resulted in growing pressure on the U.S. government to put import quotas and/or heavy tariffs on Japanese goods coming into the United States unless the Japanese did a lot more to increase sales of U.S. goods in Japan. President Bush and his advisers resisted those pressures, partly on the ground that free trade is the best economic policy and partly on the ground that as the Japanese are the United States' most important allies in the Far East, the United States should not jeopardize friendly relations with Japan. The trade imbalance continued, and the issue of what to do about it was prominent in the 1992 presidential election.

Foreign aid has been an important tool of foreign policy for the United States only since 1945. It became significant in 1947 with the creation of the Marshall Plan to assist the economic recovery of the European nations after the devastation of World War II, and it has subsequently become a major foreign policy instrument not only for the United States but also for Japan, Great Britain, France, Germany, and other nations.

Foreign aid is generally intended to accomplish two main goals: (1) to strengthen the economies and military capabilities of friendly nations so as to ensure their continuing strength and political support; and (2) to strengthen the economies and military capabilities of neutral nations so as to increase their support. Those goals are pursued through outright grants of money, food, machinery, and other goods; through technical assistance, mainly in the form of expert advice on how to increase productivity; and through supplying military weapons, materiel, and advisers. In 1991, for example, the United States gave a total of $16.5 billion in foreign aid, $4.8 billion of which was in military aid and the remaining $11.7 billion in nonmilitary aid. The biggest recipients were Israel ($1.9 billion), Egypt ($783 million), Philippines ($328 million), Turkey ($250 million), and Nicaragua ($215 million). The most controversial issue in foreign aid in the 1980s was a series of efforts by the Reagan administration to give massive aid, both military and nonmilitary, to the Nicaraguan *contras*. In the 1990s a big question in the United States and the other Western democracies was how much and what kind of aid should be given to the newly independent republics of the former Soviet Union.

There has never been general agreement on the effectiveness of foreign aid as a device for winning friends among neutral nations, and it seems that in the United States every year the requested appropriations for foreign aid are harder to get through Congress. That results in part from the fact that of all the things on which the federal government spends money, foreign aid is the least popular with the general public (see Table 17.1), and it is therefore especially vulnerable to cuts. Still, as long as adversaries are dispensing aid, it seems unlikely that the United States or any other major power will abandon it altogether. So foreign aid seems likely to remain a major weapon of foreign policy—at least for relatively rich nations—for some time to come.

FOREIGN AID AND FOREIGN POLICY. An American instructs Russian cooks on how to prepare canned chicken soup donated by the United States.

TABLE 17.1   American Public Opinion on Foreign Aid versus Other Kinds of Spending

Question: "We are faced with many problems in this country, none of which can be solved easily or inexpensively. I'm going to name some of these problems, and for each one I'd like you to tell me whether you think we're spending too much money on it, too little money, or about the right amount."

	PERCENTAGE SAYING GOVERNMENT IS SPENDING		
SPENDING ON	Too Much	About Right	Too Little
Improving the nation's education system	3	24	73
Improving and protecting the environment	5	20	75
Halting the rising crime rate	11	31	58
Improving the condition of blacks	16	44	40
Welfare	39	38	23
Military, armaments, defense	44	45	11
Foreign aid	70	25	5

Source: General Social Surveys (1990), The Roper Center for Public Opinion Research, Storrs, CT.

Propaganda and Subversion

Diplomacy and foreign aid are direct efforts to induce the public officials of other nations to act as desired. Propaganda and subversion are indirect efforts in that they are intended to change political conditions in the target nations in such a way that the leaders of those nations will be forced to adopt the desired policies.

Propaganda in this context means the use of mass communications to influence public opinion in the target nation so that its people will insist that their officials act as the propagandizing nation wishes. Most major powers use propaganda. The United States, for example, maintains the U.S. Information Agency to organize broadcasts, libraries, film showings, and other programs in friendly and neutral foreign nations, in order to present the U.S. point of view in the most favorable light. The Voice of America beams radio broadcasts all over the world, and Radio Marti broadcasts especially to Cuba. The former Soviet Union long used posters, films, and radio broadcasts to spread accusations that the United States had used germ warfare in Korea and Vietnam, that it was conspiring to overthrow other governments, and that it was preparing to start World War III. The United States countered with its own radio broadcasts beamed at the USSR. The technological improvement of mass communications and the increasing importance of public opinion (see Chapters 6 and 7) made propaganda of this sort far more common than it was before World War I.

Sometimes nations try to influence the policies of other nations by **subversion**, which is *covert action designed to overthrow an established government*. Subversion can take many forms, including secret financial and military help to rebel forces in the target nation and efforts to damage the reputations and popularity of the target government's leaders. The built-in secrecy of those operations makes it difficult to obtain and analyze accurate data in a scholarly way, and so much of what is written on subversion today is journalistic, often sensational, and impossible to verify.

Nevertheless, it is now well established that in the 1920s and 1930s the Soviet Union, operating through the Communist International (Comintern), used espionage, sabotage, infiltration of other nations' governments, and even assassination to promote Soviet foreign policy objectives. There is also considerable evidence that during the cold war between the United States and the Soviet Union (1946–1989), the American Central Intelligence Agency (CIA) mounted a number of secret operations intended to overthrow hostile regimes (e.g., in Cuba and Nicaragua) and support friendly regimes (e.g., in Italy and Israel).

Most students of subversion also agree that a classic instance was Nazi Germany's campaign in the 1930s to overthrow the government of Austria and replace it with a pro-Nazi government, a campaign that achieved complete success in 1938 when the Austrian Nazi party took power, invited in German troops, and brought about the *anschluss* (the complete absorption of Austria into the Third Reich). More recent instances have been the secret efforts of the communist government of Cuba to aid rebel forces in Bolivia, Peru, El Salvador, and Guatemala and the quasi-secret efforts of the United States (1981–1987) to support the *contra* rebels against the communist-leaning government of Nicaragua. In short, distasteful though subversion may be when compared with such respectable techniques as diplomacy and foreign aid, it seems likely that some nations will continue to use subversion some of the time to pursue foreign-policy goals.

Terrorism

In the 1980s Americans became acutely conscious of another method of foreign policy: **terrorism**, which is *the systematic use of violence or the threat of violence against civilians to achieve political objectives*. The term is taken from the "reign of terror" in the French Revolution in 1793–1794, when the Committee of Public Safety, led by Maximilien Robespierre, sought to eliminate the opposition by using mass executions to terrify and intimidate all those who opposed them (in just over a year more than three hundred thousand persons were arrested and over seventeen thousand were sent to the guillotine). Terrorism is used today by nations and political groups that cannot accomplish their objectives by diplomacy and that are too weak to use conventional military force. Immediate targets of terrorism are ordinary, unsuspecting persons such as passengers on airliners, patrons of airports, or diners at restaurants. Terrorist tactics are to harm or threaten to harm victims by seizing them as hostages or killing them with guns and bombs. Terrorism's object is to terrify the people and the officials of the target government so that they will alter their policies as the terrorists wish.

There is no shortage of recent examples of terrorism. Perhaps Americans are most conscious of the use of terror by various Muslim groups in the Middle East— especially the Shi'ite Muslims of Lebanon—to force the United States to end its support of Israel. In 1979, for instance, Iranian Shi'ites, with the full approval of the Ayatollah Khomeini's Iranian government, stormed the U.S. embassy in Teheran and held sixty diplomatic employees prisoner for over a year before they were finally released. In 1985, Shi'ite Muslim terrorists hijacked a U.S. airliner and held over seventy passengers hostage, demanding that Israel release seven hundred Shi'ites being held in Israeli jails. In 1988 a Pan American 747 flying out of London was destroyed by a bomb planted by Arab terrorists, killing 270 people. In 1993 a band of Arab terrorists exploded a car bomb in New York City's World Trade center, killing six persons and doing extensive damage to the building.

Americans have by no means been the only targets of terrorists. In 1983 the Provisional Irish Republican Army (IRA), a terrorist organization seeking to force the removal of British troops and influence from Northern Ireland, exploded a bomb at Harrod's, one of London's leading department stores. In 1983 the IRA exploded a bomb in a hotel in Brighton, where the Conservative party's annual conference was being held, killing four people, wounding thirty-two, and narrowly missing Prime Minister Margaret Thatcher. In 1986, terrorists exploded a bomb in a Paris café killing eight and wounding over two hundred. In Peru since the 1980s the *Sendero Luminoso* ("Shining Path") guerillas have used kidnapping, sabotage, and murder in their effort to overthrow the established regime.

Terrorism is perpetrated in extreme secrecy by small numbers of terrorists, such as the Lebanese Shi'ite Muslim bands, Hizbollah and Islamic Jihad, which kidnapped a number of Westerners in 1984–1986 and held them hostage until 1991. Secrecy makes it difficult to be certain which governments are using terrorism as a matter of policy. Even so, U.S. and NATO intelligence agencies concluded that a number of nations—especially Libya, Iran, Cuba, Syria, North Korea, and the former Soviet Union—have given training, weapons, and money to terrorists and have sometimes deliberately used terrorism as an instrument of foreign policy.

Whether directed by governments or not, terrorism is extremely difficult for the target nations to deal with. Those nations would like to reject all terrorist demands, and yet the consequence might well be the murder of innocent hostages. Targeted nations would like to take swift and devastating military reprisals against the terrorists, but usually they cannot be sure precisely who the terrorists are or who supports them. As President Reagan said in 1985, if in taking reprisals against terrorists the United States were to kill innocent non-terrorists, then "we would become terrorists ourselves."

So far, terrorism has not won any major political victories comparable to those won by diplomacy or victory in war. Nevertheless, for those nations with no scruples about using it terrorism is a low-cost, low-risk technique, and the odds are that it will be used more rather than less in the years ahead.

War

War has long been regarded by many people as perhaps the worst disease in the whole grim pathology of human affairs, and for good reason. Even before the advent of nuclear weapons, wars exacted a price in death and suffering too enormous for the imagination to grasp. It is estimated, for example, that in World War I an incomprehensible total of 37 million human beings died either on the battlefield or as a direct result of the famine and disease brought on by the war. In World War II, another 22 million perished. Wars have also devastated the human race in other ways. Not only have the volunteers and first casualties been some of the finest of the nations' youths and potential leaders, but the moral, social, and economic deterioration that infects both winners and losers after most wars has also left the world much poorer. Paying for past, present, and future wars is by far the greatest single economic burden born by any large modern nation. All those things were true of war before nuclear weapons were available, and what the costs of war are likely to be now that a growing number of nations have such weapons we can only guess.

Yet scarcely any generation in the history of any modern nation has lived out its time in peace, and many generations in many nations have endured as many as two or three major wars. Thus we have to face the fact that, terrible though they may be, wars continue to happen (for example, as recently as 1990–91 in the Persian Gulf). Wars, in fact, are as normal as peace in the modern world. Consequently, one of the most baffling and increasingly urgent questions confronting students of governing is, How can something so terrible happen so often?

Some theologians believe that war is a divine punishment laid on humanity for its sins, and so it may be. Social scientists, however, proceed from the assumption that war is not imposed on people by divine intervention but is an activity nations and their peoples engage in voluntarily for purposes of their own. Many political scientists regard war much as did the great Prussian student of war, Karl von Clausewitz, who declared that "War is a political instrument, a continuation of political relations, a carrying out of the same by other means."[5]

To the political scientist, then, war is best seen as one of the methods that nations in fact use to achieve their ends. For most nations a war's tremendous costs and great risks make it the method of last resort. Most nations turn to war only when one of their most cherished goals—such as preserving their independence or protecting their basic institutions—appears to be in mortal danger and all other means of achieving their goal seem to have failed. Only such a goal in such circumstances can justify the costs and risks of war.

Yet we cannot talk *only* of the costs and risks of war, for the fact is that many nations have won highly valued goals through war when they might not have done so by other means. The United States and Israel, for example, established their very national existence by fighting and winning wars of independence. Great Britain and the United States may not have made the world "safe for democracy" by fighting World War II, but at least they preserved their independence, helped to end Hitler's Third Reich, a regime that as a matter of deliberate policy had murdered 6 million Jews in the never-to-be-forgotten Holocaust, and helped to save the world from Hitler's demonic plans for the future. Many of the world's great religions—notably Christianity and Islam—have been spread among the heathen and defended against heretics and infidels by the sword. We are clearly not justified in calling *all* wars totally futile and barren of accomplishment. One of the most eminent students of war sums it up thus:

> War, then, has been the instrument by which most of the great facts of political national history have been established and maintained. . . . The map of the world today has been largely determined upon the battlefield. The maintenance of civilization itself has been, and still continues to be, underwritten by the insurance of an army and navy ready to strike at any time where danger threatens.[6]

Great questions face all nations in the nuclear age: Is war still a thinkable instrument of national policy, or do nuclear weapons mean that there can be no "winners" in modern war, that war will destroy everything and achieve nothing for any nation, and that *anything* is better than war? Can war be avoided or limited? In several senses, these are truly the final questions in a study of governing in the modern world, and we will consider them in the next and final chapter.

For Further Reading

DUCHACEK, IVO D. *The Territorial Dimension of Politics: Within, Among, and Across Nations.* Boulder, CO: Westview Press, 1986. A defense of the state system and national sovereignty as a rational organizing principle for world politics.

*FROMKIN, DAVID. *The Independence of Nations.* New York: Praeger, 1981. Analysis of the differences between domestic and international politics, with emphasis on the consequences of the state system.

*GILPIN, ROBERT. *War and Change in World Politics.* New York: Cambridge University Press, 1981. Study of the impact of war on societies and international relations.

GURR, TED ROBERT, AND BARBARA HARFF. *Ethnic Conflict in World Politics.* Boulder, CO: Westview Press, 1994. Analysis of intensified role of ethnic differences in contemporary international conflict.

*HOWARD, MICHAEL. *The Causes of War.* Cambridge, MA: Harvard University Press, 1983. Innovative analysis of what causes wars.

KEEGAN, JOHN. *A History of Warfare.* New York: Alfred A. Knopf, 1993. Historical account of the origins, weapons, and politics of war from prehistory to the present.

KISSINGER, HENRY. *White House Years.* Boston, MA: Little, Brown, 1979. Reflective memoirs by a scholar who became a key maker of foreign policy.

MORGENTHAU, HANS J., AND KENNETH W. THOMPSON. *Politics Among Nations,* 6th ed. New York: Alfred A. Knopf, 1985. Most recent version of influential survey of international politics.

ROSECRANCE, RICHARD, AND ARTHUR A. STEIN, eds. *The Domestic Bases of Grand Strategy.* Ithaca, NY: Cornell University Press, 1993. Essays on the domestic political forces shaping foreign policy.

*ROSENAU, JAMES N. *Turbulence in World Politics: A Theory of Change and Continuity.* Princeton, NJ: Princeton University Press, 1990. A reconceptualization of world politics in the light of the revolutions in communications, economics, and ethnography.

SEABURY, PAUL, AND ANGELO CODEVILLA. *War: Ends and Means.* New York: Basic Books, 1989. Argument that, despite nuclear weapons, war continues to be an instrument of foreign policy under some conditions for some nations.

TREVERTON, GREGORY F. *Covert Action: The Limits of Intervention in the Postwar World.* New York: Basic Books, 1987. Critical study of the use of covert actions in peacetime international politics.

WALTZ, KENNETH N. *Theory of International Politics.* Reading, MA.: Addison-Wesley, 1979. Innovative conceptualization and explanation of international politics.

WARDLAW, GRANT. *Political Terrorism: Theory, Tactics, and Counter Measures,* 2nd ed. New York: Cambridge University Press, 1989. Leading study of terrorism as a tactic in international politics.

Notes

1. Excerpts from *All Quiet on the Western Front* by Erich Maria Remarque, *Im Westen Nichts Neues,* copyright 1928, by Ullstein E.G.; copyright renewed 1956 by Erich Maria Remarque; *All Quiet on the Western Front,* copyright 1929, 1930 by Little, Brown & Company; copyright renewed 1957, 1958 by Erich Maria Remarque.

2. See Lewis F. Richardson, *Statistics of Deadly Quarrels* (Pittsburgh, PA: Boxwood Press, 1960), pp. 32–50.

3. Harold Nicolson, *The Congress of Vienna* (New York: Harcourt Brace Jovanich, 1946), pp. 19–20.

4. Here as elsewhere, *de jure* means as a matter of law, but not necessarily as a matter of fact; *de facto* means as a matter of fact, but not necessarily as a matter of law.

5. Karl von Clausewitz, *On War* (London: Routledge and Kegan Paul, 1940), vol. 3, p. 122.

6. James T. Shotwell, *War as an Instrument of National Policy* (New York: Harcourt Brace Jovonovich, 1929), p. 15.

18

There is such a thing as a man being too proud to fight.
Woodrow Wilson (1915)

But the right is more precious than peace, and we shall fight for the things which we have always carried nearest our hearts. . . .
Woodrow Wilson (1917)

Older men declare war. But it is youth that must fight and die. And it is youth who must inherit the tribulation, the sorrow, and the triumphs that are the aftermath of war.
Herbert Hoover

Unconditional war can no longer lead to unconditional victory. It can no longer serve to settle disputes. It can no longer be of concern to great powers alone. For a nuclear disaster, spread by winds and waters and fear, could well engulf the great and the small, the rich and the poor, the committed and the uncommitted alike. Mankind must put an end to war or war will put an end to mankind.
John F. Kennedy

As long as there are sovereign nations possessing great power, war is inevitable.
Albert Einstein

The Quest for Peace in the Thermonuclear Age

The New World Order: Good News and Bad News ───────

Since 1989 the structure of international politics has seen one of its greatest changes in history. As President George Bush proclaimed in 1991, humanity is creating a "new world order." We cannot yet be sure of the new order's final configuration, but some of its features are already clear; and, as in so many aspects of life, they bring both good news and bad news.

GOOD NEWS: THE COLD WAR IS OVER

From the late 1940s to the late 1980s international politics was dominated by the conflict between the world's two most powerful nations, the United States and the Union of Soviet Socialist Republics (USSR). The struggle was called the "cold war": "war" because the two nations and their allies opposed each other in economics, diplomacy, world opinion, and almost everything else; "cold" because the two superpowers stopped short of direct armed conflict.

Each superpower, however, was well prepared for war with the other. Each spent vast resources to make its armed forces superior to the other's. Each developed thousands of nuclear weapons and deployed them in bombers, intercontinental ballistic missiles, and nuclear-powered submarines targeted on the other. Each had the capacity to destroy the other (and perhaps the whole world) many times over, and the main deterrent to thermonuclear World War III was the prospect of "mutually assured destruction," the knowledge that if one side launched a nuclear attack, then the other would respond with an equal or greater nuclear counterattack.

The United States and the USSR became leaders of international military alliances created to resist each other. The United States headed the North Atlantic Treaty Organization (NATO), an alliance of sixteen Western nations, formed in 1948 and headquartered in Brussels, to coordinate its members' armed forces under one supreme commander (usually but not always a U.S. general) against the threat of armed invasion of Western Europe by the Soviet Union. The Soviet Union headed the Warsaw Pact, an alliance of eight Eastern European Communist nations formed in 1955 to coordinate their armed forces against NATO.

Although the two sides never directly faced each other in an all-out war, on several occasions when one superpower used military force against a third nation the other superpower gave military and diplomatic support to its enemy's enemy. For example, the Soviet Union supported North Korea against the United States and South Korea in the 1950s and North Vietnam against the United States and South Vietnam in the 1960s, while the United States supported Afghanistan against the Soviet invasion in the 1980s.

However, the early 1990s saw what millions of people in both blocs had longed for but feared would never come: the end of the cold war. The process began in the late 1980s, when Mikhail Gorbachev decided that the Soviet economy could no longer support the staggering costs of developing and maintaining its nuclear arsenal or even such non-nuclear ventures as fighting the anti-Communist rebels in Afghanistan. He signed treaties with U.S. Presidents Reagan and Bush that sharply reduced nuclear weapons on both sides and asked for Western help to bolster the Soviet economy. He raised no objections to the absorption of Communist East Germany by democratic West Germany in 1990. He supported the U.S.-led military expulsion of Iraq from Kuwait in 1990–1991. And in 1990–1991, as we noted in Chapter 2, the Soviet Union dissolved into fifteen independent republics, eleven of which formed the new Commonwealth of Independent States (CIS).

Many questions about the future of world politics remained unanswered by the end of 1994, but one thing was clear: The cold war was over.

BAD NEWS: NUCLEAR WEAPONS ARE PROLIFERATING

If it comes, what will World War III be like? Figure 18.1, which shows the damage range of a hypothetical thermonuclear bomb detonated over the center of Washington, DC, suggests part of the answer. According to data from official tests, on which the figure is based, *one* 20-megaton thermonuclear bomb (1 megaton equals the destructive force of 1 million tons of TNT) is more powerful than *all* the bombs dropped on Germany and Japan in World War II put together. One 10-megaton bomb obliterates everything within a radius of 5 miles around the blast point and leaves only a poisonously radioactive crater more than 500 feet deep. The blast sets off a suffocating firestorm for a radius of 25 miles or more. More than 200 different radioactive compounds are created and attached to particles of debris, which are swept into the air and form the familiar mushroom cloud. Those deadly particles float back to earth at varying speeds, depending upon their weight and, if spread uniformly, produce lethal levels of radioactivity over about 5,000 square miles.[1]

However, that is only what one bomb can do. Some experts estimate that a 20,000-megaton attack with multiple "dirty" warheads (those with high-fission yields) would, within 60 days, kill by fallout every American who had survived the original blasts and firestorms. Others believe that "only" 70 percent of the popula-

FIGURE 18.1   Damage Range of a Thermonuclear Bomb

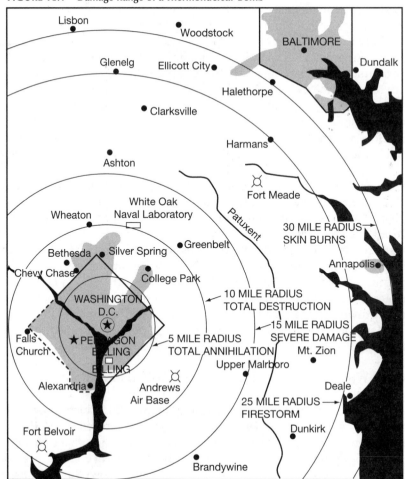

tion would be killed.[2] Many scientists believe that even worse would be the long-range effects of the "nuclear winter" that would follow: They predict that after a major nuclear attack, much of the earth would be covered with a cloud of radioactive soot that would block the sun, push temperatures far below freezing, and prevent the growing of most kinds of food. Others fear still more the breakdown of the ozone layer that now protects the earth from the full power of the sun's rays; the nuclear cloud would destroy the ozone, and when the cloud cleared there would be no protection against death from sunburn and skin cancer. Still others fear most of all the long-range genetic effects of the exposure to radiation poisoning, which, by massively altering the genes of humans and animals, might produce generations of mutants, with unpredictable consequences.

Some commentators believe that such predictions are far worse than the reality will be, that with proper measures for bomb shelters and first aid, preattack evacuation from cities, and postattack medical assistance, millions of people would survive. No one knows for sure.

Only two atomic bombs have so far been used in war, both by the United States against Japan in 1945: The 12.5-kiloton bomb (1 kiloton equals the force of 1,000 tons of TNT) dropped on Hiroshima killed 70,000 persons, and the 35-kiloton bomb dropped on Nagasaki killed 35,000. However, those bombs were primitive by present-day standards: Modern intercontinental ballistic missiles (ICBMs) are "MIRVed" (an acronym for "multiple independently targeted reentry vehicle"); that is, each missile can carry a number of nuclear warheads, each of which is independently guided to a separate target. But no matter how much some experts may disagree on the likely total damage from a nuclear attack, all experts believe that a thermonuclear war would be by far the greatest catastrophe ever experienced by the human race.

For those reasons, then, the ICBM with a thermonuclear warhead is the "absolute weapon" with which humanity and most other living things on the planet can be literally exterminated. The thermonuclear age may very well be our last if we decide to fight World War III with thermonuclear weapons. The grim fact dominating our time is that the quest for peace has become a quest for the means of sheer physical survival for all people in all nations.

It is further complicated by the "Nth-country problem." At present the United States and four republics of the former Soviet Union (Russia, Belarus, Ukraine, and Kazakhstan) have by far the most nuclear weapons, but at least four other nations—Great Britain, France, the People's Republic of China (PRC), and India—also have nuclear weapons and some means of delivering them. Many other nations (for example, Germany, Iraq, Japan, Israel, North Korea, Pakistan, South Africa, and Sweden) have the scientific knowledge and the engineering capability necessary to make nuclear weapons. If the possession of such weapons by the United States and the Soviet Union made the world nervous during the cold war, then how about the possession of nuclear weapons by, say, Libya and Israel, or Iran and Iraq, or India and Pakistan, or, for that matter, by the four republics of the former Soviet Union? For World War III might be touched off not by the original nuclear powers, but by the Nth country to possess the atomic bomb.

Precisely this apprehension induced the Soviet Union and the United States to take the lead in drawing up and pressing for the adoption of the general Nuclear Nonproliferation Treaty in 1968. The treaty provides, first, that nations now possessing nuclear weapons will not transfer them to any other nation; second, that non-nuclear nations will not manufacture or acquire nuclear weapons; third, that the International Atomic Energy Authority is authorized to conduct inspections in the various participating nations to ensure compliance; and, fourth, that all signatory nations will have access to information about peaceful uses of atomic energy. By early 1970 a total of ninety-seven nations had signed the treaty. However, the signers included only three of the six nations then possessing nuclear weapons (Great Britain, the Soviet Union, and the United States): France, the PRC, and India refused to sign. Israel and North Korea, both potential nuclear powers, also refused to sign. In 1995 the treaty was renewed and signed by over 170 nations. However, India, Israel, and Pakistan—all current or potential nuclear powers—refused to sign. Consequently, while the treaty is far from being a complete solution to the nth-country problem, it at least gives the world some hope that the problem will eventually be brought under control.

What, then, are the world's chances of survival? Some analysts believe that the chances depend mainly upon the nations' ability to keep World War III from being fought with thermonuclear weapons and to confine nations to the use of non-nuclear "conventional" weapons, which, however destructive, do not have the capacity to wipe out all life on earth. Those analysts believe that there is a strong possibility that nations will refrain from using thermonuclear weapons by mutual consent. Other analysts argue that the best chance lies in keeping all future wars limited, in both geographic area and the number of nations involved, as wars in Korea, Indochina, the Persian Gulf, the South Atlantic, and the Middle East have been limited since 1945. Still others insist that depending on limited wars is risky at best. If the world fails just once, then the whole game is lost. The only real chance for survival is to find a way to prevent *all* international wars, limited or general.

Whatever policies they think we should adopt, however, most present-day students of international affairs believe that the thermonuclear age has transformed the ancient quest for peace from a search for a utopia of tranquility into a hunt for the minimum conditions of human survival. This hunt, moreover, must take place in an age in which nuclear power makes it urgent while the political fission characteristic of the state system may still prevent people—as it has for centuries—from finding a way to eliminate war.

Wars, as we noted in Chapter 17, have almost always been both costly and risky, and few nations' leaders have ever engaged in war for its own sake because they thought it would be invigorating or would improve their nations' moral character. Yet, under the state system, just about every nation has fought wars when its leaders and people came to believe that not fighting would bring even greater disasters than the horrors of war. It would be dangerous to assume that the enormously greater costs of thermonuclear war have basically altered this historic general attitude toward international violence.

As Albert Einstein, the great physicist whose letter to President Franklin

DO NUCLEAR WEAPONS MAKE WAR OBSOLETE? Test explosion of a hydrogen bomb in the Pacific, 1952.

Roosevelt in 1939 launched the creation of the first nuclear weapons, said: "The unleashed power of the atom has changed everything except our modes of thinking."[3]

If peace is to prevail in our time, it will come either because modern nations do not desire *any* national goal enough to go to war for it or because modern nations believe their goals can be achieved by means other than war. The quest for peace in our age is thus a search for a world political structure that will incline peoples and leaders to adopt either attitude or both toward war.

Accordingly, we now examine the nature and record of some of the more prominent approaches to conducting international political conflict without war that have been tried or considered in the past.

Approaches to Peace within the State System

The state system, as we learned in Chapter 17, is deeply rooted in the fact that most people give their basic political loyalties to their nations rather than to their races, genders, economic classes, religious institutions, or other group affiliations. Although the leaders of nations have long sought ways of achieving national goals without resorting to war, most have had no hope or desire of eliminating such basic features of the state system as the sovereign independence of nations and the legal right of each nation to make its policies without interference from outside. Our first category of approaches to peace therefore includes those that assume the continuation of the state system and rely on the voluntary cooperation of independent sovereign nations.

Each of these approaches rests on a set of ideas about what causes wars and how those causes can be alleviated or eliminated. Accordingly, we will consider the rationale as well as the record of each suggested approach to peace within the existing state system.

BALANCE OF POWER

Description

The term *balance of power* is used in several different senses by analysts of international politics. In a purely descriptive sense, balance of power simply means the distribution of power among nations at any given moment and does not mean equal shares. As an approach to peace, however, **balance of power** means *a distribution of power among nations that is sufficiently equal to maintain security and peace.* Following a policy of balance of power means striving for such a distribution.

The balance-of-power approach to peace is based on the assumption that war breaks out when a particular nation feels sufficiently stronger than its antagonists to believe that it can threaten or attack them with assurance of success, or feels sufficiently weaker that it must strike now while it still has a chance. Analysts who take this approach propose to keep the peace by preventing any nation from feeling that much stronger or weaker than any of its rivals.

Methods

Many nations have tried both to protect their national interests and to avoid war by pursuing balance-of-power policies calculated to keep themselves and their allies strong enough to prevent opposing nations or combinations of nations from becoming too strong. Among the traditional methods have been *domestic measures,* such as building up their armaments and strengthening military organizations; *alliances,* including both acquiring allies for themselves and splitting off their opponents' allies in the ancient strategy of divide and conquer; *compensations,* including dividing up colonial areas among the major powers so that those powers will be satisfied and thus feel no need for aggression against other major powers; and *war,* used as a last resort to prevent the rival nation or bloc of nations from becoming unacceptably powerful. A classic example of a balance-of-power policy is that followed by Great Britain for centuries, in which it put its weight against whatever was the single most powerful nation in Europe: first Spain, then the Netherlands, then France, then Germany, and then the Soviet Union.

Evaluation

Most political scientists believe that, whatever balance-of-power policies may have done for the interests of particular nations, those policies have not kept the peace. Failure has resulted partly from the impossibility of accurately measuring what the distribution of power actually is, which means that no nation can ever be sure when power is sufficiently "balanced" to pose no threat. Another deficiency is that most nations believe that prudence requires them to leave a margin for error in their calculations; so they build up their armaments and their alliances to a level higher than what they estimate is the necessary minimum. The trouble is that a nation's antagonists feel the same need for a safety margin, and those nations in turn build up *their* armaments to a level beyond that of the rival nations. And so on and on in a process familiarly known as an arms race.

The whole idea of a balance of power thus rests upon an oversimplified and mechanical conception of international relations, which assumes that relative national power can be calculated precisely and assumes that all nations wish only to maintain their existing situations, not to improve them. Both assumptions are wrong. Balance of power has never succeeded in keeping the peace in the past, and it seems likely that it will not succeed in the future despite the possibility that fear of thermonuclear weapons may make nations more hesitant to resort to war than in the past. Always before in history some nation or group of nations has sooner or later come to believe that the only way to restore the balance is to go to war before it is too late. Is there any good reason to suppose that balance of power will work any better in the new world order?

COLLECTIVE SECURITY

Meaning and Rationale

As we have seen, those who seek peace through balance-of-power policies assume that no nation will launch an attack on any other nation unless it is confident that it has the preponderance of power necessary for victory. Peace can be maintained, balance-of-power advocates reason, by keeping any nation from acquiring enough extra power to feel that kind of confidence.

A major extension and reorientation of this point of view is the concept of **collective security**, which is *an arrangement by which nations agree in advance to take collective action against any nation that commits aggression against one or more of them.* Thus the collective-security approach seeks peace by making it clear *in advance* to any would-be aggressor that its contemplated aggression will be met with overwhelming force and therefore cannot possibly succeed. This has been one of the most widely taken of all approaches to peace within the state system, and, as we will see, it is one of the main elements in the United Nations approach to peace.

Collective security is sometimes confused with defensive military alliances such as NATO and the Warsaw Pact or the twenty-nine-nation U.S.-led coalition that drove Iraq out of Kuwait in 1991. Those coalitions differ from true collective-security arrangements, however, in that coalitions are not intended to be universal in their membership, while universality is a goal of all genuine collective-security agreements. The NATO and (former) Warsaw Pact alliances are examples of defensive military alliances that nations often form as part of a balance-of-power strategy. The nearest approximations to a genuine collective-security system in the twentieth century have been embodied in the Covenant of the League of Nations and the Charter of the United Nations (UN), both of which we will consider later.

Preconditions

The collective-security approach to peace does not propose any alteration in the basic structure of the state system, in the sense of establishing a world government with the legal and physical power to *make* nations come to one another's defense whether they want to or not. Rather, it depends upon the willingness of the nations to do so voluntarily. This approach does, however, require a number of drastic changes in the attitudes of nations and the makers of their foreign policies. For, if collective security is to work as intended, most people in most nations must fully accept at least the idea of "the indivisibility of peace," which is the notion that a nation's destiny is inextricably intertwined with the security and welfare of all nations. Furthermore, the people and the policy makers of each nation must put the requirements and obligations of collective security ahead of their own narrow national interests. Finally, each nation must voluntarily surrender to some kind of international body a considerable portion of its power over its own foreign policy.

To illustrate the differences between balance-of-power and collective-security arrangements for meeting aggression, let us consider the case of U.S. policy toward Korea in the early 1950s. When North Korea attacked South Korea in 1950, the United Nations, under U.S. leadership, declared that North Korea was the aggressor and called for all member nations to come to South Korea's defense. The United States, which had already started to fight the North Koreans, complied with the resolution by sending large numbers of troops, although many other UN members did not. The United States thus acted just as every member of a collective-security agreement should.

However, let us suppose that some time in the future anti-Communist South Korea attacks Communist North Korea. Let us suppose, further, that the UN declares that South Korea is the aggressor and calls upon all member nations to go to the Communists' defense. What would the United States do? What *should* it do? On the one hand, many Americans would feel that any aggression *by* Communists is dangerous to U.S. security, whereas any aggression *against* Communists is helpful. On the other hand, under a collective-security agreement, the United States would be bound to help the Communists just as diligently as it helped the anti-Communists in the early 1950s. If the United States were to honor its collective-security commitments, American troops would stand shoulder to shoulder with Communists killing non-Communists. If such a situation were actually to arise, it is not likely that the United States would join in any collective-security defense of communism, and we know that in 1950 the Soviet Union not only did not join the collective-security defense of an anti-Communist victim of aggression but actively opposed what the UN was doing.

Collective-Security Alliances in the Cold War

The cold war generated two noteworthy examples of collective-security alliances, both of which have changed markedly since the cold war ended. In 1949 twelve Western democratic nations (Belgium, Canada, Denmark, France, Iceland, Italy, Luxembourg, the Netherlands, Norway, Portugal, the United Kingdom, and the United States) signed a treaty establishing the North Atlantic Treaty Organization (NATO) and provided that "the parties agree that an armed attack against one or more of them in Europe or North America shall be considered an attack against them all." The treaty was later also signed by Germany, Greece, Turkey, and Spain. The signatories established a headquarters in Brussels and appointed a Supreme Allied Commander Europe (SACEUR) to command contingents from the armed forces of each member nation (France declined to contribute forces) to conduct joint military exercises to prepare for a possible attack on Western Europe by the Soviet Union, and some U.S. forces were stationed in several member countries, including Germany, Spain, and the United Kingdom.

In 1955, under the leadership of the Soviet Union, the Communist bloc of nations in Eastern Europe (Albania, Bulgaria, Czechoslovakia, East Germany, Hungary, Poland, Romania, and the USSR) signed a treaty (the Warsaw Pact) establishing a collective security alliance to counter NATO. Under the pact Soviet military units were stationed in Czechoslovakia, East Germany, Hungary, and Poland.

After the dissolution of the USSR in 1991, the Warsaw Pact was disbanded. Afterward some of its former members (notably the Czech Republic, Hungary, and Poland) applied for membership in NATO. Russia announced that it would regard such memberships as a threat to Russia's security, and in 1993 the NATO leaders, who wished to support and strengthen President Yeltsin, invited all former Communist regimes to participate in NATO, for the time being not as full members but as associated "partners for peace" who would participate with the member nations in limited joint military exercises, limited joint peace-keeping missions, and the exchange of military and diplomatic information. The Czech Republic, Hungary, and Poland accepted immediately, and in 1994 Russia also joined.

In the mid-1990s it is not yet clear whether the new NATO will be a collective-security organization like the old NATO; but its metamorphosis from a Western alliance facing the Warsaw Pact's Eastern alliance to an organization including some or all of the former members of the Warsaw Pact is one of the more striking signs that the cold war is indeed over.

Hans J. Morgenthau and Kenneth W. Thompson have neatly summed up the difference between the national attitudes required by genuine collective security and those that actually prevail under the state system:

> Collective security as an ideal is directed against all aggression in the abstract; foreign policy can only operate against a particular concrete aggressor. The only question collective security is allowed to ask is, "Who has committed aggression?" Foreign policy cannot help asking, "What interest do I have in opposing this particular aggressor, and what power do I have with which to oppose him?"[4]

Until such time as the United States can be counted upon to rush to the defense of communists against anti-communist aggression and North Korea to fight communist aggression against non-communists, no global collective-security system in the strict sense can exist for the good and sufficient reason that the national attitudes necessary for it to work do not exist. We will return to this problem in our discussion of the UN.

DISARMAMENT

Rationale

Disarmament is *the reduction or elimination of the personnel and/or equipment of national armed forces.* Closely associated concepts are *arms limitation,* which is a degree of mutual disarmament agreed to by two or more nations; and *arms-control agreements,* which are agreements among nations for certain mutual arms limitations.

Since the end of the Napoleonic wars in 1815, every major nation has from time to time publicly declared itself in favor of some kind of disarmament. Nations advance disarmament proposals for various reasons. One is the desire to reduce the heavy economic burdens of large military establishments. Another is the wish to reduce the destructiveness of future wars. A third is the wish to polish up the nation's image as a "peace-loving nation" and pin the label of "warmongers" on antagonists. The motive for disarmament proposals that concerns us here, however, is the desire to prevent war.

The theory of disarmament as an approach to peace is based upon the assumption that if there is no restriction on how heavily the major powers are armed, then those powers will inevitably engage in arms races. Because national leaders cannot be trusted not to use huge military establishments if they have them, sooner or later arms races bring on wars. Thus one way of approaching peace, not necessarily the only way but often complementary to other ways, is to persuade all nations either to limit the total quantities of their weapons or to forswear the use of certain weapons (for example, poison gas, bacterial bombs, thermonuclear weapons), or both.

Record

Since 1815 many attempts have been made at both general and regional disarmament. There have been a few successes with regional disarmament. The best known is the Rush-Bagot Agreement of 1817 between Canada and the United States, which limits naval forces on the Great Lakes and has come by informal extension to mean the demilitarization of the entire Canadian-U.S. border, which, at 3,000 miles, is the longest undefended international boundary in the world.

The most notable efforts at general disarmament have been the Holy Alliance of the immediate post-Napoleonic period in the 1820s, the Hague peace conferences of 1899 and 1907, the Washington naval conference of 1922, the world disarmament conference of 1932, and the many efforts made by the disarmament commissions of the League of Nations and the UN. Generally speaking, such efforts have failed to accomplish anything remotely approaching their stated objectives, for reasons we will review shortly.

Nuclear Weapons: Control and Disarmament

We noted earlier in this chapter that the development of thermonuclear weapons has forced the age-old quest for peace into a new atmosphere of great urgency. Much the same can be said for the problem of disarmament, which since 1945 has centered mainly upon the problem of reducing or abolishing nuclear weapons and the control of materials and facilities for nuclear fission and fusion. A brief review of those negotiations illuminates not only the special difficulties in nuclear disarmament but also the continuing difficulties of any effort at general disarmament under the state system.

In 1946 the United States—which at that time had a world monopoly of nuclear weapons—laid before the Atomic Energy Commission of the UN a proposal that an international atomic-development authority be created as a body affiliated with, but independent of, the UN. This agency would be given a worldwide monopoly on the ownership and operation of all mines and plants producing fissionable materials and of all research and testing of nuclear weapons. The agency would also be empowered to license nations to use nuclear materials for peaceful purposes and would make unrestricted inspections of all nations' scientific and industrial establishments to detect illicit supplies of fissionable materials and misuse of licenses for their peaceful use. When such an authority was established and working to U.S. satisfaction, the United States would surrender to the authority its national stockpiles of atomic bombs and fissionable materials.

The USSR found the proposal unacceptable, however. It insisted that the establishment of any international control of atomic energy must be preceded by the legal prohibition of all nuclear weapons and by the U.S. destruction of its stocks of such weapons. The Soviet Union also insisted that the proposed international authority should have no power to own, operate, or license atomic facilities and that even the authority's rather vague inspecting functions should operate in clear subordination to the Security Council, over whose operations the Soviet Union and four other great powers have a veto.

In 1948 the UN General Assembly approved a somewhat revised version of the U.S. plan, but the Soviets were so hostile to it that no serious attempt has ever been made to implement it.

Since 1946, however, several nuclear arms-control treaties have been signed. The first came in 1963, when more than one hundred nations, including the United States and the Soviet Union, agreed to end the testing of nuclear weapons in the atmosphere, in outer space, and under water. The treaty provided for no system of inspection (it was considered unnecessary because the development of sensitive detection devices has made it almost impossible to conduct such tests without the other signatories' knowledge). However, France and the PRC—both of which had just developed their own nuclear weapons—refused to sign it. During the next thirty years there was an informal moratorium on nuclear weapons testing, but in 1993 the PRC tested a new weapon and President Clinton ordered preparations for the United States to resume testing.

From the 1960s to the 1980s the United States and the Soviet Union engaged in on-again-off-again bilateral negotiations called the "strategic arms limitation talks" but better known by the acronym SALT. In 1972 the two nations signed a treaty, known as SALT I, which limited each nation to deploying only two antiballistic missile systems (ABMs), which was later reduced to one each; and it was understood that compliance with the agreement would be monitored by the earth-orbiting surveillance satellites of both nations. There were also accompanying executive agreements freezing for five years the deployment of strategic missile launchers and establishing a Standing Consultative Commission to formulate procedures for destroying or dismantling weapons in excess of the agreements or replacing old weapons with newer, improved weapons (which were allowed by the agreements).

Even greater progress has been made since the late 1980s. In 1987 the United States and the Soviet Union agreed to limit the number and deployment of intermediate nuclear missiles (those with ranges between 315 and 3,125 miles). The Soviets agreed to destroy about 400 SS-20 missiles aimed at Western Europe, and the United States agreed to destroy about 325 Pershing II missiles aimed at the Soviet Union. In another major departure from past policies, each nation agreed to permit inspectors from the other to oversee and verify the destruction of the missiles. The treaty was signed by Presidents Gorbachev and Reagan at a summit meeting in Washington in December 1987 and was ratified by the U.S. Senate in 1988. The actual destruction of the weapons in both countries, watched by inspectors from the other countries, began in September 1988.

In 1991 the first Strategic Arms Reduction Treaty (START I) was signed by Presidents Gorbachev of the USSR and Bush of the United States, and ratified by the U.S. Senate in 1992. However, many questions for further nuclear arms reduction were soon thereafter raised by the breakup of the Soviet Union. One of the most urgent questions was what entity, if any, would control the defunct union's nuclear weapons and assume its treaty obligations. The weapons (an estimated 27,000 nuclear warheads) and the missile launching sites were located in only four of the newly independent republics: Russia, Ukraine, Belarus, and Kazakhstan. After a good deal of negotiation among the republics, several agreements were reached. Control of the weapons together with the obligation to honor the treaty obligations would pass to the Russian republic. The codes necessary to launch the missiles would pass to Boris Yeltsin, the president of Russia; but he could order a launch only with the approval of the presidents of the other three republics. By late 1993 Belarus, Kazakhstan, and Ukraine ratified START I and acceded to the nonproliferation treaty. And just before President Bush left office in January 1993, he and President Yeltsin signed the START II treaty, which called for both nations to reduce their long-range arsenals to about one third of their then-current levels and entirely eliminate land-based multiple-warhead missiles, all by the year 2003. Thus, nuclear weapons control, which had seemed so hopeless in 1946, was well started by 1994.

INTERNATIONAL LAW

As an Approach to Peace

The peculiar nature and problems of international law are suggested by the fact that legal theorists and political scientists disagree about whether or not it is really law. This dispute turns on the question of whether or not "real law" must emanate from an authoritative legislative source, be enforced by an authoritative executive, and be applied by authoritative courts, so we need not linger over it here. Certainly, international law is not law in the same sense as domestic law is (see Chapters 2 and 14), yet international law plays some role in international relations. Thus, for our purposes, **international law** may be defined as *the body of rules and principles that nations usually accept as binding in their relations with one another.*

Before World War I, war was entirely legal under international law, and the law was useful as an approach to establishing peace only in the sense that it provided a body of rules and principles for the settlement of international disputes and therefore helped to avoid or limit war. Since 1918, however, war—at least war waged for any purpose other than self-defense—has become illegal in international law. The Covenant of the League of Nations severely restricted the circumstances in which its members could legally go to war; and nearly all the nations in the world ratified the Kellogg-Briand Pact of 1928, which declared that all the nations "condemn recourse to war for the solution of international controversies and renounce it as an instrument of national policy." The Charter of the United Nations requires that all its members "shall settle their international disputes by peaceful means" and "refrain . . . from the threat or use of force against the territorial integrity or political independence of any other state" (Article 2). Thus international law now seeks to prevent war by making war illegal as well as by providing rules and procedures for settling the disputes that lead to war.

Scope and Content

The rules of international law fall into four main categories: (1) The *law of peace* includes rules such as those affecting the legal creation of sovereign nations and their recognition by other nations, the definition of national boundaries, the extent of nations' legal jurisdictions over their territories, and the status of alien persons and property. (2) The *law of war* regulates the declaration and termination of war; the conduct of hostilities; the treatment of enemy civilians and their property, prisoners of war, and spies; and exclusion of certain weapons (such as poison gas). (3) The *law of neutrality* includes the definition and protection of the mutual rights and obligations of neutral and belligerent nations in time of war. (4) The *laws concerning resort to war*, as we have noted, now consist of prohibitions against war except for purposes of self-defense.

Structure

The differences between domestic and international law, all of which relate to the utility of the latter as an approach to peace, are most clearly shown by examining the legislative, judicial, and executive structure of international law.

INTERNATIONAL LEGISLATION   The rules of international law arise from two principal sources. Some rules come from customs, which are regular ways of handling certain types of situations followed by nations over a long period of time (such as the custom that a nation will not arrest, try, or imprison official diplomatic representatives from other nations). Other rules arise from treaties (formal agreements between two or more nations). It is important to note that *no* rule of international law is formally binding upon any nation that has not voluntarily accepted that rule, and no custom is binding unless the nation voluntarily adheres to that custom. For example, from 1979 to 1981, Iran did not let the diplomatic-immunity rule deter it from capturing the U.S. embassy in Teheran and holding over sixty U.S. diplomats hostage for well over a year. Furthermore, no treaty is legally binding on a nation unless the treaty has been officially ratified by that nation. Thus no new rule of international law can legally be forced upon a nation by any outside agency, for that would violate the nation's sovereignty (see Chapter 17).

Once a nation has accepted a custom or ratified a treaty, how binding are the treaty's rules *legally*? Two equally valid but contradictory legal maxims apply: *pacta sunt servanda* ("agreements are to be observed"), which means that a nation cannot legally free itself unilaterally from treaty obligations; and *rebus sic stantibus* ("in this state of affairs"), meaning that a treaty ceases to be legally binding as soon as the conditions under which it was negotiated and signed have substantially changed. Who, then, is to say which treaty obligations are binding upon a nation and which are not? Who is authorized to interpret international law? There is only one realistic answer: Each nation interprets the law *for itself*. However, if it wishes, it may submit questions of disputed interpretation to an international judicial body.

INTERNATIONAL ADJUDICATION   Some nations sometimes submit disputed legal questions to *arbitration*, in which they agree to have a third party settle their dispute. However, the only body that resembles a world court is the International Court

THE INTERNATIONAL COURT OF JUSTICE IN SESSION.

of Justice (ICJ). This tribunal sits in The Hague in the Netherlands, and consists of fifteen judges, each selected from a different nation for a nine-year term by concurrent action of the UN Security Council and General Assembly.

The ICJ, however, is a pale image of a "world supreme court." It has no compulsory jurisdiction; that is, there is no legal way in which the ICJ can compel any nation to appear before it. The Statute of the Court declares in Article 36 that its jurisdiction covers "all cases which the parties refer to it." The statute's often-mentioned "optional clause," to be sure, allows the parties to a dispute to make unilateral declarations "that they recognize as compulsory *ipso facto* and without special agreement, in relation to any other state accepting the same obligation, the jurisdiction of the Court" in certain kinds of cases. Yet over half of the members of the UN have not made such declarations, and most that have (including the United States and Great Britain) have hedged their declarations with so many qualifications and reservations that those nations are legally quite free to refuse to participate in any kind of dispute before the Court (as the United States did, with full legality, in 1984 when it refused to appear before the Court and answer a charge brought by Nicaragua that it was illegally trying to overthrow the Nicaraguan government). The ICJ cannot legally compel any nation to appear before it, nor can any nation legally "arraign" another nation against the latter's desires. This lack of any effective compulsory jurisdiction sharply differentiates the ICJ from the domestic courts of a nation.

EXECUTION   The execution of international law is also decentralized and feeble, and for the most part the rules are enforced only by the voluntary compliance of nations. Before World War I the only way in which a nation could legally be compelled to obey international law was through breaking diplomatic relations, boycotts, blockades, and even military intervention. The collective-security provisions of the League of Nations Covenant and the UN Charter permit the use of collective sanctions for the enforcement of international law; but, as we have seen, those provisions have been little used for this purpose. For the most part, accordingly, the enforcement of international law depends upon the willingness of nations to abide by it rather than upon compulsion by any international police force.

Record

There is a widespread impression that international law is a kind of political joke and that nations ignore it all the time as a matter of course. However, this impression is inaccurate, for, as J. L. Brierly has pointed out:

> [International] law is normally observed because . . . the demands that it makes on states are generally not exacting, and on the whole states find it convenient to observe it; but this fact receives little notice because the interest of most people in international law is not in the ordinary routine of international legal business, but in the occasions, rare but generally sensational, on which it is flagrantly broken. Such breaches generally occur either when some great political issue has arisen between states, or in that part of the system which professes to regulate the conduct of war.[5]

The rules of international law that apply to technical and nonpolitical matters are thus usually observed by nations for the excellent reason that those nations find such observance to be in their interest, and those rules constitute the great bulk of international law. This service to humanity, as Brierly points out, should not be over-looked or undervalued.

By the same token, however, the few areas in which international law is largely impotent are precisely those in which conflicts generally lead to war. International law in the current state of world politics thus makes many valuable contributions but is of little use as a barrier against war. The value and limitations of its contribution have been well summed up by Gaetano Anzilotti, a former justice of the ICJ:

> The interests protected by international law are not those which are of major weight in the life of states. It is sufficient to think of the great political and economic rivalries to which no juridical formula applies, in order to realize the truth of this statement. International law develops its true function in a sphere considerably circumscribed and modest, not in that in which there move the great conflicts of interest which in-duce states to stake their very existence in order to make them prevail.[6]

Perhaps that is why the often-heard charges that U.S. participation in the Vietnam War and U.S. aid to the Nicaraguan contras were illegal had no effect on ending either activity and why, by the same token, the alleged U.S. violations of in-ternational law in its border disputes with Mexico in the 1970s were settled amica-bly out of court.

Approaches to Peace through the United Nations

The UN, like its predecessor, the League of Nations (1919–1946), is not intended to achieve world peace by abolishing the state system. The UN Charter explicitly states that "the Organization is based on the principle of the sovereign equality of all its Members" (Article 2), which, as we noted in Chapter 17, is the basic legal principle of the state system. The UN is clearly not, as the term is used in this book, a world *government*.

What is it, then? Perhaps the most accurate answer is that the UN is an inter-national *organization* that tries to do two things. First, it tries to draw together in one world organization the various agencies and efforts for seeking peace *within* the state system just outlined, so that those agencies can operate with maximum effec-tiveness. Second, the UN tries to encourage and administer international coopera-tion on many largely nonpolitical matters. The UN is not committed to any one approach to peace but attempts to facilitate all approaches that do not involve basic alterations of the state system.

The UN is thus an international organization, not a world government. In this discussion we will not attempt to examine all of its many and varied organs and ac-tivities but will concentrate on the nature and results of those charter provisions and organs most directly related to efforts to maintain peace and security.

FOUNDING

The label "united nations" was first applied to a loose association of the nations fighting against Germany and Japan in World War II (1939–1945). On or after January 1, 1942, all of those nations signed the Declaration of the United Nations, a document that proclaimed some general war aims and pledged the signatories not to make a separate peace with the enemy. Preliminary plans for a permanent peacetime organization of those nations were drawn up at two conferences in Washington in 1944. The Charter of the United Nations was written at the UN conference on international organization in San Francisco in 1945. The UN was launched in 1946, when the first General Assembly and Security Council met in London. Since 1950 the organization has had its permanent headquarters in New York City.

STRUCTURE

Membership

The UN consists of the fifty-one nations that originally signed the charter and the nations that have subsequently applied and been admitted by votes of the General Assembly upon recommendations by the Security Council. As of 1994 there were 184 members, including almost all of the nations of the world. Only one nation (Indonesia) has withdrawn (it later rejoined), and one (the Chinese Nationalist government of Taiwan) has been expelled.

Organs

According to the charter (Article 7) the UN has six principal organs: the General Assembly, Security Council, Secretariat, Economic and Social Council, International Court of Justice, and Trusteeship Council (see Figure 18.2). We will consider only the first three here.

GENERAL ASSEMBLY   The General Assembly is the only organ of the UN that includes all the member nations, and it holds annual sessions. Each nation has one vote, although each can send a delegation of up to five members. The General Assembly exercises powers and functions that may be called *deliberative* (discussing any matters within the scope of the Charter); *supervisory* (controlling and regulating other organs by receiving annual reports from those organs and establishing certain administrative procedures for those organs to follow); *financial* (making up the UN budget and apportioning expenses among the members); *elective* (admitting new members and choosing members for the other organs); and *constituent* (proposing amendments to the Charter). Several of those powers, as we will see, are exercised jointly with the Security Council. The General Assembly decides "important questions" (as defined in Article 18) by two-thirds majorities of the members present and voting and decides all other matters by simple majorities.

SECURITY COUNCIL   The Security Council is composed of fifteen member nations, divided into two classes: five permanent members (the PRC, France, Russia,[7] Great Britain, and the United States) and ten nonpermanent members, which are

FIGURE 18.2 The Structure of the United Nations

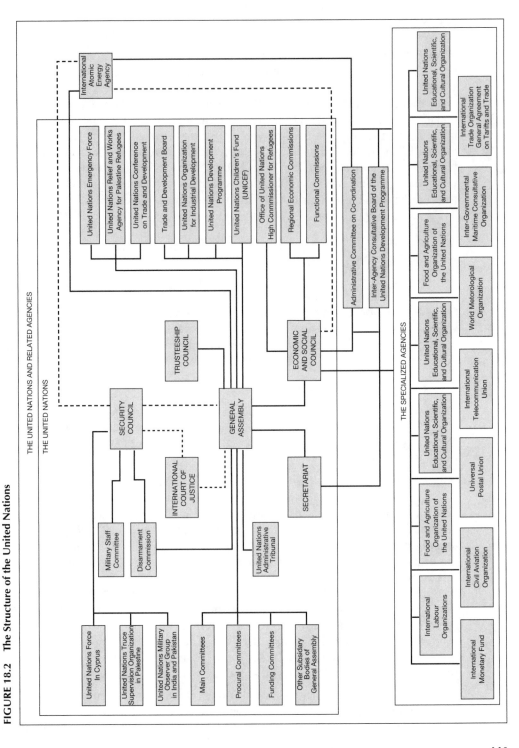

THE UNITED NATIONS GENERAL ASSEMBLY IN SESSION.

elected for two-year terms by the General Assembly. The terms of the elected members are staggered so that five new members are elected each year, and no nonpermanent member may serve two consecutive terms. The Security Council was originally intended to bear the main responsibility for and control over UN machinery for maintaining peace and security, but it has come to share a good deal of its power in this area with the General Assembly.

The most noteworthy feature of the Security Council is its voting procedure, which provides for a veto by each of the five permanent members. Article 27 of the charter stipulates:

1.   Each member of the Security Council shall have one vote.
2.   Decisions of the Security Council on procedural matters shall be made by an affirmative vote of nine members.
3.   Decisions of the Security Council on all other matters shall be made by an affirmative vote of nine members including the concurring votes of the permanent members.

Thus the Security Council, which is supposed to be the UN's main organ, cannot act unless the five permanent members unanimously agree that it should act (or at least abstain from voting no). This veto provision and its frequent use, especially by the former Soviet Union and the United States, has often been blamed for the failure of the organization to live up to its promise, but it has simply recognized the facts of international life. No resolution *for action* adopted by the UN could possibly have been effective if either of the two superpowers, the former Soviet Union and the United States, had believed that such action would threaten its vital interests and had strongly opposed it. In short, the veto has not created the present nature of world politics. It has merely reflected it.

SECRETARIAT AND SECRETARY-GENERAL   The UN Secretariat is the organization's civil service and performs many secretarial, research, and other administrative chores for the various agencies. It is headed by the secretary-general, who is appointed by the General Assembly on the recommendation of the Security Council. In addition to acting as the organization's chief administrative officer, the secretary-general plays a significant political role. Article 99 of the charter authorizes the secretary-general to "bring to the attention of the Security Council any matter which in his opinion may threaten international peace and security." All occupants of the office to date—from Trygve Lie (1946–54) to Boutros Boutros-Ghali (1992–)—have made full use of this power, and the office of secretary-general has come to be one of the most powerful agencies in the UN structure, exercising a major influence on its operations.

Those are the UN's principal organs for maintaining international peace and security. Let us now review the Charter's provisions for handling peace and security matters and see how those provisions have worked out in practice.

MAINTAINING INTERNATIONAL PEACE AND SECURITY

The UN Charter incorporates many of the approaches to peace we have been considering. The General Assembly and Security Council are forums in which international issues can be discussed and "world public opinion" can be expressed. The Economic and Social Council and affiliated specialized agencies provide opportunities for cooperation on many nonpolitical and technical matters, to the benefit of most nations. The UN also has agencies for the mediation and conciliation of international disputes, the adjudication of international legal controversies (the ICJ), and the reduction and regulation of armaments.

However, the UN relies upon collective security as its main approach to preventing war. The relevant provisions are stated principally in the charter's Chapter VII, Articles 39–51, and may be briefly summarized as follows: The Security Council is charged with determining "the existence of any threat to the peace, breach of the peace, or act of aggression" and with deciding what measures will be taken when such threats arise (Article 39). The Security Council may decide to adopt measures not involving the use of armed force and may call upon the members to apply them. "These may include complete or partial interruption of economic relations and of rail, sea, air, postal, telegraphic, radio, and other means of communication, and the severance of diplomatic relations" (Article 41). If the Security Council decides that those measures are inadequate, then it may adopt others "to maintain or restore international peace and security. Such action may include demonstrations, blockades, and other operations by air, sea, or land forces of Members of the United Nations" (Article 42). And the members are obligated to respond to the Security Council's requests that they take such action (Articles 48–50).

Those charter provisions are clearly intended to create a strong collective-security system centered upon the Security Council as the decision-making body. How have they worked out in practice?

CHANGING THE UNITED NATIONS

From the founding of the UN to 1989, the basic fact of international life, as we have seen, was the cold war between the United States and its allies on the one hand and the Soviet Union and its allies on the other (see Chapter 17). During this period (1946–1989) the fundamental prerequisite for the successful operation of the UN collective-security system—unanimity among the permanent members of the Security Council—was rarely present. In those instances of aggression or breaches of the peace in which the Soviet Union and the United States favored different sides, the Security Council was unable to take any action because one of the superpowers used or threatened to use its veto; and on occasion other permanent members did the same.

The most notable exception prior to 1990 was the Korean action of 1950. In June 1950, Communist North Korea launched an armed invasion of non-Communist South Korea, a clear instance of aggression in violation of the charter. By an ironic twist of fate, the Soviets at that moment were boycotting the UN in protest against the UN's failure to admit the PRC, and the U.S.-sponsored resolution in the Security Council to invoke Article 42 against North Korea was passed. The Soviets returned too late to veto it. However, the response of the member nations to the Security Council's call for troops to help repel the invasion was somewhat less than unanimous enthusiastic cooperation. Of the sixty member nations, only sixteen sent armed forces of any kind, and only the United States, Great Britain, Canada, and Turkey sent more than token forces. The war ended with an uneasy truce in 1953, and the episode while not a total collapse, was certainly not a great success for the UN's collective-security system.

On several other occasions the UN has sent small peace-keeping forces or truce-supervising teams into some of the world's trouble spots to observe, report, and try to prevent violations of truce agreements among warring factions or nations (the forces sent to Cambodia, Somalia, and Bosnia-Herzegovina are recent examples). However, prior to 1991 UN forces were sent only when the Soviet Union and the United States agreed that they should be sent or when the General Assembly acted to bypass the Security Council.

The UN in the 1990s is different from the organization created in the 1940s, and its changing nature has had a lot to do with the considerable fluctuations in its importance as an agency for maintaining peace and security. Its history has so far seen four main phases. The basic facts about each phase are shown in Table 18.1, and the story of each is as follows.

TABLE 18.1   Changing Membership of the United Nations, 1965–1994

	1945–1954	% of Votes 1954	1955–1964	1965–1989	1990–1994	Total 1994	% of Votes 1994
			BY PERIOD OF ADMISSION				
African-Asian	10	17%	35	21	4	70	38%
Eastern Europe	6	10	5	0	18	29	16
U.S. and Western Europe	10	17	6	1	4	21	11
British Commonwealth	4	7	1	10	0	15	8
Latin America	20	34	1	2	0	23	13
Middle East (Muslim)	7	12	2	4	0	13	7
Other	2	3	4	5	2	13	7
Totals	59	100%	54	43	28	184	100%

Source: *The World Almanac and Book of Facts 1994* (Mahwah, NJ: Funk & Wagnalls, 1994), pp. 834–35.

Decline of the Security Council, Rise of the General Assembly, 1946–1954

In its first decade the membership of the UN was little changed, and most of its proceedings were dominated by a coalition led by the United States. On most issues the United States could count on the support of the nations in Western Europe, the British Commonwealth, and Latin America. In the Security Council the Soviet Union often vetoed actions proposed by the United States, but in the General Assembly the U.S.-led coalition could usually muster thirty-nine of the sixty members, and this majority enabled the United States to carry most of the resolutions it wished. The most notable of those resolutions was the uniting-for-peace resolution passed over Soviet opposition in 1950. This resolution provided that in instances in which there appeared to be acts of aggression that threatened peace and in which the Security Council, because of a veto by one of its permanent members, failed to recommend action under Articles 41 and 42, the General Assembly would immediately consider the matter. If two thirds of the members agreed, then the General Assembly would recommend that the member nations use whatever measures, including armed force, seemed appropriate to maintain or restore international peace and security.

Thus, in 1950 the General Assembly assumed a good deal of the power in the collective-security area originally reserved for the Security Council, and that power was used several times after 1955. In 1960, for example, the General Assembly, over strong Soviet-bloc opposition, sent 23,000 troops from UN members to the Congo to prevent expansion of the civil war in that newly independent nation, and Secretary-General Dag Hammarskjöld was killed in the crash of a UN plane flying a reconnaisance mission over the fighting area. In 1956 the UN sent an emergency force of 6,000 troops to the Middle East to supervise the armistice lines established

THE UN AS PEACEKEEPER. A soldier of the UN peacekeeping force in Bosnia.

after the war between Egypt and Israel. The force remained in place for years afterward but was unable to prevent the outbreak in 1967 of the Six-Day War between Israel and the Arab nations and later was unable to prevent violations of the postwar cease-fire agreements, and a new war broke out in 1973.

Third World Dominance, 1955–1964

The first two decades after World War II saw the breakup of most of the prewar colonial empires, particularly the British, French, and Dutch. The result was a great expansion in the number of independent sovereign nations, almost all of which applied for membership in the UN. The dam burst in 1955–1956, when the UN admitted twenty new members. Over the next nine years it added thirty-four more members. Thus by 1964 the UN had 113 members, compared with the original 59, and the organization's politics changed radically. The United States added only six new members to its coalition and the Soviet bloc added only a dozen or so. The great gainers were the countries, mainly in Africa and Asia, called "Third World" because they claimed to be politically as well as geographically and economically separate from the Western bloc and the Communist bloc.

At first, with the Security Council still stymied by the superpowers' vetoes, most issues were fought out mainly in the General Assembly. By the early 1960s the Western bloc could regularly muster a coalition of only about one third of the members, the Soviet bloc could do about the same, and the remaining third consisted of the new nations. Both the Western and Soviet blocs sought the Third World bloc's support, and each won a few and lost a few.

In 1964, however, the General Assembly's new ascendance received a major setback. By a two-thirds vote under the uniting-for-peace resolution, the General Assembly ordered UN peace-keeping forces into the Congo in Africa and the Gaza Strip in the Middle East. Both France and the Soviet Union denounced those orders and refused to pay the special assessments voted by the General Assembly to support the UN forces. The consequences seemed perfectly clear: The ICJ ruled that the operations were lawful and that all members were obligated to pay. Article 19 of the charter provides that any member nation more than two years in arrears of its financial obligations as voted by the General Assembly will be deprived of its vote in the UN. However, when it came time to enforce this rule, the General Assembly—and most of the Third World countries—backed down. In its 1964 session no formal votes were taken at all,[8] France and the Soviet Union were not expelled, and the principle was established that in fact the General Assembly cannot force a major power to abide by any of its decisions calling for action unless that nation volunteers to do so. In short, a quasi-veto power came to operate in the General Assembly as well as in the Security Council.

Much Talk, Little Action, 1965–1989

Table 18.1 shows that from 1965 to 1989 the UN admitted forty-three new members, of which twenty-one are located in Africa and Asia. By 1989 the African and Asian nations constituted nearly half of the entire membership, and Third World nations together controlled well over two-thirds of the votes in the General Assembly. Of course, the Third World nations did not and do not vote together on all questions, and they continued to split sometimes into several caucuses: the African-Asian caucus, the African caucus, the Latin American caucus, the "nonaligned nations" caucus, and so on. From 1955 to 1989, the Third World nations regularly united on resolutions condemning Israel, South Africa, U.S. actions in Central America, and indeed any resolution dealing with what the Third World nations regarded as the vestiges of colonialism. The Soviet bloc invariably supported such resolutions, and the Western bloc was usually a small minority. Occasionally, many Third World nations joined the Western bloc in resolutions criticizing the Soviet Union (for example, a 1980 resolution condemning Soviet armed intervention in Afghanistan, and a 1983 resolution condemning the Soviets for shooting down a South Korean civilian airliner). Third World nations could also get near-unanimous support (joined by both the Western and Soviet blocs) urging warring nations, such as Iran and Iraq, to cease fire and settle their differences by peaceful means. However, the General Assembly could get a two-thirds vote for a resolution calling for real action under the uniting-for-peace precedent only when such a resolution was not strongly opposed by either the Western or the Soviet bloc, and that did not happen very often.

From 1990 to 1994 twenty-eight new nations emerged. The dissolution of the Soviet Union in 1991 created fifteen, (the republics of the former USSR), there were four new nations in Africa and Asia (Eritrea, Namibia, North Korea, and South Korea), four in Western Europe (Andorra, Liechtenstein, Monaco, and San Marino), and two in the Pacific (the Federated States of Micronesia and the Marshall Islands). In addition, the breakup of the former Yugoslavia added two new nations (Bosnia-Herzegovina and Croatia), and Czechoslovakia split into two nations, the Czech Republic and Slovakia. The UN admitted all twenty-eight new nations to membership.

The UN's record in preventing or stopping major aggression and war was not impressive before 1989. As we have seen, the UN did play a minor role in monitoring a truce between Israel and Egypt after their war in 1973 but played no role of any significance in the wars between the United States and North Vietnam (1964–1973), India and Pakistan (1971), Israel and Syria in Lebanon (1978–1985), Ethiopia and Somalia (1978–   ), Libya and Chad (1979–1981), or Great Britain and Argentina (1982), or in the Soviet invasion of Aghanistan (1979–1989) and the seemingly endless conflicts in Central America (1979–).

Revival: 1985–1994 and Beyond

The end of the cold war has had many consequences, not least of which has been a revival of the UN as a significant factor in world politics. The growing cooperation between the United States and the republics of the former USSR is also reflected in their activities inside the UN. Since 1989 neither the United States nor the formerly communist nations have made a move in the Security Council or the General Assembly that was totally unacceptable to the other, and each used its veto sparingly (from 1989 to 1994 Russia used its veto only three times, and the United States did not use its veto at all). As a result, Secretary-General Javier Perez de Cuellar (1982–1992) and his successor, Boutros Boutros-Ghali (1992), were able to take several initiatives that would have been impossible during the cold war. For example, Perez de Cuellar mediated the end of the long (1980–1988) and bloody war between Iran and Iraq, oversaw the independence of Namibia, helped to arrange the Soviet withdrawal from Afghanistan, and in 1991 he played a key role in securing the release of a number of American, British, French, and German hostages kidnapped by pro-Iranian terrorist organizations in Lebanon. Boutros-Ghali successfuly pressed for sending UN peace-keeping forces to Cambodia, Bosnia-Herzegovina, and Somalia.

The revival of the UN was further marked by the fact that when the United States started building its coalition to oppose Iraq's invasion and occupation of Kuwait in 1990, President Bush and his advisers chose to work through rather than outside of the UN. The United States sponsored a number of resolutions in the Security Council and General Assembly condemning the invasion and authorizing the use of force to expel Iraq. Neither the Soviet Union nor the Russian republic vetoed or even opposed the resolutions, and the military units that drove Iraq out of Kuwait in 1991, while consisting mainly of U.S., British, French, and Saudi Arabian forces commanded by U.S. General H. Norman Schwarzkopf, were formally a United Nations force acting under Article 41 of the UN Charter.

This does not mean that the UN has moved closer to becoming a world government. In legal theory and political fact the UN is still based on total acceptance of the state system. Its ability to get things done has been significantly increased by the end of the cold war, but the UN still can take significant action only when its powerful member nations want it to. It is too early to be certain what will happen to the international politics and the UN as the result of the dissolution of the Soviet Union, the new members added as a result of that dissolution, the increasing integration of the European Community, and the replacement of the Soviet Union by the Russian republic on the Security Council. However, it is clear that the UN is a more significant factor in world politics in the 1990s than it has been since the early 1950s.

Even so, the UN remains a part of the state system. If the state system is, as some believe, the basic cause of war between nations, then the UN is powerless to prevent it. But if, even within the state system, there is some real hope of preventing World War III, then the organization will continue to make a useful contribution to keeping that hope alive.

On the other hand, since 1990 the world has seen in nations as different as Yugoslavia and Rwanda the growing passions of ethnic groups to win recognition for their unique traits and/or to fight for "ethnic cleansing" by driving other groups out or slaughtering them. Some observers, indeed, say that the new tribalism has already replaced the old global cold war with many local hot wars, and neither the one remaining superpower, the United States, nor the United Nations can prevent or contain them.

Does Humanity Have a Future?

In several parts of this book we have noted the enormous changes in the structure of world politics, the prospects for war, and the clash of ideologies resulting from the disbanding of the Soviet Union and its replacement by fifteen independent republics. Let it be confessed that no political scientist publicly predicted this immense change and that it caught almost all of us, certainly including the author of this book, by surprise.

This should not surprise anyone. In the present state of political science, there are many questions that cannot be answered with any degree of confidence beyond that of the educated guess. The most important question of all is certainly an example: Does humanity have a future?

Political scientists usually regret their inability to make reliable predictions on such matters, but perhaps in this instance it is just as well. For, if the answer is that thermonuclear world war is inevitable and humanity has no future, then most of us would prefer not to know it until we have to.

DOING A GOOD JOB?

Since 1970, the Gallup poll has often asked its respondents, "In general, do you think the UN is doing a good job in trying to solve the problems it has had to face?" The percentages replying "a good job" are shown in the table:

YEAR	PERCENTAGE REPLYING "A GOOD JOB"
1970	44
1975	33
1980	31
1985	28
1990	54

Source: *The Gallup Poll, 1990* (Wilmington, DE: Scholarly Resources, Inc., 1991), p. 123.

In any case, the best answer political scientists (or anyone else) can give has two parts: First, there is every reason to suppose that international and civil wars at some level will continue for many decades to come and perhaps forever. Let us remember that since Germany surrendered in 1945 there have been at least sixteen major international and civil wars and over thirty lesser wars.

Second, however, humanity's chances of avoiding World War III seem better in the mid-1990s than at any time since 1945. During most of those decades there was a very real possibility that the struggle between the two great superpowers and their allies would escalate into a nuclear holocaust, and for a few fearful days in 1962 it looked as though the Cuban missile crisis would trigger just such an Armageddon. But it didn't happen. For whatever reason, the only nuclear weapons yet used in combat were the bombs dropped on Hiroshima and Nagasaki by the United States in 1945.

In the 1990s the probability of a thermonuclear World War III is far smaller than it was in 1962 or at any other time from 1945 to 1989. The Soviet Union has dissolved and the cold war has ended. To be sure, thousands of nuclear warheads are still stored in the United States, Kazakhstan, Russia, and Ukraine, and hundreds are stored in China, France, Great Britain, and India; but, by bilateral agreements, all these nations are reducing their nuclear arsenals. The United States is giving substantial economic assistance to Russia and other former enemies in Eastern Europe. The Warsaw Pact has been terminated, and many of its former members are seeking membership in NATO. Yes, combat with conventional weapons continues in Bosnia-Herzegovina, Rwanda, Somalia, and other areas, and civilians as well as soldiers continue to die in those places. But there appears to be little chance that such localized conflicts will lead to thermonuclear World War III.

Truly, as former President George Bush said in 1991, the peoples of the earth live today in a new world order. Political scientists *can* predict with confidence at least some of the features of that order. Most political scientists, for example, believe that, at least in the immediate future, a growing number of nations will face demands for secession and independence from some of their ethnic groups that may

PEACEMAKERS. Israeli Prime Minister Itzhak Rabin shakes hands with Palestine Liberation Organization Chairman Yasir Arafat after negotiations mediated by U.S. President Bill Clinton, 1994.

escalate into civil wars as they have in Northern Ireland and parts of the former Soviet Union and the former Yugoslavia.

Paradoxically, however, there will be an increase in the activities and role of multinational organizations such as the UN, the European Community, and the Organization of American States. The UN will continue to have its greatest successes in nonpolitical and technical matters, such as combatting illiteracy and disease. The UN will also continue to play a role of some significance in efforts to prevent aggression and maintain peace by facilitating collective security, disarmament, and peaceful settlement of disputes. But the staggering burden of preventing international and civil wars from escalating into a thermonuclear world war will continue to be borne, as it has been in the past, by the rickety old structures and processes of the state system.

That much the political scientist can foretell. Does humanity have a future? Our chances certainly look better today than they have for a long time, but no one can be certain that those chances will look as good or better in the twenty-first century. I, personally, am an optimist. But as thermonuclear-age humor has it, "An optimist is one who believes that the future is uncertain."

For Further Reading

INTERNATIONAL POLITICS

JACOBSON, HAROLD K. *Networks of Interdependence*, 2nd ed. New York: Alfred A. Knopf, 1984. Calm and balanced survey of governmental and nongovernmental international organizations, and their achievements, limitations, and problems.

JERVIS, ROBERT. *The Meaning of the Nuclear Revolution: Statecraft and the Prospect of Armageddon*. Ithaca, NY: Cornell University Press, 1989. Analysis of the impact of nuclear weapons on diplomacy and foreign policy.

MUELLER, JOHN. *Retreat from Doomsday: The Obsolescence of Major War*. New York: Basic Books, 1989. Argument that nuclear weapons have minimized the possibility of all-out World War III.

NYE, JOSEPH S., JR. *Bound to Lead: The Changing Nature of American Power*. New York: Basic Books, 1990. Analysis by a leading academic and former assistant secretary of state of the new context for U.S. foreign policy created by the decline of the USSR as a superpower.

SUGANAMI, HIDEMI. *The Domestic Analogy and World Order Proposals*. New York: Cambridge University Press, 1989. Analysis of two sets of ideas for developing a new order of world politics: those proposing abolition of the state system and construction of a true world government and those accepting the inevitability of the state system and proposing to improve its war-preventing institutions.

BALANCE OF POWER

DEHIO, LUDWIG. *The Precarious Balance*. New York: Alfred A. Knopf, 1962. Analysis of balance-of-power policies in modern conditions.

RIKER, WILLIAM H. *The Theory of Political Coalitions*. New Haven, CT: Yale University Press, 1962. Leading formal-theory study of political coalitions, with many applications to international power relations.

COLLECTIVE SECURITY

BEATON, LEONARD. *The Reform of Power: A Proposal for an International Security System*. New York: Viking, 1972. Argument in favor of collective security as the main path to peace.

NUGENT, NEIL. *The Government and Politics of the European Community*. Durham, NC: Duke University Press, 1989. Useful description of one of the increasingly important actors in international politics.

DISARMAMENT

CARTER, APRIL. *Success and Failure in Arms Control Negotiations*. New York: Oxford University Press, 1989. Detailed examination of arms-control negotiations between the United States and the Soviet Union from the late 1950s to the late 1980s.

EPSTEIN, WILLIAM. *The Last Chance: Nuclear Proliferation and Arms Control*. New York: Free Press, 1976. Study of nuclear disarmament, with special attention to the *n*th-country problem.

Harvard Nuclear Study Group. *Living with Nuclear Weapons*. New York: Bantam, 1983. Widely read

study of problems and possibilities for nuclear disarmament.

WALKER, JENNONE. *Security and Arms Control in Post-Confrontation Europe*. New York: Oxford University Press, 1993. Analysis of NATO and other collective security possibilities after the disintegration of the USSR and the termination of the Warsaw Pact.

WIESELTIER, LEON. *Nuclear War, Nuclear Peace*. New York: Holt, Rinehart & Winston, 1983. Study of consequences of nuclear war and of possibilities for nuclear arms management and control.

INTERNATIONAL LAW

BRIERLY, J. L. *The Law of Nations*, 6th ed. New York: Oxford University Press, 1963. A leading survey of the nature, principles, and applications of international law.

VON GLAHN, GERHARD. *Law Among Nations*, 5th ed. New

York: Macmillan, 1986. Updated version of a standard text on international law.

O'BRIEN, WILLIAM V. *The Conduct of Just and Limited War*. New York: Praeger, 1981. Study of philosophical attitudes toward war and international law.

THE UNITED NATIONS

GATI, TOBY T., ed. *The U.S., the U.N., and the Management of Global Change*. New York: New York University Press, 1983. Essays by various authors on the changing nature of the UN, its place in U.S. foreign policy, and its future problems and possibilities.

MURPHY, JOHN P. *The United Nations and the Control of International Violence*. Totowa, NJ: Allanheld, Osmun, 1983. Mainly legal analysis of UN authority to prevent international violence and descriptions of main instances in which the power has been used.

PETERSON, M. J. *The General Assembly in World Politics*. Winchester, MA: Allen & Unwin, 1986. Study of the Third-World's domination of the UN General Assembly.

WEISS, THOMAS G., DAVID P. FORSYTHE, AND ROGER A. CONTE. *The United Nations and Changing World Politics*. Boulder, CO: Westview Press, 1994. Survey of the changing structure and role of the United Nations.

Notes

1. The authoritative public account is still Samuel Glasstone, ed., *The Effect of Nuclear Weapons*, rev. ed. (Washington, DC: U.S. Atomic Energy Commission, 1962).

2. Harrison Brown and James Real, *Community of Fear* (Santa Barbara, CA: Center for the Study of Democratic Institutions, 1960), pp. 14–20.

3. Quoted in Ralph E. Lapp, "The Einstein Letter That Started it All," *The New York Times Magazine*, August 2, 1964.

4. Hans J. Morgenthau and Kenneth W. Thompson, *Politics Among Nations: The Struggle for Power and Peace*, 6th ed. (New York: Alfred A. Knopf, 1985), p. 454.

5. J. L. Brierly, *The Law of Nations*, 6th ed. (New York: Oxford University Press, 1963), pp. 71–72.

6. Quoted in H. Lauterpacht, *The Function of Law in the International Community* (New York: Oxford University Press, 1933), p. 169.

7. The breakup of the Soviet Union (see Chapter 2) necessitated some changes in its position as a member of the UN and a permanent member of the Security Council. Belorussia and Ukraine retained the seats they already held in the General Assembly, and the former USSR's permanent seat on the Security Council was taken by Russia. Each of the other twelve newly independent republics applied for membership, and all were given seats in the General Assembly in 1991–1992.

8. When an issue had to be decided, General Assembly President Alex Quaison-Sackley of Ghana would invite the members to give him their opinions privately, after which he would announce the Assembly's consensus.

Photo Credits

Index

Aaron, Henry J., 402
Aberbach, Joel D., 317
Abernathy, Ralph, 386
Abortion
   conflict over, 8, 34–39, 362
   lifting of "gag rule," 271
Abraham, Henry J., 347, 492
Absolute majority election systems, 169
Access, 9
Action, political:
   in democratic theory, 8–9
   in different political cultures, 64–67
   lobbying, 9
   tactics, 8–17, 197–98
   varying levels in modern democracies, 189
   working inside political parties, 9–10
Adams, John, 25
Adjudicating disputes, 297
"Administocracy," 309–10
Administrative discretion, 308
Administrators:
   accountability and responsibility, 309–14
   administrative rules, 306
   in authoritarian regimes, 314–15
   conforming to professional standards, 310
   control by courts, 315
   control by elected officials, 311–14
   defined, 289
   direct relations with citizens, 288
   distinguished from executives, 288–90
   functions, 293–97
   intervention by ombudsmen, 316
   oversight by legislators, 312–13
   partisan political activity, 299–300
   policy making by, 303–309
   politics and administration dichotomy, 302–303, 309
   proportion selected by merit system, 298–99
   proportions of work forces, 290–91
   representation of general population, 310–11
   selection by patronage, 297–98
   size, 290–91
   spoils system and merit system, 298–99
   structure, 291–93
   unions and strikes, 300
Adversarial justice systems, 327–28
Advertising, political, 139–41

Affect, 47–48
Affirmative action:
   Bakke case, 346
   conflict over, 5, 364
   reverse discrimination?, 395
Afghanistan, 415, 429, 453
African-Americans:
   and affirmative action, 5, 8, 368
   antidiscrimination and affirmative action, 392–96
   and "blacks," 384
   civil rights movement, 15, 384–92
   discrimination against, 352, 353, 382–83
   ideology, 126
   lynching, 352, 359
   registration and voting, 388–89
   segregation in schools, 343
   status compared with whites, 385
   urban riots, 16
   voting preferences, 21, 22, 54
African National Congress (South Africa), 399
Age, 57, 95
Agnew, Spiro T., 141
Agresto, John, 347
AIDS, 16
Ailes, Roger, 208
Air traffic controllers' strike, 301
Alabama, 389
Albania, 437
Algeria, 101, 110
Allensbach Institut für Demoskopie, 118
Alliances, 420–21
Almond, Gabriel A., 44fn, 68, 69fn
al-Qaddafi, Muammar, 45, 78, 106, 268
Altheide, David, 141
American Association of Retired Persons (AARP), 10
American Bar Association (ABA), 345
American Institute of Public Opinion (*see* Gallup polls)
American Medical Association (AMA), 31, 34, 202
"Americanization" of election campaigns, 199
Amicus curiae briefs, 346
Andorra, 453
Andrews, William G., 285
Anne of Austria, 375
Anne, Queen of England, 375
Anthony, Susan B., 367
Antigua and Barbuda, 356

Anzilotti, Gaetano, 444
Apparatchiks (Soviet bureaucrats), 314
Appleby, Sir Humphrey, 318fn
Apportionment of legislative districts:
  defined, 177
  general principles, 177–78
  in other democracies, 178–79
  in the United States, 100, 177–79
Aquino, Corazon, 377
Arafat, Yasir, 456
Arendt, Hanna, 91, 112
Argentina, 19, 228, 260, 264, 277, 359
Aristide, Jean-Bertrand, 268
Armenia, 51, 356
Arms limitation and control, 418, 438–40
Armstrong, Scott, 344
Arterton, F. Christopher, 156
Asher, Herbert R., 131
Asian-Americans, 21, 51
Assassination, 15–16, 236
Association of Trial Lawyers of America (ATLA), 6
Australia, 40, 101, 165, 181, 217, 219, 238, 254, 260, 264,
  283, 323, 396, 419
Austria, 40, 48, 125, 217, 236, 260, 283, 424
Austro-Hungarian Empire, 41
Authoritarian regimes:
  authoritarianism defined, 105
  characteristics, 106–107
  classifying actual governments as, 109–110
  control of bureaucracies, 314–15
  control of mass communications, 144–45
  cultivation of public opinion, 113
  distinguished from dictatorships, 107–108
  one–party or no–party systems, 221–24
  (*see also* Dictatorships)
Authority, 28–30
Azerbaijan, 356, 418
Azocar, Patricio Aylwin, 110

Bachrach, Peter, 111
Backbenchers, 244–45
"Backgrounders," 152–53
Bahrein, 356
Bakke, Allan, 395
Balance of power:
  definition, 434
  evaluation, 434–35
  methods, 434
Baldwin, Stanley, 280
Balladur, Edouard, 277
Bangladesh, 377, 408
Barber, Benjamin R., 111
Barber, James David, 247
Barghoorn, Frederick C., 69fn
Bartels, Larry, 152, 157fn, 187
Baudoin, King of Belgium, 261
Bealey, Frank, 111
Beaton, Leonard, 457

Beck, Paul Allen, 200
Becker, Carl L., 112fn
Begin, Menachem, 199
Belarus, 43, 356, 418, 431, 440
Belgium, 19, 137, 164, 172, 217, 260, 261, 282, 283, 412
Benin, 110, 356
Bentley, Arthur F., 43
Beregevoy, Pierre, 276, 277
Berelson, Bernard, 149, 150, 157fn, 200
Berger, Raoul, 347
Berlusconi, Silvio, 284
Bernstein, Carl, 157fn
Bhutan, 356
Bhutto, Benazir, 377
Biological basis of political behavior, 45–46
Bird, Rose, 334
Black, Benjamin D., 226
Black, Gordon S., 226
Blackmun, Harry, 345, 395
Blackstone, Sir William, 337, 348fn
Blair, Philip M., 347
Blair, Tony, 270
Bogdanor, Vernon, 69fn, 112fn, 186
Boland amendment, 305,
Bolivia, 424
Bonaparte, Napoleon, 298, 324
Borgia, Cesare, 78
Bork, Robert H., 234
Bosnia-Herzegovina, 449, 450, 453, 455
Botswana, 64
Boutros-Ghali, Boutros, 448, 453
Bowles, Samuel, 91
Boycotts, 16
Boyer, Ernest L., 127
Brady, Henry E., 185, 187fn
Brazil, 28, 152, 182, 228, 235, 260, 264, 277, 356, 359
Brennan, William, 345, 395
Breyer, Stephen G., 345
Brezhnev, Leonid, 60, 84, 314
Bribery, 9
Brierly, J.L., 443, 444, 457, 458fn
Brigham, John, 366
British Broadcasting Corporation (BBC), 138, 313
Brody, Richard A., 285
Brokaw, Tom, 148
Brown, Harrison, 458fn
Brown, H. Rap, 16
Brown, Linda, 344
Brown v. *Board of Education* (1954), 322, 342–43, 389–90
Brundtland, Gro Harlem, 377
Brunei, 158
Brzezinski, Zbigniew, 91, 92fn, 112fn
Buchan, John, 1
Buchanan, Pat, 141
Buchanan, William, 247, 256
"Bugging," 372–73
Bulgaria, 87, 159, 356, 437
Bureaucracy, 289–90
Burdick, Eugene L., 24

Burger, Warren, 337, 395
Burke, Edmund, 250, 256, 257fn
Burke, John P., 317
Burstein, Paul, 402
Burundi, 51
Busing issue, 343, 390–91
Buthelezi, Mangosutha Hatsha, 399
Butler, David, 156, 157fn, 182, 186, 187, 200
Butler, R. A., 262
Bush, Barbara, 266
Bush, George, 1, 3, 21, 46, 54, 115, 132, 155, 159, 165,
    171, 265 190, 197, 254, 266, 267, 268, 271, 272, 274,
    337, 345, 421, 429, 440, 454, 553

Cabinet and ministry (Great Britain), 278–82, 279–80
Cable television, 155
Cahill, Fred V., Jr., 348fn
Cain, Bruce E., 186, 187fn, 256, 256fn
California, 183, 204, 247, 334
Caligula, 78
Callaghan, James, 280
Cameron, Louise, 401
Campaigns, election:
    advertising in the mass media, 139–41
    changing nature of, 151–52, 155
Campbell, Angus, 68fn, 69fn, 200, 201fn
Campbell, Colin, 317
Campbell, Kim, 173, 377
Camus, Albert, 24
Canada:
    acid rain, 3
    candidate selection and nominations, 167, 213
    Kim Campbell, first women prime minister, 377
    common law, 323
    durability of political parties, 192
    education, 295
    judicial review, 327
    legislative committees, 238
    low party fractionalization, 217, 219, 264
    organization and regulation of mass media, 138
    political parties, 212
    referendums, 182
    regulation of mass media in election campaigns, 141
    Roman law in Quebec, 324
    Senate, 236
    stability of governments, 282, 283
    support with troops for UN intervention in Korea
      (1950), 449
    unprecedented shifts in 1993 general election,
      173–74
Candidate orientation, 197–200
Candidate selection, 165–68
Canon, Bradley C., 248
Cantril, Albert H., 131
Cape Verde Islands, 110, 356
Capitalism, 70, 79–80, 81
Cardenas, Cuanthemoc, 225
Carmichael, Stokeley, 403fn

Carter, April, 457
Carter, James C., 338, 348fn
Carter, Jimmy, 54, 198, 254, 265, 266, 270, 274, 345, 413
Carter, Rosalynn, 266
Castro, Fidel, 106, 108, 109
Categoric groups, 7–8
Catherine the Great, Queen of Russia, 375
Caucus, 242
Ceaucescu, Nicolae, 87
Cecil, Lord Robert, 282
Center for Political and Social Studies (CPSS), 47, 63,
    69, 118
Central Intelligence Agency (CIA), 306, 424
Cermak, Anton, 15
Chaban–Delmas, Jacques, 275
Chad, 110
Chamberlain, Neville, 245, 280
Chamorro, Violeta Barrios de, 110, 377
Chaplinsky v. *New Hampshire* (1942), 366fn
Charles I, King of England, 262
Charles, Mary Eugenia, 377
Checks and balances, 230
Cheney, Dick, 266
Childrens' political development, 55–56
Chile, 110, 152, 182, 277
Chirac, Jacques, 275, 276, 277
Choper, Jesse H., 347
Christina, Queen of Sweden, 375
Churchill, Winston S., 1
Cincinnatus, Lucius Quinctius, 107
Cirino, Robert, 141, 156
Citizenship:
    acquisition and loss, 39
    obligations of, 66–67
    and voting, 161
Civil disobedience, 14–15, 386–87
Civil liberties:
    conflict with security, 359–61
    in criminal trials, 355, 371–72
    defined, 349
    listed, 354–55
    nations categorized by degrees of, 357–58
    philosophy of, 350–54
    U.S. Supreme Court standards for limits of, 360–61
Civil rights:
    defined, 350
    listed, 355–56
Civil Rights Act of 1964 (U.S.), 197, 271, 390, 391, 392
Civil rights movement, 383–92
Civil War, American (1861–1865), 16, 65, 269, 383
Claire, Guy S., 309, 318fn
Classes, (social), 53–54
Clausewitz, Karl von, 427
Clear and present danger test, 360–61
Clifford, Clark, 266
Clinton, Bill, 1, 2, 5, 45, 46, 54, 63, 115, 132, 139, 152,
    155, 159, 165, 166, 171, 190, 195, 197, 213, 254, 255,
    265, 266, 268, 271, 272, 337, 345, 418, 439, 456
Clinton, Hillary Rodham, 266

Clouthier, Manuel, 225
Coalition governments, 217
Code Napoleon, 324
Codevilla, Angelo, 427
Coercion, 32–34
Cognitive maps, 46–48
Cohen v. *California* (1971), 366fn
Colbert, Jean Baptiste, 79
Cold war (1945–1991), 408, 413, 424, 428–29
Coleman, James S., 68
Collective security:
  as an approach to peace, 437
  defined, 435
  military alliances, 436–37
  preconditions, 436
Collor de Mello, Fernando, 235
Colombia, 217, 228, 260, 264, 277
Commonwealth of Independent States (CIS), 43
Communications:
  basic social process defined, 133–34
  elements, 134–35
  impact on mass publics, 133–34
  interpersonal and mass media, 136
  paid media and free media, 139–40
  past and future "revolutions" in, 153–56
Communism (*see* Marxism–Leninism)
Communist International (Comintern), 452
Comparable worth, 381–82
Compromise, 34
Compulsory voting laws, 164
Conceptual frameworks, 47
Confidence in institutions, 66
Conflict among nations, 408–10
Conflict within nations:
  characteristics, 18–21
  defined, 4
  role of groups in, 5–7
  role in human life, 4–5
  tactics, 8–18
Congo, 110
Congress of Racial Equality (CORE), 387
Conover, Pamela Johnston, 402
Conrad, Roan, 157fn
Conservatism:
  criticism of big government, 90–91
  criticism of schools, 53
  criticism of U.S. Supreme Court decisions, 337, 340
  economic doctrines, 90
  moral and social doctrines, 90
  relation to "liberalism" and "Toryism" before the
    1930s, 89–90
  wins and losses in referendums, 183
  (*see also* Laissez faire)
Conservative party (British), 10–11, 262
Constitutional convention (proposal for), 338
Constitutionalism:
  arguments for, 74–75
  defined, 74
  relation to classical liberalism, 74–75
  relation to democracy, 74–75
  "watchdogs" for, 351–52
Consuls, 416–17
Conte, Roger A., 458
Converse, Philip E., 68fn, 69fn, 200, 201fn
Conway, M. Margaret, 23
Coors, Joseph, 266
Costa Rica, 228, 260, 264
Courts:
  control of administrators, 317
  criticisms of, 343
  dispute-settling function, 326
  evolution from kings' advisers, 325
  hierarchies of appeal, 329–31
  high esteem for, 321–22
  judicial legislation, 340–43
  judicial review, 327
  law enforcement function, 326
  mechanical conception of courts' activities, 338–39
  origins, 325
  part of the political process, 343–47
  relations with executives and legislators, 335–36
  role in policy making, 336–43
  role in protecting civil liberties, 351–52
  (*see also* Judges)
Craxi, Bettino, 239
Cresson, Edith, 276
Crewe, Ivor, 201fn
Crime, 368–71
Croatia, 51, 64, 409, 453
Cuba, 101, 106, 108, 109, 111, 159, 209, 223, 285, 356,
  415, 417, 424, 425
Cuban missile crisis (1962), 455
Culture, political:
  cognitive orientations, 62
  components, 62–64
  confidence in institutions, 65–66
  defined, 62
  in different nations, 64–67
  trust in other people, 60
cummings, e.e., 1
Customs (social), 320
Customs unions, 412
Cyprus, 260
Czechoslovakia (Czech Republic), 86–87, 159, 185, 356,
  366fn, 413, 437, 453

Dahl, Robert A., 23, 111, 303
Dalton, Russell J., 18, 48, 59, 123, 131fn, 189, 200, 201fn
Danaska, Mirjan R., 347
Daniels, Jonathan, 312, 318fn
Dart, Justin, 266
Davidson, Roger H., 255
Davis, Dennis, 157
Dawisha, Karen, 43
Dawson, Richard E., 68
Debre, Michel, 275

Declaration of Independence (U.S.), 75, 76
"Deep throat," 157fn
Deering, Christopher J. 256
Defendants' rights, 371–75
de Gaulle, Charles, 275
Dehio, Ludwig, 457
De jure and *de facto,* 427fn
de Klerk, Frederik Willem, 399–401
de Medici, Catherine, 375
De Mito, Ciriaco, 239
Democracy:
    accountable-elites model, 103–104
    classifying governments as, 100–10l, 109–10
    defined, 94
    election campaigns in, 151–52, 155, 207–208
    free elections as key institutions, 159–60
    majoritarian and consensual types, 104–105
    participatory model, 101–102
    plebiscitary, 117
    popular participation, ideal and actual, 102–103
    presidential and parliamentary types, 104, 228–32
    principles, 94–97
    proportional election systems, 170–73
    recent surge of, 110–111
    relation to constitutionalism, 351
    relation to socialism, 82
Democratic party (U.S.):
    discipline and cohesion, 243
    ideologies of identifiers and activists, 204–205
    newspaper support, 145
    party identification and electoral strength, 191, 198
    perceived differences from Republican party, 211
    shares of party identifications, congressional votes,
        and presidential votes (1952–1992), 198
    women delegates, 379
Demonstrations, 12–13,
Deng Xiaoping, 83, 315
Denmark, 95, 137, 152, 167, 181, 182, 217, 237, 260, 282,
    283, 377, 412
Dennis v. *United States,* 361, 366fn
Denver, D.T., 201fn
de Poitiers, Diane, 375
Dewey, John, 87
Diamond, Edwin, 142, 156
Dictatorships, 107–108
Dini, Lamberto, 284
Di Palma, Giuseppe, 68
Diplomacy, 416–18
Diplomatic immunity, 442
Direct primaries, 167–68
Disarmament and arms control:
    as an approach to peace, 438
    defined, 438
    efforts at, 153–54
    record, 438–39
    special problem of nuclear weapons, 438–39
Divided government:
    "cohabitation" in France, 196, 276–77
    in the U.S. national government 193–94

in U.S. state governments, 194
in Venezuela, 196
Dole, Robert, 244, 255
Dominant party systems:
    in democratic nations, 224
    in developing nations, 224–26
Dominica, 377
Dominican Republic, 356
Donnelly, Jack, 366
Dostoyevsky, Fyodor, 24
Douglas-Hume, Alec, 262
Duchacek, Ivo D., 427
Dukakis, Michael, 270, 387
Dummet, Michael, 186
Dunne, Finley Peter, 45
Dupeux, Georges, 69fn
Duverger, Maurice, 226
Dworkin, Ronald, 366

Eckstein, Harry, 68
Ecuador, 260, 264
Edelman, Murray, 23
Eden, Anthony, 262
Edley, Christopher, Jr., 317
Education, in U.S. compared with other nations, 295
Edwards, George C., III, 285
Egalitarianism, 89
Egypt, 181, 356, 417, 422
Ehrenhalt, Alan, 23
Ehrlichman, John, 266
Einstein, Albert, 428, 431–32
Eisenhower, Dwight D., 265, 268, 270, 273, 274
Eldersveld, Samuel J., 226
Elections:
    absolute majority electoral systems, 169
    advantages and vulnerability of incumbents, 248
    American congressional (1992), 62
    American congressional (1994), 1, 22, 218, 248
    American congressional and presidential
        (1968–1988), 194
    American presidential (1948), 120
    American presidential (1980), 54
    American presidential (1992), 50, 54, 63, 69, 118–19,
        132, 171
    British general (1992), 174
    Canadian general (1993), 173–74
    changing nature of campaigns, 151–52, 155
    electoral systems, 168–70
    essential characteristics of free elections, 159–60
    "first–past–the–post" electoral systems, 168–69
    fixed and optional dates, 280–81
    French presidential (1995), 169–70
    German general (1990), 177
    German hybrid system, 175–77
    Italian general (1994), 284
    Italian shift away from proportional representation,
        175
    key role in democracy, 158–59

New Zealand switch to proportional representation, 175

nominations and candidate selection, 165–68

nonvoting and compulsory voting, 162–65

political effects of electoral systems, 173–77

proportional election systems, 170–73

qualifications for voting, 160–62

Venezuelan presidential (1993), 171

Electoral College (U.S.), 233

Elizabeth I, Queen of England, 375

Elizabeth II, Queen of Great Britain, 73, 262, 263, 279

Ellis, Richard J., 68

El Salvador, 424

Environmental Protection Agency (U.S.), 323

Epstein, Edward Jay, 142

Epstein, Leon D., 226, 227fn

Epstein, William, 457

Equal Employment Opportunity Commission (EEOC), 308, 392

Equal protection of the laws, 322–23

Equal Rights Amendment (ERA), 381–82

Equality, political, 95

Environmental Protection Agency (EPA), 3

Erickson, Robert S., 131, 201fn

Eritrea, 453

Estonia, 42, 43, 51, 356

"Ethnic cleansing," 454

Ethnic groups, 19

Etzioni, Amitai, 366

Eulau, Heinz, 247, 256

European Community, 412

Evans, Bergen, 92fn

Evans, Sarah P., 402

Exclusionary rule, 374–75

Executives:

    ceremonial functions, 261–62

    as chiefs of state, 259–63

    core of government, 258–59

    defined, 259

    distinguished from administrators, 288–90

    as heads of government, 259

    hereditary monarchs and elected "monarchs," 260

    in nondemocratic systems, 285

    popular focus on, 258

    presidential and prime ministerial types, 264

    reigning, 262–63

    separation versus mingling of ceremonial roles, 263

    Swiss plural executive, 228–29, 261

    symbolic and ceremonial functions, 259–61

Exit polls, 119, 121

Fabius, Laurent, 276

Fahd, King of Saudi Arabia, 93

Fairness doctrine, 142–43

Families:

    influence on political attitudes, 50–51

    as socializing agents, 58–59

Farah, Barbara G., 379

Federal Bureau of Investigation (FBI), 369

Federal Communications Commission (FCC), 136–37, 142–44, 306–307

Federal Trade Commission (FTC), 311

Federalism, 39

Feinstein, Diane, 7

Fenno, Richard F., 256

Ferejohn, John, 256, 256fn

Ferguson, LeRoy C., 247, 256

Ferraro, Geraldine, 377

Fesler, James W., 317

Festinger, Leon, 67

Fifteenth Amendment to the U.S. Constitution, 373

Fifth Amendment to the U.S. Constitution, 388

Fighting words test, 361

Finer, Herman, 263, 286f, 287fnn

Finer, Samuel E., 108, 112fn

Finifter, Ada W., 23, 43, 67

Finland, 167, 217, 228, 260, 264

Fiorina, Morris, 194, 256, 256fn

"First-past-the-post" election systems, 168–69

Fishkin, James S., 155, 156, 157fn

Flanagan, Scott C., 200, 318fn

Flanigan, William H., 200

Foley, Tom, 62, 270

Force, 30

Ford, Gerald H., 254, 265, 266, 268, 269, 274, 286fn, 345

Foreign aid, 421–22, 423

Foreign policy:

    agencies, 416–17

    goals, 410–15

    methods, 417–27

    process, 415–16

Forster, E. M., 24

Forsythe, David P., 458

Fourteenth Amendment to the U.S. Constitution, 322–23, 341–42, 352, 367

Fourth Amendment to the U.S. Constitution, 372–73

Fowler, Mark, 142

Fractionalization, party:

    defined, 215

    and executive tenure, 282–84

    impact, 216–17, 219–20

    measurement, 215–16

France:

    administrative courts, 315

    apportionment of election districts, 178–79

    Assemblée Nationale, 236, 253

    avoués, avocats, and *notaires*, 332

    candidate selection and nomination, 167

    Centre National d'Études Judiciares, 333

    changing parties and alignments, 192

    commissions and *rapporteurs* in the *Assemblée Nationale*, 240, 241

    constitution, 322

    court system, 331–32

    divided government and "cohabitation," 196, 276–77

different tracks for lawyers and judges, 333
EC membership, 412
Edith Cresson, first woman premier, 377
education, 295
election campaigns, 152
families' influence on attitudes toward government,
    60
foreign affairs ministry, 416
ideological awareness in, 48
inquisitorial system of justice, 328–29, 330
interpellations, 314
judges and prosecutors, 335–36
judicial review, 327
organization and regulation of mass media, 137
origins of merit system, 298
partisan political activity by civil servants, 299–300
political involvement level, 58
possession of nuclear weapons, 431, 455
presidency, 228, 260, 275–77
presidential election (1995), 169–70
public opinion polling, 118
referendums, 181, 275
refusal to pay UN assessment for peacekeeping
    forces, 452
refusal to sign nuclear test ban treaty, 439
semi-fractionalized party system, 217, 283
strikes, 14
student protests, 56
woman suffrage (1946), 378
women in politics, 377
Franco, Francisco, 65
Franco, Itamar, 235
Frank, Jerome, 348
Frankfurter, Felix, 367
Franks, Gary, 21
Freedom House, 356–58
Friedan, Betty, 402
Friedman, Milton, 80, 90, 91
Friedrich, Carl J., 43, 91, 92fn, 112, 303, 310, 318fn
Fromkin, David, 427
Fusion of powers in parliamentary democracies,
    230–31

Gabon, 110
Gallagher, Michael, 187
Gallup polls, 119, 120, 123, 124, 125, 131fn, 146, 195,
    421, 455
Gandhi, Indira, 16, 199, 377
Gandhi, Mohandas K., 14
Gandhi, Rajiv, 16
Gans, Herbert J., 156
Garfield, James, 15
Garry, Patrick, 156
Garth, Davis, 208
Gati, Toby T., 458
Gaynes, Martin J., 318fn
Gebhardt, Richard, 109
Gehlen, Michael F., 227

Gelb, Joyce, 402
General Agreement on Tariffs and Trade (GATT), 410
Genghis Khan, 78
George III, King of England, 263
Georgia (American state), 389
Georgia (former Soviet republic), 51, 185
Gerbner, George, 138
German Democratic Republic (East Germany), 87, 176,
    437
Germany, Federal Republic of:
    American public opinion of, 421
    constitution, 322
    court system, 331–32
    EC membership, 412
    election campaigns, 152
    foreign affairs ministry, 416
    hybrid electoral system, 175–77, 190
    ideological awareness in, 47
    impossibility of divided government, 196
    judicial review, 179, 327
    national legislature, 231
    NATO membership, 437
    nuclear weapons potential, 431
    party identifications of children and parents, 59
    president, 260
    Prussian origin of professional civil service, 298
    public opinion polling, 118
    reunification with East Germany, 87, 356, 429
    semi-fractionalized party system, 217, 283
    women in politics, 377
Germany (Third Reich, 1933–1945), 28, 71, 78, 105, 108,
    181, 223, 413, 424, 426
Germany (Weimar Republic, 1919–1933), 216
Gerrymandering, 178
Ghana, 64, 458fn
Gingrich, Newt, 55, 209, 220, 244, 255, 258
Ginsberg, Benjamin, 186
Ginsburg, Ruth Bader, 345, 377
Gintle, Herbert, 91
Giscard d'Estaing, Valery, 275
Glasnost, 84, 85
Glass, David, 163
Glasstone, Samuel, 458fn
Goebbels, Joseph, 93
Goldman, Alan H., 402
Goldwater, Barry, 197
Goodnow, Frank J., 302, 304, 317, 318fn
Goodsell, Charles T., 317
Gorbachev, Mikhail, 1, 42, 43, 63, 64, 84, 85, 87, 184,
    315, 429, 440
Gore, Al, 152
Gormley, William T., Jr., 317
Government:
    in advanced/industrial societies, 26–27
    basic tasks and tools, 31–34
    defined, 27
    differences from other social organizations, 28–31
    in primitive societies, 25–26
    as synonym for "administration," 287fn

Governors general (British commonwealth), 260
Graber, Doris A., 142, 156
Graham, Hugh Davis, 24fn, 402
Gravity of evil test, 361
Gray, John, 92
Great Britain (*see* United Kingdon)
Greece, 217, 218, 412, 437
Greene, Kathanne W., 402
Greenstein, Fred I., 67, 68
Grenada, 268
Grofman, Bernard, 186, 187fn
Groups, political:
    categoric, 7–8
    conflict among, 5–7
    conformity pressures in, 48–49
    ethnic, 50–51
    impact on individual's political behavior, 54
    imperfect mobilization, 20–21
    occupational, 53–54
    overlapping memberships, 20
    peer, 51, 52–53, 60–61
    pressure, 8
    primary, 48
    religious, 51
Gruber, Judith E., 317
Guatemala, 424
Guinea, 158
Guinea-Bissau, 110
Gulick, Luther, 303, 317fn
Gurr, Ted Robert, 24fn, 427
Guyana, 356
Gwyn, Nell, 375

Habeas corpus, 371
Hacker, The Right Honourable James, 318fn
Hagopian, Mark N., 91
Haiti, 268
Haldeman, H.R., 266
Hallett, George H., 186
Hamilton, Charles V., 403fn
Hamilton, Lee, 306
Hammarskjöld, Dag, 451
Hansen, John Mark, 201
Harald V, King of Norway, 263
Harff, Barbara, 427
Hargrove, Erwin C., 286
Harrington, Michael, 91
Harris, Louis, and Associates, 118, 251, 321
Hart, Gary, 387
Hassan II, King of Morocco, 108
Hawke, Bob, 254
Hayek, Friedrich von, 80, 90, 91
Held, David, 111
Hennessy, Bernard C., 131fn
Hennessy, Peter, 317
Henry, Antony, 247
Herring, E. Pendleton, 226, 286
Hierarchy, principle of, 291–92, 329–31

Himmelstein, Jerome L., 92
Hispanic–Americans, 51
Hitler, Adolf, 71, 78, 105, 108, 147, 181, 221
Hoadly, Benjamin, 341
Hoag, Clarence G., 186
Hochschild, Jennifer L., 402
Hochstein, Madelyn, 69fn
Hofstetter, Richard, 142
Holmes, Leslie, 43
Holmes, Oliver Wendell, Jr., 319, 349
Holocaust, 426
Homosexuals, 90
Honduras, 356
Honecker, Erich, 87
Hoover, Herbert, 428
Hoover, Kenneth R., 91
Horowitz, Donald, 23
Hostages, 453
Howard, Michael, 427
Howe, Irving, 91
Hugo, Victor, 70
Huitt, Ralph K., 255
Human rights:
    civil liberties and civil rights, 349–50
    conflict between freedom and security, 359–61
    and constitutionalism, 351
    defined, 349
    degrees of protection in modern nations, 357–58
    government as enemy and friend of, 350–54
    list of, 354–56
    philosophical foundations of, 349–54
    political conflict over, 364–65
    rights of some versus rights of others, 361–64
    (*see also* Civil liberties; Civil rights)
Humphrey, Hubert H., 389
Hungary, 8, 159, 182, 185, 356, 413, 437
Huntington, Samuel P., 68
Hussein, Sadam, 45, 78, 106, 107, 414
Hyneman, Charles S., 303, 310, 312, 317, 318fn

Iceland, 260
Ideology:
    among college students and teachers, 126–27
    awareness levels, 48
    conservatism versus liberalism in the U.S., 87–91
    conservatives versus liberals in the Supreme Court,
        337
    defined, 71
    dispute over government control of the economy,
        79–87
    dispute over proper limits on government, 74–79
    in foreign policy, 411–12
    intellectual components, 71–73
    in political parties, 208–10
    in public opinion, 125–26
    types, 73–74
Impeachment, 234–35, 254, 274, 334
Imperialism, 411

Independent voters, 193
India, 15, 40, 217, 229, 260, 323, 377, 408, 419, 431, 455
Inglehart, Ronald, 68
Inkatha party (South Africa), 399, 400
Inquisitorial systems of justice, 328–29
Intercontinental ballistic missiles (ICBMs), 431
Interests, political:
   aggregation of, 32
   articulation of, 31–32
   defined, 5
Interior, U.S. Department of, 292–93
International Court of Justice, 408, 442–43
International trade, 419–20
Inuit (Eskimo) societies, 25–26, 28
Iran, 72, 78, 109, 110, 144, 181, 182, 356, 370, 417, 425, 442
Irangate, 252, 304–306
Iran–Iraq war, 409, 453
Iraq, 78, 106, 109, 110, 268, 356, 412, 431
Ireland, 137, 172, 181, 182, 217, 283, 295, 412
Irish Republican Army (IRA), 425
Irvine, Reid, 141
Islam, 51, 52, 72
Israel:
   aid from U.S., 422
   candidate selection, 206
   child rearing in *kibbutzim*, 58
   coalition governments, 264
   early recognition by U.S., 417
   fractionalized party system, 215, 217–18
   Golda Meir, first woman prime minister, 377
   nuclear weapons potential, 431
   proportional representation, 174
   stability of governments, 282, 283
Issue orientation, 195–96
Italy:
   administrative courts, 315
   changing electoral system, 171, 172, 174, 175
   court system, 331–32
   EC membership, 412
   under fascism (1922–1943), 223
   fractionalized party system, 217
   frequent use of referendums, 181
   ideological awareness in, 47, 48
   judicial review, 327
   powerful upper legislative house, 237
   presidency, 260
   secret voting in the Chamber of Deputies, 239
   student protests, 56
   weakness of premiers, 264, 282–83, 284
   women in politics, 377
Ivory Coast, 110, 356
Iyengar, Shanto, 156

Jackman, Robert W., 163–64, 187fn
Jackson, Jesse, 386, 387, 388, 393–94, 403fn
Jacobs, Herbert, 347
Jacobson, Gary, 195, 201

Jacobson, Harold K., 457
James, William, 87–88, 92fn
Japan, 40, 56, 64, 118, 167, 174, 217, 218, 229, 260, 295, 300, 327, 416, 419, 421, 431
Jefferson, Thomas, 75, 76, 79–80, 92fn, 162, 350
Jennings, M. Kent, 68, 201
Jennings, Peter, 148
Jensen, Jay W., 157fn
Jervis, Robert, 457
Jesse, Eckhard, 201fn
Jews:
   discrimination against, 353
   holocaust, 426
   voting preferences, 22
"Jim Crow" laws, 341–42, 384, 391
John Paul II, Pope, 17
Johnson, Charles A., 348
Johnson, Lyndon B., 15, 197, 198, 266, 268, 271, 272, 389
Johnson, Samuel, 319
Jones, Charles O., 286
Jordan, Hamilton, 266
Jordan, Vernon, 386
Judge, David, 255
Judges:
   appointment and removal, 333–34
   criticisms of, 336–37
   election and recall, 334–35
   ideal of independence, 335–36
   insulation from political pressures, 336
   judicial legislation, 340–43, 342
   and lawyers, 332–33
   partisan affiliations, 345
   as part of the political process, 343–47
   relations with legislatures and executives, 335–36
   role in governing, 336
   seen as nonpolitical technicians, 337–39
   selection and tenure, 345
   separation from prosecutors, 335
Judicial review, 98, 351
Judiciary Act of 1789 (U.S.), 322
J–shaped curve, 117

Kaase, Max, 187fn
Kampuchea (Cambodia), 78, 411, 449
Kaplan, Cynthia S., 186, 187fn
Kazakhstan, 431, 440, 455
Keegan, John, 427
Keith, Bruce E., 201
Kellerman, Barbara, 286
Kelley, Walt, 45
Kendall, Willmoore, 24fn, 111, 112fn
Kennan, George F., 411
Kennedy, Edward, 258
Kennedy, John F., 15, 236, 247, 268, 428
Kennedy, Robert, 15
Kenya, 110, 356
Kernell, Samuel, 286
Kettl, Donald E. 317

Key, V. O., Jr., 113, 114–15, 131fn, 201
Khomeini, Ayatollah, 52, 72, 78, 109, 147, 305, 424
Khrushchev, Nikita, 84
Kibbutzim, 58
Kim Il Sung, 223
Kim Jong Il, 109, 223
Kinder, Donald R., 156
King, Anthony, 255, 259, 286, 286fn
King, Larry, 134
King, Martin Luther, Jr., 14, 15, 236, 367, 386, 393
King, Richard H., 403
Kirbo, Charles, 266
Kirghizia, 356
Kirk, Russell, 92
Kirkpatrick, Jeane J., 402
Kirp, David L., 403
Kissinger, Henry, 427
"Kitchen cabinet," 266
Klein, Ethel, 402
Koestler, Arthur, 24
Koh, B.C., 317
Kohl, Helmut, 45
Kohut, Andrew, 201
Korea, North, 109, 110, 144, 159, 223, 268, 356, 409, 425, 431, 449, 453
Korea, South, 14, 101, 268, 409, 419, 449, 453
Korean War (1950–1953), 268, 406, 411, 419, 423, 429, 435, 449
Kostrich, Leslie I., 157
Kraus, Sidney, 157
Ku Klux Klan, 16, 361
Kuwait, 111, 268, 409, 412, 453

Labor unions, 14
Labour party (British), 10–11, 82, 145, 199, 213, 224
Ladd, Everett Carll, Jr., 131fn
Laissez faire:
    defined, 79
    as a political ideology, 80–81
    (*see also* Conservatism)
LaPalombara, Joseph, 227
Lapp, Ralph E., 458fn
Lasswell, Harold D., 38, 44fn
Latvia, 42, 43, 51, 356
Lau, Richard R., 67
Lauterpacht, H., 458fn
Laver, Michael, 226
Law, domestic:
    administrative, 323
    civil (from *Code civil*), 324
    civil (not criminal), 324, 325
    common, 323
    constitutional, 322–23
    criminal, 325
    defined, 321
    equity, 324
    Roman, 324
    statutory, 323

    voluntary compliance with, 33–34, 66–67
Law, international:
    as an approach to peace, 440–41
    content, 441–42
    defined, 441
    differences from domestic law, 441–43
    formation and enforcement, 442–43
    role in war and peace, 443–45
Lawyers, 6, 332–33
Lazarsfeld, Paul F., 200
League of Nations, 435, 441, 443
"Leaks," 152–54
Lebanon, 17, 424
Left, 68–69fn (*see also* Commuism; Socialism; Liberalism)
Legislators:
    Americans' mixed feelings about, 251–52
    "independent operators" in the U.S. Congress, 236–49
    "party soldiers" in the British parliament, 243–46
    proposals for limiting terms, 252
    relations with constituents, 249–51
Legislatures:
    arena and transformative, 253
    bicameral and unicameral, 236–37
    changing role in democracies, 252–55
    committees, 238, 240–42
    conference committees, 238–39
    constitution–making functions, 232–33
    debate in, 238
    defined, 232
    functions, 232–36
    procedures for handling bills, 237–39
    party organization, cohesion, and displine, 213–14
    organization and power of legislative parties, 242
    overriding executive vetoes, 239
    oversight of administrators, 312–13
    relations with executives, 229–32, 233–34
    upper houses, 237
Legitimacy, 30
Lenin, V.I., 83, 84, 86, 221, 314
Lesbians, 90
Lewis, Anthony, 402
Lewis, Drew, 301
Liberalism:
    classical, 72, 74–76, 88
    of college students and teachers 126–27
    contemporary doctrines, 88–89
    criticism of schools, 53
    criticism of Supreme Court decisions, 336, 343
    in public opinion, 125–26
    public understanding of the concept, 126
    two meanings of, 88
    welfare state advocacy, 88
    wins and losses in American referendums, 183
Liberia, 17
Libertarian party (U.S.), 71, 80
Libya, 78, 101, 106, 107, 268, 425
Licensing, 297

Lie, Trygve, 448
Liechtenstein, 453
Light, Paul C., 286
Lijphart, Arend, 104, 111, 112fn, 186, 187fn, 256fn
Lilburne, John, 249
Lincoln, Abraham, 15, 158, 265, 267, 269, 287fn
Lincoln-Douglas debates (1858), 155
Line and staff functions, 292–93
Lippmann, Walter, 131
Lipset, Seymour Martin, 69fn, 131, 201
Lithuania, 42, 43, 51, 356
Litigation:
    defined, 12
    as a tactic of political action, 12
Lobbying, 9
Locke, John, 76, 80, 92fn, 162, 350, 351
Longley, Lawrence D., 255
Loomis, Burdett A., 23
Louis XIV, King of France, 78, 260
Louisiana, 389
Lovenduski, Ethel, 402
Lowery, Joseph, 386
Lowi, Theodore J., 286
Luttbeg, Norman R., 13, 201fn
Luxembourg, 412

Maastricht accords (European community), 412
Macklin, Charles, 319
Macmillan, Harold, 262
Macridis, Roy C., 71, 91, 92fn
Madison, James, 228, 267
Mafia, 369
Magleby, David B., 201
Major, John, 199, 279, 280
Majorities and pluralities, 112fn
Majority rule:
    defined, 97
    and human rights, 98
    limited, 97–99
    as a principle of democracy, 96–99
    self-limited, 97–98
Malbin, Michael J., 187, 255, 257fn
Mali, 101
Mandela, Nelson, 63, 110, 399–401
Mann, Thomas E., 187, 201, 257fn
Mansbridge, Jane J., 402
Mao Zedong, 78, 82, 108, 315
Marcuse, Herbert, 366
Market and Opinion Research International (MORI),
    118
Marsh, Michael, 187
Marshall Islands, 453
Marshall, John, 340
Marshall, Thomas R., 347
Marshall, Thurgood, 345, 389, 395
Martel, Myles, 157
Martens, Wilfried, 261

Martin, Curtis H., 68
Marx, Karl, 53, 70, 73, 83, 91, 221
Marxism-Leninism, 72, 221
    analysis of causes of war, 410–11
    concept of class conflict, 82
    conflict with democratic socialism, 82
    decline, 83–87
    defined, 82
    remnants in Cuba, North Korea, and China, 83–84,
        87, 223
    in the Socialist Workers party (U.S.), 209–10
    tactics for overthrowing capitalism, 82
Mass communications:
    impact on mass publics, 146–51
    impact on political and governmental leaders,
        151–56
    impact on political socializaton, 61–62
    interpersonal and mass media defined, 136
    newspapers, 144–45
    paid media and free media, 139–40
    radio, 146
    as sources of political information, 147
    television, 136–44
    types of impacts, 135–36
Masters, Roger D., 23, 43
Mauritania, 110, 158
Mayhew, David, 195, 201, 256
McAllister, Ian, 24fn
McCarthy, Larry, 201
McClellan, David, 91
McClosky, Herbert, 68
McGovern, George, 197, 198
McIlwain, Charles H., 91
McInnes, Neil, 227
McKinley, William, 15, 272
McLuhan, Marshall, 157
McPhee, William H., 200
Meese, Edwin, 70, 305
Meir, Golda, 377
Merit system, 298
Merkl, Peter H., Jr., 23
Mexico, 17, 40, 101, 118, 225–26, 228, 264, 277, 444
Mickelson, Sig, 157fn
Micronesia, Federated States of, 453
Miliband, Ralph, 43, 91
Mill, John Stuart, 91, 366
Miller, Warren E., 68fn, 69fn, 200, 201, 201fn
Milton, John, 77, 92fn, 349, 366
Miranda rights, 373–74
Mississippi, 389
Mitchell, George, 62
Mitterand, François, 275, 276, 277
Models:
    defined, 99
    of democracy, 102–105
    of the free market, 99–100
    normative and descriptive, 100
    uses in social science, 99–102
Moldova, 356

Monaco, 453
Monarchism, 72
Monarchs, hereditary and elected, 259–60
Mondale, Walter F., 198, 270, 387
Mongolia, 110
Moore, Barrington, Jr., 366
Moos, Malcolm, 411
Moral precepts, 320
Morgenthau, Hans J., 411, 427, 437, 458fn
Morin, Richard, 157fn
Moyers, Bill, 266
Mozambique, 110
Mueller, John E., 187fn, 457
Mulroney, Brian, 173, 199
Multiple independently targeted reentry vehicle
    (MIRV), 431
Murphy, Frank, 353
Murphy, John P. 458
Mussolini, Benito, 93
Myanmar (Burma), 101

Namibia, 453
Nathan, Richard P., 43
National Abortion Rights Action League (NARAL),
    35, 379, 381
National Association for the Advancement of Colored
    People (NAACP), 308, 344, 384–85, 389, 395
National Opinion Research Center, 118
National Organization for Women (NOW), 35, 379,
    381
National Security Agency (NSC), 306
National Urban League, 386
Nationalism, 39–41
Nations:
    birth and death of, 41–43
    diplomatic recognition of, 417–18
    foreign policy goals, 410–14
    nature of, 39–41
    new nations created since 1945, 41, 451
    noncumulative conflict among, 405–406
    sovereign equality of, 405
Nebraska, 201fn
Nelson, Barbara J., 402
Nelson, Candice J., 201
Nelson, Michael, 286
Nepal, 110
Netherlands, The, 28, 48, 125, 174, 181, 217, 264, 283,
    295, 377, 412
Neustadt, Richard, 267, 286, 286fn, 287fn, 312, 318fn
New England town meetings, 117, 180
New Jersey, 247
New World Order:
    end of the cold war, 428–29
    proliferation of nuclear weapons, 429–30
New York, 220
New Zealand, 167, 175, 212, 217, 218, 219, 233, 237,
    264, 283, 378
Newspapers:

American, 144
    in authoritarian regimes, 144–45
    circulation and readership, 145–46
    number of readers in various nations, 132
Nicaragua, 110, 252, 254, 304–306, 377, 422
Nicolson, Harold, 415–16, 427fn
Nie, Norman H., 201
Nieburg, H. L., 131
Niemi, Richard G., 68
Niger, 110, 158
Nigeria, 64, 110, 356
Nisbet, Robert, 92
Nixon, Richard M., 154, 197, 235, 254, 266, 274, 413
Nominations, 165–68
Noriega, Manuel, 268
North Atlantic Treaty Organization (NATO), 14, 412,
    425, 429, 435
North, Oliver P., 252, 305, 306, 307, 374
Norway, 64, 137, 207, 216, 217, 218, 260, 283, 295, 377, 378
Nozick, Robert, 92
Nth country problem, 431
Nuclear weapons:
    destructive force of, 41, 429–31, 433
    Nuclear Nonproliferation treaty, 432
    proliferation of, 431–32
    Strategic Arms Limitation treaties (SALT), 439–40
    test ban treaties, 439–40
    UN declarations, 439
    use of in World War II, 431, 455
Nugent, Neil, 457
Nye, Joseph S., Jr., 457

O'Brien, William V. 458
O'Connor, Edwin, 24
O'Connor, Sandra Day, 377
O'Donnel, Guilermo, 111
Office of Personnel Management (U.S.), 298
Ohio, 247
Oleszek, Walter J., 255
Oligarchy, 106, 107
Oman, 93, 109, 158, 260
Ombudsmen, 316
Omnibus Crime Control and Safe Streets Act of 1968,
    373, 374
O'Neil, Robert M., 403
O'Neill, Thomas P., 270
Ornstein, Norman J., 187fn, 201, 247, 256fn, 257fn
Orr, Elizabeth, 201
Orwell, George, 24, 78, 96
Ostrogorski, M.I., 226
Ottoman Empire, 41, 79

Page, Benjamin I., 286
Pakistan, 64, 408, 431
Palme, Olof, 17
Panama, 14, 268
Paraguay, 110, 377

Parks, Rosa, 14
Parliamentary democracies, 230–31
Parrott, Bruce, 43
Participation, political, 18, 207
Party identification:
    changes in, 57, 192
    defined,191
    development, 191–92
    distinguished from party membership, 203
    distribution in U.S., 1960–1992, 191
    impact on voting behavior, 192–93
    parents' influence on children's party
        identifications, 58–59
Passman, Otto, 273
Pateman, Carole, 112
Paterson, William, 249, 257fn
Paton, Alan, 24
Patriotism, 64 (see also Nationalism)
Patronage, 297–98
Patterson, Bradley H., Jr., 286
Patterson, Thomas E., 157
Peace, international:
    as a goal of nations' foreign policies, 414
    prospects for, 454–55
    through balance of power, 434–35
    through collective security, 435–37
    through disarmament, 438–40
    through international law, 440–44
    through the United Nations, 448–49
Peel, Sir Robert, 114
Pempel, T.J., 227
Penniman, Howard R., 186
Perez de Cueller, Javier, 453
Perlmutter, Amos, 112
Perot, Ross, 1, 63, 132, 134, 155, 159, 165, 171, 284
Peltason, J. W., 343, 344, 348, 348fn
People's Republic of China (PRC):
    changing alliances, 406
    communist regime, 83–84, 111
    conquest of Tibet, 41
    control of bureaucracy, 315
    education, 60
    executive power, 285
    human rights, 356
    invasion of Vietnam, 411, 415
    Marxist-Leninist-Maoist ideology, 209
    monoparty system, 221, 222, 223
    one-candidate-per-office elections, 159
    possession of nuclear weapons, 431, 455
    recognition by U.S., 417
    refusal to sign nuclear test ban treaty, 439
    Tiananmen Square protests, 13, 84, 223
    totalitarian regime of Mao Zedong, 78, 108
People United to Save Humanity (PUSH), 387
Perceptual screens, 46
Perestroika, 84, 85, 315
Perry, Barbara, 402
Perry, Michael I., 348
Persian Gulf War (1991), 1, 268, 406, 409, 411, 412, 413,

426, 429
Peru, 17, 424, 425
Peterson, M.L., 458
Peterson, Theodore, 157fn
Petracca, Mark P., 286
Petrocik, John R., 201
Philip V, King of Spain, 260
Philippines, 377, 422
Pinochet, Augusto, 110
Pitkin, Hanna Fenichel, 250, 256, 257fn
Pitt, William the Elder, 319
Planned Parenthood, 35, 44
Plato, 44
Plessy v. Ferguson (1896), 342, 389
Pluralities and majorities, 112
Poindexter, John, 252, 305, 306, 374
Poland, 86, 159, 185, 356, 413, 437
Police:
    conflict over powers, 368–71
    and crime, 368–70
    discretion in law enforcement, 308
    secret, 370
Political action tactics, 8–18
Political efficacy, 60
Political parties, in authoritarian systems:
    communist and fascist monoparty stems, 220
    dominant party systems, 224–26
Political parties, in democracies:
    activities, 206–208
    "broker" and "missionary," 209–11
    candidate selection, 206–207
    centralization and decentralization, 212–13
    characteristics of less fractionalized systems, 219–20
    cohesion, 214–15
    defined and distinguished from pressure groups,
        202
    discipline, 213–14
    fragmentation, degrees and consequences, 215–19
    identification and membership, 203–205
    in legislatures, 208, 242–43
    nature and role of ideologies, 208–12
    pressure groups inside, 9–10
Political parties in U.S.:
    activists and identifiers, 204–205
    "broker" major parties, 210
    cohesion and discipline, 213, 214, 243
    decentralization of power, 206–207, 212
    differences between Democrats and Republicans,
        205, 220
    legal membership rules, 204
    liberal and conservative members, 210
    minimum role in candidate selection, 204, 206–207
    perceived handling of issues, 211
Political science:
    clouded crystal ball, 455–56
    defined, 1, 26
Politics:
    action tactics, 8–13
    conflict as the essence, 4–7

contrasted with administration, 300–303, 309
defined, 2
in everyday conversation, 1–2
international and domestic compared, 405–408
Politics/Administration dichotomy, 302–303, 309
Polity, 92fn
Pol Pot, 78
Polsby, Nelson W., 23, 67, 226, 253, 255, 256fn, 257fn, 267, 286, 286fn
Pomper, Gerald M., 187fn
Pompidou, Georges, 275
Ponce de Léon, Ernesto Zedilla, 118
Pope, Alexander, 288
Popular consultation, 96
Popular sovereignty, 94–95
Portugal, 174, 217, 412
Powell, G. Bingham, Jr., 44fn, 112fn
Powell, Jody, 266
Powell, Lewis, 395
Pragmatism, 87–88
Presidencies:
    American, 254, 263–74
    compared with prime ministers, 264–65, 282–83
    French, 275–77
    other, 277–78
President of the United States:
    chief diplomat, 267
    chief executive, 265–66
    chief legislator, 271–73
    chief of state, 265
    commander-in-chief, 267–68
    compared with prime ministers, 282–83
    control of administrators, 311–14
    emergency leader, 269–70
    executive departments and cabinet, 265
    Executive Office of the President, 266
    "kitchen cabinet," 266
    mingling of ceremonial and political roles, 263
    party leader, 270–71
    power and problems, 273—74
    relations with Congress, 254–55
    veto and threat of veto, 272–73
    war-making powers, 267–68
    world leader, 267
Presidential democracies, 228–30
Pressure groups, 8
Prewitt, Kenneth, 68
Primary groups, 48–49
Prime ministers:
    in coalition governments, 282–85
    compared with presidents, 264–65, 282–83
    party leadership as source of power, 280
    relations with ministry and cabinet, 278–79
    selection, 278, 279
Pritchett, C. Herman, 402
Pro–choice advocates, 35–36
Professional Air Traffic Controllers Organization (PATCO), 301
Pro–life advocates, 35

Propaganda:
    by domestic pressure groups, 11
    in foreign policy, 423
Proportional representation, 170–73, 174, 216
Psychology, political, 45–55
Public opinion:
    on abortions, 115
    changes in concerned publics from issue to issue, 114
    characteristics, 114
    on comparable worth, 381–82
    comparisons among nations, 124, 125, 129–30
    cultivation in both democratic and authoritarian polities, 113
    defined, 114–15
    dimensions (preference and intensity), 115–16
    on foreign aid, 423
    on foreign policy, 130
    general opposition to government spending, support of most spending programs, 127–30
    on ideologies, 125–26
    levels of information, 62–63
    main matters of public concern, 123–25
    measurement by polls, 116–23
    on prayer in schools, 116
    presidential appeals to, 273
    relation to college education, 126–27
    on the UN, 455
    on the USSR, 407
Public opinion polls:
    accuracy of, 119–21
    how they work, 118–19
    impact of question phrasings on answers, 120–21
    increasing prominence, 118
    influence, 121–23
Pye, Lucian W., 68, 227fn

Qatar, 158
Quaison-Sackley, Alex, 458
Quayle, Dan, 62
Qube interactive television system, 135
Question time, 313

Rabin, Yitzhak, 172, 456
Racism, 71, 382–83
Radio:
    number of sets in various nations, 132
    and specialized programming, 146
Rae, Douglas W., 173, 186, 187fn, 215–16, 227fn
Random sampling, 118
Ranney, Austin, 112fn, 149, 156, 157, 182, 186, 187, 226
Rather, Dan, 148
Rawls, John, 92
Rayburn, Sam, 247
Reagan, Nancy, 266
Reagan, Ronald, 37, 54, 127, 142, 147, 153, 154, 197, 198, 199, 254, 265, 266, 268, 270, 271, 272, 273, 274, 301, 305–306, 321, 337, 345, 413, 425, 429, 440

Real, James, 458fn
Red tape, 289–90
Reedy, George R., 286
Referendums:
  defined, 179
  and legitimacy, 184
  liberal versus conservative results, 183–84
  organization, 180–81
  rationale, 179–80
  results, 181–84
  role in changing governments after dissolution of
    USSR, 184–86
  sample of recent referendums, 182
Regulation, government, 294–97
Rehnquist, William, 62, 395
Reigning, 262
Remarque, Erich Maria, 404, 427fn
Representatives' relations with constituents:
  "independence" theory, 249–51
  "mandate" theory, 249
Republican party (U.S.):
  discipline and cohesion, 243
  ideologies of identifiers and activists, 204–205
  newspaper support, 145
  party identification and electoral strength, 21, 191, 198
  perceived differences from Democratic party, 211
  shares of party identifications, congressional votes,
    and presidential votes (1952–1992), 198
  women delegates, 379
Republicanism, 73
Restrictive covenants, 391
Reverse discrimination, 395
Richards, Ann, 377
Richards, Peter G., 256fn
Richardson, Bradley M., 318fn
Richardson, Lewis F., 427fn
Riding, Alan, 403fn
Riff, M.A., 91
Right, 68–69 (*see also* Conservatism)
Riker, William H., 23, 112, 457
Rivers, William L., 157
Robertson, Pat, 35, 90
Robespierre, Maximilien, 424
Robinson, Michael J., 142, 147, 149, 157, 157fn
Rocard, Michel, 276
Rockman, Bert A., 286
Roe v. *Wade* (1973), 37, 38, 44fn, 363, 381
Roman Catholic Church, 35, 51
Romania, 87, 437
Roosevelt, Franklin D., 2, 15, 88, 212, 213, 267, 271, 272,
  274, 336, 432
Roosevelt, Theodore, 15, 267
Roper poll, 157fn
Rose, Richard, 23, 24fn
Rosecrance, Richard, 427
Rosebery, Lord, 280
Rosen, Bernard, 317
Rosenau, James N., 427
Rosenstone, Steven J., 201

Rossiter, Clinton, 274, 287fn
Rourke, Francis E., 303, 317
Rousseau, Jean Jacques, 21–22, 24fn, 117, 162, 179, 249,
  256
Rumsfeld, Donald, 266
Rush, Mark E., 186
Russia, 43, 51, 182, 184–85, 356, 418, 421, 431, 440, 455
Rwanda, 51, 64, 455

Saavedra, Daniel Ortega, 110
Safire, William, 24
Salinas de Gortari, Carlos, 225
Sample surveys, 118 (*see also* Public opinion polls)
Sanctions, 30
Sandinistas, 305
San Marino, 453
Sao Tome and Principe, 110
Sartori, Giovanni, 112, 227
Saudi Arabia, 51, 59, 93, 101, 109, 111, 158, 260, 268,
  356, 413
Scalfaro, Oscar Luigi, 284
Schattschneider, E.E., 227, 227fn
Schauer, Frederick, 366
Schenk v. *United States,* 360, 366fn
Schick, Allen, 255
Schlafly, Phyllis, 35, 380
Schlozman, Kay Lehman, 23
Schmidt, Helmut, 199
Schmitter, Phillipe C., 111
Schneider, William, 69fn
Schofield, Norman, 226
Schools:
  as agencies of political socialization, 52
  desegregation/integration/busing controversy, 5
Schumpeter, Joseph, 112
Schwarz, John E., 256
Schwarzkopf, H. Norman, 412, 454
Scott, Paul, 24
Seabury, Paul, 427
Searing, Donald, 256, 256fn
Sears, David O., 67
Security:
  in domestic politics, 359–60
  in international politics, 410, 414
Segregation, racial:
  doctrines, 342–43
  in education, 389–91
  in employment, 392
  in housing, 391
  in public accommodations, 391–92
  in public schools, 323
  struggle against, 384–87
Select committees, 235
Separation of powers:
  classical doctrine, 228–30
  modern criticisms, 231–32
Serbia, 51, 64, 409
Services provided by governments, 293–94, 295

Sexism, 375–78
Shapiro, Ian, 366
Shapiro, Martin, 344, 347, 348fn
Shaw, George Bernard, 148
Shaw, L. Earl, 256
Sheehan, Margaret A., 157
Shefter, Martin, 186
"Shining Path" guerillas (Peru), 425
Shotwell, James T., 427
Shugart, Matthew Soberg, 186
Shultz, George, 154
Sierra Club, 308
Silberman, Bernard S., 317
Simon, Herbert A., 317
Sindler, Allan P., 403
Six-day war (Israel and Arab nations, 1967), 451
Sixth Amendment to the U.S. Constitution, 367
Sloman, Anne, 255
Slovakia, 185, 453
Slovenia, 64
Smith, Adam, 80, 81
Smith, Arthur K., Jr., 112
Smith, Hedrick, 157fn
Smith, Steven S., 256
Sniderman, Paul M., 67
Snow, C.P., 24
Social democratic parties (Western Europe), 73
Socialism:
    conflict with communism, 82
    core doctrine, 81–82
    defined, 81
    relation to democracy, 82
Socialist Workers party (U.S.), 210–11
Socialization, political:
    agents, 58–62
    defined, 55
    process, 55–57
Société Française pour Études Sondages (SOFRES), 118
Society, defined, 4
Soltau, Roger H., 89, 92fn
Somalia, 110, 111, 453, 455
Soper, Philip, 347
South Africa:
    apartheid policy, 383, 397–99
    "bantustans," 398–99
    ending of apartheid, 110, 399–401
    mulit–racial election of 1994, 400–401
    nuclear weapons potential, 431
    referendum (1991), 182, 398, 400
South Carolina, 389
Southern Christian Leadership Conference (SCLC), 386–87
Sovereignty:
    in international politics, 405, 444
    popular, 94–95
Spain, 51, 65, 174, 182, 217, 260, 377, 412, 437
Spitz, Elaine, 112
Spoils system, 297–98
Spring, Howard, 234

Squier, Robert, 208
Squire, Peverill, 163
Sri Lanka, 40
Stalin, Joseph, 60, 78, 83, 84, 105, 314
Standing and select committees, 240
Star Chamber, 335
Stare decisis, 323
State, U.S. Department of, 416
State system:
    anarchy, 407–408
    approaches to peace within, 433–44
    characteristics, 433
    defined, 405
    (see also Nations; United Nations)
Statutes, distinguished from laws, 232
Stein, Arthur A., 417
Stevens, John Paul, 395
Stimson, James A., 131
Stokes, Donald E., 68fn, 69fn, 200, 201fn
Strikes as political action tactic, 14
Stroessner, Alfredo, 110
Stronach, Bruce, 68
Stumpf, Harry P., 348
Subversion, 423–24
Suez Crisis (1956), 245
Suganami, H., 457
Sullivan, Louis W., 21
Sundquist, James, 194, 201
Supreme Court (U.S.), 332
Survey Research Center, 118
Swaziland, 356
Sweden, 40, 64, 152, 217, 260, 315, 316, 377, 431
Switzerland:
    appointment and election of judges, 334
    durability of political parties, 192
    heaviest user of referendums, 181, 182
    ideological awareness in, 48, 125
    judicial review, 179
    landsgemeinde,103, 117, 180
    low voting turnout, 163–64
    Nationalrat, 236
    plural executive, 228–29
    political parties, 212–13, 217
    popular initiative, 181
    powerful upper legislative house, 237
    woman suffrage, 378
Syria, 19, 356, 413, 425

Taagepera, Rein, 186
Tadjhikistan, 356
Tajfel, Henri, 67
Taney, Roger B., 340
Tannenbaum, Frank, 411
Tannebaum, Percy H., 157
Taxes, 67
Taylor, Frederick W., 393
Tedin, Kent L., 131, 201fn
Teeter, Robert, 208

Television:
bias, political and structural, 141–42
cable, 155
most consumed and trusted, 132
number of sets in various nations, 133
ownership and organization, 134–39
political and structural bias, 141–42
presentation of political news and information, 139–41
Qube interactive system, 155
regulation in the U.S., 142–44, 263
Tennessee, 247
Term limits, 252, 277
Terrorism, 424–25
Thatcher, Margaret, 63, 199, 254, 279, 377, 425
Thayer, Lee, 157fn
Third World, 19, 451–52
Thomas, Clarence, 195, 234, 339, 402fn
Thompson, Kenneth W., 427, 437, 458fn
Thompson, Michael, 68
Tibet, 41
Ticket–splitting and divided government in the U.S., 193–95
Tierney, John T., 23
Tilly, Charles, 17, 24fn
Tito, Marshall (Josip Broz), 64
Togo, 110
Torts, 369
Totalitarianism, 77–79
Tracking polls, 119
Treverton, Gregory F., 427
Trollope, Anthony, 24
Trudeau, Pierre Elliott, 199
Truman, David B., 44
Truman, Harry S., 120, 263, 267, 274
Tummala, Krishna K., 317
Tunisia, 64
Turkey, 260, 422, 437, 449
Turkmenistan, 356
Tuttle, Holmes, 266
Twenty-fourth Amendment to the U.S. Constitution, 388
Twenty-sixth Amendment to the U.S. Constitution, 54

Ukraine, 43, 51, 184, 356, 418, 431, 455
UNESCO, 112fn
Union of Soviet Socialist Republics, (USSR) 1917–1991:
Apparatchiks, 314
changing alliances, 406
collapse of communism, 84–85
control by the Communist Party of the Soviet Union (CPSU), 84, 221–22
dissolution, 1, 41–43, 429
elections after 1991, 159
first free election in 1990, 85, 222
invasions of Afghanistan, Czechoslovakia, Estonia, Hungary, Latvia, and Lithuania, 411, 413, 415, 429, 453

monoparty system, 216, 221–22
penal code, 319
refusal to pay UN assessment for peacekeeping forces, 452
role of families in resisting ideology, 60
secret police, 370
Stalin as dictator, 106
support of terrorists, 425
totalitarianism, 78
use of Communist International, 424
use of Warsaw Pact, 437
Unitary governments, 39–40
United Kingdom of Great Britain and Northern Ireland (Great Britain, U.K.):
American public opinion of, 421
apportionment of parliamentary constituencies, 178
barristers and solicitors, 332
cabinet dominance of Parliament, 279, 280–81
changing alliances, 406
classification as a democracy, 101
Conservative party, 10–11, 199, 204, 262, 279
durability of political parties, 192
European Community membership, 412
Foreign Office, 416
general election of 1992, 175
government bills and private members' bills, 237
high cohesion and discipline in parliamentary parties, 242–43
House of Commons, 236
House of Lords, 235, 236, 322
ideological awareness in, 48
Labour party, 10–11, 145, 199, 213, 224
Leader of Her Majesty's Loyal Opposition, 270–71
Lord Chancellor, 348fn
low party fractionalization, 217
Margaret Thatcher, first woman prime minister, 377
mass media in election campaigns, 140
ministry, 278
NATO membership, 437
nomination and candidate selection, 166–67, 207, 213
Northcote–Trevelyan report and origins of professional civil service, 298
occasional party revolts, 254
organization and regulation of mass media, 138
Parliament Act of 1911, 322
parliamentary standing and select committees, 240
partisan political activity of civil servants, 299
patriotism, 64
possession of nuclear weapons, 455
prime minister, 278, 281–82
prosecutors, 335
public opinion polling, 118
question time, 313
racial tensions, 396
role of monarch, 260, 262, 263
Scottish and Welsh nationalism, 64
selection of prime ministers, 241
stable governments, 282
statutory instruments, 313

strong party discipline and cohesion, 213–14
student protests, 56
traditional balance–of–power foreign policy, 434
two-party system, 264, 283
unwritten constitution, changed by Parliament, 233, 322
women in Parliament, 377
United Mine Workers (UMW), 31
United Nations:
    agencies, 445–46
    American public opinion of, 455
    changing nature, 449–54
    charter, 414, 435, 441, 443
    collective security provisions, 448–49
    founding, 445, 449
    future prospects, 454
    General Assembly, 408, 439, 445, 450
    in the Korean war, 435, 449
    membership, 445, 451–52
    not a world government, 407, 444
    peacekeeping forces, 449, 450, 452
    Secretary General, 448
    Security Council, 408, 445–47, 448
    structure, 446
    uniting–for–peace resolution, 450
    veto by permanent members of the Security Council, 447, 450
Universal Declaration of Human Rights, 77, 92fn
University of California Regents v. *Bakke* (1978), 395
Uruguay, 110
U-shaped curve, 116
Uzbekistan, 356

Values:
    defined, 4
    in ideologies, 71–72
Van Dyke, Vernon, 92
Variables, 112fn
Venezuela, 152, 196, 217, 260, 264, 277
Verba, Sidney, 68, 69fn, 201
Vermont, 103
Veto and item veto, 272
Victoria, Queen of Great Britain, 375
Vietnam, 111, 159, 411, 415, 417
Vietnam War (1963–1975), 19, 406, 411, 423, 444
Viguerie, Richard, 11
Violence, 15–16
von Glahn, Gerhard, 457
Voting:
    candidate orientation, 197–200
    impact of issue orientation, 195–97
    impact of party identification, 191–95
    nonvoting and compulsory voting, 162–65
    qualifications for, 160–62
    registration for, 161–62
Voting Rights Act (1965), 271, 388–89
Voting turnout:
    Gallup formula for predicting, 120

related to age groups, 57
turnout rates in various democracies compared, 162–65

Wahlke, John C., 247, 256
Walensa, Lech, 86, 185
Walker, Geoffrey deQ., 187fn
Walker, Jennone, 457
Wallace, George C., 15
Waller, Michael, 227
Walsh, Lawrence E., 305
Walters, Ronald W., 403
Waltz, Kenneth N., 427
War:
    causes of, 426
    consequences of, 425
    contrary to international law, 441
    as an instrument of foreign policy, 426
    persistence of, 426
Wardlaw, Grant, 427
Warren, Earl, 337
Warren, Robert Penn, 24
Warren, Robert W., 362
Warsaw Pact, 429, 435, 437, 455
Washington, George, 2, 154
Watergate scandal, 235, 254
Wattenberg, Martin P., 201fn, 227
Weaver, Paul H., 157
Webb, Thomas G., 458
Weiner, Myron, 227
Welfare state, 88, 353
Westin, Av, 157
Westlye, Mark C., 201
Weyrich, Paul, 35
Whips, 242
White, Byron, 345, 395
Whitehead, Alfred North, 70
Whitehead, Lawrence, 112
Whitman, Christine Todd, 377
Wiatr, Jerzy, 227fn
Wieseltier, Leon, 457
Wildavsky, Aaron, 68, 317
Wilkins, Roy, 386
Wilson, James Q., 311, 317, 318fn, 402
Wilson, Woodrow, 241, 256fn, 267, 272, 302, 318fn, 428
Wiretapping, 373
Wisconsin, University of, 349, 362
Wolff, Robert Paul, 366
Wolfinger, Raymond E., 163, 201
Women:
    abortion controversy, 34–39
    and affirmative action, 394
    "comparable worth" controversy, 381–82
    employment and pay, 376
    Equal Rights amendment (ERA), 380–81
    in political science, 376
    in politics and government, 376–78
    women's rights movement, 378–82

Women's Equity Action League (WEAL), 379
Women's Political Caucus, 379
Woodward, Bob, 157fn, 344
World Trade Organization (WTO), 419
World War I (1914–1918), 425
World War II (1939–1945), 411, 413, 425
Wright, Jim, 270
Wylie, Laurence, 60, 68, 69fn

Yankelovich, Daniel, 131
Yankelovich, Skelly, and White, 121
Yeltsin, Boris, 42, 85, 184–85, 418, 440
Yemen, 110

"Yes, Minister," 318fn
Young, Whitney M., Jr., 386
Yugoslavia, 41, 51, 64, 185

Zaire, 109, 110
Zaller, John, 68
Zambia, 110
Zedilla, Ernesto, 225
Zero-sum games, 38
Zhivkov, Todo, 87
Zia, Khaleda, 377
Zingale, Nancy, 200
Zuckerman, Harvey L., 318fn